D1084365

Cold War Exiles and the CIA

Cold War Exiles and the CIA

Plotting to Free Russia

BENJAMIN TROMLY

OXFORD
UNIVERSITY PRESS

Great Clarendon Street, Oxford, OX2 6DP,
United Kingdom

Oxford University Press is a department of the University of Oxford.
It furthers the University's objective of excellence in research, scholarship,
and education by publishing worldwide. Oxford is a registered trade mark of
Oxford University Press in the UK and in certain other countries

First Edition published in 2019

Impression: 1

Published in the United States of America by Oxford University Press
198 Madison Avenue, New York, NY 10016, United States of America

British Library Cataloguing in Publication Data
Data available

Library of Congress Control Number: 2019934650

ISBN 978-0-19-884040-4

DOI: 10.1093/oso/9780198840404.001.0001

Printed and bound by
CPI Group (UK) Ltd, Croydon, CR0 4YY

For Maxim and Sasha, with love and pride.

Acknowledgments

This book has been made possible through the help of many kind, helpful, and intellectually stimulating people. I owe my gratitude to several people who have offered feedback on different parts of the manuscript in different phases of development: Oleg Beyda, Katharine Etsell, Norman J. W. Goda, Johanna Granville, Anne-Christine Hamel, John Lear, Simo Mikkonen, Igor' Petrov, Per Anders Rudling, and Nina Tumarkin. Editors at and anonymous reviews for Contemporary European History, Intelligence and National Security, and Journal of Cold War Studies provided useful comments on parts of the text that were first published in article form. I have also benefitted greatly from the comments offered and questions posed by scholars at the different venues at which I have presented work from the project: the Center for European Studies at Lund University; the East European History Seminar at the Institute for Historical Sciences at Humboldt University, Berlin; the Ellison Center for Russian, East European and Eurasian Studies at University of Washington; the Harriman Institute for Russian, Eurasian and East European Studies, Columbia University; the Kennan Institute at the Woodrow Wilson Center; and the Research Center for East European Studies at University of Bremen. Of course, flaws in the text are my responsibility alone.

I also thank the many people who have offered support and advice of various kinds, without which this book would not have taken shape. I have benefitted from the efforts of several archivists who have answered queries and offered kind assistance, especially Tanya Chebotarev at Columbia University Rare Book and Manuscript Library, Christian Dellit at the Federal Commission for the Records of the State Security Service of the former German Democratic Republic, Maria Klassen at the Archive of the Research Center for East European Studies at the University of Bremen, Lisette Matano at Georgetown University Archives, Anatol Shmelev at the Hoover Institution, and Kathy Shoemaker at the Stuart A. Rose Manuscript, Archives, and Rare Book Library at Emory University. Gelinada Grinchenko, Eleonora Narvselius, Benjamin Nathans, Matthew Rojansky, Susanne Schattenberg, and Olga Sveshnikova were supportive of my project and helped make research on it possible. Catherine Andreyev, Richard Cummings, Anna Holian, A. Ross Johnson, Andrei Popov, Joshua Sanborn and Pavel Tribunskii have helped me with locating or acquiring sources. I thank Columbia University Libraries, Gerda Henkel Stiftung, and University of Puget Sound for providing funding for research trips related to the project. Last but certainly not least, I would like to thank my colleagues and students at University of Puget Sound, who have been supportive of my research.

My family has been incredibly supportive during work on this project. Katya, Maxim, and Sasha have been my constant inspiration, and they have been kind enough to let me descend to the basement to write this book. My parents, Fred and Annette, have my love and limitless gratitude for reading through my manuscript with pen in hand. Much love goes to Luke, Stephanie, and Henry in Winnipeg; Aleksei Nikolaevich and Zinaida Iakovlevna in St. Petersburg; Dirk-Jan, Masha, and Mateo in Amsterdam; and my other wonderful family in different locales.

Chapter 3 of this book appeared in slightly different form as "Reinventing Collaboration: The Vlasov Movement in the Postwar Russian Emigration," in Eleonora Narvselius and Gelinada Grinchenko (eds.), *Traitors, Collaborators and Deserters in Contemporary European Politics of Memory: Formulas of Betrayal* (New York: Palgrave Macmillan, 2017). Part of Chapter 4 appears as "Émigré Politics and the Cold War: The National Labor Alliance (NTS), United States Intelligence Agencies and Post-War Europe", in *Contemporary European History* (published online in January 2019). A version of Chapter 7 was published as "The Making of a Myth: The National Labor Alliance, Russian Émigrés, and Cold War Intelligence Activities," *Journal of Cold War Studies* 18, no. 1 (2016): 80–111. Chapter 9 is based on "Ambivalent Heroes: Russian Defectors and American Power in the Early Cold War," *Intelligence and National Security* 33, no. 5 (2018): 642–58.

Contents

PART IV. THE END OF THE AFFAIR: THE DECLINE OF ÉMIGRÉ ANTI-COMMUNISM

List of Figures

List of Abbreviations

Note: I provide the full Russian or German names of the following entities only in the first reference in the text, thereafter identifying them in English translation or by acronym.

AFL	American Federation of Labor
AFRF	American Friends of Russian Freedom; a US charitable organization supporting Soviet defectors
Amcomlib	American Committee for Liberation of the Peoples of Russia, Inc. (from 1953, American Committee for Liberation from Bolshevism, Inc.); a CIA front organization that carried out psychological warfare projects against the USSR
ATsODNR	Anti-Bolshevist Center of the Liberation Movement of the Peoples of Russia (*Antibol'shevitskii tsentr osvoboditel'nogo dvizheniia narodov Rossii*); a rightist-Vlasovite émigré anti-communist organization based in Munich
BfV	Federal Office for the Protection of the Constitution (*Bundesamt für Verfassungsschutz*); a counterintelligence agency of West Germany
BMG	Federal Ministry of Intra-German Affairs (*Bundesministerium für gesamtdeutsche Fragen*), West Germany
BND	Federal Intelligence Service (*Bundesnachrichtendienst*), West Germany
BOB	Berlin Operations Base
CCF	Congress of Cultural Freedom
CDU	Christian Democratic Party (*Christlich Demokratische Union*)
ChK	All-Russian Extraordinary Commission (*Vserossiiskaia Chrezvechainaia Komissiia*)
CIA	Central Intelligence Agency
CIC	Counter Intelligence Corps; a US military intelligence agency
CIG	Central Intelligence Group
DP	Displaced person
FBI	Federal Bureau of Investigation
FRG	Federal Republic of Germany
FSO	Research Center for East European Studies at the University of Bremen (*Forschungsstelle Osteuropa an der Universität Bremen*)
GDR	German Democratic Republic
GRU	Main Intelligence Directorate of the Soviet armed forces (*Glavnoe Razvedyvatel'noe Upravlenie*)
IO Division	International Organizations Division
IRC	International Rescue Committee
IRD	(British) Information Research Department
IRO	International Relief Organization

KGB	Committee for State Security (*Komitet Gosudarstvennoi Bezopasnosti*)
KgU	Combat Group against Inhumanity (*Kampfgruppe gegen Unmenschlichkeit*); a CIA-supported German anti-communist group
KONR	Committee for Liberation of the Peoples of Russia (*Komitet osvobozhdeniia narodov Rossii*); a Russian liberation committee formed by Russian collaborationist general A. A. Vlasov under Nazi auspices
KTsAB	Coordinating Center for Anti-Bolshevik Struggle (*Koordinatsionnyi tsentr antibol'shevitskoi bor'by*); an iteration of the CIA-supported anti-communist émigré united-front organization
KTsONR	Coordinating Center for the Liberation of the Peoples of Russia
LBNS	League of Struggle for the People's Freedom (*Liga bor'by za narodnuiu svobodu*); a democratic anti-communist exile organization based in New York
MfS	Ministry for State Security (*Ministerium für Staatssicherheit*), usually known as the Stasi, East Germany
MGB	Ministry of State Security (*Ministerstvo Gosudarstvennoi Bezopasnosti*), in 1954 reorganized as part of the *Komitet Gosudarstvennoi Bezopasnosti* (or KGB)
NATO	North Atlantic Treaty Organization
NATsPRE	National Representation of the Russian Emigration (*Natsional'noe predstavitel'stvo rossiiskoi emigratsii*); an organization representing Russian exiles in postwar West Germany
NCFE	National Committee for a Free Europe
NSC	National Security Council
NTS	National Labor Alliance of Russian Solidarists (*Natsional'no-trudovoi soiuz (rossiiskikh solidaristov)*; from 1957, *Narodno-trudovoi soiuz (rossiiskikh solidaristov)*; a rightist anti-communist émigré organization headquartered in West Germany (for the sake of brevity, I leave out "Russian Solidarists" in the text)
OMGUS	Office of Military Government, United States
OPC	Office of Policy Coordination
OSS	Office of Strategic Services
PPS	Policy Planning Staff
RIAS	Radio in the American Sector (*Rundfunk im amerikanischen Sektor*)
RND	Russian National Movement (*Russkoe narodnoe dvizhenie*)
RNTS	Russian National Labor Alliance
ROA	Russian Liberation Army
RONDD	Russian National Popular State Movement (*Rossiiskoe obschenatsional'noe narodno-derzhavnoe dvizhenie*); a far-right monarchist anti-communist émigré organization
ROVS	Russian All-Military Union (*Russkii obshche-voinskii soiuz*)
SAF	Union of Andrew's Flag (*Soiuz Andreevskogo flaga*); a far-right monarchist anti-communist émigré organization
SBONR	Union for the Struggle for the Liberation of the Peoples of Russia (*Soiuz bor'by za osvobozhdenie narodov Rossii*); an anti-communist émigré organization representing Vlasovite exiles

SBSR	Union of Struggle for the Freedom of Russia (*Soiuz bor'by za svobodu Rossii* or SBSR); a liberal anti-communist émigré organization
SD	Security Service (*Sicherheitsdienst*)
SED	Socialist Unity Party of Germany (*Sozialistische Einheitspartei Deutschlands*)
SONR	Council for the Liberation of the Peoples of Russia (*Sovet osvobozhdeniia narodov Rossii*); an iteration of the CIA-supported anti-communist émigré united front organization
SPD	Social Democratic Party of Germany (*Sozialdemokratische Partei Deutschlands*)
SR Division	Soviet Russia Division
SRs	Socialist Revolutionary Party
SS	Protection Squadron (*Schutzstaffel*), Nazi Germany
SSU	Strategic Services Unit
TsOPE	Central Representation of Postwar Emigrants (*Tsentral'noe ob'edinenie poslevoennykh emigrantov*; a CIA-created anti-communist organization, originally consisting of Soviet defectors. Later renamed the Central Representation of Political Emigrants
TsPRE	Central Russian Representation of the Russian Emigration (*Tsentral'noe predstavitel'stvo rossiiskoi emigratsii*)

Note on Transliteration
and Russian Names

I use the abbreviated American Library Association–Library of Congress system for translation from Russian into English. This holds when rendering Russian names into English, even in cases where the individuals transliterated them differently. Thus, I refer to Boris Ivanovich Nikolaevskii despite the fact that he published widely in English as Boris Nicolaevsky. I offer first names and patronymics ("Boris Ivanovich") when referring to an individual for the first time (when available); thereafter in the text, I provide a shortened form ("B. I." in the case of Nikolaevskii).

Many Russian émigrés who exited the USSR during World War II changed their names after arriving in the West, a practice connected to their attempts to escape repatriation to the USSR. To indicate such shifts, I render both surnames when first referring to an individual, with the individual's original name coming first; in subsequent references to an individual, I employ only the surname more widely used at the time. For simplicity's sake, I use only the first names and patronymics that individuals adopted after emigration.

Introduction

In 1949, Harper & Brothers published *Thirteen Who Fled*, a book purporting to be about "typical Russian men and women – all recently escaped – [who] tell their personal stories."[1] The authors told of tragic lives that had inspired them to flee their homeland, recalling starving peasants, despotic commissars in the Red Army, loved ones who disappeared during the Great Terror of the 1930s, and the ubiquitous threat of denunciation. The book's editor, the American writer and former communist fellow traveler Louis Fischer, drew the logical conclusion from the testimonies: Soviet society was mired in poverty, fear, and corruption, and "the moment the door opens Russians escape to the West."[2]

With its political geography of the free West and totalitarian East, *Thirteen Who Fled* was emblematic of American Cold War culture. But the volume's rousing narrative papered over more complex historical realities. The book's various authors had escaped during World War II, which meant that the land they crossed over to was Nazi-occupied Europe, not the democratic West of the Cold War. The notion of "escape" to freedom that the book advertised was also questionable. Some of the authors had been slave laborers brought by force to the Third Reich or Soviet prisoners of war captured on the battlefield.[3] The book did not mention another inconvenient fact: at least one, and probably more, of the memoirists had collaborated with the Germans during the war.[4] Clearly, the volume obfuscated the wartime pasts of the thirteen, imposing on them a misleading narrative of Cold War boundary-crossing.

Like the tales of its authors, the volume itself had a backstory that American readers could never have guessed. *Thirteen Who Fled* was a product of unlikely cross-cultural contacts during the early Cold War. Louis Fischer's son George had grown up in Moscow in the 1930s before moving to the United States, his father's

---

[1] Louis Fischer and Boris A. Yakovlev (eds.), *Thirteen Who Fled* (New York: Harper, 1949).

[2] Ibid., 243.

[3] In the case of "Peter Gornev"—the authors took pseudonyms—flight was clearly a misnomer. He had served as a loyal officer in the Red Army and had only become hostile to Soviet rule after being incarcerated in German POW camps. Ibid., 39.

[4] Cooperation with the wartime enemy is nowhere mentioned in *Thirteen Who Fled*. However, another source confirms that "Gregory Ugryumov" had served in the Dabendorf training camp for Russian propaganda workers under the Wehrmacht Supreme Command of the Armed Forces, an institution tied to the collaborationist Vlasov movement (to be discussed at length in this book). Harvard Project on the Soviet Social System, schedule A, vol. 10, case 131, 56.

Cold War Exiles and the CIA: Plotting to Free Russia. Benjamin Tromly, Oxford University Press (2019). © Benjamin Tromly.
DOI: 10.1093/oso/9780198840404.001.0001

home country; he learned of the Russians eking out a living in war-torn Germany from Russian exiles he knew in New York. Soon Louis's wife, the Russian-born Bertha "Markoosha" Fischer, encountered the uprooted Russians while working in Germany as European representative of the International Rescue Committee (IRC).[5] Markoosha, a former supporter of communism turned American patriot like her husband, marveled at the displaced Russians' "desire of bloody revenge" against Stalin, and periodically attached anti-communist manifestos penned by her new Russian friends to the letters she sent home to the United States. Here, she explained to Louis, was "a Soviet Russia we had never known," a generation of Russians who had come of age under Stalin yet were eager to fight his tyrannical regime.[6]

Soon more powerful Americans replicated the Fischers' discovery and patronage of the Russian anti-communists in Germany. In the late 1940s, the Truman administration, amidst fears of communist expansionism and subversion, launched a program of covert operations against the USSR and its newly formed bloc of satellite states in Europe. As part of this effort to go on the offensive in the Cold War, the new Central Intelligence Agency (CIA) offered covert assistance to "underground resistance movements, guerrillas and refugee liberation groups" representing the peoples under communist rule.[7] The Russian communities championed by the Fischers appeared to be ideal recruits for such "combat on the clandestine front."[8] Indeed, the Russian co-editor of *Thirteen Who Fled*, Boris Aleksandrovich Troitskii-Iakovlev, became the head of the Institute for the Study of the History and Culture of the USSR in Munich, funded by the Central Intelligence Agency. Other Russians, many of whose biographies resembled those of the "thirteen," would carry out US-funded covert operations aimed at destabilizing the USSR, which included producing anti-communist propaganda in Russian, sending agents on secret missions into the USSR, and seeking to convince Soviet soldiers and administrators in East Germany to defect to the West.

This book tells the story of Russian exiles' roles in the Cold War in Europe. What were the agendas of Russian anti-communists, and how did the US government seek to promote them as part of the Cold War? What forms did their collaboration take and how did the Soviet state seek to thwart these subversive

[5] The IRC had emerged in the 1930s as an organization to help leftists escape from Nazi-dominated Europe and settle in the United States. It served an analogous function vis-à-vis exiles from communist lands in the postwar period, benefitting from close ties to the US intelligence establishment. Eric Thomas Chester, *Covert Network: Progressives, the International Rescue Comemittee, and the CIA* (Armonk, NY: M.E. Sharpe, 1995).

[6] Markoosha Fischer to family, March 25, 1948, 2, in Seeley G. Mudd Manuscript Library, Princeton University, Louis Fischer Papers, box 42, fol. 1.

[7] National Security Council Directive on Office of Special Projects, June 18, 1948, document 292, in Foreign Relations of the United States, 1945–1950, Emergence of the Intelligence Establishment, retrospective volume.

[8] Office of Policy Coordination, 1948–1952, CIA Historical Study, February 1973, 7, in CIA FOIA Electronic Reading Room.

activities? These lines of inquiry bring into focus a distinct political sphere that took shape within the wider Cold War in Europe. The Russian émigrés were the symbols and potential architects of an anti-Soviet Russia, and therefore they became the object of the designs of policymakers and intelligence officials from different countries. As conveyed by the publication history of *Thirteen Who Fled*, anti-communist Russians in Europe became actors in a Cold War enterprise that involved secret intelligence operations, deceptive propaganda and the forging of unexpected alliances.

An Anti-Communist Troika: Russian Exiles, Americans, and Germans

A central theme of this book is the interaction of ideas and identities among different actors involved in Cold War plots to free Russia. The approach adopted here is transnational, meaning one that focuses on "connections, borrowings, exchanges, and influences" across borders and national categories.[9] Political emigrations are inherently transnational in nature, as they serve as nodes of physical, intellectual, and cultural exchange among their country of origin, their land of exile, and sometimes third countries embroiled in their affairs, such as the United States in the case discussed here.[10] The American-émigré project to liberate Russia created an institutional and political framework in which different national brands of anti-communism interacted, producing ambitious political agendas as well as chronic strains and misunderstandings. What follows is an introduction to the three main political contexts from which US plans to subvert Soviet rule in Russia emerged: American anti-communism, the Russian diaspora, and Cold War conflict in divided Germany.

American support for anti-communist Russian exiles was, to an extent, a logical development of the Cold War. As early as the Russian Civil War (1918–22), the Wilson administration had not only participated in the Allied military intervention in Soviet Russia but also launched the kind of covert political measures against the Bolshevik regime that would become common during the Cold War.[11] Little wonder that soon after the anti-Hitler alliance of World War II collapsed in the 1940s and East-West tensions set in, Washington turned to the task of subverting the Soviet regime from abroad. At root, US support of the

---

[9] Editors, "Across and Beyond: Rethinking Transnational History," *Kritika* 17, no. 4 (2016): 716.

[10] I use exile and émigré interchangeably to denote emigrants who refused to return home for political reasons and attempted to maintain their national culture abroad rather than seeking assimilation into their host societies. Yossi Shain, *The Frontier of Loyalty: Political Exiles in the Age of the Nation-state* (Middletown, CT: Wesleyan University Press, 1989), 13–17.

[11] David S. Foglesong, *America's Secret War against Bolshevism: U.S. Intervention in the Russian Civil War, 1917–1920* (Raleigh: University of North Carolina Press, 2001).

Bolsheviks' exiled opponents was an example of the proverbial befriending of one's enemy's enemy.

The Russian exiles' participation in America's Cold War, however, was more meaningful—and also more complicated—than the framework of a pragmatic marshaling of assets against the USSR would suggest. To gain a fuller picture, one can turn to an episode recounted in the memoir of a CIA officer from the period, William Sloane Coffin (a civil-rights activist in the 1960s). Coffin recalled a conversation with the CIA Chief of Station in Frankfurt in 1950, during which the Russian-speaking Coffin was tasked with seeking out Russians in Germany for use in the Agency's nascent program of covert action. Coffin and "Dave," as the higher official was called, were "simultaneously drawn to the [Russian] people and repulsed by the tyranny of their rulers," and agreed that supporting Russian rebels against communism would be a noble endeavor. Soon the conversation between the two Americans switched into Russian, and Dave's "face relaxed, he warmed up several degrees, he began to gesticulate energetically." The CIA official, it turned out, had studied Russian history and literature at Berkeley, and for him "Russians were something of an obsession."[12]

Dave's concern for the well-being of the Russian people, let alone his excitement about Russian culture, were hardly a preoccupation for most Americans fighting the Cold War in Europe. But his "obsession" was not an isolated case. A driving force of American involvement with the anti-communist Russians examined in this book was "liberationism," an intellectual and political position that advocated US support for the freeing of Russians from communist rule. The purveyors of this view, sometimes dubbed "liberationists," included not just some CIA officers but also Russian experts in the diplomatic service, journalism, and academia. Far from a monolithic group, they had divided views of the Russian people and their history: some liberationists viewed Russians as a democratically-minded and European people, while others thought they were neither.[13] Yet they were united by the conviction that behind the Soviet façade there existed "another Russia," which awaited "an opportune moment to assert itself, weapons in hand if necessary, in the name of national freedom"—and that supporting it should be a major goal of US foreign policy.[14]

In an important study, David Foglesong has argued that liberationism had deeper roots than Cold War confrontation. Instead, dreams of rousing the Russian people against communism were "part of a century-long American drive to

[12] William Sloane Coffin, *Once to Every Man: a Memoir* (New York: Atheneum, 1977), 93.
[13] David S. Foglesong, *The American Mission and the "Evil Empire": The Crusade for a "Free Russia" since 1881* (New York: Cambridge University Press, 2007), 114–19, and David Engerman, "William Henry Chamberlin and Russia's Revolt against Western Civilization," *Russian History* 26, no. 1 (1999): 45–64.
[14] Eugene Lyons, *Our Secret Allies: The Peoples of Russia* (New York: Duell, Sloan and Pearce, 1953), 253.

penetrate, open, and remake Russia."[15] In Foglesong's formulation, Americans had long viewed Russia as an "imaginary twin," a country that was somehow similar to the United States but badly in need of American missionary zeal, liberal institutions, and capitalist development.

Foglesong's account has done a great service by revealing the American cultural, religious, and also racial assumptions on which belief in Russian liberation rested. However, seeing liberationism as a projection of American identities fails to capture the transnational character of the phenomenon. The liberationists' embrace of Russia was hardly imaginable without their relationships—intellectual, political, and often social—with Russian émigrés.[16] Russians who had fled communism (or were driven from it) appeared to Americans as prima facie evidence that Russia was both capable and worthy of liberation. The liberationists' embrace of émigrés reflected the prominence of the latter in Russian studies in the United States.[17] As was presumably the case with "Dave" at Berkeley, Russian liberationists received from their Russian instructors not just knowledge of a language and culture but also exposure to the distinctly émigré conviction that the *true* Russia was that of pre-communist vintage.

At first glance, the influence of liberationism on US foreign policy during the early Cold War would seem to be an unlikely development. As the liberationists themselves stressed, their view of Russia ran against the grain of much American public opinion at the height of the Cold War, when hatred for "the Russians" and a demonization of them as a people prone to "Asiatic despotism" were common.[18] However, the liberationists had the advantage of belonging to the small pool of Americans who had expertise about the new Cold War opponent, or at least the USSR's Russian core. Moreover, they had one of their own at the nerve center of US foreign policy during the onset of the Cold War. As the head of the Policy Planning Staff at the Department of State from 1947 to 1950, George F. Kennan was not just the author of the policy of containing the Soviet Union but also a crucial figure in institutionalizing the apparatus for pursuing "organized political

[15] Foglesong, *The American Mission and the "Evil Empire"*, 118.
[16] Note that Foglesong refers to émigrés at numerous points but does not incorporate them into his account of liberationism. Ibid., 93, 111, 123, 144, 273. Likewise, a recent overview of transnational contacts between the United States and Russia passes over émigré anti-communism in America. I. I. Kurilla, *Zakliatye druz'ia: Istoriia mnenii, fantazii, kontaktov, vzaimo(ne)ponimania Rossii i SShA* (Moscow: Novoe literaturnoe obozrenie, 2018), 233–80.
[17] For exiles and Russian studies in the United States, see David C. Engerman, *Know Your Enemy: The Rise and Fall of America's Soviet Experts* (New York and Oxford: Oxford University Press, 2011), 13–23; I. I. Kurilla and V. Iu. Zhuravleva (eds.), *Russian/Soviet Studies in the United States, Amerikanistika in Russia: Mutual Representations in Academic Projects* (Lanham: Lexington Books, 2016), and E. L. Nitoburg, *Russkie v SShA: Istoriia i sud'by, 1870–1970: Etnoistoricheskii ocherk* (Moscow: Nauka, 2005), 145–8. The émigré role was similar in Britain: E. V. Petrov, "Rol' russkikh istorikov-emigrantov v stanovlenii 'rossievedcheskoi traditsii' v Velikobritanii," in O. B. Vasilevskaia (ed.), *Kul'turnoe i nauchnoe nasledie rossiiskoi emigratsii* (Moscow: Russkii put', 2002), 254–64.
[18] Martin E. Malia, *Russia under Western Eyes: From the Bronze Horseman to the Lenin Mausoleum* (Cambridge, MA: Belknap Press of Harvard University Press, 1999), 370.

warfare" as a component of US foreign policy.[19] His influence was crucial for launching the different secret projects involving Russian exiles.

Liberationism, along with its indispensable corollary of reliance on émigrés, shaped US covert action projects against the Soviet Union. There were practical reasons for the US intelligence establishment to cultivate Russian exiles, who promised to provide the Americans with otherwise unavailable resources with which to fight the Cold War: intelligence on the secretive and closed Soviet bloc and footholds in their homeland that might prove crucial if a hot war were to break out in Europe (as many feared was imminent). But the liberationists pursued an altogether bolder strategy of utilizing Russian exiles to foment "disaffection" in the USSR.[20] As politically minded members of a fundamentally anti-Soviet nation, it was hoped, exiled Russians were uniquely poised to challenge the legitimacy of the Soviet state from abroad. A 1950 policy recommendation from the OPC (Office of Policy Coordination), a covert operations agency which was housed in the CIA, explained that "the greatest menace to Soviet Communism" was Russian nationalism. Covert support of Russian exiles was a way to leverage the Russian masses in the USSR, "a most valuable ally" of the United States, against the Soviet state.[21] A direct outgrowth of this strategy was the American Committee for Liberation of the Peoples of Russia, Inc., a CIA-funded front organization made up of liberationist intellectuals that worked to mobilize exiles as agents of national revolution from abroad. In this and other projects, US geopolitical agendas merged seamlessly into a transnational anti-communist mission to regenerate the Russian nation.

As this book will show, the task of reconciling US foreign policy and exile nationalism proved an exceedingly complicated matter. The Russian exiles were a problematic set of covert proxies for US authorities, most of all because of a set of seemingly incontrovertible political and even geographical facts. Ethnic Russians were the state-carrying people of a Soviet state that was then extending its power in Europe. And the Russians showed no signs of rebelling against Soviet rule—or, at least, none that could be detected from across the Iron Curtain. On the contrary, the Russians had actually rallied behind Stalin during World War II to defeat the Axis invaders.[22] The apparent stability of Soviet rule put a dent in the

---

[19] A work that correctly stresses Kennan's central role in the initiation of psychological warfare operations is Peter Grose, *Operation Rollback: America's Secret War behind the Iron Curtain* (Boston: Houghton Mifflin, 2000).

[20] CIA (OSO & OPC)/State Department Talks with SIS/Foreign Office: VI. Russian Emigre Groups, April 24, 1951, 1–2, in National Archives and Records Administration (NARA), RG 263, Entry ZZ-19, 230/86/25/02, box 13, AERODYNAMIC: OPERATIONS, vol. 20.

[21] Recommendations with Regard to the Utilization of the Russian Emigration, April 26, 1950, 1, in History and Public Policy Program Digital Archive at the Woodrow Wilson Center, Radio Free Europe and Radio Liberty: Cold War International History Project e-Dossier no. 32.

[22] Scholarship on the Russian question in the period stresses the USSR's fusion of Soviet patriotism and Russian nationalism. See Geoffrey A. Hosking, *Rulers and Victims: the Russians in the Soviet Union* (Cambridge, MA: Harvard University Press, 2006), and David Brandenburger, *National Bolshevism:*

national legitimacy of Russian exiles in the West. Indeed, the Russians were at a disadvantage vis-à-vis corresponding émigré populations from Eastern European satellite states and the non-Russian areas of the USSR. While the latter could make the claim that their more or less recently annexed or Sovietized nations dreamed of independence, the displaced Russians were compelled to make the more difficult argument that the Russian people, thirty years into the communist period, remained unreconciled to rule from the Kremlin.[23] Such stubborn realities cast doubt on the exiles' claim that the Russian nation was fundamentally opposed to Soviet communism, leaving them no recourse but to rail against Western commentators who saw the Cold War enemy as being "the Russians."[24]

A no less important problem for the exiles was the actual state of political life in the Russian diaspora. Russians abroad had no leaders with recent pasts of political relevance, let alone a government in exile that could unify the diverse collection of Russians stranded outside Soviet borders. Unfortunately, the Russian émigré leader with the greatest cachet abroad and at least some trappings of historical legitimacy—Aleksandr Federovich Kerenskii, the premier of Russia in 1917 who was toppled by the Bolsheviks—had a poor reputation among many Russian émigrés. Unlike some East European exile leaders who had recently been ejected from government by communists, Kerenskii's authority was based on a political career from the distant past, to say nothing of the fact that he was commonly blamed for failing to prevent the Bolsheviks' seizure of power.

The émigrés' lack of authoritative leaders was symptomatic of the deep internal dissension within the Russian diaspora. To be sure, internal divisions have been common to all political emigrations, a product of the powerlessness and frustration of exile as well as the constant struggle to maintain their national cultures abroad.[25] Following this pattern, infighting plagued US plans to organize East European exiles in the late 1940s, particularly the Poles.[26] Nevertheless, the Russian political scene was distinctive in its extreme internal acrimoniousness, which was mostly a result of the diversity of the Russian communities on which it was based. The Russian diaspora or "emigration" (*emigratsiia*) was composed of

---

Stalinist Mass Culture and the Formation of Modern Russian National Identity, 1931–1956 (Cambridge, MA: Harvard University Press, 2002).

---

[23] This point is also made in Simo Mikkonen, "Exploiting the Exiles: Soviet Émigrés in U.S. Cold War Strategy," *Journal of Cold War Studies* 14, no. 2 (2012): 106.

[24] The American liberationists blamed the common conflation of Russia and the USSR in the west on ignorance, while émigrés often attributed it to "anti-Russian propaganda." Compare R. Gordon Wasson, "A Second Look at Some Popular Beliefs about Russia," *The Commercial and Financial Chronicle* 173 (Feb. 1951): 820, with A. V. Antoshin, *Rossiiskie emigranty v usloviiakh "kholodnoi voiny" (seredina 1940-kh–seredina-1960-kh gg.)* (Ekaterinburg: izd. Ural'skogo universiteta, 2008), 395.

[25] Robert C. Williams, "European Political Emigrations: A Lost Subject," *Comparative Studies in Society and History* 12, no. 2 (1970): 140–8.

[26] Anna Mazurkiewicz, "'Join, or Die' – The Road to Cooperation among East European Exiled Political Leaders in the United States, 1949–1954," *Polish American Studies* 69, no. 2 (2012): 5–43.

successive population outflows resulting from Russia's twentieth-century political catastrophes.[27] The staggered flow of emigration from Russia created a pattern of distinct exile generations or "waves," as they are usually called. The so-called first wave of Russian émigrés exited the country during the Russian Civil War, while the second wave—that of "the thirteen"—consisted of Soviet citizens displaced during World War II, typically as prisoners of war, slave laborers, or collaborators of various kinds. During the early Cold War, exiles from these two waves frequently clashed, a pattern that reflected their distinctive memories of the country they had left behind as well as their post-emigration experiences. Making matters worse, the political forces of the two waves were not themselves cohesive entities but rather conglomerations of clashing organizations and interests. As a result of its intricate composition, the Russian diaspora's expressions of national identity tended to fracture into plural and conflicting visions.[28]

Deepening the troubles of Russian anti-communists was the problem of empire. Alongside the Russians, exiles from the various minority peoples of the USSR were also active in exile and competed for US government support. The sharply contrasting national identities of Russian and non-Russian exile groups complicated CIA projects against the Soviet Union.[29] While Russian exiles with virtual unanimity envisioned post-Soviet Russia as a multiethnic entity with borders similar to those of the Soviet Union, political exiles representing the non-Russian minorities of the USSR just as vehemently pursued independence for their respective nations. As a result, US intelligence operatives and CIA-affiliated intellectuals faced a balancing act in working with Russian and non-Russian exile groups which had mutually exclusive and generally inflexible national claims.

American liberationists and Russian exiles, then, struggled to find common ground due to problems of national legitimacy, Russian émigré divisions, and the national diversity of Soviet exile groups. Factoring in the third major set of players in this book, Germans on both sides of the Iron Curtain, adds to this picture of troubled cross-cultural interaction. Divided Germany served as the essential setting for early CIA operations against the Soviet bloc for a host of reasons: its

---

[27] Important studies chronicling different historical trajectories within the Russian emigration include André Liebich, *From the Other Shore: Russian Social Democracy after 1921* (Cambridge, MA: Harvard University Press, 1997), and Paul Robinson, *The White Russian Army in Exile, 1920–1941* (Oxford: Clarendon Press, 2002).

[28] For a path-breaking analysis of the multiplicity of national ideas in the first-wave Russian diaspora, see Laurie Manchester, "How Statelessness Can Force Refugees to Redefine Their Ethnicity: What can be Learned from Russian Émigrés Dispersed to Six Continents in the Inter-war Period?" *Immigrants & Minorities* 34, no. 1 (2016): 70–91.

[29] This study differs from Anna Holian's valuable account of divergent Russian and Ukrainian nationalisms in exile by treating them in a Cold War context. Anna Holian, *Between National Socialism and Soviet Communism: Displaced Persons in Postwar Germany* (Ann Arbor: University of Michigan Press, 2011).

location at the center of Cold War Europe, the geographical anomaly of joint Allied sovereignty over Berlin, the presence of large populations of anti-communist displaced persons (including the Russians) in the country's west, and the stationing of Soviet troops in the east.[30] In the vocabulary of Russian anti-communists, West Germany and Austria (at least until the withdrawal of occupation forces from that country in 1955) constituted "the front" of the struggle, places of political opportunity, intrigue, and also danger.

Rather than just providing their battleground, German contexts and problems shaped the Russian exile movements. As already suggested, many exiles active in the CIA's projects had collaborated with Nazi Germany in some capacity, whether by choice or—as was especially common for Soviet soldiers detained in horrific conditions in prisoner-of-war camps—in pursuit of mere survival.[31] Not surprisingly, Cold War Russian exiles derived from these and other wartime experiences a wide range of attitudes toward the German population. Russian émigrés were embittered at the brutal treatment Germans had meted out to their countrymen during the war, and they resented the hostile attitude of many postwar West Germans toward the presence of extensive displaced populations in their midst.[32] Moreover, Russians who had collaborated during the war had a strong incentive to distance themselves from the defeated and discredited Germans. At the same time, some former collaborators hoped that their past ties to the wartime Hitler state might prove useful in the current struggle, with the new West Germany serving as an anti-communist patron distinct from the powerful yet unfamiliar Americans.

To some extent, such ambitions bore fruit. West Germany was not only an anti-communist state but, at least on the level of rhetoric, a revanchist one, as the government of Konrad Adenauer espoused the goals of reuniting Germans in the Soviet occupation zone to West Germany and returning Germans expelled from Eastern Europe after the war to their homelands.[33] Moreover, the West German state employed many former servitors of the Third Reich whose hostility to the USSR matched that of the Russian exiles. Indeed, an early player in Russian émigré politics was the Gehlen Organization, a spy organization consisting of the holdovers from Hitler's intelligence organization on the Eastern Front, *Fremde Heere Ost* (Foreign Armies East), which was revived by the US army and then

---

[30] The importance of Berlin for Cold War intelligence is stressed in Paul Maddrell, "The Western Secret Services, the East German Ministry of State Security and the Building of the Berlin Wall," *Intelligence and National Security* 21, no. 5 (2006): 829–47.

[31] Chapters 1 and 2 explore debates over collaboration during the early Cold War.

[32] Cf. V. G. Fursenko, "Di-Pi: dni i gody," in V. S. Karpov et al. (eds.), *V poiskakh istiny: puti i sud'by vtoroi emigratsii. Sbornik statei i dokumentov* (Moscow: Rossiiskii gos. Gumanitarnyi universitet, 1997), 111.

[33] For an account of lingering war grievances from WWII in West Germany, see G. Moeller, *Robert War Stories: The Search for a Usable past in the Federal Republic of Germany* (Berkeley: University of California Press, 2001) and Pertti Ahonen, *After the Expulsion: West Germany and Eastern Europe, 1945–1990* (Oxford and New York: Oxford University Press, 2003).

passed to the CIA. The following pages will explore the contacts between exile and West German anti-communists and the tensions to which they gave rise, particularly with regard to divided war memories and national identities as well as to CIA operations carried out on West German territory.

The Cold War project to liberate Russia, then, was based on transnational flows of power, ideas, and memories, all of which were sometimes constructive but usually frictional in nature. The primary actors were the Russian exiles, who were divided into groupings with disparate and often mutually exclusive ideologies, notions of history, and political affiliations. The Russians competed with other exile communities from the USSR, whose political programs and geopolitical visions were often diametrically opposed to theirs. Surrounding the exiles of all stripes were powerful outside political actors in the Cold War West, including American and West German policymakers, administrators and intelligence officers, who were all hostile to communism but pursued their own interests toward the exiles. The result was a kaleidoscopic anti-communist sphere in which not just the intentions and actions of different actors but even the Russian nation that the exiles purported to represent took on shifting shapes.

The Secret War: Spy Services and the Émigrés

A crucial framework for the Russian anti-communist enterprise remains to be explored: the activities of clashing intelligence services in Cold War Europe. In order to undertake anti-communist activities on a serious scale, Russian exiles had no choice but to operate in the murky world of espionage agencies. The Truman and Eisenhower governments were loath to admit that they were backing Russian and other East European exile organizations that attempted to violate the sovereignty of Soviet bloc states during a time of peace, a course of action that might pose risks for US diplomacy and national security. For this reason, the task of cultivating the exiles fell to US intelligence agencies, or sometimes to ostensibly private bodies that were hidden fronts for them. In spy argot, the émigrés operated primarily into the sphere of "covert action," or activities undertaken to influence conditions abroad that could not be traced to—or, at least, might be "plausibly denied" by—the US government.

For the United States, the adoption of covert action as a regular tool of state was a Cold War phenomenon. Quickly emerging as a superagency for intelligence and covert action after its creation in 1947, the CIA was the first peacetime entity of its kind for the United States. For the emergent US security establishment, the expansive new paradigm for understanding covert action was "psychological warfare" or "political warfare," terms often used interchangeably to signify the use of all political instruments short of war against an enemy (in this case, world communism).[34] Although the US government waged political warfare across the globe, a crucial target was the Soviet bloc, against which the CIA undertook what has rightfully been called a "secret war" that included propaganda operations (both those involving "black" disinformation and unattributed but ostensibly truthful or "gray" information), subversion, sabotage, espionage, and, at least in the case of operations toward Albania, even the training of paramilitary forces.[35]

Bold US psychological warfare plans against the Soviet bloc bore very meager results. As Stephen Long has recently argued convincingly, the US political warfare campaign against the Soviet bloc was marred by "strategic confusion." Bureaucratic infighting bogged down political warfare agendas, as the State Department, the CIA, and the Department of Defense clashed over the shape of covert action and control over it. In the process, essential questions about political warfare went unanswered. Was the objective to topple communist governments or to spur them to reform? How were aggressive attempts to weaken communist states via covert action to connect to the policy of containment, which isolated the Soviet bloc and therefore might work to strengthen the USSR's control over its European empire?[36] And how could the US government utilize its new covert action capacities without provoking the Soviet Union into a military response?[37] None of these questions found conclusive answers, with the result that grand plans for political warfare gave way to a haphazard collection of operations that did little to weaken Soviet rule.[38]

Paradoxically, a political warfare program that produced futile and costly results dragged on for years with little oversight.[39] Continued covert operations against the USSR held an obvious appeal for US policymakers in the Cold War: they were seen as "a third option between doing nothing and engaging in full-scale warfare," and they were conveniently free of congressional oversight.[40] A change in course only came after mass unrest emerged in the Soviet bloc and was

---

[34] Gregory Mitrovich, *Undermining the Kremlin: America's Strategy to Subvert the Soviet Bloc, 1947–1956* (Ithaca, NY: Cornell University Press, 2000), 8–10; Kenneth Osgood, *Total Cold War: Eisenhower's Secret Propaganda Battle at Home and Abroad* (Lawrence: University of Kansas, 2006); and Lowell Schwartz, *Political Warfare against the Kremlin: US and British Propaganda Policy at the Beginning of the Cold War* (Basingstoke: Palgrave Macmillan, 2009), 11–14.

[35] Grose, *Operation Rollback*; Bernd Stöver, *Die Befreiung vom Kommunismus: amerikanische Liberation Policy im Kalten Krieg 1947–1991* (Cologne: Böhlau, 2002), and Beatrice Heuser, "Covert Actions within British and American Concepts of Containment, 1948–1951," in Richard J. Aldrich (ed.), *British Intelligence, Strategy and the Cold War, 1945–1951* (London: Routledge, 1992), 65–84.

[36] Stephen Long, *The CIA and the Soviet Bloc: Political Warfare, the Origins of the CIA and Countering Communism in Europe* (London and New York: I.B. Tauris, 2014), 292–3.

[37] The strategic nuclear balance as a factor in political warfare plans is a theme of Mitrovich, *Undermining the Kremlin*, 57–69.

[38] Long, *The CIA and the Soviet Bloc*; Mitrovich, *Undermining the Kremlin*, 42. Lack of strategy is also the theme of Sarah-Jane Corke, *US Covert Operations and Cold War Strategy: Truman, the CIA and Secret Warfare* (London: Routledge, 2007).

[39] Long, *The CIA and the Soviet Bloc*, 157–9; Richard Immerman, *The Hidden Hand: A Brief History of the CIA* (Chichester, England: Wiley-Blackwell, 2014), 42–4.

[40] John Prados, *Safe for Democracy: The Secret Wars of the CIA* (Chicago: Ivan R. Dee, 2006), 19.

suppressed by Soviet troops, first in East Germany (in 1953) and then in Hungary (in 1956)—an outcome that finally exposed the flawed strategic assumptions of the program.[41]

If the policy formulation of US psychological warfare toward the Soviet bloc is fairly well researched, the same cannot be said about its implementation on the ground. It has long been known that the CIA pursued political warfare against the Soviet bloc by recruiting non-state actors (or "outside instigators"), and that exiles from the communist countries were foremost among them.[42] However, work on different exile communities, especially by scholars with knowledge of the national histories involved, is only now appearing.[43] Zeroing in on the émigré agents of political warfare will uncover a transnational political sphere through which US power flowed. It will also reveal an aspect of political warfare that is rarely studied: its embeddedness in an ongoing competition between spy services of the Cold War adversaries.

Soviet policymakers and intelligence operatives are essential actors in the story of exile anti-communism. From the early months of the Bolshevik regime, the Soviet intelligence and security complex had fought anti-Soviet conspiracies from abroad.[44] After the Bolsheviks emerged triumphant from the Civil War, they pursued and harassed the remnants of the anti-Soviet forces that had scattered across the globe. One of the Soviets' many coups on the émigré front was "the Trust" in the 1920s, a Soviet counterintelligence operation which involved creating a sham anti-communist organization in order to disrupt exile networks and penetrate British and French intelligence services.[45] Battling anti-communist émigrés became a permanent function of Soviet counterintelligence efforts in the West and even something of an *idée fixe* for Iosif Vissarionovich Stalin. In his final years, the dictator issued "instructions to annihilate minor figures in

[41]   Walter L. Hixson, *Parting the Curtain: Propaganda, Culture, and the Cold War, 1945–1961* (New York: St. Martin's Press, 1997), 87–119.

[42]   Long, *The CIA and the Soviet Bloc*, 9–10.

[43]   For valuable work on Russian exiles, see Antoshin, *Rossiiskie emigranty*; Mikkonen, "Exploiting the Exiles"; P. A. Tribunskii, "Fond Forda, Fond 'Svobodnaia Rossiia,' Vostochno-Evropeiskii Fond i sozdanie 'Izdatel'stva imeni Chekhova,'" *Ezhegodnik Doma Russkogo zarubezhiia imeni Aleksandra Solzhenitsyna 2014–2015*, Moscow, 2015, 577–600; and E. V. Kodin, *Miunkhenskii institut po izucheniiu istorii i kul'tury SSSR, 1950–1972 gg.: evropeiskii tsentr sovetologii?* (Smolensk: Izd. SmolGU, 2016). For other East European exile communities, see Katalin Kádár Lynn (ed.), *The Inauguration of Organized Political Warfare: Cold War Organizations sponsored by the National Committee for a Free Europe/Free Europe Committee* (Saint Helena, CA: Helena History Press, 2013), and Anna Mazurkiewicz (ed.), *East Central Europe in Exile*, vols. 1–2 (Newcastle upon Tyne, UK: Cambridge Scholars Publishing, 2013).

[44]   John Costello and Oleg Tsarev, *Deadly Illusions* (New York: Crown, 1993).

[45]   See Natalie Grant, "Deception on a Grand Scale," in *International Journal of Intelligence and Counterintelligence* 1, no. 4 (1986): 51–77, and Karl Schlögel, *Berlin, vostochnyi vokzal: Russkaia emigratsiia v Germanii mezhdu dvumia voinami, 1919–1945* (Moscow: Novoe Literaturnoe Obozrenie, 2004), 421–30.

émigré circles," as his police chief Lavrentii Pavlovich Beriia apparently later complained.[46] Such offensive operations against émigré anti-communists actually intensified after Stalin's death, when an insecure Soviet leadership drew on the gamut of "active measures" (*aktivnye meropriiatia*)—which included the recruitment of agents of influence, unattributed propaganda and misinformation, and targeted violence—against its opponents in exile.[47]

The Soviets played a strong hand in the internal affairs of the Russian diaspora, taking advantage of their extensive counterintelligence and security system, their long experience of thwarting exile groups and the considerable resources they devoted to the task.[48] As a result, the CIA had great difficulty fending off Soviet interference in the Russian diaspora. In contrast to their Soviet counterparts, American intelligence officials knew little about the exiles with whom they became entangled. Even worse, they were neophytes who had to "learn by doing" in the realm of covert action, as a report observed.[49] Not surprisingly, the CIA's operations involving Russians bore few tangible results from either an intelligence or a psychological warfare perspective. In fact, the former head of the SR (Soviet Russia) Division admitted to the CIA having had in the mid-1950s "almost no assets, in terms of agents, within the borders of the USSR or the Baltic states."[50]

The clash of superpower intelligence agencies within the Russian diaspora was not as simple as the undeniably considerable failures of the CIA suggest. Instead, involvement in Russian diasporic communities produced unforeseen and unwanted consequences for the spy services of both superpowers. For the CIA, one such outcome of exile politics was the surprising room for maneuver that their émigré allies sometimes exercised. The CIA often established fairly loose liaison relationships with existing émigré anti-communist organizations in the hope that they knew best how to cause trouble for the Soviet state. In this arrangement, the exiles functioned as covert proxies of American power as much as intelligence assets—and, as in proxy wars proper, they exercised a degree of autonomy from their bankrollers who were distant from the battlefield.[51] Going further, the exiles

---

[46] Pavel Sudoplatov et al., *Special Tasks: The Memoirs of an Unwanted Witness, a Soviet Spymaster* (Boston: Little, Brown, 1994), 359. During the Cold War, an entire department of Soviet foreign counterintelligence was devoted to infiltrating émigré groups. See Oleg Kalugin, *Spymaster: My Thirty-Two Years in Intelligence and Espionage against the West* (New York: Basic Books, 2009), 168.

[47] Jonathan Haslam, *Near and Distant Neighbors: A New History of Soviet Intelligence* (New York: Farrar, Straus and Giroux, 2015), 19–26, 42–3. Notably, policies toward anti-communist exiles did not follow the wider reconsideration of Soviet ideological positions on the United States that took place under the Khrushchev regime. Rósa Magnúsdóttir, *Enemy Number One: The United States of America in Soviet Ideology and Propaganda, 1945–1959* (New York: Oxford University Press, 2019).

[48] For a description of Soviet counterintelligence, see Robert W. Stephan, *Stalin's Secret War: Soviet Counterintelligence against the Nazis, 1941–1945* (Lawrence: University of Kansas Press, 2004), 55–120.

[49] This characterization comes from a later evaluation of the Office of Policy Coordination (OPC), an early agency devoted to such activities. Office of Policy Coordination, 26.

[50] Peer De Silva, *Sub Rosa: The CIA and the Uses of Intelligence* (New York: Times Books, 1978), 56.

[51] On the role of proxies in starting and shaping military conflicts, see Andrew Mumford, *Proxy Warfare* (Oxford: Wiley, 2013), 18–23.

proved to be ambitious and sometimes clever political operators who sought to maximize the political agency imparted on them by the Cold War. The reader of this book will encounter émigrés fighting among themselves for the favor of their superpower patrons, lobbying powerholders in the US government, and disseminating mendacious propaganda to Western onlookers and journalists.

Soviet foreign intelligence also experienced unwelcome headwinds in their battle with anti-communist exiles. Ironically, Soviet efforts to diminish the stature and influence of its émigré enemies in the West sometimes had the opposite effect. The Soviets' persistent efforts to neutralize or destroy émigré groups, the Americans concluded, were proof that their proxies were being taken seriously by the enemy and therefore had strategic value in the Cold War. In this manner, conflict between superpowers and especially their spy agencies transformed Russian anti-communists abroad from unexceptional members of a marginalized and destitute diasporic group into political and intelligence operators on an international stage.

US plans to subvert the USSR created a Russian political sphere that constituted a sub-front in the Cold War, one that had its own distinctive dynamics. In tracing this outcome, this book situates the exiles in recent literature that stresses the unanticipated political consequences of the CIA's disparate Cold War undertakings.[52] In a broader sense, it confirms the value of examining the Cold War from the perspective of low-level and non-state actors, whose "alternative projects" became entangled with the wider geopolitical contest of the era.[53]

Piecing Together Mayhem: Methodologies

Émigré politics of the Cold War presents historians with multiple layers of controversy. As the encounter between the US government and the exiles was often handled through the CIA, one confronts the wider challenges inherent to the study of that agency. Writing on Cold War intelligence is too often marred by sensationalism and a preference for "anecdote instead of analysis."[54] Such shortcomings reflect not just the public fascination with spies but also the difficulty of making sense of historical events which hinged on secrecy and deception. As this book will show, all parties connected to the émigré political milieu in Germany marshaled the telling of untruths or partial truths as a political practice: émigré

[52] Cf. Hugh Wilford, *The Mighty Wurlitzer: How the CIA Played America* (Cambridge, MA: Harvard University Press, 2008), and Helen Laville and Hugh Wilford (eds.), *The US Government, Citizen Groups and the Cold War: The State-private Network* (London: Routledge, 2012).

[53] Jadwiga E. Pieper Mooney and Fabio Lanza (eds.), *De-centering Cold War History: Local and Global Change* (London and New York: Routledge, 2013).

[54] John Ferris, "Coming in from the Cold War: the Historiography of American Intelligence, 1945–1990," in Michael J. Hogan (ed.), *America in the World: The Historiography of American Foreign Relations since 1941* (Cambridge and New York: Cambridge University Press, 1995), 577.

organizations sought to mislead intelligence agencies on all sides about the scale of their activities, specific exiles engaged in mutual denunciation as part of their internal struggle for power, and spies on both sides of the Iron Curtain carried out devious psychological operations against each other (and sometimes tried to hoodwink the spies of their ostensible allies, as well). As a result of these multiple forms of subterfuge, a hall-of-mirrors effect took hold in exile circles which makes separating fact from fiction difficult.

A related and particularly contentious question is how to present the dramatis personae of the current study, particularly CIA personnel and their Russian clients. Not surprisingly, in Soviet (and sometimes in post-Soviet) Russia, scholars and propagandists savaged the exiles as mercenaries of the imperialists, fascists, traitors, and war criminals.[55] Perhaps surprisingly, such a perspective found echoes in historical work on the subject in the West and especially in the United States, which attacked the CIA for engaging émigrés who were collaborators and fascists.[56] In a recent iteration of this approach, David C. S. Albanese condemns what he sees as "Western democratic sponsorship of hate-based nationalism," claiming that US intelligence planners "purposely" drew on extremist elements on the logic that they had the most potential as "paramilitary actors."[57] Such a perspective is heavily influenced by the spirit of moral censure often present in the study of espionage and covert operations in the Anglosphere, which the late D. Cameron Watt lambasted as the "politically correct doctrine according to which anything the CIA turned to was morally wrong and legally contrary to the laws and ethos of the United States."[58]

This book attempts a more balanced approach to the CIA and the exiles. Issuing a normative verdict on historical actors is perhaps inevitable but not the end goal; instead, an attempt must be made to understand them in the context of their time. It is beyond doubt that US national-security officials engaged some groups and individuals that had integral nationalist and anti-Semitic ideas as well as compromising records of association with Nazism. Yet while the CIA acted on quite cold-blooded ("operational") considerations, there is no evidence that they

[55] The post-Soviet situation saw more polarization. Some authors continued the Soviet-era line on exiles, while other works, sometimes written by people associated with the émigré groups discussed in this book, lionize exiles as national heroes and freedom fighters. Compare S. A. Krivosheev, *KGB protiv NTS* (Moscow: Trovant, 2015), and Andrei Okulov, *V bor'be za Beluiu Rossiiu: Kholodnaia grazhdanskaia voina* (Moscow: Veche, 2013).

[56] Christopher Simpson, *Blowback: America's Recruitment of Nazis and its Effects on the Cold War* (New York: Weidenfeld & Nicolson, 1988); Prados, *Safe for Democracy*, 43–77; and Mark Aarons and John Loftus, *Ratlines: How the Vatican's Nazi Networks Betrayed Western Intelligence to the Soviets* (London: William Heinemann, 1991).

[57] David C. S. Albanese, "In Search of a Lesser Evil: Anti-Soviet Nationalism and the Cold War," PhD thesis, Northeastern University, 2015, 12–13.

[58] D. Cameron Watt, "The Proper Study of Propaganda," *Intelligence and National Security* 15, no. 4 (2000): 144. I should note that I do not subscribe to Watt's dismissive treatment of the literature he reviewed, which includes important studies of Cold War propaganda, including Gary D. Rawnsley (ed.), *Cold-War Propaganda in the 1950s* (New York: St. Martin's Press, 1999).

embraced "hate-based nationalism." Turning to the exiles, one must present facts about individuals' wartime actions and affiliations as fully as possible while also recognizing that evidence on these matters is often murky; specific charges of war crimes generally remained unsubstantiated in the legal systems of the West,[59] while some Soviet sources remain problematic due to the bias outlined above.[60] To address these dilemmas, the book hews close to available evidence, ambiguous as it often proves.

A related challenge is that of addressing the question of historical actors' motivations—perhaps a difficult task for all historians but one that is especially thorny given the shadowy and divisive world under examination here. To what extent did historical actors—whether exiles or their varied allies, enemies, or interlocutors—speak honestly about their intentions? In particular, are we to believe the exiles' own accounts of their motives, in which ideological anti-communism is invariably the standard theme, or should we lay emphasis on the pursuit of self-interest or opportunism? This study rejects one-sided approaches that would present exiles as either anti-communist heroes or cynical mercenaries, instead positing that both anti-communist ideas and the pursuit of self-interest shaped the émigré enterprise. To deny the purely materialistic aspects of émigré politics would be unwise, as made clear by a letter from a Russian anti-communist who complained that "the object and the limits of the desires" of his comrades were "a car, money," and, at least for one individual, "broads."[61] Yet it would be equally incorrect to discount ideology in driving the exiles' activities in divided Europe. In a phenomenon seen in many diasporic communities, the Russians compensated for their distance from the homeland by clinging all the more firmly to their convictions about it.[62] It makes most sense to posit that high-minded nationalism and unprincipled self-promotion coexisted among the exiles and sometimes fed into each other.

The secretive and scandal-filled nature of exile politics demands careful recon-struction of events using varied sources. Invaluable is documentation from US intelligence agencies, including recently declassified files of the CIA and the US army's Counter Intelligence Corps (CIC).[63] An equally important (and widely dispersed) body of sources comes from the émigré side and includes correspond-ence, the minutes of meetings of political organizations, and propaganda mater-ials, as well as published journals, newspapers, and memoirs. Finally, this study

---

[59] For a useful discussion, see Andrew Paul Janco, "Soviet 'Displaced Persons' in Europe, 1941–1951," PhD diss., University of Chicago, 2012, 85–6, 173–8.

[60] In particular, this study gives little credence to memoirs written by émigrés after being arrested by Soviet security forces. Cf. E. I. Divnich, *NTS, nam pora obiasnit'sia!* (New York: Izd. "Sootechestven-niki," 1968).

[61] This is from a letter of A. G. Nerianin-Aldan, as cited in Antoshin, *Rossiiskie emigranty*, 138.

[62] Robin Cohen, *Global Diasporas: an Introduction* (Hoboken, NJ: Taylor & Francis, 1997), 180.

[63] Many of the CIA sources employed here were released in response to the 1998 Nazi War Crimes Disclosure Act. See the list of archives cited in the bibliography.

draws on German state archives—mostly the holdings of West German state bodies that interacted with the exiles and of the East German Ministry of State Security that combatted them—as well as a much smaller range of British and Soviet archival sources.

Inevitably, a historian's source base poses distinctive challenges. CIA sources consist mostly of operational plans and reports from the field, both of which were shaped by bureaucratic interests—which, one might add, are themselves hard to reconstruct given the frequent redaction of documents. Unlike the CIA, the CIC in Germany focused on gathering information on the émigrés rather than utilizing them for covert operations, and therefore its files allow better reconstruction of the exile scene. Yet the information conveyed in CIC sources is often inconclusive or ambiguous.[64] After World War II, agents of the CIC were overburdened by the momentous tasks of denazifying German society, fighting crime, and screening immigrants to the United States. In this context, investigating the secretive and fast-changing émigré scene was difficult, especially as most CIC agents did not speak Russian.[65]

No less problematic are sources generated by the exiles themselves. While providing a much-needed counterpoint to the perspectives of non-exile observers and actors, documents penned by exiles are flavored with the conflictual and sometimes defamatory style of émigré politics. For their part, Soviet intelligence documents pertaining to the Russian exiles remain largely inaccessible, meaning that one is often compelled to make educated guesses about Soviet espionage activities in the anti-communist émigré organizations.[66] Avoiding overreliance on any one source base and juxtaposing the different kinds of sources available are essential tasks in order to provide a reliable account.

This book is structured around the different stages of the Russians émigrés' interaction with US power.[67] The first chronological–thematic section explores activities of the main movements of Russian exiles in occupied and war-torn Germany in the late 1940s: the Whites (old-regime figures who left Russia after the revolutions of 1917), old socialists (former rebels against both the tsars and Lenin), Vlasovites (followers of A. A. Vlasov, a Soviet general who formed a Russian liberation army under Hitler), and "Solidarists" (members of the

---

[64] On the CIC International Records Repository sources, see Richard Breitman and Norman J. W. Goda, *Hitler's Shadow: Nazi War Criminals, U.S. Intelligence, and the Cold War* (Washington, DC: National Archives and Records Administration, 2010), 1–3.

[65] Holian, *Between National Socialism and Soviet Communism*, 50–1, and James L. Gilbert, et al., *In the Shadow of the Sphinx: A History of Army Counterintelligence* (Belvoir, VA: History Office, Office of Strategic Management and Information, US Army Intelligence and Security Command, 2005), 90, http://permanent.access.gpo.gov/lps103181/GPO_Army_318-530.pdf, accessed February 27, 2016.

[66] I learned of the availability of some KGB sources relevant to the topic in the Sectoral State Archive of the Security Service of Ukraine (*Haluzevyi derzhavnyi arkhiv Sluzhby Bezpeky Ukrainy*) after completing this book.

[67] It is worth stressing that the book does not aspire to provide a complete history of émigré life in the decades in question and passes over crucial questions such as intellectual developments and the Orthodox Church abroad. For a more comprehensive approach, see Antoshin, *Rossiiskie emigranty*.

Natsional'no-trudovoi soiuz or National Labor Alliance, a far-right exile group of interwar origins). As sustained backing for émigré anti-communists was not yet forthcoming from a US intelligence system that was in a state of postwar transformation, important roles in exile affairs fell to transnational intermediaries, people able to connect exiles to outside communities such as the German intelligence operatives of the already mentioned Gehlen Organization and elderly Russian socialists in America.

The narrative then moves to exploring the major US covert actions that utilized Russian and Soviet exiles. Receiving extended treatment is a major US project to unify Russian and other Soviet exiles into a single political center in order to challenge the legitimacy of the Soviet regime from abroad. Separate chapters reconsider different aspects of this project: émigré influence on the generation of OPC-CIA plans (which produced the already mentioned Amcomlib), the negotiations between émigré groups that broke down amid debates over Russian nationhood and empire, and the subsequent development of a more US-centered approach to Russian-language psychological warfare, as seen in Radio Liberty, the CIA-backed radio broadcaster to the Soviet Union. The narrative then turns to other CIA covert operations that drew on the Russians in Germany, including the infiltration of parachuted agents into the USSR, propaganda operations based in divided Berlin, and the recruitment and utilization of Soviet defectors. Taken together, these chapters present the exile operational front as a quagmire, as heady plans to subvert the USSR from abroad gave way to more calibrated efforts to harass, confuse, and merely embarrass the Soviet opponent.

Part IV explores the reasons for the sharp, although not complete, curtailment of CIA funding for Russian exile organizations in the late 1950s and early 1960s. Chapters examine two factors that damaged the political fortunes of the Russian exiles: the Soviet "return to the homeland" campaign that served as a psychological warfare offensive to intimidate and demoralize anti-communist Russians, and the shifting positions of the West German state toward CIA operations carried out on its soil. In the 1960s, émigré anti-communism in Germany was in decline, increasingly viewed by outsiders as irrelevant to a Cold War that, at least in Europe, had taken on a more institutionalized and consolidated form.

*   *   *

The non-communist Russia that the émigrés embodied and sought to forge with American support did not come to fruition, at least not during the political careers—and sometimes lifetimes—of most of the exiles who championed it. To some extent, the US project of supporting and utilizing Russian anti-communists against their homeland was a mirage from the outset, a marriage of the Russocentric and overambitious schemes of a subset of American cold warriors and overheated émigré political passions. This would seem to situate the story in a common narrative that presents exile politics as an exercise in futility. As scholarly literature shows, political exiles in different places and times face a set of common problems: vulnerability to the whims of international affairs, the unrealistic schemes of émigré groups, the sometimes hollow claims of exiles to "speak for their fellow citizens at home," and the internal squabbling that has existed "within all political emigrations from time immemorial."[68]

Such a pessimistic verdict on exile politics is hardly satisfying. There is a degree of truth to the claim that diasporas are prone to a politics of unrealism and acrimony, a product of their powerlessness and distance from the homeland. However, stressing the predetermined nature of émigré failures means engaging in what Andre Liebich calls "anticipation," a reading of historical events only "in light of their future success" that prevents one from seeing them "from the inside."[69] When severed from a teleological perspective, events take on greater complexity. In the story that follows, the exiles' engagement with American, German, or other backers and sympathizers contained moments of mutual influence as well as conflict, of resilience together with hopelessness, and of adaptation along with disaster—all of which render the appeal to "immemorial" dilemmas out of place.

Stressing the political impotence of diasporas also overlooks the underlying significance of émigré anti-communism in the Cold War. Whether treating it with enthusiasm, hostility, or mistrust, an array of policymakers, spies, and public figures on both sides of the Iron Curtain took exile politics seriously and invested resources in it. And for good reason. The controversies and struggles within and surrounding the Russian émigré milieu went to the core of the Cold War situation and potential means of resolving it: the allegiance (or lack thereof) of the Russian people toward communism, the viability of Russian empire in an imagined post-Soviet space, the legacies of revolutions and wars in twentieth-century Russia, the status of divided Germany as a playing field for competing superpowers, and, more basically, the promise and pitfalls of pursuing covert action and psychological warfare as part of great power policy. That these problems caused acrimony and political paralysis demonstrated the exiles' importance rather than their marginality. The exiles and their visions of liberated Russia constituted a meaningful sub-front in the wider Cold War, as the superpowers became entangled in the internal concerns of a troubled diaspora.

---

[68] A. Ross Johnson, *Radio Free Europe and Radio Liberty: The CIA Years and Beyond* (Washington, DC: Woodrow Wilson Center Press, 2010), 18. Useful literature includes Kirsty Carpenter and Philip Mansel (eds.), *The French Émigrés in Europe and the Struggle against Revolution, 1789–1814* (New York: St. Martin's Press, 1999), and Shain, *The Frontier of Loyalty*.

[69] Liebich, *From the Other Shore*, 2.

PART I

THE MANY FACES OF RUSSIAN ANTI-COMMUNISM

1

A Fissile National Community

The Political World of Russian Émigrés

Andrei Georgievich Nerianin-Aldan was a product of the sharp historical turns of twentieth-century Eastern Europe. Born into a working-class family in the Ural region, Nerianin fought in the Civil War as a Red Army soldier and rose up the military ranks in the interwar years, reaching the position of Chief of Staff in the 22nd Army in 1941. After being captured by German forces in November 1941 during the chaos of Operation Barbarossa, Nerianin eagerly took up work for the Germans, doing analytical work for the Wehrmacht and later for the Abwehr intelligence agency.[1] After the war, Nerianin came to the attention of Soviet repatriation officials while in a displaced-persons camp in Germany. To evade extradition to the Soviet authorities, he forged his birth certificate to adopt the identity of M. A. Aldan, a Polish farmer, and went undercover. Within a few years, Nerianin-Aldan had taken up work for "U. S. intelligence agencies in [the] capacity of instructor, researcher, and consultant on questions pertaining to the Armed Forces of the USSR."[2]

The dramatic twists in Nerianin's story reflected the chaotic history that forged the post-Second-World-War Russian diaspora. Regardless of when and why they had left the homeland, Russian exiles were products of war, revolution, and upheaval in Russia during the first half of the twentieth century. Having come of age either in revolutionary Russia or in the fully developed Stalinist state, the émigrés were then transplanted abroad—sometimes voluntarily and sometimes not—and forced to adapt to trying conditions in foreign lands which were themselves undergoing great instability in the period. Nerianin's experience of serving the Soviet, Nazi, and American military government regimes in the course of a mere decade was only one variant of the ways conflicts within and outside

---

[1] See the published interrogations of Nerianin by the Germans in Igor' Petrov and Oleg Beyda, "Pervyi god plena polkovnika Nerianina," pts. 1–2, *Live Journal*, March 1, 2015, at http://labas. livejournal.com/1097511.html, accessed July 1, 2017. See also the list of war criminals and persons who collaborated with the enemy in the US zone of occupation in Germany, translated note from General Chuikov, May 13, 1949, 9, in Georgetown University Archives and Special Collections, Robert F. Kelley Papers (hereinafter Kelley Papers), box 5, fol. 6.

[2] Charles T. O'Connell, "The Munich Institute for the Study of the USSR: Origin and Social Composition," *The Carl Beck Papers in Russian and East European Studies*, no. 808., Pittsburgh, 1992, 18–19.

Cold War Exiles and the CIA: Plotting to Free Russia. Benjamin Tromly, Oxford University Press (2019). © Benjamin Tromly.
DOI: 10.1093/oso/9780198840404.001.0001

their homeland shaped the exiles' biographies. Indeed, the exiles understood that they lived in extraordinary times, and sometimes even grew used to it. As an émigré political activist commented, "we [the émigrés] are the children of an abnormal life, so we cannot strive for a normal existence here abroad." He continued that it was "easier on one's soul" that one lived without being able to foresee the future beyond a few months.[3]

This chapter presents the ideologies and parties that dominated the émigré milieu as well as the myriad historical pathways that gave rise to them. Although many members of the Russian diaspora did not engage in organized politics— whether out of a focus on immediate problems or because they preferred cultural, mutual aid or civil society activities—a determined minority always strove to fight communism from abroad.[4] Within this politicized émigré substrata, four ideological camps figured most prominently during the Cold War: the Whites, socialists, Vlasovites, and Solidarists. One cannot refer to these categories using more concrete terms such as "organizations" or even "movements," as each included multiple and sometimes mutually hostile organizations at various points of time. As one American observer explained, the Russian émigré scene was a political "morass" marked by "a bewildering array of splinter groups and splinters off splinter groups."[5] Nevertheless, the four camps reflected distinct ideological positions, which differed according to both left–right considerations customary to modern politics as well as to less commonly known positions on Russia's national identity and position in the world.[6]

Why were these specific ideologies dominant in the Russian anti-communist milieu? As Laurie Manchester has argued, the identities of Russian exiles were dynamic, as individuals were "forced to continually reassess their ethnicity" in light of experience abroad and contact with other ethnic groups.[7] Following this insight, this chapter explores how émigré political movements and ideologies reflected the makeup and experiences of the Russian diaspora. Each political

---

[3] Unidentified NTS member in Germany to A. N. Artemov, Archiv der Forschungsstelle Osteuropa an der Universität Bremen (hereinafter FSO), 01–098 Tarasova, kor. 38–40.

[4] On the determination of some Russian organizations to "stay out of politics," see Negotiations for an Effective Partnership: Study of the Negotiations between the American Committee for Liberation from Bolshevism and Leaders of the Emigration from the USSR to Create a Central Émigré Organization for Anti-Bolshevik Activity, 2–3, in Hoover Institution Archives and Library (HILA), Arch Puddington Collection, box 27, fol. 5.

[5] Sig Mickelson, America's Other Voice: The Story of Radio Free Europe and Radio Liberty (New York: Praeger, 1983), 63.

[6] The four trends discussed here do not represent an exhaustive list of anti-Soviet positions available to Russian exiles, let alone take account of pro-Soviet perspectives in the emigration. For instance, I bypass anarchist and Trotskyist movements, which had no influence in the US-funded sphere under discussion here. On the remnants of Russian anarchism, see A. V. Antoshin, Rossiiskie emigranty v usloviiakh "kholodnoi voiny" (seredina 1940-kh-seredina-1960-kh gg.) (Ekaterinburg: Izd. Ural'skogo universiteta, 2008), 132–4, 656–7.

[7] Laurie Manchester, "How Statelessness Can Force Refugees to Redefine Their Ethnicity: What can be Learned from Russian Émigrés Dispersed to Six Continents in the Inter-war Period?" Immigrants & Minorities 34, no. 1 (2016): 83.

trend examined here had its own bases of supporters in the Cold War period, people who often (but not always) shared similar formative experiences of Russia prior to emigration, departure from the homeland, and experiences once abroad. Connecting ideologies to émigré experiences is a difficult but necessary task, for it sheds light on the emigration's defining trait of political division. The awkward collective moniker of the "Russian emigration" papered over the simultaneous existence of several Russias in exile, whose interplay and conflict sometimes gave émigré politics of the Cold War period the appearance of being a displaced civil war.

The First Wave: The Whites

The Russian emigration was born of tragedy. The Russian Revolution and Civil War (1918–22) sparked a massive exodus of subjects from the old tsarist empire, who refused to live under a hated communist regime.[8] This so-called "first wave"—sometimes also dubbed the "White emigration" because it included many fighters and sympathizers of the anti-Bolshevik armies of the Civil War period—scattered for the most part across France, Germany, Czechoslovakia, the Baltic States, the Balkans, and Manchuria.[9] While experiences differed widely based on local conditions, most émigrés faced a common lot of statelessness, impoverishment, social isolation, and the nostalgia-ridden sense of despair peculiar to exiles. For years, the Russians believed that their exile was temporary, as conveyed by the (probably) apocryphal stories about émigrés who kept their suitcases packed in anticipation of the Bolsheviks' imminent overthrow. When the communist regime unexpectedly stabilized, the exiles were left with little more than hazy "hopes of future redemption" and "myths of past happiness."[10]

The cultural achievements of the exiles in interwar Europe tempered their growing pessimism somewhat. Precisely because they hoped to return home, the first wave struggled valiantly to maintain Russian culture abroad. The first wave produced a panoply of influential writers, philosophers, and cultural figures.[11]

---

[8] A well-reasoned estimate places the outflow of Russians from these years at roughly 800,000 people. Marc Raeff, *Russia Abroad: a Cultural History of the Russian Emigration, 1919–1939* (New York: Oxford University Press, 1990), 202–3.
[9] Given the existence of Russian communities abroad before 1917, it is a misnomer to call the revolutionary-period exiles the *first* wave. However, I follow convention by using the term. Notably, Russians in the United States hailed mostly from the pre-1917 period, as strict immigration quotas and the émigré desire to stay close to Russia lowered the numbers of first-wave immigrants to the country. Raeff, *Russia Abroad*, 4–5.
[10] Robert C. Williams, "European Political Emigrations: A Lost Subject," *Comparative Studies in Society and History* 12, no. 2 (1970): 142.
[11] While the literature on Russian émigré culture is too vast to cite, important recent work includes Matthew Lee Miller, *The American YMCA and Russian Culture: The Preservation and Expansion of Orthodox Christianity, 1900–1940* (Lanham: Lexington Books, 2013).

Seen more broadly, the Russian exiles developed colonies that could claim to continue and even develop different directions in pre-revolutionary life and culture: Berlin served as a base for the far-right and far-left political movements in exile, in particular in the 1920s; Belgrade was the center for old regime elites and especially former combatants of the Civil War; Prague continued Russian academic traditions; and Paris was the hub for Russian arts and culture, gaining the reputation of the capital of "Russia abroad."[12] In part due to these well-developed centers of Russian life, the first wave gave rise to the notion of a single Russian "emigration" (*emigratsiia*) as an alternative, anti-communist nation beyond Soviet borders.[13]

Given the first wave's distinctive mission of maintaining an uncorrupted, un-Sovietized Russian nation, it is only natural that some exiles pursued anti-communist political activities. However, in contrast to the first wave's cultural and intellectual achievements, émigré political life was filled with crisis and disappointment. As Robert Williams has explained, the passage of time is toxic to all political émigrés, who succumb to "the pressure of old issues, abrasive personalities, and new movements" during a protracted sojourn from the homeland.[14] Even against this background, the Russians were poorly equipped for exile. The closing of borders and growing xenophobia of Stalin's rule severed the exiles' ties to the homeland almost completely.[15] Moreover, the exiles lacked a government-in-exile or even a commonly accepted center of authority. In practice, exile politics reproduced the bitter political divisions of late tsarist Russia and the revolutions of 1917 in their far-flung colonies abroad, even as new political movements emerged to create new rifts.

The fractured state of first-wave politics becomes clear when one considers the monarchist movement in exile. Although a majority of the first-wave exiles probably supported a restoration of the Romanov dynasty, it was unable to agree on what form it should take. In the 1920s, the Russian monarchist camp broke into factions surrounding dueling Romanov claimants to the throne, a rift which invoked both European allegiances (German vs. French orientations) and political principles (the "legitimist" stance of supporting a Romanov pretender as emperor versus the "non-predeterminist" position that constitutional matters should be decided in the future).[16] And if their internal divisions were not strong

---

[12] On these different émigré communities, see Karl Schlögel (ed.), *Der Grosse Exodus: Die Russische Emigration und ihre Zentren, 1917 bis 1941* (Munich: C. H. Beck, 1994); Robert C. Williams, *Culture in Exile: Russian Emigres in Germany, 1881–1941* (Ithaca, NY: Cornell University Press, 1972), and Catherine Andreyev and Ivan Savický, *Russia Abroad: Prague and the Russian Diaspora, 1918–1938* (New Haven: Yale University Press, 2004).

[13] General studies are Raeff, *Russia Abroad*, and John Glad, *Russia Abroad: Writers, History, Politics* (Tenafly, NJ, and Washington, DC: Hermitage Publishers & Birchbark Press, 1999).

[14] Williams, "European Political Emigrations": 144.

[15] On the isolation of the USSR in the Stalin years, see Eric Lohr, *Russian Citizenship from Empire to Soviet Union* (Cambridge, MA: Harvard University Press, 2012), 132–76.

[16] See Williams, *Culture in Exile*, 159–80.

enough, monarchists of all stripes had difficulty shaking the impression that they pursued a "program of a simple restoration without innovation or even analytic reflection," which convinced many exiles, including significant numbers of veterans of the White armies, that monarchism was a blind alley for Russian political development.[17]

Despite their lack of cohesion, the Whites attempted to fight back against the communist regime. Plans hatched to foment revolution in Russia from abroad, though, were thwarted by Soviet spy networks abroad, which abducted and spirited to the Soviet Union two successive heads of the main association of White veterans, the Russian All-Military Union (*Russkii Obshche-Voinskii Soiuz* or ROVS).[18] In the face of such fiascos, most of the first wave held to the cultural task of preserving Russian life abroad rather than pursuing the dangerous and chimerical goal of toppling the Bolsheviks. Expressing the same sense of demoralization, some political thinkers of the first wave responded to the surprising tenacity of the Bolshevik regime and its successful reconstitution of a multiethnic empire by pursuing ideological reconciliation with communism.[19]

The Whites' mission of overthrowing communism gained new impetus with World War II. Already during the march to war in the late 1930s, a boisterous debate emerged in émigré circles over where Russian interests would lie in the anticipated conflict. Disillusioned by the perceived betrayal of the White forces by their French and British allies after the First World War, increasing numbers of émigrés looked to Nazi Germany as a potential supporter of Russian interests.[20] These so-called "defeatists" saw the anticipated war between Germany and the USSR as an opportunity to revive the White cause of the Civil War under German auspices, unfurling figurative banners that had long since gathered dust. In stark contrast, a host of considerations inspired other émigrés to take a "defensist," pro-Soviet position toward the war: an aversion to

---

[17] Claudia Weiss, "Russian Political Parties in Exile," *Kritika* 5, no. 1 (2004): 228. See also Paul Robinson, *The White Russian Army in Exile, 1920–1941* (Oxford: Clarendon Press, 2002), 113–29.

[18] Ibid., 131–48. The two figures were Aleksandr Pavlovich Kutepov (abducted in 1930) and Evegenii-Ludvig Karlovich Miller (kidnapped in 1937).

[19] Sergei Glebov, "The Mongol–Bolshevik Revolution: Eurasianist Ideology in Search for an Ideal past," *Journal of Eurasian Studies* 2, no. 2 (2011): 103–14; Hilde Hardeman, *Coming to Terms with the Soviet Regime: The "Changing Signposts" Movement among Russian Emigrés in the Early 1920s* (DeKalb: Northern Illinois University Press, 1994), and Mirey Massip, *Istina—doch' vremeni. Alexandr Kazem-Bek i russkaia emigratsiia na zapade* (Moscow: Iazyki slavianskoi kul'tury, 2010).

[20] On the perception of betrayal among the Whites, see Anatol Shmelev, "Gallipoli to Golgotha: Remembering the Internment of the Russian White Army at Gallipoli, 1920–3," in Jenny Macleod (ed.), *Defeat and Memory: Cultural Histories of Military Defeat in the Modern Era* (New York: Palgrave Macmillan, 2008), 195–213. Russian engagement with the European far right took many forms other than support of Nazism, a point underscored in pieces by Marlene Laruelle and Martin Beisswenger in Marlene Laruelle (ed.), *Entangled Far Rights: A Russian-European Intellectual Romance in the Twentieth Century* (Pittsburgh: University of Pittsburgh Press, 2018), 47–82.

fascism, the rejection of foreign intervention as such, or hope that the war would spark a liberalization of Stalin's rule.[21]

The Axis invasion of the USSR in 1941 gave a strong advantage to the defeatist position within Russian communities in Europe. In Paris, a small minority of Russian exiles hewed to defensism, for instance by joining anti-Nazi resistance movements, but the clear majority hoped to take advantage of what seemed to be the impending collapse of the hated communist regime.[22] The White officers who volunteered in droves to take part in the liberation of their homeland were quickly disappointed. The Nazis rebuffed Russian exile volunteers for the same reasons they had refused the advances of pro-German and fascist Russian exile organizations prior to the war: they saw Russians as racial inferiors and had no intention of allowing the restoration of a strong Russian state.[23] That perhaps some 20,000 old émigrés nevertheless collaborated with Germany in various capacities—as appointed leaders of Russian populations in different countries, translators in the Wehrmacht, intelligence operatives for the Abwehr military intelligence organization, or even in specially formed military units—was testimony to their anti-Soviet zeal and, in a minority of cases, sympathy for Nazi ideological goals.[24]

The failure of émigré collaborationism soon became overshadowed by the reversal of fortunes on the Eastern Front, which brought about a widespread uprooting of the Russian diaspora. One by one, interwar centers of Russian settlement came under Soviet control and sent streams of their exile populations to the West: the Baltic States in the first stage of the war, and Eastern Europe, Southern Europe, and Harbin in Manchuria in its final months. Meanwhile, Russian life in Western Europe went into decline after the war, with the Paris colony suffering from the destruction of the Russian Jewish population as part of the Holocaust

[21]   Robert H. Johnston, "The Great Patriotic War and the Russian Exiles in France," *Russian Review* 35, no. 3 (1976): 303–21, and Sergei Karpenko, *Mezhdu Rossiei i Stalinym: rossiiskaia emigratsiia i vtoraia mirovaia voina* (Moscow: RGGU, 2004), 9–21.

[22]   Mikhail Iakunin and D. Iu. Guzevich, *Zakat Rossiiskoi emigratsii vo Frantsii v 1940-e gody: istoriia i pamiat'* (Paris-Novosibirsk: Assosiatsiia "Zarubezhnaia Rossiia," 2012), 22. Pro-German moods were even stronger in the Russian colony of Yugoslavia. Aleksei Belkov, "Nachalo Velikoi Otechestvennoi voiny v otrazhenii russkoi emigrantskoi pressy v Iugoslavii," in A. Martynov (ed.), *Istoriia otechestvennoi kollaboratsii: materialy i issledovaniia* (Moscow: Staraia Basmannaia, 2017), 274–83.

[23]   Iu. S. Tsurganov, *Neudavshiisia revansh: belaia emigratsiia vo vtoroi mirovoi voine* (Moscow: Intrada, 2001), 56.

[24]   Ibid., ch. 5; Wim Coudenys, "Russian Collaboration in Belgium during World War II: The Case of Jurij L. Vojcehovskij," *Cahiers Du Monde Russe* 43, no. 2/3 (2002): 479–514; Oleg Beyda, " 'Iron Cross of the Wrangel's Army': Russian Emigrants as Interpreters in the Wehrmacht," *Journal of Slavic Military Studies* 27, no. 3 (2014): 430–48, and K. L. Kotiukov, "Rossiiskie voennye emigranty i 'porazhencheskoe' dvizhenie v period vtoroi mirovoi voiny," in Iu. A. Poliakov et al. (eds.), *Istoriia rossiiskogo zarubezh'hia: emigratsiia iz SSSR-Rossii, 1941–2001 gg.: sbornik stat'ei* (Moscow: Rossiiskaia akademiia nauk, Institut rossiiskoi istorii, 2007), 24–43. Explicitly fascist Russian movements were strongest in Japanese-occupied Manchuria and the United States, not in Europe. John J. Stephan, *The Russian Fascists: Tragedy and Farce in Exile, 1925–1945* (New York: Harper & Row, 1978). On the *Aufbau Vereinigung* ("Reconstruction Organization") that was close to Hitler in the early 1920s, see Michael Kellogg, *The Russian Roots of Nazism: White Émigrés and the Making of National Socialism, 1917–1945* (Cambridge, UK, and New York: Cambridge University Press, 2004).

and the surge of Soviet influence in the now left-leaning country.[25] Although small communities of old émigrés remained in Paris, Brussels, and elsewhere in Western Europe after the war, the interwar emigration as a coherent community was increasingly a "vanished world," with New York eventually replacing Paris as the center of first-wave culture.[26]

Despite their woeful wartime experiences, the Whites would become a backbone of postwar Russian anti-communism. In the immediate wake of victory, it is true, some émigrés in Western Europe considered repatriation to the USSR—or, less radically, some form of ideological reconciliation with it. According to a French police report, even many "irreconcilable anti-communists" in Russian Paris "could not resist admiring the successes of the Red Army."[27] But such moods were short-lived. The onset of the Cold War and the sorry fate of Soviet repatriates—many of whom were subjected to repression upon return—soon swung exile opinion back toward its traditional anti-communism. In Europe, the center of the émigré right became West Germany, where the Russian monarchist and conservative circles had long had a presence and whose ranks were now bolstered by White exiles fleeing from the Soviet advance into the Baltic countries, East-Central Europe, and the Balkans. Here first-wave exiles met a very different cohort of Russians: former Soviet subjects who had also been displaced by the war.

The Old Socialists

The Whites were not the only Russians to oppose Lenin's communist regime or to find themselves in exile after the Civil War. When the Bolsheviks took power in 1917 and solidified it during the Civil War, they overthrew a panoply of democratic movements, some of which had become active during the brief period of constitutional rule in that year between Nicholas II's abdication and the October Revolution. Important in the Cold War scene were exiles belonging to the two major socialist movements banished from Lenin's fledgling state: the Menshevik

---

[25] Iakunin and Guzevich, *Zakat Rossiiskoi emigratsii*, 13–14. The understudied destruction of Russian-Jewish exiles during the war is discussed in Leonid Livak, "The Two Solitudes of Russia Abroad: Russian and Russian-Jewish Writers in the Aftermath of World War II," paper presented at the National Convention of the Association for Slavic, East European, and Eurasian Studies, Philadelphia, PA, November 2015.

[26] The Russian population of France was 175,000 in 1930, but just 35,000 Russians remained in Paris in 1951. Raeff, *Russia Abroad*, 203, and Robert H. Johnston, *New Mecca, New Babylon: Paris and the Russian Exiles, 1920–1945* (Kingston: McGill-Queen's University Press, 1988), 182.

[27] D. Iu. Guzevich et al. (ed. and comp.), "Russkaia emigratsiia vo Frantsii v 1940-e, 1 chast': Politseiskii otchet 1948 goda 'La colonie russe de Paris' ('Russkaia koloniia v Parizhe')," *Diaspora*, vol. 8 (2007): 412. On the pro-Soviet Union of Russian Patriots and first-wave exiles in France, see A. V. Antoshin, *Russkii Parizh za Sovetskii Soiuz? Ideinye iskaniia russkikh emigrantov vo Frantsii (vtoraia polovina 1940-kh gg.)*. Ekaterinburg: Izd. Ural'skogo universiteta, 2017).

faction of the Russian Social Democratic Labor Party, which had espoused a more gradualist alternative to Leninism after the Russian Marxists' split early in the century, and the Socialist Revolutionary Party (SRs), an organization distinguished from the Russian Marxists by its attachment to the peasantry as participants in a "toilers' revolution." Famously assigned by Lev Davidovich Trotskii to the "dustbin of history," the Russian democratic socialists rose from the ashes to reassert their political importance during the Cold War, albeit now from outside the homeland.

The continued existence of a Russian democratic movement in exile was anything but inevitable. In the 1920s, democratic émigrés had failed to construct a unified front against Bolshevism.[28] Moreover, during the Civil War and beyond the exiled socialists struggled to find a way to oppose Bolshevism without siding with the counterrevolutionary Whites, one example of which was the Mensheviks' futile attempt to organize legal opposition to the Bolsheviks through the grassroots democracy of the Soviets.[29] Even after being persecuted and then driven from Russia by the Bolsheviks, the Mensheviks and Socialist Revolutionaries continued to resist breaking ranks with the communist experiment decisively on the plane of ideas, with the Mensheviks holding to the so-called "Martov line" of espousing reformism rather than revolution in the USSR for virtually the entire interwar period.[30]

The leftists showed considerable tenacity abroad, nevertheless. Most of all, the socialists distinguished themselves in intellectual discourse and publishing. Prominent SRs were active in organizing and editing émigré journals, while the Mensheviks offered sophisticated analyses of the Soviet scene in their redoubtable journal *Sotsialisticheskii vestnik* ("The Socialist Herald").[31] While such activities hardly threatened the Kremlin, they still ensured the survival of the non-Bolshevik Russian socialists. The same effect came from the socialists' allegiance to the international left. Help from socialists or democrats in countries of exile helped ease the myriad difficulties posed by the first-wave socialists' uprooted existence.[32] Most of all, alliances with the American left helped many Russian socialists to escape the European continent to the United States in the early phases of World War II, and to adjust to their new place of exile once they arrived. In contrast to

---

[28] Jane Burbank, *Intelligentsia and Revolution: Russian Views of Bolshevism, 1917–1922* (New York & Oxford: Oxford University Press, 1989), 113–69.

[29] André Liebich, *From the Other Shore: Russian Social Democracy after 1921* (Cambridge, MA: Harvard University Press, 1997), 73–80. On the SR leader Viktor Mikhailovich Chernov's call for a "Third Way" between Lenin and the Whites, see Scott B. Smith, *Captives of Revolution: The Socialist Revolutionaries and the Bolshevik Dictatorship, 1918–1923* (Pittsburgh, PA: University of Pittsburgh Press, 2011), 214.

[30] This position was associated with Menshevik leader Iulii Osipovich Martov. Liebich, *From the Other Shore*, 83–4.

[31] On the role of different SRs in émigré publishing, see Weiss, "Russian Political Parties", 224.

[32] While the SRs lacked close ties to socialist parties in Germany and elsewhere, they cooperated with democrats in Czechoslovakia. Andreyev and Savický, *Russia Abroad*, 74–9.

the myriad sufferings and disappointments of their co-nationals in Europe, the socialists who managed to flee the continent had the privilege of viewing World War II from afar.

The relevance of the non-Bolshevik left to the Cold War came not just from survival but from ideological evolution. In particular, several socialists moved steadily to the right in the interwar and wartime years, setting the stage for participation in the American Cold War. Most important were a trio of Mensheviks who would play particularly important roles in US émigré plans: Boris Ivanovich Nikolaevskii, David Iul'evich Dalin, and Rafael Abramovich Rein (commonly known as Rafael Abramovich). Despite their common political trajectories, the three were very different. Nikolaevskii was the son of a Siberian parish priest and a self-taught archivist and historian; Dalin, from a wealthy Jewish family, earned a doctorate degree in Germany and spent years outside the Menshevik orbit; and Abramovich, initially a member of the Yiddish-speaking Marxist General Jewish Labor Bund in Lithuania, Poland, and Russia, was renowned for his personal and diplomatic skills.

What united the three men was their uncompromising hostility to the Soviet state. The trio's shift to the right had personal sources: all of them had been incarcerated in and then expelled from Soviet Russia in the early 1920s, while Abramovich's son was kidnapped and killed by communists during the Spanish Civil War.[33] More fundamentally, the three thinkers had developed anti-communist positions in response to Stalinist policies of the 1930s, particularly the Great Terror and the Nazi–Soviet pact of 1939. By the time of World War II, the three thinkers, though not rejecting social democracy as such, had decided that the USSR was "totalitarian" and therefore comparable to fascism.[34]

American exile gave Russian socialists a new lease on life in the postwar period. The Mensheviks and SRs took positions during World War II that bolstered their reputations in the United States. While supporting the Allied war effort and the alliance with Stalin, Nikolaevskii and Dalin offered criticisms of the Soviet dictator in the late phases of the war, a period when US governing circles and public opinion were still committed to peaceful relations with the Soviets.[35] When tension set in between the US and the USSR soon after the war, the émigrés' criticisms of Stalin appeared to be prophetic, helping to cement their reputations

[33] Ladis K. Kristof, "B. I. Nicolaevsky: The Formative Years," in Boris I. Nicolaevsky et al., *Revolution and Politics in Russia: Essays in Memory of B.I. Nicolaevsky* (Bloomington, IN: Indiana University Press, 1973), 22–32 and Liebich, *From the Other Shore*, 261–3.

[34] Liebich, *From the Other Shore*, 270–86, and Iu. G. Fel'shtinksii and G. I. Cherniavskii, *Cherez veka i strany: B. I. Nikolaevskii. Sud'ba men'shevika, istorika, sovetologa, glavnogo svidetelia epokhal'nykh izmenenii v zhizni Rossii pervoi poloviny XX veka* (Moscow: Izd. Tsentr-poligraf, 2012), 356–74.

[35] A. V. Antoshin, "Men'sheviki v emigratsii posle Vtoroi mirovoi voiny," *Otechestvennaia istoriia* 1 (2007): 102–3, and A. A. Goloseeva, "Sotsial'no-politicheskaia pozitsiia eserov v gody Vtoroi mirovoi voiny (po materialam emigrantskoi pressy v SShA)," *Klio* no. 10 (106) (2015): 33–40.

in American diplomatic and Russian-expert circles in their adoptive country.[36] The socialists' role in the postwar emigration would stem from their connections and reputations in the distant and, to exiles in Europe, unfamiliar superpower.

The Vlasovites

If World War II destroyed much of the first-wave diaspora in Europe, it also created a "second wave" of Russians abroad. Similar to their exile elders twenty years before, the new émigré generation owed its existence to political upheaval in the homeland—in this case, the bloodshed and turmoil of the Eastern Front in World War II. In numerical terms, the major tributaries of the wartime Russian cohort were Soviet prisoners of war and slave laborers (*Ostarbeiter*) taken from occupied territories, along with citizens of the USSR who had survived the brutal Nazi occupation there and then retreated to the West with the German armies.[37] Clearly, many second-wave exiles were victims rather than purveyors of Nazi actions in the East. However, the subset of second-wavers who took part in US-backed postwar exile politics stemmed overwhelmingly from the ranks of "collaborators," understood here in a loose and value-neutral sense of people who served a wartime enemy in an institutional or organized setting.[38]

By this definition, the scale of wartime collaboration by Soviet citizens was vast. The total number of Soviet citizens who joined German army and police organs alone was perhaps 1.6 million over the course of the war, a figure that included an unknown but surely substantial component of ethnic Russians.[39] Despite Hitler's rejection of the practice, the Wehrmacht began employing Soviet citizens from the very first weeks of Operation Barbarossa, mainly as support personnel (the so-called *Hiwis* or voluntary assistants). Within months, several uncoordinated experiments were being pursued by German officers to utilize the huge population

[36] André Liebich, "Mensheviks Wage the Cold War," *Journal of Contemporary History*. 30, no. 2 (Apr., 1995), 247–64.

[37] Estimates hold that less than half of the 5.7 million Soviet POWs in Axis custody survived the war. The best discussion of these victims of the Nazis is P. M. Polian, *Zhertvy dvukh diktatur: zhizn', trud, unizhenie i smert' sovetskikh voennoplennykh i ostarbaiterov na chuzhbine i na rodine* (Moscow: ROSSPEN, 2002).

[38] The term collaboration is a problematic one, as it carries powerful negative connotations of fascist ideology and unprincipled self-seeking. See Jan. T. Gross, "Themes for a Social History of War Experience and Collaboration," in István Deák et al. (eds.), *The Politics of Retribution in Europe: World War II and Its Aftermath* (Princeton, NJ: Princeton University Press, 2000), 23–32.

[39] For different calculations, see Rolf-Dieter Müller, *An der Seite der Wehrmacht: Hitlers ausländische Helfer beim "Kreuzzug gegen den Bolchewismus" 1941–1945* (Frankfurt: Fischer, 2010), 242, and A. V. Okorokov, *Antisovetskie voinskie formirovaniia v gody Vtoroi mirovoi voiny: monografiia* (Moscow: Voennyi Universitet, 2000), 59.

of Soviet POWs in such endeavors as anti-partisan formations and propaganda undertakings.[40] As the German war effort dragged on, the scope and range of institutional settings for such initiatives spread, with Soviet POWs coming to serve in auxiliary police units, in armed combat as Eastern troops of the Wehrmacht (*Osttruppen*), and in intelligence and propaganda work in institutions such as the Abwehr, Goebbels's Propaganda Ministry and Alfred Rosenberg's Ostministerium.[41]

The most important and also emblematic manifestation of Russian collaboration was the so-called Vlasov movement. Andrei Andreevich Vlasov was a Soviet general who participated in the defense of Moscow in 1941 and was taken prisoner months later when his army was surrounded on the Volkhov Front. Vlasov agreed to serve his captors, hoping to create a fighting force of POWs that might form the basis for Russian statehood in the event of Axis victory. However, Hitler's hostility to arming Russians meant that Vlasov's projected Russian Liberation Army (ROA) remained "mythical" for much of the conflict, a fiction the Germans exploited in their propaganda toward Russians in the Reich and, to a lesser extent, on occupied Soviet territories.[42] Only in 1944, with the Red Army moving toward German borders, did Hitler agree to give Vlasov the trappings of legitimacy in the form of a "Committee for Liberation of the Peoples of Russia" (KONR) and a few military divisions attached to it that were never brought to full capacity—one of several "pathetic and totally fictitious governments set up well past their sell-by date" by a Nazi leadership desperate to turn the tide on the Eastern Front.[43] Even then, the Nazis did not abandon racial hatred of their Russian helpers: a Russian propaganda worker attached to Army Group Center recalled that Russian soldiers were formed into Labor Battalions where they suffered hunger, disastrous living conditions, and frequent beatings.[44] While they served the Germans in far greater numbers than the first-wavers could, the displaced Soviet citizens

---

[40] Oleg Beyda and Igor Petrov, "The Soviet Union," in David Stahel (ed.), *Joining Hitler's Crusade: European Nations and the Invasion of the Soviet Union, 1941* (Cambridge and New York: Cambridge University Press, 2018), 369–425.

[41] Overall accounts of Soviet Russian collaboration are Müller, *An der Seite der Wehrmacht*, 204–26, and B. N. Kovalev, *Kollaboratsionizm v Rossii v 1941–1945 gg.: tipy i formy* (Novgorod: Novgorodskii Gosudarstvennyi Universitet imeni Iaroslava Mudrogo, 2009).

[42] Catherine Andreyev, *Vlasov and the Russian Liberation Movement: Soviet Reality and Émigré Theories* (New York: Cambridge University Press, 1987).

[43] Mark Mazower, *Hitler's Empire: How the Nazis Ruled Europe* (New York: Penguin Press, 2008), 466, and K. M. Aleksandrov, *Protiv Stalina: Vlasovtsy i vostochnye dobrovol'tsy vo vtoroi mirovoi voine: sbornik stat'ei i materialov* (St. Petersburg: Iunventa, 2003), 89–91. Future debates about Vlasov will be shaped by the recent publication of documents pertaining to the Vlasov Movement: A. N. Artizov et al. (eds.), *Vlasov: istoriia predatel'stva*, tom 1–2 (Moscow: ROSSPEN, 2015).

[44] I use the term Vlasovites (*vlasovtsy*) because it was often utilized at the time, including by the followers of Vlasov themselves. See the letter from Lt. Colonel Riehl to Commander in Chief, Group "Mitte," n.d. (1944), located in Special Investigation and Interrogation Report, Military Intelligence Service in Austria, December 16, 1946, 8–9, in National Archives and Records Administration (NARA), RG 319, Entry 134A, 22348387, 270/84/20/02, box 68 (hereinafter Vlassow Group).

faced the same exploitation and lack of agency that were the invariable fate of Russian collaborators under Hitler.

Why had Soviet citizens, including those who eventually ended up as cold warriors in the West, collaborated with such an odious wartime opponent as Nazi Germany? Writing after the war, anti-communist exiles stressed that collaboration had emerged from the widespread "defeatism" of Soviet society in 1941, the casting off of the hated Stalinist regime in favor of a yet unknown German one.[45] In the retelling of the war by postwar exiles, collaboration was a continuation of anti-communist resistance by other means, an attempt to "use" the Germans to pursue the struggle "against the Stalinist regime to liberate the homeland."[46]

The émigrés' narrative of defeatism needs to be approached critically. To be sure, defeatist and specifically anti-Soviet moods were a reality during the early phase of the German–Soviet war, as parts of Russian-Soviet society greeted the invading Germans eagerly, acting on previously concealed anti-Soviet convictions.[47] In a recent study, Mark Edele shows that defeatism also plagued the Red Army, as Soviet soldiers were more likely to desert to the opposing side of the front than any other combatants in World War II.[48] Yet defeatism and its concrete manifestations, such as willing surrender on the battlefield or deliberately falling under German occupation, did not necessarily translate into taking up active service of the Axis invaders. Moreover, the émigrés' emphasis on defeatism obscured a perhaps more important reason for active collaboration: the pursuit of self-preservation in the brutal conditions of POW camps and Nazi-occupied territory more generally. Simply put, many captured soldiers who collaborated with the Germans did so out of "fear" and "desire to avoid death by hunger," not due to ideological considerations—motivations, it is true, which were not mutually exclusive.[49]

For the people who would make up the second wave, the struggle for survival that characterized the war years extended far into the time of peace. At war's end, the western zones of Germany and Austria contained millions of Soviet citizens who had arrived there by any number of paths: as *Ostarbeiter*, as prisoners of war,

[45] Chapter 3 provides a critical discussion of second-wave historical memories of World War II.

[46] O. V. Budnitskii and G. S. Zelenina (eds.), *Svershilos'-prishli Nemtsy! Ideinyi kollaboratsionizm v SSSR v period Velikoi Otechestvennoi Voiny* (Moscow: ROSSPEN, 2014), 61.

[47] See the insightful discussion in O. V. Budnitskii, "The Great Patriotic War and Soviet Society: Defeatism, 1941–42," *Kritika* 15, no. 4 (2014): 767–97. Budnitskii sees defeatism as having been more widespread than previous scholarship has credited. Compare with the pieces collected in Robert W. Thurston and Bernd Bonwetsch (eds.), *The People's War: Responses to World War II in the Soviet Union* (Urbana, IL: University of Illinois Press, 2000).

[48] Mark Edele, *Stalin's Defectors: How Red Army Soldiers became Hitler's Collaborators, 1941–1945* (New York and Oxford: Oxford University Press, 2017), 21, 31–2.

[49] Beyda and Petrov, "The Soviet Union," 375; The Harvard Project on the Soviet Social System Online (hereinafter HPSSS), schedule B, vol. 11, case 382, 3, and Special investigation and Interrogation Report, Military Intelligence Service in Austria, December 16, 1946, 4, in Vlassow Group, fol. 1. Survival is a major theme of recent research on collaboration on the Eastern Front. Cf. Leonid Rein, *The Kings and the Pawns: Collaboration in Byelorussia during o* (New York: Berghahn Books, 2011), 17.

as collaborators of various kinds, or simply as refugees escaping with German forces toward the end of the conflict. Registered as displaced persons and confined to camps, the Soviet citizens in Germany were expected to return to their home country. Indeed, Stalin placed a high priority on the repatriation of displaced Soviet citizens after the war, convincing his allies in the anti-Hitler coalition at the Yalta Conference to return all such persons located on territory under their control.[50] Stalin surely had many reasons to pursue such an uncompromising position, including the need to address the massive death toll of the Soviet population during the war. Also indisputable is the fact that repatriation constituted an effort to enact vengeance against those who had served the enemy or had shown insufficient patriotism by merely falling into enemy hands. Accordingly, the Soviet authorities placed particular emphasis on repatriating members of the Vlasov forces and other Russians who had donned German uniforms, sending out teams of spies across Germany and Austria to locate them.[51] The punitive aspect of repatriation shaded into a wider effort on Stalin's part to shape postwar political realities abroad. As one repatriation officer told a US counterpart off the record, a high Soviet priority was bringing back to the homeland people who were "creating bad feelings against Russia not only among the Americans and British but also among all nations in Europe."[52] In other words, the Stalinist state sought to prevent the emergence of a postwar émigré population similar to that of the interwar period.

The anti-exile thrust of Stalinist repatriation was successful only in part. Within months of the armistice, well over two million Soviet DPs in Europe returned to the USSR, mostly voluntarily.[53] However, many others sought to avoid repatriation at all cost. Indeed, during several episodes when the US or British military forces rounded up and forcefully repatriated Soviet nationals to the East, some desperate individuals tried to take their lives before falling into the hands of Soviet authorities.[54]

Why were these Soviet citizens so eager to escape return to their homeland? Without a doubt, people who had collaborated in various capacities feared punishment. Recent research has shown that DPs' fears that return meant an automatic sentence to the Gulag were overblown, as administrative exile rather than incarceration in camps was a common punishment even for Soviet combatants

---

[50] P. M. Polian, *Deportiert nach Hause: Sowjetische Kriegsgefangene im "Dritten Reich" und ihre Repatriierung* (Munich: Oldenbourg, 2001), 60–9.

[51] See ROA officers' testimony in Report on non-Repatriates, CIC, n.d. (1945), 4–5, in NARA, RG 319, IRR, XEO22248, Russian non-Repatriates, obtained through FOIA request.

[52] Extract for File No. 700/4, Report # 18, 18 May 1946, in Vlassow Group, fol. 3. See also Polian, *Deportiert nach Hause*, 50, and Antoshin, *Rossiiskie emigranty*, 40.

[53] Janco, "Soviet 'Displaced Persons,'" 57.

[54] Anna Holian, *Between National Socialism and Soviet Communism: Displaced Persons in Postwar Germany* (Ann Arbor: University of Michigan Press, 2011), 108–19 and Mark R. Elliot, *Pawns of Yalta: Soviet Refugees and America's Role in their Repatriation* (Urbana, IL: University of Illinois Press, 1982).

in the Wehrmacht.[55] Yet collaborators' fear of retribution was well warranted, especially in light of the nature of Soviet repatriation, which featured the processing of returners through "filtration camps" run by security organs at the Soviet borders. Combined with fears of political persecution were quite different motivations to remain in the West, such as the expectation that postwar living standards would be better there than at home.[56] Finally, anti-communist organizations agitated against repatriation and might well have persuaded some DPs to remain in the West. For its part, the Soviet bureaucracy placed blame for DPs' refusal to return solely on anti-communists, drawing on the ideologically tinted argument that Soviet people would naturally wish to return to the USSR if only left to their own devices.[57] In fact, many Soviet "non-returners" (*nevozvrashchentsy*), as they came to be called, were driven by some combination of fear, the lure of capitalist wealth, and hostility to communism.

Much clearer than the motivations for non-return was its outcome. By evading repatriation, Soviet Russians defied the socialist state and became its enemies. Faced with the threat of repatriation, the second-wavers resorted to subterfuge, refusing to register as displaced persons and, especially important if they were already in the camps, adopting false identities. As suggested by the case of Nerianin discussed at the start of the chapter, some claimed citizenship of interwar Poland or the Baltic States, which spelled exemption from mandatory repatriation, while others claimed the identities of first-wave Russian émigrés.[58] After witnessing DP resistance, US and British military government officials became wary of the repatriation provisions of the Yalta agreements and some-times failed to enforce them, mostly by overlooking the DPs' strategies of evasion and imposture.[59] In any case, the American military government in Germany had difficulty keeping track of the various populations of displaced persons in its zone; surprisingly, US military intelligence agencies were not even in possession of a full roster of Vlasov's soldiers in late 1946.[60] Thanks to these circumstances, many Soviet DPs managed to remain in the West, although their number remains

[55] See a detailed rendering of the process of repatriation in V. N. Zemskov, "K voprosy o repatriatsii sovetskikh grazhdan, 1944–1951," *Istoriia SSSR*, no. 4 (1990): 26–41, and the useful overview in Edele, *Stalin's Defectors*, 41–3. The lives of returners to the USSR are poorly studied, with an important exception being Laurie Manchester, "Repatriation to a Totalitarian Homeland: The Ambiguous Alterity of Russian Repatriates from China to the USSR," *Diaspora: A Journal of Transnational Studies* 16, no. 3 (2007): 353–88.

[56] Zemskov argues that material considerations were the most important factor driving "non-returnism," but offers no evidence for the claim. V. N. Zemskov, " 'Vtoraia emigratsiia' i otnoshenie k nei rukovodstva SSSR, 1947–1955," in Iu. A. Poliakov et al. (eds.), *Istoriia rossiiskogo zarubez'hia: emigratsiia iz SSSR-Rossii, 1941–2001 gg.: sbornik stat'ei* (Moscow: Rossiiskaia akademiia nauk, Institut rossiiskoi istorii, 2007), 76–7.

[57] Janco, "Soviet 'Displaced Persons,' " 173–4.

[58] On DP imposture strategies, see ibid., 159–66.

[59] Elliot, *Pawns of Yalta*, 172.

[60] HQ, US Forces, European Theater, Office of the Assistant Chief of Staff to Director of Intelligence, OMGUS, November 12, 1946, in Vlassow Group, fol. 2.

obscure due to the very practices of imposture and evasion through which they did so. According to Soviet repatriation authorities, the size of the second wave in early 1952 was 451,000 persons, of whom 31,704 were ethnic Russians.[61] The Soviet DPs who avoided repatriation eked out a stressful and trying existence. The second-wavers lived in a "harrowing atmosphere of uncertainty, dread and enervating rumors," as one émigré wrote to fellow Russians in the United States in 1946.[62] Records from the Office of Military Government, United States (OMGUS) bear out this characterization: while DPs in Landshut believed that the Americans "will send back anyone with Soviet citizenship," their counterparts in Passau reached the very different conclusion that former Vlasovites would be enlisted soon in the US army.[63] Even after forced repatriation had ground to a halt amid rising East–West tensions, the position of the second-wave exiles in Germany remained tenuous. The Soviet government never relinquished the goal of repatriating its war-displaced citizens and continued to contest their status as refugees.[64] Meanwhile, their future in the West was unclear. The prospect of remaining in West Germany, a war-torn country where the local population looked at DPs with hostility, was unappealing, while prospects for emigration overseas were uncertain.[65]

The second wave was shaped by its distinct experiences of the Soviet period, war, and repatriation. Living through danger and instability for a prolonged period of time—Stalinist famine and terror, battlefield capture and incarceration (sometimes under both the Soviets and Germans), and flight from repatriation—took a heavy psychological toll. Merle Fainsod, a scholar from Harvard University who interviewed Soviet DPs in Germany in 1949, reported that some had been reduced to "pitiful pathological cases as the result of their worries and sufferings in the last years."[66] For those in better shape, "great suspiciousness" and "political

[61] Zemskov, "'Vtoraia emigratsiia'": 71–2.
[62] This anonymous quotation appears in Eugene Lyons, "Orphans of Tyranny," *Plain Talk* 2 (March 1948): 44.
[63] Extract, CIC Report Region V Passau Sub Region, May 20, 1946, in Vlassow Group, fol. 3, and Robert A. Shepanek, Special Investigator Region V CIC to Commanding Officer, Hqs, 970th CIC Department, December 18, 1946, in Vlassow Group, fol. 2.
[64] Hans-Erich Volkmann, "Die politischen Hauptströmungen in der russischen Emigration nach dem Zweiten Weltkrieg," *Osteuropa* 4 (1965): 242. On international law on refugee status and the Cold War context, see Gerard Daniel Cohen, *In War's Wake: Europe's Displaced Persons in the Postwar Order* (Oxford: Oxford University Press, 2011), 13–34, and Andrew Janco, "'Unwilling': The One-Word Revolution in Refugee Status, 1940–51," *Contemporary European History* 23, no. 3 (2014): 429–46.
[65] On German attitudes to Soviet DPs, see Janco, "Soviet 'Displaced Persons,'" 109–10, 122–3, and Holian, *Between National Socialism and Soviet Communism*, 44.
[66] Merle Fainsod, "Controls and Tensions in the Soviet System," External Relations Staff, Department of State, Series 3, No. 2, October 18, 1949, 2, in Georgetown University Archives and Special Collections, Robert F. Kelley Papers, box 4, fol. 1. This speech to State Department officials was printed in partial form as Merle Fainsod, "Controls and Tensions in the Soviet System," *The American Political Science Review* 44, no. 2 (1950): 266–82.

distrust" were nevertheless common.[67] Simply put, the second-wavers were conditioned to expect the worst from those around them, and this applied not only to Soviet officials but also to US and British powerholders whom they saw as being accomplices of Stalin during repatriation.[68]

Years spent at the mercy of brutal regimes and their armies compelled second-wavers to resort to survival strategies of flight, deception, and the taking of false identities. Even after the Western allies had stopping executing the Yalta repatriation provisions, the DPs retained the false names they had adopted during or after the war, making imposture the second wave's birthmark of sorts. Moreover, the majority of second-wavers—including many of those who became involved in fighting the Cold War in anti-communist organizations—sought to emigrate as far away from their estranged homeland as possible. According to Soviet estimates, by 1952 only 27 percent of the Russian second-wavers remained in Germany, with 18 percent having already relocated to Australia, 15.7 percent to the UK, 8.2 percent to Canada, and 6 percent to the United States, with smaller pockets located elsewhere in Western Europe or in South America.[69] To a far greater extent than for the first wave, the new cohorts of exiles were driven by long-fostered survival instincts as much as anti-communist agendas.

The backgrounds of the second wave produced another of its distinctive characteristics: the amorphous intellectual and cultural state of many of its members. Again, comparison with the older émigré generation is instructive. Both waves derived from their disastrous experiences an uncompromising hatred of Soviet communism. However, émigrés of the first wave had stronger political identities than those of the second. After all, members of the first wave had often left Russia of their own volition, and invariably brought into exile many of the leaders, intellectual and political traditions, and sometimes institutions of late imperial Russia.[70] In contrast, many second-wavers had left the homeland due to forces beyond their control, and they arrived in the West with little more political baggage than the distinctive habits of living under Stalinism and the Nazi racial empire.[71] One second-wave exile, B. A. Filistinskii-Filippov, described the thinking and identities of Russian DPs as being in total upheaval: they were cynical due to circumstances yet in search of ideological certainty, they supported the Church but had no religious faith, and they were hostile to Marxism–Leninism while still thinking in Marxist categories.[72] Less charitable were the first-wavers who viewed the younger exiles as irredeemable Stalinists, who followed their fallen leader Vlasov

[67] HPSSS, schedule A, vol. 5, case 59, 56.
[68] B. M. Kuznetsov, *V ugodu Stalina: gody 1945–1946* (London, ON: Izdatel'stvo SBONR, 1968).
[69] Zemskov, "'Vtoraia emigratsiia'": 70.
[70] D. Iu. Guzevich et al. (ed. and comp.), "Russkaia emigratsiia": 402–3.
[71] On this point, see Antoshin, *Rossiiskie emigranty v usloviiakh "kholodnoi voiny"*, 61–4.
[72] B. A. Filistinskii-Filippov to B. I. Nikolaevskii, July 6, 1950, published as Igor' Petrov (ed.), "V kotle emigrantskogo proziabaniia," *Live Journal*, February 2, 2014, https://labas. livejournal.com/1055917.html, accessed June 30, 2018.

in much the same way as they had Stalin.[73] If such a dismissal of the Vlasovites as unreformed communists was uncharitable, it was not entirely incorrect. How could people who had no political education outside totalitarianisms of the left and right be expected to shed their pasts overnight?

The second wave, then, was traumatized by the war and repatriation, prone to tactics of dissimulation, eager to flee Europe, and ideologically unformed—all traits that would complicate their participation in the Cold War. The lot of the DPs might have been easier if they had integrated into the existing communities of Russian émigrés in Europe. Unfortunately, the differences between the second-wave Vlasovites and the first-wavers created a wall of mistrust. Most immediately, the two waves were of very different backgrounds, a point driven home by examining their social origins prior to emigration. The first wave had been dominated by the landowning class, educated elites, urban bourgeoisie, skilled workers, and Cossacks.[74] In contrast, the second wave was more plebian. One estimate of the social makeup of Soviet non-returners holds that 47 percent were white-collar workers (or *sluzhashchie* in Russian), 35 percent were workers, and 14 percent were peasants (following the official classification of social groups in the USSR).[75] The second-wave was the product of Stalin's USSR—a politically monochrome, scarcity-driven, and socially leveled society—and therefore quite different than the status-conscious and differentiated pre-revolutionary social world that the first wave still represented.

More fundamental than social backgrounds were the divergent experiences of the first- and second-wavers during the interwar and wartime periods. The defeated opponents of early Bolshevism, whether on the right or left, and the uprooted subjects of the Stalinist USSR were products of different historical worlds. If both generations were Russian, the homeland they remembered, and that to which they longed to return, differed radically. Underlying differences in national identity had already found expression during World War II, when collaborators of the two age cohorts had frequently expressed mutual hostility. First-wave collaborators had been suspicious of the Soviet-born soldiers who made up the bulk of the Vlasov forces, seeing them as "Reds" who were not worthy of trust any more than the Germans were—or, some thought, were actually less so.[76] Among the old émigrés, perceptions of the second-wavers as

---

[73] On postwar perceptions of Vlasov, see Chapter 3. The ongoing hold of Soviet culture on the second wave was the dominant theme of the major work that emerged from the Harvard Project on the Soviet Social System, which will be discussed in Chapter 4. Alex Inkeles and Raymond Bauer, *The Soviet Citizen: Daily Life in a Totalitarian Society* (Cambridge, MA: Harvard University Press, 1961).

[74] Raeff, *Russia Abroad*, 26–71.

[75] These data come from a sample of Soviet DPs gathered by the Harvard Project on the Soviet Social System, as cited in Janco, "Soviet 'Displaced Persons,'" 81.

[76] Tsurganov, *Neudavshiisia revansh*, 167, 172–98.

"valueless, Soviet, incomprehensible, ignorant and almost half-savage" lived on in the postwar years.[77]

Conversely, the Soviet-born Vlasovites derived from their upbringing a negative view of the old émigrés, who had lost touch with their homeland and could not claim to speak for it.[78] The generational gap was even visible in the exiles' comportment and culture. Some DPs dubbed the first-wavers "knights of the old orthography," a reference to the fact that many of them still rejected the postrevolutionary reforms of the Russian language.[79] Quite possibly, mistrust of the old émigrés expanded after the war, when second-wavers who feared repatriation looked with envy at the first-wave exiles who faced no such tribulations and sometimes found employment in the DP camps and other relief organizations.[80]

The generational divide of exiles, therefore, carried social, cultural, and political inflections. Not surprisingly, the rift between exile waves would cause misunderstandings and mutual recriminations during the Cold War, when exiles sought to create a unified anti-communist movement.

The Solidarists

The group that would become the most important client of US power during the Cold War, the National Labor Alliance (NTS), was unlike the other political camps already discussed. In contrast to the Whites, socialists, and Vlasovites, the NTS was a single and centralized political organization for much of its existence. And if the other dominant political trends were largely built on the experiences of a single émigré cohort, the NTS drew on both the first and second waves. Most importantly, the NTS was distinct in being a right-radical, fascist-influenced organization, even though it sought to obscure its extremist origins in the postwar years. The right-wing and collaborationist pasts of the "Solidarists," as NTS members were dubbed, helped to account for their influence and also infamy during the Cold War.

The founders of the NTS, established as the National Alliance of the New Generation in 1931, belonged to the younger cohorts of the White emigration. The early Solidarists envisioned their movement as a forward-looking counter-reaction to what they saw as the weakness and archaism of their White elders.[81]

---

[77] D. V. Konstantinov, *Cherez tunnel' 20-go stoletiia* (Moscow, IAI RGGU, 1997), 365.

[78] Andreyev, *Vlasov and the Russian Liberation Movement*, 89–158.

[79] "Spory o 'Vlasovtsakh,'" *Sotsialisticheskii vestnik* no. 6/609 (June 26, 1948): 120.

[80] B. A. Filistinskii-Filippov to B. I. Nikolaevskii, July 6, 1950.

[81] The Alliance's interwar origins remains poorly explored by scholars. See Liudmila Klimovich, "Narodno-trudovoi soiuz rossiiskikh solidaristov: rannye stranitsy istorii," *Neprikosnovennyi zapas*, no. 91 (May 2013), at http://magazines.russ.ru/nz/2013/5/14k.html, accessed 14 March 2019; Robinson, *The White Russian Army*, 157–64, 202–5; and V. S. Varshavskii, *Nezamechennoe pokolenie* (New York: Izd-vo im. Chekhova, 1956), 68–91.

Their search for a muscular political ideology fit to counter Bolshevism led them to embrace the politics of the ascendant European radical right. The NTS's conception of a pan-Russian, quasi-imperial nationalism and its pronounced anti-Semitism placed the movement firmly in the context of rightist movements of late imperial Russia. In contrast, the NTS's ideology of "national labor Solidarism" drew on several ideological aspects of Italian fascism and German National Socialism: national revolution, the transcendence of class divisions through corporatist institutions, a cult of action, and the forging of a new elite tasked with moving the masses through history.[82] The NTS also adopted much of the distinctive political style of European fascism, such as doctrinal texts, organizational hierarchy, and inspirational symbols and songs.[83]

The NTS was unable to gain sustained foreign backing for its anti-communist politics in the interwar period, at least outside of its headquarters in Yugoslavia. Nevertheless, it entered the murky world of intelligence agencies and international intrigue with energy and resolve. Some of the NTS's leaders worked for French and perhaps British intelligence, and later in the 1930s the Alliance gained backing from Poland, Japan, and Romania for operations designed to penetrate Soviet borders with propaganda and agents.[84] The results were disappointing and, for the NTS agents captured trying to cross Soviet borders, tragic. Indeed, the NTS's interwar activities had no effect on the USSR apart from lending substance and credence to Stalin's narrative that hidden enemies threatened the Soviet state.[85] Nevertheless, the motivation and cohesion of the Solidarists were impressive, at least against the backdrop of the divisions and demoralization of other Russian exile groups.

The NTS's émigré activities gained newfound importance with the Axis invasion of the USSR. Documents from the German Foreign Office show that the NTS had tried and failed to win support from Nazi Germany in the late 1930s, with a Gestapo official expressing skepticism over a "meaningless Russian émigré organization."[86] However, in 1941, the Nazis' need for Russian-speaking personnel during Operation Barbarossa led a part of the Hitler state to actively cultivate the NTS. Acting with the support of the Reich Ministry for the Occupied Eastern Territories (Ostministerium), V. M. Despotuli, the editor of Berlin's sole (and Nazi-funded) Russian newspaper *Novoe Slovo* ("New Word"), invited the NTS to

[82] See Boris L. Dvinov, *Politics of the Russian Emigration* (Santa Monica, CA: Rand Corp., 1955), 115–18.
[83] B. V. Prianishnikov, *Novopokolentsy* (Silver Spring, MD: Multilingual Typesetting, 1986), 39–44, 113–18.
[84] Ibid., 75–108, 137–46.
[85] A surprisingly candid account appears in the memoirs of NTS's longstanding leader. V. M. Baidalakov, *Da vozvelichits'ia Rossiia, da pogibnut nashi imena: vospominaniia predsedatelia NTS: 1930–1960 gg.* (Moscow: Avuar Konsalting, 2002), 1–17.
[86] National-Sozialer Bund der Neuen Russischen Generation, Geheime Staatspolizei to Auswärtiges Amt, June 7, 1938, 1–3, in Auswärtiges Amt-Politisches Archiv, R-104377.

relocate its headquarters from Belgrade to Berlin.[87] With the defeat of the Soviet Union appearing almost certain in 1941, NTS leaders, with few exceptions, cast their lot with Nazi Germany and "pursued an unmistakably fascist course" during the war, in the later opinion of a West German diplomat.[88] Several NTS activists took up employment in bureaucracies active on the Eastern Front, including Alfred Rosenberg's above-mentioned ministry, the Abwehr (military intelligence), the Anti-Comintern agency in the Propaganda Ministry, the sabotage outfit Unternehmen Zeppelin, which was formed by the SS (*Schutzstaffel* or Protection Squadron, the Nazi security superagency), and local police organs in occupied Soviet areas.[89] In these varied institutional settings, NTS activists spread Nazi propaganda to Soviet collaborators and prisoners of war, contributed to anti-partisan warfare, and, in some cases, participated in the mass killing of the Holocaust.[90]

The Solidarists saw collaboration as a path to national revolution in Russia. Most of the NTS members assembled in Germany hoped that Hitler, pressed by "the very logic of events" on the Eastern Front after Stalingrad, would embrace a new policy recognizing Russian national interests.[91] In the meantime, the NTS members sought to utilize their positions under the Nazis to their own political advantage. Solidarists working as propagandists in POW camps recruited new members for the Alliance, while those employed as administrators or spies on occupied Soviet territory established temporary and probably quite weak footholds in Russia.[92] Nonetheless, it is clear that some Soviet citizens under German

[87] Georg Leibbrandt of the *Ostministerium* had approved of the invitation extended to the Russians. Baidalakov, *Da vozvelichits'ia Rossiia*, 26. On Despotuli's closeness to the Nazis, see Beyda and Petrov, "The Soviet Union," 381–2.
[88] Ausarbeitung über die russische Emigration (Stand März 1954), no author indicated, 34, in AA-PA B12, Akte 455.
[89] Prianishnikov, *Novopokolentsy*, 27–9; "NTS–The Russian Solidarist Movement," US Department of State External Research Staff, Series vol. 3, no. 76 (January 10, 1951), 1–5, and S. G. Chuev, *Spetssluzhby Tret'ego Reikha*, book 1 (Moscow: Neva, 2003), 254–73, and ibid., book 2, 232–5 and 242–8.
[90] See Dmitrii Zhukov and Ivan Kovtun, "Boris Khol'mston-Smyslovskii i NTS: istoriia sotrudnichestva i protivostoianiia," in A. Martynov (ed.), *Istoriia otechestvennoi kollaboratsii: materialy i issledovaniia* (Moscow: Staraia Basmannaia, 2017), 297–338; Yuri Radchenko, "'We Emptied our Magazines into Them': The Ukrainian Auxiliary Police and the Holocaust in Generalbezirk Charkow, 1941–1943," *Yad Vashem Studies* 41, no. 1 (2013): 64, 74–6; Beyda and Petrov, "The Soviet Union," 393–5, and Iz direktivy NKVD SSSR no. 136 ob aktivizatsii agenturno-operativnoi raboty po prosecheniiu podryvnoi deiatel'nosti zarubezhnoi antisovetskoi organizatsii NTSNP, March 19, 1943, in S. V. Stepashin and V. P. Iampol'skii (eds.), *Organy gosudarstvennoi bezopasnosti SSSR v Velikoi Otechestvennoi voine: sbornik dokumentov*, vol. 4, part 1 (Moscow: Kniga i biznes, 1995), 311.
[91] Prianishnikov, *Novopokolentsy*, 158–9.
[92] For evidence of hostility to the NTS among Soviet citizens living under Nazi occupation, see Vera Pirozhkova, *Poteriannoe pokolenie: vospominaniia o detstve i iunosti* (St. Petersburg: Zhurnal Neva, 1998), 164–5, and Petrov and Beyda, "Soviet Union," 394. See also Prianishnikov, *Novopokolentsy*, 146–81, and Andrei Kutakov and Sebastian Stopper, *Nelegal'nyi Briansk, 1941–1943. Nelegal'naia deiatel'nost' razlichnykh sil v okkupirovannykh Brianske i Ordzhonikidzegrade s 6 oktiabria po 17 sentabria 1943* (Briansk: "klub liubitelei rodnogo kraia," 2014).

rule were drawn to the NTS's stridently nationalist and anti-Semitic ideology.[93] At the same time, the NTS activists won influence among the masses of Soviet Russians interned in the Third Reich as prisoners of war, often for the simple reason that joining the organization might offer a path out of the squalor of the camps.[94] Regardless of their motivations, the very willingness of some Soviet citizens to join the NTS was an accomplishment, especially considering the common suspicion that soured relationships between the émigré waves discussed above.

The NTS's pro-German position, however, became untenable after Stalingrad, when Russians on both sides of the front reacted to the success of the Red Army by rallying to the Soviet cause. In an effort to maintain influence, the NTS issued propaganda that stressed its independence from German agendas, but ran afoul of their patrons in the process. The Gestapo arrested over one hundred Alliance members in 1944 (although other Solidarists remained at large and participated in the Vlasov movement).[95]

Against the wider backdrop of the Hitler state's cynical exploitation of collaborators of all stripes, the NTS's political failure and near-destruction were hardly surprising.[96] Rather more impressive was what had preceded it. The NTS had expanded its influence by siding with a state in armed conflict with the Soviets, pursuing their own national agendas behind the façade of loyal service to it. No less importantly, such a duplicitous strategy had yielded some results, most concretely in the form of the Solidarists' contact with co-nationals from a long-estranged homeland.

The immediate postwar situation formed a stark contrast to the Solidarists' heady agendas of the wartime years. Like other Soviet DPs, Solidarists escaped the advance of the Red Army by fleeing West, settling in DP camps in the Western-administered zones of Germany and Austria. However, Soviet authorities peppered their wartime allies with demands for the extradition of members of the NTS, both on the grounds that they were traitors and war criminals and, for

---

[93] For the published memoirs of wartime recruits of the NTS, see O. V. Budnitskii and G. S. Zelenina (eds.), *Svershilos'-prishli Nemtsy! Ideinyi kollaboratsionizm v SSSR v period Velikoi Otechestvennoi Voiny* (Moscow: ROSSPEN, 2014), and P. D. Il'inskii, "Tri goda pod nemetskoi okkupatsiei v Belorussii (Zhizn' Polotskogo okruga 1941–1944 godov)," in K. M. Aleksandrov (ed.), *Pod nemtsami: vospominaniia, svidetel'stva, dokumenty* (St. Petersburg: Skriptorium, 2011), 42–138.

[94] See the recollections of an NTS figure who worked in a German propaganda camp in Igor' Petrov (ed.), "Vustrau," *Live Journal*, August 22, 2014, https://labas. livejournal.com/1078806.html, accessed June 30, 2018; Alexander Dallin, *German Rule in Russia, 1941–1945: a Study of Occupation Policies* (New York: St. Martin's Press, 1957), 526, and Antoshin, *Rossiiskie emigranty v usloviiakh "kholodnoi voiny"*, 206.

[95] See SI-05606 (1944), NARA, RG 263, Entry ZZ-18, 230/86/23/04, box 77, Viktor Larionoff (hereinafter Larionoff), vol. 1. See also an NTS report from 1944 or 1945, seemingly genuine, that is reproduced in S. A. Krivosheev, *KGB protiv NTS* (Moscow: Trovant, 2015), 26–36. Another version of events is that the German crackdown was triggered by suspicion of NTS ties to British intelligence. Zhukov and Kovtun, "Boris Khol'mston-Smyslovskii i NTS," 327.

[96] For an overview, see István Deák, *Europe on Trial: The Story of Collaboration, Resistance, and Retribution during World War II* (Boulder, CO: Westview Press, 2015), 67–80.

second-wave Solidarists, as part of the mandated repatriation of Soviet citizens. Nor did the NTS seem well situated to earn the favor of American or British authorities. The organization had never had much of a presence in the United States and the UK, and many of the Solidarists held a decidedly negative view of the Anglo-Americans—a product, no doubt, of the White emigration's longstanding bitterness over its lot in Europe as well as the Alliance's fascist-influenced disdain for liberal democracy.[97] Of more immediate concern to the exiles, in the chaos of 1945–6 a few NTS leaders were taken into custody and underwent interrogation by US and British security forces before being released—a move that placed the émigré organization in the sights of military occupation authorities.[98]

The NTS confronted the difficult terrain of occupied Germany with skill and even creativity, drawing on the political practices it had developed in the past years. From the outset, the NTS's contact person with the Americans was Konstantin Vasil'evich Boldyrev, a White émigré who had learned fluent English while working at a British firm in Yugoslavia before the war. By courting military government (the Office of Military Government, United States, or OMGUS) officials, Boldyrev secured permission to establish a DP camp at Mönchehof near Kassel, where NTS members settled en masse.[99] Mönchehof quickly came under the protection of the local American military brass, which was impressed by the orderly, hard-working, and conservative Russians who had fled communism.

Courting the Americans paid dividends. In 1946, OMGUS arrested Boldyrev and his assistant Irina Vergun on charges of carrying out anti-Soviet activity and collaboration with the SS during the war.[100] The charges were eventually dropped due to lack of evidence, even though both were probably true. US Counter Intelligence Corps (CIC) agents discovered that Boldyrev had headed a construction firm called Erbauer, which operated first in occupied Minsk and then, after the German retreat, took up work under SS supervision at a V-2 rocket factory in Niedersachswerfen in Thuringia. Recent scholarship identifies Erbauer as a cover

[97] For postwar NTS criticism of the "cacophony" of liberal democracy, see A. Kolin, "Strategiia Solidarizma," *Volia*, no. 2 (1949): 19.

[98] V. D. Poremskii, who had worked under the Germans as an instructor of Russian-language propagandists, was arrested by the US military government but quickly released in 1945. The Soviet side concluded that US authorities "instructed" Poremskii to reorganize the core of the NTS at that time, a charge that is unsubstantiated and flies in the face of available evidence. Information zu der Emigrantenorganisation NTS, no author indicated, February 19, 1968, 4, in Federal Commissioner for the Records of the State Security Service of the former German Democratic Republic, Central Archive (Bundesbeauftragte für die Unterlagen des Staatssicherheitsdienstes der ehemaligen Deutschen Demokratischen Republik, Zentralarchiv), MfS-AFO 1187, 000084. On the detention and interrogation of N. F. Shits by British field police in 1946, see NARA, RG 319, IRR, XE065662, Sheets, Nikolai, obtained through FOIA request.

[99] The creation of this camp followed a dramatic evacuation from Thuringia when the territory was handed over to the Soviets. A work on the camp by a former resident and NTS member is S. V. Tribukh, *Menkhegof—lager' russkikh DiPi, 1945–1949* (US, n.p., 1986), in Hoover Institution Library and Archives (HILA), Constantin W. Boldyreff Papers (hereinafter Boldyreff), box 3.

[100] Memorandum for the Officer in Charge, Su: Constantin Boldyreff, CIC Special Agents Robert H. Swezey and William K. Russell, May 5, 1948, 2–3, in Boldyreff Papers, box 7.

organization for the counterespionage outfit "Ingvar," formed in 1944 in Minsk by security police and the SD Security Service (*Sicherheitsdienst des Reichsführers-SS*, Security Service of the Reichsführer SS).[101] Decisive in the exoneration of Boldyrev and Vergun was the spirited defense offered by US military officials to the court, and particularly the testimony of Lieutenant Colonel Robert Cameron, whom a CIC agent characterized as being "deeply biased" in Boldyrev's favor. Here was a palpable sign that the NTS's strategy of cultivating American ties had not been in vain.[102]

Boldyrev also took the lead in a campaign to shield Russian DPs, and especially those under his authority at Mönchehof, from repatriation. He lobbied senior OMGUS officials for the purpose, sending a memorandum to then military governor Dwight D. Eisenhower through Boldyrev's military government contacts that drew a tragic picture of the fate that awaited the DPs in the USSR.[103] The approach, it would seem, was successful. Detailed to Mönchehof, Major Philip Steers stood his ground in two tense meetings with Soviet repatriation officers visiting the camp, who warned the American that "force would have to be applied to return the DPs" and threatened to report the incident to Moscow.[104] When the camp passed to the jurisdiction of the United Nations Relief and Rehabilitation Administration (UNRRA), Steers instructed the organization's staff at the camp to not be "too exacting" about the registration of the DPs—aware, no doubt, that the Russians were doctoring their paperwork to escape repatriation.[105] Boldyrev had saved the Russians from a vindictive homeland, in the process expanding the influence of the NTS among the Russian DPs.

Boldyrev and his fellow Solidarists utilized Mönchehof as a vehicle for re-establishing the NTS, even while convincing the Americans that they were refraining from political activity (technically illegal in DP camps). Boldyrev and his companions located and reassembled Alliance leaders strewn across the different

[101] S. G. Chuev, *Spetssluzhby Tret'ego reikha*, Book 1 (Moscow: Neva, 2003), 267–8, and Zhukov and Kovtun, "Boris Khol'mston-Smyslovskii i NTS," 325. One CIC investigator suspected that Erbauer was involved in espionage. See collated information from CIC document marked "Internal Review Slip" on Boldyrev, dated August 22, 1946, in Boldyreff Papers, box 7.

[102] Memorandum for the Officer in Charge, Seymour Gilbert, Special Agent of the 75th CIC Department, August 2–3, 1948, 7, in Boldyreff papers, box 7.

[103] See Memorandum re. Repatriation of Russians, M. F. Iuriev, A. V. Lampe, F. V Danilov, M. A. Meandrov, and C. W. Boldyreff to General Dwight Eisenhower, Commander in Chief, Allied Expeditionary Force, June 16, 1945, Boldyreff papers, box 7. The list of signatories includes at least two prominent military collaborators, White general A. V. von Lampe and Vlasovite commander M. A. Meandrov.

[104] Major Philip Steers, Jr, QMC, contacts with Russian Liaison Officers, Counter Intelligence Corps (CIC) Investigation, George N. Liske to Kassel CIC Subdistrict, September 29, 1945, in Boldyreff, box 7. Documents suggest that Steers was acting in the spirit if not perhaps the letter of instructions from above during the encounter. According to CIC agents, Steers was "instructed in person on the 17 July 1945 [sic] by General Woods, of General Eisenhower's Staff, to permit the Russian Liason [sic] officers to visit only certain parts" of Mönchehof. Memorandum for the Officer in Charge, Seymour Milbert, Sp. Agent, August 1, 1945, in Boldyreff, box 7.

[105] Tribukh, *Menkhegof*, 38.

zones of Germany and Austria, bypassing the ubiquitous checkpoints in a German medical truck with "Typhus" written on the sides.[106] Meanwhile, the NTS leadership at Mönchehof placed the residents firmly in the orbit of the Solidarists, with Boldyrev running the camp as "a kind of dictator," CIC investigators reported. DPs quickly "found out that they live better by becoming members of the organization," while opponents of the NTS might find themselves expelled or barred from entry to the camp.[107] The combination of privilege and pressure toward DPs at Mönchehof amounted to a calculated strategy for creating a postwar political cadre for the NTS. Against considerable odds—and, notably, at the same time Vlasovites were being deported to the East—the NTS had reconstituted its political center under the sympathetic eye of US military officials.

* * *

The postwar scheming of the NTS was just one manifestation of the anti-communist passions that characterized the lives of the political émigrés. Whatever twisted historical paths they traversed over the decades since 1917—whether combat in the White armies, underground opposition to Lenin, exile in interwar Europe, internment on the Eastern Front, collaboration with Nazi Germany, or the relatively advantageous position of life in the United States—émigré anti-communists struggled to maintain their faith that Soviet rule could be toppled. Indeed, they also attempted to pass on this conviction to their offspring in exile. For instance, the ever enterprising NTS developed an elaborate program of education for the offspring of Russian exiles, centering on scout organizations whose motto was "for Rus', for faith!"[108] Commenting on NTS work in the early postwar years, the second-generation White émigré Mikhail Viktorovich Slavinskii recalled his belief that the overthrow of Soviet rule in the immediate future was quite possible.[109]

The exiles' existential confrontation with Soviet communism, however, was only the primary struggle of several in which the exiles engaged. While seeking to win the support of the societies and states in which they lived, the exiles often viewed the latter suspiciously, drawing on memories of Western betrayal such as the abandonment of the White army after the Civil War (for the first wave) and forced repatriation after the Second World War (for the second wave). The exiles were also badly divided among themselves for a wide array of reasons: the distinct socialization of different émigré cohorts; divergent memories of the Russian political past during the periods of late tsarism, revolution, constitutional rule, and communism; ideological principles which ranged from fascism and conservative monarchism on

---

[106] Prianishnikov, *Novopokolentsy*, 226.

[107] Memorandum for the Officer in Charge, Su: Constantin Boldyreff, 1, 6.

[108] R. V. Polchaninov, *Molodezh' russkogo zarubezh'ia* (Moscow: Posev, 2010).

[109] Liudmila Klimovich, "Po tu storonu sovetskoi vlasti: k istorii Narodno-troduvogo soiuza," *Neprikosnovennyi zapas*, no. 5/67 (May 2009), at http://magazines.russ.ru/nz/2009/5/kl12.html, accessed July 2018.

the right to social democracy on the left; and party politics and personal feuds, which sometimes made bitter enemies out of exiles who had similar ideological positions.

While it was often petty and even sometimes pathetic, infighting in Russia abroad reflected a deeper truth: the exiles embodied different visions of Russian identity and history. When they imagined a future Russia free of communism, the Whites looked to the Russian old regime, the leftists to democratic socialism of the revolutionary period in Russia, the Vlasovites to the promises of a liberation movement that existed under Nazi auspices, and the Solidarists to a conservative, Orthodox, and corporatist idyll. In the postwar period, however, pressing questions emerged about national representation. Which, if any, of these visions of Russianness might find support among the Russian population in the Soviet Union? And which varieties of Russian anti-communism would the Western powers, and particularly the United States, want to back in the Cold War? The imperative of representing the nation, the driving force of all modern exile politics, became a central concern as the Cold War set in and foreign interests began to survey the landscape of the émigré anti-communists in Europe.

2

"A Political Maze Based on the Shifting Sands"

The Vlasov Movement and the Gehlen Organization in postwar Germany

In 1949, a group of Russian monarchists called the Union of Andrew's Flag (*Soiuz Andreevskogo flaga* or SAF) announced that it was establishing an "Institute for Study of the Record of the 1941–1945 War" in Munich. The institute, which was designed to "elevate and expand the military and military-political proficiency of the SAF officer staff," evidently produced a military regiment called the "Varangians," a title harkening back to the first rulers of Rus' a millennium before. Soon after, the Romanov pretender Grand Duke Vladimir Kirilovich placed a message of support in the SAF's newspaper, stating that he hoped he could rely on the regiment "when the time comes."[1]

The image of an exile army led by a Romanov invading Moscow in 1949—unfurling the "banner of St. Andrew over the walls of the ancient Moscow Kremlin"—was far-fetched, to say the least.[2] Of course, tsarist autocracy was far from either Western democracy or Soviet communism, the hegemonic ideological polarities of the early Cold War; in any case, Vladimir Kirilovich dabbled in politics only intermittently from his adopted home of Spain.[3] Yet the revival of monarchist dreams among Russian exiles in Germany was more than a historical curiosity. The restorationist schemes of the venerable representatives of prewar Russia rested on a certain reading of the postwar situation in Europe. If full-scale war between the USSR and its erstwhile allies was widely feared on the European continent in the late 1940s, the exiles—and certainly the organizers of the "Varangians"—viewed the prospect of a new war as carrying promise as well as danger.[4] Should the Cold War become hot, the White émigrés in the SAF might return to the field in some capacity—just as, in fact, some of them had done during World

---

[1] Boris L. Dvinov, *Politics of the Russian Emigration* (Santa Monica, CA: Rand Corp., 1955), 214–15.
[2] Ibid., 227. The St Andrews's flag was the naval ensign of the tsarist empire.
[3] The Romanov family in exile remains understudied. Robert K. Massie, *The Romanovs: The Final Chapter* (New York: Ballantine, 1996), 275–306.
[4] A. V. Antoshin, "Rossiiskaia emigratsiia i germanskii vopros v 1945–1961 gg.," *Ural'skii vestnik mezhdunarodnykh issledovanii*, ed. 3 (Ekaterinburg: Izd-o Ural'skogo universiteta, 2005), 171.

Cold War Exiles and the CIA: Plotting to Free Russia. Benjamin Tromly, Oxford University Press (2019). © Benjamin Tromly.
DOI: 10.1093/oso/9780198840404.001.0001

War II under German auspices.[5] Moreover, the Varangian unit suggested that potential recruits for a new campaign in the East existed in the form of the second-wave exiles, a new cohort of staunchly anti-Soviet transplants from Stalinist Russia, some of whom had also collaborated with the Germans during the war.

The SAF institute, and the Russian monarchist cause more generally, also found sources of external material support, an essential ingredient of any émigré political initiative. When the exiles began to organize themselves in the displaced persons (DP) camps of occupied Germany and Austria in the late 1940s, the United States had yet to turn to actively harnessing anti-communist Russians against the Soviet regime. However, the exiles found an indirect connection to US power and money through German intermediaries. As part of the opportunistic remarshaling of wartime German resources by the country's conquerors, the US army funded the Gehlen Organization, an intelligence outfit assembled from Hitler's military intelligence unit *Fremde Heere Ost* (Foreign Armies East or FHO). Reinhard Gehlen, the FHO's chief, resurrected his intelligence enterprise directed against the postwar Soviet bloc, and drew on the Russian and other Soviet exile communities in Germany to recruit informants and agents. In the convoluted proxy arrangement that emerged, American money flowed covertly through Nazi-era intelligence officers to Russian monarchists. As the Russian-born American commentator Isaac Deutscher commented on the late 1940s émigré milieu in Germany, "not only outsiders but even Russians find it now hard to penetrate this strange political maze based on the shifting sands of DP camps and other refugee colonies."[6]

This chapter examines the emergence of exile politics in Germany in the late 1940s, situating the "strange political maze" that it became in both the internal divides of the exiles and the espionage world of the early Cold War. Russian émigré communities in Germany were deeply divided along lines of generation and historical memory, as the monarchist organizations active among the Whites clashed with the Vlasovite cohorts of the second wave. Rather than overcoming this rift, the involvement of the Gehlen Organization only complicated the exile camp further, as secretive factions of intelligence agents fought over leadership and influence within the DP camps. Perhaps worst of all, the divided state of the émigrés provided an opening for Soviet counter-intelligence agents, who unleashed operations to deepen the already considerable strife within the nascent exile anti-communist milieu in West Germany. In the situation that emerged, virtually all émigré groups and their different initiatives within the DP camps—including the SAF and its plans for taking the Kremlin—came under suspicion of

[5] Oleg Beyda, "'Re-Fighting the Civil War': Second Lieutenant Mikhail Aleksandrovich Gubanov," *Jahrbücher für Geschichte Osteuropas* 66, no. 2 (2018): 245–73.
[6] Isaac Deutscher, "Strange World of Russian 'Non-Returners'," *The New York Times*, 24 July 1949, SM9.

being elaborate Soviet-hatched provocations. The result was the fracturing of the Russian anti-communist milieu in Germany, which set a troubling precedent for US patronage of the exiles.

Out from the Shadows

The re-emergence of anti-communist Russian groups in Germany seemed unlikely against the backdrop of the war. As described in Chapter 1, the repatriation drive at the end of the war made second-wave exiles into virtual fugitives, hiding their identities as they struggled for survival in war-torn Germany. Yet the situation for exiles changed within a few years of the peace, as the forced repatriation of Soviet citizens ground to a halt amid the collapse of superpower relations.[7] Meanwhile, the breakdown of relations among the wartime allies also raised hopes for a renewed conflict with the Soviet Union. An exile who visited the DP camps in early 1947 reported that Russian communities were awash with rumors that "some drastic change towards the Russian refugees" was forthcoming, which would involve the creation of Russian military units, the uniforms of which would bear arm patches "with the Russian Imperial colors, white, blue, and red, with the former Russian eagle."[8]

Such wishful thinking was tempered by seemingly intractable realities on the ground. As part of its occupation policies in Germany and Austria, the US military government imposed a ban on political activities among DPs, and especially on those directed against the Soviet government.[9] As late as fall 1947, US military authorities in Austria "outlawed" a Russian anti-communist group when they discovered anti-Soviet leaflets created by it floating in bottles on the Enns River, destined for the country's Soviet occupation zone.[10] If the onset of the Cold War generated interest in the exiles on the part of US intelligence agencies in Germany, plans to utilize them for political warfare operations would emerge much more slowly than many émigrés hoped and anticipated. Foreign-policy considerations were at work: colluding with the sworn enemies of the Soviet state would poison the already badly deteriorating relations between the erstwhile allies. Institutional factors limited American involvement as well. The US intelligence establishment was in flux, as the wartime Office of Strategic Services was sharply downsized and placed under army control.[11] The US army's Counter Intelligence Corps (CIC) became more closely involved with the

---

[7] On the link between the Cold War and the DP question, see Gerard Daniel Cohen, *In War's Wake: Europe's Displaced Persons in the Postwar Order* (Oxford: Oxford University Press, 2011), 13–34.

[8] Henry C. Newton, Col. Inf. to Colonel C. F. Fritzsche, Asst. Deputy Director of Intelligence, Hqs, European Command, April 23, 1947, 5, in National Archives and Records Administration (NARA), RG 263, Entry ZZ-18, 230/86/23/06, box 88, Gerhard von Mende, vol. 1.

[9] Anna Holian, *Between National Socialism and Soviet Communism: Displaced Persons in Postwar Germany* (Ann Arbor: University of Michigan Press, 2011), 50–3.

[10] Su: Russian Anti-Bolshevik Organizations, 430th CIC det., September 9, 1947, in NARA, RG 319, IRR, XA039276, Russian Anti-Bolshevik Organizations, obtained through FOIA request.

[11] Cf. Peter Grose, *Operation Rollback: America's Secret War behind the Iron Curtain* (Boston: Houghton Mifflin, 2000), 22–7.

émigrés, keeping a close watch on anti-communist organizations and recruiting informants from among their ranks. While the CIC's efforts constituted a means of sizing them up in view of their potential roles in a new war in Europe, the agency shied away from engaging exile anti-communists in ways that might be interpreted as support for their cause.[12]

The first chapter of postwar émigré politics, then, unfolded with little direct participation of the US government. Of necessity, initial anti-communist activities in the DP milieu took a shadowy and semi-underground shape. The first organizations to operate among the DPs were those of the first wave, namely the People's Labor Alliance (NTS) and the Supreme Monarchist Council (VMS).[13] Several factors made it possible for anti-communists of the older generation to mobilize: their possession of Nansen passports (documents that had been granted to stateless persons before the war by the League of Nations which usually exempted them from mandatory repatriation to the USSR), knowledge of foreign languages, ties to German civilians, in some cases employment by the United Nations Relief and Rehabilitation Organization, and, not least, longstanding social networks and organizations in Germany and elsewhere, which a second-waver called disparagingly their "aristocratic cohesion."[14]

Such language reflected the main stumbling block for the monarchists: the émigré generational divide, already discussed in Chapter 1. Many Vlasovites refused to join the first-wave organizations, such that the monarchist meetings were mostly attended by the white-haired representatives of the Russian old regime.[15] Instead, many Vlasovites looked to the wartime Russian liberation movement as a template for postwar anti-communism. As discussed in Chapter 1, the Vlasovites lacked clear ideological positions beyond an emotive bond to their wartime leader—and the execution of Vlasov and his chief officers in Moscow in 1946 only cemented their martyr status for members of his armies remaining in the West.[16] Above all, the Vlasovites' refusal to merge with the monarchists showed the two waves' divergent formative experiences. Vlasov and many of his postwar followers had been apparently loyal members of the Stalinist

---

[12] One documented exception, perhaps a local initiative, was the support of CIC officials in Austria for anti-communist "leaflet operations" by the émigré organization NTS. Narrative Summary of AIS Relationship with NTS, n.d., 1–2, in NARA, RG 263, Entry ZZ-19, 230/86/25/03, box 24, AESAURUS/AENOBLE, vol. 1, pt. 1.

[13] Survey of the Russian Emigration, no author indicated (presumably Robert F. Kelley), April 1950, 26–9, in Georgetown University Archives and Special Collections, Robert F. Kelley Papers, box 5, fol. 14.

[14] Survey of the Russian Emigration, 25, and "K chemu stremitsia russkaia emigratsiia," Sotsialisticheskii Vestnik (hereinafter SV) no. 2 (605) (February 28, 1948): 45. Some first-wave collaborators were repatriated, with the best-known case being the Vlasovites and Cossack forces extradited by the British in Operation Keelhaul. Julius Epstein, Operation Keelhaul: the Story of Forced Repatriation from 1944 to the Present (Old Greenwich, CT: Devin-Adair, 1973).

[15] Survey of the Russian Emigration, 28.

[16] Early postwar Vlasovite writings featured an eclectic and confusing fusion of ideological pronouncements and historical antecedents. Cf. "Kto my?", Izdanie boevogo soiuza molodezhi narodov Rossii, n.d., 4, in Nicolaevsky Collection, box 264, fol. 5.

elite before the onset of the Second World War, and therefore adversaries of the Whites and their cause.[17]

Not surprisingly given such historical and ideological divides, postwar attempts to create a movement that would harken back to Vlasov were not long in coming. Already in mid-1946, a pamphlet ostensibly released by Vlasov's Russian Liberation Army appeared in Munich, calling on Russians to combat the Soviet state and to resist repatriation.[18] In the same year, CIC began to monitor efforts to bring together surviving members of Vlasov's wartime committee (*Komitet Osvobozhdeniia Narodov Rossii* or KONR) in the DP camps of occupied Germany.[19] Spearheading the project was Colonel Konstantin Grigor'evich Kromiadi, an old émigré who had driven a taxi in interwar Berlin before joining the Wehrmacht and then serving as chief of chancellery in the short-lived KONR.[20] As soon as the Western powers had stopped extraditing Soviet citizens to the USSR, Kromiadi brought his project to revive the movement into the open by holding organizational meetings in the Schleissheim DP camp outside Munich.

Kromiadi's effort to reboot Vlasovism quickly ran up against the divisions of the Vlasovites in Germany. In March 1948, Kromiadi called a unification congress of anti-communist Russians in Germany, the diverse guest list of which included the Union for the Struggle for the Liberation of the Peoples of Russia (*Soiuz bor'by za osvobozhdenie narodov Rossii* or SBONR), an organization stemming from an embryonic wartime Vlasovite youth organization,[21] as well as conservative groups such as the VMS, the main organization of White army veterans (the Russian All-Military Union), the NTS, and a group of Kuban' Cossacks. However, several rightist Vlasovites protested and tried to stop the proceedings, claiming that Kromiadi "was not entitled to call such a meeting."[22] In part, a struggle for leadership was at work; many of Kromiadi's opponents were members of the wartime KONR who feared being sidelined by the creation of a new Vlasovite organization. More decisive was the generational cum ideological rift between émigré waves. Although Kromiadi himself was an old émigré with monarchist proclivities, his base of support were the Vlasovites in SBONR who refused to be

[17] Scholars still dispute Vlasov's own political views prior to his capture on the Eastern Front. A largely hagiographic work is K. M. Aleksandrov, *Mify o generale Vlasove* (Moscow: Posev, 2010).

[18] Richard A. Nelson, Munich Sub-Region, CIC to Chief, CIC, Region IV, July 13, 1946, in NARA, RG 319, Entry 134A, 22348387, 270/84/20/02, box 68 (hereinafter Vlassow Group), fol. 1.

[19] MOIC, January 9, 1948, in NARA, RG 319, Entry 134A, XE182853, 270/84/20/02, box 23 (hereinafter AZONDER), vol. 1, fol. 1.

[20] Col. Kromiadi, personal history, no author indicated, February 9,1950, in Kelley Papers, box 5, fol. 7.

[21] SBONR was created in 1947 as the Militant Union of Youth of the Peoples of Russia (*Boevoi soiuz molodezhi narodov Rossii*), a youth organization apparently mandated by Vlasov himself in 1945. F. M. Legostaev, "Kak eto bylo: u istokov SBONRa," V. S. Karpov et al. (eds.), *V poiskakh istiny: puti i sud'by vtoroi emigratsii: sbornik statei i dokumentov* (Moscow: Rossiiskii gos. gumanitarnyi universitet and Istoriko-arkhivnyi institut, 1997), 89–90.

[22] MOIC, Su: ODNR, Special agent Rea M. Pyle, CIC, March 9, 1948, 2, in AZONDER, vol. 1, fol. 1.

associated with the White cause. The deep divides between exile waves threatened to derail postwar Vlasovism before it had begun.

The divide between first- and second-wave émigrés would continue to hamper the Russian anti-communist circles. In April 1948, after managing to sink their differences, pro-Vlasov exiles from both waves created an anti-communist organization called the Anti-Bolshevist Center of the Liberation Movement of the Peoples of Russia (*Antibol'shevitskii Tsentr Osvoboditel'nogo Dvizheniia Narodov Rossii* or ATsODNR).[23] However, the unwieldy acronym suggested the political difficulties awaiting the organization. Kromiadi was out as the main leader, replaced by a council with a rotating chairmanship—hardly a recipe for decisive action.[24] Likewise, the organization settled on a bland platform. Beyond calls to prepare for the "decisive encounter" on the battlefield with the Bolsheviks, the organization's program was non-committal, dodging constitutional questions through the principle of "non-predeterminism" that put off the task of defining the political complexion of post-communist Russia into the future.[25] Symptomatic of the muddle was the organization's ambiguous position on monarchism. While "non-predeterminism" signaled a rejection of openly monarchist politics, ATsODNR's newspaper nonetheless published a statement of support from aspirant to the throne Vladimir Kirilovich.[26]

Despite its indeterminate shape and *raison d'être*, ATsODNR was an accomplishment of sorts. It brought together the varied subgroups of former collaborators in Germany under the universally respected mantle of Vlasov. Most importantly, US military government tolerated the new émigré initiative by allowing ATsODNR to hold meetings and release publications—in the process, ignoring its legal obligation to prevent political activities in the DP camps.[27] A postwar exile movement had begun, and soon attracted outside political forces, both wanted and unwanted.

---

[23] Notably, the Vlasovites only managed to form ATsODNR after heading off a conservative counter-rally to the Kromiadi initiative. B. Dvinov, "Sredi 'ob'edinitelei' i 'osvoboditelei,'" *SV* no. 1–2/616–17 (February 15, 1949): 12.

[24] Survey of the Russian Emigration, 47.

[25] National Committee for a Free Europe, "Political Trends among Russian Exiles," in George Fischer (ed.), *Russian Emigre Politics* (New York: Free Russia Fund, 1951), 3, and Uchreditel'nyi S'ezd uchastnikov ODNR, April 24, 1948, in AZONDER, vol. 1, fol. 2.

[26] Dvinov, *Politics of the Russian Emigration*, 216–20.

[27] The Americans justified their hands-off attitude by legal sleight of hand. Rather than being anti-Soviet, KONR was labelled as anti-communist, and therefore deemed not to be in violation of Military Government laws. Summary report of investigation, Su: KONR, HQ CIC Region IV, February 4, 1948, 3, in AZONDER, vol. 1, fol. 1.

Operation Rusty and Émigré Espionage

Historians point to strong continuities across the 1945 divide in Europe. As Mark Mazower argues, there was "No Year Zero, no clean break between hot and cold war."[28] Adherents of this view need look no further than the postwar career of Reinhard Gehlen, who headed Foreign Armies East of the German Army High Command, the Wehrmacht's agency charged with collecting intelligence on the Soviet Union. The clever and ambitious Gehlen had foreseen Hitler's defeat and the coming Cold War as early as 1942, and began planning for it.[29] Fired by Hitler in the final weeks of the war for submitting reports acknowledging the strength of the Red Army, Gehlen left Berlin for Bavaria in order to surrender to the US army, taking wartime files with him to spark the interest of his captors.[30] The plan worked. After being brought to Washington for interrogation, Gehlen received a green light to reactivate his wartime intelligence-gathering networks, which he claimed extended into the East European countries that would make up the Soviet bloc and even into the USSR itself.[31] In the early stages of occupation, amid policies of denazification and fears of Nazi underground resistance, the US army was bankrolling a reactivation of the Nazis' intelligence apparatus on the Eastern Front.

The Gehlen organization did not live up to the expectations of its sponsors. Known as Operation Rusty while it operated through the American military, Gehlen's outfit was elaborate, with an annual budget of $2.5 million in 1946—at the time much larger, one should note, than the German budget of the Central Intelligence Group, the forerunner of the CIA.[32] And yet the "operation" was never free from scrutiny in Washington. CIA officials in Germany were concerned that the Gehlen Organization was abusing denazification laws—not an unreasonable assumption given that the new structure amounted to a virtually "intact unit" of the Wehrmacht's General Staff.[33] More importantly for the Americans, the Gehlen Organization's performance as an intelligence operation was highly doubtful. Operation Rusty recruited agents haphazardly and without necessary security checks, producing an intelligence organization with "poor cohesion and mixed

---

[28] Mark Mazower, *Dark Continent: Europe's Twentieth Century* (New York: Vintage Books, 2000), 213.

[29] Magnus Pahl, *Hitler's Fremde Heere Ost: German Military Intelligence on the Eastern Front, 1942–45*, trans. Derik Hammond (Solihull, West Midlands: Helion & Company Ltd, 2016), 287.

[30] James H. Critchfield, *Partners at the Creation: The Men behind Postwar Germany's Defense and Intelligence Establishments* (Annapolis, MD: Naval Institute Press, 2003), 28–9.

[31] Kevin C. Ruffner, "A Controversial Liaison Relationship: American Intelligence and the Gehlen Organization, 1945–49," *Studies in Intelligence* (1997), CIA History Staff, 70 in CIA Electronic Reading Room.

[32] Ibid., 72–3.

[33] Ibid., 77, and Pahl, *Hitler's Fremde Heere Ost*, 287.

allegiances." As a later evaluation by an in-house CIA historian put it, "throughout the Western Allied zones of Germany, men and women openly claimed to be working for American intelligence"—even as Gehlen shielded information about its agents from his US army overseers.[34] And though not known at the time, senior ranks of the Gehlen Organization were infiltrated by Soviet intelligence.[35] For several years, the CIA refused to take over control of Operation Rusty, seeing it as an institutional anomaly and an espionage boondoggle.

One aspect of the Gehlen Organization's troubles was its recruitment of East European exiles to spy on their respective homelands. In particular, Operation Rusty actively recruited intelligence assets among the Russian populations in West Germany, taking advantage of its wartime contacts with Vlasov circles.[36] Gehlen hoped that the Russians could help detect Soviet spies in Germany and also provide information from across the Iron Curtain, presumably via "stay-behind" agents who remained on Soviet territory during the advance of the Red Army. At first glance, raw counterintelligence reports that the émigrés produced for Operation Rusty seem to bear out Gehlen's assumptions, as they covered such topics as Soviet intelligence agencies in East Germany and a Soviet counterintelligence officer operating in the US zone.[37]

The quality of the émigré intelligence take was doubtful, though. The CIA's so-called Critchfield Report investigating Operation Rusty found that the Gehlen Organization "habitually extract[ed] 50–60%" of the comments made in reports emanating from its Russian nets as being "unreliable."[38] The meager results of the Gehlen Russian networks in intelligence terms had much to do with the exile scene in which they operated. Among Russian communities in West Germany after the war, spying had a decidedly mercenary nature, as down-and-out exiles tried to get ahead by selling valueless or entirely fraudulent information about the homelands they had recently (or not so recently) departed. A CIA official described postwar Munich as an "intelligence jungle" in which "padding reports to improve one's payments of cigarettes, coffee, and such was virtually standard

---

[34] Ruffner, "A Controversial Liaison Relationship," 72–3.

[35] On Heinz Felfe, a former SS officer and senior Gehlen official recruited by Soviet intelligence, see James H. Critchfield, "The Early History of the Gehlen Organization and its Influence on the Development of a National Security System in the Federal Repubic of Germany," in Heike Bungert et al. (eds.), Secret Intelligence in the Twentieth Century (London: Frank Cass, 2003), 164. In his memoirs, Gehlen boasted of the security of his organization. Reinhard Gehlen, The Service: The Memoirs of General Reinhard Gehlen (New York: World Pub., 1972), 129–30, 158–61.

[36] Gehlen's contacts with the Vlasovites are mentioned in Jürgen Thorwald, The Illusion: Soviet Soldiers in Hitler's Armies (New York: Harcourt Brace Jovanovich, 1975), 35–9, 146–7.

[37] See Counterintelligence Reports no. 258 and 260, Operation RUSTY, April 10, 1947, in NARA, RG 319, IRR, D137584, Russian Émigré Anti-Soviet, obtained through FOIA request.

[38] Report of Investigation-RUSTY, Chief, MO [Critchfield] to Chief, OSO, December 17, 1948, in Kevin C. Ruffner, ed., Forging an Intelligence Partnership: CIA and the Origins of the BND, 1945–1949, vol. II (CIA History Staff, Center for the Study of Intelligence, European Division 1999), 95, released 2002, CIA FOIA Electronic Reading Room.

procedure for émigré practitioners of the intelligence game."[39] Reliable sources of intelligence were hard to come by in this environment, and the Gehlen Organization's poor recruitment practices only added to the problem.

The Gehlen Organization's involvement in émigré affairs went beyond intelligence into party politics. On paper, Operation Rusty's activities were limited to gathering "positive intelligence," screening for security threats, and protecting other operations.[40] However, the émigré recipients of Gehlen money utilized their funding for explicitly political ends, with the result that intelligence networks led double lives as pressure groups within the Russian anti-communist organizations in Bavaria. The blurring of intelligence and politics had doubly unfortunate consequences. While political considerations marred the gathering of intelligence, the reverse was also true, as covert money flows gave the exile milieu an opaque and conspiratorial character.

The espionage networks of Operation Rusty played a direct, if also surely inadvertent, role in undermining the postwar Vlasovite efforts at unification. As discussed above, Kromiadi's initial effort to create a new Vlasov organization met with opposition from members of Vlasov's wartime KONR. Kromiadi complained that his opponents were being backed by "various intelligence organizations," and CIC documentation shows that he was correct.[41] In particular, Kromiadi's opponents belonged to two Gehlen Organization émigré intelligence networks, those surrounding Nikolai Aleksandrovich Baranovskii and Lieutenant General Petr Vladimirovich Glazenap (in German, von Glasenapp).[42]

The two exile intelligence operatives were hard-nosed competitors, even though they both pursued the goal of expanding monarchist influence among Vlasovites in the DP camps. Baranovskii, a White émigré intelligence operative closely tied to the Supreme Monarchist Council, was a secretive individual who worked behind the scenes.[43] In contrast, Glazenap, the scion of a Baltic German aristocratic family, was a notorious figure in Russian circles. After serving as a commander in the Russian Civil War, Glazenap had moved to Germany and become a naturalized citizen.[44] The general claimed to be in possession of a mysterious stock of silver, the Petersburg Loan Exchequer, which had been taken out of the country by White leader P. N. Vrangel' and then passed to Vlasov and eventually

[39] David E. Murphy, Sergei A. Kondrashev, and George Bailey, *Battleground Berlin: CIA vs. KGB in the Cold War* (New Haven: Yale University Press, 1997), 471, n. 26.

[40] Report of Investigation-RUSTY, 95.

[41] MOIC, Su: ODNR, 2.

[42] Of the figures involved in the dispute over KONR, Iu. A. Pis'mennyi-Muzychenko, G. K. Meier, and Vsevolod Grechko belonged to the Baranovskii group, while V. V. Pozdniakov and V. P. Artem'ev worked for Glazenap. Ibid., 3.

[43] S. V. Volkov, *Russkaia voennaia emigratsiia: izdatel'skaia deiatel'nost'* (Moscow: "Pashkov Dom," 2008), 202.

[44] On Glazenap's biography, see Dvinov, *Politics of the Russian Emigration*, 216–17.

US officials.[45] Perhaps drawing on these funds, Glazenap was able to finance a new arch-conservative political organization, the already mentioned SAF. That Glazenap's organization doubled as an intelligence network was an open secret among the exiles. Worse still, large numbers of the DPs distrusted the White officer, whom they saw as an aspiring autocrat bent on seizing control of the Vlasovite project in Bavaria.[46]

Boosting the political agenda of the unpopular Glazenap was one way that Operation Rusty destabilized the exile scene. Just as disruptive was the confusion spawned by espionage networks. The roster of Gehlen's Russian spy nets did not overlap with the membership of the émigrés' political organizations. To take one example, Baranovskii's network included figures from rival political organizations such as the VMS, SBONR, and NTS.[47] Not surprisingly, the presence of covert networks within the anti-communist organizations confused lines of allegiance among the exiles. Strikingly, the leadership council of ATsODNR actually consisted of three separate "political camps": the Baranovskii and Glazenap spy webs, as well as Kromiadi's own circle. Each of them vied for power, operating independently and hoarding information from each other.[48] In one particularly egregious case, the Vlasovite V. V. Pozdniakov used Gehlen funds to run surveillance against his enemy in the émigré world, B. A. Troitskii-Iakovlev.[49] Clearly, the intertwining of politics and espionage networks added to both the confusion and internal tensions within the nascent Vlasovite political organizations.

The warring intelligence groups soon led to an open split of the Vlasov camp. In September 1948, ATsODNR expelled Glazenap and several of his followers from its ranks, alleging that they were guilty of a "breach of discipline and collaboration with elements contrary to the best interests of the liberation movement."[50] Soon after Glazenap's expulsion, Vlasovites made clear what this vague formulation meant when they claimed that the general was a stalking horse for German interests in the emigration. Glazenap, an unidentified ATsODNR

---

[45] Ibid., 218–19. The murky story of these funds is given in "Russkie den'gi na Russkoe Delo," *Nabat*, February 18, 1951, 1, 3. Thanks go to Igor' Petrov for providing me with this source. The Loan Exchequer is distinct from the moneys chronicled in O. V. Budnitskii, *Den'gi russkoi emigratsii: kolchakovskoe zoloto, 1918–1957* (Moscow: Novoe Literaturnoe Obozrenie, 2008).

[46] Subj: AZODNR, author not indicated, June 21, 1948, 2, in AZONDER, vol. 1, fol. 1.

[47] According to Baranovskii himself, in late 1950 his "organization" included Kromiadi, monarchists A. V. Turkul and Iu. A. Pis'mennyi-Muzychenko, NTS leaders G. S. Okolovich and V. D. Poremskii, and SBONR figures A. G. Nerianin-Aldan and Iu. V. D'iachkov-Dikov. Chief of Station, Karlsruhe, to Chief, Foreign Division M, November 1, 1950, in NARA, RG 263, Entry ZZ-18, 230/86/23/04, box 77, Viktor Larionoff, vol. 1.

[48] Annex, Munich Military Post Weekly Intelligence Summary #87, December 14, 1948, 2, in AZONDER, vol. 2, fol. 1.

[49] Delo V. V. Pozdniakova, D. P. Kandaurov, January 3, 1955, in Stuart A. Rose Manuscript, Archives, and Rare Book Library, Emory University, Isaac Don Levine Papers, box 7, and Nikolai Troitskii, *Ty, moe stoletie*—(Moscow: Institut politicheskogo i voennogo analiza, 2006), 346.

[50] Munich Military Post Weekly Intelligence Summary #75, September 21, 1948, 2, in AZONDER, vol. 2, fol. 2.

member informed the CIC, had worked for the Gestapo in Prague during the war.[51] If allowed to gain power, ATsODNR warned, Glazenap would grant a future German government "control of the anti-Communist movement of the Russian emigrants."[52]

The discrediting of Glazenap showed how toxic the internal politics of the Vlasovites had become. There was some truth to the charge that Glazenap was close to German power structures: his connection to the Gehlen organization seems to have run through his son-in-law Rudolph Maeker, who had been a *Sturmbannführer* (assault-unit leader) in Himmler's SS. However, there is no clear evidence that Glazenap himself had been particularly close to the Nazis during the war, let alone that he had been employed by the Gestapo.[53] Instead, the Vlasovites used questions of German ties as a convenient way to besmirch their political rival. Casting out a pro-German figure, moreover, served as a way for the Vlasovites to obscure their own collaborationist pasts. As CIC informants recruited among the Vlasovites reported, Kromiadi's above-mentioned decision to jettison the wartime KONR in favor of a new and wider political front was grounded in the realization that the older organization had "been founded with the assistance of the German Nazi government" and therefore "might be viewed unfavorably in the West."[54] As with many émigré conflicts, Glazenap's fall saw the entangling of controversies over wartime collaboration with cynical power politics.

The Gehlen Organization, then, was doubly detrimental to the exiles. It infiltrated the anti-communist milieu with secretive clans that heightened the already considerable distrust that reigned among the exiles. Indeed, Glazenap was cut from the Gehlen Organization later in 1948 at the request of the Americans for submitting "inaccurate information" and mishandling funds—perhaps charges that were tied to the personal feuds playing out in the organization's Russian networks.[55] At the same time, Operation Rusty confronted the Vlasovites with the

---

[51] Agent report, Edward W. Shick, 7970th CIC Group, Region V, August 6. 1948, in AZONDER, vol. 2, fol. 2.

[52] Agent Report: AZONDR, Albert F. Werner, S/A, CIC, Region IV, August 16, 1948, in AZONDER, vol. 2, fol. 2.

[53] Glazenap claimed that he had rejected collaboration with the Germans. However, one intelligence source claims that Glazenap was a reserve officer in the German General Staff during the war. Igor' Petrov, "Vneshnepoliticheskoe vedomstvo NSDAP: vzgliad iznutri," *Live Journal*, December 1, 2012, https://labas. livejournal.com/, accessed 30 June 2018, and document marked Translation, n.d., in Kelley Papers, box 7, fol. 5. Apparently, some Vlasovites believed that Glazenap had been hostile to Vlasov—a plausible scenario given mistrust between collaborators of the different waves during the war. Organization Summary Report, Su: SAF, to HQ, 66th Intelligence Corps Detachment, December 5, 1949, 4, in AZONDER, vol. 2, fol. 1.

[54] MOIC, Su: ODNR, 4.

[55] Aktennotiz über die Besprechung mit General von GLASENAPP, November 1, 1948, in Bundesarchiv, Digitalisierte Bestände, B 206-Bundesnachrichtendienst, 2.2.1, B 206/3016, Umorganisation der Organisation 8500 unter der Leitung von General von Glasenapp, http://www.bundesarchiv.de/DE/Navigation/ Finden/Digitalisierte-Bestaende/digitalisierte-bestaende.html, accessed November 15, 2018. See also Hermann Zolling and Heinz Höhne, "Pullach intern: Die Geschichte des Bundesnachrichtendienstes," *Der Spiegel* no. 19 (May 3, 1971): 156. I thank Igor' Petrov for bringing these sources to my attention.

question of wartime allegiances, exposing the difficulty of creating an anti-communist organization in the Cold War West that drew directly and explicitly on a collaborationist exemplar.

The Specter of Betrayal

The vilification of Glazenap was part of a wider wave of mutual recriminations and slander that overwhelmed the Vlasovite milieu. If Glazenap was probably unfairly accused of being a war criminal, he also resorted to slander by alleging that Kromiadi's entourage was littered with Soviet agents.[56] Continuing the trajectory further, months before Glazenap's death in 1951, the general himself came under attack from within his own coterie, as an opposition arose in SAF claiming that the organization had been taken over by "former members of the repressive institutions of the USSR."[57]

Denunciations were tools in the hands of ambitious exile operators, fed in this case by the personal hostility between Kromiadi and Glazenap. However, accusations about Soviet enemies in anti-communist circles were more than just a product of the émigrés' ambitions, egos, and overheated imaginations. Already well developed in the interwar years, Soviet counterintelligence operations against exile organizations continued apace during World War II. As declassified documents show, the Soviet security organs sent spies across the front lines to infiltrate the Vlasov movement and German intelligence agencies working against the USSR. For example, the operational group "Aktivnye" was dispatched in mid-1943 with a mission of "corrupting" the ROA and carrying out unnamed "special measures" directed at Vlasov himself and his close associate V. F. Malyshkin.[58] In all likelihood, informants and agents in the Vlasov circles recruited by Soviet intelligence during the war offered a foothold for postwar operations against the anti-communist forces consolidating in West Germany.

What is beyond doubt is that émigrés in Germany remained a priority target for Soviet counter-espionage efforts in the postwar years, despite it being a period of reorganization and bureaucratic struggles in Soviet foreign intelligence.[59]

[56] Agent report, Edward W. Shick and Su: Dissident Russian Groups, Lt. Col. Ellington D. Golden to Commanding Officer, 970th CIC Detachment, May 3, 1948, in AZONDER, vol. 1, fol. 1.

[57] Dvinov, *Politics of the Russian Emigration*, 221–3.

[58] Iz dokladnoi zapiski NKGB BSSR v NKGB SSSR ob itogakh agenturno-operativnoi raboty v tylu protivnika v 1943 g., no later than February 4, 1944, in S. V. Stepashin and V. P. Iampol'skii (eds.), *Organy gosudarstvennoi bezopasnosti SSSR v Velikoi otechestvennoi voine: sbornik dokumentov*, vol. 5, part 1 (Moscow: Kuchkovo pole, 2007), 136, n. 5, 140–1.

[59] In 1947, the foreign intelligence directorates of the Ministry of State Security (MGB) as well as the military's Main Intelligence Directorate (GRU) were merged in the Committee of Information, but as early as 1948 the MGB had clawed back authority over officers responsible for Russian émigré and "Soviet colonies abroad" operations. Christopher M. Andrew and Vasilii Mitrokhin, *The Mitrokhin Archive: The KGB in Europe and the West* (London: Allen Lane, 1999), 187–91.

Moreover, the postwar occupation of Germany offered Soviet intelligence agencies a favorable environment in which to operate. As was common knowledge among Western intelligence agents, the Soviet military liaison offices in West Germany mandated for repatriation purposes engaged widely in espionage.[60] Indeed, the liaison missions, which were allowed a degree of access to the DP camps, provided cover for Soviet spies to recruit Russian and other Soviet exiles as intelligence assets. One such recruit was Ivan Koval'-Kolos, a Soviet national arrested by the CIC in 1946 due to reports that he had been visiting a Soviet repatriation mission and had spread Soviet propaganda in the DP camps. A Red Army deserter who had fought in the Wehrmacht and served in Vlasov's KONR, Kolos had sought to create a Vlasov Committee near Augsburg in 1945 with the evident goal of gathering information on "VLASOV men, SS, SD, and Gestapo collaborators for Soviet Repatriation officers."[61] Although Kolos was not in a position to do extensive damage to the exiles, fears that better-hidden Soviet agents lurked in the Vlasovite ranks were voiced by Kromiadi and others.[62]

Russians in West Germany, including the Vlasovites such as Kolos, constituted an easy target for traditional intelligence-recruitment strategies. In 1946, a German intelligence officer provided the CIC with a rich account of the recruitment methods employed by Soviet agents. The simplest approach to exiles, he explained, was to offer them money, which would "alleviate their rather miserable existence." When attempting to recruit tougher human material such as committed anti-communists, the Soviets resorted to more individualized and sometimes sophisticated strategies, such as "making use of political frictions among the émigrés" and resorting to blackmail—typically, by threatening to denounce exiles to occupation authorities for any wrongdoings in which they might have been implicated.[63] Such schemes hinged on the exploitation of the myriad troubles facing postwar émigré populations in West Germany: sometimes unsure legal status, poverty, records of collaboration, vulnerability to claims for repatriation, frequent involvement in illegal smuggling and black-market schemes, and also the "atmosphere of personal jealousies, professional gossip, and the fight for physical and political survival" that plagued the anti-communist exile milieu (an illustration of which is Figure 2.1).[64]

[60] See the results of a CIC surveillance of Soviet Repatriation Missions: NARA, RG 319, IRR, D169274, Russia Repatriation Mission at Bad Wildunger, obtained through FOIA request and also Peer De Silva, *Sub Rosa: The CIA and the Uses of Intelligence* (New York: Times Books, 1978), 10–12.
[61] Kolos was also closely associated with "known Soviet agent" Il'ia Iakushev. CIC Work Sheet Annex, Su: Kolos, Iwan, November 23, 1951, in NARA, RG 319, Entry 134B, 270/84/01/01, XE160579, box 421, Ivan Kolos.
[62] MOIC, Su: ODNR, 2.
[63] Russian Emigration and the Soviet Intelligence Service, US Forces European Theater Military Intelligence Service Center, September 19, 1946, 3–4, in NARA, RG 319, IRR, XE 152740, Russian Emigration Soviet Intelligence Service, obtained through FOIA request.
[64] Harry Rositzke, *The KGB: The Eyes of Russia* (Garden City, NY: Doubleday, 1981), 102.

Figure 2.1 "I am a Vlasovite!" "No, I am a Vlasovite!" A caricature from 1950 that appeared in the émigré journal *DP-Satirikon* captures the acrimony of exile politics among the Vlasovites. Both members of the wartime Vlasovite movement, Iurii Aleksandrovich Pismennyi-Muzychenko (left) sided with monarchists while Boris Aleksandrovich Troitskii-Iakovlev (right) adopted a democratic political agenda. A poem attached to the cartoon depicted the men as two soldiers in a regiment who fight each other instead of the enemy—a characterization that conveyed the disgust with which many exiles viewed the chronic infighting in their ranks.
Source: Archiv der Forschungsstelle Osteuropa an der Universität Bremen.

Western counterintelligence services were at a distinct disadvantage when it came to operating among the émigrés. The general chaos of the war-torn country, a shortage of Russian-speaking intelligence officers, and a lack of urgent interest limited the efforts of the CIC (and later the CIA) to counter Soviet penetration efforts within the Russian anti-communist organizations in Germany.[65] The

[65] Both US intelligence officers and émigrés understood the Americans' disadvantage operating in the émigré milieu. Ibid., 105, and *Organizovannoe pokushenie na emigratsiiu* (Munich: Izdanie SBONR, 1956), 8–9.

Gehlen organization was much more engaged in the exile milieu, it is true, but it had little success in carrying out "mole hunts" within its ranks.

The failure of the Gehlen organization and the CIC to counter Soviet penetration became clear in 1947, when a scandal emerged around A. F. Chikalov-Almazov, a second-wave émigré leading an intelligence network for Operation Rusty. A high-ranking state security official in the USSR before World War II, Chikalov was captured by the Germans in 1943 and later became the head of an embryonic counterintelligence service under Vlasov.[66] As a DP after the war, Chikalov continued his career as an enterprising spy, offering to provide "excellent information about Soviet arms and about a new powerful secret weapon in the hands of the Soviets" to any intelligence service willing to pay for it.[67] Soon Chikalov was heading a Gehlen Organization network in Munich, which produced intelligence on Soviet military installations in the East zone and on alleged Soviet spies in the Russian emigration.[68] In a 1947 operation called "Operation Hagberry," the CIC arrested Chikalov and his fellow Rusty agent V. P. Tukhol'nikov-Sokolov for espionage carried out "with the mission of penetrating American intelligence networks."[69]

Chikalov's case demonstrated the difficulty of combatting Soviet intelligence in the émigré milieu. By all accounts, "Operation Hagberry" was a failure. The Americans never gathered enough evidence to try the two individuals in court, and it remains questionable whether they were actually "Soviet penetration or confusion agents," as the theory went, or not.[70] Indeed, sources suggest that the US counterintelligence case might have emerged from the exiles' suspicion of Chikalov or even his feuding with another highly controversial émigré operator in the Gehlen Organization, Vladimir Vasil'evich Pozdniakov.[71] Adding further mystery to the story, Chikalov disappeared from West Germany in 1949 without a trace. Chikalov's rivals assumed that he had been recalled by his Soviet paymasters, but B. I. Nikolaevskii was convinced that Chikalov was a genuine anti-communist kidnapped by the Bolsheviks. Although a verdict on Chikalov's intelligence career remains elusive, Nikolaevskii was probably closer to the truth: declassified Soviet documents show that Chikalov was interned in a repatriation camp in the USSR soon after his disappearance and was then condemned to death as a traitor by the Military Collegium of the USSR Supreme Court.[72]

---

[66] According to some reports, Chikalov had been a commander in the partisan movement in wartime Ukraine prior to being captured on the battlefield. On Chikalov's murky biography, see Igor' Petrov, "Odin agent i try razvedki: avtobiografiia A. F. Chikalova i kommentarii k nei," *Live Journal*, December 31, 2013, https://labas.livejournal.com/1052599.html, accessed June 30, 2018.

[67] Memorandum to col. Schmidt, Su: Tucholnikov, Wjatscheslav, no author indicated (CIC agent), n.d., 5, in NARA, RG 319, Entry 134B, 270/84/01/01, G8167289, box 810, Wjatscheslaw Tucholnikov (hereinafter Wjatscheslaw Tucholnikov).

[68] Some intelligence reports produced by the network are found in Wjatscheslaw Tucholnikov.

[69] See card labelled Tucholikow, Wjatscheslaw, 1954, in Wjatscheslaw Tucholnikov.

[70] Memorandum to Col. Schmidt, 1.

[71] Henry C. Newton to Colonel C. F. Fritzsche, 4–8.

[72] Igor' Petrov, "Tainstvennoe izcheznovanie maiora Chikalova," *Live Journal*, July 14, 2016, https://labas.livejournal.com/1152407.html, accessed 30 June 2018.

Regardless of whether Chikalov or people in his entourage were Soviet spies, Operation Hagberry demonstrated the problems facing the Gehlen Organization and its use of émigré networks. Operation Rusty had taken up with feckless intelligence operatives (or worse), and had proven unable to cleanse its own ranks without prodding from the CIC. Army counterintelligence also came out poorly from the episode. The CIC's failure to prosecute Chikalov and Tukhol'nikov suggested that the Americans were incapable of distinguishing true anti-communists from exiles working for the enemy, a fact that did not bode well for the émigré political sphere that was emerging in occupied Germany.

Perhaps the most damaging aspect of the Chikalov case was what it suggested about the Russian émigré anti-communists as a whole. An intelligence operative appointed by Vlasov himself appeared to have been a traitor, feeding speculation about other enemies lurking undetected in the émigré political organizations. In his 1948 review of the Gehlen Organization, CIA officer James C. Critchfield posited that all the Vlasovite organizations—including ATsODNR, SAF, and SBONR—had been "fairly well penetrated by the Soviets."[73] There were grounds for such a suspicion. The Vlasovite organizations gave little attention to internal vetting procedures, with SBONR admitting to its ranks "almost anyone professing anti-Soviet sympathies."[74] Such lax practices were the product of the ideological myopia of the exiles as well as the cutthroat competition between exile groups, which made it imperative to build up the ranks of one's organization by all means possible. Making matters worse, the exiles were unwilling to cooperate fully with the Western counterintelligence agencies which *might* have been able to carry out successful mole hunts in their ranks.[75] Such resistance reflected the exiles' ingrained mistrust of Westerners, to be sure, but also their touchy national pride. As self-styled Russian liberation fighters, they could not allow foreigners to act as judges of national loyalty and betrayal in their ranks.[76] In this sense, the nationalist mission of the émigrés as well as their deeply rooted suspiciousness of outsiders weakened their defense against Soviet infiltration, with anti-communist fervor taking the place that counterintelligence mechanisms should have occupied.

Facing little opposition, Soviet intelligence agents exploited the exiles' considerable weaknesses with well-developed tactics. The goal of Soviet "active measures" against the exile political organizations was their "corruption" (*razlozhenie*),

---

[73] Report of Investigation-RUSTY, 98.

[74] MOIC, Su: KONR, special agent Michael Farr, April 21, 1948, in AZONDER, vol. 1, fol. 1. This report was evaluated B-2, meaning the source was deemed "usually reliable" and the information "probably true."

[75] Of course, the high-level Soviet penetration of MI6 and the Gehlen Organization in this period makes even this assumption uncertain.

[76] In this spirit, Kromiadi refused to allow ATsODNR members to work for the CIC—an instruction, it is true, that was routinely ignored. MOIC, Subject: ODNR, Special Agent Erick J. Talvia, April 12, 1948, in AZONDER, vol. 1, fol. 1.

to be achieved through spurring confusion and mistrust within them.[77] A common practice was the spreading of forgeries and fake documents in the émigré milieu. In 1948 a broadsheet ostensibly written by rank-and-file Vlasovites appeared in Munich, which accused several ATsODNR members of having served Nazi security agencies and currently working as Soviet spies. In this specific instance, the strategy of inciting animosity and confusion fell short. The exiles identified the broadsheet as a ruse, with ATsODNR going so far as to republish the mysterious document with the words "An Example of Soviet Provocation" written over it.[78] However, the exiles could rarely find definitive evidence of whether the hidden hand of the Soviets was at work in any specific situation or not, meaning that even badly camouflaged Soviet actions might feed the lingering sense of doubt and suspicion in émigré ranks.

More damaging still for the exiles were disruption agents or agents provocateurs, moles tasked with generating controversy, mistrust, and feuds within the anti-communist organizations. While the identity of such moles was typically unclear and often remains so to this day, there can be no doubt as to their existence in the postwar Vlasovite circles. Probably one such agent was Vladimir Petrovich Vasilaki, a Ukrainian of Greek ancestry who had been captured on the Eastern Front and then joined Vlasov's Committee for the Liberation of the Peoples of Russia. Vasilaki aroused suspicion of having been a long-term Soviet provocateur after he redefected to the USSR in 1955. In the postwar anti-communist milieu in Germany, Vasilaki had behaved for years in ways that seemed calculated to instill confusion and discord among the émigrés, or to act as a source of "disintegration and destruction," in one characterization.[79] In 1948, he accused Boris Iakovlev-Troitskii of being a Soviet spy, a move that probably represented an effort to compromise, in Iakovlev, an exile who had developed extensive ties with American journalists, academics, and other anti-communists.[80] If this was the objective, the Soviets may have had a degree of success. In 1950, Iakovlev resigned from leadership of SBONR after clashing with the organization's other leaders, a rift that might have been deepened by the atmosphere of suspicion

[77] See the discussion of *razlozhenie* in an internal 1977 textbook on the history of the KGB. V. M. Chebrikov, *Istoriia Sovetskikh organov gosudarstvennoi bezopasnosti: uchebnik* (Moscow: Vysshaia Krasnoznamennaia Shkola Komiteta Gosudarstvennoi Bezopasnosti pri Sovete Ministrov SSSR imeni F.E. Dzerzhinskogo, 1977), 521.

[78] Otkrytoe pis'mo rukovoditeliam Antibol'shevitskogo Tsentra Osvoboditel'nogo Dvizheniia Narodov Rossii (A.Ts.O.D.N.R.) i Glavnomu Upravleniiu Soiuza Andreevskogo Flaga, in HILA, Boris I. Nicolaevsky Collection, Series 201, box 264, fol. 1. On the origins of this document, see Agent Report, Su: Ukrainian activities, special agent Thomas V. Mullen, October 21, 1948, in AZONDER, vol. 2, fol. 2.

[79] Gerhard von Mende to Dr Bräutigam, Auswärtiges Amt, Betr: Ukrainischer Re-Emigrant Wladimir Petrowitsch Wassilakij, April 29, 1955, in Auswärtiges Amt-Politisches Archiv (AA-PA), B 12, Akte 455.

[80] MOIC, Su: AZODNR, special agent Thomas V. Mullen, July 6, 1948, 3, in AZONDER, vol. 1, fol. 1.

that enveloped the anti-communist exiles in Germany.[81] More directly, Iakovlev lost the trust of the CIA in the course of the 1950s, most likely as a result of Soviet efforts at compromising him.[82]

The Iakovlev case suggested the almost free rein that exile politics gave to Soviet disruption strategies. In an environment in which mistrust was universal, virtually any émigré was a suitable target for defamation. Indeed, the very fact that the exiles routinely accused each other of improprieties and betrayals of all sorts created a kind of cover for Soviet provocations. Given constant émigré infighting, could one really be sure that Vasilaki—or even, for that matter, Iakovlev—was *not* a Soviet agent? The Soviet side had created a vicious circle of universal suspicion and accusation that nearly paralyzed the exiles' activities.[83]

The Kremlin's Fascist

One exile widely suspected to be a Soviet disruption agent in the Russian anti-communist scene was Evgenii Nikolaevich Artsiuk-Derzhavin. His was a remarkable life, even by the standards of the Russian emigration. Hailing from a first-wave family that settled in Paris, Artsiuk worked as a dancer and costume designer for a ballet troupe in in the interwar years.[84] During the German occupation of France, Artsiuk joined a pro-Nazi collaborationist group, spied on the émigré community for the Gestapo, served as an interpreter for the Wehrmacht, set foot in occupied Western Russia, and entered the Vlasov camp by the end of the war. Dark rumors accompanied him throughout: a fellow Vlasovite alleged that Artsiuk disappeared during the German retreat from Russia under suspicious circumstances.[85]

[81] According to one source, some SBONR leaders had come to express doubts in Iakovlev's "political trustworthiness." Deiatel'nost' "Amerikanskogo Komiteta Bor'by za Svobodu Rossii," (report, evidently for French intelligence), n.d. (1951), in HILA, Ryszard Wraga Papers, box 4, fol. 1. See also E. V. Kodin, *Miunkhenskii institut po izucheniiu istorii i kul'tury SSSR, 1950–1972 gg.: evropeiskii tsentr sovetologii?* (Smolensk: Izd-o SmolGU, 2016), 15.

[82] Notably, the Chief of the CIA Munich Base expressed doubt about Iakovlev's allegiances in 1958 after being sent a denunciation of the exile that was clearly slanderous. Chief, Munich Base to Chief, IO, March 31, 1958 in NARA, RG 263, Entry ZZ-19, 250/86/26/01, box 55, QKACTIVE, vol. 1.

[83] Soviet infiltration of the émigrés bears resemblance to the counterinsurgency strategy discussed in Jeffrey Burds, "Agentura: Soviet Informants' Networks & the Ukrainian Underground in Galicia, 1944–48," *East European Politics & Societies* 11, no. 1 (1996): 89–130.

[84] L. A. Mnukhin et al., *Rossiiskoe zarubezh'e vo Frantsii: 1919–2000: biograficheskii slovar'* (Moscow: Dom-muzei Mariny Tsvetaevoi, 2008), 81.

[85] On Artsiuk's alleged work for the Gestapo in the Russian colony of Paris, see Vermerk, betr: russische Organisationen, May 9, 1953, in B 137, Akte 1021. A description of Artsiuk's disappearance in 1944 comes from the Vlasovite Boris Wolff-Lüdinghausen. Apparently, Artsiuk aroused German suspicion when he disappeared from his unit for a few weeks and then reappeared in civilian clothes and carrying false identity papers. Agent Report, Su: Artsyuk, Eugenij, W. E. Hermann, 66th CIC det., October 6, 1952, 1–2, in NARA, RG 319, Entry 134B, 270/84/01/01, XE 312364, box 23, Yeugeny Artsuk (hereinafter Yeugeny Artsuk).

Artsiuk's postwar activities were just as murky. In the period just after German capitulation, he was involved in a crime ring that stole aid packages destined for DPs and resold them on the open market.[86] Once the émigré political world resurfaced in Germany, he became an active if also highly controversial participant. In 1948, Artsiuk founded the Russian National Popular State Movement (*Rossiiskoe Obshchenatsional'noe Narodno-Derzhavnoe Dvizhenie* or RONDD), a far-right monarchist group that splintered from ATsODNR. Soon Glazenap and his SAF, also banished from the Vlasovite center, joined forces with Artsiuk to form a small but tightly organized radical-right flank of the emigration.[87]

Artsiuk's enterprise was unlike all others in the Russian anti-communist sphere. As shown by the Glazenap affair, Russian exiles who collaborated with Germany were eager to obscure their war records by all means possible, not least by stressing their fealty to Western-style democracy. Not so Artsiuk, who openly embraced the neo-Nazi parties that appeared in the Federal Republic.[88] If other émigrés sought to establish ties with the United States, Artsiuk denounced the country as a "Jew capitalist system" and sent the 1952 Republican National Convention a special English-language edition of RONDD's publication *Nabat* ("the Tocsin") claiming that Eisenhower was a tool of the Kremlin.[89] And while other émigré organizations saw the need to work toward some form of mutual cooperation, Artsiuk claimed to represent the only genuine anti-Soviet force in the emigration and denounced virtually all exiles outside it as traitors, Jews, and freemasons—all people who would be hanged in post-Soviet Russia, he declared on one occasion.[90]

Western intelligence services suspected that Artsiuk was playing a double game. As observers on all sides noted, his scandal-courting political moves in the 1950s were consistent with a strategy of discrediting Russian émigrés and their American and German backers. In 1952, the CIC investigated Artsiuk and his associates, evidently at the behest of the German Federal Office for the Protection of the Constitution (*Bundesamt für Verfassungsschutz* or BfV) and the British MI6.[91] As was often the case, the CIC was unable to prove Artsiuk's link to Soviet

[86] Agent Report, Re: Artsyuk, Eugenij, Special Agent W. E. Hermann, October 6, 1952, in Yeugeny Artsuk.

[87] Aufzeichnung, Betr: Die Emigration aus der Sowjetunion und den von ihr beherrschten Gebieten, Ref. Scholl, January 19, 1956, 68–70, in AA-PA, B 12, Akte 455.

[88] Artsiuk's activities are described in Agent report, Artsyuk, Eugenij, October 6, 1952, 61, in Yeugeny Artsuk and the Activity of TsPRE and RONDD, report from LfV to BfV, J. H. Lez, Reports Section, AMCOMGEN, Munich to Hq 66th CIC Group, June 27, 1953, 5, in AZONDER, vol. 2, fol. 1.

[89] LfV agent report from source V, March 6, 1952, 2, in Yeugeny Artsuk and Agent Report, Su: Artsyuk, Eugenij, W. E. Hermann, 66th CIC det., October 6, 1952, 1–2, in Yeugeny Artsuk.

[90] For RONDD's denunciation of ATsODNR, see Otvet politicheskim mistifikatoram i koldunam iz TsIK'a ATsONDR i CC'a SBONR, byvsh. SMNR, gruppa narodno-derzhavnikov, August 20, 1948, in AZONDER, vol. 2, fol. 2. Artsiuk threatened hanging for those exiles who signed an American-sponsored 1952 manifesto on the February Revolution. Agent Report, Artsyuk, Eugenij, October 6, 1952, in Yeugeny Artsuk.

[91] Hq., British Intelligence Organization (Germany) to British Liaison Office, Hq. EUCOM, August 1, 1952, in Yeugeny Artsuk.

intelligence agencies, perhaps because the investigation had failed to get close enough to the entourage of the isolated and suspicious Artsiuk to "furnish accurate information."[92] In hindsight, it seems very likely that Artsiuk was indeed the Kremlin's fascist, an interpretation lent credence by the fact that a convicted Soviet spy identified him as a fellow agent.[93] Also suspicious were Artsiuk's waning years, which, by one account, he spent visiting the Soviet Union, praising communism, and proudly driving a Soviet car through the streets of Munich.[94]

At first glance, one might question the effectiveness of Artsiuk's campaign of disruption. Virtually all the émigrés outside Artsiuk's orbit suspected him of treachery, while his tactics were perhaps counterproductive: in 1954, Artsiuk and his associate V. K. Kudinov-Mosichkin, a second-wave Vlasovite, were convicted in a German court of inciting racial prejudice and national hatred after publishing an anti-Semitic tract. (During the proceedings, Artsiuk attempted to call US Senator Joseph McCarthy as a witness to defend his stance that Jewish bankers had created Bolshevism.)[95] It would appear that Artsiuk had provoked too many outrages and blown his cover in the process.

Artsiuk inflicted damage on the Russian emigration nevertheless. In particular, his RONDD was at the center of a scandal surrounding the creation of a representative body for Russian DPs in Germany. Relative to other DP populations, the Russians were slow to create a central body to represent their interests in the western zones of Germany, a situation that reflected their extreme internal division.[96] In early 1947, the International Relief Organization (IRO) recognized the Central Russian Representation of the Russian Emigration (*Tsentral'noe Predstaviteľ'stvo Rossiiskoi Emigratsii* or TsPRE) as a body that would represent the legal and economic interests of Russians in the US zone as well as deal with the matter of their eventual resettlement. Two years later, however, RONDD and SAF launched an elaborate and well-funded campaign to seize the majority at a TsPRE congress, allegedly offering émigré representatives substantial monetary sums if they agreed to join their list of delegates.[97] Artsiuk and his fellows then proceeded to use control of TsPRE to embezzle its funds and to sell exiles fraudulent identity

[92] Bernard Tormey, col., CIC to Assistant Chief of Staff, G-2, Intelligence, EUCOM, January 23, 1953, in Yeugeny Artsuk.

[93] The agent was Darko Čirković, who gave this information to self-confessed Soviet spy and fellow Yugoslav Wojislav Memedović. Agent report, Artsyuk, Eugenij, October 6, 1952, 61, in Yeugeny Artsuk.

[94] The source of this information, Grigorii Petrovich Klimov, is a controversial figure, as will be discussed in Chapter 9. Grigorii Klimov, *Otkrovenie*, ch. 5, http://g-klimov.info/, accessed July 11, 2017.

[95] See the translation of the Munich *Abendzeitung* in Agent Report, Special Agent William J. Jones, 66th CIC Group, July 29, 1954, in NARA, RG 319, Entry 134B, 270/84/01/01, H8002378, box 535, Wsewolod Mositschkin (henceforth Wsewolod Mositschkin).

[96] Holian, *Between National Socialism and Soviet Communism*, 112.

[97] Document entitled Glasenap, George Meyer, n.d., in Georgetown University Archives and Special Collections, Robert F. Kelley Papers, box 6, fol. 7. RONDD was said to have held control of the "Petersburg Pawn Exchequer" mentioned above with regard to Glazenap. Aufzeichnung, Betr: Die Emigration, 61.

cards at exorbitant prices.[98] The fact that an internationally recognized welfare agency for Russian exiles had fallen into the hands of a fascist and likely Soviet spy was a sad commentary on the Russian diaspora, a population for which political infighting made the articulation of collective interests all but impossible.

The Artsiuk takeover of TsPRE was a coup for his agenda of disrupting and discrediting the wider Russian diaspora in Germany. Neo-fascist control over an official representative body compromised the Russian exiles en masse in the eyes of non-Russian observers. According to a CIC agent, RONDD's paper *Nabat*, apparently due to the organization's control of TsPRE, was "considered by most people to be the official publication of all Russian emigrant organizations." By extension, the agent remarked, the émigrés as a whole came across as rabid anti-Semites.[99] In 1949 a group of exiles, with the support of a US military intelligence agent, responded to the hostile seizure of the representative body by creating a counter-organization called the National Representation of the Russian Emigration in West Germany (*Natsional'noe Predstavitel'stvo Rossiiskoi Emigratsii* or NATsPRE).[100] However, the existence of warring émigré welfare organizations itself demoralized the exiles. And understandably so, for a constant motif of the Artsiuk camp was scandal: witness a fistfight between Mosichkin and a NATsPRE leader after an Orthodox Church service in Stuttgart, during which the former had apparently screamed, "I will kill you, you Communist bastard."[101] Clearly, Artsiuk had succeeded in stoking hostilities among the exiles.

Artsiuk's strategy of provocation was directed at a much wider target than his many émigré opponents. In the early 1950s, the integration of West Germany into the NATO alliance and its planned rearmament were central issues in the Cold War. In this respect, Artsiuk's relationship with unreformed Nazis served Moscow's purposes. As already intimated, Artsiuk was tireless in his efforts to associate his political cause with that of the resurgent right in Germany. Sources suggest that Artsiuk and RONDD were quite close to two neo-Nazi organizations, the *Deutscher Block* of Karl Meissner and the League of German Youth (*Bund deutscher Jugend*).[102] Such associations tarred the exiles with the Nazi brush, while also contributing to Soviet propaganda depicting West Germany as a country of unreformed fascists.

---

[98] Su: Dzersavin-Artiuk, Eugenie, agent report from BfV, June 5, 1954, 3–4, in Wsewolod Mositschkin.

[99] Agent Report, Re: Artsyuk, Eugenij.

[100] Ibid., 27. The new body was financed by Aleksei Mikailovich Mil'rud, a Russian employed by US Military Intelligence whose efforts in organizing Russian émigrés are discussed in Chapters 4 and 9. Agent report, Su: Mositschkin, Wsewolod, Arthur P. Jastrzebski, Special Agent, CIC, February 14, 1953, in Wsewolod Mositschkin.

[101] Ibid.

[102] RONDD ties with German groups are mentioned in Bernd Stöver, *Die Befreiung vom Kommunismus: amerikanische Liberation Policy im Kalten Krieg 1947–1991* (Cologne: Böhlau, 2002), 340, 360.

Artsiuk's attempts to taint West Germany also extended to the government and the ruling Christian Democratic Party (CDU). As Christopher Andrew and Vasilii Mitrokhin have written, a goal of Soviet intelligence agencies throughout the Cold War was to "discredit as many West German politicians as possible as neo-Nazis and 'revenge seekers.'"[103] Likely in pursuit of this end, Artsiuk persistently tried to build links to offices of the Federal Republic, including the Federal Ministry of Intra-German Affairs (*Bundesministerium für gesamtdeutsche Fragen* or BMG), the German agency charged with carrying out psychological warfare against East Germany. Ewert Freiherr von Dellingshausen, the BMG official in charge of ties with exiles, was in discussions with Artsiuk in 1952, and even wrote that he hoped to "present" the RONDD leader in Bonn at some undetermined date.[104] Perhaps after receiving warnings from his other exile contacts, von Dellingshausen soured on the divisive exile.[105]

If Artsiuk failed to tie his organization to German power structures, he created the *impression* that he had. For instance, a 1953 report from the West German BfV on a TsPRE conference hypothesized that Artsiuk's organization received funding not just from the small fascist parties noted above but also from a host of establishment political forces: a powerful organization of German expellees from the East (the All-German Bloc/League of Expellees and Deprived of Rights or *Gesamtdeutscher Block/Bund der Heimatvertriebenen und Entrechteten*), the Gehlen Organization, the BMG, and the West German Ministry of the Interior.[106] The intelligence seems doubtful, and one might suspect that it was based on rumors spread by Artsiuk and his entourage. Nevertheless, that a BfV informant would pass on such information showed that Artsiuk had at least created the illusion of being connected to the West German state.

The possibility that RONDD was tied to the nascent Federal Republic concerned German political elites as well. In 1953, CDU Bundestag member Hermann A. Eplée wrote the BMG asking for information on which Russian groups the ministry supported, while warning that a "false path" on this question could have "unforeseen consequences" (and mentioning RONDD by name).[107] The spectacle of Russian fascists working alongside German elites would be an obvious embarrassment during the early Cold War. As the Eplée letter suggested, RONDD's antics could easily damage the reputation of the Russian exile groups as a whole, driving a wedge between the latter and their potential German

---

[103] Andrew and Mitrokhin, *The Mitrokhin Archive*, 573.
[104] Von Dellingshausen to Artsiuk, June 20, 1952, in BA B 137, Akte 1021.
[105] Auszugsweise Abschrift aus "Deutscher Informationsdienst," April 8, 1953, 2, in BA B 137, Akte 1021.
[106] The Activity of TsPRE and RONDD, report from LfV to BfV, J. H. Lez, Reports Section, AMCOMGEN, Munich to Hq 66th CIC Group, June 27, 1953, 6, in AZONDER, vol. 2, fol. 1.
[107] Hermann A. Eplée to Jacob Kaiser, March 12, 1953, in BA B 137, Akte 1021.

or US sponsors. For all his buffoonery and unpopularity, then, Artsiuk was a valuable asset.

*   *   *

By the start of the 1950s, dreams of planting royalist flags on the Kremlin walls had proven hollow. While some Whites continued to hope for a chance to return to the field, the rightist cause as a whole had splintered into hostile factions. Several factors had conspired to frustrate the political ambitions of the émigré right, and particularly of the monarchists. The White forces of the older generation had failed to cement leadership over the second-wave Vlasovites, a circumstance that hinged on the cohorts' different generational experiences. The activities of the Gehlen Organization inserted an element of chaos into this already complex picture, as intelligence networks clashed behind the façade of exile political organizations. Infiltration by Soviet intelligence networks added to the already considerable divisiveness of the exile political milieu in Germany. The Chikalov affair conveyed to all parties concerned that hidden enemies lurked among the anti-communists, while Artsiuk showed the extensive damage a Soviet agent could accomplish, even one as universally mistrusted as he. The rightist path had collapsed—even though many first-wave exiles, and even a portion of the second wave, still favored the restoration of the Russian monarchy.[108]

The distinctive feature of Russian anti-communist politics in the DP camps, as well as the major cause of its troubles, was its connection to espionage. As a diasporic community attempting to influence the homeland, the exiles found themselves at the intersection of different intelligence services, mainly the Gehlen Organization, the CIC, and Soviet foreign intelligence. The poverty, demoralization, and unsettled nature of Russian communities in West Germany facilitated the covert moves made by these different spy agencies. So too did the very anti-communism that drove the exiles' political agendas, as the exiles saw espionage matters through the distorting ideological categories of national loyalty and betrayal.[109] In the situation that resulted, intelligence tasks and politics were often indistinguishable: recall the Gehlen agents who used their funds to pursue political power or the Soviet disruption agents burrowing into anti-communist organizations. The cross-fertilization of politics and espionage gave émigré political activism its byzantine and unpredictable character, as organizations coalesced and then disintegrated—amid personal feuds, clan battles, and demoralization—in rapid succession.

---

[108] Aufzeichnung, Betr: Die Emigration, 47.

[109] On the impact of ideology on counterintelligence in a very different context, see Reg Whitaker, "Cold War Alchemy: How America, Britain and Canada transformed Espionage into Subversion," *Intelligence and National Security* 15, no. 2 (2000): 177–210.

The early postwar adventures of the Russian anti-communists demonstrated the need for foreign sponsorship of their liberationist cause. Even after the Western allies ended the mandatory repatriation of Soviet citizens and offered de facto permission for their political activities, the exile anti-communists had limited room for political action and remained vulnerable. However, the governments with the power and ability to support the anti-communist exiles—those of the United States and, to a lesser extent, Britain—were reluctant to do so and largely watched from the sidelines until the end of the 1940s. The defeated Germans had more experience with anti-communist exiles of all stripes, but were hardly in a position to pursue a more assertive role. The Gehlen Organization bridged the gap between American power and the Russians to an extent, but its entry into émigré affairs brought new problems. As both the Glazenap and Artsiuk episodes showed, most Russian exiles in Germany resisted close association with the occupied Germans, fearful of drawing attention to their own collaborationist pasts. Meanwhile, the security failures of the Gehlen Organization encouraged the spread of crippling suspicions of betrayal among the exiles.

Time was on the side of the exiles, however. While Vlasovites clashed among themselves, policymakers, journalists, and academics in the United States began to turn their attention to anti-communist causes in Europe and beyond. The mobilization of anti-communism across the Atlantic would bring new political influences to the emigration in Germany, which included familiar voices from the Russian past.

3

Socialists and Vlasovites

War Memories and a Troubled Cross-Continental Encounter

In 1949, *The New York Times* reported on a meeting of Russian émigrés that had taken place at a Jewish community center on Eighty-Ninth Street. The paper described the meeting as the first effort to create "an amalgam of all anti-Soviet émigrés seeking the overthrow of the Soviet regime," and added that related initiatives were afoot in Paris and West Germany. While the New York meeting was billed as a new endeavor, its leaders were well known. Headlining the event was Aleksandr Federovich Kerenskii, the head of the Provisional Government toppled by the Bolsheviks in Petrograd in 1917. Like the New York event itself, Kerenskii's message was a mixture of timeworn and newfangled ideas. Predictably, he proclaimed that Russians sought to regain the constitutional rule and "life of a free people" that Lenin had stolen from them in 1917. At the same time, Kerenskii urged the émigrés to "forget the past and start anew," overcoming their past conflicts in order "to build after the desires and wishes of the new generation" in Russia.[1]

The meeting in New York marked the entry of a new force onto the world of postwar Russian anti-communism in Europe: democratic socialists of the first wave who had left Russia during and sometimes after the Russian Civil War (1918–22). As discussed in Chapter 1, the exiled left had experienced thirty years of often repeated flight prompted by European political catastrophes: first the Russian Revolution and then Hitler's conquest of the continent. After decades of limited political relevance, exile in the US during the early Cold War brought Kerenskii and other figures from Russia's revolutionary past into the spotlight again. Branding themselves as moderate social democrats rather than revolutionaries, the men speaking in New York in 1949 had become "soldiers in the Cold War" in their new place of exile.[2]

Despite its fanfare, the meeting in New York revealed the difficulties posed by the political resurgence of the Russian socialists in Cold War America. Kerenskii's

---

[1] "'Free Russia' Move is Organized Here: Kerensky, Premier in 1917, Asks Emigres to 'Start Anew'—Unit Set up in Paris Also," *The New York Times*, March 14, 1949, 19.

[2] André Liebich, "Mensheviks Wage the Cold War," *Journal of Contemporary History* 30, no. 2 (1995): 247–64.

Cold War Exiles and the CIA: Plotting to Free Russia. Benjamin Tromly, Oxford University Press (2019). © Benjamin Tromly.
DOI: 10.1093/oso/9780198840404.001.0001

call to "start anew" alluded to the deep rifts among the different groupings of first-wave émigrés, which dated back to 1917 or before but had deepened during the long history of infighting in exile. An even more profound problem raised at the meeting was the cross-generational nature of Kerenskii's enterprise. The leftists in New York directed their efforts at courting the second-wave exiles in Germany, and particularly the Vlasovites, who were then still associated with the conservative Whites. In a complicated generational courtship, the old socialists attempted to woo the second-wave Vlasovites away from the monarchists and conservatives who held influence in the immediate postwar years. In this competition between putative ideological parents, the socialists had an advantage: they had the goodwill of powerful circles in the United States, the anti-Soviet juggernaut whose support exile groups on all points of the political spectrum sought out.

The leftists, however, experienced considerable headwinds in their Cold War project. As with the White émigrés, the old socialists would find that exerting influence on the second wave was difficult. Unlike the elderly socialists, the second-wavers were thought to be authentic specimens of Stalinist society, and therefore more relevant to the anti-communist struggle. As Kerenskii conceded in an article in the American press, the first-wavers had superior "political experience and organizing ability," but "the destiny of the country" lay in the hands of the younger émigré cohort.[3] More important still, the two generations of exiles had different views of Russian history, and these divergences were perhaps even starker than those between the Whites and Vlasovites discussed in Chapter 2.[4] In particular, the issue of World War II and Russian collaborationism proved intractable for Kerenskii's postwar Russian project. While the socialist democrats rejected collaboration with Nazism in any form, the Vlasovites defended their wartime actions heatedly. As Kerenskii and his companions in American exile would discover, efforts to bring together the two cohorts of exiles eventually drove them apart by sparking intergenerational debates over war, revolution, and the Russian nation.

Finding the New Russian Democrats

Coverage in *The New York Times* signaled the crucial political asset of the Russian socialists: their sure-footed position in American exile. Within the Russian

[3] Leonard J. Schweiter, "There's Hope for Russia: This man makes bold predictions, but he is confident they will come true," unidentified magazine article in Columbia University Rare Book and Manuscript Library, Bakhmeteff Archive of Russian and East European History and Culture (hereinafter Bakhmeteff Archive), Mikhail Mikhailovich Karpovich Correspondence, box 2.

[4] This chapter builds on previous work on the socialist–Vlasovite interaction. See A. V. Antoshin, "Men'sheviki v emigratsii posle Vtoroi mirovoi voiny," *Otechestvennaia istoriia* no. 1 (2007): 102–15, and André Liebich, *From the Other Shore: Russian Social Democracy after 1921* (Cambridge, MA: Harvard University Press, 1997), 291–5.

diaspora, the first-wave socialists' path to integration into American society was an anomaly. Generally speaking, many Russians in the United States, like East European minorities more generally, espoused a conservative anti-communist ideology.[5] Many first-wave Russians in America were skeptical of what they saw as a disorganized and ineffectual liberal order, casting doubt on whether such a society had the willpower to stop communist expansion. Often, the political activists followed exiled philosophers in developing a Slavophilic juxtaposition between the mechanical and egotistic West and the supposedly more spiritualistic and communalistic Russians.[6] More immediately, some looked for American figures who might stiffen the spine of the United States: both Senator Joseph McCarthy and General Douglas MacArthur developed strong fan bases among rightist Russian Americans.[7]

The leftists had an altogether more positive perception of the United States. To be sure, many of the exiles fell on hard times in New York, finding "little work or support" beyond their own tight milieu.[8] A case in point was Vasilii Federovich Butenko, associated with an offshoot of the Socialist Revolutionaries abroad, who lived in the office of an émigré political organization in New York and complained of hunger in his letters.[9] On the whole, however, the Russian socialists were distinctive among exiles in their ability to find a place in American society. The tireless organizer Rafael Abramovich became connected to anti-communist American labor, receiving funds for the Menshevik Foreign Delegation through the American Federation of Labor's (AFL) Labor Conference on International Affairs.[10] Meanwhile, the exiles found common ground with "liberal anti-communism," the democratic and cosmopolitan strand in American anti-communism that had mobilized against the Roosevelt-era accommodation with the Soviet Union.[11] In particular, Mensheviks found natural allies among the so-called New York intellectuals, disillusioned fellow-traveler intellectuals such as Melvin Lasky and Sidney Hook, with whom they shared a history of struggle against communism from leftist positions.[12] Meanwhile, Kerenskii's close associate

---

[5] See Ieva Zake (ed.), *Anti-communist Minorities in the U.S.: Political Activism of Ethnic Refugees* (New York, NY: Palgrave Macmillan, 2009).

[6] A. V. Antoshin, *Rossiiskie emigranty v usloviiakh "kholodnoi voiny" (seredina 1940-kh-seredina 1960-kh gg.)* (Ekaterinburg: Izd. Ural'skogo universiteta, 2008), 328–400.

[7] Ibid., 395, 546.

[8] George Uri Fischer, *Insatiable: A Story of my Nine Lives* (Philadelphia: unpublished TS, 2000), 74. I thank David Engerman for providing me with a copy of this rare text.

[9] Butenko refused to take a job as a dishwasher in order to devote all his energies to anti-Soviet politics. V. F. Butenko to R. B. Gul', March 17, 1949, in Bakhmeteff Archive, Vasilii Fedoseevich Butenko Papers (hereinafter Butenko Papers), box 1, fol. 1.

[10] Liebich, "Mensheviks Wage the Cold War": 248–9.

[11] Richard Gid Powers, *Not without Honor: The History of American Anticommunism* (New York: Free Press, 1995), 199–212.

[12] Hugh Wilford, *The Mighty Wurlitzer: How the CIA Played America* (Cambridge, MA: Harvard University Press, 2008), 70–98, and Larry Ceplair, *Anti-Communism in Twentieth-Century America: A Critical History* (Santa Barbara, CA: Praeger, 2011), 153–70.

Mikhail Mikhailovich Karpovich used his position on the faculty at Harvard University to widen émigré contacts with the growing host of American Russia experts.[13] All these cross-cultural contacts represented a remarkable expansion of influence for personalities who had fallen into obscurity during exile.

The most important means of émigré access to American life was the pen. In particular, the Mensheviks B. I. Nikolaevskii and D. Iu. Dalin became leading Soviet specialists in the United States, people to whom Russia experts and American anti-communist activists of various stripes turned for knowledge on the Stalinist regime and how to fight it. Especially influential was their jointly written *Forced Labor in Soviet Russia*, the first detailed exposé of Stalin's Gulag in English, which made waves in international public opinion and prompted verbal assaults from Soviet representative Aleksandr Ianuarevich Vyshinskii on the floor of the United Nations General Assembly.[14] In this way, the first-wave socialists acted on a political stage alongside American journalists, academics, and foreign-policy experts—and, as soon would become clear, spies.

Russian revolutionaries, then, found an unexpected niche in the capitalist United States, where they formed a pro-Western and cosmopolitan strain in the wider Russian diaspora.[15] Yet the primary interest of the old socialists—and, paradoxically, the very basis of their integration into American society—was the political situation in Russia. The émigrés' continued struggle against Stalin pointed them toward the second wave of war-displaced Russians in Germany. Early information on the Soviet displaced persons (DPs) arrived in New York via émigré letters across the Atlantic, after the Russians who had been lucky enough to escape Europe before the war re-established contact with their friends who had not. Witnessing the tragedy of the war from afar, Russian exiles in America of all ideological types threw themselves into charitable work for their co-nationals in Europe, including the second-wave "non-returners" who were under risk of repatriation to the USSR.[16] These efforts to save the new cohorts of exiles became an expression and also a test of the national spirit of the American branch of "Russia abroad."

The old revolutionaries in America were quick to see the political significance of the émigrés in Europe. In 1947, Nikolaevskii traveled to Europe in order to

---

[13] In part, Karpovich founded *Russian Review*, which printed articles by émigré scholars alongside their American colleagues. N. N. Bolkhovitinov, *Russie uchenye-emigranty (G. V. Vernadskii, M. M. Karpovich, M. T. Florinskii) i stanovlenie Rusistiki v SShA* (Moscow: ROSSPEN, 2005), 47–64.

[14] David J. Dallin and Boris I. Nicolaevsky, *Forced Labor in Soviet Russia* (New Haven: Yale University Press, 1947). On the public resonance of the book in the United States, see Susan L. Carruthers, *Cold War Captives: Imprisonment, Escape, and Brainwashing* (Berkeley, CA: University of California Press, 2009), 267–72.

[15] On cosmopolitanism and exile, see the Introduction to Susanne Lachenicht and Kirsten Heinsohn (eds.), *Diaspora Identities: Exile, Nationalism and Cosmopolitanism in Past and Present* (Frankfurt and New York: Campus Verlag, 1999), 8–9.

[16] See T. I. Ul'iankina, *"Dikaia istoricheskaia polosa..." sud'by Rossiiskoi nauchnoi intelligentsii v Evrope (1940-1950)* (Moscow: ROSSPEN, 2010).

retrieve archives he had left behind during his flight from France, a trip arranged through the Central Intelligence Group, the immediate predecessor to the CIA.[17] Utilizing this protection, Nikolaevskii visited the DP camps of Germany, where he met with the different circles of émigré anti-communists organizing themselves there. During his travels, Nikolaevskii developed a high opinion of the second-wave Vlasovites who formed the majority of the anti-communist activists in Europe.[18] The DPs in Europe were promising "reinforcements" for the anti-communist cause, he reasoned, for they had not only "first-hand knowledge of Stalinist Russia" but also a recent record of fighting it.[19] Nikolaevskii also took to the second wave because of its supposedly "deeply democratic" social compos-ition, which, he thought, contrasted with the White exiles, whose sole concern was their loss of "wealth, estates, and privileges" during the Revolution.[20] The decision of Nikolaevskii and others to court the second-wave displaced persons also had a personal dimension. The elderly social democrats saw the Soviet citizens uprooted by the war as a potential channel through which to subvert Stalin's rule over their long-estranged homeland. In this sense, the DPs seemed to constitute a last path to political relevance for people who had devoted their lives to revolution in Russia.

Nikolaevskii's trip to the German DP camps, which Dalin replicated a year later, was a turning point in Russian émigré politics.[21] The appearance of exiles from distant America sent shock waves through the DP camps. Arriving with the goodwill of US occupation forces, Nikolaevskii and Dalin appeared to their fellow Russians to be no less than emissaries of the American superpower. Rumors swirled through Russian circles that the newcomers were offering visas to the United States as the reward for political association, information that was surely false but reflected the extent to which immigration to America was the dream of

---

[17] HQ, Sub-Region Frankfurt, CIC Region III, Su: Rurr, Fred, September 22, 1947, in National Archives and Records Administration (NARA), RG 319, IRR, D211036, Nikolaewskij, Boris, acquired through FOIA request. See also Memorandum for the Record, February 27, 1948, in Crafting an Intelligence Community: Papers of the First Four DCIs, CIA FOIA Electronic Reading Room.

[18] MOIC, Su: ODNR, March 9, 1948, 13, in AZONDER vol. 1, fol. 1.

[19] This is a reconstruction of Nikolaevskii's thinking from his American associate Professor Philip Moseley. Philip E. Mosely, "Boris Nicolaevsky: The American Years," in Boris I. Nicolaevsky et al., *Revolution and Politics in Russia: Essays in Memory of B.I. Nicolaevsky* (Bloomington, IN: Indiana University Press, 1973), 36.

[20] "Liga bor'by za narodnuiu svobodu," *Sotsialisticheskii vestnik* (hereinafter *SV*) no. 3 (618) (March 25, 1949): 44. Here Nikolaevskii oversimplified the social composition of the second wave, which included substantial numbers of Stalin-era elites. See comments on the social makeup of the two waves in Chapter 1, pages 39.

[21] Like Nikolaevskii, Dalin toured occupied Germany with at least the prior knowledge and goodwill of the Military Government and perhaps the CIA. According to one CIC informant, he gave lectures at the US European Theatre Intelligence School at Oberammergau during his trip. HQ CIC Region IV to Commanding Officer, 7970th Counter Intelligence Corps Group, November 19, 1948, in NARA, RG 319, Entry 134B, X8185228, box 146, Dallin, David (hereinafter David Dallin).

the mass of DPs.[22] Finally, some exiles in Germany concluded, the US government was involving itself in the Russian anti-communist cause.

The leftists, though, met with pushback from the conservative political groups that held sway over exile politics in Germany in the 1940s. True, Nikolaevskii established a solid rapport with Vlasovite leader K. G. Kromiadi during his trip, and it is possible that the two very different émigré leaders discussed future collaboration.[23] Ultimately, though, the ideological gulf between the two sides made cooperation impossible. During his trip, the undiplomatic Dalin attended a meeting of the Central Committee of the Anti-Bolshevist Center for the Liberation Movement of the Peoples of Russia (ATsODNR), the conservative Vlasovite organization which was discussed in Chapter 2. There Dalin declared that he was creating a "republican-democratic bloc" in which monarchists and the far-right National Labor Alliance (NTS) would not be welcome.[24] If Dalin predicated intra-diaspora collaboration on acceptance of democracy, the Whites did the same with anti-Marxism. The conservatives viewed Marxism as inherently evil—a "criminal and deprived conception of the world," in one evaluation—and refused to deal with individuals who were unwilling to renounce their past and present ties to Marxist thought.[25]

If political ideology and historical memory prevented cooperation between the two camps of first-wave exiles, the struggle for power in the diaspora made their relationship downright antagonistic. The Whites in Germany now saw the New Yorkers not just as anti-Russian Marxists but as dangerous rivals eager to break their already shaky hold on the second-wave Vlasovites. Such a view of the socialists' intentions was not inaccurate. In correspondence, Roman Borisovich Gul', an ally of the socialists who spent the war in occupied France, criticized the Whites in Germany as "reactionary scum that has seized the commanding posts everywhere [in the DP camps] and holds in terror all those they find disagreeable."[26] In return, ATsODNR tried to discredit the New York leftists as dangerous radicals whose only gripe with communism was the fact that "the Bolshevics [sic] refused to acknowledge them as partners in a coalition government."[27] Another

[22] Intelligence report: Russian socialists, Hq. EUCOM, APO 403 to CIC Region IV, June 14, 1948, in David Dallin. See also A. V. Antoshin, *Rossiiskie emigranty v usloviiakh "kholodnoi voiny" (seredina 1940-kh–seredina-1960-kh gg.)* (Ekaterinburg: Izd. Ural'skogo universiteta, 2008), 55–6.
[23] Survey of the Russian Emigration, no author indicated (presumably Robert F. Kelley), April 1950, 41, in Georgetown University Archives and Special Collections, Robert F. Kelley Papers, box 5, fol. 14.
[24] Survey of the Russian Emigration, 52.
[25] This was Nikolaevskii's summary of the typical émigré view of Marxism, which he made in a letter that was intercepted by an FBI informant. Nikolaevskii to V. V. Pozdniakov, February 4, 1950. Records of the Federal Bureau of Investigation, Boris Nicolaevsky, FOI/PA# 1357485–8, obtained through FOIA request.
[26] V Ligu bor'by za narodnuiu svobodu, Hoover Institution Library and Archives (HILA), Boris I. Nicolaevsky Collection (henceforth Nicolaevsky Collection), Series 204–4, box 264, fol. 15.
[27] AZODNR and Its Attitude toward the Newly Formed KERENSKI Committee in New York, April 18, 1949, 2, in NARA, RG 319, Entry 134A, XE182853, 270/84/20/02, box 23 (hereinafter AZONDER), vol. 2, fol. 1.

tack was to present Nikolaevskii and Dalin as cynical powerbrokers. The NTS's Aleksandr Rudol'fovich Trushnovich claimed to exile acquaintances that Dalin had boasted of his American contacts while using "threats and repressions" to bring exiles under their influence. In any case, Trushnovich added in an anti-Semitic vein, the name Dalin was "believed to be a pseudonym."[28] (Dalin's original surname was Levin.) The exchange of denunciations and insults highlighted how the pursuit of power within the emigration deepened wider ideological and historical divides.

Deepening the troubles of the exiles from New York were the schemes of Soviet espionage operatives. Eager to sever any transatlantic bonds that might involve US power more actively in the émigré scene, Soviet counter-intelligence kept a close eye on the Russian socialists and probably sought to discredit them. Both Nikolaevskii and Dalin came under scrutiny from US Military Intelligence for associating themselves with suspected Soviet spies during their German travels. In particular, Nikolaevskii was in close communication with A. F. Chikalov, the Gehlen Organization agent whose arrest on charges of Soviet espionage was discussed in Chapter 2. In the wake of the Chikalov scandal, the American Counter Intelligence Corps (CIC) reported up the chain of command that Nikolaevskii was himself "suspected of being a Bolshevist instigator."[29] A year later, Dalin—who, ironically, became a foremost academic expert on Soviet espionage in the United States—also appeared in CIC card files as a "suspected Soviet agent."[30] While Nikolaevskii and Dalin were able to clear their names in US government, association with suspected spies deflated their reputations among the Russian colony in Germany.[31]

Despite their setbacks in Europe, Nikolaevskii's and Dalin's foray into the Russian scene in Germany set in motion a project to establish a cross-continental and cross-generational movement of anti-Soviet exiles. For their part, the socialists formed the League of Struggle for the People's Freedom (*Liga bor'by za narodnuiu svobodu* or LBNS) with much publicity in New York in 1949. Its membership included several prominent Mensheviks, small numbers of other first-wave socialists (including Kerenskii), a circle of liberals in Paris called the Russian National Movement, and a handful of second-wave émigrés in New York and Europe. True to the American nature of the project—and also cognizant of the stringent anti-communism of the DPs—the new organization's leaders eschewed all talk of socialism. Instead, the League proclaimed itself to be fighting

---

[28] Agent report, Su: David Dalin, January 4, 1949, 2, in David Dallin.

[29] Su: Counterintelligence Report No. Z-173, CIC to Deputy Director of Intelligence, EUCOM, December 6, 1947, in NARA, RG 319, IRR, D211036, Nikolaewskij, Boris, obtained through FOIA request.

[30] CIC sources connected Dalin to Ilia Iakushev, an individual suspected of espionage for the Soviets. Dallin, fnu, n.d., and Su: Russian Menshevik Party, October 28, 1948, 2, in David Dallin.

[31] Su: Russian Menshevik Party, Marvin L. Rissinger, Special Agent, CIC, October 28, 1948, 2, in David Dallin.

for the rebirth of democratic politics in Russia that had arisen and then been thwarted by Lenin in 1917, an approach marked symbolically by founding the organization on the anniversary of the February Revolution.[32]

The League would have to draw on the energies of the second-wave exiles in Europe if it were to constitute itself as a serious anti-communist organization. Luckily, the leftists had been handed an opportunity to do just that, as the Vlasovites, especially those grouped in the organization Union for the Struggle for the Liberation of the Peoples of Russia (*Soiuz bor'by za osvobozhdenie narodov Rossii* or SBONR), were moving away from the influence of their White elders in Europe. To take advantage of this situation, Nikolaevskii led an effort starting in late 1948 to establish deeper relations with SBONR, hoping that the Vlasovites would either enter into the League directly or establish a permanent alliance with it. The fruit of this strategy was SBONR's mid-1949 adoption of an explicitly democratic–republican platform, a step that soon led to the organization's exit from the wider Vlasovite organization ATsODNR.[33]

The notion that the Vlasovites had become principled defenders of liberal democracy overnight is unsustainable. Rather, the democratic transformation of SBONR was a result of strategic calculation, as the Vlasovites determined that they should shift from the patronage of one set of émigré elders to that of another—that is, from the White exiles in Europe to the socialists in New York. Indeed, the search for US sinecures was an essential backstory to the left–Vlasovite relationships. Despite their best efforts, the conservatives in ATsODNR failed to receive the patronage of the US government, and the new CIA in particular.[34] Against this backdrop, younger Vlasovites turned to the League, recalling the impression made by the recent trips of Nikolaevskii and Dalin to the DP camps. As the League's negotiator Gul' wrote to his colleagues in New York, SBONR's main reason for seeking an alliance with the LBNS was the perception that the latter had "a direct and CLEAN entry to Washington" and would therefore be able to "do something."[35] The circumstances of the Vlasovites' ideological metamorphosis also suggested that pragmatic motives were at work. SBONR remained within the monarchist-leaning ATsODNR for some time even after adopting a democratic

---

[32] "Liga bor'by za narodnuiu svobodu," *SV* no. 3 (618) (March 25, 1949): 44.

[33] Survey of Russian Emigration, 1950, 63, in Kelley Papers, box 5, fol. 14.

[34] In 1949, a CIA source recommended that the Agency not fund ATsODNR because two of its leading figures, G. K. Meier and N. A. Baranovskii, were employed by the Gehlen operation—a further example of the disruptive effects of the German agency in émigré circles. See Richard Helms, ADPS to ADSO, Su: ATsODNR, May 10, 1949, in NARA, RG 263, Entry ZZ-18, 230/86/23/06, box 90, Georg Meyer. See also MOIC, Su: AZODNR, Special Agent Albert F. Werner, June 14, 1948, 2, in AZONDER, vol. 1, fol. 1 and Report of Investigation-RUSTY, Chief, MO [Critchfield] to Chief, OSO, December 17, 1948, in Kevin C. Ruffner, ed., *Forging an Intelligence Partnership: CIA and the Origins of the BND, 1945–1949*, vol. II (CIA History Staff, Center for the Study of Intelligence, European Division 1999), 98, released 2002 in CIA FOIA Electronic Reading Room.

[35] V Ligu bor'by za narodnuiu svobodu.

program—in essence, hedging its bets while the concrete benefits of associating with the League remained unclear.[36]

They would wait in vain. The socialists never managed to create a dynamic anti-communist organization, let alone recruit significant numbers of second-wavers into the League. In part, their political tactics were flawed: Nikolaevskii decided not to admit new members to LBNS while negotiations with SBONR were underway, a decision that translated into the League's failure to establish a foothold among the DPs in Europe.[37] More fundamentally, the socialists were not as tightly connected to American power as they appeared. While Nikolaevskii, Dalin, and Abramovich were public authorities on Bolshevism in the United States, they lacked serious influence in the intelligence establishment, the part of US government that really mattered for exile politics in Europe.[38] In short, money flows from intelligence agencies—which always constituted a "hidden transcript" in émigré politics—go far in explaining why an alliance between the old socialists and Vlasovites never fully materialized.[39]

Historical Visions

If the absence of CIA support damaged the socialist–Vlasovite flirtation, the question of historical memory was a more basic impediment. In particular, the question of wartime collaboration sparked heated polemics in exile journals and letters across multiple continents. This should hardly surprise given the different experiences and ideological attitudes held by the leftists and the Vlaso-vites. As described in Chapter 1, the Russian leftists who managed to reach the United States in the late 1930s backed the alliance with Stalin against Hitler, even if sometimes they did so with gritted teeth. In contrast, the Vlasovites had taken up arms for the Germans. Both sides defended their past positions as having been in Russian national interests. Accordingly, both parties faced the dilemma of how to forge a common anti-communist front with partners whose notion of national history was drastically different than their own.

Nikolaevskii spearheaded the attempt at reconciliation. According to one émigré CIC informer, Nikolaevskii arrived in the DP camps in 1947 believing that many of the Vlasovites had become "true Nazis at heart" during the war, but left with the conviction that many were in fact incipient democrats.[40] Upon his

[36] A useful account of the complicated relations between these groups, albeit one written by a participant in the events, is Dvinov, *Politics of the Russian Emigration*, 285–302.

[37] See V. M. Zenzinov to A. F. Kerenskii, May 17, 1949, in Bakhmeteff Archive, Vladimir Mikhai-lovich Zenzinov Papers, box 1.

[38] As Chapter 4 will explain, when the new Office of Policy Coordination crafted an operation to forge a Russian émigré center, the Russian leftists would find themselves in a subordinate role. Survey of Russian Emigration, 61–2.

[39] Here I draw on a term used by James C. Scott to analyze popular conflicts. James C. Scott, *Domination and the Arts of Resistance: Hidden Transcripts* (New Haven, CT: Yale University Press, 2008).

[40] MOIC, Su: ODNR, March 9, 1948, 13, in AZONDER vol. 1, fol. 1.

return to the United States, Nikolaevskii set about telling the history of the Vlasovites in a way that would provide a basis for Cold War political cooperation. Nikolaevskii argued that the Vlasov movement was the product of widespread "defeatism" (*porazhenchestvo*) in the wartime Soviet Union, as Soviet soldiers and citizens supported a relatively unknown invading power rather than fighting for a hated one. Crucially, "defeatism" situated the origins of Vlasovism in anti-Stalin moods among the Soviet masses. In temporal terms, it drew a clear line between Stalin's crimes of the 1930s, the alleged refusal of soldiers to fight in 1941, and the subsequent taking up of arms on behalf of the German invader. In this sense, defeatism was a conceptual alternative to "collaboration," which carried connotations of treachery and opportunism in the postwar world.[41]

Nikolaevskii's conceptualization of defeatism cleared the way to make a more controversial claim. Unlike all other collaborationist groups in World War II, Nikolaevskii argued, Vlasov's Russian liberation movement was, "from the very start," "an attempt to create an anti-Bolshevik movement on the basis of a democratic program."[42] In this view, the Germans had sabotaged the Vlasov movement precisely because the latter had tapped into the "massive and elemental pull of democracy" in the "popular masses" of Russia.[43] Nikolaevskii's articles constituted an effort to rehabilitate the Vlasovites—in the wider Western public sphere, in the emigration, and among his immediate comrades—by establishing their democratic credentials.

Nikolaevskii never finished his planned series of articles on Vlasov, perhaps as a result of the backlash he received from his socialist comrades (soon to be discussed). But his conceptualization of Vlasovism would become influential among exiles and US cold warriors alike. Indeed, when the Vlasovites set about telling their own story, they hewed close to the themes of Nikolaevskii's historical narrative: defeatism, democratic ideas, and Vlasovism's mass appeal.

Crucial to the Vlasovites' own historical narrative was the claim that siding with Hitler against Stalin had been a purely tactical move. As a 1947 article in SBONR's publication *Bor'ba* ("The Struggle") explained, Stalin had always been enemy number one, and fighting on the German side had been "the only existant [*sic*] possibility of organizing armed warfare against the STALIN clique."[44] In order to substantiate this argument, the Vlasovites depicted collaboration with the enemy as a reaction to Stalin's crimes of the 1930s—while, it should be noted, leaving virtually undiscussed those of Hitler's Germany during the war. As the wife of a

[41] For Russian socialists, defeatism had the added benefit of suggesting associations with past "defeatist" revolutionary movements during the Russo-Japanese and First World Wars. George Fischer, *Soviet Opposition to Stalin: A Case Study in World War II* (Cambridge: Harvard University Press, 1952), 212–13 (n. 8).
[42] B. I. Nikolaevskii, "O 'staroi' i 'novoi' emigratsii," SV no. 2 (605) (February 28, 1948): 33.
[43] Ibid.: 35.
[44] Su: KONR (Committee for the Liberation of the Russian Peoples, Memorandum for the Officer in Charge by CIC special agent Rea M. Pile, January 9, 1948, 19 in AZONDER, vol. 1, fol. 2.

KONR commander asserted, "There was no other choice... Think of the millions of deaths the Soviet [*sic*] caused in the 1930s."[45] Focusing attention on the 1930s instead of the war allowed the Vlasovites to depict their movement as a home-grown movement of resistance to Stalinism rather than a collaborationist project. As a corollary of this position, the Vlasovites connected their movement to prior manifestations of opposition to the Soviet state, asserting that their comrades forcefully repatriated by Western armies after the war belonged to the line of victims of Soviet rule that included rebels slain on "the fields of the Civil War, [in] the forts of Kronstadt and the forests of Tambov," and in "the basements of the ChK."[46]

Unlike these other anti-communist insurgents, of course, the Vlasovites had fought on the side of a brutal invader. All the more crucial, then, was another aspect of SBONR's account of the war: the claim that the Vlasov movement, while serving the Hitler state, had actually struggled against it. In this rendition of the past, Vlasov had agreed to a "temporary and tactical" alliance with Germany in the name of Russian interests, but had been deceived by a Nazi regime bent on pursuing an anti-Russian policy.[47] Faced with this putative betrayal, Vlasov and his commanders pursued a behind-the-scenes fight against the Nazis to defend the Russian people, an example being his efforts to intervene on behalf of the mistreated Eastern workers in the Reich. Vlasov, then, had championed Russian interests against both Stalin and Hitler. As his postwar followers argued, the general had paid the price for this independent line, particularly when he was confined to virtual house arrest in 1943 after carrying out a Wehrmacht-organized tour of occupied Soviet regions that had drawn Hitler's ire.[48]

The founding of the Committee for the Liberation of the Peoples of Russia (KONR) in 1944 with the support of Nazi police leader Himmler seemed to contradict this postwar rendering of the past. If the Nazis had tricked Vlasov, why would the Russian general continue and indeed deepen his collaborationist course? In fact, SBONR publicists insisted, KONR actually proved the wisdom of Vlasov's wartime agenda. The new liberation committee, the Vlasovites alleged, was never a simple creature of the Nazis, as shown by a statement in the Prague Manifesto, the programmatic document of KONR composed in 1944: KONR would welcome German support only "on conditions leaving unscathed the

---

[45] The Harvard Project on the Soviet Social System Online (henceforth HPSSS), schedule A, vol. 23, case 468, 15–16.

[46] *Pervyi s'ezd SBONR: materialy sekretariata s'ezda* (Munich: Izdatel'stvo Bor'ba, 1950), 6, 17. The events mentioned are the Tambov peasant rebellion in 1920–1 and the Kronstadt Rebellion of 1921. ChK is short-form for the All-Russian Extraordinary Commission (*Vserossiiskaia Chrezvechainaia Komissiia*), the first incarnation of the Soviet political police.

[47] Su: KONR (Committee for the Liberation of the Russian Peoples), 19 in AZONDER, vol. 1, folder 2.

[48] For one account of this episode, see Catherine Andreyev, *Vlasov and the Russian Liberation Movement: Soviet Reality and Émigré Theories* (Cambridge and New York: Cambridge University Press, 1987), 47–55.

honor and independence of our peoples."[49] In essence, Vlasov remained an independent leader who "wasn't afraid of Hitler," as one DP put it, and this found expression, paradoxically enough, both in the general's early failures to gain German support and in his later success in doing precisely that.[50]

The thrust of SBONR's arguments—that Vlasov and his troops had pursued collaboration for high-minded reasons and had also fought against Germany in all but name—was that the general's movement had been (and, by implication, still was) democratic and, at least *in potentia*, popular among Soviet Russians. To support this political message, SBONR adopted a new interpretation of the Prague Manifesto. Instead of depicting it as a "non-predeterminist" document as they had when they had belonged to the conservative ATsODNR, the Vlasovites now saw the manifesto as thoroughly democratic, emphasizing its call to "return to the peoples of Russia the rights that had been won in the people's revolution of 1917."[51] SBONR argued that the democratic essence of Vlasovism had endeared it to the Russian people, generating mass enthusiasm not just within the POW camps—allegedly, even at the end of the war when being associated with the Germany war machine was dangerous—but also among the wider population on occupied Russian territory.[52] In this view, Vlasovism was nothing less than an embodiment of the will of the Russian people. Here the Vlasovite memory project diverged from Nikolaevskii's framework. The Menshevik had tempered his praise of Vlasov with the comment that it had been "inherently fallacious" to collaborate with Hitler.[53] In contrast, SBONR propagandists countenanced no criticism of their wartime position, taking as an article of faith that collaboration had been necessary and even noble.

There can be no doubt that the new line on Vlasov involved historical falsification. The depiction of him and his men as uniformly anti-Soviet in ideology, anti-Hitler in word and deed, and democratically supported, could only be sustained if uncomfortable facts were passed over. Indeed, correspondence between exiles shows that the Vlasovites were actively shaping historical narratives to fit postwar political strictures. In 1948, the Vlasovite Igor' Andreevich Efimov wrote to SBONR leader F. M. Legostaev with sharp criticism of *Bor'ba*. In recollections of the Vlasov movement, he complained, "too many German names are mentioned," while the size of a detachment was given as only fifty-five men. "Censorship is needed," Efimov concluded.[54] The Vlasovites' story was being

[49] Su: KONR (Committee for the Liberation of the Russian Peoples), 19.

[50] HPSSS, schedule A, vol. 35, case 386/(NY) 1495, 90.

[51] Iu. S. Tsurganov, *Neudavshiisia revansh: belaia emigratsiia vo vtoroi mirovoi voine* (Moscow: Intrada, 2001), 180.

[52] For instance, see Konstantin Kromiadi, *Za zemliu, za voliu* (San Francisco: "Globus," 1980), 101–7.

[53] Nikolaevskii, "O 'staroi' i 'novoi' emigratsii": 35.

[54] Igor' Efimov to F. M. Legostaev, letter intercepted by CIC, n.d. (1947), in NARA, RG 319, Entry 134B, 270/84/01/01, XE216081, box 460, Philip Legostayew.

constructed to appeal to critical constituencies, most of all US policy planners—and Chapter 4 will show that it hit the mark. As émigré stories went, the Vlasovites' retelling of the war was a good one.

The Narrative Comes Apart

The Vlasovites' presentation of their past, and Nikolaevskii's account of the movement that had underpinned and promoted it, gave rise to a wide-ranging debate over historical memories on both sides of the envisioned socialist–Vlasovite alliance. In particular, prominent Menshevik allies of Nikolaevskii rejected key parts of the pro-Vlasov narrative.

The most trenchant criticism of Nikolaevskii's attempt at the rehabilitation of the Vlasovites came from the Menshevik Grigorii Iakovlevich Aronson. In a piece entitled "What one needs to know about the Vlasov Movement," Aronson questioned whether the democratic statements of the Vlasovites during the war had been genuine or were rather an effort to court the Western powers in the face of certain German defeat. With regard to the Prague Manifesto, Aronson asked, "What other program was imaginable in November 1944 than that of democracy, even for the stunned and hopeless partners of Hitler?" Most controversially, Aronson suggested that members of the Vlasov movement had held an affinity for Nazism. Citing fascist and anti-Semitic statements attributed to Vlasov in wartime Russian-language publications, he wondered, "In what measure in 1943–1944 the Vlasov Movement was used by the Germans for the destruction of the Jews and suppression of the resistance movement in Europe."[55]

The other Mensheviks and leaders of the New York League refrained from making allegations about the war record of the Vlasovites. No doubt they understood that doing so would scuttle any hope of common action with the new emigration—and, by extension, bring their own Cold War political agendas to a halt. However, the Menshevik Boris L'vovich Dvinov offered a different line of attack on the Vlasovites that proved even more damaging than Aronson's. Eschewing innuendo and unfounded charges, Dvinov set out to prove his assertions by publishing and commenting on a series of newly available German documents pertaining to Russian collaborators.

---

[55] G. Aronson, "Chto nado znat' o Vlasovskom dvizhenii?" *SV* no. 3 (606) (March 29, 1948): 61–3. The question of whether Vlasov forces engaged in Nazi war crimes seems to hinge on questions of definition. The Vlasov forces proper (the KONR divisions formed very late in the war) probably did not. However, sources leave no doubt that Soviet collaborators affiliated with the ROA prior to the formation of KONR engaged in brutality against Soviet civilians, for instance in the so-called Kaminskii Brigade in occupied Russia. Cf. HPSSS, schedule B, vol. 10, case 143, 8–9, and D. Zhukov and I. Kovtun, "Repressivnaia deiatel'nost' brigady Kaminskogo na okkupirovannykh territoriakh SSSR v 1941–1944 gg.," in A. Martynov (ed.), *Istoriia otechestvennoi kollaboratsii: materialy i issledovaniia* (Moscow: Staraia Basmannaia, 2017), 123–81.

In the relentless picture Dvinov drew, Vlasovism was a German affair from start to finish, a "propaganda trick" designed by Goebbels to further Nazi goals in the East.[56] Rather than being a naïve Soviet "defeatist," Dvinov stressed, Vlasov knew what kind of regime he was volunteering to work for: by the time of Vlasov's capture in mid-1942, it was no secret that Hitler was pursuing an "organized and merciless destruction" of the Russian people.[57] That Russian collaborators would be "powerless pawns" of the Germans and would be forced to do their bidding was inevitable.[58] In this context, even if Vlasov and other captured commanders had pursued an independent and at times even anti-Nazi agenda, they were to be blamed for undertaking what had been an "irresponsible and unintelligent adventure."[59] Moreover, Dvinov suggested, Vlasov and his commanders were at least indirectly complicit in Nazi crimes, for they had generated propaganda that willfully misled their Russian compatriots in Germany and in occupied Soviet lands about the nature of the Hitler regime.

Dvinov's anti-Vlasov line presented the socialists with a political dilemma. Virtually all the active League members, including Dvinov himself, thought that the task of fighting Stalin necessitated cooperation with at least some second-wavers associated with the wartime Vlasov movement. But which Vlasovites were the uncompromised and therefore politically acceptable ones? Dvinov and Abramovich called on the Vlasovites to admit their mistakes, suggesting that public repentance would serve as something of a litmus test of their "democratic-mindedness."[60] Nothing of this nature was forthcoming from the solidly unrepentant Vlasovites, however. Accordingly, Nikolaevskii faced the daunting task of finding a justification for the alliance with SBONR that would satisfy his skeptical comrades in New York without alienating their projected allies in the DP camps of Europe.

A solution to this balancing act seemed to emerge with the drafting of a set of theses on the Vlasov question by the Menshevik Foreign Delegation of the Russian Social Democratic Labor Party in early 1949. The document made a significant concession to Aronson, Dvinov, and Abramovich by condemning Vlasov's wartime actions. However noble had been Vlasov's goal of creating an independent and democratic Russia, collaboration had been "deeply mistaken," as the Vlasovites had been "doomed from the very start not only to failure but to constant compromises with their conscience."[61] At the same time, the theses neglected to pass judgment on the mass of former collaborators as they did on Vlasov and

---

[56] Boris L. Dvinov, *Vlasovskoe dvizhenie v svete dokumentov (s prilozheniem sekretnykh dokumentov)* (New York, 1950), 69.

[57] Ibid., 23–5.

[58] Ibid., 47.

[59] Ibid.

[60] R. Abramovich, "O chem my vse-taki sporim? (Otvet vlasovtsu)," *SV* no. 4–5 (607–8) (May 20, 1948): 89, and Dvinov, *Vlasovskoe dvizhenie*, 70.

[61] The theses were only published over a year later. "K voprosu o 'Vlasovskom dvizhenii,'" *SV* no. 10 (637) (October 1950): 191.

other collaborationist Red Army commanders. Instead, they criticized Dvinov for failing to account for the "tragic situation" that had led Soviet people to defeatism during the war. Victimized by Stalin, "cut off from any contact with the outside world for half a century," and "systematically poisoned by mendacious Soviet propaganda," former Soviet citizens could not be blamed for clinging to the "disastrous illusion" that they could side with Hitler against Stalin.[62] And if one needed to evaluate the Vlasovites' wartime actions with empathy, the same applied to the present as well. Implicitly rejecting the calls by several Mensheviks for the former collaborators to publicly distance themselves from the Vlasov episode, the theses argued that the Vlasovites' refusal to criticize their wartime actions served a "psychologically understandable need."[63] In short, the Vlasov movement had been a tragic mistake (or worse), but its survivors had not compromised themselves through association with it—and, therefore, should not be expected to come to terms with their wartime choices.

As suggested by their elaborate logic, the theses were a hard-won compromise. And while the theses did clear the way for the formal creation of the New York League, they papered over a deep split over the Vlasov question that had emerged among the tight-knit group of Russian social democrats in New York.[64] Clearly, core issues were at stake. Given the fact that all the old socialists had taken a "defensist" position in favor of Soviet victory during World War II, the willingness and even eagerness of Nikolaevskii, Kerenskii, and others to ally with former collaborators seemed to be sheer opportunism or even ideological betrayal.[65] Characterizing his comrades' views, Dvinov quipped that a *Vlasovshchina*, an "age of Vlasov" perhaps comparable to the hyper-patriotic *Zhdanovshchina* then underway in the Soviet Union, had taken hold in the League.[66] The charge that Nikolaevskii and his followers embraced Vlasov uncritically was unfair, but it was true that their unwillingness to confront the Vlasovites over collaboration had a political and pragmatic aspect. Demanding that Vlasovites repent was unreasonable and counterproductive, Nikolaevskii held, for such forced penance would alienate the entire second-wave Russian emigration from democracy—and, in so doing, make certain the Russian emigration's political irrelevance in the Cold War.

The dilemma facing all the socialists, then, was how to balance democratic principles—which they thought were incompatible with accepting collaboration with Hitlerism in any form—with the demands of struggle against Stalin. Here was a specific rendition of a problem that resounded widely in the thought and culture

[62] Ibid.: 192.

[63] Ibid.: 191.

[64] Nikolaevskii and Dvinov broke off all contact with each other for some time over the Vlasovism debate. See "Vyderzhka iz chastnogo pis'ma," August 3, 1949, evidently written by Nikolaevskii, in HILA, Nicolaevsky Collection, box 264, fol. 7.

[65] Dvinov, *Vlasovskoe dvizhenie*, 70.

[66] "Liga, SONR i prochee," October 19, 1951, International Institute of Social History Archive, Amsterdam, Boris L'vovich Dvinov Papers, fol. 7.

in the Cold War West, and particularly on the left: what means were justified in fighting communism?[67] For the Mensheviks, who had long existed in a closed world where ideas mattered most of all, the problem was a particularly tortured one.

Back to 1917

The debate over Vlasovism in Russian New York had a disastrous impact on the transatlantic alliance Nikolaevskii and others sought to create. As the socialists' internal discussions revealed, the leftists and Vlasovites had fundamentally different views on the admissibility of wartime collaboration, which rested on different evaluations of the Hitler regime. The Mensheviks held Nazism to be an absolute evil and made frequent reference to the Holocaust in the debate with their erstwhile partners in Europe. By contrast, the Vlasovites claimed that Hitler had been the lesser of two evils during the war—and, one senses, by a wide margin. Indeed, some of the Vlasovites' postwar writing places in doubt whether they even acknowledged the enormity of Nazi violence. An example is a SBONR proclamation that excoriates Nazism not for its crimes but for its "mistakes": Hitler's "incomprehension" of the Russian people's anti-communism, it argued, allowed Stalin to rally Russians behind the Soviet regime and to win the war.[68] To the socialists, such statements were morally reprehensible. As Abramovich wrote in his published "answer to a Vlasovite," "at the time that was most difficult for all of us, we remained, at least morally, on different sides of the front."[69]

The socialists' outrage at defense of collaboration was connected to a certain condescension toward the Vlasovites. In effect, the aging leftists claimed the status of being the true Russian democrats in the emigration, whose task was to guide the thinking of the second wave. Indeed, even Nikolaevskii saw the Vlasovites in a paternalistic manner, for his "defeatism" construct depended on the position that the collaborators, as subjects of Stalin, had known no better than to side with Germany. At its most extreme, such a position absolved the Vlasovites of moral responsibility for their wartime actions on principle. In a letter, Gul' responded to allegations that an unnamed second-waver had collaborated with the Germans with the thought that "even if something like that happened," he could be forgiven. The new émigrés "had a right to a big allowance" in such matters, Gul' explained.[70]

The Vlasovites responded to the criticisms leveled by their putative partners across the Atlantic by going on the offensive themselves. They did so by attacking

[67] For an example of a thinker consumed with this problem, see Arthur Koestler, *Bricks to Babel: A Selection from 50 Years of His Writings, Chosen and with New Commentary by the Author* (New York: Random House, 1981).
[68] "Liniia Vlasova," *Bor'ba* no. 3 (November 1947): 12.
[69] Abramovich, "O chem my vse-taki sporim?": 89.
[70] R. B. Gul' to V. F. Butenko, December 15, 1948, 2, in Butenko Papers, box 1, fol. 1.

the political pasts of the socialists. Here it should be recalled that, somewhat like the postwar Vlasovites, the Mensheviks had undergone a path of self-transformation to arrive at their present political coloration. If the former now downplayed their wartime collaboration with Nazi Germany, the latter had moved away from belief in Marxist revolution—which, as Chapter 1 noted, had always inserted a degree of ambivalence into Menshevik evaluations of Bolshevism—in order to become left-wing American anti-communists. A discursive strategy soon emerged. If the socialists criticized the Vlasovites over their war records, the latter might repay in kind by highlighting their ostensible partners' pasts in the Russian Revolution—no small matter, of course, given that the socialists lived in a United States roiled by McCarthyism.

The Vlasovites did not have to invent the tactic of weaponizing memories of the Russian Revolution. Rightist exile groups took every opportunity to tarnish the socialists with the Marxist brush. ATsODNR, by then a rump of conservatives, depicted Nikolaevskii and Dalin as representatives of a "Politburo" in New York who sought to carry out another violent Marxist revolution in Russia.[71] More surprising, perhaps, was the willingness of the Vlasovites to criticize their supposed partners across the Atlantic. In October 1949, a decidedly hostile article appeared in *Za Rodinu* ("For the Homeland"), an Austrian SBONR publication. Evidently based on rumors, the piece reported on a meeting of the League in New York at which the Menshevik Solomon Meerovich Schwartz had allegedly demanded to "check everyone who wants to join the League to see if he is a 'Vlasovite' who destroyed (!) the Jews [*sic*]."[72] The editors of *Za Rodinu* commented that Schwartz's speech suggested "inevitable parallels" with communism, with Schwartz and his allies "pouring dirt" on the fighters of Vlasov's Russian Liberation Army just as the Kremlin exploited the Russian people. If the comparison of elderly socialists to Stalin's regime was absurd, it represented a clear rhetorical strategy. The League activists had no right to pass judgment on collaborators if they had "totalitarian" tendencies themselves. In this sense, the cross-continental alliance spearheaded by Nikolaevskii confronted a dynamic in which both sides accused the other of past anti-democratic sins, whether of a Marxist or fascist mold.

If their pasts in revolutionary Marxism and collaboration drove the two parties apart, the socialists and Vlasovites would seem to be on common ground with another historical marker: the February Revolution. As noted above, the activists of the New York League trumpeted the heritage of democratic revolution as a counterpoint to communism, while Vlasov's KONR had done the same. And since

---

[71] AZODNR and its Attitude Toward the Newly Formed KERENSKI Committee in New York, April 18, 1949, 2, in NARA, RG 319, Entry 134A, XE182853, 270/84/20/02, box 23 (hereinafter AZONDER), vol. 2, fol. 1.

[72] "Neprilichnaia isterika," *SV* no. 10 (625) (October 31, 1949): 175.

it represented the brief moment of democratic ascendancy in Russia, the February Revolution was a fitting founding myth for any Russian organization fighting the Cold War on the Western side.

As so often happened in the exile milieu, however, the marshaling of historical memories created new debates. The February Revolution proved a difficult historical marker for the League, since some Vlasovites pointed out that it had paved the way for the Bolshevik seizure of power in October. As many League activists had been important actors in the brief window between February and October, they were vulnerable to the accusation that they were "responsible for the preparation of the Bolshevist revolution," as the conservative ATsODNR alleged.[73]

More damaging still was the prominent role in the League played by Kerenskii, who, whether fairly or not, had come to symbolize the failure of non-Bolshevik Russia (see Figure 3.1). He had long been the bête noire of the White émigrés, as seen in the willingness of ATsODNR to repeat the canard that the premier had fled the Winter Palace in 1917 in a dress.[74] As their relationship with the socialists soured, the Vlasovites also turned to critical examination of 1917. The SBONR paper Bor'ba carried an article sharply criticizing Kerenskii for his political failures, going so far as to label him a "traitor" for his role in the Kornilov Affair, the failed counterrevolutionary coup that had set the stage for Lenin's seizure of power. The article prompted a testy response from Abramovich, who accused the SBONR paper of straying into "historical apologies for restorationism and reaction."[75]

Despite Abramovich's angry rebuttal, the League members were well aware of their Kerenskii problem. The League needed Kerenskii, whose reputation in US government circles, buttressed by his personal charm, gave their émigré organization an air of political legitimacy.[76] However, claiming the cachet of Kerenskii came at the cost of the League's position in the emigration. As Vasilii Federovich Butenko commented in April 1949, the League lost authority among exiles due to the "repulsion" (ottalkyvanie) widely felt toward the former Russian premier.[77] Making matters worse, Kerenskii had strained relationships with Nikolaevskii and Abramovich—both of whom, it is worth mentioning, had been "Menshevik internationalist" critics of the Provisional Government in 1917.[78] In any case, Kerenskii did not seem particularly committed to the League, apparently seeing it

---

[73] AZODNR and Its Attitude toward the Newly Formed KERENSKI Committee, 2.

[74] Ibid.

[75] R. Abramovich, "Grekhi fevralia ili otsy i deti," SV no. 1–2 (616–17) (February 15, 1949): 10–12.

[76] Indeed, financial arrangements for publishing the New York League's Bulletin ran through Kerenskii. Unfortunately, documents do not clearly identify the source of these funds, although given Kerenskii's extensive ties in Washington, it seems possible that the State Department was involved. V. F. Butenko to R. B. Gul', June 22, 1949, 2, in Butenko Papers, box 1, fol. 1. On Americans taken by the gallant and "warmhearted" Kerenskii, see Isaac Patch, Closing the Circle: A Buckalino Journey around Our Time (Wellesley, MA: Wellesley College Printing Services, 1996), 236–41.

[77] V. F. Butenko to R. B. Gul', April 3, 1949, in Butenko Papers, box 1, fol. 1.

[78] Antoshin, Rossiiskie emigranty, 127.

Figure 3.1 The historical mishmash of the émigrés is on display at a commemoration at the Russian Cemetery in Berlin, 1952. Aleksandr Federovich Kerenskii is at the center flanked by the White Army veteran Nikolai Potapovich Zolotarenko on his right and the National Labor Alliance's Vladimir Dmitrievich Poremskii behind and to his left. To the left of Poremskii are the Vlasovite Georgii Il'ich Antonov and a recent defector, F. A. Arnol'd. Kerenskii is an awkward fit for the event held at a monument dedicated to the fallen soldiers of the White armies. The Whites and often the Vlasovites were hostile to Kerenskii and his Provisional Government of 1917, blaming them for setting the stage for the October Revolution.
Source: Archiv der Forschungsstelle Osteuropa an der Universität Bremen.

only as a path toward his own historical rehabilitation.[79] In short, Kerenskii drew exile attention back to 1917 in unwanted ways while complicating the internal workings of the League.

Still more troubling to the cross-continental alliance was another factor in their polemics: anti-Semitism. As all could see, the debate within the left in New York over Vlasov seemed to conform to a religious or racial pattern, with the non-Jewish Nikolaevskii and Kerenskii taking a more positive attitude to the Vlasovites, while Mensheviks of Jewish background such as Aronson, Dvinov, and Abramovich came out in opposition. Anti-Semitism also arose in the polemics between the socialists and Vlasovites. While the Vlasovites did not mention the origins of many of the Mensheviks explicitly, Jewishness seemed to lurk behind many of

[79] V. F. Butenko to R. B. Gul', April 3, 1949.

the Vlasovites' criticisms of them.[80] As mentioned above, Aronson had asked whether Vlasov forces had participated in the Holocaust. In response to this article, *Bor'ba* questioned Aronson's sources and also criticized the author. Aronson, "sitting in distant America," had "long ago forgotten how to understand the Russian people (*russkii narod*)," seeing them only as plebian "Ivan Ivano-viches."[81] These accusations associated Aronson's alleged elitism and the privilege of American exile with his essential otherness, a quality described in ethnic terms (*russkii*). For Aronson's comrades, such polemics confirmed views of the Vlasovites as unreformed fascists—though *Bor'ba*'s depiction of the Mensheviks as ineffectual theorizers who had sat out the war smarted almost as much as the article's anti-Semitic subtext. The Mensheviks' *Sotsialisticheskii vestnik* ("Socialist Herald") intoned in response to the SBONR publication that Aronson had "fearlessly struggled against the Bolshevik dictatorship in Russia itself" at a time when Vlasov had still been faithfully serving Stalin.[82]

The association of the League with the Jewish socialists detracted from its influence, as some of its members clearly understood. In correspondence with a new émigré in Europe, Butenko confronted the common "objection" that among the socialists there were many Jews, who "cannot be trusted." Butenko responded that it was better for the liberation movement to have Jews on their side than to oppose them. The "Jewish influence in the world press is so great" that one would have to be a "political idiot" to refuse an alliance with them.[83] Butenko's defensive position on the Jews—and his utilization of Jewish stereotypes in the process—suggested just how widespread anti-Semitism among the Russian emigration was, and how much it damaged the prospects of the exile left.

* * *

The League's project of creating a cross-generational bloc to forge Russia's future stumbled upon visions of its past. With the help of Nikolaevskii, the Vlasovites in Europe constructed an image of their movement as a principled, democratic, and anti-Nazi endeavor. Yet Nikolaevskii's comrades among the Russian socialists criticized the Vlasovite account of the war, instead asserting that Vlasov and his companions had been witting agents of the Nazi regime and, by implication, traitors against an imagined democratic Russia. The Vlasovites responded with their own allegations of national treachery, accusing their putative allies in the United States of being crypto-Bolsheviks or, as one NTS member put it, mere

---

[80] The role of Jewish identity in the disputes was noted by a German Foreign Ministry official. Aufzeichnung, Betr: Die Emigration aus der Sowjetunion und den von ihr beherrschten Gebieten, Ref. Scholl, January 19, 1956, 55, in Auswärtiges Amt-Politisches Archiv, B 12, Akte 455.

[81] V. S., "O chem zabyl gospodin Aronson," *Bor'ba* no. 7–8 (March–April 1948): 27. Aronson had referred to Vlasovite officers as "Ivan Ivanoviches" and the "mostly plebian origin" of Soviet intellectuals in passing. Aronson, "Chto nado znat'": 62.

[82] "Bran' ne dovod," *SV* no. 1–2 (628–9) (February 20, 1950): 46.

[83] V. F. Butenko to I. I. Alcheev, February 14, 1949, 2, in Butenko Papers, box 1, fol. 1.

"political corpses" dating from the February Revolution of 1917.[84] In the end, the clash between alternative renderings of Russian history unraveled the common agenda of forging a common anti-Soviet front among the exiles.

The historical debates of the exiles over wartime collaboration and betrayal can be fruitfully compared to similar processes elsewhere in postwar Europe. As a rule, the Cold War provided a context for Europeans to create unifying national war memories that ameliorated the divisive experiences of defeat and occupation.[85] In contrast, the construction of a single wartime narrative proved impossible for the Russian emigration—an entity, indeed, that held no overarching identity apart from being the accidental byproduct of successive cataclysms in modern Russian history. In an émigré milieu badly divided along generational and ideological lines, national history could be marshaled in multiple ways, with the Vlasovites raising the socialists' alleged betrayal during 1917 as a counterpoint to criticism of their own record of collaboration with Hitler.

There was an all-important if silent third party in the socialist–Vlasovite disputes: the United States government. As already noted, the Vlasovites were interested in the old socialists as seemingly influential Americans, not for their reputation as Russian politicians. It was only the promise of American patronage and money that convinced the New York League and SBONR to sink their differences uneasily, and it was the inability of the League to win the support of US intelligence that rendered the coalition hollow. It was to the Americans that the different exile anti-communists now looked, with apprehension as well as expectation.

---

[84] Unidentified NTS member in Germany to A. N. Artemov, n.d., Archiv der Forschungsstelle Osteuropa an der Universität Bremen (hereinafter FSO), 01–098 Tarasova, kor. 38–40.

[85] Cf. Sarah Farmer, *Martyred Village: Commemorating the 1944 Massacre at Oradour-sur-Glane* (Berkeley: University of California Press, 1999).

PART II
THE TRANSNATIONAL QUEST
FOR RUSSIAN LIBERATION

4

American Visions and Émigré Realities

The American Project to Unify the Russian Exiles

In 1951, George Frost Kennan's "America and the Russian Future" appeared in *Foreign Affairs*. Kennan, who had articulated the US policy of containing the USSR years before, now posed a no less far-reaching question of grand strategy: What kind of Russia would Americans eventually like to see in the future and to have as a "partner in the world community?" Kennan cautioned against the notion that Russia should be remade in the American image as a "capitalistic and liberal-democratic" country. The imposition of such a blueprint, which was foreign to Russian "character" and "national realities," was impossible. Instead, America should set less ambitious goals for Russian development: the abandonment of Stalinist xenophobia and the Iron Curtain, an end to the state's efforts to "enslave its own working population"—which, Kennan thought, led inexorably to its hostility toward the outside world—and the cessation of "the ancient game of imperialist expansion and oppression." Beyond these demands, Kennan stated, Americans must let the Russians "be Russians" and "work out their internal problems in their own manner."[1]

On one level, Kennan's call to respect Russia's national traditions appears to be hypocritical. In the late 1940s, Kennan had spearheaded a secret US program of "organized political warfare" aimed at subverting the Soviet bloc.[2] Just months before "America and the Russian Future" went to press, Kennan, at the time State Department Counsellor, set in motion a covert project to organize Russian exiles into an anti-Soviet organization, called alternatively a "united front" or a "political center."[3] The endeavor, organized by the recently-created OPC (Office of Policy Coordination), an agency for psychological warfare and paramilitary action housed within the CIA, was a direct effort to shape Russia's future from abroad,

---

[1] George F. Kennan, "America and the Russian Future," reprinted in George Fischer (ed.), *Russian Émigré Politics* (New York: Free Russia Fund, 1951), 11–32.

[2] National Security Council Directive on Office of Special Projects, Washington, June 18, 1948, document 292, in Foreign Relations of the United States (hereinafter FRUS), 1945–1950, Emergence of the Intelligence Establishment, retrospective volume.

[3] Office of Policy Coordination Memorandum on Russian Emigration, August 7, 1951, 1, in History and Public Policy Program Digital Archive at the Woodrow Wilson Center, Radio Free Europe and Radio Liberty: Cold War International History Project e-Dossier no. 32 (hereinafter Radio Free Europe and Radio Liberty).

Cold War Exiles and the CIA: Plotting to Free Russia. Benjamin Tromly, Oxford University Press (2019). © Benjamin Tromly.
DOI: 10.1093/oso/9780198840404.001.0001

with exiles serving as "a vehicle" to pry the Soviet population away from communism.[4] The US government masked its support for the project through the creation of the American Committee for Freedom for the Peoples of the USSR, Inc. (Amcomlib), ostensibly a nonprofit organization run by private citizens with no governmental connection but in fact a front organization created by the OPC-CIA.[5]

Kennan, it would seem, was engaged in precisely the kind of nation-building vis-à-vis Russia against which he warned in his *Foreign Affairs* article. Developing this perspective, David Foglesong sees in US support for liberating Russia from communism a longstanding project of transforming the country to fit American ideals by imposing its "moral values and religious beliefs," reproducing US economic development models and imposing a "racial definition of Russians as white Europeans."[6]

This chapter offers a broader, transnational understanding of American plans to liberate Russia during the height of the Cold War. Kennan's call to take heed of Russian "character" and "national realities" was not entirely disingenuous. For while the liberationist mission of Amcomlib stemmed from the beliefs of its American members, it was to be articulated, developed, and acted on primarily by Russian and other Soviet exiles, who had their own ideas about communism and freeing their country from it. Kennan and other OPC planners held a conservative and Russophilic reading of Russian history, from which they derived the notion that exiles were not just vital parts of the Russian nation but also harbingers of the country's non-communist future. As a result, political warfare plans against the USSR were not only or mainly a matter of American Cold War passions or projections but, rather, emerged from the interactions of influential Americans and Russian émigrés.

The transnational nature of US-exile relationships are particularly important for understanding the origins and also the limitations of the OPC plans for covert action against the USSR, and the united-front project in particular. Convinced as they were that the exiles held the key to Russia's future, Kennan and other OPC planners determined the united-front project's form and dramatis personae based on émigré politics, not on grounded evaluations of the moods of the Soviet population. The discussion traces the impact of exile politics on three aspects of

---

[4] Ibid.

[5] Previous accounts include Simo Mikkonen, "Exploiting the Exiles: Soviet Émigrés in U.S. Cold War Strategy," *Journal of Cold War Studies* 14, no. 2 (2012): 98–127, and A. Ross Johnson, *Radio Free Europe and Radio Liberty: The CIA Years and Beyond* (Washington, DC: Woodrow Wilson Center Press, 2010), 30–3.

[6] David S. Foglesong, *The American Mission and the "Evil Empire": The Crusade for a "Free Russia" since 1881* (New York: Cambridge University Press, 2007), 114–19. For another work that connects psychological warfare to the projection US identities, see Philip M. Taylor, "Through a Glass Darkly? The Psychological Climate and Psychological Warfare of the Cold War," in Gary D. Rawnsley (ed.), *Cold-War Propaganda in the 1950s.* New York: St. Martin's Press, 1999), 225–42.

the united-front project: the Vlasovites' role, favoritism toward the NTS (National Labor Alliance), and the weak position granted to the exile left. As subsequent chapters will show, the OPC-CIA's empowering of exiles as political actors had damaging consequences, as émigré dogmas and misconceptions would provide a faulty basis for political warfare against the USSR.

The Classroom, the Embassy, and the Emigration

At the origins of the united-front campaign were two State Department Russia specialists: Kennan and Robert F. Kelley. As a young diplomat in the 1930s, Kennan watched from inside the new US embassy in Moscow a country convulsed by terror.[7] In part as a result of his impressions, Kennan found himself on the outside of established opinion in Washington during World War II, "openly critical" of the Grand Alliance Franklin Delano Roosevelt pursued with the Soviet Union and cognizant of the danger of Soviet expansion after the war.[8] With the onset of the Cold War, Kennan's warnings about Soviet foreign policy came to be seen as prophetic in Washington, and the previously isolated and controversial diplomat shot to the forefront of the US foreign-policy establishment. Appointed in 1947 as the head of the new Policy Planning Staff (PPS), a committee designed to give strategic advice to the Secretary of State, Kennan exerted unparalleled influence on US foreign policy during the beginning of the Cold War.[9]

Kennan's agenda toward the USSR at this early stage was far more aggressive than suggested by the doctrine of containment, at least as it is often portrayed.[10] Kennan's PPS pushed the government to engage in "organized political warfare" as a regular instrument of state policy, particularly against the Soviet Union. National Security Council Directive 10/2, adopted in June 1948, authorized the OPC to undertake "preventive direct action" against the Soviet bloc, "including sabotage, anti-sabotage, demolition and evacuation measures" as well as "assistance to underground resistance movements, guerrillas and refugee liberation groups."[11] As part of this agenda, Kennan focused governmental attention on displaced Soviet and East European citizens in Europe, which he saw as crucial for

---

[7] George F. Kennan, *Memoirs, 1925–1950* (Boston: Little, Brown, 1967), 58–86.

[8] Walter L. Hixson, *George F. Kennan: Cold War Iconoclast* (New York: Columbia University Press, 1989), 18–19.

[9] John Lewis Gaddis, *George F. Kennan: An American Life* (New York: Penguin Press, 2011), 265–71.

[10] In Kennan's thinking, there was no contradiction between containment and aggressive political warfare, for he expected the latter to contribute to the former by raising the cost of Soviet aggression abroad. Ibid, 235.

[11] National Security Council Directive on Office of Special Projects, Washington, June 18, 1948, document 292, in FRUS, 1945–1950, Emergence of the Intelligence Establishment.

"politico-psychological operations" as well as for "official intelligence" and "public information."[12]

The first OPC gambit at carrying out this program involved exiles from the satellite states of Eastern Europe. The model for Amcomlib was the National Committee for a Free Europe (NCFE), the American front organization that OPC created as a conduit for funding East European National Councils. The logic of engaging émigrés via an ostensibly independent committee of American citizens was to provide the US government with "plausible deniability" for its support of anti-communist exiles, while also creating the impression of public enthusiasm for the liberationist cause on the American home front. The major difference between the East European and Soviet projects was that NCFE's National Councils, made up of expelled Eastern European politicians and diplomats, had a major presence in the United States. In contrast, the Soviet project was to take place in Europe, where the Soviet anti-communists of greatest interest to the OPC were located.[13]

The recruitment of American go-betweens differed from the East European precedent, as well. The NCFE had been headed by a high-powered lineup of former government officials and diplomats including Allen Dulles, soon to become Director of Central Intelligence. When it turned to organizing the Russians, however, the OPC recruited a somewhat less prominent group of anti-communists: journalist and *Reader's Digest* editor Eugene Lyons; Russian historian and writer for *The Wall Street Journal* William H. Chamberlin; vice president of Time Inc. Allen Grover; Harvard professor and Washington insider William Y. Elliot; writer and publisher William L. White; and former New Jersey mayor Charles Edison.[14] Presumably, the OPC opted for such a roster in order to avoid the difficulties it had experienced in controlling the NCFE. Amcomlib was to remain "strictly a 'front,'" the planners decided, in order to avoid any "misunderstanding" over its prerogatives at a later date.[15]

The OPC Russian project also had distinct historical and intellectual origins. When Kennan and OPC head Frank Wisner authorized work with "refugee liberation groups" among Russians, they placed the project in the hands of Robert F. Kelley. As head of the State Department East European Affairs Division from 1926 to 1937, Kelley had trained a generation of Russia experts, including Kennan, who would go on to influence and conduct American foreign policy during the

---

[12] Peter Grose, *Operation Rollback: America's Secret War behind the Iron Curtain* (Boston: Houghton Mifflin, 2000), 7.

[13] Katalin Kádár Lynn, "At war while at peace: United States Cold War policy and the National Committee for a Free Europe, Inc.," in Katalin Kádár Lynn (ed.). *The Inauguration of Organized Political Warfare: Cold War Organizations sponsored by the National Committee for a Free Europe/Free Europe Committee* (Saint Helena, CA: Helena History Press, 2013), 1–15.

[14] Hugh Wilford, *The Mighty Wurlitzer: How the CIA Played America* (Cambridge, MA: Harvard University Press, 2008), 40–4.

[15] Memorandum for Deputy Director (plans), Frank Wisner, Assistant Director for Policy Coordination, August 21, 1951, 2, in Radio Free Europe and Radio Liberty.

Cold War. However, his career at State was cut short. A vocal proponent of the early US policy of denying diplomatic recognition to the Soviet Union, Kelley saw his division dismantled after Roosevelt established relations with the USSR. Kelley would leave the diplomatic service altogether in 1945 amid a scandal involving currency operations at the US Embassy in Ankara. With the onset of the Cold War, Kelley re-entered the policy world, now as an employee of the political warfare agency that would undertake some of the United States' most provocative anti-communist policies.[16]

A primary context for the anti-communist project spearheaded by Kennan and Kelley was their view of Russian history. Kelley, who was doing doctoral work in Russian history at Harvard University when he was drafted into the army in 1917, implemented an ambitious program of training State Department Russian hands by sending them to universities in Europe for three years of study in Russian language, culture, and history.[17] Only some years later would Kennan establish his credentials as a professional historian. But his sponsorship of the Russia project derived from his romantic fascination with historical Russia, which stemmed in part from his nineteenth-century ancestor and namesake who had explored Russian Siberia and popularized its exiles for a US audience.[18] And as a young diplomat in the 1920s, Kennan read thirty volumes of the collected works of Anton Pavlovich Chekhov, seeing them as a portal to "the atmosphere of pre-revolutionary Russia," and hoping to write a manuscript on the subject.[19]

Kennan's choice of words was important. Daniel Yergin has criticized Kelley's training program for Washington's Russia hands, calling their immersion in what is now called area studies as an "exercise in nostalgia." American diplomats, he alleged, came to view Russia through the prism of the past and held a caricatured and inflexible "image of the Soviet Union as a world revolutionary state."[20] This verdict is hardly satisfying: why should one fault Kelley for requiring that diplomats be exposed to serious study of Russia, especially in light of the poor state of American knowledge about the country at the time? Nevertheless, the liberationists' belief that historic Russia was the genuine one did distort their thinking. As Foglesong comments, theirs was an "optimistic or wishful reading of Russian history," which posited that an "inextinguishable passion for freedom" churned "under the lid of tsarist and Soviet oppression."[21] Perhaps the most naïve

---

[16] Kelley applied for work in the CIA in early 1949. Jody Lee Peterson, *Ideology and Influence: Robert F. Kelley and the State Department 1926–1937*, PhD diss., Washington State University, 1998, 24.

[17] Many Russian specialists in the State Department completed this training at the École Nationale des Langues Orientales Vivantes at the University of Paris, where Kelley had himself studied for a time, while Kennan was sent to the Oriental Institute at the University of Berlin. Peterson, *Ideology and Influence*, 23–6, 73–8.

[18] Gaddis, *George F. Kennan*, 48, 81.

[19] Kennan, *Memoirs, 1925–1950*, 49.

[20] Daniel Yergin, *Shattered Peace: The Origins of the Cold War and the National Security State* (Boston: Houghton Mifflin, 1977), 20–2.

[21] Foglesong, *The American Mission and the "Evil Empire"*, 112.

expression of this belief came from Eugene Lyons, the first chairman of Amcomlib. Born to a Jewish family on the periphery of the Russian Empire, Lyons had been a communist fellow traveler in the United States, employed for a time as a correspondent for the Soviet news agency Tass. After working as a Moscow correspondent for United Press during Stalin's Great Break (1928–34)—during which he interviewed Joseph Stalin—Lyons turned sharply against Soviet communism.[22] Despite, or perhaps because of his long association with the left, Lyons took up the cause of yesterday's Russia. In *Our Secret Allies: the People of Russia*, he argued that émigrés and defectors were prima facie evidence that "the traditional Russian," "with his primordial leanings to the spiritual and idealistic," still survived behind *Homo Sovieticus* and eagerly awaited the opportunity to "break through."[23]

The almost messianic conviction that the "traditional Russian" would one day cast off his or her artificial communist casing was a distorted reading of the Soviet Union in the early Cold War. It woefully exaggerated the instability of Stalinist rule, and particularly the extent to which the Russian nation operated outside the strictures of Soviet power.[24] In fact, the unreality of the OPC planners went much deeper than Yergin and Foglesong suggest. Kelley, Kennan, and Lyons were not just biased toward traditional Russia but specifically toward exiles as representatives of it. In their view, what could be more indicative of the illegitimacy of communism in Russia than the huge numbers of Russians who had fled or been banished from their homeland? And who could better articulate a vision of anti-communist Russia than the exiles, who were living purveyors of the anti-Soviet movements of the past?

The OPC's almost boundless enthusiasm for the exiles determined the structure of the united-front project. In order to become "an effective anti-Communist political force," Kelley reasoned, the political center should not be "an 'artificial' creation imposed from without, but something evolved by the Russian émigrés themselves."[25] Accordingly, the blueprint for the operation was remarkably simple: the American Committee would assemble the leaders of several hand-picked exile organizations in Germany and let them pursue concerted action against the Soviets with only loose guidance.[26] Indeed, Kelley's view of émigré

---

[22] Lyons's influential account of his experience of the USSR and crisis of faith is *Assignment in Utopia* (New York: Harcourt, Brace, 1937).

[23] Eugene Lyons, *Our Secret Allies: The Peoples of Russia* (New York: Duell, Sloan and Pearce, 1953), 373.

[24] Worth mentioning, though, is the fact that the view of the USSR as an adulteration of historic Russia represented the standard approach of historians of Russia in the United States at the time. On the historiography of Russia during the early Cold War, see Engerman, *Know Your Enemy*, 153–79.

[25] Recommendations on Utilization of the Russian Emigration, April 26, 1950, 3, in Radio Free Europe and Radio Liberty.

[26] American Friends of the Freedom of the Russian Peoples, n.d. (1950), 1–2, in Georgetown University Archives and Special Collections, Robert F. Kelley Papers (hereinafter Kelley Papers), box 5, fol. 3.

anti-communism was so sanguine that he rejected organizational schemes for the project that might have afforded the OPC more control behind the scenes, such as Kennan's and Wisner's suggestion that the united front might begin operations as a Russian Welfare Committee before undertaking anti-Soviet activities.[27] The Americans would bring together the exiles and then serve as their relatively distant bankroller—perhaps an expression of what Kennan meant when he called for Russians to be themselves and work out their problems in the pages of *Foreign Affairs*.

Assigning such a world-historic role to the exiles was a recipe for disaster. The conviction that émigrés would be effective instruments of political warfare rested on the view that Russian populations abroad and at home were basically the same in culture, outlook, and even political convictions. The virtual closure of the USSR to outside contacts in Stalin's last years meant that exiles took on a status as the virtually unchallenged window on Russian Soviet public opinion for US policymakers and intelligence officials.[28]

Reading domestic affairs in the Soviet Union through the prism of exiles, however, was a deeply problematic exercise. In practical terms, the virtual black-out on independent information from inside the USSR affected the exiles as much as Western intelligence officers. Even the NTS, the most developed of the émigré groups, lacked a courier service for communicating with Soviet citizens.[29] Clearly, the exiles could not provide a picture of Soviet society that would serve as the basis for an effective program of political warfare against the USSR.

The situation was worse still. More than just physically isolated from their homeland, the exile anti-communist groups represented rigid ideological positions that were in no way representative of Russian Soviet society under late Stalinism—a point which, as this book will show, would come to be recognized in Washington gradually as contacts with defectors and other Soviet citizens increased. And as already seen in previous chapters, the exiles were engaged in a brutal internal competition, often involving tactics of misinformation and defamation of their opponents. As a result, the united front took shape in direct relation to the chaotic internal struggle of the exiles and would bear its imprint. In particular, the OPC's core task of identifying which groups from the émigré

[27] Kelley rejected the idea for security considerations, pointing out that the makeup of the committee would immediately demonstrate its political purpose. Kennan authorizes Russian Émigré Broadcasting Project, September 13, 1949, in Radio Free Europe and Radio Liberty.

[28] This wider point is made forcefully in Matthew W. Aid, "The National Security Agency and the Cold War," in Matthew W. Aid and Cees Wiebes (eds.), *Secrets of Signals Intelligence during the Cold War and beyond* (London and Portland, OR: Frank Cass, 2001), 30–1.

[29] NTS (National Labor Union), 11, in NARA, RG 263, Entry ZZ-19, 230/86/25/03, box 24, AESAURUS/AENOBLE (hereinafter AESAURUS), Vol. 1, pt. 1. An enterprising CIA officer, working as diplomatic courier to the USSR in 1949, attempted to set up a letter exchange between DPs and their Soviet contacts at home, but was soon detected and denied re-entry to the country. Peer De Silva, *Sub Rosa: The CIA and the Uses of Intelligence* (New York: Times Books, 1978), 20–36.

milieu deserved to take part in the project would prove hopelessly intertwined with exile politics.

General Vlasov Goes to Washington

If Kelley and Kennan looked to imperial history to find the building blocks of an anti-Soviet Russia, it is no less true that they found them in World War II. The architects of the OPC united-front project gained inspiration from Russian wartime collaboration and its central symbol, General A. A. Vlasov. The Eastern Front provided Kelley and other leaders of the project with both a precedent and a cautionary tale about political warfare against Soviet rule. As Kelley believed, the "mass surrender of Soviet soldiers and their willingness to join the invaders to fight the Soviets" in 1941—in other words, the "defeatism" discussed in Chapter 3 of this book—demonstrated that the national feeling of ethnic Russians was directed against Soviet rule, not in support of it.[30] In Kelley's verdict, Hitler had squandered a golden opportunity to exploit a Russian national movement by fighting a war against the Russian people. The United States could learn from Hitler's mistake if only it recognized that its enemy was "not Russia but the Communist rulers of Russia."[31]

The OPC's reading of the Eastern Front translated into enthusiasm for the second-wave Vlasovites who had remained in the West. The new exiles had "personal knowledge of communist methods" and of "the psychology of their fellow citizens," Kelley pointed out, and therefore were uniquely qualified to carry out political warfare against the USSR. No less important, the second-wavers had "a more intense hatred of Communism" than the old émigrés and, in general, were "a tougher and much more ruthless breed." Following this judgment, Kelley called for leaders of the Union for the Struggle for the Liberation of the Peoples of Russia (SBONR), the major Vlasovite organization, to make up a "majority of the members, including the head of the Directing Center of the united front."[32]

Kelley's vision of the Vlasovites was surely a manifestation of wishful thinking about Russian history. *Pace* Foglesong's analysis, the American liberationists' writing on the Vlasovites was rife with religion-infused language about the "free Russian spirit" and its suffering and martyrdom, both at the hands of Stalin and, tragically, of the Americans who shipped the Russians back to the USSR after the war.[33] But reducing the liberationists' perspective on Vlasovism to their

[30] Memorandum for the Record, Su: Psychological Warfare against the Soviets (Utilization of Emigration Groups), no author (perhaps Robert F. Kelley), March 6, 1952, 7, in Kelley Papers, box 5, fol. 1.
[31] Recommendations on Utilization, 4.
[32] Ibid.
[33] Lyons, *Our Secret Allies*, 248–53.

ideological preoccupations is unsatisfying. For in constructing the political-center project, Kelley adopted ideas about the Vlasovites that were in wide circulation among the exiles in Germany. As Kelley's archive shows, he read reports written by individuals associated with the wartime Vlasov movement, both its Russian participants and German overseers, which substantiated the pro-Vlasov narrative.[34] Kelley's adoption of the Vlasov movement as a model for political warfare was a product of émigré politics as much as American ideals.

The Vlasov myth passed from the exiles in Europe to Washington elites through more circuitous ways than Kelley's intelligence reports. The crucial figure in popularizing Vlasov was George Fischer. The son of formerly pro-Soviet journalist Louis Fischer and his Russian-born wife Markoosha (discussed in the Introduction), the younger Fischer was drawn to the Russian exiles by an unlikely personal path. George grew up as Iurii in 1930s Moscow and arrived in the US late in the decade when his parents fled from Stalinist terror. In the United States, Fischer was equally at home among the liberal elites to which his father belonged—he dined with the Roosevelts in the White House—and among communities of down-and-out Russian and German socialists in New York. From contact with both his father's and mother's American milieus, George came to reject the communism of his upbringing with all the zeal of a convert, a trend which deepened when he came face to face with Soviet military men in Europe during his service in the Second World War.[35] Fischer's obsession with the Vlasovites emerged from his varied origins. In a 1946 letter to an old relation, Fischer explained that:

> the Vlasov case appeals to me most because it deals with a young Soviet hero-general and because in Germany he gathered around him not only White Guards etc [sic] but also high officers who talked and dreamed not about race and Hitler but about democracy in Russia.[36]

From the beginning, then, Fischer saw Vlasov through the prism of his own ideological commitments, as a figure from inside the Soviet system who sought to bring American-style democracy to Russia.

Remarkably, Fischer channeled his discovery of the Vlasovites into serious scholarly and political agendas in his adopted American homeland. Then a graduate student at Harvard's Russian Research Institute, the first institution of its kind in the United States, Fischer sought out the real-life Vlasovites in

---

[34] A Study in Political Psychology, no author indicated (Vlasovite commander), n.d., 8, in Kelley Papers, box 5, fol. 6. The unidentified author claimed to have known Vlasov personally. See also testimony from Gunter d'Alquen, SS liaison to ethnic units in the Wehrmacht, January 5, 1949, in Kelley Papers, box 3, fol. 12.

[35] George Uri Fischer, *Insatiable: A Story of my Nine Lives* (Philadelphia: unpublished TS, 2000), 71–94.

[36] Ibid., 155.

Germany. Receiving his contacts via B. I. Nikolaevskii, who had done the same a year before, Fischer met the Vlasovites in Germany in 1948. He found in the "bedraggled refugees" both "people hot to fight Stalin" and "typical and likable Soviet people"—in other words, the purveyors of the democratic Soviet Russia he imagined.[37] The 23-year-old graduate student convinced scholars at the Russian Research Institute of the need to study the Russian DPs systematically, taking advantage of "a rare chance to question Soviet people away from the terror of their own country."[38] Fischer's initiative produced the Harvard Project on Soviet Social System, a mammoth project for interviewing Soviet DPs that received funding from the US Air Force.[39] Just as Kelley was drawing up plans for the OPC united front in Washington, a small army of American researchers descended on Munich to interview the Vlasovites and other second-wavers, forging contacts that would eventually contribute to US psychological warfare operations.

Perhaps as important as Fischer's organizational efforts was his scholarship on the Vlasov issue. In two 1949 articles published in *Russian Review*, a new journal edited by Harvard émigré historian M. M. Karpovich, Fischer provided some of the first and most influential English-language accounts of Vlasov and wartime collaboration. While approaching the subject with a degree of scholarly detachment, Fischer's pieces conveyed the common exile picture of Vlasovism as a bona fide "anti-Soviet movement" that emerged from the groundswell of "defeatism" on the Soviet home front during World War II.[40] Fischer had brought the pro-Vlasov narrative from the obscurity of an émigré community in Germany to the attention of American intellectual and policy elites.

The pro-Vlasov orientation of OPC's exile action, therefore, involved a transfer of ideas from exiles in Europe to the new American intelligence establishment through multiple passageways: reports from Wehrmacht veterans, émigrés in the United States such as Nikolaevskii and Karpovich, and especially the organizing efforts of an enterprising Russian-American graduate student in Fischer. If news of Vlasov certainly fell on fertile soil in the thinking of US policymakers, the Russian exile political world was a crucial ingredient in American schemes to liberate Russia.

---

[37] Ibid., 156.

[38] Ibid. See also Dzh. Iu. Fisher [George Fischer], "Dve strasti," in V. S. Karpov et al. (eds.), *V poiskakh istiny. Puti i sud'by vtoroi emigratsii: sbornik statei i dokumentov* (Moscow: RGGU, 1997), 199–202.

[39] Engerman, *Know Your Enemy*, 56–69. A recent study that overstates the place of American governmental policies in the project is E. V. Kodin, "*Garvardskii Proekt*" (Moscow: ROSSPEN, 2003).

[40] George Fischer, "The New Soviet Emigration," *The Russian Review* 8, no. 1 (1949): 11–13, and "General Vlasov's Official Biography," *Russian Review* 8, no. 4 (1949): 284–301. By the time Fischer published a manuscript on the topic, he had arrived at the more nuanced position that wartime defeatism stemmed from the "political inertness" that dominated Soviet political life. George Fischer, *Soviet Opposition to Stalin: A Case Study in World War II* (Cambridge: Harvard University Press, 1952). See also Mark Edele, *Stalin's Defectors: How Red Army Soldiers became Hitler's Collaborators, 1941–1945* (New York and Oxford: Oxford University Press, 2017), 152–60.

Exile realities not only helped to shape the OPC united front but also contributed to its deficiency, namely the overly optimistic and even wrong-headed character of its scheme for Russian liberation. However one interprets the history of the Vlasov movement, there can be no doubt that the pro-Vlasov narrative the émigrés espoused—and which Kelley endorsed—provided a flawed precedent for the OPC project to unify the emigration during the early Cold War. Given the patriotic upsurge of World War II in the USSR, appealing to Vlasov was hardly a winning strategy for political warfare in the Cold War.[41] In fact, the point was not lost on OPC chief Wisner, who would caution Amcomlib's Radio Liberation against mentioning Vlasov's name on air.[42]

Kelley's seemingly boundless faith in the political possibilities of the Vlasovites was yet another manifestation of wishful thinking that surrounded the united-front project. As seen in previous chapters, second-wave exiles were plagued by traumatic pasts, unclear ideological commitments, a lack of acknowledged leaders, and chronic Soviet infiltration operations—all of which prevented them from becoming the determined activists Kelley imagined them to be. In this way, the émigré-derived Vlasov myth that liberationists imbibed added to the unrealistic expectations of the OPC psy-war agenda.

The NTS: Revolutionary Simulation

If Kelley placed the Vlasovites at the core of plans for the OPC project, the NTS was not far behind. Kelley's April 1950 memorandum on the united front asserted that it was of "the greatest importance that the Solidarists be represented in the anti-Communist center." And for a simple reason: the NTS was "the best organized and the most active in anti-Communist work of all the Russian émigré organizations."[43] Although seemingly straightforward, Kelley's bullish appraisal of the NTS had its own complex backstory. Like his thinking about the Vlasovites, Kelley's confidence in the political prowess of the NTS had its origins in the émigré scene in Europe. In large part, the OPC-CIA's embrace of the NTS was a product of the concerted political efforts of the organization's members, the "Solidarists" themselves.

The emergence of the view that the NTS was an anti-Soviet force to be reckoned with was a seemingly unlikely development. As discussed in Chapter 1, after

---

[41] On the abusive treatment of Vlasovites in Soviet custody, see Catherine Merridale, *Ivan's War: The Red Army 1939–45* (London: Faber, 2005), 304–6.

[42] Office of Policy Coordination requests State Department Views on Radio Liberty, June 2, 1952, 5, in Radio Free Europe and Radio Liberty.

[43] Recommendations on Utilization, 4. Here I disagree with David C. S. Albanese's position that the CIA deliberately courted the NTS and other xenophobic elements with the aim of "stoking the flames of ethnic and national hatreds." David C. S. Albanese, "In Search of a Lesser Evil: Anti-Soviet Nationalism and the Cold War," PhD thesis, Northeastern University, 2015, 24.

Figure 4.1 The NTS Council in 1949, Limburg, Germany. The NTS leaders had collaborated in various capacities with the intelligence, propaganda, and security agencies of Nazi Germany. Now they looked to the new anti-communist superpower across the Atlantic as a potential patron. From right to left: V. D. Poremskii, A. N. Artemov, N. N. Rutchenko, E. R. Romanov, A. R. Trushnovich, E. E. Pozdeev, N. F. Shits (in front), M. L. O'lgskii, R. N. Redlikh.
Source: Arkhiv Narodno-trudovogo soiuza, Frankfurt am Main.

collaborating with the Germans and then being persecuted by them, the NTS activists managed to survive and remobilize with the intermittent benevolence of the US military government, establishing their own DP camp and shielding second-wavers in their orbit from repatriation. Nevertheless, the NTS had very little presence in the United States or Britain, and its far-right, anti-Semitic leaders viewed the Atlantic democracies with suspicion. At a 1952 meeting, NTS leader Viktor Mikhailovich Baidalakov listed his grievances against the United States, such as "excessive democracy," "Semitophilism," and the tendency of Americans to equate Stalinism with tsarism, which he called "shitting on" historical Russia. However, Baidalakov pointed out that anti-communists had no serious alternative to working with the United States in the struggle against communism.[44] Following this logic, from the very outset of the postwar period the leaders of the NTS, depicted in Figure 4.1, undertook a concerted effort to win the support of the Western superpower for its anti-communist activities.

---

[44] Protokoly s'ezda Soveta NTS v ianvare 1952 g., 4, in Georgetown University Archives and Special Collections, Victor M. Baydalakoff Collection (hereinafter Baydalakoff Collection), box 1, fol. 1.

NTS members had worked with multiple intelligence services in their ill-starred efforts to penetrate the Soviet Union in the interwar period, and some Solidarists were probably engaged in spying for multiple services at once.[45] Given such a background, it was to be expected that the organization would seek to exploit US intelligence structures in occupied Germany. Already in 1946, the NTS began to operate a rudimentary intelligence service that drew on "occasional agents in the Soviet occupied zone, German black market dealers from the Soviet zone, German PW [sic] repatriates, and liaison with Yugoslav and Ukrainian elements in Germany which have their individual sources of information."[46] Although information from these haphazard sources was probably of little quality, the NTS was soon engaged in ongoing "cooperation" with army intelligence officials in the US occupation zone.[47] In the process, the NTS used intelligence channels to further its own political goals. For instance, in 1946 the charismatic NTS leader K. V. Boldyrev sent Joe Osborne of the Intelligence Branch (G2) of the Third US Army a "list of positive war criminals still at large" and a "list of persons confirmed in American prisons and deserving release." The first list included several long-standing opponents of the NTS, and the second carried the names of incarcerated NTS members, including one figure widely thought to have collaborated with the Gestapo during the war.[48]

While seeking to manipulate American military intelligence to its advantage, the NTS also undertook a massive public-relations campaign designed to obscure its collaborationist and radical-right past.[49] Similar to the Vlasovite efforts discussed in Chapter 3, the NTS constructed its own historical myth, presenting itself as a "Third Force" that had fought against both the USSR and Nazi Germany for

[45] In the early 1950s, it seems that NTS leader V. D. Poremskii worked for the CIA, the Gehlen Organization, and perhaps also French intelligence. Chief of Station, Karlsruhe to Chief, Foreign Division M, November 1. 1950, in NARA, RG 263, Entry ZZ-18, 230/86/23/04, box 77, Viktor Larionoff, vol. 1, and Memorandum, Su: REDBIRD/Summary of projects for [redacted], June 30, 1951, in AESAURUS, vol. 1, pt. 1.

[46] Office of the Assistant Chief of Staff, G-2, Su: Interview of White Russian Leaders, April 25, 1948, in NARA, RG 319, Entry 134A, 22348387, 270/84/20/02, box 68, Vlassow Group, fol. 1.

[47] 1st Lt. Sig C Joe Oswald to HQ, 3rd United States Army, Office of the Assistant Chief of Staff, G-2, July 1, 1946, in NARA, RG 319, IRR, D137606, Russian Dissident Groups in US Zone, released by FOIA request.

[48] Ibid. The first list included K. A. Voss (alias B. A. Foss), an opponent of the NTS from the 1930s whom the latter had accused of being a Soviet spy, and S. L. Voitsekhovskii, who competed with the NTS for German patronage during World War II as head of the Russian Representation (*Vertrauens-stelle*) in Warsaw. See Paul Robinson, *The White Russian Army in Exile, 1920–1941* (Oxford: Clarendon Press, 2002), 151–63. On V. M. Grechko's collaborationist past, see Su: KONR, Lt. col. Ellington D. Golden to Commanding Officer, 970th CIC Detachment, January 13, 1948, 11, NARA, RG 319, Entry 134A, XE182853, 270/84/01/01, box 22, Azonder, vol. 1, fol. 2.

[49] For a similar effort at historical revisionism in the Ukrainian nationalist movement in the final stages of the war and beyond, see Per Anders Rudling, "Historical Representation of the Wartime Accounts of the Activities of the OUN–UPA (Organization of Ukrainian Nationalists—Ukrainian Insurgent Army)," *East European Jewish Affairs* 36, no. 2 (2006): 163–89.

the duration of the war—a basically mendacious historical narrative in light of the extensive collaboration of NTS members with Nazi Germany.[50]

Complementing the Alliance's new presentation of the past was its simultaneous ideological transformation. Soon after the war ended, the NTS sought to redefine its doctrines in such a way that the organization might be allowed to operate in occupied Germany and, more broadly, in a postwar West that was dominated by the democratic and centrist political spectrum fostered by American hegemony. Starting with its 1946 program, the NTS began purging its doctrinal statements of fascistic and anti-liberal terminology—plans for "national dictatorship" and condemnation of "the comedy of parliamentary elections"—as well as its call for anti-Semitic ethnic cleansing, namely the demand that Jews either leave Russia without capital or settle in a "territory specially designated for them."[51] According to the postwar party line, Solidarism was (and always had been) a moderate and even democratic doctrine that opposed totalitarianism in both its fascist and Marxist variants.[52]

The NTS's ideological facelift, however, might have been unnecessary. All evidence points to the fact that Kelley and other OPC-CIA planners viewed the NTS's potential to contribute to covert operations as being far more important than its ideology or wartime activities.[53] Kelley's thinking on the matter was probably redolent of the sentiment expressed by Michael Burke, a CIA official who worked with the NTS in Germany for a time, who opined that there could be "no shilly-shallying about morality" in the Cold War.[54]

Kelley's placing of expediency over democratic politics created an opening for the NTS to propagandize its image of political prowess. Starting almost immediately after the war, the NTS loudly advertised its supposed ability to penetrate the Iron Curtain. In its propaganda, the NTS claimed that it had "dozens" of secret cells in the USSR, which were active in low-level protest such as scrawling the NTS trident symbol on walls and fences.[55] Again, leading the charge was the resourceful

[50] Anne Kuhlmann-Smirnov, "'Stiller als Wasser, Tiefer als Gras': Zur Migrationsgeschichte der Russischen Displaced Persons in Deutschland nach dem Zweiten Weltkrieg," *Arbeitspapiere und Materialien—Universität Bremen*, no. 68, Forschungsstelle Osteuropa an der Universität Bremen, 2005, 42.

[51] See the sixteenth chapter of "Skhema natsional'no-trudovogo stroia 1942," at http://www.ntsrs.ru/content/programmnye-dokumenty.nts, accessed April 24, 2013. Efforts of NTS members to attribute this clause from the war period to Nazi pressure are unconvincing given the numerous anti-Semitic references found in prewar Alliance writings. Boris L. Dvinov, *Politics of the Russian Emigration* (Santa Monica, CA: Rand Corp., 1955), 139–40, 157–67 and Ivan Dorba, *Svoi sredi chuzhikh: v omute istiny* (Moscow: Veche, 2012), 40–2, 160–2.

[52] For an example of how the Solidarists constructed the right and left as external and equidistant entities, see A. Kolin, "Strategiia Solidarizma," *Volia* no. 2 (1949): 25.

[53] Survey of the Russian Emigration, no author indicated (presumably Robert F. Kelley), April 1950, 32–6, in Kelley Papers, box 5, fol. 14.

[54] Michael Burke, *Outrageous Good Fortune* (Boston: Little, Brown, 1984), 155.

[55] Bernd Stöver, *Die Befreiung vom Kommunismus: amerikanische Liberation Policy im Kalten Krieg 1947–1991* (Cologne: Böhlau, 2002), 523–4.

K. V. Boldyrev, who had arrived in the United States in 1948 (almost surely with CIA help).[56] The charismatic émigré unleashed a remarkable publicity campaign: he appeared as the author of pieces in *Reader's Digest* and *Look* magazine, befriended the staunchly anti-communist congressman Charles J. Kersten of Wisconsin, and delivered lectures on Russian affairs to State Department staff—an engagement that morphed eventually into a career at Georgetown University's School of Foreign Service. More quixotically, Boldyrev interested Hollywood producers in his plans for a television program about the "struggle of the NTS," apparently to be based on "real episodes."[57]

Boldyrev and other Solidarists not only created a sensational picture of the NTS's revolutionary exploits but also tailored their messages to their American audience. To the wider public, Boldyrev stressed that the NTS could win the Cold War for the United States without bloodshed by carrying out a revolution in Russia.[58] When lobbying US capitalists, an NTS publication recommended, one should talk dollars and cents, stressing that after the fall of the Bolsheviks "you will supply us with refrigerators and cars and we will send you oil and manganese."[59] The NTS tried to tell Americans frightened by the Soviet threat—or lured by its market—what they wanted to hear.

The results of the NTS's propaganda blitz in the United States should not be exaggerated. Boldyrev overplayed his hand with his lurid depiction of the NTS freedom fighters in Russia. When *Newsweek* published a piece on a news conference held by Boldyrev, it also solicited the opinions of the NTS's émigré opponents who cast doubt on the NTS's claims.[60] Nor did friendship with Kersten yield benefits. Boldyrev fell out with the congressman after Kersten introduced a resolution in the House of Representatives expressing friendship toward the minority peoples of the Soviet Union—a move that the Russian saw as a precedent for the eventual dismemberment of the Russian state.[61] Meanwhile, American audiences were deprived of the opportunity of watching real scenes of the NTS

---

[56] Boldyrev was clearly close to the CIA at this time. He met with powerful figures in the CIA, including Michael Josselson and, most impressively, Director of Central Intelligence Roscoe Hillenkoetter, in July 1950. Protokoly S'ezda Soveta NTS v dekabre 1950 g., 6, in Baydalakoff Collection, box 1, fol. 1. See also the entry for Friday, July 7, 1950, in Special Collection: Intelligence, Policy, and Politics: The DCI, the White House, and Congress, Document Number (FOIA)/ESDN (CREST): 5166d49399326091c6a604c4, CIA FOIA Electronic Reading Room.

[57] Boldyrev discusses his television and movie plans in K. V. Boldyrev to V. D. Poremskii, October 7, 1951, in FSO, 01–098 Tarasova, kor. 41.

[58] Constantine W. Boldyreff, as told to Edward B. Paine, "The Story of One Russian Underground Organization Attempting to Overthrow Stalin," *Look* 12, no. 22 (October 26, 1948): 25–7.

[59] S. Rozhdestvenskii, "Iz opyta raboty s inostrantsami," *Za Rossiu* no. 9–10 (1953): 4, as cited in Antoshin, *Rossiiskie emigranty*, 364.

[60] "Man from Russia," *Newsweek*, October 25, 1948: 38.

[61] Boldyrev's confrontation with Kersten foreshadowed the difficulties that Russian nationalism would pose for émigré involvement in the Cold War. K. V. Boldyrev to V. D. Poremskii, November 25, 1951. Kersten's resolution is found in United States Congressional Record, 1951, 82nd Congress, vol. 97, session 1, A530, AG347.

underground on their television screens, perhaps because other Solidarists seem to have been skeptical that Hollywood could convey the organization's image with the needed gravitas.[62] After observing his erratic plans, the CIA determined not to "deal with the infamous Boldyrev" at all, and he was soon replaced as leader of the NTS's chapter in the United States.[63]

Boldyrev's fall from grace reflected an underlying problem. NTS claims to hold influence in the USSR, at least in the early 1950s, were false. When CIA officials examined the matter, they concluded that the "NTS has not had any post war penetration of the Soviet Union, nor do they have many contacts within the Soviet Union who are actively sending out information."[64] The NTS responded to the massive gap between its boasts and actual abilities to cross the Iron Curtain with its characteristic resourcefulness. Starting in 1947, the NTS, "whenever the opportunity presented itself," attempted to distribute anti-Soviet leaflets and literature in the Soviet zones of Germany and Austria.[65] These undertakings were self-financed, small-scale, and basically ineffective, as they relied on such crude distribution methods as stowing copies of the NTS's newspaper *Posev* ("The Sowing") and leaflets in Soviet military trains, mailing them directly to military units in East Germany, and "assigning elderly, inconspicuous Germans to carry and distribute copies."[66]

If these shoestring propaganda activities did little to challenge the communist enemy, they did serve the ancillary goal of winning patronage from the US intelligence establishment. As NTS leader Vladimir Dmitrievich Poremskii commented while describing the organization's German activities to his fellow Solidarists, "The path to Washington lies through the occupied zone."[67] The NTS publicity strategy worked, at least as far as courting the CIA was concerned. If it was perhaps inevitable that US spies empowered to launch covert operations against the USSR would turn to the NTS, the exiles' tireless propaganda efforts surely helped to tip the scales in their favor. For instance, the OPC-CIA operated on the conviction that the NTS was an active and relatively large organization. Kelley's 1950 survey of the emigration estimated that the NTS had a membership of roughly 2,000 worldwide in 1948, but internal documents from the émigrés show that the true number was a mere 764 persons.[68] Based on such flawed impressions, the US anti-communist and governmental circles that embraced

---

[62]   V. D. Poremskii to K. V. Boldyrev, October 13, 1951, in FSO, 01–098 Tarasova, kor. 41.

[63]   Chief FDS/West to Chief, FDS, December 15, 1950, in AESAURUS, vol. 1, pt. 1. Boldyrev's stock with the CIA also fell due to his role in an abortive project to infiltrate agents into the Soviet Far East (cryptonym WARNACK). Memorandum, SR/West to Chief, SR Division, January 7, 1952, 1, in AESAURUS, vol. 3, pt. 1.

[64]   Chief FDS/West to Chief, FDS, December 15, 1950, in AESAURUS, vol. 1, pt. 1.

[65]   Evgenii Romanov, *V bor'be za Rossiiu: vospominaniia* (Moscow: Golos, 1999), 106.

[66]   NTS (National Labor Union), 12, in AESAURUS, vol. 1, part 1.

[67]   Protokol utrennogo zasedaniia, 12-go ianvaria 1949 g., in Baydalakoff Collection, box 1, fol. 1.

[68]   Compare Survey of the Russian Emigration, 35, and Otchetnyi doklad Predsedatelia Soiuza za trekhletie svoikh polnomochii, ot 24-1-1952 goda, 12, in Baydalakoff Collection, box 1, fol. 9.

Kennan's liberation project brought the NTS directly into their orbit. Whether in the DP camps or in the halls of power in Washington, the NTS proved adept at writing its own story, misleadingly depicting itself as a large, disciplined, and dynamic anti-communist force.

Ironically, the NTS had limited interest in the political-center project that Kelley so urgently wanted it to join. Generally speaking, Russian exiles embraced the goal of unifying their efforts, not only in order to strengthen their political authority but also to avoid the perception that they were pursuing "narrow party interests."[69] In contrast, a debate about the American political center at the NTS Council in late 1950 showed that considerations of party realpolitik reigned supreme in the organization. Baidalakov suggested that the NTS give in to the "strong pressure" it received from US circles to take part, commenting that there existed "no third position" apart from those of the superpowers from which to act on the international stage. A. R Trushnovich agreed, warning that "if we resist, they will simply throw us in jail"—a sentiment, no doubt, colored by the NTS's fall from grace under the Third Reich.[70] But other NTS leaders were hesitant to agree to the united front. Roman Nikolaevich Redlikh opined that the NTS did "not need" a unification of Russian anti-communists. Time was on the side of the NTS, he argued, as it was the most effective exile force and "would do more than others on the same allocation" (obviously, of American dollars).[71] In his view, the NTS should avoid the unification effort, which would only limit the Solidarists' freedom of action and tie them to weaker émigré groups.

The different positions articulated at the NTS Council had a common denominator. The NTS leaders wanted American support and, especially, largesse, but did not want to share it with rival exile organizations. Moreover, as some of them must have known, the OPC-CIA was in the process of establishing contact with anti-communist groups in Germany, which held out the prospect that the NTS might receive direct support for its operations.[72] In light of this development, taking part in the united front seemed unnecessary and perhaps harmful. Ultimately, the NTS leaders adopted a compromise position, agreeing to join the united front as a "tactical maneuver" to maximize the organization's clout.[73] As will be seen in the coming chapters, Kelley's efforts to include the power-hungry NTS in the united front at all costs would prove to be a bad miscalculation—another example, like the Vlasov question, of how émigré politics not only shaped but also hampered US liberation policies.

---

[69] Nikolai Troitskii, *Ty, moe stoletie*—(Moscow: Institut politicheskogo i voennogo analiza, 2006), 318.

[70] Protokoly S'ezda Soveta NTS v dekabre 1950 g., 7, 10, 51.

[71] Ibid., 10.

[72] Project Outline, 4, August 28, 1950, NARA, RG 263, Entry ZZ-19, 230/86/26/01, box 58, QKDROOP.

[73] Report on NTS, Ryszard Wraga, October 11, 1951, in HILA, Ryszard Wraga Papers, box 4, fol. 6.

The Fight for the Mantle of Democracy

Kelley's determination to work with the Vlasovites and the NTS set the basic parameters of the united front but raised new questions. At root, the OPC was engaged in creating a counter-polity to Soviet rule in miniature, a "center of national hope" in Kennan's original formulation. Therefore, Kelley had the daunting task of adjudicating national claims among different émigré organizations. Who were the exiles with the best national credentials, meaning those whose programs for fighting communism would appeal to the masses of Russians in the USSR assumed to be awaiting deliverance from abroad?

Kelley adopted a consistent approach to the problem of national representation. The political center was an entity that would include "all the worthwhile political elements of the Russian emigration." According to Kelley, this meant that the united front should carry a "centrist" complexion, with only the far left ("Mensheviks") and far right ("reactionary monarchists") excluded from participation.[74] Kelley's justification for excluding what he saw as ideological extremes had little to do with democracy per se—indeed, Kelley and also Kennan sometimes questioned whether Russians were even capable of democratic rule.[75] Rather, Kelley was convinced that monarchists and socialists had "programs which do not appeal to the Russian masses in the Soviet Union," and therefore were not worthy of American support.[76] Estimates of Soviet realities, not American ideological preferences, dictated the exclusion of the political left and right.

The problem was that Kelley's understanding of the state of Soviet Russian opinion—and, therefore, his determination of the proper political complexion of the united-front organization—stemmed from his reading of émigré politics. Indeed, it seems probable that various Russian exiles had Kelley's ear during the united-front project's gestation. Kelley's archive contains several exile proposals for how to carry out its impending Russian psychological warfare action, news of which must have spread by word of mouth in exile circles in Germany. A few weeks before penning an important April 1950 memorandum on the united front, Kelley received a memorandum from V. V. Pozdniakov, a former Red Army colonel who worked as a propagandist in POW camps during World War II and then served on Vlasov's staff. Boldly presenting his own plan for American utilization of the exiles, Pozdniakov called for the exclusion of both conservative monarchists and socialists, declaring that "only centrist groups" represented

---

[74] Survey of the Russian Emigration, 73.

[75] The question of the feasibility of democracy in Russia divided the American proponents of Russian liberation. Foglesong, *The American Mission and the "Evil Empire"*, 121–3.

[76] Recommendations on Utilization, 5.

"a genuine force capable of rallying the emigration and directing its energies toward a real struggle with Bolshevism."[77]

One might doubt how effective émigré input could have been in shaping the policies of the young CIA. In particular, Kelley might have cast doubt on a memorandum from Pozdniakov, a divisive figure among the Vlasovites, an alleged war criminal, and an intelligence operative who had recently been removed from the Gehlen Organization for "over-evaluation of information and excessive expenditures."[78] More fundamentally, Kelley had his own reasons for excluding the far right and left. Without a doubt, the OPC's negative view of the monarchists stemmed from observation of their troubled postwar politics (see Chapter 2). And with regard to the left, Kelley himself was predisposed to reject Marxists as such. In a 1951 letter to State Department official Robert G. Hooker, Kelley opposed the idea of utilizing socialist language in US political warfare toward the Soviet Union. As he opined, Marxism, "preaching as it does the class struggle and advocating the rule of a small elite group, is fundamentally a totalitarian system … ".[79]

The anti-leftist design of the united front was not merely a product of American prejudices, though. Indeed, in the same letter to Hooker, Kelley explained that he based his opposition to Marxist themes in propaganda on "the views both of new defectors and of older members of the Russian emigration in Germany." More-over, OPC documents on the united front tended to echo the views of the émigré. As Chapter 3 showed, exiles of the rightist and Vlasovite camps routinely (and falsely) alleged that the New York-based League of Struggle for the People's Freedom (LBNS) consisted of unreformed Marxists and other radical socialists masking themselves as democrats.[80] A survey of the emigration commissioned by the OPC reproduced this anti-League rhetoric almost verbatim, casting doubt on the organization's own claims to represent a "strictly democratic and anti-Bolshevist party."[81] There is every reason to assume that the anti-leftism

---

[77] V. Pozdniakov, Nekotorye voprosy problem bor'by s bol'shevizmom, April 11, 1950, 3, in Kelley Papers, box 5, fol. 6. The major difference between Pozdniakov's and Kelley's recommendations on the groups to be included were the former's recommendation to exclude leaders of the NTS from the united front.

[78] Survey of the Russian Emigration, 42. According to the Soviet government, Pozdniakov had served as chief of police in a POW camp. List of war criminals and persons who collaborated with the enemy in the US zone of occupation in Germany, translated note from General Chuikov, May 13, 1949, 10 in Kelley Papers, box 5, fol. 6, and Igor' Petrov and Andrei Martynov, "'Neprigliadnaia kartina kulis vlasovskogo dvizheniia': Mikhail Samygin i ego kniga," in Martynov (ed.), Istoriia otechestvennoi kollaboratsii: materialy i issledovaniia (Moscow: Staraia Basmannaia, 2017), 27.

[79] Robert F. Kelley to Robert G. Hooker, East European Affairs, Department of State, May 9, 1951, in Kelley Papers, box 5, fol. 1.

[80] The ideological face of the League is conveyed in Roman Gul', Ia unes Rossiiu: Apologiia emigratsii (New York: "Most," 1981), vol. 3, 85–8. On the reformist character of postwar Menshevism, see A. V. Antoshin, "Men'sheviki v emigratsii posle Vtoroi mirovoi voiny," Otechestvennaia istoriia no. 1 (2007): 104.

[81] Survey of the Russian Emigration, 42.

dominating the émigré scene in Germany at least contributed to the OPC's mistrust of socialists.

Compounding the difficulties of the exile leftists were challenges from other democratic political forces. The New York League encountered a major competitor for democratic credentials in the form of the Paris-based Union of Struggle for the Freedom of Russia (*Soiuz bor'by za svobodu Rossii* or SBSR), which derived from the old Russian liberal movement.[82] The head of this organization was Sergei Pavlovich Mel'gunov, a first-wave historian widely respected in the emigration for his hostility to both communists and Nazis.[83] The SBSR was safely to the right of the New York League—an advantage Mel'gunov set out to exploit. In a 1948 document that crossed Kelley's desk, the historian claimed that both monarchism and socialism were "hopelessly compromised" in the eyes of the second-wave exiles. Along the same lines, he contrasted his party's embrace of "non-predeterminism" with the New York League's call for a future Russian republic, deriding the latter as "an effort to comply with old party slogans."[84] In this manner, Mel'gunov depicted his own movement as the true voice of democratic Russia, while presenting the League as being outside the émigré mainstream. And not, it would seem, without success: Mel'gunov's outfit would take part in the united front on equal footing with the League, despite the fact that SBSR never "counted more than a handful of members" and lacked the League's constellation of respected anti-Soviet intellectuals and commentators.[85]

The New York League tried to parry these attacks by making its own claims to national representation and by exploiting its own channels to American power. In April 1950, Nikolaevskii sent to Carmel Offie, Wisner's deputy, an outline of what he called a US "Russian action" very different to that of Pozdniakov. Nikolaevskii stressed that the Russian masses had "broad democratic sympathies," implicitly suggesting that the League's program and ideology were more in tune with Soviet public opinion than those of other émigré organizations.[86] Rafael Abramovich offered a much blunter version of the same argument in a memorandum he sent to Kelley a year later: the only plausible exile leaders were those "in whose moral

---

[82] For the background of the organization, see Aufzeichnung, Betr: Die Emigration aus der Sowjetunion und den von ihr beherrschten Gebieten, Ref. Scholl, January 19, 1956, 49–50, in Political Archive of the Foreign Ministry (Auswärtiges Amt-Politisches Archiv, hereinafter AA-PA), B 12, Akte 455.

[83] On Mel'gunov's work in Russia and in his early years of exile, see Iu. N. Emel'ianov, *S. P. Mel'gunov: v Rossii i emigratsii* (Moscow: Editorial URSS, 1998).

[84] Memorandum Submitted by the "Union of Struggle for the Freedom of Russia," S. P. Mel'gunov and A. Zagolo, October 5, 1948, 2, in Kelley Papers, box 5, fol. 6.

[85] Negotiations for an Effective Partnership: Study of the Negotiations between the American Committee for Liberation from Bolshevism and Leaders of the Emigration from the USSR to Create a Central Émigré Organization for Anti-Bolshevik Activity, 10, in HILA, Arch Puddington Collection, box 27, file 5.

[86] Russian Action and its Tasks, Nicolaevsky to C. Offie, April 10, 1950, 12, in Kelley Papers, box 5, fol. 1.

integrity and political honesty" the Soviet people had "absolute confidence" (read: the leaders of the League).[87]

The leftists' claims to national credibility had limited purchase in the context of the OPC operation. One doubts whether substantial numbers of Soviet citizens even knew the names of the Mensheviks, to say nothing about whether they approved of them. In this sense, the League members were engaged in posturing and projection, which was exactly what its members accused the NTS of doing. The League's efforts were to little effect, though, as the OPC planners were predisposed to doubt the political relevance of the old socialists. As already mentioned, OPC-CIA planners held émigrés of the second wave to be more representative of the mindset of Soviet people than those of the first, a position articulated by Lyons's characterization of the second-wavers as a virtual "'poll' of Soviet popular opinion."[88] In contrast, the old socialists and liberals seemed to be anachronisms with little connection to Russian-Soviet realities.

The disadvantage of the leftists only deepened when operational matters came into consideration. For the OPC-CIA, the national credentials of the various exile groups found clearest expression in their ability to carry out covert operations against the USSR. Here the elderly socialists and liberals were at a clear disadvantage. The League members or Mel'gunov might be distinguished voices in the émigré press, but the NTS and SBONR were the only Russian groups "active in anti-Communist work," Kelley opined, presumably in reference to the two groups' propaganda operations in East Germany.[89] In response, the first-wavers sought to deflate the Americans' views of the "revolutionary" activities of the NTS. As Nikolaevskii pointed out, communication with Soviet citizens in the USSR was unreliable at best, rendering underground work in the USSR impossible.[90] Abramovich went further, making an obvious reference to the NTS by claiming that any exiles who claimed to be able to stage a revolution in the USSR were "irresponsible fakers or, still worse, tools in the hands of the NKVD."[91]

The leftists' sober diagnosis of the limited possibilities of émigré penetration of the Soviet bloc was well warranted, as future chapters will show. However, pessimism about breaching the Iron Curtain was not what Kelley and others, bullish on the prospects of an émigré offensive, wanted to hear. Meanwhile, given their failure to establish a serious presence among second-wavers in Germany, the League leaders were open to the charge of being "generals without an army."[92] Old

---

[87] Memorandum on the formation of a Russian political center, Rafael Abramovich, n.d. (November 1951), 2, in Kelley Papers, box 5, fol. 1.

[88] Lyons, *Our Secret Allies*, 259.

[89] Recommendations on Utilization, 4.

[90] Russian Action and its Tasks, 11.

[91] Abramovich used the outdated name for Russia's security services, the People's Commissariat for Internal Affairs (*Narodnyi Komissariat Vnutrennikh Del*). Memorandum on the formation, 2.

[92] Agent Report: Dalin, David, August 3, 1950, in NARA, RG 319, Entry 134A, X8185228, box 146, David Dallin.

men whose link to the homeland belonged to a different epoch, the socialists were bound to lose the competition to represent Russia abroad.

If the leftists had little to offer on the covert operations front, they had one card left to play: their credentials as opinion-shapers in the United States. In his note to Offie, Nikolaevskii appealed to his own reputation as a foremost Soviet expert by boasting that the book he coauthored with D. Iu. Dalin on slave labor in the USSR was "the only major victory over communism on the ideological front" in recent years.[93] The League also stressed its ties to those parts of the American labor movement that were involved in fighting the Cold War with CIA help. In the same letter, Nikolaevskii proposed the creation of an Institute for the Study of Bolshevism and the USSR in the United States, stressing that Jay Lovestone, the head of the American Federation of Labor's anti-communist Free Trade Union Committee, "fully approved" the idea.[94] Unfortunately, the undeniable achievements of Nikolaevskii, Dalin, and Kerenskii in courting American public opinion proved of limited value for the OPC's Russian exile plans. As perhaps Nikolaevskii did not understand, the CIA faced legal limits on operating on US soil, making Germany—where the leftists had little influence—the key arena for émigré political warfare.

The weakness of the émigré left, then, stemmed from exile politics as much as from American distaste for Marxists. Striking was the degree to which exile groups competed in the struggle to win the OPC's favor, seeking to shape their encounter with US power—a reminder of the transnational nature of the émigré project and OPC's pro-exile agenda itself. The way the OPC project was finally launched would further demonstrate how US policies had become interwoven with émigré conflicts.

A Monarchist Plot and a Convoluted End Game

Amid jockeying among the exile organizations, the OPC's united front took shape. The different movements in the emigration had made their various cases to American policymakers, whether directly (as in the case of memoranda from Pozdniakov, Mel'gunov, Nikolaevskii, and probably others) or indirectly (the elaborate publicity stunts of the NTS). Then the unexpected happened, as it often did in the political world of the Russian diaspora.

Not content to be passed over in the exile competition for US patronage, Russian monarchists in Germany took matters into their own hands. In 1950, a series of congresses of Vlasovites took place in Munich, held in halls

---

[93] Russian Action and its Tasks, 11.

[94] Ibid., 12. It is unclear to what extent Lovestone was actually supportive of Nikolaevskii's plans. On Lovestone's role in the Cold War, see Ted Morgan, *A Covert Life: Jay Lovestone, Communist, Anticommunist, and Spymaster* (New York: Random House, 1999).

conspicuously adorned with portraits of Vlasov, White general Lavr Georgievich Kornilov, and Emperor Nicholas II.[95] Amid solemnity and martial pomp, one such meeting called for the dissolution of all existing émigré organizations, with a keynote speaker mocking their endless acronyms. The congress then proclaimed White general Anton Vasil'evich Turkul, the highest-ranking Russian military figure in exile at the time, as "heir" to Vlasov and the tradition of armed opposition to Bolshevism in its different manifestations.[96]

The new rightist unification effort represented a sharp detour in exile politics in Germany. Turkul was an unlikely figure to lead the exiles, as he was an arch-conservative who had belonged to the pro-fascist Russian National Union in the 1930s and then worked for German intelligence during the war. (Turkul was also most likely a Soviet spy, something his supporters could hardly have suspected.)[97] The majority of the Vlasovites, who had already rejected monarchism, wasted no time in denouncing the new monarchist-Vlasovite initiative in Munich for falsely re-appropriating the name of their fallen leader. Nonetheless, the new unification effort in Munich created an imposing image, in large part because it drew on the all-important lifeblood of émigré politics: foreign backing. The Munich conferences were bankrolled by US intelligence officials, most importantly Aleksei Mikhailovich Mil'rud, a second-wave exile who—remarkably enough, given his Jewish origins—had worked as a Russian-language propagandist in German-occupied Latvia during the war before becoming an employee of American military intelligence after the war.[98] Exiles on the ground had little doubt of American involvement, noting that Turkul's committee received a villa in Munich, an automobile, and "practically unlimited financial support."[99] The émigré right had not only reversed its fortunes but had won the support of the Americans, or so it seemed.

The leaders of the League in New York reacted with panic to the rightist resurgence in Germany, which threatened to marginalize the democratic forces

[95] Dvinov, *Politics of the Russian Emigration*, 229.

[96] Turkul became the highest-ranking émigré officer when P. V. Glazenap, the White leader discussed in Chapter 2, died in early 1950. Turkul was the head of a planned third division of Vlasov's Committee for Liberation of the Peoples of Russia (KONR) during the war. Memorandum on the Fake Congress of Russian Refugees in Germany, no author indicated, n.d. (1950), in Kelley Papers, box 5, fol. 1.

[97] Igor' Petrov, "Kak general Turkul byl agentom NKVD," *Live Journal*, January 26, 2013, https://labas.livejournal.com/997663.html, accessed June 30, 2018. A less reliable account of Turkul's career is Mark Aarons and John Loftus, *Ratlines: How the Vatican's Nazi Networks Betrayed Western Intelligence to the Soviets* (London: William Heinemann, 1991), 158–221.

[98] On Mil'rud's role, see Renewal of Project AEVIRGIL, no author indicated, n.d. (1962), 2–3, in NARA, RG 263, Entry ZZ-19, 239/86/25/04, box 25, AEVIRGIL, vol. 2. His biography is gleaned from Beseda A. M. Mil'ruda s prof. L. Fleishmanom, 1995, 4, 9 in HILA, Aleksei Milrud Papers, box 2. It was also likely that Gehlen-operation money was involved, for several of the participants in the initiative were members of the Baranovskii network discussed in Chapter 2, including Turkul himself, Iu. A. Pis'-mennyi-Muzychenko, and V. M. Grechko. Chief of Station, Karlsruhe to Chief, Foreign Division M.

[99] The History, Leadership and Activities of the so-called Vlassovite Association, no author indicated, December 21, 1950, 1, in Kelley Papers, box 5, fol. 1.

of the diaspora entirely. Nikolaevskii hastily developed a plan to convene a "democratic congress" of Russian exiles in Europe, hoping to finance the endeavor through his contacts in the Congress of Cultural Freedom (CCF), the CIA-funded initiative to mobilize anti-communist intellectuals in Europe.[100] Abramovich was skeptical of Nikolaevskii's plan for a counter-congress, instead offering the bold suggestion that one should "lean on" Walter Bedell Smith, recently appointed CIA director, to end "the fabrication of the 'führerdom' of Turkul." "Policy in the Russian question," he opined in a letter to a comrade, should be carried out by the State Department and the White House, not "self-proclaimed 'politicians'" from the CIA.[101] Though it was surely far-fetched, Abramovich's call to influence US policies at the highest level offered some sense of the leftists' political resourcefulness and their Washington connections.

Abramovich's hope for a change of course in Washington, in fact, soon came to pass. Mil'rud and other bankrollers of the Turkul initiative in Munich, it turned out, had not received the green light from the OPC-CIA in Washington. In fall 1950, the OPC finally launched Kelley's united-front project by sending to Germany the journalist and former Moscow correspondent Spencer Williams as Amcomlib representative. The envoy torpedoed Mil'rud's monarchist experiment, not surprisingly finding it to be "incompatible" with Amcomlib's "program."[102] The ostentatious Turkul initiative disappeared without a trace—so fast, in fact, that rumors spread in the far-right fringe of Russian Munich that Turkul and Nikolaevskii were in fact in cahoots (predictably, as representatives of a Jewish conspiracy in America).[103] Events in the emigration were indeed dramatic and even baffling. Different parts of the US intelligence system had undertaken clashing plans to unify the Russian emigration, a striking example of the bureaucratic confusion surrounding psychological-warfare projects in the early Cold War.[104]

Williams's arrival finally inserted some order into the exile scene by initiating the long-planned OPC action. But the potential weaknesses of the project were immediately evident. Following decisions made at OPC–State Department discussions months before, Williams arrived with a mandate to begin negotiations

---

[100] V. F. Butenko to R. R. Abramovich, August 20, 1950, 1, in Butenko Papers, box 1, fol. 1. Nikolaevskii had taken part in the Congress's famous 1950 rally in Berlin. Iu. G. Fel'shtinksii and G. I. Cherniavskii, *Cherez veka i strany: B. I. Nikolaevskii. Sub'da men'shevika, istorika, sovetologa, glavnogo svidetelia epokhal'nykh izmenenii v zhizni Rossii pervoi poloviny XX veka* (Moscow: Izd. Tsentr-poligraf, 2012), 389–91.

[101] R. R. Abramovich to V. F. Butenko, August 24, 1950, 1, in Butenko Papers, box 1, fol. 1.

[102] Renewal of Project AEVIRGIL, 3 and Betr: Die Amerikanische Initiative in der Ostemigration, Gerhard von Mende, Büro für Heimatsvetriebene Auslander, January 20, 1954, 3–4, in AA-PA, B 11, Akte 605.

[103] See Bachmanov to S. E. Ionin, letter intercepted by CIC, June 29, 1951, in NARA, RG 319, Entry 134B, 270/84/01/01, XE001758, box 812, Anton Turkul, vol. 1, fol. 1.

[104] On this point, see Stephen Long, "Strategic Disorder, the Office of Policy Coordination and the Inauguration of US Political Warfare against the Soviet Bloc, 1948–50," *Intelligence & National Security* 27, no. 4 (2012): 459–87.

with four parties: the NTS, SBONR, Mel'gunov's SBSR, and the New York League.[105] The arrangement pleased the NTS which, given the monarchists' exclusion, would monopolize the right wing of the united front. The Solidarists were also flattered by the OPC's determination to secure their participation in the political center; one émigré emerged from a meeting with Williams at NTS headquarters in Limburg so enthused that he proclaimed, "We have an Ameri-Solidarist!"[106] No doubt, SBONR and SBSR were content to be at the (American-built) table, as well.

The New York League, though, was far less happy with the shape of the Amcomlib project. Although no doubt relieved by the unraveling of the Turkul initiative, the League members were discouraged that the united front was to be based in Germany, where their influence was minimal, rather than in the United States. Most of all, the leftists were horrified at the prospect of working with the NTS, which they viewed as an organization of unreformed fascists seeking to erect a totalitarian regime in the homeland.[107] In fact, the inclusion of the NTS reactivated the painful debate within the émigré left over wartime collaboration (see Chapter 3), and several Mensheviks now left the League in disgust.[108] Only the unstinting Nikolaevskii kept the League together by convincing a critical mass of the socialists to go along with the Amcomlib scheme.[109] Clearly, the OPC plan rested on the flawed assumption that archenemies such as the NTS and the socialists could work together, a byproduct of Kelley's idealized perspective on the exiles.

*   *   *

During the cross-Atlantic clash over the united front in late 1950, Dalin sent a letter to SBONR leaders in Germany. He complained about US policies toward the exiles, declaring that because "the American government has not set its line," "little bureaucrats" on both sides of the Atlantic were taking it upon themselves to deal with the exiles in a "personal, casual and ignorant" manner. In Dalin's damning presentation, the Americans who were engaging the exiles were simultaneously immature, fickle, and even slightly pathetic: he claimed to know of one US official in Europe whose "policies" toward the exiles were shaped by the views of his White émigré cook.[110]

---

[105] Office of Policy Coordination History of American Committee for Liberation, memorandum for Deputy Director (Plans), Frank Wisner, August 21, 1951, 3, in Radio Free Europe and Radio Liberty.

[106] Unidentified author to G. S. Okolovich, October 22, 1950, in Archiv der Forschungsstelle Osteuropa an der Universität Bremen, fond 98, kor. 38–40.

[107] Letter from D. Iu. Dalin to SBONR leaders, September 3, 1950, 2–3, in HILA, Ryszard Wraga Papers, box 4, fol. 6.

[108] The Mensheviks B. L. Dvinov, G. Ia. Aronson, and B. M. Sapir exited, while Abramovich and Shvarts stayed in the League, vainly hoping that the State Department might realize the government's errors and intervene to banish the NTS from the unity talks. R. A. Abramovich to I. M. Lazarevich, March 21, 1951, in International Institute of Social History Archive, Amsterdam, Boris Lvovich Dvinov Papers, fol. 7.

[109] A. F. Kerenskii to M. M. Karpovich, August 23, 1951, in Karpovich Correspondence, box 2.

[110] Letter from D. Iu. Dalin to SBONR leaders, 6.

Dalin exaggerated the dysfunctional nature of American schemes vis-à-vis the exiles, which took shape with the OPC united-front project soon after he penned his letter. In a wider sense, though, Dalin's letter is instructive. The émigré felt it to be entirely within his rights to criticize his US patrons for their blunders. In other words, Dalin saw himself and the other exiles as parts of a single political space with their superpower patrons, one in which the exiles wielded some degree of agency—even if, of course, they were the far weaker party, as his own inability to prevent the Americans from working with the NTS showed.

Dalin's belief that exiles had some say in the formation of the US-exile political sphere, moreover, was basically accurate. The architects of the OPC united-front plan, and Kelley in particular, were committed to a view of exiles as harbingers of an anti-communist regeneration of the Russian nation. As a result, the views, clashes, and schemes of Russian exile organizations had a formative impact on psychological warfare and espionage operations generated in Washington. Several aspects of the united-front project were a direct product of Russian émigré politics: the central role of Vlasovism, the privileged position of the NTS, and the limited position of the émigré left. While surely imagining the freeing of Russia from Bolshevism on their own terms, the Americans involved nevertheless viewed the exiles as crucial actors in their own right.

The rooting of American ideas in émigré realities did not bode well for their realization, however. In its basic contours, the OPC united-front project rested on a series of problematic assumptions: that Russian exiles, who had lost virtually all direct contact with their homeland, nevertheless had their fingers on the pulse of public opinion in the Soviet Union; that exile organizations could effectively combat Soviet power; and, not least, that émigré rivals could bury their differences in the name of the common struggle against communism. And as the chaos and infighting that marked the onset of the united-front operation showed, the Americans had difficulty coordinating and planning their own actions vis-à-vis the exiles. Significantly, outside observers such as the British Foreign Office harbored a skeptical view of the Amcomlib's united-front approach, an indication of its origins in the distinctive intellectual framework of the American liberationists and the exiles they patronized.[111]

The problems of flawed assumptions and inconsistent strategy would plague the American effort to create an exile political center. They were especially damaging with regard to the most urgent challenge faced by the united front, one to which the American planners had given surprisingly scant thought: how groups of émigrés representing different Soviet nations in exile would collaborate in the political center.

---

[111] See V. D. Poremskii to K. V. Boldyrev, October 19, 1951, in FSO, 01–098 Tarasova, kor. 41, and CIA (OSO & OPC)/State Department Talks with SIS/Foreign Office: VI. Russian Emigre Groups, April 24, 1951, 2–3, in NARA, RG 263, Entry ZZ-19, 230/86/25/02, box 13, Aerodynamics: Operations, vol. 20.

5

Builders and Dissectors

Émigré Unification and the Russian Question

In 1951, a group of Russian exiles wrote an angry letter to *The New York Times*. A. F. Kerenskii, B. I. Nikolaevskii, Rafael Abramovich, and others—all members of the New York-based League of Struggle for the People's Freedom (LBNS)—complained of a recent speech by Secretary of State Dean Acheson that the paper had excerpted. Acheson had tied the Stalinist regime's aggression abroad to an "imperial Russian tradition" of expansion and aggression.[1] The émigrés countered that Acheson had got Russian history wrong. The Soviet regime was far more expansionist and brutal than the old empire of the tsars, making any comparisons between them inappropriate. In any case, before 1917 Russia had been moving away from the worst aspects of its imperial tradition, with "progressive and liberal elements" coming to the forefront of Russian life.[2]

The exiles' defensive, if not touchy, letter to the American daily laid bare the dilemma they faced when discussing multinational empire. It was only natural that anti-communist exiles should turn to the past to substantiate their vision of a free Russia. Yet drawing on historical Russia meant defending it from the charge of being an imperial "prison of peoples," as Lenin had famously dubbed it. All of them pre-revolutionary socialists, the authors of the letter argued that the true Russia was not the tsarist empire per se but rather a Russia of "progressive and liberal elements" that was associated with the constitutional period of 1906 to 1917—of course, the Russia which the authors had been part of prior to their exile. The liberalizing Russia the exiles embraced had existed for only a short period, though, sandwiched chronologically between centuries of unreformed autocracy and three decades of communist rule. Why was this supposed democratic and non-imperial interregnum a more genuine version of the national past than what came before or even after?

This chapter explores the national problems that plagued the project to unify Russian exiles, covertly funded by the Office of Policy Coordination (OPC) within the CIA. Émigré negotiations to forge a political center, sponsored by the

---

[1] This was the editorial board's paraphrase of recent comments made by Secretary of State Acheson in Congress.

[2] "Russia's History: Equating Kremlin Policies with National Traditions Criticized," *The New York Times*, July 8, 1951: 112.

Cold War Exiles and the CIA: Plotting to Free Russia. Benjamin Tromly, Oxford University Press (2019). © Benjamin Tromly.
DOI: 10.1093/oso/9780198840404.001.0001

American Committee for Freedom for the Peoples of Russia, Inc. (Amcomlib), stumbled on the national question, with ethnic Russians and exiles from the national minorities of the USSR proving unable to work together. No doubt because of its ultimate failure, the OPC-CIA's effort to unify Russian and non-Russian Soviet exiles has received little attention from scholars. Several studies of Radio Liberty mention the émigré origins of the radio while providing only perfunctory analysis of the exiles' political disputes.[3] A recent article by Simo Mikkonen provides a much fuller account of US policy toward the Soviet exiles. Yet Mikkonen's piece offers an incomplete account of the crucial issue of competing nationalisms in the undertaking.[4]

Russian national identity provides an illuminating framework with which to reappraise the united-front project. The CIA-sponsored negotiations to form an exile united front gave rise to a far-reaching debate about Russian nationhood and statehood, as the immediate struggle against the Soviet state became overshadowed by arguments about what kind of structure would replace it after communist rule had been toppled. Starkly different national claims found expression. Most non-Russian exiles demanded the immediate recognition of their nations' independence from Russia. In contrast, the Russians sought to create a multinational state similar in size to that of the USSR or the Romanov Empire, even though they were willing to endorse a future Russia as a looser federation rather than a centralized state. In this manner, the CIA plan to create a voice of the Russian and Soviet peoples abroad had the unexpected consequence of animating and rehearsing core dilemmas about the meaning of national identity in modern Russia.

Russia of Yesteryear

The starting point for exile discussions of Russian identity is what one might call the "empire complex" that has complicated Russians' sense of their collective identity in the modern age of nationalism and nation-states. As Geoffrey Hosking has argued, the predominance of imperial statehood throughout modern Russian history hindered the creation of a cohesive Russian *nation*. Tsarist rule limited the emergence of an ethnic national identity in Russia by promoting an essentially non-national form of state legitimacy, while also preventing the emergence of the kind of middle-class civil society that was the typical champion of modern

---

[3] Sig Mickelson, *America's Other Voice: The Story of Radio Free Europe and Radio Liberty* (New York, NY: Praeger, 1983), 63–70; Arch Puddington, *Broadcasting Freedom: the Cold War Triumph of Radio Free Europe and Radio Liberty* (Lexington: University Press of Kentucky, 2000), 158–62, and A. Ross Johnson, *Radio Free Europe and Radio Liberty: The CIA Years and Beyond* (Washington, DC: Woodrow Wilson Center Press, 2010), 30–3.

[4] Simo Mikkonen, "Exploiting the Exiles: Soviet Émigrés in U.S. Cold War Strategy," *Journal of Cold War Studies* 14, no. 2 (2012): 98–127.

nationalism in other European contexts. As a result, Russianness remained a fragmented notion, caught between civic and ethnic polarities conveyed tidily in the Russian language by the distinct adjectives *rossiiskii* ("statist Russian" or "civic Russian") and *russkii* ("ethnic Russian").[5]

That Russian identity has carried different civic and ethnic idioms is a crucial insight. It goes far toward explaining the position on the national question of liberals in the late empire, who were confident that the advent of democratic rule would solve the empire's interlocking national problems by uniting its peoples in a *rossiiskii* identification.[6] To be sure, Soviet rule reframed the Russian problem. Already rejected by many national minorities before 1917, the democratic, pan-Russian model was dashed during the Russian Revolution and Civil War, when the empire shattered into nationally defined fragments. The communist dictatorship regathered the empire, but did so in a way that institutionalized multi-ethnicity in the guise of an ostensibly federative Soviet state.[7] Yet Russian "imperial consciousness" in its tsarist form lived on in Russia abroad, and was perhaps even strengthened as ethnic Russians interacted with other ethnic groups which had left the empire either before or after 1917.[8]

Imperial and revolutionary-era history and identities would occupy the exile united-front project for a simple reason: many of the exiles active in the Cold War episode had been political actors during the late imperial period and maintained a strong identification with the civic and multiethnic notion of Russia that had been commonplace at that time. In fact, all the Russian exiles involved in the united front believed that Russia's proper borders extended far beyond areas of predominantly ethnic Russian settlement, while steadfastly denying that such a future state would represent an empire. Instead, they held, Russia was a coherent multiethnic nation, a "family of peoples" bound together by a shared past and future. The non-Russian peoples currently inside Russia—with the exception of the Baltic peoples, whom the Russians admitted were victims of Soviet aggression and therefore could leave—would remain there after the Soviet Union fell.[9] S. P. Mel'gunov, the émigré historian who was one of the exiles' main leaders,

---

[5] Geoffrey A. Hosking, *Russia: People and Empire, 1552–1917* (Cambridge, MA: Harvard University Press, 1997), and *Rulers and Victims: the Russians in the Soviet Union* (Cambridge, MA: Harvard University Press, 2006).

[6] Theodore R. Weeks, *Nation and State in Late Imperial Russia: Nationalism and Russification on the Western Frontier, 1863–1914* (DeKalb, IL: Northern Illinois University Press, 1996), ch. 1.

[7] On the Bolsheviks' response to rising nationalisms, see Terry Martin, *The Affirmative Action Empire: Nations and Nationalism in the Soviet Union, 1923–1939* (Ithaca and London: Cornell University Press, 2001). On multiethnicity as a defining trait of mature Soviet rule, see Rogers Brubaker, "Nationhood and the National Question in the Soviet Union and Post-Soviet Eurasia: An Institutional Account," *Theory and Society* 23, no. 1 (1994): 47–78.

[8] Laurie Manchester, "How Statelessness Can Force Refugees to Redefine Their Ethnicity: What can be Learned from Russian Émigrés Dispersed to Six Continents in the Inter-war Period?" *Immigrants & Minorities* 34, no. 1 (2016): 75–7.

[9] The exiles' willingness to let go of the Baltic states paid fealty to the US policy of non-recognition of their annexation.

called it "a historical absurdity" that non-Russian peoples of the Soviet Union would want to separate from the Russian core.[10]

If all the exiles shared the *rossiiskii* position, they nevertheless articulated variations on it. On the right of the exile political spectrum was the National Labor Alliance (NTS), which was in the process of casting off its interwar semi-fascist complexion. The Alliance leaders tended to view Russia as an imperial nation in the most direct sense, one that would naturally fuse together the different "peoples of Russia"—as they envisioned Soviet non-Russians—through its more advanced culture.[11] This position harkened back to the conservative nationalism of the tsarist period that is commonly associated with the term "Russification," understood as the imposition of the Russian language and culture on other peoples of the empire.

The other organizations taking part in the united-front negotiations espoused Russian unity but did so in ways that stressed civic values rather than the NTS's ethnic Russian cultural domination. Closest to the Solidarists was Mel'gunov's Union of Struggle for the Freedom of Russia (SBSR), which stressed that democracy would bring about the fusing of the peoples of Russia.[12] The strongest alternative to the NTS came from the émigré left organized in the New York League, which espoused a more federative vision of Russia. The prominent Menshevik Rafael Abramovich defended the unity of Russia, but did so on the grounds that the separation of non-Russian peoples would bring about "an endless chain of inter-national and inter-tribal wars and the 'Balkanization' of the whole Eurasian sub-continent."[13] If, on the contrary, the liberated peoples of the USSR could hold free plebiscites to decide their fate, Abramovich and other leftists assumed, they would surely stay with Russia, forging a progressive form of multiethnic statehood shorn of its imperial associations. The remaining Russian group in the united front, the Vlasovite Union of Struggle for the Liberation of the Peoples of Russia (SBONR), stood close to the League on the national question, though some members embraced the more rigid NTS or Mel'gunov positions.[14] However important these political differences were, all the ethnic Russians participating in the deliberations to create an American-funded united-front organization sought to remake Russia as a multiethnic, *rossiiskii* state.

---

[10] Excerpts from a speech of S. P. Mel'gunov made at the Starnberg Conference, June 19, 1952, 2, in Georgetown University Archives and Special Collections, Robert F. Kelley Papers (hereinafter Kelley Papers), box 5, fol. 1.

[11] Protokoly s'ezda Soveta NTS v dekabre 1950 goda, 26, in Georgetown University Archives and Special Collections, Victor M. Baydalakoff Collection (hereinafter Baydalakoff Collection), box 1, fol. 1.

[12] Excerpts from a speech of S. P. Mel'gunov.

[13] Memorandum on the nationality problem in the USSR, Rafael Abramovich, n.d. (1950), in Kelley Papers, box 6, fol. 1.

[14] SBONR's divisions on the national question were anticipated by the wartime Vlasov movement, which struggled to gain influence among non-Russian collaborators. A Brief History of the Vlasov Army, Office of the Assistant Chief of Staff, G-2, Military Intelligence Section, US Army, February 9, 1946, 2, in NARA, RG 319, Entry 134A, 22348387, 270/84/20/02, box 68, Vlassow Group, fol. 1.

When they began their deliberations, the exiles had reason to feel that Amcomlib's position on the national question was similar to their own. The OPC's initial framework for the united front seemed to harken back to the unitary and pan-Russian ideas predominant in the tsarist empire. Indicative was Amcomlib's name change from the American Committee for Liberation of the Peoples of the USSR to *the Peoples of Russia* in a clear concession to the Russian émigré groups [italics added].[15] On an organizational level, the OPC decided to begin negotiations to create a united front with meetings of exclusively Russian groups, with the intention of bringing in non-Russian organizations at a later date. Original plans stated merely that it was "of the greatest importance that the Political Center should include representatives of ethnic groups other than the Great Russians," a formulation that suggested that the participation of non-Russian groups would be limited and selective.[16] In this sense, the united-front operation carried a pro-Russian complexion which reflected the conservative and Russophilic proclivities of its architects, George Kennan and Robert F. Kelley. Indeed, in his memoirs written years later Kennan would recall his exasperation at non-Russian exile groups, which seemed to want to wage war "not against the Soviet Union, as such, but against the Russian people."[17]

Amcomlib's position was ambiguous and poorly thought out, however. To be sure, the OPC's plan to organize the Russian organizations first made some sense, as it would have been hard to develop a "spirit of mutual confidence" and habits of "joint work" if Russians and non-Russian exiles were lumped together from the outset.[18] However, early plans penned by Kelley provided surprisingly little consideration of non-Russian exile organizations, suggesting that the OPC planners did not understand how difficult it would be to persuade their exile clients to work across national lines.[19] Insofar as Amcomlib had a coherent approach to the national question, it was encapsulated by the concept of "non-predeterminism," according to which future political systems and borders would be determined democratically only after the end of Soviet rule.[20] Some Russians hoped that non-predeterminism would dissuade non-Russian exiles from agitating for immediate

[15] Johnson, *Radio Free Europe and Radio Liberty*, 28. Notably, in 1953 the committee would change its name yet again to the American Committee for Liberation from Bolshevism, Inc., a sign of its difficulty in approaching the émigré national problem.

[16] American Friends of the Freedom of the Russian Peoples, n.d. (1950), 1–3, in Kelley Papers, box 5, fol. 3.

[17] George F. Kennan, *Memoirs, 1950–1963* (Boston: Little, Brown, 1972), 98.

[18] Handwritten notes on Political Center, Robert F. Kelley, n.d. (1950 or 1951), in Kelley Papers, box 5, fol. 3.

[19] In his 1950 memorandum, Kelley mentions merely that it would be "extremely desirable" to have "representatives" from non-Russian nationalities join at a later date. Recommendations on Utilization of the Russian Emigration, April 26, 1950, 3, in History and Public Policy Program Digital Archive at the Woodrow Wilson Center, Radio Free Europe and Radio Liberty: Cold War International History Project e-Dossier no. 32 (hereinafter Radio Free Europe and Radio Liberty).

[20] Negotiations for an Effective Partnership: Study of the Negotiations between the American Committee for Liberation from Bolshevism and Leaders of the Emigration from the USSR to Create

recognition of independent statehood for their peoples. But such a reading of the tea leaves was misplaced: above all, the Americans embraced non-predeterminism in the hopes that it would allow them to skirt entirely the issue of competing nationalisms in the united front. In sum, Amcomlib hinted at support for Russian ideas of a future *rossiiskii* state without explicitly endorsing them, a position that invited false hopes and eventual discord.

Even a cursory view of non-Russian exiles in Germany should have disabused Kelley of his ambiguous position on national questions in the emigration. The major émigré organizations representing the non-Russian peoples, and particularly the Ukrainian DP population in Germany—which, one should note, was several times larger than the ethnic Russian one—saw Soviet rule as tantamount to Russian imperialism and demanded immediate recognition of their independence from it.[21] Such a national liberationist agenda was particularly common among organizations led by old émigrés who claimed to represent governments that had gained and then lost independence during the Russian Civil War.[22] Granted, the second-wave non-Russian exiles were sometimes less committed to pursuit of the independence of their people at all costs. Nevertheless, the wartime cohorts also included fiercely nationalistic West Ukrainians and West Belarusians who had fought against Soviet power in guerilla movements during and after the war, before fleeing west.[23] Not surprisingly, when word leaked out about meetings of Russian organizations in remote locations in Germany that were sponsored by a mysterious American organization, the non-Russian exile press wasted no time in lashing out at what they saw as a capitulation of Americans to the Russian imperialists.

The Veil Drops: Amcomlib and the Exiles

The nationalist strivings of the non-Russians formed the context in which Amcomlib and the Russian exiles fell out over the national question. The first meeting of Russian groups in January 1951 in the small Bavarian town of Füssen ended in acrimony. In virtual unison, the Russian organizations demanded that

a Central Émigré Organization for Anti-Bolshevik Activity, 9 in Hoover Institution Archives and Library (HILA), Arch Puddington Collection, box 27, fol. 5.

---

[21] On the Ukrainian DPs and their politics, see Volodymyr Kulyk, "Ukrainian displaced persons in Germany and Austria after the Second World War," in Karen Schönwälder et al. (eds.), *European Encounters: Migrants, Migration, and European Societies since 1945* (Burlington, VT: Ashgate, 2003): 214–37.

[22] Negotiations for an Effective Partnership, 191.

[23] Works on these wars include Alexander Statiev, *The Soviet Counterinsurgency in the Western Borderlands* (Cambridge and New York: Cambridge University Press, 2010), and Jeffrey Burds, *The Early Cold War in Soviet West Ukraine, 1944–1948* (Pittsburgh, PA: Russian and East European Studies Program, University of Pittsburgh, 2001).

the united front should pursue "the preservation of the unity of the family of free peoples of Russia"; they also pushed for organizational measures that would give the Russian groups control within the united front they were in the process of creating, including in the matter of recruiting non-Russian organizations.[24] Belatedly realizing that such moves would make non-Russian participation in the united front virtually impossible, Amcomlib rejected both demands. Perhaps unexpectedly to the émigrés, the American Committee had shown that it would not allow the Russians to dominate the US project and impose on it their great-Russian agenda. Feeling that they had been tricked, the Russians responded to Amcomlib's ultimatum at Füssen by breaking off the talks.

As it turned out, the unsuccessful outcome of Füssen was just the beginning of Amcomlib's troubles. Intervening in the exile affair was another problem: public opinion in *Russian* émigré communities in the West. In particular, a scandal surrounding D. Iu. Dalin, the longstanding Menshevik and member of the New York League, politicized the united front within the Russian diaspora. The brouhaha began with misunderstandings and inflated egos, as was often the case for exile conflicts. Dalin's reputation as commentator on Soviet affairs in Cold War America seemed to make him well suited for a role in the united front. In fact, Dalin was *too* American in a literal sense. In its attempt to ensure the united front's Russian national credentials, Amcomlib had barred US citizens from taking part in the Füssen meeting. Dalin, a naturalized American citizen, ignored this stipulation and traveled to Füssen, only to be turned away at the door by Amcomlib representative Spencer Williams.[25]

The cost of this rebuff was not long in coming. A month after Füssen, Dalin launched a frontal attack on Amcomlib in an article in the influential American left-of-center magazine *The New Leader*. Pulling no punches, Dalin blasted "U.S. 'intelligence' officers" for embracing tsarists, reactionaries, and fascists such as the NTS—whom he collectively dubbed "the wrong Russians"—at the expense of "the large masses of pro-democratic Russians."[26] Dalin also detailed the failure of the Füssen meeting, which he blamed on the meddling Americans who gave "orders by cable" from Washington. In Dalin's devastating verdict, Amcomlib was conniving, naïve, and incompetent at the same time.

Dalin's article was an open challenge to Amcomlib. It broke the gentleman's agreement the exiles made with Amcomlib to keep the united front talks secret until progress was made.[27] Even more taboo, Dalin exposed Amcomlib's connection to intelligence agencies, which was an open secret among many exiles but would have come as a shock to the American public. The Dalin scandal also

---

[24] The clearest overall picture of the twists and turns in the negotiations comes from a later study produced by Amcomlib. Negotiations for an Effective Partnership, 29.

[25] Report by Dr Leo Dudin, Secretary of the Füssen meeting, 3, in Kelley Papers, box 5, fol. 1.

[26] David Dallin, "The Wrong Russians again," *The New Leader*, vol. 34 (February 12, 1951): 11–12.

[27] Negotiations for an Effective Partnership, 30–1.

suggested that divisions existed among American anti-communists, as the émigré had managed to publish his rebuke in *The New Leader*, whose former editor was none other than Amcomlib head Eugene Lyons. Perhaps worst of all, news of the scandals and clashes in Germany created the impression in Washington that the operation had veered out of control. In September 1951, officials at the State Department expressed skepticism as to "whether it was reasonable to expect the groups forming the Political Center to continue to work together with any cohesion."[28] The concern was a valid one, even though Amcomlib had brought some of the trouble upon itself with its clumsy handling of Dalin.

If the turmoil surrounding Dalin and Füssen created doubts in Washington, its effects on the Russian emigration were even more drastic. It was perhaps inevitable that some parts of the diaspora would react with scorn to news of the mysterious events in Bavaria. Dalin's article now gave émigrés grounds to dismiss the unity effort as a foreign enterprise—what's more, a back-room intelligence operation—rather than the genuine undertaking of exiles that Amcomlib presented it as being. Russian monarchists, who had been bypassed by the American project, wasted no time in attacking the exiles gathered at Füssen as "impostors claiming to speak from the whole Russian (*rossiiskaia*) emigration illegally."[29] From the perspective of some monarchists, the émigré action was trebly treacherous, for it represented an illegitimate power grab in the emigration, a subordination of Russian national interests to a foreign power and, at least potentially, an enterprise that might lead to the territorial dissection of Russia in the future.[30]

For different reasons, Dalin's revelations also damaged the reputation of the project among democratic and leftist Russian exiles, who were mostly located in the United States. For them, Dalin's allegations drove home the message that the exiles involved in the Amcomlib project were making unpalatable alliances with the much-hated NTS. Dalin also confirmed émigré suspicions that the unity effort was a nefarious enterprise directed behind the scenes by the US government. After his article, criticism of the united front emerged in *Novoe russkoe slovo* ("New Russian Word"), the longstanding New York publication which catered to democratic political circles. Why, one exile asked, had supposedly "democratic representatives" employed "Politburo methods" of secrecy and conspiracy at Füssen?[31] Going further, the first-wave socialist Ekaterina Dmitrievna Kuskova opined that the negotiations were an endeavor with "no foundation" in Russia abroad other

---

[28] CIA-State Department Reservations about Broadcasting to the Soviet Union, September 6, 1951, in Radio Free Europe and Radio Liberty.

[29] This is a paraphrase from S. M. Mel'gunov, "Razbitye illiuzii (fakty i dokumenty)," *Rossiiskii democrat*, vol. 21, no. 2 (1951): 2.

[30] In a sign that such accusations rankled, Mel'gunov claimed that the front had originally been the initiative of the émigré groups—a falsehood that émigré readers probably discounted given Dalin's portrayal of the meeting's American controllers. Ibid.

[31] "Tainy Madridskogo dvora," *Novoe russkoe slovo*, January 11, 1952.

than a search for financial sinecures.[32] In this manner, the émigrés taking part in the united front emerged with compromised reputations in virtually all parts of the diaspora—of course, the exact opposite of what Amcomlib hoped to achieve.

If blowback in the Russian press were not enough, the scandal surrounding Dalin created fissures within the united-front project. Not surprisingly, Amcomlib members were furious at Dalin. As discussed in Chapter 4, the revolutionary background of many of the New York League's members was a political liability from the outset. Dalin's broadside against the united front soured the Americans on the League even further. Sensing blood in the water, the League's rivals in the united front, and most of all the NTS, launched an effort to undermine the League by demanding that it formally renounce their companion Dalin. The NTS seized on a murky episode in which League leaders, with Dalin in the lead, had sought to organize a "Democratic Conference" in Germany a few months after Füssen, seeking thereby to take the united front into their own hands.[33] These accusations were perhaps overblown: the League members, for their part, accused their enemies of cynically creating the specter of a "Menshevik Plot" against the American unification effort.[34] Wherever the truth lay, the Dalin scandal inflicted lasting damage on the émigré left—particularly when Kerenskii, who had always felt marginalized in the League, left the organization to head a small party called the Russian National Movement (*Russkoe narodnoe dvizhenie* or RND), to which Amcomlib offered a seat at the table for the next round of talks.[35] Clearly, the conflict had taken on a destructive dynamic common to many Russian exile conflicts, as ideological disputes and personal rifts intertwined and spiraled out of control.

Kelley's plan to create a political center that would bring together anti-communist exile communities had done the opposite. Dalin's public airing of debates over ideology, wartime collaboration, and US leadership heightened the ongoing clashes among émigré groups within the American-sponsored front and caused some émigrés to entertain doubts about the wisdom of working with the American Committee. Bickering among themselves and isolated from the wider

[32] E. Kuskova, "Bez fundamenta," *Novoe russkoe slovo*, January 27, 1952.
[33] Negotiations for an Effective Partnership, 35.
[34] The clashing left and right interpretations of the Democratic Conference are conveyed in V. F. Butenko to I. I. Alcheev, December 22, 1951, 1, in Columbia University Rare Book and Manuscript Library, Bakhmeteff Archive of Russian and East European History and Culture, Vasilii Fedoseevich Butenko Papers, box 1, fol. 1, and Protokoly s'ezda Soveta NTS v ianvare 1952 g., 4, in Baydalakoff Collection, box 1, fol. 1. Notably, the League's partners in SBONR participated in the Democratic Conference reluctantly, fearing the loss of Amcomlib's favor. Peripheral: Meeting of Russian "Democratic" Émigré Groups in Munich, n.d., in Stuart A. Rose Manuscript, Archives, and Rare Book Library, Emory University, Isaac Don Levine Papers (hereinafter Levine Papers), box 6.
[35] Negotiations for an Effective Partnership, 34.

diaspora, the Russians in the united front looked nothing like the "center of national hope" Kennan had hoped it would become.[36]

Dissecting Russia: the Wiesbaden Conference

The uproar created by the Dalin scandal did not obscure a basic fact: the United States was the main and even irreplaceable source of funding for émigré anti-communist projects of all kinds. No doubt in recognition of this reality, the exile organizations that had cast their lot with Amcomlib proved willing to come back to the table. Most importantly, the NTS, which had adopted divisive tactics at Füssen and even stormed out of the proceedings before they had finished, now made concessions in their position on the national question in order to restart the negotiations.[37]

The Solidarists' conciliatory stance had much to do with the appearance of a new Amcomlib representative in Europe: Isaac Don Levine. Levine seemed to be a uniquely qualified figure for the task of managing the doctrinaire and proud exiles. After growing up in Ukraine in the family of a Zionist, Levine had returned to his land of birth as the first "bourgeois" US correspondent in revolutionary Russia, and told stories of his ride in L. D. Trotskii's famous armored train during the Civil War.[38] After a brief period as a communist fellow traveler, Levine found his calling as a staunch anti-communist writer for Hearst papers. He was at the center of several US anti-communist causes célèbres, ghostwriting the memoirs of Soviet defectors Walter Krivitskii and Victor Kravchenko (before and after the war, respectively) and supporting Whittaker Chambers's accusations of espionage against State Department official Alger Hiss.[39] Levine was a publicist, not a politician—a fact that would soon make itself felt. But his anti-communist passions matched those of the émigrés, and the NTS leader V. M. Baidalakov embraced Levine as a friend of the organization who "cannot stand socialists and Marxists."[40]

A desire for compromise was on display when the Russian exiles met again under Amcomlib auspices in August 1951, now in Stuttgart. The exile organizations finally managed to reach a collective position on the issue of Russia's future statehood that met with American approval, albeit only after painfully slow

[36] George F. Kennan on Organizing Political Warfare, April 30, 1948, in Radio Free Europe and Radio Liberty.

[37] In particular, the NTS adopted the principle that non-Russian peoples could separate from Russia after the overthrow of Bolshevism by holding national plebiscites. Negotiations for an Effective Partnership, 34.

[38] Isaac Don Levine, *Eyewitness to History: Memoirs and Reflections of a Foreign Correspondent for Half a Century* (New York: Hawthorn Books, 1973), 35–50.

[39] See his obituary: "Isaac Don Levine, 89, Foe of Soviet," *The New York Times*, February 17, 1981, D15.

[40] V. M. Baidalakov to K. V. Boldyrev and N. I. Bevad, May 16, 1951, in FSO, 01–098 Tarasova, kor. 41.

horse-trading over the wording of specific documents. The meeting called into creation a body called the Council for the Liberation of the Peoples of Russia (*Sovet osvobozhdeniia narodov Rossii* or SONR). The new organization's program included language on the national question that was liberal by any definition: all "peoples of Russia" had "the right to determine freely, on the basis of a national vote, their own destiny."[41] At the same time, the exiles adopted a separate, non-binding resolution on the national question that called for the "preservation of the unity of the family of the free peoples of Russia" on the basis of "federation and cultural-national unity."[42] A compromise seemed to have emerged that maintained Amcomlib's free hand on national problems while still allowing the Russians to advocate for a quasi-imperial, *rossiiskii* future.

The weeks after Stuttgart, however, exposed the deep gulf that still existed between Russians and their American patrons on the national question. Decisions reached at Stuttgart mandated that the five Russian organizations making up SONR would initiate negotiations with non-Russian organizations in order to include the latter in the united front. Not unsurprisingly, the Russians delegated to draw non-Russians to the negotiating table had little success. Sent to Paris as SONR envoy, Kerenskii acted in an "extremely imperious" manner, presenting "the invitation extended to the nationalities as a privilege which the latter must earn by being properly respectful of the Russians," a later Amcomlib report alleged.[43] At least one of the Russian participants in SONR agreed that the Russians' attitude toward the non-Russians was flawed. SBONR leader B. A. Troitskii-Iakovlev complained that the Russians acted as if they were the "older brothers" of the non-Russians, a patronizing attitude that infuriated the latter and embarrassed their American patrons.[44]

Eventually, an exasperated Levine took matters into his own hands, luring several non-Russian organizations to engage in the negotiations with the Russians, in part by promising to pay regular subsidies to every organization taking part. (Even then, all the Ukrainian organizations refused to participate.) Meanwhile, Levine's active involvement in recruiting non-Russian organizations sparked "resentment" among the Russians, who felt that by carrying out separate negotiations with the separatist groups he was "exceeding his authority" as Amcomlib representative.[45] The Russians had a point. Amcomlib stressed that the united front was to be "a genuine creation of the Soviet emigration," and that American-exile relationships should befit those "between allies, between partners, who

---

[41] Decree on the Formation of the Council for the Liberation of the Peoples of Russia, August 1951, 2, in Kelley Papers, box 5, fol. 1.

[42] Negotiations for an Effective Partnership, 45–6.

[43] Ibid., 53.

[44] Stenograficheskii protokol piati russkikh politicheskikh organizatsii s predstaviteliami natsional'nostei, Visbaden, smena 125, 1, in Levine Papers, box 6.

[45] Peripheral: Present Status of Efforts to Unite Russian Emigration, November 28, 1951, 1, in Kelley Papers, box 5, fol. 1.

are associated in a common enterprise."[46] Such rhetoric would prove to be a serious design flaw of the project, for it allowed the exiles to claim that Amcomlib interventions—such as the hapless Levine's deliberations with the non-Russians— were violations of the entire project's national legitimacy.

Such were the inauspicious origins of the Wiesbaden conference that convened in November 1951, at which non-Russians first entered the CIA-funded united-front project. The fragile compromise reached at Stuttgart between Amcomlib and its Russian exile clients became irrelevant as the Russian exiles entered into conflict with the Georgians, Belarusians, Azerbaijanis, Armenians, North Caucasians, and Central Asians who gathered in the Hessian town.[47] Although Russian was the lingua franca at the meeting, the Russians and non-Russians found that they were speaking different languages. According to the delegate for the North Caucasian Peoples Alliance, Abdurakhman Genazovich Avtorkhanov-Kunta, Kerenskii showed a "tragic misunderstanding of the mentality of the 'nationals.'" While profusely defending the honor of Russia, Avtorkhanov complained, Kerenskii expressed mere "puzzlement" when the non-Russians complained of their peoples' dependence on Moscow.[48]

The Wiesbaden Conference deteriorated into a cold war between the self-styled representatives of Soviet nations, with Russians facing off against a bloc of the minority peoples. In tense and fitful talks, disagreements emerged over every conceivable topic: whether the current conference constituted a "sovereign" meet-ing that superseded the Russians' agreements at Stuttgart (the non-Russian perspective) or was a continuation of them (the Russian view); whether the platform of the united front should automatically restore independence to "free peoples who lost their independence as a result of occupation by Soviet power" (as the Georgian delegation insisted) or rather should maintain a strict "non-predeterminism" toward matters of future sovereignty (the Russian position); and whether the organization to be created should grant parity to the Russians and non-Russians (the non-Russian demand) or should follow a tripartite struc-ture involving separate baskets of Russians, non-Russians, and "public figures" (as the Russians called for).[49]

Emblematic of the impasse at Wiesbaden was the failure to name the organ-ization the assembled exiles were attempting to create. Non-Russians refused to belong to an organization with "Russia" in the title, while the Russians were equally unwilling to part with that descriptor.[50] In the painfully negotiated joint

[46] Radio Liberty Broadcasting Policy, March 28, 1952, 2, in Radio Free Europe and Radio Liberty.

[47] The six nationality organizations were the Georgian National Council, the Azerbaijani Committee of National Unity, the North Caucasian Peoples Alliance, the Armenian Fighters for Freedom, the Turkeli Organization, and the Belorusian National Rada. Negotiations for an Effective Partnership, 48–64.

[48] Abdurakhman Avtorkhanov, O sebe i vremeni: memuary (Moscow: Dika-M, 2003), 668.

[49] Negotiations for an Effective Partnership, 56–60.

[50] Boris L. Dvinov, Politics of the Russian Emigration (Santa Monica, CA: Rand Corp., 1955), 312–26.

statement produced at the end of the conference, the name of the organization was left blank. This seemingly petty detail represented a matter of principle: the non-Russians refused to accept their designation as "peoples of Russia" in the first place. In this manner, the non-Russians had rejected Russian primacy in the united front as well as the multiethnic definition of Russia that justified it.

During the tension-filled talks, the Russians gave ground to a surprising degree. Faced with Levine's refusal to back their demands—and amid much handwringing and lamentation—the Russians eventually made crucial concessions to the non-Russians. Ultimately, the Russian exiles agreed to the principle of numerical parity in the united-front organization between Russian organizations, on the one hand, and non-Russians, on the other—a move that buried hopes that the Russians could exert control over the project.[51] In a symbolic sense, then, the Russians had sacrificed their special role as leaders of a multiethnic Russian nation, receiving in return only the formal representation that came with being the most numerous ethnic group in the USSR. In fact, the Russians seemed to acknowledge that they represented a merely ethnic nation, as when Kerenskii called the Russian five-organization Bureau a "Russian (*russkaia*) group," not a *rossiiskaia* one.[52] Without a doubt, the situation that resulted must have been frustrating and even baffling to the Russian delegates. As the SBSR delegate V. P. Nikitin lamented during the Wiesbaden proceedings, "We must reexamine fundamental matters and admit that all that we wanted to do, everything we thought was somehow unshakable has fallen apart."[53]

During their slow capitulation to non-Russian and Amcomlib demands, the Russian leaders struggled to find convincing arguments to make in favor of multiethnic Russia. One common position was to appeal to public opinion in the USSR, claiming that the separatist nationalism of the exile groups jarred with the more harmonious state of national coexistence in the homeland.[54] Most likely, the Russians' argument had some merit: the national liberation rhetoric of the non-Russian exile groups was probably not widely shared by the masses of minority peoples in the USSR in the early postwar period.[55] However, these arguments fell flat, and not only because it was awkward for anti-communists to praise current developments in the Soviet Union. The Iron Curtain

---

[51] Also, the Russians abandoned their plan for a tripartite structure for SONR after their opponents denounced it as a backdoor mechanism to ensure Russian dominance. Negotiations for an Effective Partnership, 99, and Stenograficheskii protokol piati russkikh politicheskikh organizatsii, smena 113, str. 2.

[52] Ibid., 1.

[53] Ibid., 2.

[54] The émigré V. P. Nikitin referred to unspecified recent defectors as evidence of his view. Stenograficheskii protokol piati russkikh politicheskikh organizatsii, smena 113, str. 3.

[55] Scholars view non-Russian nationalism in the USSR as being connected to gradual processes of modernization and administrative decentralization. See Ronald Grigor Suny, *The Revenge of the Past: Nationalism, Revolution, and the Collapse of the Soviet Union* (Stanford, CA: Stanford University Press, 1993).

meant that Russians could not marshal evidence for their claims about Soviet popular opinion. In the circumscribed world of the American-sponsored conferences, the national sentiments of the Soviet peoples were gauged by the voices of their exiled representatives, and these added up to a loud chorus of national grievances.

As the Soviet present was problematic territory, the Russian exiles turned to history to substantiate their belief in a multinational, *rossiiskii* future. At Füssen, Mel'gunov had proclaimed that the peoples of Russia were united by the country's "historic past, its tragic fate under Bolshevism, and its future."[56] The historian's ringing proclamation found little traction in the united-front initiative. Even if one leaves aside the hostile audience on the other side of the negotiating table, Mel'gunov had difficulty articulating an edifying history of multiethnic Russia. Rather than solidifying a single nationhood, the "tragic fate" of communism might well have divided the exiled representatives of Soviet peoples into their own national memories of victimization.[57] No clearer was Mel'gunov's appeal to the "historical past" of the pre-Soviet period as a basis for multiethnic nationhood. As described at the beginning of the chapter, the imperialism of the tsars was discredited, while the democratic revolution of 1917 had failed to create a viable democratic, multiethnic state. Thus it proved difficult to draw on the historical record to give shape to the exiles' vision of a future multiethnic Russia, let alone make arguments about it that might convince the non-Russians and Amcomlib.

The Russians thought that the situation they found themselves in at Wiesbaden was deeply unfair. The terms in which they articulated their grievances spoke to the issue of the Russian imperial complex. For instance, the Russians complained that full parity between Russians and non-Russians in SONR was unjust. While the Russian groups included numerous Russified Ukrainians, Georgians, and so on, there were no ethnic Russians in the non-Russian groups, a circumstance that seemed to give the minority peoples an overall numerical advantage in the united front.[58] If such a complaint reflected hard-nosed negotiating tactics, it cannot be dismissed as mere casuistry. As one might expect, some assimilated, Russian-speaking Ukrainians or others did join the Russian groups, in part because they rejected the rhetoric of national liberation that predominated in the organizations of their own peoples.[59] In a real sense, the Russian émigré organizations were *rossiiskii*, not *russkii*, in terms of their ethnic makeup, and this fact seemed to disadvantage ethnic Russians in the united front's politics of national representation.

---

[56] Negotiations for an Effective Partnership, 30.

[57] On the distorting effect of victim narratives among Ukrainians abroad, see John-Paul Himka, "War Criminality: A Blank Spot in the Collective Memory of the Ukrainian Diaspora," *Spaces of Identity* 5, no. 1 (2005): 9–24.

[58] Stenograficheskii protokol piati russkikh politicheskikh organizatsii, smena 110, 2.

[59] Negotiations for an Effective Partnership, 191.

The Russian organizations were *rossiiskii* in rhetoric and ideology, as well. Albeit to varying degrees, all the non-Russian organizations railed against Soviet-Russian domination and demanded an unconditional right to independence.[60] In contrast, the Russian organizations were organized around political ideologies, and, as the Dalin episode highlighted, they were prone to debilitating internal debates. In this sense, too, the Russian organizations were *rossiiskii*, as their agendas could not be reduced to ethnic nationalism. As Nikolaevskii pointed out at Wiesbaden, the Russian organizations were "psychologically" unable to forge a cohesive Russian front in the way their non-Russian counterparts had— ironically enough, given the incredible ethnic diversity the minorities represented.[61] In a sense, the *rossiiskii* nature of the exile organizations came at the expense of their ability to articulate ethnic national demands, an echo of the process discussed by Hosking by which imperial statehood stunted Russian ethnic nationality throughout Russian history.[62] The Russian exiles were at an impasse at the negotiations, no longer able to impose their vision of Russia as a multiethnic nation yet not fully comfortable with their status as mere representatives of one of many ethnic nations.

Ultimately, the Russian representatives proved unable to live with the sacrifices on the national question they had made. The immediate fallout from the conference was a clash between the Russians and Amcomlib representative Levine over the standing of the conference and the bodies that were supposed to continue its work.[63] The communique signed at Wiesbaden mandated the creation of an "Internationality Commission" to continue discussions, but the Russian organizations refused to send delegates to it, instead continuing to meet in their five-party Bureau. A furious Levine announced that the Russian organizations had violated the conference's decisions and cut off Amcomlib funding to them, prompting Mel'gunov and Kerenskii to respond with scathing attacks on their erstwhile American sponsors in the émigré press.[64] The Russians' objections were at least partially justified, as Levine's line at the conference had been downright inconsistent if not erratic.[65]

---

[60] Differences in the non-Russian organizations hinged on the question of how self-determination should be understood. More moderate organizations were content to be granted the *right* to declare national self-determination in the future, while the more radical groups made the quixotic demand that their independence be acknowledged immediately. For an overview, see Negotiations for an Effective Partnership, 10–17.

[61] Stenograficheskii protokol, smena 110, 2.

[62] Compare with Hosking, *Rulers and Victims*, 80–2.

[63] Negotiations for an Effective Partnership, 65.

[64] Protokoly s'ezda soveta NTS v ianvare 1952 g., 5, in Baydalakoff Collection, box 1, fol. 1 and S. M. Mel'gunov, "Razbitye illiuzii": 20.

[65] In particular, there is no documentary evidence to support Levine's contention that an agreement had been reached that the Russian Bureau would disband after the Wiesbaden Conference. The Starnberg Conference for the Unification of Russian and National Minority Émigré Political Organizations, Joseph T. Kendrick, Jr, Peripheral Reporting Unit, n.d. (1952), 1, in Kelley Papers, box 5, fol. 1.

The underlying reason for the Russian backlash against Amcomlib, of course, was dissatisfaction with its approach to the national question. From the Russian perspective, Levine's backing of separatist minority groups in the political center constituted betrayal on both personal and national levels. The Russians were quick to draw inferences about long-range American intentions from the conference. As a US intelligence report put it, the Russian groups felt that "the Committee has taken too strong a position in favor of the minorities and they are quick to infer from this action that the American Committee, and probably the United States Government as well, favors a policy of dividing the territories of the Soviet Union."[66] The conceptual dismemberment of the Russian nation that took place at Wiesbaden, the exiles feared, had set the stage for its real partition in the future.

The sacrifices made to Amcomlib on the national question were all the more painful given the state of public opinion in the Russian diaspora, where the *rossiiskii* identity was hegemonic. As Kerenskii voiced during the conference, Russians associated with the US risked being seen as "dismantlers (*raschleniteli*)" of Russia, which would "draw the fury" of other exiles.[67] His prediction came true. In the aftermath of Wiesbaden, rightist exiles in Paris gathered over a thousand signatures—no mean feat in the fissiparous emigration—for an open letter to Amcomlib that defended a Russian multiethnic state and denounced separatism.[68] The intelligence agent Ryszard Wraga describes how news of the deliberations had created "a flood of acute chauvinism and great-power thinking (*edinoderzhavnost'*) not only among the right (monarchist) emigration but also among more moderate circles."[69] Of course, the Russian émigrés would have rejected the label of chauvinism. Instead, they saw their people as the victims of American designs, sometimes alleging that the new superpower was replicating the promotion of Soviet minorities pursued by Hitler's Ministry for the Occupied Eastern Territories.[70]

An even more categorical reaction to the Wiesbaden debacle came from the stridently nationalist NTS. As described in Chapter 4, the NTS had agreed to take part in the united front reluctantly, and only as a means to boost its power. Working from this agenda, the Solidarists undertook aggressive tactics throughout the negotiations. At the Stuttgart conference weeks before, the NTS leaders worked to bring Kerenskii's RND over to their side in order to secure a

---

[66] Peripheral: Present Status, 3.

[67] Kerenskii was addressing a Georgian demand that their independence be automatically restored. Stenograficheskii protokol piati russkikh politicheskikh organizatsii, smena 109, str. 1.

[68] Memorandum for the Chairman from TK, Su: Receipt of open letter and petition addressed to Admiral Kirk, June 10, 1952, in Levine Papers, box 9.

[69] Deiatel'nost' Amerikanskogo Komiteta Bor'by za Svobody Narodov, in HILA, Ryszard Wraga Papers, box 4, fol. 1. Wraga had worked with émigrés while on the Polish General Staff before World War II and maintained numerous ties to the Russian political emigration after the war.

[70] Antoshin, *Rossiiskie emigranty*, 389–90.

three-to-two majority within the Russian camp, allegedly manipulating the former premier of Russia like a "marionette" by playing on his "vanity."[71] While the NTS stayed at Wiesbaden until the end and even signed its final communique, they soon split ranks with the other Russian groups, denouncing the other exiles' willingness to make cause with the separatists as "impotence" and "loss of faith in themselves."[72] In the end, the NTS was only willing to return to the united front if Amcomlib handed control of it to the Russian organizations. As this was a political impossibility after Wiesbaden, the Solidarists—the group, it will be recalled, the OPC had courted assiduously—exited the stage acrimoniously.[73]

The NTS leaders now turned on Amcomlib itself. They had developed a strong dislike of Levine, which was sustained by their traditional anti-Semitism. The intoxicated wife of a prominent Solidarist once asked why "the Dons" were being allowed to represent "the Russians."[74] At the same time, the crafty Solidarists sought to turn the tables on Amcomlib by cultivating other contacts in Washington, apparently on the conviction that George Kennan and State Department Russian hand Charles Bohlen had turned on "Lyons and co." for driving the united front into the ground. Apparently, Poremskii based his hopes for changes in Amcomlib on discussions with Nicholas Nabokov (cousin of the famous Russian-American writer), who had recently become Secretary General of the CIA-backed Congress for Cultural Freedom.[75] While this effort to bypass Amcomlib did not shift the politics of the united-front project, the NTS's feud with Levine did open up divisions within the American Committee. In particular, Levine expressed anger at other Amcomlib members who had allegedly undercut his authority by adopting a "policy of appeasement" toward the NTS.[76] The conflicts among different exile factions had triggered divisions in US liberationist circles, a stark reminder of how Americans and émigrés were part of a common political field.

---

[71] Visbadenskoie soveshchanie, November 10, 1951, in Wraga Papers, box 4, fol. 25.

[72] Protokoly S'ezda Soveta NTS v iiune 1952 g., 140.

[73] Memorandum of Conversation: Mr Baidalakov, Mr Poremski, of NTS; Mr Davis, Department of State; and Francis B. Stevens, November 26, 1951, in Kelley Papers, box 5, fol. 1.

[74] N. Koriakin to V. M. Baidalakov, May 10, 1952, 2, in Archiv der Forschungsstelle Osteuropa an der Universität Bremen (hereinafter FSO), 01–098 Tarasova, kor. marked V. D. Poremskii, i. a. perepiska.

[75] V. D. Poremskii to K. V. Boldyrev, June 26, 1951, in FSO, 01–098 Tarasova, kor. 41. Evidently, there was some basis to the NTS's hopes. In October 1951, Nabokov wrote to Kennan complaining of "certain steps" in the Russian émigré problem that were "erroneous, even dangerous," citing a discussion with Bohlen on the matter (the NTS is not mentioned). Kennan's response to the letter did not refer to Amcomlib specifically, though. Nicholas Nabokov to George Kennan, October 19, 1951, in Seeley G. Mudd Manuscript Library, Princeton University, George F. Kennan Papers, box 32, fol. 13.

[76] See Isaac Don Levine to Henry Chamberlin, December 16, 1951, in Levine Papers, box 8. Don Levine also drafted a letter of resignation to Chamberlin dated the same day, which was apparently not sent.

Prolonged Agony: The Unity Campaign Re-doubled

Despite the embarrassing ruckus at and after Wiesbaden, Amcomlib was not willing to give up on the united-front project. To be sure, the initial optimism that underlay the OPC-CIA plan was gone. Levine emerged from the conference furious at the Russian exiles, who "do not show any interest in the struggle against Bolshevism," "live and work in total detachment from Soviet life and think in some sort of obsolete anachronisms," and even engage in "fraud," presumably a reference to incessant émigré requests for money. Levine now expressed more faith in the non-Russian groups, although he also added that they were gripped by "mad chauvinism."[77]

Levine's grumblings foreshadowed a stronger approach to future collaboration. An Amcomlib attempt to force the exiles back to the negotiating table through indirect means—namely, by publishing a "Non-Partisan Appeal" signed by exiles not associated with the political organizations—fell on deaf ears.[78] However, Levine managed to reassemble the Wiesbaden participants in the town of Starnberg near Munich in June 1952 by issuing a clear incentive for them to cooperate.[79] Amcomlib announced that it would launch a large-scale radio operation broadcasting to the USSR in a matter of months; should an émigré political center not be created by that time, the committee would be "obliged to hire its own personnel from the ranks of the emigration without respect to political affiliation."[80]

The gambit to tie exile participation in the united front to a concrete anti-Soviet operation had some effect. For the exiles, the radio was important for the possibilities it might offer for anti-Soviet work and also for its potential to become a major employer. Indeed, the demand that the exiles have control over staffing the proposed radio operation was virtually the only thing the Russian and non-Russian exile groups could agree upon at the united-front meetings.[81] In large part due to this consideration, the united front took on a new incarnation after several meetings in 1952, this time as the Coordinating Center for Anti-Bolshevik Struggle (*Koordinatsionnyi tsentr anti-bol'shevitskoi bor'by* or KTsAB), a body that now included equal participation from Russian and non-Russian groups. Again, US largesse bought the exiles' willingness to cooperate. Amcomlib granted

---

[77] Mnenie don Levina o sozyve po soveshchaniiu SONR v Visbadene, Ryszard Wraga, November 25, 1951, 1, in Wraga Papers, box 4, fol. 16.

[78] Negotiations for an Effective Partnership, 80–3.

[79] NTS leaders met the Russian delegates at the train station to try to convince them to abandon Amcomlib. Memorandum, Su: TK's Memorandum on Kurganov's Questions to Admiral Kirk and Spencer Williams, June 2, 1952, in Levine Papers, box 8.

[80] Peripheral: Present Status of Efforts to Unite Russian Emigration, November 28, 1951, 3, in Kelley Papers, box 5, fol 1.

[81] The Starnberg conference for the Unification of Russian and national minority émigré political organizations, n.d. (1952), 8, in Kelley Papers, box 5, fol. 1.

regular subsidies to the organizations participating in KTsAB, funds that were all the more important to exiles due to the hardship accompanying the closure of the DP camps by the International Relief Organization in 1952.[82] Nevertheless, the new organization was a weak body, as its name implied: it was a loose holding tank of organizations ("Coordinating Center") with a hazy mission (an "anti-Bolshevik struggle," but whose, and in the name of what?).[83]

The reason for the united front's malaise was unchanged: the incompatible national claims articulated by the Russians on the one hand and the non-Russians on the other. Complicating matters, Amcomlib had come to see participation in the project by Ukrainians as essential. The Ukrainian DP population in Germany was relatively large, and the constant criticisms of Amcomlib being aired by the Ukrainian diaspora in North America rankled.[84] Meanwhile, Ukrainians had become important to American Cold War agendas. As Amcomlib leaders perhaps fathomed, the CIA was engaging Ukrainian exiles in Germany for intelligence and psy-war operations—which, it is worth noting, were larger in scale than the Agency's corresponding Russian-centered endeavors.[85]

The problem for Amcomlib was that the dominant forces in the Ukrainian emigration all rejected overtures to join the united front. Groups such as the Organization of Ukrainian Nationalists, the Ukrainian Supreme Liberation Council, and the Ukrainian National Council declared that they could cooperate only with groups that gave "prior acknowledgment" of Ukrainian independence.[86] Only two courses of action were available to Amcomlib on the Ukrainian question, and both were undesirable. The political center could have attempted to draw in established Ukrainian groups, but such a move would have angered the Russian émigrés and probably led to their departure from the political center. Alternatively, the Russians involved in the united front sought to fill the Ukrainian void in the political center by admitting "federalist" organizations into KTsAB, meaning groups that acknowledged their nation's right to self-determination but hoped to remain connected to Russia in some federal structure after the hypothetical fall of communism.

---

[82] Memorandum, Su: Views of a Recent Arrival from Germany (Milrud), Leo Dudin to Eugene Lyons, January 30, 1952, 1–2, in Levine Papers, box 8.

[83] Negotiations for an Effective Partnership, 96.

[84] Ibid., 123. On the Ukrainian diaspora and the Cold War, see Myron B. Kuropas, "Fighting Moscow from Afar: Ukrainian Americans and the Evil Empire," in Ieva Zake (ed.), *Anti-communist Minorities in the U.S.: Political Activism of Ethnic Refugees* (New York: Palgrave Macmillan, 2009), 43–66.

[85] See Taras Kuzio, "U.S. Support for Ukraine's Liberation during the Cold War: A Study of Prolog Research and Publishing Corporation," *Communist and Post-Communist Studies* no. 45 (2012): 51–64. DOI:10.1016/j.postcomstud.2012.02.007, accessed June 3, 2014 and Richard Breitman and Norman J. W. Goda, *Hitler's Shadow: Nazi War Criminals, U.S. Intelligence, and the Cold War* (Washington, DC: National Archives and Records Administration, 2010), 81.

[86] Negotiations for an Effective Partnership, 13.

At face value, the Russian position seemed reasonable. As the Russians stressed, demanding recognition of Ukrainian independence in the present contradicted Amcomlib's longstanding "non-predeterminist" position, which put off claims for sovereignty until the post-Soviet future. The Russians also questioned the legitimacy of the Ukrainian nationalist groups in emigration, pointing out with some reason that they had a largely West Ukrainian membership and did not represent the less nationalistic East Ukrainians.[87]

Supporting the Russian-backed federalist Ukrainians, however, seemed politically toxic. Amcomlib was determined to include "the greatest mass of the USSR emigration" in the common front, and admitting Ukrainian federalists would close the door to participation of the much larger and better-organized separatist organizations.[88] Moreover, Amcomlib leaders became skeptical of the viability of the small and internally divided federalist groups.[89] As the Americans complained, many Ukrainian federalists actually belonged to Russian organizations and seemed to be moonlighting as "nationals" for political gain.[90] The Russians' insistence on the participation of the federalists, even at the cost of torpedoing the entire united front, is only comprehensible when one considers the wider dilemma of Russian identity.[91] Pro-Russian Ukrainians were tangible proof of the multi-ethnic nation that the Russians endorsed—and the existence of which Ukrainian nationalists denied on principle.

The American Committee found itself "between Scylla and Charybdis" on the Ukrainian question, as its new head Admiral Alan G. Kirk explained to Kerenskii.[92] Personnel changes in the American Committee made the situation worse. The circumstances of the exit of the first Amcomlib chief Eugene Lyons in early 1952 are not entirely clear, but his hostility to "anti-Russian" Ukrainian groups placed him out of step with the direction of the united-front project.[93] Kirk, former Ambassador to the USSR, took the helm, but resigned half a year later citing health reasons. His successor was another military man with extensive knowledge of Russia: Vice Admiral Leslie C. Stevens, who had recently served as US Naval

---

[87] The fundamental obstacle to the creation of the United Front of the anti-communist emigres for Russia (U.S.S.R.), memorandum by A. F. Kerenskii, December 15, 1953, in Kelley Papers, box 5, fol. 1.

[88] Draft: Brief History of the Munich Organizational Activities of the American Committee for Liberation from Bolshevism, Inc., November 10, 1953, 2, in Kelley Papers, box 5, fol. 1. See also Memorandum, Su: Diki Group's position in Ukrainian Federalists' Quarrel, Spencer Williams to Alan G. Kirk, June 16, 1952, in Levine Papers, box 9.

[89] Airgram No. 50, Su: Position of Amcomlib with reference to the problem of Ukrainian admissions to Coordinating Center, Admiral Kirk, February 19, 1953, in Levine Papers, box 8.

[90] On SBONR members who were cross-listed in the federalist Ukrainian groups, see Memorandum for the Chairman, Spencer Williams, Su: Conversation with Ivan P. Lapko, June 11, 1952, in Levine Papers, box 9.

[91] The Russians made the promise to admit federalist groups a condition of their "finalizing" of KTsAB. Unidentified draft document, Robert F. Kelley, n.d. (1952), in Kelley Papers, box 5, fol. 3.

[92] Beseda s Adm. Kirkom, transcription of May 13, 1952, meeting between RND and Amcomlib leaders, 2, in Levine Papers, box 8.

[93] Memorandum from EL, Su: New York League Projects, February 13, 1952, in Levine Papers, box 9.

Attaché in Moscow and consultant of the Joint Chiefs of Staff to the OPC.[94] Amcomlib's office in Munich underwent similar overhaul. Levine returned to the United States after declaring victory upon the creation of KTsAB, no doubt with a sense of relief. His position passed first to the radio specialist Forrest McCluney and then to diplomat Otis B. Swift, neither of whom spoke Russian or had extensive knowledge of matters Soviet.[95] The replacement of Russian-born anti-communists Lyons and Levine with "persons of prominence" such as soldiers and diplomats weakened Amcomlib's already limited ability to navigate the exile milieu.[96] It also lent credence to Soviet propaganda alleging that Amcomlib was a cover for government activity—which, of course, it was.[97]

The new Amcomlib leadership proved unequal to the task of leading the united-front project, and not just because some of them needed interpreters. Stevens was prone to public gaffes, such as when he announced to a room of exiles in New York that "every Russian comes up with a different solution to the Russian problem," an impolitic if perhaps not totally inaccurate statement.[98] More serious was Amcomlib's inability to produce a clear position on the divisive question of federalist and nationalist Ukrainian groups. Amcomlib pursued a "balanced admissions" principle of promising to admit federalist *and* separatist Ukrainians to the united-front organization, a position that amounted to an attempt to "duck the question indefinitely," as Amcomlib's Spencer Williams put it.[99] Under Stevens's watch, Amcomlib pursued two contradictory policies at once, with its New York headquarters sending a delegation of Ukrainian Americans to Europe to court Ukrainian nationalists, while its Munich office made promises to Russian exiles about federalist participation.[100] When Stevens visited Munich in March 1953, he managed to confuse everyone by "admit[ing] the justice of having both federalist and separatist Ukes [*sic*]" in the center but also proclaiming that "the Committee does not approve of federalists."[101]

---

[94] Gregory Mitrovich, *Undermining the Kremlin: America's Strategy to Subvert the Soviet Bloc, 1947–1956* (Ithaca, NY: Cornell University Press, 2000), 68.

[95] Negotiations for an Effective Partnership, 123.

[96] CIA, State Department, American Committee for Liberation Discussion of Radio Liberty Broadcasting, March 15, 1952, 1, in Radio Free Europe and Radio Liberty. On a wider process of "professionalization" underway in CIA-funded political warfare operations of the period, see Hugh Wilford, *The Mighty Wurlitzer: How the CIA Played America* (Cambridge, MA: Harvard University Press, 2008), 70–98.

[97] Replies to questions on images of émigrés, RL images, and regime reaction, Manager, Audience Research and Evaluation Department to Director of Planning, December 16, 1959, 6, in Kelley Papers, box 5, fol. 4.

[98] V. S. Makarov to Vice Admiral L. C. Stevens, February 18, 1953, in HILA, Constantin W. Boldyreff Papers, box 1.

[99] Airgram No. 50 and Memorandum for the Chairman, Su: Letter to EL from Dr F. Bohatirchuk, Spencer Williams, June 11, 1952, in Levine Papers, box 9.

[100] The delegation, which represented the Ukrainian Congress Committee of America, was unable to influence the Ukrainian organizations in Europe. Negotiations for an Effective Partnership, 114–24.

[101] Prist Visit to Europe, March 9–24, 1953, Chief of Base, Munich to Chief EE, April 4, 1953, 2, in NARA, RG 263, Entry ZZ-19, 230/86/26/01, QKACTIVE, box 55, vol. 1.

Stevens's inconsistency, not to speak of his use of ethnic slurs, were self-inflicted wounds for Amcomlib. His failure to resolve the federalist–separatist conundrum was perhaps more forgivable. It is unclear how the question of admitting Ukrainians to the united front could have been resolved, for it went to the core of different variants of Russian national identity. Was Russia a multiethnic or an ethnic nation? Here was a problem that no amount of American money and power could fix.

* * *

The OPC-CIA project for a united front, then, had badly misfired. It aimed to galvanize émigré political activists, but instead left them weakened and demoralized. It sought to build up Russian nationalism as a foil to Soviet communism, but instead created fissures over national interests among the exiles. It sought to cross divides between different Soviet exile communities, but, if anything, hardened them. To some extent, Amcomlib was to blame for these dismal results. The original OPC plan had made the unrealistic assumption that exile political organizations could sink their differences and form a cohesive anticommunist bloc, which was a tall order for Russian organizations left to their own devices and a virtually impossible one for émigré groups representing different nationalities. Faced with infighting among the exiles, the improvised efforts of Amcomlib figures to right the ship tended to make matters worse; consider Spencer Williams's handling of the Dalin affair, Levine's clash with the exiles before and after Wiesbaden, and Stevens's incomprehensible course over the Ukrainian issue.

Amcomlib's blunders were surely less important than the more fundamental issue plaguing the united front: the contentious nature of multiethnic nationhood in Russia. The Russians were devoted to the cause of recreating Russia as a "family of peoples," but discovered that their ideas were steadfastly opposed by non-Russian exiles as well as by Amcomlib. Faced with the inability to push through this agenda, the Russians found themselves outflanked and mired in fruitless conflicts in the wider émigré milieu.

Rather than being obscure exile squabbles, the arguments in Bavarian hotels and meeting halls reflected crucial historical debates about Russian nationhood. The failure of the Russian exiles to impose their will on the united-front project was a belated echo of developments in Russian and Soviet history. The Russian exiles remained wedded to the notion of a multiethnic Russian nation, one rooted historically in the intelligentsia of the imperial period and the country's brief experiment with democracy in 1917. A democratic and multinational state, however, had been removed from the stage—and then pushed into exile—by Civil War and communist power, which fused Russian nationalism to a multi-ethnic Soviet state. In this sense, the united-front project inadvertently provided a space in which Russians rehearsed debates over the past.

The backward-looking nature of the exiles' view of Russia found expression in a curious exchange at a 1950 Council meeting of the NTS—the most nationalistic, it will be recalled, of the Russian groups involved in the united front. The old exile R. N. Redlikh, himself of Baltic German origins, commented to his fellow Solidarists that "the national consciousness" of the Russians had diverged from contemporary realities. "There is no Russian (*rossiiskoi*) nation," he opined, as "they [non-Russian peoples] either want to leave or become Russians (*russkimi*)."[102] Redlikh's expression of pessimism about the the the viability of a multi-ethnic Russian nation that could integrate other ethnicities of the empire struck a nerve with the other Solidarist leaders. NTS leader V. M. Baidalakov commented that "earlier, Russians [*rossiiane*] gave themselves up," by which he clearly meant that non-Russians in the tsarist period had defined themselves as part of a multiethnic Russian nation. Baidalakov held himself up as an example, as he was a "Ukrainian" (he was of Cossack origin) who wanted to "stay in Russia." If this was a rebuttal of Redlikh's point, its invocation of the tsarist past was telling. By espousing a multiethnic notion of Russian identity, the exiles were working against history.

---

[102] Protokoly s'ezda Soveta NTS v dekabre 1950 goda, 26–7.

6

Reluctant Chieftains

The Ascendance of the American Committee for Liberation from Bolshevism

> Fellow countrymen! For a long time the Soviet regime has concealed from you the very fact of the emigration's existence...We have been covered with a gravestone of silence, but we have not died. We are well aware why the Soviets have decided not even to rail against us in written or verbal attacks. That would mean constantly reminding the people about the existence of an anti-Bolshevik Russia which did not find a place in the motherland, about a Russia which took arms against Bolshevism and to this day awaits its hour.[1]

So ran the first Russian broadcast on March 1, 1953, of Radio Liberation from Bolshevism. A project of the CIA front organization American Committee for Liberation of the Peoples of Russia, Inc. (Amcomlib), the radio presented itself as an exile affair, the mouthpiece of "anti-Bolshevik Russia" abroad. In fact, the broadcast claimed to be speaking in the name of the "Coordinating Center for anti-Bolshevik Struggle" (known by its Russian acronym as KTsAB), and left obscure the matter of its American sponsorship.[2] In the radio we find the embodiment of Amcomlib's strategy of psychological warfare, that of using exiles as instruments with which to pry the Soviet people away from their communist rulers.

The first broadcast soon became a curious historical relic. Radio Liberation, renamed as Radio Liberty in the late 1950s, developed into a major propaganda effort against the USSR that would last, in modified forms, to the end of the Cold War and beyond. Yet the connection of the radio to exile political causes became obscured. KTsAB, the organization produced by Amcomlib's united-front project, fell apart after just months of existence due to émigré infighting, prompting

---

[1] Gene Sosin, *Sparks of Liberty: An Insider's Memoir of Radio Liberty* (University Park, PA: Pennsylvania State University Press, 1999), 15.

[2] Tass on Voice of America Broadcast citing Radio Liberation Appeal to Soviet Military in Germany, June 26, 1953, in History and Public Policy Program Digital Archive at the Woodrow Wilson Center, Radio Free Europe and Radio Liberty: Cold War International History Project e-Dossier no. 32 (hereinafter Radio Free Europe and Radio Liberty).

Cold War Exiles and the CIA: Plotting to Free Russia. Benjamin Tromly, Oxford University Press (2019). © Benjamin Tromly.
DOI: 10.1093/oso/9780198840404.001.0001

Amcomlib to take direct sponsorship of the radio and other political-warfare projects. While it would always rely on exiles for its operations, Radio Liberty would no longer claim to speak for an "anti-Bolshevik Russia" awaiting its day to take up arms. Instead, the radio presented itself as a surrogate free press for the Soviet Union, and stressed its adherence to Western journalistic standards.[3]

Over the decades, the shift from the intended exile to US leadership over Radio Liberation has received distinctly partisan treatment. After the collapse of the united front project, Amcomlib members criticized the exiles for failing to "put unity above partisanship, and victory over Bolshevism above personal spleens," squandering the opportunity for political action that the Americans had offered them.[4] In contrast, the Russians lambasted Amcomlib for siding with non-Russian separatists and treating the Russians as subordinates, not equals. Historical accounts have echoed these polarized charges from the 1950s. English-language literature, including several studies written by former employees of the radio or of Radio Free Europe, its sister operation broadcasting to Eastern Europe, presents a relatively unproblematic process in which Amcomlib stepped in to replace the hopelessly ineffectual émigrés in managing Radio Liberation.[5] In stark contrast, a recent Russian account rehabilitates the exile argument that the Americans seized control over Russian initiatives imperiously.[6]

Both these perspectives oversimplify the transformation of Amcomlib–exile relations in the 1950s. The Amcomlib view of exiles as being inept and politically toxic is hardly satisfactory, not least because it distracts attention from the American Committee's own role in sinking the united front. Conversely, the émigrés' charge that Amcomlib was a ruthless exploiter of the exiles flies in the face of documentary evidence presented here, which paints a picture of an organization that stuck to its exile program despite considerable external pressures within the US government.

---

[3] The best analysis of the editorial line of Radio Liberation-Liberty, and one that distinguishes it from the approaches of other Western media broadcasting to the USSR, is Lowell Schwartz, *Political Warfare against the Kremlin: US and British Propaganda Policy at the Beginning of the Cold War* (Basingstoke: Palgrave Macmillan, 2009), 124–36. On the important roles of exiles in Radio Liberation and Radio Free Europe throughout the Cold War, see Friederike Kind-Kovács, "Voices, letters, and literature through the Iron Curtain: exiles and the (trans)mission of radio in the Cold War," *Cold War History* 13, no. 2 (2013): 193–219.

[4] Although the comment was written in 1951, this analysis carried over into later Amcomlib evaluations as well. Statement for Novoye Russkoye Slovo, Eugene Lyons and Isaac Don Levine, n.d. (late 1951 or 1952), 2, in Stuart A. Rose Manuscript, Archives, and Rare Book Library, Emory University, Isaac Don Levine Papers (hereinafter Levine Papers), box 9.

[5] A. Ross Johnson, *Radio Free Europe and Radio Liberty: The CIA Years and Beyond* (Washington, DC: Woodrow Wilson Center Press, 2010), 17–20; Arch Puddington, *Broadcasting Freedom: the Cold War Triumph of Radio Free Europe and Radio Liberty* (Lexington: University Press of Kentucky, 2000), 158–62; Sig Mickelson, *America's Other Voice: The Story of Radio Free Europe and Radio Liberty* (New York: Praeger, 1983), 66–71; Richard H. Cummings, *Cold War Radio: The Dangerous History of American Broadcasting in Europe, 1950–1989* (Jefferson, NC: McFarland & Co., 2009), 27; and Sosin, *Sparks of Liberty*, 31, 57.

[6] A. V. Popov, "Miunkhenskii institute po izucheniiu istorii i kul'tury SSSR i vtoraia emigratsiia," *Novyi istoricheskii vestnik* no. 1 (10): 54–70.

This chapter eschews these polarized views with the goal of providing a new account of the end of the united front and Amcomlib's move away from exiles in the mid-1950s. Rather than being a clean break, Amcomlib's decision to take over direct control of political warfare from the exiles was a slow and faltering process. Members of the American Committee remained convinced that the exiles served a crucial legitimizing function for political warfare, a perception that remained operative even after the united front had broken down. In the event, Amcomlib gradually drifted away from work with exiles under the weight of US power and wealth, as its radio staff in Munich and its overseers in the Central Intelligence Agency pressed for a more straightforwardly top-down approach. The definitive turn against the exiles only came later in the 1950s, when the changing shape of the Cold War in Europe delegitimized exile anti-communism. Thus, collaboration between Amcomlib and Russian exile politicians was more tenacious than has previously been thought, a product of the American liberationists' persistent commitment to a pro-émigré political line as the centerpiece of its psychological strategy against the USSR.

Death Throes of the United Front

If Amcomlib's divorce from the exiles would prove protracted and difficult, the fall of the political center itself occurred with seemingly inexorable momentum. Writing decades later, the top American negotiator, the diplomat Isaac "Ike" Patch, remembers more than a year of a "never-ending succession of fruitless meetings in smoke-filled rooms or parks with representatives of émigré political parties," all dressed in their Sunday best and prone to "acting like dictators."[7]

One can appreciate Patch's anguish. With very few exceptions, both the Russian and non-Russian émigré camps eschewed compromise. As discussed in Chapter 5, KTsAB veered into chaos soon after the exiles founded it due to divisions over which Ukrainian groups deserved a seat at the table. After a tortuous conference at the beginning of 1953 ended with minimal compromise, the Russian and non-Russian factions dug in their heels. Led by the Georgian delegation, the so-called Paris Bloc of non-Russian organizations consolidated itself with the agenda of forcing Amcomlib to recognize non-Russian claims for national independence.[8] After another failed KTsAB plenary session in the Bavarian town of Tegernsee in May 1953, the Russian exile organizations broke off to form what they claimed

---

[7] Isaac Patch, *Closing the Circle: A Buckalino Journey around Our Time* (Wellesley, MA: Wellesley College Printing Services, 1996), 244.

[8] Negotiations for an Effective Partnership: Study of the Negotiations between the American Committee for Liberation from Bolshevism and Leaders of the Emigration from the USSR to Create a Central Émigré Organization for Anti-Bolshevik Activity, 135–6 in Hoover Institution Archives and Library (HILA), Arch Puddington Collection, Box 27, File 5.

was the true coordinating center, a "Russian KTsAB." This body, soon rejoined by the National Labor Alliance (NTS) and several obscure federalist groups claiming to speak for non-Russian peoples, returned to the position they had held at the outset of the negotiations: the defense of the "unity of historical Russia as an organic state entity."[9] In essence, the united front had divided into two halves, both of which attempted to present Amcomlib with a fait accompli that would force it to recognize their side instead of the other.[10] If the Russians and non-Russians disagreed about much, they both used a common playbook of employing "high pressure tactics" vis-à-vis their American patrons.[11]

The Russian exiles, it is true, faced a nearly impossible situation during the waning days of the united front. Continuing collaboration with the Americans seemed to require taking positions that ran against Russian national interests. The dilemma was apparent in the turmoil that gripped the Russian exile organization most heavily subsidized by Amcomlib: the Vlasovite Union for the Struggle for the Liberation of the Peoples of Russia (SBONR).[12] During the final weeks of KTsAB, B. I. Nikolaevskii, the old émigré socialist who proved the most determined proponent of the united-front project, broke ranks with his fellow Russians and joined the national minority camp. Nikolaevskii's attempt to save the American project earned him the unremitting hatred of most of the Russian exiles, who railed at the national "renegade" and refused to sit with him at the same table. Even worse, his defection split SBONR in two, as some of the Vlasovites sided with Nikolaevskii and others opted for solidarity with the Russian camp.[13] Ironically, Amcomlib's commitment to lumping together different national groups in a single body had cast one of its exile allies (Nikolaevskii) into the role of national traitor and sabotaged its favored Russian anti-communist group (SBONR).

If the rupture of SBONR damaged a pillar of Amcomlib's envisioned united front, the collapse of KTsAB brought down the entire edifice. Particularly disruptive was Amcomlib's decision after Tegernsee to discontinue the monthly subsidies it had been paying out to the different exile groups participating in the negotiations. The payments were the lifeblood of the exile organizations, for they covered the costs of publishing in-house journals that were seen as the litmus test of a serious émigré political outfit. Another major, if not officially admitted,

---

[9] Notably, although they claimed to represent the "true" KTsAB, they now changed their name to KTsONR—Coordinating Center for the Liberation of the *Peoples of Russia* (emphasis added). Negotiations for an Effective Partnership, 184.

[10] Agenda: outstanding problems affecting QKACTIVE, Chief of Base, Munich to Chief, EE, March 5, 1953, 9, in NARA, RG 263, Entry ZZ-19, 230/86/26/01, QKACTIVE (hereinafter QKACTIVE), box 56, vol. 1.

[11] Isaac Don Levine to Forrest McCluney, June 20, 1952, in Levine Papers, box 8.

[12] SBONR received monthly payments of $9,000 until August 1952, compared to $3,500 received by the other Russian groups. Memorandum on émigré publications, no author indicated, n.d. (1954), 1 in Levine Papers, box 8.

[13] Negotiations for an Effective Partnership, 135–52.

reason to grant the exile organizations funds had been to coax them to join the center, what a CIA report characterized as "sweetening for sweetening's sake."[14] As suggested by the breakdown of KTsAB, such financial "sweetening" had exerted less influence on the exiles than Amcomlib had hoped. The exiles thought that they could press their interests without losing American funding—perhaps a rational assumption given the role that Amcomlib assigned exiles as freedom fighters and representatives of their respective nations.

The break over subsidies demonstrated that the exiles had misjudged their US patrons. While the collapse of the united front was the main reason for Amcomlib's canceling of its payments, the Americans had also become convinced that the émigrés were misusing them. A later Amcomlib report charged that the exiles were placing the monthly stipends into "slush fund[s] which corroded and demoralized the émigré leaders themselves." "Older émigrés drank champagne, the young ones bought themselves camel's hair coats and new briefcases," the report alleged.[15] A CIA report elaborated on the exiles' extravagant lifestyles: A. G. Avtorkhanov-Kunta, the leader of the North Caucasian anti-Communist People's Alliance and later a widely known historian in the West, allegedly "entertain[ed] lavishly at local bars and remark[ed], 'God gives, we drink.' "[16]

However venal the émigrés were—and Amcomlib perhaps had reason to belabor the point—the cutting of American subsidies to the exile organizations created "a mounting wave of criticism throughout the entire emigration" against Amcomlib and, in many cases, against the United States more generally.[17] Not surprisingly, leading the attack were the rightist and monarchist groups, who resented having been left out from the united front negotiations years before. With patriotic pathos, White officer Vasilii Vasil'evich Orekhov, the head of the United Vlasovite Council in Europe, declared that all the Americans' efforts had come to naught because they assumed that "everything including conscience and honor can be bought for dollars."[18]

While the émigré far right had always opposed Amcomlib, the collapse of the united front—and, no less important, the end of payouts that it portended—now expanded the ranks of exiles who saw themselves as slighted by the committee. To take one example, A. S. Zagolo-Bogdanov had taken active part in the united-front project as a member of the Union of Struggle for the Freedom of Russia (SBSR). In 1955 he denounced Amcomlib as a nest of crypto-communists that had deliberately torpedoed exile unification, dubbing it "Lattimore in the Russian question,"

[14] Memorandum, Su: Discussion of AmComLib policy on émigré publication activities, W. Cates to the President, December 17, 1953, 2, in Levine Papers, box 8.

[15] Negotiations for an Effective Partnership, 194–6.

[16] Agenda: outstanding problems affecting QKACTIVE, 2–3.

[17] Chief of Mission, Frankfurt to Chief, EE, Su: AEACTIVE/Comments on apparently new developments AEAFFIRM policy, October 20, 1953, 2, in QKACTIVE, box 55, vol. 1.

[18] See the account of Orekhov's piece in the Brussels monthly *Chasovoi* ("The Sentinel") in Review of the Russian Émigré Press, vol. IV, no. 6, April 9, 1956, 2, in Levine Papers, box 15.

evoking the scholar of China tarred by Joseph McCarthy.[19] This clumsy gambit to draw on domestic American anti-communism underscored the extent of Russian anger as Amcomlib pulled the rug out from under its erstwhile clients.

The fall of KTsAB, then, seemed to destroy the Russian nation in exile that Amcomlib had tried so exhaustively to build, or perhaps even mobilized it against the United States. Making matters worse, the committee also found itself under scrutiny from the CIA, as the constant crisis that surrounded the political center undercut Amcomlib's position in Washington. In February 1953, C. Tracey Barnes, recently appointed Chief of Political and Psychological Warfare, offered his superior Frank G. Wisner a scathing take on QKACTIVE, the CIA project encompassing Amcomlib's activities.[20] QKACTIVE was three years old and had absorbed over two million dollars to date, but it had accomplished "little or nothing." One reason for the debacle, Barnes argued, was the CIA's weak involvement. Amcomlib head Admiral Leslie C. Stevens resisted close CIA control, meaning that "command channels are ambiguous and appropriate management controls do not exist"—an understandable criticism given Amcomlib's dance over the federalist issue, as discussed in Chapter 5.[21] A few months later, Dana Durand, head of the CIA Soviet Russia Division, reached an even more categorical verdict. Referring to a six-month review of the project, Durand opined to the Deputy Director of Plans that the creation of an émigré center was "probably not feasible" given the "irreconcilable differences" among the exile groups and also "Soviet penetration of the Coordinating Center," which he called "effective and damaging." Going further, Durand called into question the very premise of using exiles for political warfare against the USSR, arguing that "experience of the Agency" had showed that "the political validity, and effectiveness within the target country, of any émigré grouping has been over-estimated in the past."[22]

Despite this anti-exile evaluation from Amcomlib's purseholders, the committee continued its political approach unchanged. Stevens proved resilient in defending Amcomlib's conception of the émigré center. In May 1953, when the Coordinating Center was already in the process of dissolution, the CIA called for Amcomlib to cut political subsidies to the exile political organizations and move Radio Liberation to Paris, away from the troublesome exiles in Munich. Admiral Stevens shot back that these steps were "unnecessary or undesirable," and the

---

[19] See the overview of the publication *Rossiia* in Review of the Russian Émigré Press, vol. III, no. 44, November 15, 1955, 2, in Levine Papers, box 15.

[20] According to one employee of the time, the Amcomlib project was on the brink of being canceled in late 1952, and many American and émigré staff members were dismissed—only to be rehired a few months later. James Critchlow, *Radio Hole-in-the-head/Radio Liberty: An Insider's Story of Cold War Broadcasting* (Washington, DC: American University Press, 1995), 8–9.

[21] Memorandum, C. Tracy Barnes, Chief, Political and Psychological Warfare to Deputy Director (plans), February 27, 1953, 1, in QKACTIVE, vol. 1.

[22] CIA Criticizes American Committee for Liberation Policies, May 18, 1953, 1, in Radio Free Europe and Radio Liberty.

matter of relocating Amcomlib—though, evidently, not that of cutting funding for the exiles—apparently stopped there.[23]

In order to understand the survival of Amcomlib's pro-émigré line in the face of criticism in Washington, one must consider that the American Committee had already initiated psychological operations against the USSR, including Radio Liberation. While views on exiles in Washington were souring, the effectiveness of Amcomlib's political operations remained an open question. In June 1953, a Committee on Internal Information Activities convened by President Eisenhower criticized the political-center concept—referring to "the futility" of trying to force émigrés to work together—while still advising the American Committee to continue work on its broadcasting operation.[24] The emergence of a new arsenal for psychological warfare added urgency to the question of Amcomlib's relationships with the émigrés.

The Munich Institute and Amcomlib Institution-Building

Two Munich-based CIA–Amcomlib operations came to the forefront of exile politics. Housed in several rooms at Amcomlib headquarters at 46 Augustenstrasse was the Institute for the Study of the History and Culture of the USSR (often known as the Munich Institute), and Radio Liberation was located at a half-destroyed former Luftwaffe base on the outskirts of town. Both initiatives were supposed to be subordinate to the united-front organization, and from the outset both employed many émigrés affiliated with the different exile organizations involved in the negotiations. As a result, the two operations were flashpoints for Amcomlib–exile politics during the long demise of the united-front project and beyond.

The Munich Institute's importance for émigré politics overshadowed its role in political warfare. A byproduct of the Harvard Project on the Soviet Social System, the sociological study of Soviet refugees discussed in Chapter 4, the Munich Institute was a research operation staffed by second-wave exile scholars from the USSR that published research materials, held conferences, and ran a research library.[25] In later writings, the institute's chairman B. A. Troitskii-Iakovlev falsely claimed that the institute was an independent exile initiative that remained free of

---

[23] Radio Liberty Broadcasting Reviewed, July 24, 1953, in Radio Free Europe and Radio Liberty.

[24] "Report to the President by the President's Committee on International Information Activities," Foreign Relations of the United States, 1952–1954, National Security Affairs, vol. 2, part 2, 1829–31.

[25] In 1954, the institute employed roughly eighty people. The American Committee for the Liberation from Bolshevism, no author indicated, n.d. (1954), 2 in Georgetown University Archives and Special Collections, Robert F. Kelley Papers (hereinafter Kelley Papers), box 5, fol. 3. The research institute began its existence as a Russian library that served as the legal headquarters for the Harvard Project. See E. V. Kodin, *Miunkhenskii institut po izucheniiu istorii i kul'tury SSSR, 1950–1972 gg.: evropeiskii tsentr sovetologii?* (Smolensk: Izd-o SmolGU, 2016), 16.

American involvement for several years.[26] In fact, Amcomlib stepped in to support the enterprise soon after the Harvard Project ended, an arrangement that reflected a confluence of interests between impoverished refugee academics and the American cold warriors of Amcomlib.[27]

Eager to bolster the status of their endeavor, Iakovlev and other exiles involved in the Institute later described it as a "large and respectable institution" that won considerable influence in the Western world.[28] Amcomlib evaluated the organization it supported quite differently. In March 1952, CIA officer William Cates stated that the Institute seemed "long ago to have died a natural death of stagnation" and pondered a fundamental restructuring of it.[29] As he explained, the Institute's publications were not scholarship but rather propaganda rife with "habitual flat prejudiced-sounding statements."[30]

The politicized character of the Institute's activities was inevitable given its design. Amcomlib had assumed that former Soviet citizens uprooted during the war were "uniquely qualified" to produce research that evaluated "the significance of changing conditions within the USSR" and forecasted its future.[31] Yet the exiles, many of whom were political activists with doubtful academic credentials, were hardly well positioned to offer unbiased evaluations of Soviet affairs.[32] Its director was a case in point. Iakovlev's prewar work at a Moscow architecture institute in the 1930s was questionable preparation for leading an institute on Soviet affairs.[33] As well, the wartime pasts of the Institute's leaders damaged the credibility of the Institute in the West. A scandal arose when Amcomlib forced the Institute to fire Konstantin Feodoseevich Shteppa, a Kiev University historian who collaborated with the Soviet secret police in the 1930s and then the Nazi SD (Security Service of the Reichsführer SS) during the war.[34] Rather than being a serious academic institution or even a research unit for Radio Liberation, as some Amcomlib

[26] Nikolai Troitskii, *Ty, moe stoletie*—(Moscow: Institut politicheskogo i voennogo analiza, 2006), 304.

[27] Evidence of the Institute's early funding comes from a document marked 1. History and purpose, no author indicated, n.d., in Kelley Papers, box 5, fol. 4. On the transition from the Harvard Project to the Munich Institute, see Kodin, *Miunkhenskii*, 40–9, and Sigmund Diamond, *Compromised Campus: The Collaboration of Universities with the Intelligence Community, 1945–1955* (New York: Oxford University Press, 1992), 99–101.

[28] Troitskii, *Ty, moe stoletie*, 341.

[29] William Cates to Isaac Don Levine, Su: The Institute, March 27, 1952, 1, in Levine Papers, box 9.

[30] Ibid.

[31] Statement of Mission and Operating Objectives, Deputy to President, Europe (Robert F. Kelley) to All Division Heads, Headquarters and Europe, September 1, 1954, 11 in Levine Papers, box 10.

[32] See the document marked Appendix I: Who's Who of Members of Council of Institute for Research on the History and Institutions of the USSR, n.d., in Kelley Papers, box 5, fol. 4. The same document shows that several institute members earned incomes as instructors at the "U. S. School," presumably the European Command Intelligence School at Oberursel near Frankfurt.

[33] Troitskii, *Ty, moe stoletie*, 331–3.

[34] Oleg Beyda and Igor Petrov, "The Soviet Union," in David Stahel (ed.), *Joining Hitler's Crusade: European Nations and the Invasion of the Soviet Union, 1941* (Cambridge and New York: Cambridge University Press, 2018), 418. Troitskii, *Ty, moe stoletie*, 349–51.

officials hoped it might become, the Munich Institute served primarily as an anti-communist propaganda agency in the West—and one of questionable usefulness, at that.[35]

Compounding the Institute's problems were the chaotic politics of the united-front project. In particular, the Institute was the site of one of Amcomlib's many political scandals. In 1953, the "Russian KTsAB," the Russian-only rump of the defunct united front, announced a boycott of the Institute's upcoming conference entitled "The USSR Today and Tomorrow." According to Amcomlib, the NTS and its allies "circulated rumors to the effect that the American Committee was planning to use this conference to create an organization that would replace the Coordinating Center as a sponsor for Radio Liberation." When the Institute announced that it would limit discussion of the conference's reports, Russian exiles gathered a petition denouncing the event as "undemocratic" and non-academic.[36] In his memoirs, Iakovlev criticized the boycott as an effort to "sub-ordinate the institute to party functionaries."[37] Such a conclusion was misleading, for the Munich Institute was already home to "party functionaries," including Iakovlev himself. Rather, the protest against the Institute was an expression of the Russian exiles' anger toward their US patrons, who were seen to have betrayed the exiles on the national question.

The rise in tensions between Amcomlib and the Russian political organizations placed the exiles who straddled both camps in a difficult position. In the wake of the boycott, Amcomlib imposed an informal employment blacklist on members of the NTS, the organization that had been most aggressive in opposition.[38] Not surprisingly, this move deepened the rifts between Amcomlib and the Russian exile groups. In late 1953, S. P. Mel'gunov and A. F. Kerenskii protested the expulsion of an NTS member from the Munich Institute and the "dismissal" of two more directly by Amcomlib to Robert F. Kelley, who was in Munich negoti-ating with the exiles. If Amcomlib "contemplated a reconciliation with the Russian emigration," Mel'gunov intoned, it should not "go about deliberately antagonizing Russian public opinion." As this exchange makes clear, the exiles believed they had the right to a voice in Amcomlib's operations even after the center had fallen. Moreover, Kelley's denial that Amcomlib was following a policy of retaliation showed that the Americans still took "Russian public opinion" seriously.[39] In

[35] Observations on "Statement of Mission, Operating Objectives and Policy Guides," Andre Yedigaroff, n.d. (early 1956), 4, in Levine Papers, box 10.
[36] Negotiations for an Effective Partnership, 198. A study of the Russian emigration produced by the West German Foreign Ministry provides a similar account of the event. Referat 508, Betr: Ausarbeitung über die russische Emigration, March 1954, 17 in Auswärtiges Amt-Politisches Archiv, B 12, Akte 455.
[37] Troitskii, Ty, moe stoletie, 346–8.
[38] Mickelson, America's Other Voice, 70–1.
[39] The fired NTS figures were Ia. V. Budanov, Derugin, and Grachev. Su: Conversation with Mel'gunov and Kerenskii, European Representative to the President, December 15, 1953, 2, in Kelley Papers, box 5, fol. 1.

other words, the political center hung over Amcomlib as a political framework, if not as an existing institution.

The national issue that had undermined the united front soon confronted the Munich Institute as well. The Institute, which had emerged during the early days of the united-front project, had remained Russian-dominated long after the united-front deliberations had become mired in national questions. In October 1953, Amcomlib changed course, deciding that the Munich Institute was not to be a "Russian Institute but an All-Nationality Institute for Study of USSR [sic]," and began negotiations with the Ukrainian Free Academy of Sciences to bring Ukrainian scholars into the fold.[40] Only a year later, the Institute had brought in non-Russian members and was operating in several Soviet languages in addition to Russian. As with the united front, the attempt to balance national claims proved demoralizing and destructive. Iakovlev and some other Russian members resigned, a move that turned yet another segment of the Russian émigré milieu against Amcomlib.[41] Moreover, the Munich Institute's non-Russian recruits did nothing to boost its claim to scholarly respectability. As the intelligence agent Ryszard Wraga reported, the non-Russians brought into the institute consisted of "journalists," politicians, or "simply graphomaniacs" rather than scholars.[42]

The Munich Institute, then, proved to be of limited use to the CIA, even prior to its exposure to the bruising national polemics of the united front. The really important institution for both the exiles and their Agency patrons was Radio Liberation, and it was there that the future of Amcomlib's émigré entanglements would be decided.

Radio Liberation and the Phantom Center

"Radio Liberation from Bolshevism" began its fiery calls for the overthrow of communist rule on March 1, just days before Stalin's death. It is unclear if anyone was listening. In its early months, the radio's short-wave transmitters were

[40] See Telegram from Stevens and Kelley to W. B. Ballis and Otis B. Swift, October 16, 1953, in Kelley Papers, box 5, fol. 1. The Ukrainian Academy had been lobbying for such changes for some time before. See Memorandum, Su: Conversation of the Ukrainian Free Academy of Sciences with the Institute, G. A. (unidentified), March 14, 1952, in Levine Papers, box 9.

[41] Analiticheskaia zapiska o reorganizatsii Institute po izucheniiu istorii i kul'tury SSSR i sostoianii raboty v nem, January 25, 1955, in V. S. Karpov et al. (eds.), V poiskakh istiny: puti i sud'by vtoroi emigratsii. Sbornik statei i dokumentov (Moscow: Rossiiskii gos. gumanitarnyi universitet, 1997), 349–54.

[42] See Polozhenie i dal'neishie vozmozhnosti de l'Institut pour l'étudie de l'histoire et de la culture d l'URSS, n.d. (1955), 1–2 in HILA, Ryszard Wraga Papers, box 4, fol. 3. An Amcomlib document contained a chart which designated Institute members as either "political" or "non-political." Virtually all the non-Russian scholars belonged to the first category, but many in the "Russian line" were labelled "non-political." Organizational chart for Munich Institute, n d. (1955 or later), in Kelley Papers, box 5, fol. 4.

probably within range of only East Germany, although broadcasts from US facilities in Taiwan might have reached the USSR's Pacific maritime provinces. In any case, Soviet jammers targeted the radio two minutes after it went on air.[43]

As the strong Soviet response suggested, the beginning of broadcasts was a major escalation of American psy-war efforts against the USSR—and therefore a crucial juncture for Amcomlib and its united-front project. From Amcomlib's inception, CIA and State Department planners were insistent that the radio's effectiveness as an instrument of psychological warfare depended on its sponsorship by an émigré political center. As the argument ran, a radio station that operated on behalf of the US government, or even one that expressed an American viewpoint, would be demonized by Soviet propaganda and therefore rejected by the vast majority of Soviet citizens. "In order to win the listener's confidence," Amcomlib's Isaac Patch asserted, "it must be clearly established by terminology and by attitude, that the émigré speaking on Radlib is 'one of us.'"[44] If the station hewed too closely to US government informational policies, it would become an ineffective institution and, given the already existing Russian-language broadcasts of Voice of America, a redundant one.[45] Accordingly, the radio was closely bound up with the political center from the outset.

Amcomlib had little notion of how to proceed once the united front had collapsed. The first instinct of the American Committee's members was to maintain that a political center sponsoring the radio could be revived. At the 1953 meeting with Mel'gunov and Kerenskii mentioned earlier, Kelley claimed that Amcomlib was acting as a "trustee pending the establishment of a political Center."[46] However, Kelley's principled support of the émigré nature of Radio Liberation was already coming under challenge on the ground in Munich, where Amcomlib was hastily constructing a functioning radio station with a team of trained radio personnel brought in from the United States. The Americans pressed their own control over the radio at the expense of exile input, bypassing an exile Radio Commission that had been created at the June 1952 Starnberg Conference. Amcomlib director Stevens approved of marginalizing émigré participation, dubbing the Radio Adviser Manning Williams "dictator of the radio"—a formulation so much at odds with Amcomlib's espoused policy toward exiles that it drew criticism from members of the organization and CIA officials alike.[47]

[43] Johnson, *Radio Free Europe and Radio Liberty*, 32.
[44] Memorandum, Émigré Relations Advisor to Deputy to the President, Europe, January 26, 1955, in Kelley Papers, box 5, fol. 4.
[45] Draft: Brief History of the Munich Organizational Activities, 3, and CIA, State Department, American Committee for Liberation Discussion of Radio Liberty Broadcasting, March 15, 1952, 2–3, in Radio Free Europe and Radio Liberty.
[46] Su: Conversation with Mel'gunov and Kerenskii, 3.
[47] Prist Visit to Europe, March 9–24, 1953, Chief of Base, Munich to Chief EE, April 4, 1953, 3 in NARA, RG 263, Entry ZZ-19, 230/86/26/01, QKACTIVE, box 55, vol. 1.

Stevens's appointment of an American "dictator" to Radio Liberation was not a matter of capriciousness. Under pressure from Washington to produce tangible results, Amcomlib committed to getting the radio on the air at breakneck speed. When the American radio specialists refused to work with the émigrés—finding them to be "without firm leadership or any idea whatsoever about radio operation"—Amcomlib sided with the former rather than the latter.[48] Out of the same need for quick results, Amcomlib utilized radio scripts sent from New York that were produced by a team of writers under Boris Shub, the Russian-American son of a Menshevik, rather than those written by exiles in Munich.[49] Worst of all from the Russian exile perspective, Amcomlib, no longer encumbered by the united front, soon turned to the separatist Ukrainian National Council and Belarusian National Council in order to create and staff national desks at Radio Liberation.[50] The development of the radio showed that Amcomlib would—and, in lieu of the united front, perhaps had to—take a direct role in its political warfare activities, despite its talk about exiles as allies and partners.

The abrupt turn toward American control of Radio Liberation deepened the already pronounced bitterness toward Amcomlib in Russian exile communities. "None of the émigrés have any respect for the American chiefs" at the station, an American Radio Liberation employee overheard in Russian from a nearby table in a Munich restaurant.[51] According to Liberation employee James Critchlow, the exiles employed at the radio saw the Americans as a distant class of power holders, dubbing them *nachal'stvo* (the "bosses") just as they had called their superiors in the Soviet elite.[52] And no wonder. The exiles had been demoted from ostensible controllers of the radio to mere employees of it.

Adding insult to injury was the influx of Americans who took up work at Radio Liberation, part of the rapid growth of the radio's staff in Germany and New York from 23 in 1951 to 320 a year later.[53] The Americans were paid more than the émigré employees, and many of them had neither the genuine interest in Russian culture nor the sense of the exiles' national importance that Amcomlib officials held. In 1953, Kelley complained that many American employees of the radio had come to believe that the "émigré programming staff is intended merely as a façade and that the real programming is to be done by the Americans." Going further, the flown-in Americans, "consciously or unconsciously," saw the exiles

[48] Draft: Brief History of the Munich Organizational Activities, 3.

[49] Mickelson, *America's Other Voice*, 66.

[50] Notably, Amcomlib bypassed the federalist Ukrainian groups that the Russians had sought to include in the political-center project the year before. Memorandum, Robert F. Kelley, n.d. (1955 or later), in Kelley Papers, box 5, fol. 3.

[51] Elizabeth Golden to Isaac Patch, January 5, 1953, in Kelley Papers, box 5, fol. 4.

[52] James Critchlow, *Radio Hole-in-the-head/Radio Liberty: An Insider's Story of Cold War Broadcasting* (Washington, DC: American University Press, 1995), 34.

[53] Mickelson, *America's Other Voice*, 67.

as "second-rate people" or even "punks."[54] Kelley opined that the Americans' attitudes imperiled the radio's entire mission, namely its distinctive identity as an "émigré voice."

The situation, perhaps, was not as starkly negative as Kelley suggested. Certainly, there was no shortage of Russian exiles willing to work in Amcomlib operations. If many were drawn by the promise of a steady income, some exiles also reached the sober realization that they could carry out more meaningful anti-Soviet work in the mammoth American operation—whose yearly budget by the end of the 1950s approached five million dollars—than outside it.[55] Nevertheless, Kelley's criticism of the radio's creeping Americanization was telling, not least because it demonstrated that he was still struggling to maintain the principle of an émigré radio despite the imposition of US control.

The perception that the radio needed to represent the exiles spurred Amcomlib efforts to find some suitable substitute for the united front. To be sure, Amcomlib's conception of working with the émigrés hardened with the fall of the political center. The committee's eleventh-hour gambit at reassembling a political center, a "Working Alliance" proposal in early 1954, attempted to bypass political organizations entirely while also vesting in Amcomlib veto power over exile decisions—strictures the exile politicians rejected point-blank.[56] Despite the collapse of the united front and the ongoing Americanization of the radio, the exile leaders refused to be subordinate themselves to Amcomlib on the grounds that it was a betrayal of their national mission.

The failure of the ill-conceived Working Alliance plan, perhaps surprisingly, still did not exhaust Amcomlib's commitment to the united front. True, Kelley, whose faith in the exiles seemed inexhaustible, did not win support for his proposal that Amcomlib restart the united front talks along lines very similar to the pre-Working Alliance status quo ante.[57] However, another approach seemed more promising. In late 1954, Isaac Patch, whose "perennial optimism" about émigré unification amazed his American colleagues, championed the idea that the Americans should fund two separate exile political centers, one for Russians and one for non-Russians, with only a loose "roof" coordinating their activities.[58] After sending out informal feelers in the different parts of the emigration, Amcomlib staff in Munich discovered that there existed widespread support for the "dual

[54] Confidential: Situations requiring corrective action, no author indicated [Kelley], n.d. (1953), 2–4, in Kelley Papers, box 5, fol. 4.

[55] Cf. Liudmila Flam, "V rakurse proshlogo," in Liudmila Flam (ed.), Sud'by pokoleniia 1920-1930-kh godov v emigratsii: ocherki i vospominaniia (Moscow: Russkii put', 2006), 121. For budget figures, see Briefing Material for Meeting with Howland Sargaent, Cord Meyer, Chief, International Organizations Division to Director of Central Intelligence, February 14, 1957, in QKACTIVE, box 55, vol. 1.

[56] Draft letter to Kelley, 4 and Negotiations for an Effective Partnership, 175–86 and 234–7.

[57] In particular, Kelley pushed for reverting to the older pattern of approaching political organizations and offering them financial support. Robert F. Kelley to L. C. Stevens, June 4, 1954, 2.

[58] Memorandum to the President, Isaac Patch, Su: Suggestions for Action, December 1, 1954, in Levine Papers, box 8. On Patch, see Critchlow, Radio-hole-in-the-Head, 18.

center" approach, largely because it would allow the Russian and non-Russian exile blocs to engage the Americans without cooperating with each other.[59] As Patch saw it, the two-camp framework would allow Amcomlib to continue its patronage of the exile organizations and thereby to achieve the longstanding goal of enlisting exile political forces in its anti-Soviet operations.[60]

Amcomlib's leadership rejected the dual-center plan. Paradoxically, however, opposition to Patch's plan only demonstrated Amcomlib's faith in exile anti-communism. In part, Amcomlib head Stevens was set against Patch's "roof" approach because acknowledging the two exile fronts—which, after all, had formed in contravention of the committee's wishes—would have represented an acceptance of Amcomlib's failure. More importantly, as Stevens had already stated to émigré organizations a year before, "the existence of two centers would solidify differences among partners in a common struggle, perpetuate and probably exacerbate existing animosities and cripple the conduct of an effective struggle against the Bolshevik regime."[61] In addition, the two-centers model would also discredit psychological-warfare projects directed at the Soviet population by giving "formal American recognition to a sharply defined and unbridgeable chasm between Russian and non-Russian peoples which does not in fact exist in the Soviet Union."[62] Clearly, Stevens blocked the two-center approach out of an ongoing belief in the original model of the united-front concept, not because he had come to reject it. Despite repeated failures, Amcomlib remained committed to Kennan's initial vision of sponsoring exile organizations as "centers of national hope" abroad, long after it had become clear that the interests of Russian and non-Russian exile groups were essentially incompatible.

Amcomlib's stubborn attachment to exile politics was even more remarkable given the shifting moods of the committee's backers in Washington. A watershed in this respect was the October 1953 transfer of the Amcomlib project from the CIA's SR Division to its International Organizations (IO) Division. IO head Thomas W. Braden had no sympathy for the political-center idea in general, holding the opinion that Amcomlib's program of using exiles to "weaken and eventually disintegrate" Soviet power "verge[d] on the ridiculous."[63] By mid-1954, Braden had pushed through a revised mission for Amcomlib that decoupled the issue of the radio's effectiveness from its exile sponsorship. Despite the end of the

[59] Memorandum to the President, Su: Views of the Emigration on the Formation of an Anti-Bolshevik Political Center, Émigré Relations Officer, Munich, November 22, 1954, 4–6.

[60] Patch also hoped that the two halves of the united front might eventually move closer together as a result of their practical activities. Memorandum to the President, Isaac Patch, Su: Suggestions for Action, December 1, 1954, 3.

[61] L. C. Stevens to seven organizations, May 4, 1953, 3, in Kelley Papers, box 5, fol. 1.

[62] This is Patch's characterization of a common criticism of his plan. Memorandum to the President, Su: Attached paper entitled "Suggestions for Action," Isaac Patch, December 2, 1954, in Levine Papers, box 8.

[63] CIA Criticism of American Committee for Liberation Mission Statement, April 12, 1954, in Radio Free Europe and Radio Liberty.

united front, the document read, Radio Liberation had become a "hard hitting, direct, tactical weapon in our psychological warfare arsenal."[64] Far from lamenting the demise of the political center, the mission statement identified it as a blessing in disguise, for it freed Amcomlib and its radio "from interference and control of émigré politics."[65] The new anti-émigré line came to a head in late 1954, when the CIA removed Amcomlib director Stevens from the project. His replacement, former Assistant Secretary of State for Public Affairs Howland Sargaent, entered the position with a clear goal of distancing Amcomlib from the exiles. He only accepted the job on the condition that he would not be heading "an organization for the care and feeding of exiles," as he put it in a later interview.[66] Clearly, a stark gulf existed between the visions of Sargaent and Kelley, pictured together in Figure 6.1.[67]

The Amcomlib members' defense of its policy line in the face of CIA opposition underscored how important the exiles were to American notions of liberation. Stevens, Kelley, Patch, and others remained convinced that Russian exiles could issue a more powerful rebuke to the Soviet state than Americans could, and this position was perhaps tempered but not extinguished by the negligible results of the political-center project. As late as 1954, Russian historian and Amcomlib member William Henry Chamberlin still maintained that the "embittered rebels" against Stalin "might someday yield an unexpected harvest," while calling on his readers not to grow discouraged by the "rather naive intrigues and juvenile personal quarrels that crop up in the atmosphere of refugee politics."[68] Ironically, the very anti-communism of Amcomlib's leaders led them to clash with their funders in Washington.

The Changing Soviet Landscape

While Amcomlib was developing its radio operation and negotiating its ties to the exiles, the Soviet target for psy-war was itself shifting. Radio Liberation was born of the unwavering anti-communism of the early Cold War, both émigré and American. Yet by the time it went on the air, the Soviet bloc was set to enter a period of change and instability sparked by the death of Stalin. The first post-Stalin years posed unforeseen challenges to the liberationist program of Amcomlib, while marginalizing the exiles from American power more fundamentally than had the failure of the united front.

---

[64] American Committee for Liberation's Mission Redefined, July 30, 1954, 1–2.
[65] Ibid.
[66] Mickelson, *America's Other Voice*, 70.
[67] Surprisingly, Kelley stayed on as Amcomlib deputy in Europe until his retirement in 1967.
[68] William Henry Chamberlin, "Emigre Anti-Soviet Enterprises and Splits," *Russian Review* no. 2 (1954): 98.

Figure 6.1 Howland Sargaent (left), President of Amcomlib, and Robert F. Kelley, his deputy for Europe, examine incoming news items at the monitoring station in Radio Liberation's Munich offices. Kelley designed the radio as a voice of the anti-communist émigrés, but Sargaent rejected the concept.
Source: Hoover Institution Libraries and Archives.

The months after Stalin's death marked a formative stage for US strategies for fighting the Cold War. Dwight Eisenhower had championed liberationist slogans during the 1952 presidential campaign, lambasting the Truman administration for refusing to fight communism in earnest—quite unfairly, in fact, in light of the program of covert operations it had launched.[69] Once in power, however, Eisenhower moved toward a more "cautious and balanced approach," sidelining the administration's proponents of liberating communist lands through covert operations.[70] The prime cause of this shift was the Kremlin's moderated foreign-policy course. The post-Stalin collective leadership backpedaled from the dictator's collision course with the Western powers, and even showed new flexibility on the German problem that constituted the Gordian knot for the entire Cold War.[71] Although Eisenhower was skeptical of the possibility of negotiating an end to the Cold War, he nevertheless found that the new diplomatic situation dictated restraint.[72] When opportunities to pursue "rollback" or "liberation" in the Soviet bloc in earnest came—first with the workers' uprising in the GDR in 1953 and then with instability and revolution in Poland and Hungary three years later—the United States refused to intervene, in part out of fear that a crumbling Soviet bloc could bring war.[73]

The shifting international situation placed Radio Liberation and other political warfare projects in limbo. In fact, the radio, despite the highly militant tone of its early broadcasts, was ambivalent about how it should respond to unrest in the Soviet bloc. Initial Amcomlib broadcasting policies explained that the radio should "sow the seeds of dissatisfaction" and encourage "the spirit of resistance to exploitation and oppression" among the Soviet people.[74] However, Amcomlib's overseers in the CIA and the State Department instructed Radio Liberation to avoid calls for active unrest in the USSR, which would lead to the repression of radio listeners in the USSR, alienate West Germany, and might even start a war.[75] In theory, Radio Liberation's status as a non-attributable or "gray" propaganda instrument would limit diplomatic fallout from provocative calls to the populace of the Soviet bloc. But in practice, Amcomlib's cover as an initiative of private citizens was weak to begin with—for their part, the exiles held Radio Liberation's governmental ties to be self-evident—and became increasingly implausible as the radio operation grew in size and staff.[76]

---

[69] Peter Grose, *Operation Rollback: America's Secret War behind the Iron Curtain* (Boston: Houghton Mifflin, 2000), 193–4.

[70] Schwartz, *Political Warfare against the Kremlin*, 169. See also Klaus Larres, "Eisenhower and the First Forty Days after Stalin's Death: The Incompatibility of Détente and Political Warfare," *Diplomacy & Statecraft* 6, no. 2 (1995): 431–69.

[71] Vladislav M. Zubok, *A Failed Empire: The Soviet Union in the Cold War from Stalin to Gorbachev* (Chapel Hill: University of North Carolina Press, 2007), 86–101.

[72] At the same time, Eisenhower approached diplomacy with the Soviet Union from the perspective of psychological warfare. Kenneth Alan Osgood, *Total Cold War: Eisenhower's Secret Propaganda Battle at Home and Abroad* (Lawrence: University of Kansas, 2006), 48–66.

[73] László Borhi, "Rollback, Liberation, Containment, or Inaction? U.S. Policy and Eastern Europe in the 1950s," *Journal of Cold War Studies* 1, no. 3 (1999): 70–1.

[74] Radio Liberty Broadcasting Policy, March 28, 1952, 2, in Radio Free Europe and Radio Liberty.

[75] Radio Liberty Objectives Outlined, August 25, 1951, 2, and Radio Liberation Editorial Policies Defined, January 22, 1953, 2, in Radio Free Europe and Radio Liberty.

[76] Surprisingly, Amcomlib's pronouncements presented its goals and those of the US government as virtually one and the same. "Novoe rukovodstvo Amerikanskogo komiteta osvobozhdeniia ot bol'shevizma," *NIVA*, April 16, 1954, in Kelley Papers, box 5, fol. 4. For émigré perceptions, see Weitere

Amcomlib's uncertain approach to liberation was put to the test in June 1953, when workers in East Berlin and across East Germany revolted amidst the country's unremitting Sovietization drive. Amcomlib saw the GDR workers' revolt as an opportunity to put liberationist rhetoric into practice, and used Radio Liberation's airwaves to appeal to Soviet troops stationed in Germany to put down their arms or even to cross over to the insurgents. On June 17, Admiral Stevens sent two cables to Director of Plans Frank Wisner recommending the broadcasting of the following slogans to Soviet troops: "Who are you, soldiers or gendarmes? Who are you, sons of the people or hangmen of the people?"[77] While these highly provocative broadcasts probably did little to damage morale among their troops, they drew the alarm of Soviet authorities.[78]

The radio's chance to exploit unrest in the bloc would not come again. During the Polish and Hungarian crises of late 1956, Radio Liberation received explicit instructions to report "hard facts" and not to inflame the situation. Diplomatic interests came first, with the State Department arguing that the radio should not create the "impression to Soviets that we are counseling or abetting anti-Soviet elements" or give the Soviet military an excuse for taking "harsher repressive measures" against the Hungarians.[79] No doubt articulating the position of the radio's émigré staff on the matter, the CIA officer in charge of Radio Liberation expressed "complete disagreement" with this virtual gag order.[80] He had a point: how could a radio devoted to liberating the USSR from communist rule sit on the fence in times of political instability in the bloc?

Radio Liberation's forced restraint during the Hungarian crisis was bound up with its shift away from exile involvement. As Amcomlib's Howland Sargaent commented on the question of broadcasting on Hungary, "Radlib is so identified as an American voice" that taking an active line on the Hungarian crisis would develop among Soviet listeners "an impression of outside interference" in Soviet affairs.[81] Of course, the identification of the radio as "an American voice" was exactly what the architects of the radio had tried to prevent by creating an émigré radio. In this sense, the 1956 events signified a decisive confirmation that exile sponsorship of the radio was now a moot point.

Ergänzung zum Überblick über die Tätigkeit des "Amerikanischen Komitees für die Befreiung der Völker Russlands," April 1, 1954, 3 in Federal Archives of Germany (Bundesarchiv-Koblenz) B 137, Akte 1021.

---

[77] Memorandum for the Files, Su: American Committee Activity on the East German Riots, June 17, 1953, in QKACTIVE, box 56, vol. 1.

[78] Tass on Voice of America Broadcast. Chapter 11 discusses the impact of the June revolt for émigré covert operations.

[79] Policy Considerations for Radio Liberty Broadcasts, November 2, 1956, 1, in Radio Free Europe and Radio Liberty.

[80] International Operations Division, Guidance to Radio Liberation from New York on Satellite Situation, October 24, 1956, 1, in Radio Free Europe and Radio Liberty.

[81] International Operations Division, Guidance.

Unrest in the bloc, then, discredited the radio's liberationist position. Paradoxically, the growing *stabilization* of the bloc, and particularly of the Soviet regime itself, in the latter years of the decade had the same effect. Against the backdrop of successes of the Khrushchev leadership within the USSR—economic expansion, limited post-Stalin liberalization and an uneven opening of the country to the outside world—Amcomlib's liberation rhetoric appeared increasingly out of place if not anachronistic. In 1956, State Department Russia hand Charles E. "Chip" Bohlen, then ambassador to the USSR, offered a harsh critique of the radio during a meeting with Radio Liberation and VOA managers.[82] Soviet citizens were "accommodating" themselves to the ruling system, Bohlen asserted, and therefore Western propaganda should focus on encouraging evolutionary rather than revolutionary changes in the Soviet Union. "To suggest the possibility of anything like bloodshed or revolution would produce an adverse reaction," he warned. Not stopping at presenting liberation itself as an unrealistic agenda, Bohlen also criticized Amcomlib's reliance on exiles. Of course, Radio Liberation's *raison d'être* had been the assumption that émigrés could influence the moods of the Soviet people. The Soviet "man in the street," Bohlen now argued, "knows little about émigré groups abroad, and has little sympathy for them."[83] In one fell swoop, Bohlen had challenged the radio's self-image as an agent of overthrowing communism as well as the exile connection upon which it relied.

As if Bohlen's sharp critique were not enough, a change in thinking was also afoot within Amcomlib itself from mid-decade. With the gradual opening up of the Soviet system after Stalin's death, Amcomlib developed new sources of information on the USSR that called into question its program of supporting a liberation struggle against Soviet rule. In the late 1950s, the radio launched an Audience Research and Development Department, which employed sophisticated strategies to gain a picture of the radio's audience, including interviewing Soviet travelers abroad, debriefing foreign travelers to the USSR, and soliciting letters from Soviet listeners on air.[84] These limited sources suggested that Soviet citizens had highly divided reactions to Radio Liberation, with some praising the station and identifying with its image of an "émigré station" staffed by "real Russians" and others seeing the very notion of liberation as an "insult."[85] If its results were mixed, audience research nevertheless contradicted Amcomlib's previous view of the

[82] CIA-State Department Reservations about Broadcasting to the Soviet Union, September 6, 1951, 1, in Radio Free Europe and Radio Liberty.

[83] Notes on Conversation with Mr Charles E. Bohlen, April 17, 1956, in Kelley Papers, box 5, fol. 4 and Ambassador Bohlen's Views of Radio Liberation, May 1, 1957, in Radio Free Europe and Radio Liberty. Bohlen had long been skeptical of Kennan's view that covert action could change the Cold War. Gregory Mitrovich, *Undermining the Kremlin: America's Strategy to Subvert the Soviet Bloc, 1947–1956* (Ithaca, NY: Cornell University Press, 2000), 93.

[84] The President's Annual Report to the Board of Trustees, The American Committee for Liberation, Inc., October 7, 1959, 4, in Levine Papers, box 14.

[85] Manager, Audience Research and Evaluation Department to Director of Planning, December 16, 1959, 3, in Kelley Papers, box 5, fol. 4.

USSR as being in a state of "permanent civil war between the rulers, ideologically aliens serving as agents of an international conspiracy" and the anti-communist Soviet peoples, along with the corresponding confidence that liberation from Soviet rule was plausible or even imminent.[86]

The rise of critical voices presaged a wider transformation of Radio Liberation in the late 1950s. Already in the radio's early years, Boris Shub in New York pushed for a less uncompromising line than that of the Munich exiles, calling for the need to speak to the "loyal Soviet citizen" rather than assuming listeners were implacable enemies of the regime.[87] The decisive shift away from liberation came with a review of the radio's Russian programs in 1958, which lambasted their encouragement of "a total and massive overthrow of the Soviet system" and employment of "ironic, contemptuous, didactic, hortatory, denunciatory" and "provocative" tones on the air. Instead, the radio should deliver "more subtle, varied and non-polemic programming" that would "instruct" the Soviet population "through subtle precept and the force of reasonable analysis."[88] A few months later, revised policy guidelines for the radio enshrined this new editorial approach. Given the Soviet population's basic acceptance of the regime, it was stressed, the goal of the radio was to "stimulate independent thought among its listeners." To this end, the radio "must establish a reputation of complete reliability," presenting news and commentaries that were "scrupulously accurate."[89] The diminishment of ambition from inciting revolt to spurring freer thinking among Soviet citizens found expression in the name change from Radio Liberation to Radio Liberty in 1959.[90]

The moderation of the radio's editorial line severed the American Committee's close association with the exiles, whose role as mouthpieces for anti-communist nations was cast into doubt. By the end of the 1950s, collaboration with émigrés was almost an afterthought to the American Committee, with "émigré relations work" taking up only 3 to 4 percent of its annual budget.[91] Some American employees of the Amcomlib operations even came to see the involvement of exiles as a liability. In 1959, Francis U. Macy, then acting deputy director of the Radio Programming Division, argued that Radio Liberty should seek the "support and association of well-known and well-respected organizations and individuals in

---

[86] The World's Dilemma and a Way Out: Liberation of the Peoples of the Soviet Union, declaration by Amcomlib, n.d. (1954), 9, in Levine Papers, box 10.

[87] Sosin, *Sparks of Liberty*, 8.

[88] Radio Liberty Broadcasts Reviewed, March 6, 1958, 1, in Radio Free Europe and Radio Liberty.

[89] Radio Liberty Broadcasting Policy Guidelines, May 1, 1958, 2–3, 9, in Radio Free Europe and Radio Liberty.

[90] Cummings, *Cold War Radio*, 26–8.

[91] Meanwhile, roughly one half the work Amcomlib *did* do with exiles was "defensive" in nature—in other words, activities directed toward addressing challenges on the exile front—rather than "offensive" work aiming to influence Soviet or world public opinion. Amconfidential: A Review of ACL Émigré Relations Work: Summary, no author indicated, n.d., in Kelley Papers, box 5, fol. 4.

America and Europe" in an effort to weaken the perception that it was "a band of irresponsible, fanatic émigrés."[92]

Amcomlib's dissociation from the émigrés, to be sure, was never complete. Exiles were still the bedrock of Radio Liberty staff, even if they came to work under ever closer US control in the course of the 1950s.[93] In the new situation, however, the radio no longer stressed the exiles' national liberationist mission. Insofar as the radio's broadcasts touched on exiles, their focus had shifted from the second wave to the first and from anti-Soviet politics to cultural matters. For instance, some of the broadcast programs that radio managers deemed most effective were the work of first-wave exiles, including the Menshevik Iurii Petrovich Denike and writer Vladimir Vasil'evich Veidle—both, importantly, highly pro-Western thinkers.[94] Moreover, the second-wavers had the disadvantage of having left the country during—or, for the Vlasovites, fighting on the wrong side of—the Great Patriotic War, which became enshrined as a linchpin of Soviet ideology in the postwar years.[95] If the second-wavers had seemed to be ideal recruits for delivering anti-communist broadsides, intellectuals of the first wave seemed better equipped for the new mission of giving Soviet citizens lessons in "independent thought."

In 1960, one Radio Liberty employee took further the notion of the emigration as a cultural, non-political construct. He suggested a focus on the "common heritage" between the radio's broadcasters and listeners, positing that the radio might replicate the appeal of Irish American societies.[96] A position further from the exile anti-communist language that had gone on the air in 1953 could hardly be imagined.

*　*　*

In 1955, the NTS's Aleksandr Nikolaevich Zaitsev-Artemov called Amcomlib a "strange institution" that "does not know what it wants," despite holding endless "negotiations on agreements and agreements on negotiations."[97] Artemov's harsh verdict was perhaps unfair, especially as his NTS had itself contributed to the confusion and failure of Amcomlib's policies. Nevertheless, he was correct that

---

[92] Memorandum for the Record, Su: Radio Liberty Image and Unique Capabilities, Acting Deputy Director, RPD, December 18, 1959, in Kelley Papers, box 5, fol. 3.

[93] On the gradual imposition of tighter editorial guidelines on Radio Liberty's Russia Desk, see Radio Liberty Broadcasts Reviewed.

[94] See the praise in Radio Liberty Russian Broadcasts Reviewed, 2. On these programs, see also Critchlow, *Radio Hole-in-the-Head*, 20–3. Antoshin, *Rossiiskie emigranty*, 398–400, describes Denike and Weidle as "Westernizers."

[95] Audience Research and Development Department reports suggested that Soviet citizens were mistrustful of exiles who left during the war. East-West Report #2, Special Projects Office, Radio Liberty, January 17, 1960, 1 in Levine Papers, box 14.

[96] Proposed New Radio Image and some of its Implications, Policy and Planning Advisor to the President, January 11, 1960, in Kelley Papers, box 5, fol. 4.

[97] Review of the Russian Émigré Press, Radio Liberation, vol. III, no. 42, October 26, 1955, 3, in Levine Papers, box 15.

Amcomlib was confused about its own mission and how to pursue it. Amcomlib's agenda had rested on several assumptions that proved to be flawed and even naïve: that exiles on the right and left could be coaxed into burying their differences; that the Russian and non-Russian exile groups could cooperate; that the committee would or even could treat exiles as allies rather than underlings; and that radio broadcasting carried out under US auspices could nevertheless express a "Russian" point of view. Soon these different positions were undermined as the united front broke down and the radio came to function independently of émigré organizations. Yet the American Committee sought to maintain its original pro-exile positions, leading to the flurry of proposals and initiatives that Artemov ridiculed.

Amcomlib's slow and uncertain turn away from its original mission was even more remarkable when considered in the context of US policies. The doubts voiced by Washington officials grew after months of fruitless exile negotiations, with the CIA placing in doubt the entire rationale of pursuing psy-war through émigrés. Yet the American Committee only abandoned the united-front plan conclusively when faced with unalterable facts on the ground: the emergence of a distinctly American radio operation in Radio Liberation, the appointment of a new Amcomlib head with little interest in exile matters, and, ultimately, the ebbing of the liberationist cause with the shifts of the Cold War.

The uneasiness of Amcomlib's divorce from the exiles derived from the agenda of its members, anti-communist activists whose conviction that exiles could challenge the Soviet state persisted even when circumstances, and perhaps common sense, dictated a new approach. The Amcomlib members' faith in the émigré center and the plausibility of a Russian radio had a doctrinaire quality that bore some resemblance to the thinking of the anti-communist exiles with whom they were engaged. An example of this commonality came in 1958, when Amcomlib veteran Isaac Don Levine wrote a scathing report on the radio's Russian broadcasts, accusing them of turning a broadcaster "designed as the voice of militant anti-Communism" into "an effective adjunct of the [Soviet] Voice of Moscow."[98] In the course of the 1950s both Amcomlib members and Russian exiles found their anti-communist stances blunted by a more sober US foreign policy, itself a product of an increasingly stabilized bipolarity in Cold War Europe.

Amcomlib's political course calls into question common narratives on the CIA's role in Cold War psychological warfare. As noted above, existing English-language accounts have tended to stress the deft strategies of Radio Liberation in countering Soviet power as well as the harmonious cooperation between the American Committee and the CIA.[99] Rather more fitting is the perspective offered

---

[98] Isaac Don Levine to Howland Sargaent, March 15, 1958, 20, in CREST: General CIA Records, Document Number (FOIA)/ESDN (CREST): CIA- CIA-RDP80B01676R004200090037-9.
[99] See the literature referenced in note 5 of this chapter.

by recent literature on the role of networks and civil society in US political warfare.[100] The CIA often operated through fronts such as Amcomlib during the Cold War, an arrangement that both granted the Agency plausible deniability and provided an appealing cover of popular support for the agendas it supported. As Lowell Schwartz has posited, the CIA acted somewhat like a philanthropic foundation rather than an intelligence agency in its handling of false-front operations, dispersing money to what it deemed worthy causes while exercising fairly loose oversight.[101] The predictable result of such an indirect approach to psychological warfare was that fronts tended to act quite independently, pursuing their ideological agendas without strict top-down control. The resistance of Amcomlib to giving up its pro-exile line in the face of pressures from Washington provides an illustration of the agency wielded by CIA fronts, in this case by the anti-communist activists and intellectuals who championed Russian liberation.

Amcomlib's émigré project, it is true, was eventually discredited. Yet this did not exhaust the relevance of Russian exiles for advancing American interests in the Cold War. While plans for a Russian liberation committee abroad proved chimerical, exiled anti-communists, including some who had been involved with Amcomlib, occupied roles within more secretive CIA projects against the Soviet bloc. The development of a covert operational front in Germany would bring both new opportunities and new dangers for the Russian anti-communists as well as for their US patrons.

---

[100] Helen Laville and Hugh Wilford (eds.), *The US Government, Citizen Groups and the Cold War: The State-private Network* (London: Routledge, 2012).
[101] Schwartz, *Political Warfare against the Kremlin*, 124.

PART III
THE CIA OPERATIONAL FRONT

7

From Revolution to Provocation

The NTS and CIA Covert Operations

In December 1950, V. M. Baidalakov delivered a report to the Council of the National Labor Alliance (NTS) in Germany. He offered his fellow exiles a glowing account of the progress of the NTS's fight against communism on Soviet soil. The influence of the NTS in the USSR was growing, he explained; after being exposed to its message through radio or print propaganda, Soviet citizens were spontaneously affiliating themselves (*"samopriemom"*) to the organization. Meanwhile, the NTS was creating a network of more structured cells in the USSR that he called the "Carcass," which would carry out propaganda operations and eventually act as a "detonator" for an uprising against the Soviet regime.[1]

Baidalakov's claims about the existence of underground NTS cells in the USSR became a leitmotif in the years that followed, when the organization he headed carried out covert operations for the CIA and British MI6. Yet the NTS leader's account of the organization's exploits in the homeland was strikingly misleading. Contrary to Baidalakov's claims, in the early 1950s the organization had virtually no presence in the USSR and only a limited ability to operate in East Germany.[2] Baidalakov's boasting belonged to an NTS tradition of using posturing and misinformation about its capabilities as a strategy for building its reputation in exile and for gaining hard-won subsidies from foreign intelligence services.

The gap between assertion and reality is crucial for understanding the NTS's activities on the covert operational front during the early Cold War. The infusion of CIA money and operational abilities did not help the NTS construct the underground network on Soviet soil that Baidalakov heralded. In particular, the "Carcass," which was in fact a codename for a CIA operation that infiltrated the Alliance's agents into the USSR, resulted in complete failure as successive waves of air-dropped agents were seized by Soviet security services. Making matters worse, the NTS plunged into internal disarray, as the Solidarists divided along generational and ideological lines amid widespread fears of internal betrayal.

---

[1] Protokoly S'ezda Soveta NTS v dekabre 1950 g., 2, in Georgetown University Archives and Special Collections, Victor M. Baydalakoff Collection (hereinafter Baydalakoff Collection), box 1, fol. 1.

[2] Chief FDS/West to Chief, FDS, December 15, 1950, in National Archives and Records Administration (NARA), RG 263, Entry ZZ-19, 230/86/25/03, box 24, AESAURUS/AENOBLE (hereinafter AESAURUS), vol. 1, pt. 1.

Cold War Exiles and the CIA: Plotting to Free Russia. Benjamin Tromly, Oxford University Press (2019). © Benjamin Tromly.
DOI: 10.1093/oso/9780198840404.001.0001

The distance between the claims and achievements of the NTS had a paradoxical outcome. The CIA responded to the disappointing results of its NTS operations by rethinking its use of the Russian organization as an instrument of psychological warfare. Paradoxically, the new CIA strategy embraced the kind of bluffing and boasting in which the NTS leaders such as Baidalakov customarily engaged. In the new arrangement, the CIA attempted to boost the reputation of the NTS and its supposed revolutionary exploits as a means of putting the Soviet government on the defensive and provoking it into costly reactions. In the situation that resulted, the NTS came to play a role in the Cold War as a myth, an image of a powerful anti-Soviet Russian organization that bore little resemblance to reality.

Subversive Adventures

The CIA's decision to back the NTS was hardly inevitable. The organization had never been fully trusted in intelligence circles. In 1946, an agent of the Strategic Services Unit (SSU), the immediate predecessor to the CIA, asserted that Soviet agents had penetrated the NTS to some extent and even exercised "a certain amount of control" over it.[3] The CIA's thinking shifted drastically in 1949–50 in the context of the heating up of the Cold War, marked by communist victory in China, the first Soviet nuclear tests, and then the onset of the Korean War. With war potentially around the corner, the Truman administration, and particularly the Pentagon and commanders in Europe, pressed for improving the CIA's very limited intelligence on the USSR and creating subversion plans for wartime.[4] And despite its checkered reputation, the NTS seemed capable of providing a rare resource: Soviet exiles who were willing to undertake illegal agent missions to the USSR.[5] For these reasons, the CIA agreed in 1951 to fund an NTS project (carrying the cryptonym AEROSOL, later changed to AESAURUS) that included several initiatives: propaganda activities designed to encourage defection among Soviet forces in occupied Germany and Austria, the establishment of an anti-Soviet radio station, and—what was of paramount interest to the Americans – "Operation Carcass," which infiltrated agents directly into Soviet territory.[6]

The American experience of supporting the NTS was conflict-ridden from the outset. Perhaps distrust was to be expected between the intelligence operatives of

[3] Front Saint to Saint, Amzon, August 12, 1946, in NARA, RG 263, Entry ZZ-18, 230/86/23/04, box 77, Viktor Larionoff, vol. 1. See also Stephen Dorril, *MI6: Inside the Covert World of Her Majesty's Secret Intelligence Service* (New York: Free Press, 2000), 422–3.

[4] Harry Rositzke, "America's Secret Operations: A Perspective," *Foreign Affairs* 53, no. 2 (1975): 336.

[5] In espionage argot, an "illegal" agent is one operating without official cover. Discussions with Mr Angleton and [ ] regarding NTS, a report sent to Chief, FDS on September 14, 1950, 1 in AESAURUS, vol. 1, pt. 1.

[6] Narrative Summary of AIS Relationship with NTS, n.d., 1 in AESAURUS, vol. 1, pt. 1.

the new democratic superpower and exiles connected to a far-right ideological movement. Moreover, the Solidarists fought to maximize CIA funding while minimizing outside control—or, as one Agency official put it bluntly, to "take us for all they can get."[7] Meanwhile, a dispute arose over the intended use of NTS Carcass agents on Soviet soil. Self-styled revolutionaries, the NTS leaders refused to let their members engage in what they saw as the demeaning enterprise of traditional intelligence-gathering. Conversely, the CIA was dubious about the NTS's intention to use infiltrated agents to create revolutionary cells in the USSR. CIA officials did not believe that the NTS would pose a serious threat to Soviet power anytime soon.[8] If Carcass agents were to begin "laying on a leaflet campaign," the Americans reasoned, they would immediately be captured. In the end, a compromise emerged, with the agents instructed to focus on legalizing themselves in the USSR and collecting "operational intelligence" while refraining from revolutionary agitation until a more promising political environment emerged.[9]

What did the CIA-NTS operations accomplish? Evaluating the results of AESAURUS is complicated by the NTS's dishonest accounts of its own activities—what one knowledgeable observer, Ryszard Wraga, called a deliberate "misinformation campaign" pursued against its foreign backers.[10] The most poignant NTS fabrication was the "molecular theory" of revolution that V. D. Poremskii unveiled in 1949, which held that the NTS center abroad was creating revolutionary "molecules" of two to three individuals in the homeland whose only link to the foreign center would be the consumption of "one-way communications." Shielded from detection by the Soviet state, the molecules would be ready to mount a rebellion at an opportune moment.[11] Of course, the "molecular theory" was deceptive, as it held that the NTS's influence in the USSR was inherently invisible and unverifiable.

---

[7] Commentary on memoranda prepared by NTS on creation of central Carcass school, n.d. and no author indicated, in AESAURUS, vol. 1, pt. 1. It is impossible to estimate the amount of CIA expenditure on NTS operations. Monetary sums are excised from virtually all available CIA documents, along with the names of the vast majority of CIA operatives. In May 1952, roughly a year after the CIA-NTS operations had been agreed upon, some $114,000 had been spent on the sub-operations Carcass, Spain, and Radio. Su: Summary and Evaluation of the Relationship of the NTS to CIA, Chief, SR/W to Chief, SR, May 20, 1952, 3 in AESAURUS, vol. 1, pt. 1.

[8] In this sense, the operation hardly constituted a "rollback" scheme. Compare with David C. S. Albanese, "'It Takes a Russian to Beat a Russian': the National Union of Labor Solidarists, Nationalism, and Human Intelligence Operations in the Cold War," *Intelligence and National Security* 32, no. 6 (2017): 782.

[9] Discussion of Carcass with CABOCHE 7, September 10, 1951, 4 in AESAURUS, vol. 1, pt. 1.

[10] Effort to Analyse Soviet Provocation and Inspiration in Recent Years in Western Europe and Role in such Provocation Activity of Émigré Political Organisations, 7–8, August 13, 1954, in AEVIRGIL, vol. 1.

[11] V. D. Poremskii, *Strategiia antibol'shevitskoi emigratsii: izbrannye stat'i, 1934–1997* (Moscow: "Posev," 1998).

By contrast, the ineffective and tragic outcomes of the Carcass infiltration operations were clear enough. On May 27, 1953, the Soviet press announced the capture, trial for espionage, and execution of four Russian exiles who had parachuted into Soviet Ukraine from unmarked planes.[12] The four were Carcass agents, and they had been discovered soon after landing thanks to unspecified "measures taken by the Ministry of Internal Affairs."[13] Adding insult to injury, the Soviets provided a "candid exposé" of the entire Carcass operation, replete with details of the agents' recruitment and training and the identities of their American trainers and case officers.[14] (The embarrassment caused by these revelations was tempered by the American press, which responded with incredulity to truthful Soviet claims that these and other captured parachutists were, in fact, American agents.)[15] In the following years, the Soviet propaganda machine periodically "surfaced" additional CIA-infiltrated NTS agents, leaving the Agency to gradually piece together that all the Carcass agents maintaining radio contact from the USSR had been captured and "played back" to them by the Soviets.[16] Trying to gain some minimal benefit from the project, the Americans undertook lengthy radio games with these turned agents that served little purpose other than providing an opportunity to study the methods of Soviet foreign intelligence up close.[17]

The CIA was at a loss to explain the failure of the Carcass operation. Investigations after the first capture of agents posited that the low-flying planes had been spotted entering Soviet airspace, but they were unable to rule out the possibility of "internal betrayal."[18] In retrospect, the latter scenario seems almost certainly to have been the case. How else could all eight agents sent in a "cycle" of the operations, including those whose capture the Soviet government advertised, be apprehended virtually overnight? The possibility that the operations were betrayed to Moscow by British master spy Kim Philby—as many similar CIA infiltration operations of the Soviet bloc were—seems unlikely, for he was already under suspicion of betrayal in 1951.[19] Instead, the more likely scenario is that Soviet counterintelligence penetrated the operation from the émigré side.

---

[12] See the detailed reconstruction of the operation in Albanese, "It Takes a Russian to Beat a Russian."

[13] "USSR Executes four Spies of U.S.," USSR International Service, May 27, 1953, in AESAURUS, vol. 2, pt. 1.

[14] See analysis of *Izvestiia* (no. 279) of November 25, 1955, in AESAURUS, vol. 3, pt. 1.

[15] See O. J. Cutler, "4 'U.S. Spies' Tell All on Moscow TV Show," *The Washington Post and Times Herald*, February 7, 1957, A6.

[16] Memorandum for Chief, SR Division, re. Termination of Project AENOBLE, October 13, 1959, in AESAURUS, vol. 3, pt. 1.

[17] General Evaluation of Operational Intelligence Produced by AENOBLE Cases, October 28, 1955, in AESAURUS, vol. 3, pt. 1.

[18] Investigation of the Capture of CACCOLAS 10, 20, 21 and 28, Chief of Mission, Frankfurt to Chief SR, July 7, 1953, in AESAURUS, vol. 3, pt. 1.

[19] For speculations about Philby, see William Sloane Coffin, *Once to Every Man: A Memoir* (New York: Athenaeum, 1977), 112, and Grose, *Operation Rollback*, 159–60, 170–2. Similarly, the

There is no doubt that Soviet intelligence infiltrated the NTS, just as they had the Vlasovite organizations discussed in Chapter 2. In mid-1953, soon after the first group of Carcass agents was seized, the CIA uncovered a Soviet mole in the NTS leadership who was convicted by a US military court for treason. In 1948, Soviet Army Captain Nikita Khorunzhii fled from the East zone of Germany with a German bride-to-be. Soon thereafter, Soviet intelligence recruited him by threatening his new wife's relatives as well as the family he had left behind in Russia.[20] Receiving orders to penetrate the NTS, Khorunzhii, who had taken the name Georg Müller to hide his identity, quickly earned the confidence of its leaders and received an appointment as an instructor in its "cadre school," a party training establishment in Bad Homburg that funneled Alliance members to the CIA for recruitment as agents.[21] While it remains unclear whether Khorunzhii-Müller was in a position to betray the entirety of the Carcass operations, he did provide detailed information on agent candidates and instructors at the cadre school.[22] Apparently, Khorunzhii's testimony led to the identification of two more Soviet agents in the school, suggesting that the Soviet penetration of the CIA-NTS complex was extensive.[23]

Khorunzhii's exposure by a fellow agent had tumultuous consequences for the CIA-NTS collaboration. Alongside the loudly publicized capture of agents, evidence that the cadre school had been compromised forced the CIA to undertake a lengthy series of security investigations that postponed the training of future NTS agents for Carcass operations.[24] Moreover, the Khorunzhii affair raised suspicions of treason within the NTS, an organization that was already sliding into internal discord.

suggestion made by an NTS historian that Soviet agent George Blake betrayed the NTS operations is doubtful, as Blake was still in captivity in North Korea when the operations were planned. Andrei Okulov, "Polupravda s Lubianki," *Posev* no. 4 (1615) (2012): 25–6, and Roger Hermiston, *The Greatest Traitor: The Secret Lives of Agent George Blake* (London: Aurum Press, 2013), 252. This is not to deny that Philby, in particular, did betray many of the CIA's Soviet operations. By the estimate of an official CIA historian, "at least" 75 percent of the eight-five agents infiltrated into the USSR through "RED-SOX" operations (those involving the illegal return of defectors and émigrés to USSR) "disappeared from sight and failed in their missions." Kevin Conley Ruffner, "*Eagle and Swastika*: CIA and *Nazi* War Criminals and Collaborators," 15, Draft Working Paper, History Staff, Central Intelligence Agency, Washington, DC, April 2003, CIA FOIA Electronic Reading Room.

[20] Nigel West, *Historical Dictionary of Cold War Counterintelligence* (Lanham, MD: Scarecrow Press, 2007), 175.

[21] Proposals for Resumption of Cycle C, September 1953, 1–2 in AESAURUS, vol. 2 pt. 2.

[22] See a report Khorunzhii-Müller issued to his Soviet handler soon before his capture, which somehow came into the hands of NTS leaders. Avgustovskii raport G. Miullera, December 1953, in Baydalakoff Collection, box 3, fol. 5. For further evidence that the KGB had detailed knowledge of NTS agents trained by the CIA, see Nachal'nik 1 upravleniia USSR polk. Zhivaga to MVD USSR, 8 August 1953, in Haluzevyi derzhavnyi arkhiv Sluzhby Bezpeky Ukrainy fond 1, opys 1, sprava 1678137-38, Zhivaga. Thanks to Joshua Sanborn for this source.

[23] Dorogoi drug, G. Ia. Kiverov, and seven other NTS oppositionists, January 10, 1955, in Baydalakoff Collection, box 2, fol. 2.

[24] Proposals for Resumption of Cycle C, 1.

The Solidarists Divided

CIA-NTS covert operations contributed to an internal crisis brewing in the NTS. Starting in the late 1940s, groups of NTS members in different countries voiced opposition to what they saw as the authoritarianism, lack of ideological commitment, and dubious allegiances of the Alliance's leadership. In 1955, this internal rift reached a climax when Baidalakov, head of the NTS since the 1930s, made common cause with the opposition. After failing to convene a congress of the entire NTS to retake control over the reigning Executive Bureau, Baidalakov left the organization to form a splinter Russian National Labor Alliance (RNTS). This internal split dealt a serious blow to the NTS, driving away some of its most committed cadres and tarnishing its image in the Russian diaspora.[25]

As with most exile conflicts, the internal NTS battle of the 1950s had ideological, generational, and personal components. As the struggle was commonly framed at the time, a group of "pragmatic types" (*deloviki*)—which controlled the Alliance's leading bodies and eventually emerged triumphant in 1955—sought to pursue revolutionary activity against the USSR, while an oppositional camp of "spiritualizers" (*dukhovniki*) focused on ideological training and cultural work in the emigration.[26] The dominant "pragmatic" NTS faction was led by E. R. Ostrovskii-Romanov, a second-wave exile from Dnipropetrovsk who had worked for the pro-Nazi newspaper *Novoe slovo* ("New Word") in Berlin. After the war, Romanov became editor of the Alliance's main publication *Posev* (the Sowing) and a leader of the Alliance's Operational Staff, the committee that controlled secret or "operative" work. Taking advantage of the influence and control over purse strings that these two positions brought, Romanov built up his own personal power in the NTS, gradually outmaneuvering Baidalakov, the nominal head of the organization.[27]

Romanov used his role as de facto leader to press the Alliance toward pursuing revolution in Russia, a line that placed emphasis on covert work on "the front" in Germany instead of the many other chapters of the NTS around the globe. Controversially, Romanov directed the NTS and *Posev* to focus on producing propaganda materials intended for a Soviet audience. For instance, *Posev*'s ideological pronouncements eschewed Alliance traditions by de-emphasizing the

---

[25] E. R. Ostrovskii-Romanov estimated that 20 percent of the NTS joined the opposition. Even more of its members abandoned the troubled organization without taking sides in the dispute. See Ostrovskii-Romanov in "Zametki o soiuze," *Za Rossiiu*, no. 335–336 (2001), http://ntsrs.ru/con tent/zametki-o-soyuze, accessed 17 July 17, 2014.

[26] For an example of this terminology, see Iurii Slepukhin, "Krushenie odnoi kontseptsii," *Novoe russkoe slovo*, April 26, 1955.

[27] Baidalakov later alleged that Romanov conspired against him by strengthening the Operational Staff at the expense of the Alliance's other bodies and by modifying the NTS regulations (*ustav*) to strip power from the office of Alliance chairman. K istorii zakhvata NTS Evgeniem Romanovichem Romanovym-Ostrovskim, n.d., in Baydalakoff Collection, box 1, fol. 9.

organization's attachment to Orthodox Christianity and by proclaiming that Soviet elites—including secret policemen—would prove faithful servants of a post-Soviet Russia and could therefore become members of the NTS in the present.[28]

The "spiritualizers" saw the ostensibly "pragmatic" course of the postwar NTS as an abandonment of the organization's ideological purpose. In sharp contrast to Romanov's group, they were committed to Solidarism as a comprehensive world-view, arguing that only serious ideas could defeat Bolshevism and ensure the cohesion and moral stature of the Alliance itself.[29] As a 1947 letter from Solidarists in Hamburg put it, the leadership's pursuit of revolution at all costs and the principle that the NTS "exists only for the organization of the struggle" led inexorably to a "degeneration of the very essence of the Alliance" in the direction of "bureaucracy and compulsion," "party-mindedness and demagogy."[30] By the early 1950s, many Solidarists had decided that Romanov was pursuing nothing less than the construction of "Bolshevism under a different sign."[31] In seeking to explain the NTS's current crisis, "spiritualizers," many of whom hailed from the old emigration, pointed to generational differences: the Alliance had erred in accepting large numbers of Soviet citizens during the war, "littering its ranks with an element that is alien in spirit."[32] Romanov and his second-wave émigré allies appeared to them fundamentally Soviet in their culture and outlook. When Romanov addressed an NTS audience in 1952 as "comrades," a group of prominent Solidarists in New York wrote to headquarters in Frankfurt asking if *Posev* was still "ours" at all.[33]

The already familiar trend of exile waves carrying different worldviews was not the sole or even the main cause of the NTS internal crisis. The tidy division of Solidarists into *deloviki* and *dukhovniki* or second- and first-wave exiles is misleading; several of Romanov's opponents had been involved in secret work and some belonged to the second wave.[34] The very term "spiritualizers" represented an attempt by Alliance leaders to discredit their opponents as ineffectual émigré

[28] O Poseve: vyderzhki iz pisem kadrov Sev. Amerikanskogo Otdela, July 7, 1952, in FSO, 01–098 Tarasova, kor. Poremskii.
[29] Dmitrii Shul'gin, speech to Washington, DC NTS Division, September 15, 1953, 2, in Baydalakoff, box 1, fol. 3.
[30] Pis'mo pervoe, unknown author in Hamburg, July 12, 1947, in FSO, 01–098 Tarasova, kor. 6.
[31] Speech by Baidalakov to the NTS Council, June 1952, 5, in Baydalakoff Collection, box 1, fol. 1.
[32] Slepukhin, "Krushenie odnoi kontseptsii."
[33] NTS members in New York to Baidalakov, November 4, 1952, in National Alliance of Russian Solidarists: Correspondence and Photographs, 1930–1982 (M1909), Department of Special Collections and University Archives, Stanford University Libraries (hereinafter National Alliance of Russian Solidarists), box 1, fol. 2.
[34] Operational Headquarters cadres who came out against the NTS leadership included A. N. Tenson, B. B. Martino, and E. E. Pozdeev. A prominent second-wave critic of Romanov was N. I. Osipov.

intellectuals uninterested in revolution.[35] In fact, the more important context for the NTS split was the intelligence war in which the organization was engaged. The crucial basis of Romanov's power—in particular, the reason the salaried NTS activists in Germany rallied around him—was his position of power in the Operational Staff (*Operativnyi shtab*) that carried out covert operations for the CIA and British MI6.[36]

Paradoxically, the CIA paved the way for factional warfare within the organization it sponsored. To be sure, granting a small group of people, in this case the divisive Romanov and his associates, an exclusive right to handle ties to the Agency made operational sense. Whether the CIA could have pursued its relations with the NTS in any other way is doubtful given the general suspicion many Solidarists felt toward work with intelligence services. For example, a 1954 letter to Baidalakov from several oppositionists called for ensuring the NTS's "independence from foreign factors" through the subordination of the Operational Staff to the Alliance's "public opinion"—a demand that, if ever implemented, would have made further US support of the organization impossible.[37]

Even if the CIA had no other courses of action, its mode of handling the NTS deepened the Alliance's internal woes. Most of all, by limiting its support of the NTS to a small group of salaried leaders in Frankfurt, the CIA sparked recriminations among the often impecunious wider membership of the organization that pursued semi-public activities in the diaspora.[38] Making matters worse, Romanov and his allies—perhaps operating on CIA instructions—erected a wall of secrecy around the NTS Operational Staff, which hid its budget from even top-ranking Solidarist leaders.[39] All of this created the perception that the NTS leaders in Frankfurt were power-hungry and cynical bureaucrats who held the Alliance's wider membership in contempt.

The CIA's role in the NTS split was indirect and likely inadvertent, as the Agency's actions during the 1955 fracture suggest. When the opposition splintered from the parent organization to form the RNTS, the CIA funded both groupings for a time—a hedging of bets that perhaps demonstrated genuine confusion in the Agency over the political loyalties of both sides in this murky émigré dispute.[40] In

[35] For an example of the politicized use of "spiritualizer" language, see *Vestnik Ispol'nitel'nogo Biuro Soveta NTS*, March 31, 1952, 2.
[36] The Operational Staff was sometimes known as the Closed Sector (*Zakrytyi sektor*). Opposition to Romanov was most extensive in the NTS organizations in the United States, Argentina, Australia, and Morocco, far from the covert operations that were based in Germany. B. V. Prianishnikov, O revoliutsionnoi deiatel'nosti Natsional'no-trudovogo soiuza, New York, 1957, 33, in HILA, Boris V. Prianishnikov papers, box 5, fol. 13, and Iu. Chikarleev, *Tragediia NTS: epizod tainoi voiny* (New York: International University Book Exchange Service, 1987), 65.
[37] E. I. Mamukov et al. to the NTS Council, January 18, 1954, 3, in Baydalakoff Collection, box 1, fol. 3.
[38] *Dorogoi drug*, 3–4.
[39] Obsuzhdenie doklada Ispol'nitel'nogo Biuro, January 20, 1951, in Baydalakoff Collection, box 1, fol. 1.
[40] Director to Frankfurt, Munich, Berlin, Bonn, January 17, 1958, in AEVIRGIL, vol. 1.

contrast, the Soviet role in disabling the NTS was more direct and deliberate. Beyond a doubt, Soviet counterintelligence not only welcomed but actively worked to bring about the acrimonious divorce within the NTS. Following tactics discussed in Chapter 2 with regard to the Vlasovites, Soviet counterintelligence battled the NTS by promoting its internal "corruption" (*razlozhenie*) through the stoking of "mistrust and mutual accusations" within its ranks.[41]

Although many sources remain declassified, one can reconstruct the overall contours of the Soviet effort to subvert the NTS. By exposing the Carcass operations they had thwarted, Soviet counterintelligence accomplished several goals at once: fanning suspicions of the NTS leadership among its members, compromising the Alliance in the eyes of its CIA backers, and, perhaps most important, casting doubt on the ability of the US intelligence service to operate on Soviet soil.[42] Without a doubt, the Carcass mishap struck at the NTS's overall morale, and especially its reserve of idealistic young cadres willing to risk their lives for the cause. Already prior to the debacle, fear that Soviet power was unshakable meant that there was only an "insignificant percent" of Solidarists willing to volunteer for secret work, as NTS activist Ariadna Evgen'evna Shirinkina reported from Brussels in 1948.[43] The specter of Soviet infiltration in the thwarting of Carcass multiplied such doubts and fears and thereby shrank the pool of volunteers for secret work further.[44] Ironically, the exposure of Khorunzhii—on the face of things a victory for the CIA—served the same end of creating mistrust in the NTS.[45]

The NTS leadership's reactions to the widely publicized setbacks on the operational front only added to the suspicions within the organization's ranks. The official line of its leaders was that the NTS's presence in Russia was growing and revolution was near, and any questioning of the leadership was angrily rebuffed as playing into the hands of the NTS's enemies.[46] Moreover, exposure of Soviet moles in the organization was asserted to be "a normal consequence of the growth and importance of the activities of the Alliance."[47] Forced to reconcile the leadership's claim of virtual infallibility with evidence of the Alliance's failures and vulnerability to infiltration, some Solidarists decided that the entire edifice of

[41] Dienstanweisung Nr. 4/69, Ministerium für Staatssicherheit, July 30, 1969, 14, in HILA, John O. Koehler Papers, box 21, fol. 7.

[42] Prianishnikov, O revoliutsionnoi deiatel'nosti, 100.

[43] A. E. Shirinkina to V. M. Baidalakov, August 22, 1948, in FSO, 01–098 Tarasova, kor. 38.

[44] On the shortage of NTS agent candidates for AEROSOL operations in 1954, see Project Outline: AESAURUS/AENOBLE, n.d., 1 in AESAURUS, vol. 3, pt. 1.

[45] Prianishnikov, O revoliutsionnoi deiatel'nosti, 108.

[46] Zasedanie Soveta 26-12-1952, 2, in Baydalakoff, box 1, fol. 1.

[47] This characterization of the NTS's position comes from an appeal from NTS oppositionists. Dorogoi drug, 10. For an example of this rhetoric, see Vestnik Ispol'nitel'nogo Biuro Soveta NTS, December 1, 1952, 1. For the leadership's reaction to the Khorunzhii affair, see Protokol zasedaniia Soveta 23 ianvaria 1954 goda, 41–2.

the NTS-inspired underground in Russia was "a fiction," and perhaps a Soviet provocation.[48]

A feverish search for enemies within the NTS followed. Both internal NTS oppositionists and outside observers have asserted that high-ranking Soviet agents provocateurs played a role in producing the NTS's crisis and subsequent schism. Recently, a retired Committee for State Security (KGB) official claimed that Georgii Sergeevich Okolovich, the former Abwehr agent who was head of the NTS Operational Staff and the Solidarist most trusted by the Americans, was under Soviet control.[49] As the theory goes, Okolovich had been captured and turned by the Soviets during a secret NTS mission to the USSR in the 1930s.[50] Among NTS dissidents at the time, suspicion often fell on Romanov, whose mysterious origins, determined conquest of power, and seeming embrace of Soviet political language seemed tailor-made to produce strife in the NTS.[51] Another plausible candidate for the role of enemy within was Romanov's close associate Nikolai Nikolaevich Rutych-Rutchenko, a second-wave exile widely accused of committing war crimes while working for the Nazi SD (Security Service of the Reichsführer SS) in occupied Soviet territory.[52] According to one theory, Rutchenko was a Soviet agent who moved across German lines to pursue a long-term mission in the West in 1940.[53] Suspicion about Rutchenko persisted for decades. When a 1973 book mentioned the charges about his allegiance to the Soviets, Rutchenko was evidently unsettled enough to write to his old associate Romanov to plead his innocence.[54]

So long as the relevant KGB archival sources remain unavailable, it is impossible to prove or reject the allegations of top-level Soviet infiltration that engulfed the NTS. On the one hand, a CIA counterintelligence investigation after the Khorunzhii case did not uncover Soviet agents, and the oppositionists who

---

[48] S. M. Shvarts, "O krizise NTS," *Sotsialisticheskii vestnik*, no. 678, January 1955: 16, and Prianishnikov, O revoliutsionnoi deiatel'nosti, 89.

[49] According to the Soviet side, Okolovich was also a Gestapo resident in occupied Russian territory during the war. Information zu der Emigrantenorganisation NTS, no author indicated, February 19, 1968, 4, in Zentralarchiv des Bundesbeauftragten für die Unterlagen des Staatssicherheitsdienstes der ehemaligen Deutschen Demokratischen Republik (BStU, ZA), MfS-AFO 1187, 000084.

[50] S. A. Krivosheev, *KGB protiv NTS* (Moscow: Trovant, 2015), 57–8. Krivosheev posits that the organs recruited Okolovich by using his sister in the USSR as a hostage, and provides evidence of her arrest. While logically plausible, Krivosheev has not provided compelling evidence that Okolovich was a Soviet agent. Nor does his theory account for the multiple Soviet attempts on Okolovich's life in the 1950s. See also "Georgii Okolovich. Byt' s narodom...Interviu zhurnalu 'Posev,'" in V. A. Senderov (ed. and comp.), *Ot zarubezh'ia do Moskvy: Narodno-Trudovoi Soiuz (NTS) v vospominaniakh i dokumentakh 1924–2014* (Moscow: Posev, 2014), 54–5.

[51] The most detailed version of this argument is Prianishnikov, "O revoliutsionnoi deiatel'nosti," especially 29–35, 61–70.

[52] V. G. Makarov, "Poruchik SD. Nikolai Rutchenko-Rutych i ego nepredskazuemoe proshloe," *Rodina*, no. 3 (2007): 83–7.

[53] Prianishnikov, "O revoliutsionnoi deiatel'nosti," 50–8.

[54] N. N. Rutych to E. R. Ostrovskii, March 10, 1973, in National Alliance of Russian Solidarists. The book in question was Michel Slavinsky, *Ombres sur le Kremlin: une voix libre se fait entendre derriére le rideau de fer* (Paris: La Table Ronde, 1973), 108.

suspected foul play in the NTS failed to produce hard evidence on this score.[55] More broadly, accusations against Romanov, Rutchenko, and others were entangled with the web of rumor and mutual recrimination that accompanied the NTS crisis—and that Soviet counterintelligence sought to deepen. On the other hand, the charges of betrayal that surfaced during the NTS leadership struggle cannot be ruled out. It is striking that some former cadres in the Operational Staff—people who had unprecedented access to the NTS's inner secrets—remained convinced of crooked goings-on at the Alliance's headquarters in Frankfurt. One operative-turned-schismatic wrote to a colleague that he was convinced that "some third force" other than the NTS Executive Bureau or "our Western friends" [read: the CIA and MI6] had been "leading our work." He could not provide evidence of Soviet involvement, yet he thought that the repeated failure of NTS operations, and its effect in lowering morale in the NTS, was proof enough.[56] Perhaps fortunately for the Romanov group, such charges never had the chance to undergo public scrutiny. The CIA placed a gag order on discussion of the CIA-NTS collaboration, preventing the oppositionists from going beyond issuing dark hints about "hostile elements" within the organization.[57]

Complicating matters further, the CIA's position on the possibility of Soviet infiltration of the NTS was more contradictory than its clear support of the Romanov group suggested. CIA officials engaged with the NTS assumed that the organization was infiltrated by Soviet intelligence to some extent. "Theoretically," a CIA official from the Soviet Russia (SR) Division in Germany conceded in 1952, "the NTS could be penetrated from top to bottom."[58] The Agency based this pessimistic evaluation on the NTS's poor security practices, including its lack of stringent procedures for screening cadres and its use of regular mail to communicate operational secrets.[59] Protocols of top-level discussions in the Alliance reveal its vulnerability to outside infiltration. As late as May 1954, the NTS had no regular mechanism for investigating reports of Soviet penetration in its ranks,

---

[55] Su: Notes on AETNA-1 Conference, Frankfurt, February 12–17, Chief of Mission, Germany to Chief, SR, March 1, 1954, 1, in AESAURUS, vol. 3, pt. 1. A 1954 NTS investigation of Rutych-Rutchenko—initiated, a source suggests, based on information from the American military Counter Intelligence Corps (CIC)—did not establish that he was a mole. Protokol S'ezda Soveta NTS v mae 1954 goda, 8, in Baydalakoff Collection, box 1, fol. 2. Likewise, in 1954 the FBI reported that it had "no information concerning any Soviet or Communist infiltration into NTS." National Alliance of Russian Solidarists, Report made at New York, December 1954, 1, in NARA, RG 263, Entry ZZ-18, 230/86/24/04, box 122, Vladimir Sokolov. In a memoir published decades later, Baidalakov stated that "enemy provocation" had affected the NTS leadership but did not make specific allegations about individuals being recruited by the Soviets. V. M. Baidalakov, *Da vozvelichits'ia Rossiia, da pogibnut nashi imena: vospominaniia predsedatelia NTS: 1930–1960 gg.* (Moscow: Avuar Konsalting, 2002), 69–74.
[56] See the unsigned letter to A. N. Danilov dated February 28 (no year) in Baydalakoff Collection, box 2, fol. 2. The author was possibly A. A. Tenson.
[57] B. B. Martino to P. P. Kalinovskii, June 12, 1955, in Baydalakoff Collection, box 2, fol. 2.
[58] Su: Summary and Evaluation of the Relationship of the NTS to CIA, n.d., 2, in AESAURUS, vol. 1 pt. 1.
[59] CSOB Progress Report for December 1952 in AESAURUS, vol. 3, pt. 1.

perhaps because no one was trusted enough to control such a process.[60] No doubt, the laxity of NTS internal security reflected its nature as an ideological movement, much the same as in other exile organizations discussed in Chapter 2. A "small group of near-destitute and often fairly incompetent fanatics," as one of the group's CIA handlers characterized them in 1954, the NTS members could only evaluate their own cadres using the unreliable guides of ideological correctness and exile social ties.[61] In light of its inherent security weakness, the NTS was clearly vulnerable to Soviet infiltration.

The multiple known instances of Soviet penetration demonstrate the scope of the NTS's weaknesses and suggest the extent to which it may have been compromised. The Khorunzhii case showed the ease with which a Soviet agent introduced from the outside could enter NTS leadership circles—and, according to one source, Khorunzhii owed his ascent to none other than Operational Staff head Okolovich.[62] Also well documented is the case of Darko Čirkovič, a displaced Yugoslav national tried by a US military court in Germany for engaging in espionage for the Soviets. Čirkovič, whose friendship with NTS leaders originated in interwar Belgrade, received an assignment from his Soviet handler to enter the Alliance's leadership early in 1952. Although Čirkovič probably failed to gain access to NTS covert operations as Khorunzhii did, the Serb maintained close relations with its leaders while he was under Soviet control.[63] Even more damning, it emerged at his trial that NTS leader Poremskii had requested a top-secret meeting with Čirkovič *after* the latter had revealed that he had entered into contact with Soviet intelligence.[64] Assuming that Poremskii was not a Soviet agent himself, the only logical explanation is that he considered Čirkovič a real or potential double agent, an assumption that underscores the recklessness of the NTS in intelligence matters.

---

[60] Protokol S'ezda Soveta NTS v mae 1954 goda, 7–9, and Su: Notes on AETNA-1 Conference, 2.

[61] Su: Notes on AETNA-1 Conference, 2.

[62] See the CIA review of the security case of former NTS activist Aleksei Zotov. Chief, Munich Operations Group to Chief of Station, Germany, January 12, 1962, 8, in NARA, RG 263, Entry ZZ-19, 230/86/26/01, QKACTIVE, box 56, vol. 7. Soviet efforts to penetrate the NTS leadership in the West were already active during World War II, when the focus was on utilizing NTS stay-behind agents who had been left in the path of the Soviet advance and uncovered by Soviet security organs. Iz direktivy NKVD SSSR no. 136 ob aktivizatsii agenturno-operativnoi raboty po prosecheniiu podryvnoi deiatel'nosti zarubezhnoi antisovetskoi organizatsii NTSNP, March 19,1943; S. V. Stepashin and V. P. Iampol'skii (eds.), *Organy gosudarstvennoi bezopasnosti SSSR v Velikoi otechestvennoi voine: sbornik dokumentov*, vol. 4, part 1 (Moscow: Kniga i Biznes, 1995), 311.

[63] A. V. Pirang, an NTS member and Čirkovič's neighbor in Munich, met daily with the Yugoslav national and reported "everything that occurred the previous day in the Russian Organizations." The source here is Vojislav Memedovič, a Soviet agent doubled by the CIC who helped expose Čirkovič. Agent report, HQ, Reg IV, 66th CIC Det., September 18, 1952, 9, in NARA, RG 319, Entry 134B, 270/84/01/01, XE 166913, box 132, Darko Cirkovic (hereinafter Darko Cirkovic).

[64] V. D. Poremskii to A.V. Pirang, March 18, 1952, in Agent Report, special agent George J. Fedzora, Reg IV, 66th CIC Group, January 12, 1953, 4, in Darko Cirkovic. Then NTS leader Baidalakov claims that Poremskii had established contact with Čirkovič and unnamed "Titoists" against his orders. V. M. Baidalakov, *Da vozvelichits'ia Rossiia*, 71.

Perhaps just as important as the Soviets' record of penetrating the NTS was the widespread *perception* that they had. Commenting on postwar intelligence actions against the NTS, KGB archivist and later defector Vasilii Mitrokhin reported that Soviet "active measures" against the Alliance were meant to "put the thought into one's head that all the activities of the NTS fell under the control of KGB."[65] One channel through which to insinuate the existence of treachery in the NTS was Soviet agents in the émigré milieu. For instance, the fascist and likely Soviet spy E. N. Artsiuk, discussed in Chapter 2, used the pages of *Nabat* ("The Tocsin"), the organ of his Russian National Popular State Movement, to attack the NTS as a stalking horse for Soviet power. Artsiuk sought to influence the Western press, as well. In 1954, the German magazine *Deutsche Illustrierte* published a series of articles that used selective and misleading claims about the capture of Carcass agents and the Khorunzhii and Čirković cases to accuse the NTS en masse of working for the Soviets.[66] When the Solidarists investigated the issue, they found that the source for the article was Artsiuk's "Russian Information Bureau," a "dummy" organization likely under the control of Soviet intelligence.[67] Such sophisticated tools of insinuation subverted the NTS by increasing its external isolation and breaking down solidarity within it. As Paul Robinson has shown with regard to the exiled White army, Soviet foreign intelligence created an atmosphere of paranoia in the NTS in which it became "increasingly difficult to trust anybody else" and in which any setback was "invariably laid at the door of Soviet *provocateurs*."[68]

From Revolution to Cold War "Bogeyism"

Relentlessly deceptive, associated with fascism and collaborationism, and penetrated by Soviet agents to some extent—a less desirable client for US intelligence in the Cold War than the NTS is hard to imagine. Striking, then, is the fact that the

[65] History and Public Policy Program Digital Archive at the Woodrow Wilson Center, The Mitrokhin Archive: The Chekist Anthology, fol. 53, National Alliance of Russian Solidarists, http://digitalarchive.wilsoncenter.org/document/112272, accessed July 2, 2014.

[66] The mainstream émigré press relayed the *Deutsche Illustrierte* accusations at great length. Author not indicated, "Delo Sovetskogo shpiona Miullera-Khorunzhego (informatsiia iz Miunkhena), *Novoe russkoe slovo*, November 21, 1953.

[67] "Soobshchenie o provokatsionnoi deiatel'nosti organov gosbezopasnosti, napravleny protiv Natsional'no-trudovogo soiuza," *Posev*, n.d., in Columbia University Rare Book and Manuscript Library, Bakhmeteff Archive of Russian and East European History and Culture, Boris Sapir Papers, Series VI: Papers of Boris L'vovich Gurevich, box 63. See also BfV report on V. Mosichkin to the 66th CIC Group, April 20, 1954, in NARA, RG 319, Entry 134B, 270/84/01/01, XE 312364, box 23, Yeugeny Artsuk. Baidalakov and Poremskii tried to sue the magazine for libel but failed on procedural grounds. Beglaubigte Abschrift in Sachen Baydalakoff gegen Illustrierte Presse, in Baydalakoff Collection, box 3, fol. 6.

[68] Paul Robinson, *The White Russian Army in Exile, 1920–1941* (Oxford: Clarendon Press, 2002), 141.

CIA continued to support this organization, no doubt in changing ways, for the duration of the Cold War. The CIA's backing of the NTS is even more perplexing in light of other developments of the time. British intelligence had pursued its own NTS espionage operations after the war, attempting to establish a presence in the USSR by recruiting Soviet officials abroad.[69] However, MI6 curtailed its involvement with the organization in 1954 after Soviet diplomatic protests over the organization. Two years later, the British severed ties to the NTS altogether, a result of the pattern—sadly, all too familiar to the Americans—of the organization's agents coming under Soviet control or proving to have been *provocateurs* from the start.[70]

The CIA had a clear justification for maintaining support for the NTS, nevertheless. To some extent, it refused to withdraw from ties with the NTS because doing so would be an admission of defeat at the hands of the Soviet enemy, as the head of the SR Division stated in late 1954.[71] There was more to the CIA's reasoning than mere pride or institutional inertia, however. The Alliance proved to have a kind of utility for the CIA in the mid-1950s, even if it was of a far more modest kind than the Agency officials had originally envisaged. Although it had been discredited as an instrument of espionage and active subversion on Soviet soil, the NTS promised to be an effective tool of political warfare, particularly for what one CIA document called the "overt show in Germany."[72]

The CIA's new approach to the NTS developed during a period when the Alliance suffered draconian Soviet actions taken to disrupt it. In mid-1953, the post-Stalin Soviet leadership adopted an aggressive strategy of attacking anti-Soviet exile groups, a part of which was the initiation of diversion operations and "acts of terror" against the organizations' leaders.[73] (The "tacit understanding between Western and Soviet intelligence organizations" to not kidnap or kill their staff did not apply to the émigrés, who operated without official cover.)[74] Two such operations directed against the NTS proved crucial in the evolution of CIA–NTS collaboration. On April 13, 1954, A. R. Trushnovich, the head of NTS operations in Berlin, was entrapped by an East German double agent in an apartment building in the West sector of the city, kidnapped, and taken to the

[69] On the divergence in methods between the two spy services, see SHUBA 100 Penetration Operations, n.d. (1954), 1 in AESAURUS, Vol. 3, pt. 1.

[70] Project Outline, AESAURUS/AENOBLE, July 1, 1956, 2 in AUSAURUS, vol. 3, pt. 1, and Tom Bower, *The Perfect English Spy: Sir Dick White and the Secret War, 1935–1990* (New York: St. Martin's Press, 1995), 206. The British government had already scaled back liberation projects after Churchill's Conservatives returned to power in 1951. Beatrice Heuser, "Covert Actions within British and American Concepts of Containment, 1948–1951," in Richard J. Aldrich (ed.), *British Intelligence, Strategy and the Cold War, 1945–1951* (London: Routledge, 1992), 77–8.

[71] Albanese, "'It Takes a Russian to Beat a Russian'": 790.

[72] Su: Notes on AETNA-1 Conference, 4.

[73] See a September 1953 decree of the Central Committee of the Soviet Union in Russian State Archive of Contemporary History (Rossiiskii gosudarstvennyi arkhiv noveishei istorii, RGANI) f. 89, op. 18, d. 31, ll. 1–5.

[74] Michael Burke, *Outrageous Good Fortune* (Boston: Little, Brown, 1984), 163.

East. After East German radio carried a statement attributed to Trushnovich declaring that he was defecting to the Soviet side of his free will, he was never heard from again.[75] In the 1990s, the successor to the KGB stated that the kidnappers, seeking to bring Trushnovich to the East in a fake defection, had accidently killed him.[76]

Just days later the NTS made the international headlines again. In February 1954, a captain of State Security, Nikolai Evgen'evich Khokhlov, arrived in Frankfurt along with two East German agents with orders to assassinate the NTS's Okolovich (see Figure 7.1). According to the CIA's version of events,

Figure 7.1 A KGB assassin and his target share the stage at a press conference in Germany. Nikolai Evgen'evich Khokhlov (right) was sent to West Germany to organize the assassination of NTS leader Georgii Sergeevich Okolovich (left). Khokhlov presented himself at the doorstep of his intended victim and then defected to the CIA in a widely publicized Cold War drama. The story was so sensational that many exiles assumed that dark machinations were at work.
Source: Getty Images.

---

[75] The East German agent, Hans Gläske, also worked for the Gehlen Organization, the US-funded intelligence outfit of former wartime intelligence operatives in the East. For the immediate investigation of the affair, see Telegram, General Oliver to Bonn, April 15, 1954, in The National Archives of the United Kingdom (NAUK), Foreign Office (FO) 371/09320/C560762.

[76] Carey Goldberg, "KGB's True Confessions Spark Emigrants' Anger: Spy agency admits it killed former dissident. Accusations fly as documents are opened," *Los Angeles Times*, July 24, 1992. It remains an object of speculation why Soviet intelligence targeted Trushnovich instead of some other NTS leader. In 1952, the CIA head in Germany claimed that Trushnovich was a "poor security risk" and had been "cut out of all operations" in Berlin in favor of his son. Memorandum, SR/West to Chief, SR Division, January 7, 1952, 1 in AESAURUS, vol. 3, pt. 1.

Khokhlov presented himself dramatically at the doorstep of his intended victim, detailed his mission, and, after Okolovich explained that he "desired to discuss the affair with American and British friends," defected to the American side.[77] American officials first doubted Khokhlov's identity, but soon became convinced that he was not under Soviet control.[78] After an unsuccessful operation aiming to recruit Khokhlov's superior in Germany, the CIA had their high-ranking defector go public in April 1954, telling of his abandoned mission and demonstrating his exotic murder weapon—a cigarette case that shot bullets spiked with potassium cyanide—to the world at a press conference in Bonn.[79]

The NTS leaders saw both the Khokhlov defection and the Trushnovich abduction—curiously, in the second case, given the loss of their comrade—as political victories. Speaking at the NTS Council, Poremskii took a triumphant tone, declaring that the Khokhlov defection and the kidnapping of Trushnovich demonstrated that the NTS was creating a "revolutionary situation in Russia" and had put the Soviet regime on the defensive.[80] It is impossible to know whether Poremskii actually believed his own fantastical assertion that a "revolutionary situation" was at hand, although the fact that he was speaking behind closed doors to NTS leaders suggests that he was not merely engaging in the public boasting customary for the Solidarists.

Strange as it sounded, Poremskii's optimism regarding the NTS's prospects had a certain logic. The two spy scandals had brought the NTS into the international spotlight, bringing to fruition the organization's longstanding goal of courting mass opinion in the West. As NTS leader A. N. Artemov boasted, "Before we ran after each journalist, but now we are sick of them."[81] Moreover, attention in international headlines seemed to ensure the NTS new institutional footholds in the Cold War world. In Poremskii's account, the Soviets' attempts to cripple the NTS served as a kind of "recognition" of it, such that its leaders could now make a convincing claim to be "representatives of the struggling Russian people" in an

---

[77] See Okolovich, Georgi Sergeyevich, March 31, 1954, in NARA, RG 319, IRR, XE235786, Georg Okolvisch, obtained through FOIA request. In his old age in California, Khokhlov claimed that he had intended to sabotage the operation and return to Moscow. This seems unlikely, as Khokhlov must have known that his approach to Okolovich would have exposed him to great risk. "Interviu s Nikolaem Evgenievichem Khokhlovym" in A. V. Okulov, *V bor'be za Beluiu Rossiiu: Kholodnaia grazhdanskaia voina* (Moscow: Veche, 2013), 381. See also Gordon Brook-Shepard, *The Storm Birds: Soviet Post-War Defectors* (London: Weidenfeld & Nicolson, 1989), 91–112. The claim of Pavel Sudoplatov, who had been Khokhlov's boss as KGB special operations chief, that Khokhlov did not deliberately abandon his mission to kill Okolovich but was "caught and turned by the CIA" runs against all other evidence. Pavel Sudoplatov et al., *Special Tasks: The Memoirs of an Unwanted Witness, a Soviet Spymaster* (Boston: Little, Brown, 1994), 247.

[78] Boris Volodarsky, *Nikolai Khokhlov ("Whistler"): Self-Esteem with a Halo* (Vienna and London: Borwall Verlag, 2005), 42–3.

[79] Volodarsky, *Nikolai Khokhlov*, 50–1, and Christopher M. Andrew and Vasilii Mitrokhin. *The Mitrokhin Archive: The KGB in Europe and the West* (London: Allen Lane, 1999), 467.

[80] Protokol S'ezda Soveta NTS v mae 1954 goda, 9–11.

[81] Protokol S'ezda Soveta, 11.

international context. Foreign governments were now lavishing attention on the Alliance, Poremskii explained. The newly sovereign West German authorities—which had held an ambivalent position toward NTS and sometimes hindered its activities—now took a more cooperative attitude, while negotiations were under-way with Taiwan and South Korea about opening new paths to reaching the USSR in the East.[82] As the Solidarists understood, being targeted by Soviet intelligence boosted the international reputation of the NTS in a way that the meager results of its combat with the Soviet state could not. In fact, Poremskii conveyed a similar idea in 1952 when he claimed that insofar as the NTS was "in the focus of world events," "the myth about us surpasses our objective importance."[83]

The Khokhlov and Trushnovich affairs also boosted the CIA's opinion of their exile asset, helping to offset the disappointment of the Carcass operation. With the Khokhlov defection, the Agency finally saw tangible gain from its support of the NTS. By one account, the CIA's intelligence "take" from the Khokhlov defection included valuable information about the top-secret sphere of Soviet special oper-ations, the unmasking of an unnamed Soviet spy in the NTS, and the defection of Khokhlov's friend, also in foreign intelligence, to the West.[84] More basically, the CIA saw Soviet repressions as evidence of the NTS's value. In a December 1954 memorandum on NTS operations, the CIA's SR Division stressed that the attempted assassination of Okolovich confirmed "the Soviet desire to hamstring NTS operations in the USSR."[85] Moreover, the document continued, "the most recent MVD defectors"—a group that included Khokhlov himself—"all confirmed independently that the Soviet government considers NTS to be one of the most dangerous émigré anti-Soviet organizations."[86] Echoing an argument regularly made by the exiles, CIA officials determined that the Solidarists must be doing something right if they drew the ire of the Soviets.

The CIA built on this reading of events by launching elaborate psychological-warfare campaigns surrounding the Khokhlov and Trushnovich cases. In propa-ganda in the West and in broadcasts to Soviet listeners over Voice of America and Radio Liberation, the CIA used the two scandals to boost the image of the NTS as an underground movement in the USSR.[87] In testimony to the Committee on Un-American Activities in the US House of Representatives, Khokhlov claimed that he had abandoned his mission and saved Okolovich in order to serve the "Russian anti-Communist underground," which he called "enemy No. 1" of the

[82] Ibid. Chapter 11 discusses the relationship of the West German government to the NTS at length.
[83] Protokoly S'ezda Soveta NTS v ianvare 1952 g., 5, in Baydalakoff Collection, box 1, fol. 1.
[84] Volodarsky, *Nikolai Khokhlov*, 20–3.
[85] NTS Penetration Operations into the USSR, Memorandum from Chief, SR, to Chief of Oper-ations, DD/P, December 8, 1954, 2, in AESAURUS, vol. 3, pt. 1.
[86] Ibid. At the time, the foreign intelligence service was lodged in the *Ministerstvo Vnutrennykh Del* (Ministry of Internal Affairs).
[87] Prianishnikov, O revoliutsionnoi deiatel'nosti, 113.

system.[88] So confident was Khokhlov in NTS operations on Soviet territory that he asked Okolovich to help his wife and son escape from the Soviet Union. Boris Volodarsky accepts Khokhlov's explanation at face value, positing that Khokhlov was "deluded" into thinking that the "NTS was a powerful organization that could do a lot for him" by the KGB itself, which presented the Solidarists as the arch-enemies of Soviet power.[89] This theory cannot be ruled out, even though it seems odd that Khokhlov would not have gained a more realistic picture of the émigré organization prior to taking up the Okolovich mission.[90] Just as likely was the possibility that Khokhlov—who was under close CIA control at the time[91]—told his story in a manner designed to bolster the reputation of the Agency's asset.

Khokhlov's presentation of his wife, Ianina Adamovna ("Iana"), also suggested that a wider psychological-warfare campaign was at work. In public pronouncements in the West, Khokhlov claimed that Iana was a deeply religious woman who had encouraged her husband to defect, sacrificing "her happiness and the happiness of her little son in the name of the great law: 'Do not kill!'"[92] The NTS picked up on this story, calling in its propaganda for "all humanity to unite in doing all possible to save Elena Khokhlova [sic] from the hands of the Communist hangmen."[93] The habitually skeptical émigré press cast doubt on Khokhlov's account of his wife, and not just because it seemed far-fetched that a KGB special operations captain was married to a devout Christian. Why had Khokhlov sacrificed his beloved wife in favor of the unknown émigré Okolovich, and why had he then placed her in danger by drawing attention to her role in his defection?[94] Years later, Khokhlov claimed that he publicized Iana's situation from the West in order to protect her from Soviet reprisals. If this was the case, he failed: Iana Khokhlova spent five months in prison before being exiled to Syktyvkar in the Russian north.[95] Whatever the truth about Khokhlov's wife, the depiction of her as a

[88] Testimony of Nikolai Khokhlov, Thought Control in Soviet Art and Literature and the Liberation of Russia, part 8, Investigation of Communist Activities in the Los Angeles, Calif., Area hearings before the United States House Committee on Un-American Activities, Eighty-Fourth Congress, second session, on April 17, 1956, 3798, in HILA, Nikolai Evgen'evich Khokhlov papers, box 1. See also his English-language memoirs, N. E. Khokhlov, In the Name of Conscience (New York: D. McKay Co., 1959), 202.
[89] Volodarsky, Nikolai Khokhlov, 20.
[90] Khokhlov—and Volodarsky after him—have claimed that the special operations officer learned little of the organization before setting out on his mission. Ibid., 39–40.
[91] One sign of the CIA's control was FBI director J. Edgar Hoover's "strong protest" to Director of Central Intelligence Allen Dulles that FBI investigators had been granted only partial access to Khokhlov. J. Edgar Hoover to Allen W. Dulles, May 19, 1954 in CREST: General CIA Records, Document Number (FOIA) /ESDN (CREST): CIA-RDP80R01731R000800090012-6.
[92] See Appendix C, translation of Heroism of a Russian Woman, Posev, April 25, 1954, reprinted in Volodarsky, Nikolai Khokhlov.
[93] Ibid.
[94] Elena Kuskova, "Otvet g—nu N. Khokhlovu," Novoe russkoe slovo, November 27, 1955.
[95] See "Interviu s Nikolaem Evgenievichem Khokhlovym," 381, and Volodarsky, Nikolai Khokhlov, 60, 71. Apparently, when Khokhlov traveled to Moscow in the 1990s to be pardoned by the Yeltsin government, Iana refused to see him.

Christian and a "true Russian woman" functioned as a propaganda line to add emotional depth to the story of the repentant KGB assassin.

The media coverage of the Trushnovich kidnapping was, if anything, even more carefully packaged for Cold War propaganda. In contrast to the Khokhlov defection, Trushnovich's disappearance to the East spurred some negative reactions in the press, as it called into doubt security in West Berlin and fueled speculation, even in the influential *Der Spiegel*, that Trushnovich had in fact been a Soviet agent.[96] Nevertheless, the Trushnovich case became a cause célèbre for the NTS and its CIA backers. The Alliance launched a vociferous propaganda campaign to demand Trushnovich's release, while charging that the abduction had only shown Soviet impotence and "brought shame" upon the USSR in international public opinion.[97] Seeking to create a spectacle, Trushnovich's wife, Zinaida Nikanorovna, traveled to Switzerland during the Geneva Conference to demand an audience with foreign minister Viacheslav Mikhailovich Molotov about her husband's disappearance.[98] Meanwhile, the "Free Trushnovich" campaign bore the imprint of more direct US governmental, and no doubt CIA, involvement, including the creation of a "Committee to Combat Soviet Kidnapping" that included prominent Americans (including Eugene Lyons) which sent a report on the case to the UN Human Rights Commission.[99]

What did CIA operatives hope to achieve by publicizing the Khokhlov and Trushnovich cases on such a scale? While documents on these activities are still classified, one can reconstruct the CIA's goals. As their United Nations action suggests, propaganda about violence in Germany could put Soviet authorities on the defensive, something that was perhaps particularly desirable in the context of the unstable post-Stalin collective leadership.[100] The US government also used the NTS myth for domestic purposes, as the wide coverage of the Khokhlov and Trushnovich cases in the domestic press suggest. English-language publications about the Solidarists appeared in the following years, expressing the naïve populism characteristic of American Cold War propaganda by depicting Solidarists as virtuous Russian freedom fighters.[101]

[96] Telegram from Sir F. Hoyer Millar, UK High Commission in Germany to Foreign Office, April 28, 1954, in NAUK, FO 371/109320.

[97] Rezoliutsiia o novom etape bor'by, n.d., in Baydalakoff Collection, box 1, fol. 2.

[98] UK High Commission in Bonn to the United Kingdom Delegation in Geneva, May 20, 1954, NAUK, FO 371/109320. See also Aleksandr Kolpakidi and Dmitri Prokhorov, *KGB: Spetsoperatsii sovetskoi razvedki* (Moscow: AST, 2000), 208.

[99] "To Rescue Dr. Trushnovich: Formation of Committee to Combat Kidnapping is Welcomed," *The New York Times*, 26 May 1954.

[100] On Eisenhower's attempts to embarrass Soviet leaders through rhetoric and diplomacy, see Kenneth Alan Osgood, *Total Cold War: Eisenhower's Secret Propaganda Battle at Home and Abroad* (Lawrence: University of Kansas, 2006), 46–75.

[101] Cf. George Gordon Young, *The House of Secrets* (New York: Duell, Sloan, and Pearce, 1959). On populism in US Cold War propaganda, see Gary D. Rawnsley, "The Campaign of Truth: A Populist Propaganda," in Gary D. Rawnsley (ed.), *Cold-War Propaganda in the 1950s* (New York: St. Martin's Press, 1999), 31–46.

The main thrust of the CIA's strategy with the NTS, though, was to deceive and disrupt the Soviet government. CIA officials determined that the NTS had unnerved the Kremlin. In the first years after World War II, the Soviet press had avoided mentioning the NTS by name, presumably in order to avoid giving the Alliance free publicity within Soviet society. However, starting in 1953, the USSR launched "drastic and unusual measures" to discredit the NTS, such as diplomatic protests and "blasts against the NTS" in the Soviet press, while also devoting "a far greater percentage of their security effort than in reality should be necessary" to the hunt for the organization's agents within Soviet borders.[102] The CIA derived from this picture of the Soviet government's excessive responses a new approach of "tying up and harassing Soviet security organs through the use of deception."[103] In other words, while the CIA could not use the NTS to infiltrate Soviet borders, at least it could launch "a plan of attack aimed at building up the bogey of [NTS] strength in the USSR."[104]

We see the CIA's stratagem of exaggerating the NTS's influence in the Soviet Union at work in June 1954, when the Soviet press announced that two Carcass agents had been apprehended in the USSR. David E. Murphy, then Chief of the SR Division, wrote to Frankfurt with "recommendations" on how the NTS should respond to this most recent setback on the covert front. The Alliance should admit that the agents were members of the NTS, an organization that had "long conducted [the] struggle against Soviet power on Russian soil." The Soviets' charge that the two had been American spies was to be portrayed as a falsehood aimed at retaliating for the Khokhlov affair as well as an expression of "Soviet anxiety" over manifestations of "anti-Soviet activity" in the USSR.[105] At work here was an attempt to provoke the Soviet government into costly and embarrassing overreactions, in essence using its obsessive hostility toward the exiles against it.[106]

For their part, the NTS leaders understood and embraced the CIA's new political-warfare strategy. In fact, one might posit that the NTS had been pursuing precisely such a direction for years. Solidarists had long issued mistruths about their revolutionary work, and some had articulated the idea that the Soviet state might prove susceptible to hoodwinking on this score.[107] The joint CIA–NTS

---

[102] Review of SHUBA 100 Internal Agent Cases, Memorandum for Chief, SR/3, June 9, 1955, 3, in AESAURUS, vol. 3, pt. 1.

[103] Review of SHUBA 100 Internal Agent Cases, 3.

[104] SHUBA 100 Penetration Operations, 4.

[105] Director to Frankfurt, June 17, 1954, in AESAURUS vol. 3, pt. 1.

[106] How CIA use of the NTS compared with its other operations in a matter of speculation. Notably, in 1952 policymakers in the Truman administration had espoused the use of "spoiling operations" against the USSR that would seek through "disinformation and deception" to exploit the "jealousy and paranoia" of the Soviet party elite. Gregory Mitrovich, *Undermining the Kremlin: America's Strategy to Subvert the Soviet Bloc, 1947–1956* (Ithaca, NY: Cornell University Press, 2000), 72–3.

[107] See an articulation of the idea that operations against the USSR might induce Soviet propaganda to "feed and strengthen revolutionary thought" in the country: E. E. Pozdeev, Neskol'ko razroznennykh zamechanii po propagande, 3, in FSO, 01–044 Poremsky, kor. 1940-ye.

propaganda strategy found a clear if also quite radical exposition in a speech by Solidarist R. N. Redlikh to the Alliance leadership cadres in May 1954. The Soviet government, driven by its "exaggerated notion" of the NTS's presence on Soviet soil, would increasingly resort to repression in order to uproot it. In turn, mass arrests of citizens under suspicion of being tied to the NTS would create further discontent in Soviet society while "popularizing" "the fact of the existence of a revolutionary force on the territory of the Soviet Union." Redlikh envisioned a feedback loop of provocation, repression, and radicalization that would benefit the Alliance. In fact, Redlikh anticipated something like a replay of the Great Terror of the 1930s, with the NTS being a "candidate" for the role of internal enemy that Trotskyists had earlier occupied.[108]

It is unclear whether CIA officials expected or hoped to revive mass terror in the USSR as the Solidarists evidently did. However, the NTS leaders and their Agency supporters worked in tandem to pursue a strategy of incitement and provocation. In effect, the CIA had decided to utilize the NTS's longstanding practices of misinformation and posturing as weapons of psychological warfare against Soviet communism.

*   *   *

What emerged from the CIA's collaboration with the People's Labor Alliance was a paradoxical situation in which a myth of NTS power outstripped its modest reality. In the new arrangement, the CIA finally found use for its troublesome émigré asset, one that might destabilize the Soviet enemy in the long run. The motives of the Alliance leaders were also clear enough. While no doubt hoping that the strategy of provocation might further the anti-Soviet cause, the NTS leaders also saw some advantage in the new state of affairs. Trushnovich's fate showed that covert operations against the Soviet state were a dangerous business. And yet the NTS's struggle against the USSR provided an otherwise obscure outfit of exiles with money and public recognition.

A crucial set of questions remains to be answered about the exercise of power in the intelligence war surrounding the Solidarists. Was the fabricated illusion of NTS power an effective weapon in the CIA's psy-war arsenal during the Cold War? How did Soviet leaders understand the threat to their interests posed by the NTS, and were Soviet security organs really "tied up and harassed" by their enemies' deception tactics?

To some extent, the CIA's strategy of exploiting deception and the "overt show" yielded results. At the very least, the NTS managed to continue its struggle against the Soviet state and perhaps even expanded its presence on Soviet soil over time. Presumably referring to the late Soviet years, Mitrokhin noted that the NTS had

---

[108] R. N. Redlikh, Kontury griadushchego etapa (doklad na sobranii chlenov Rukovodiashchego Kruga v Frankfurte 11 iiunia 1954 g.), 1–5 in FSO, 01–098 Tarasova, kor. 41.

190 COLD WAR EXILES AND THE CIA

the special attention of the KGB as an organization that was "active, large in number," and possessing of "supporters in the USSR."[109]

One might question, however, whether Soviet counterintelligence officials were as deceived by the NTS myth as CIA operatives and the Solidarists seemed to think. Unable to infiltrate its cadres across the Iron Curtain, shorn of many of its cadres following its internal split and infiltrated at least to some extent by Soviet disruption agents, the NTS was hardly a serious threat to the USSR. And at least in the 1950s, the NTS strategy of provocation had little impact in the Soviet Union, where police controls effectively undercut underground oppositional activities. NTS print propaganda calling on Soviet citizens to form underground cells and prepare for revolution seems to have won few adherents, as suggested by Soviet Procurator's Office materials on prosecutions for "anti-Soviet and counter-revolutionary propaganda and agitation"—and understandably so, given the KGB's success in detecting and breaking up underground organizations of all kinds.[110]

Soviet counterintelligence operatives might well have understood that the NTS was not the "enemy number one" that Khokhlov claimed it was. One piece of evidence suggesting that such might have been the case is a KGB report on the organization from the late 1960s, which commented on the efforts of the NTS leaders to "create an impression" that the "center of gravity" of its activities was already in the Soviet bloc—a sign that the KGB was not necessarily taken in by the Solidarists' exaggerated claims about their exploits in the USSR.[111] More broadly, the pattern of Soviet policies toward the NTS was oddly and perhaps suspiciously ham-fisted and counterproductive. In particular, the Soviet government's highly publicized attacks on the NTS had the obvious consequence of boosting the Solidarists' standing in the West, as seen by the émigrés' eager publicizing of Soviet reprisals against them. Observing the dynamic by which the Alliance boasted of the news coverage it received in the USSR, the former Solidarist Boris Vital'evich Prianishnikov opined that "the Soviet press is the best friend of the NTS."[112]

[109] National Alliance of Russian Solidarists, 1. This view is supported by Andrei Okulov, *Kholodnaia grazhdanskaia voina: KGB protiv russkoi emigratsii* (Moscow: EKSMO: IAUZA, 2006).

[110] The NTS pointed to the existence of its cells in Soviet Russia, such as the "Young Russia" group in Leningrad that was uncovered by the KGB in 1956, as proof of the success of the "molecular theory." "Seredina 50-kh: Molekulyarnaya teoriya v deistvii," http://www.posev.ru/files/nts-about/ne7008.htm, accessed April 20, 2016. However, there are few known cases of such cells. See V. A. Kozlov and S. V. Mironenko, eds., *58–10: nadzornye proizvodstva prokuratury SSSR po delam ob antisovetskoi agitatsii i propagande: annatirovannyi katolog, mart 1953–1991* (Moscow: Mezhdunarodnyi fond "Demokratiia," 1999), 244–5, 266–7, 305, and Rob Hornsby, *Protest, Reform and Repression in Khrushchev's Soviet Union* (New York: Cambridge University Press, 2013), 164–6. For instances of Soviet citizens handing in NTS propaganda to the authorities, see RGANI, f. 5, op. 30, d. 151, l, 164.

[111] Auskunftsbericht, n.d. (not before 1967), 5, in Bundesbeauftragte für die Unterlagen des Staatssicherheitsdienstes der ehemaligen Deutschen Demokratischen Republik, Zentralarchiv (BStU, ZA), MfS-AFO 1187, 000110.

[112] B. V. Prianishnikov to R. P. Ronchevskii, May 29, 1960, 1, in HILA, Boris Prianishnikov Papers, box 3, fol. 9. See also "Effort to Analyse Soviet Provocation," 11.

One can speculate that Soviet authorities might have had some reason to bolster the NTS's stature in such an indirect manner. The ongoing existence of a Russian émigré movement against Soviet power—and especially one backed by the United States—helped Soviet intelligence and security agencies to secure bureaucratic prerogatives and resources.[113] Also, ongoing American patronage of the controversial NTS helped to fuel internecine struggles in the Russian emigration, while tying up US resources that might have been used for more effective projects. Finally, the "overt show" of publicity that the NTS specialized in was by no means a one-sided affair. The Soviet propaganda apparatus published numerous attacks on the NTS in Western languages that stressed the Alliance's fascist origins and its record of collaboration with the Nazis. This line of attack aimed to discredit the politics of the Russian emigration while adding substance to the wider Soviet position that the West was imperialist and militaristic.[114] In short, the CIA's strategy vis-à-vis the NTS relied on deception, and it possible that the Soviet side was also complicit in this game. If so, then the NTS had become the focal point for a curious struggle, one in which intelligence services of both superpowers sought to gain advantage through manipulating the fiction of a politically effective Russian émigré organization.

Better understanding of Soviet measures against the NTS awaits new archival revelations. Regardless, the highly publicized place of the NTS in the Cold War of the 1950s shows the complexity of US psychological-warfare strategies, as attempts at regime change gave way to more subtle struggles for political advantage. Having failed to make the NTS a viable organization for penetrating Soviet borders, the CIA had decided to utilize it as a propaganda piece. Yet the CIA and the exiles still had reason to hope for more direct opportunities to influence the Soviet population. If infiltrating the territory of the USSR was an overly ambitious goal, the exiles had better luck breaching the Iron Curtain at its particularly vulnerable point: divided Germany and, in particular, its jointly occupied capital of Berlin.

---

[113] "Interviu s Nikolaem Evgenievichem Khokhlovym," 372. I am grateful to A. Ross Johnson for drawing this point to my attention.

[114] For instance, see the exposé by an NTS agent who had apparently absconded to the USSR, which was translated into several languages. K. K. Cherezov, *Maska NTS, ili NTS bez maski* (Berlin: Izd. Sovetskogo komiteta po kul'turnym sviaziam s sootechestvennikami za rubezhom, 1965). See also N. N. Iakovlev, *CIA Target, the USSR* (Moscow: Progress Publishers, 1982), 96–110.

8

Spies, Sex, and Balloons

Émigré Activities in Divided Berlin

> To the soldiers, sergeants, and officers of the Soviet Occupation
> Army! Comrades! Use the opportunity afforded to you to get to
> know the local population! Try to find true friends among the
> Germans! They will help you in the common struggle, they will help
> you attain freedom![1]

In the 1950s, leaflets in Russian regularly appeared on the bases and outside the
barracks of Soviet armed forces stationed in East Germany, falling from the sky
from white balloons or strewn by furtive figures. The leaflets' authors were
Russian exiles in West Germany, and the entire operation was funded by the
CIA—although the leaflets sometimes obscured the first fact and always hid the
second. The propaganda airdrops were a psychological-warfare operation carried
out by two CIA-backed organizations, the National Labor Alliance (NTS) and the
Central Representation of Postwar Emigrants (*Tsentral'noe ob'edinenie poslevoennykh emigrantov* or TsOPE). Working from offices in the West sector of Berlin,
the émigrés released subversive scraps of paper and sent agents across the inter-
zonal border with the goal of undermining the morale of the Soviet occupation
forces and encouraging defection to the West.

This chapter analyzes the exiles' Berlin operations using the files of the GDR's
Ministry for State Security (*Ministerium für Staatssicherheit,* or MfS, usually
known as the Stasi), which fought subversion in the East zone and then GDR
under close supervision by its Soviet counterpart.[2] In some ways, these sources
confirm the picture of exile operations from Chapter 7, as security and counterintelligence practices of the Soviet bloc thwarted the CIA's offensive operations.
And as with NTS's activities on Soviet soil, exile forays onto East German territory
involved posturing and publicity more than concrete achievements.

---

[1] Leaflet beginning "Deutscher freund," n.d., in National Archives and Records Administration
(NARA), RG 263, Entry ZZ-19, 230/86/25/04, box 25, AEVIRGIL (hereinafter AEVIRGIL), vol. 1.
[2] Some of the German archival files drawn on in this chapter were first brought into scholarly
use in Bernd Stöver, *Die Befreiung vom Kommunismus: Amerikanische Liberation Policy im Kalten
Krieg 1947–1991* (Cologne: Böhlau, 2002), 525.

Cold War Exiles and the CIA: Plotting to Free Russia. Benjamin Tromly, Oxford University Press
(2019). © Benjamin Tromly.
DOI: 10.1093/oso/9780198840404.001.0001

Although they were largely unsuccessful, the émigrés' Berlin operations took on importance due to their transnational nature, as the text of the leaflet suggests. Insofar as exiles could not set foot in the GDR for security reasons, their Berlin operations were carried out by border-crossing East German civilians who served as agents, propagandists, informants, and consumers of propaganda. In the process, the Russians and their anti-communist activities became dependent on the politics of division, competition, and human movement in Germany. Indeed, the exiles' anti-communist project became a "common struggle" with Germans against Soviet power. The émigré operations in Berlin, therefore, exemplified the transnational nature of Russian anti-communist politics, as American, Russian, and German enemies of communism with quite different interests and ideas interacted within a single operational space.[3]

Stirring the Berlin Cauldron

Defection, which was at the heart of the exile operations in Berlin, was a Cold War phenomenon. If flight across borders has always held political meaning, the organized and large-scale encouragement of illegal emigration during peacetime was not accepted practice in previous periods, when Europe was dominated by nation-states preoccupied with strengthening borders.[4] In the conflict-ridden yet gridlocked state of the continent during the Cold War, however, the strategy of encouraging flight from enemy territory became a major strategic weapon.

Only gradually did the US government discover the potential value of defection, including the symbolic charge the crossing of Cold War borders carried. As late as 1949, the United States lacked a coherent policy on how to deal with defectors, despite requests from US military governments of Germany and Japan for policy guidance on the matter.[5] A major initiative for establishing a US policy toward defectors—as with plans to utilize exile communities in Europe—came from George Kennan. As argued in a February 1948 Policy Planning Staff (PPS) Paper, Soviet citizens who fled from their homeland after the war were a massive

---

[3] Interactions across national lines are mentioned but not fully explored in the fullest discussion of CIA psy-war operations in Germany: David E. Murphy, Sergei A. Kondrashev, and George Bailey, *Battleground Berlin: CIA vs. KGB in the Cold War* (New Haven: Yale University Press, 1997), 103–25. On various forms of transnational anti-communism in the Cold War, see Luc van Dongen, Stéphanie Roulin, and Giles Scott-Smith (eds.), *Transnational Anti-Communism and the Cold War: Agents, Activities, and Networks* (Basingstoke: Palgrave Macmillan, 2014), and Giles Scott-Smith, *Western Anti-communism and the Interdoc Network: Cold War Internationale* (Basingstoke and New York: Palgrave Macmillan, 2012).
[4] Susan L. Carruthers, "Between Camps: Eastern Bloc 'Escapees' and Cold War Borderlands," *American Quarterly* 57, no. 3 (2005): 915–17.
[5] PPS 54: Policy Relating to Defection and Defectors from Soviet Power, June 28, 1949, 1, in NARA, RG 59, Records of the Policy Planning Staff, Microfiche 1171, card 62.

untapped resource for the United States in fighting the Cold War.[6] Defectors were "by far the best potential source of accurate information on the Soviet world," Kennan's PPS argued, an intelligence "gold mine" that needed to be "systematically exploited."[7] In a second and no less important consideration, defectors constituted a tool for psychological warfare against the Kremlin. "Deserters from the Soviet world" were "the most effective agents to destroy the communist myth of the Soviet paradise."[8] Finally, defection promised to desta-bilize the Soviet power structure in an immediate sense by creating an "atmos-phere of distrust and suspicion." Kennan's elucidation of the purposes of defection—"intelligence and related activities," "propaganda use and value," and the fomenting of "disaffection and confusion" within the Soviet bloc—formed the basis of a "United States Policy on Soviet and Satellite Defectors" endorsed by the National Security Council (NSC 86/1) in 1951.[9]

The United States' embrace of defection as a new instrument of foreign policy left several questions unresolved. If the policy of accepting Soviet bloc defectors became uncontroversial in US government, the same was not true of programs to *encourage* defection from the Soviet bloc. Facilitating large-scale defections was a provocative act in the context of divided Europe; it also threatened to bring over people who were of little use for US Cold War efforts and whose absorption into Western societies would prove difficult and costly. As a result, the scope of efforts to secure Soviet-bloc defectors remained unclear. On the one hand, Kennan's 1949 policy paper stressed that not all border-crossers from the Soviet bloc were defectors proper and therefore deserving of American attention and care. The true defector was a narrowly defined figure: a "military deserter, a civilian official, a communist party official, a member of the intelligentsia or a technician" from the USSR or a satellite state who had left his or her country for "bona fide political reasons."[10] On the other hand, the NSC policy cast aside such an approach in calling for the spurring of "mass flows" from the Soviet bloc, an approach that blurred the lines between defectors and a catch-all category of "escapees."[11] Reconciling these imperatives, US government policy would settle on a practice of encouraging targeted defections rather than issuing indiscriminate calls for flight. The CIA-funded Radio Liberation, while maintaining that defectors would

[6] PPS 22: Utilization of Refugees from the Soviet Union in US National Interest, February 5, 1948, in NARA, RG 59, Records of the Policy Planning Staff, microfiche 1171, card 23.
[7] PPS 54: Policy Relating to Defection and Defectors, 4.
[8] Ibid.
[9] Attachment B: Absorption of Escapees through Utilization in Intelligence and Psychological Programs, December 20, 1951, 1, in CREST: 25-Year Program Archive, Document Number (FOIA) / ESDN (CREST): CIA-RDP80R01731R003200030004-4.
[10] PPS 54: Policy Relating to Defection and Defectors, 2.
[11] The US Department of Defense pushed for such an aggressive plan. Kevin P. Riehle, "Early Cold War evolution of British and US defector policy and practice." *Cold War History*, online edn (2018): 15.

be "well received" and granted political asylum, refrained from issuing blanket calls for defection.[12]

A related question was where authority for such defector inducement operations would rest. No doubt because of its inflammatory nature, encouraging defection was to be the remit not of overt government bodies but of intelligence officers. In 1952, an official in the Public Affairs Division of the Office of the US High Commissioner for Germany proposed that the State Department, and not just intelligence agencies, undertake propaganda efforts toward Soviet troops.[13] An official at the Department of State in Washington opposed the idea, however. Encouraging Soviet occupation personnel to desert would contradict America's "professed desire for peace" while also, somewhat paradoxically, alienating German public opinion by hinting at a US–USSR rapprochement.[14] In order to avoid diplomatic blowback, defection inducement would fall under the purview of the secretive CIA.

The situating of defector programs in an intelligence agency raised yet another problem: the relationship between defection and intelligence-gathering. Some CIA officials were skeptical of spurring defection for fear of exhausting potential sources of information behind the Iron Curtain.[15] Bringing intelligence assets across the Iron Curtain might produce rich sources of intelligence, but they would be one-off affairs by their very nature. Moreover, US policies treated defectors as tools of psychological warfare as well as espionage assets, roles that could pull in different directions.

From these various problems—the imperatives of limiting defection, maintaining secrecy, and keeping up the push for intelligence operations behind the Iron Curtain—emerged a CIA program carrying the cryptonym REDCAP. According to a later description, REDCAP operations involved "the planned collection of information on Soviet personnel stationed abroad for the purpose of operational exploitation, including defection inducement."[16] The plan called for facilitating the defection of selected Soviet officials and, in an evident concession to intelligence officers, maintained the goal of recruiting what were called "defectors in

[12] Radio Liberation Policy Manual, June 29, 1956, 17, in Georgetown University Archives and Special Collections, Robert F. Kelley Papers (hereinafter Kelley Papers), box 5, fol. 4.

[13] Soviet Soldiers in Germany, A Need for Increased Propaganda Effort, March 28, 1952, Gregory Henderson, Policy and Program Staff, Berlin Element, Public Affairs Division, in NARA, RG 466.4 (HICOG), box 6, Berlin Element-Classified Subject Files, 1949–1953, Po–Pr (hereinafter Berlin Element).

[14] Su: Draft paper on Soviet Soldiers in Germany, Memorandum, May 23, 1952, Lewis Revey, Information Programs Officer, to John Devine, Special Assistant to the Assistant Secretary for Public Affairs, in Berlin Element.

[15] Murphy, Kondrashev and Bailey, *Battleground Berlin*, 238.

[16] "Research Aid: Cryptonyms and Terms in Declassified CIA Files, Nazi War Crimes and Japanese Imperial Government Records Disclosure Acts," available at https://www.archives.gov/files/iwg/declassified-records/rg-263-cia-records/second-release-lexicon.pdf, accessed May 21, 2017. See the declassified collection of REDCAP documents in NARA, RG 319, Entry 134A, 230/86/26/02, box 60 (hereinafter REDCAP).

place," agents carrying out espionage assignments who planned to flee at some future date.[17]

While REDCAP operations targeted Soviet consular and other personnel around the globe, their focal point was Germany, and particularly Berlin. The divided city offered Western spy services unprecedented opportunities. It allowed relatively unfettered passage across the Iron Curtain, and therefore constituted an otherwise unavailable route for Soviet defection to the West. No less important, the enclave of West Berlin offered American spies the ability to run Eastern bloc spies with an otherwise unimaginable degree of security and ease. During face-to-face meetings in parked cars, apartments, and sometimes even in crowded bars in the West sector, spies could debrief, train, and relay instructions to German agents at regular intervals.[18] Finally, of great importance to specifically Russian operations was Berlin's proximity to the Group of Soviet Forces in Germany, the largest conglomeration of Soviet soldiers abroad and a strike force for a potential invasion of Western Europe.[19] Perhaps due to the unparalleled advantages of operations there, the CIA did not curtail its operations in Berlin after the revolt of June 1953, an event which scholars often see as having dented enthusiasm in Washington for aggressive psy-war projects in pursuit of liberation or "rollback." Just weeks after the quashed revolt, Eisenhower approved NSC Directive 158, a plan to exploit unrest in "Satellite Europe," which included calls for "the intensification of defection programs" and the "consideration of large-scale systematic balloon propaganda operations to the satellites."[20]

Enter the exiles. The REDCAP operations in Berlin required agents with Russian and German language skills and sufficient knowledge of the immediate environment. To some extent, the CIA Berlin Station met these personnel requirements with "several staff officers and some gifted contract employees – foreign-born American citizens so fluent in German and Russian that they could pose as either Germans or Russians."[21] To make up for the shortfall in such agents, the CIA turned to Russian émigré groups to carry out REDCAP operations under Agency oversight. In all likelihood, the CIA thought that the exiles' experience in East German operations—the NTS had spent years attempting to spur defections

[17] Bob Burton, *Dictionary of Espionage and Intelligence: Over 800 Phrases Used in International and Covert Espionage* (New York: Skyhorse Publishing, 2014), 6.

[18] Paul Maddrell, "British Intelligence through the Eyes of the Stasi: What the Stasi's Records Show about the Operations of British Intelligence in Cold War Germany," *Intelligence and National Security* 27, no. 1 (2012): 52.

[19] Ilko-Sascha Kowalczuk and Stefan Wolle, *Roter Stern über Deutschland: Sowjetische Truppen in der DDR* (Berlin: Links, 2001), 106–7.

[20] C. F. Ostermann (ed.), "Implementing 'Roll-back': NSC 158," *Newsletter of the Society of Historians of American Foreign Relations* 26, no. 3 (1996): 1–7. While Ostermann has argued that NSC 158 was never implemented, the émigré operations detailed here cast doubt on this theory. Christian Ostermann, "US Intelligence and the GDR: The Early Years," in Heike Bungert et al. (eds.), *Secret Intelligence in the Twentieth Century* (London: Frank Cass, 2003), 143.

[21] Murphy, Kondrashev and Bailey, *Battleground Berlin*, 239.

from the Soviet zone—would make them effective operators.[22] At the very least, CIA staff in Germany hoped, the émigré organizations would provide a degree of cover for REDCAP cases in which the "premature disclosure" of American involvement might "scotch the operation before it has fairly begun."[23]

The exile operations in Berlin were multipronged endeavors. Russian operatives in the West sector recruited East German agents, whom they tasked with spreading propaganda in the vicinity of Soviet installations—or, in the case of those who worked in close proximity to them and could speak Russian, with the more dangerous mission of establishing personal contact with Soviet personnel.[24] Alongside these REDCAP operations, the NTS and TsOPE produced propaganda and staffed teams in West Germany that distributed it through the launching of hot-air balloons to the East laden with printed material.[25] In theory, the two areas of activity carried out by the émigré organizations from Berlin were connected, for leaflets destined for the East encouraged Russian and German readers to visit the exiles' West Berlin offices or to send letters to them. In this sense, the émigré offices in Berlin were at the center of combined defection inducement, mass propaganda and espionage operations.

In principle, the Berlin operations were a continuation of Russian liberation efforts, with émigrés seeking to turn their fellow Russians in East Germany against the Soviet regime. From the outset, however, Russian-to-Russian interactions were mediated through other transnational relationships. Of course, the Americans were heavily involved in Berlin operations. Though the NTS seems to have carried out their German operations with looser oversight, TsOPE was an Agency-created and subservient unit that worked under close CIA supervision. Indeed, one CIA official reported that TsOPE's contribution was limited to placing an "AEVIRGIL-1 [TsOPE-BKT] shingle on the door" in West Berlin and delegating a "real live" representative from Munich who could "speak for the group" in the divided German capital.[26]

The fact of CIA control over the exiles' Berlin operations should not obscure the basic reality that they were largely a *German* affair. Almost exclusively, the agents and informants who spread propaganda and contacted Soviet citizens were Germans, and their recruitment depended on distinctly German conditions. The

[22] As early as 1949, the NTS operated a "Hamburg Committee for Aid to Russian Refugees" which sought to encourage Soviet personnel to defect to the West, an operation perhaps supported by British MI6. Narrative Summary of AIS Relationship with NTS, n.d., 1 in AESAURUS, vol. 1, pt. 1.

[23] Project AEVIRGIL Outline, Chief, SR to Chief of Mission, Frankfurt, February 8, 1955, 5, in AEVIRGIL, vol. 1.

[24] Struktur über die russische Emigrantenorganisation National Trudevoj Sojus=NTS, n d. (not before 1955), in Bundesbeauftragte für die Unterlagen des Staatssicherheitsdienstes der ehemaligen Deutschen Demokratischen Republik, Zentralarchiv (BStU, ZA), MfS-AFO 1187, 000032.

[25] Notably, TsOPE's ballooning team in West Berlin was staffed by "local Berlin Germans" for security reasons—a reminder of the limited ability of Russian émigrés to operate in the city. AEVIRGIL status report, Chief of Base, Munich to Chief, SR, November 7, 1955, 4 in AEVIRGIL, vol. 1.

[26] Ibid.

CIA–émigré nexus focused its recruiting efforts on the large numbers of German refugees who fled communist rule to the West via Berlin throughout the decade.[27] In the typical scenario, a recent refugee would invite relatives or acquaintances remaining in the GDR to a rendezvous in West Berlin, where exile operatives would seek to recruit them and send them back to the East with various REDCAP assignments. The refugees housed in the camps in Berlin, in limbo and usually lacking a steady means of income, often proved willing to cooperate with the exiles.[28]

Taking up with the mysterious Russian figures in West Berlin was much more dangerous for Germans remaining in the East than for the refugee go-betweens. Nevertheless, the exiles succeeded in recruiting a number of East Germans. The willingness of refugees to persuade their friends, family members, or co-workers in East Germany to take part was crucial to the recruitment of East German assets for REDCAP. So too was the wider context of divided Germany. In the 1950s, living standards were plummeting in the East, while the economy of the Federal Republic was stabilizing—en route, of course, to a level of prosperity commonly likened to a miracle.[29] In the context of the poverty of East German life and the unpopularity of its rulers, the émigrés' promise of easy money appealed to some Germans—especially as one could always flee West in case of danger, as one of the exiles' German go-betweens stressed to a potential recruit.[30] In fact, some young East Germans saw work for anti-communists in the West sector as preparation for their own flight to West Germany. Such was the case with Betina Kaiser, a young journalist in East Berlin who agreed to work for the "Russian-German Friendship Society," as the NTS was presented to her.[31] After her arrest by the Stasi, Kaiser explained that she hoped to utilize her contact with this organization to find journalistic work in West Germany.[32] Clearly, German division and its consequences—the relative wealth of the West and the hemorrhaging of population by an unpopular East German regime—made it possible for the émigrés and their German cutouts to recruit East Germans for REDCAP operations.

---

[27] According to an MfS report, the NTS Berlin Office devoted an entire "department" to screening German refugees for potentially useful contacts remaining in the East. Struktur über die russische Emigrantenorganisation, 000032. Refugees from the GDR were a major factor in other espionage operations of the period. Paul Maddrell, "The Western Secret Services, the East German Ministry of State Security and the Building of the Berlin Wall," *Intelligence and National Security* 21, no. 5 (2006): 830.

[28] Vernehmungsprotokoll, February 13, 1952, in BStU, ZA, MfS-AU 82/52, Bd. 2, 000037.

[29] For an overview, see Mary Fulbrook, *A History of Germany, 1918–2014: The Divided Nation* (Chichester, UK: Wiley-Blackwell, 2014), 142–63.

[30] Vernehmungs-protokoll, February 25, 1952, in BStU, ZA, MfS-AU 193/52, Bd. II, 000185–6.

[31] I assign pseudonyms to all individuals referred to in the Stasi files. As will be discussed in Chapter 11, the NTS did establish a Russian–German Friendship Society for the purpose of courting public opinion in West Germany. It bore no direct relation to the NTS's CIA operations in Berlin.

[32] Vernehmungsprotokoll, February 18, 1952, in BStU, ZA, MfS-AU 193/52, Bd. I, 000067.

Exile Inroads into the Soviet Bloc

The availability of German recruits did not ensure the smooth operation of the exiles' efforts to demoralize and disrupt Soviet forces in Germany and Austria. To the contrary, these operations faced counter-measures from the the the Soviet Committee for State Security (KGB) and the new East German State Security Service, whose "top priority" was the struggle against political opponents on German soil and their "enemy bases" in West Germany and the Western enclave in Berlin.[33] The MfS worked under the close supervision of advisors and instructors from the KGB on the ground in Germany, and the Soviets probably kept important operations against the CIA-backed exiles under exclusive control.[34] Nevertheless, the MfS played a major role in work against CIA–exile projects in Berlin. It recruited German agents and informants to spy on the exiles, efforts whose extent were shown by the fact that sometimes multiple informants were in attendance at a single TsOPE or NTS event. They also dangled GDR citizens as double agents to the émigrés' West sector offices.[35] As a result of these painstaking efforts, East German spies came into possession of carefully guarded information on the Berlin operations: the identity of the exile operatives, their phone numbers, and the addresses of their safe houses.[36]

The leakage of such information, of course, placed the exiles and their East German helpers directly in the crosshairs of KGB and MfS operatives. Indeed, the Soviets and East Germans also undertook active measures to undermine the émigrés' Berlin gambit. Provocations were regular occurrences at the offices of the exile organizations: bomb threats were called in, leaflets appeared in the lobby of buildings alleging that the Russians working there were common criminals, and mysterious businesses appeared nearby that were suspected of being fronts for the KGB or the MfS.[37] The Soviets also resorted to violent reprisals, "wet affairs" in Chekist parlance, in their effort to counter the exile operations in Berlin. In addition to the kidnapping of A. R. Trushnovich that was discussed in Chapter 7, the MfS "seized" the leader of TsOPE's Berlin Branch in 1956— who then, it seems, exposed the identities of his German agent network.[38] Such

---

[33] Jens Gieseke and David Burnett, *The History of the Stasi: East Germany's Secret Police, 1945–1990* (New York: Berghahn Books, 2014), 32.

[34] Ibid., 39. In one case, the MfS passed on the informant "Riegner," who was keeping tabs on TsOPE, to "Soviet friends." Monatsbericht-Oktober-1955, Verwaltung Gross-Berlin, abt. II-1, January 11, 1955, in BStU, ZA, MfS-AOP 10286/62, Bd. I, 0291.

[35] See a case in which an East German recruited by the MfS to reconnoiter TsOPE headquarters in West Berlin as an ostensible informant switched allegiances. BStU, ZA, MfS-GH 61/61.

[36] Struktur über die russische Emigrantenorganisation National Trudevoj Sojus=NTS, n.d. (not before 1955), BStU-ZA, MfS-AFO 1187, 000027–35.

[37] Unidentified testimony on TsOPE and Betr: NTS-Berlin-Grunewald, Hohenzollerndamm 98/99, November 9, 1961, in BStU-ZA, MfS-GH 9/62, Bd. II, 000071, 000090.

[38] A December 1956 document shows that the MfS was comparing the interrogation records of TsOPE member "Victor" with information gathered through two MfS *Gesellschaftliche Mitarbeiter*

operations struck fear into the émigrés in Berlin who, according to one account, received special permission to carry handguns in the city.[39] Indeed, violent retributions were a sure indication of the determination of the USSR and its German satellite to uproot the exiles from Berlin at virtually any cost—a fact that becomes especially clear when one considers that wet affairs were relatively rare expedients in post-Stalin Soviet intelligence operations.[40]

Quite independent of counterintelligence operations, the East German system posed weighty logistical obstacles to the exile defector-inducement operations— as, indeed, the closed societies of the Soviet bloc always did for opposing spy services. Recruiting East Germans who could operate in close proximity to Soviet troops was a challenge, even when the émigrés located Germans with the Russian-language skills necessary for the task. After a brief postwar period when rules against fraternization with the occupied population were lacking, Soviet forces in Germany and Austria steadily ramped up measures to isolate their troops and also Soviet civilian personnel from the local population in the late 1940s. Workplaces separated their Soviet and German employees, while the Soviet forces resettled the German inhabitants of entire urban neighborhoods and villages located close to Soviet troops.[41] Meanwhile, Soviet personnel also came under increasing surveillance, both from fellow Soviet employees and soldiers and from Germans in their midst. A Soviet Army veterinarian who defected to the West thought that he "had been under the observation of his German cook, maid, chauffeur and doorman."[42] Under such pressure, nodes of cross-cultural contact shrank to a minimum.

The extensive counterintelligence operations and security arrangements in the GDR posed serious problems for the REDCAP operations—not to speak of

---

(GMs), presumably with the goal of rolling up the TsOPE agent network. Schneider, Abteilung 5 to MfS Berlin-Abteilung II, December 27, 1956, in BStU-ZA, MfS-AOP 10286/62, Bd. I. With regard to the 1956 episode, a CIA report noted that the TsOPE operative, obviously the above-mentioned "Victor," had failed to "take the necessary precautions in going to a night meeting alone with a suspect contact," raising the possibility that he had been doubled already by the Soviets. Action Reported by the Field, no author indicated, January 1–31, 1957, 2, in AEVIRGIL, vol. 1. In 1961, the then head of TsOPE's Berlin office was beaten nearly to death in an episode mentioned only peripherally in a declassified CIA document. Chief, Munich Operations Base to Chief, SR, Chief, EE and Chief of Station, Germany, Su: Close Down of AEVIRGIL 51, February 27, 1962, in AEVIRGIL, vol. 2.

---

[39] I. V. Ovchinnikov, *Na pereput'iakh Rossii* (Moscow: Informatsionno-ekspertnaia gruppa "Panorama," 1995), 93–4.

[40] Christopher M. Andrew and Vasilii Mitrokhin, *The Mitrokhin Archive: The KGB in Europe and the West* (London: Allen Lane, 1999), 467, and Serhii Plokhy, *The Man with the Poison Gun: A Cold War Spy Story* (New York: Basic Books, 2016), 114–16.

[41] Norman M. Naimark, *The Russians in Germany: A History of the Soviet Zone of Occupation, 1945–1949* (Cambridge, MA: Belknap Press of Harvard University Press, 1995), 90–6. For a description of fully developed Soviet towns in the GDR, see Kowalczuk and Wolle, *Roter Stern über Deutschland*, 123–6.

[42] Report 1, August 1951, 3, in Hoover Institution Library and Archives, Office of External Research typescript: The Soviet Union as Reported by Former Soviet Citizens, External Research Staff, Office of Intelligence Research, Department of State (hereinafter The Soviet Union as Reported by Former Soviet Citizens).

extreme danger to the German civilians who worked as cross-sector runners and agents. The MfS case on the prosecution of Pauline Schneider, a 30-year-old schoolteacher in East Berlin, sheds light on the perilous conditions faced by German civilians. Like most other Germans who became involved in the CIA–émigré operations, Schneider came into the orbit of the NTS through a relative who had fled to the West.[43] While visiting her cousin, Schneider met a foreigner who, to her surprise, claimed to be a Soviet citizen. Soon her new Russian contact convinced her to undertake assignments for the NTS back home in the East. Hatred of communism—a desire to topple what she called the "power regime of the Soviets" (*Machtregime der Sowjets*) in Germany—seems to have motivated her to take this step. She was also impressed by her new Russian friend, who followed longstanding Solidarist practice by supplying wildly exaggerated accounts of the organization's conspiratorial feats.[44] For instance, Schneider recalled stories of German war veterans who smuggled NTS leaflets from West Berlin to the East in their prosthetic limbs and distributed them near the barracks of Soviet soldiers.[45]

Schneider's stint as an NTS agent was short, inconsequential, and tragic. She failed to carry out her first task, that of locating and contacting a Soviet civilian she had met in passing some time before. (Schneider claimed that she lacked the time or interest to execute the task, but her Stasi interrogators thought that she had simply failed to locate him.)[46] When she received an instruction to strew NTS leaflets close to several Soviet installations near Berlin's East–West demarcation line, she neglected to act again, instead burning the leaflets in the toilet in her apartment.[47]

The Schneider case was emblematic of the ineffectiveness and unreliability of the CIA's and exiles' German recruits. A Soviet newspaper editor tied to the KGB told the MfS that "most agents" employed by the NTS acted as Schneider did, destroying the leaflets they were tasked with distributing while also delivering to their Russian handlers "false reports in order to receive money."[48] Perhaps the Soviet reporter had an interest in stressing the exiles' failures, and one should add that not all Germans working for the CIA REDCAP oeperations were as inactive as Schneider. The MfS routinely discovered hand-distributed "subversive documents" penned by Russian exiles in public spaces across the GDR, such as a

[43] Schneider's cousin was a Socialist Unity Party of Germany (*Sozialistische Einheitspartei Deutschlands* or SED) official suspected of involvement in the uprising of June 1953. Arriving in the West with a cache of official documents, he quickly gained political refugee status and then received unspecified "support" from an NTS agent. See BStU-ZA, Mfs-S 357/54, Bd. II, 000037.
[44] Ibid., 000033.
[45] Ibid., 000034.
[46] Schlussbericht, Berlin, April 20, 1954, in BStU-ZA, MfS-AU 357/54, Bd. I, 000121.
[47] Ibid., 000122.
[48] Interview eines Vertreters des MfS der DDR durch einen Mitarbeiter der Zeitung "Für die Rückkehr in die Heimat," in BStU-ZA, MfS-ZAIG 30250, 0364. The publication *For Return to the Homeland* (*Za vozvrashchenie na rodinu*) was part of the KGB-controlled return campaign discussed in Chapter 10.

prominent street and an open-air theater in Halle.[49] Nevertheless, clear enough is the fact that some of the émigrés' employees were derelict in their duty—often, like Schneider, out of fear and a lack of accountability toward their West-sector employers. In 1956, Georgii Il'ich Antonov, the head of the Union for the Struggle for the Liberation of the Peoples of Russia (SBONR), alleged that agents hired by "some organizations" to spread anti-Soviet propaganda—though, of course, not those tied to his own—burned hundreds of thousands of leaflets in furnaces while announcing that they had distributed them all over East German territory.[50]

Schneider's story underscored not only operational misfires but also the perils of exile operations for the Germans who took them up. One of the few assignments that Schneider actually carried out resulted in her arrest.[51] Schneider brought her friend, a high-ranking German engineer with whom she had held "intimate relations," to the West sector to meet her NTS contact. Allegedly, her lover had taken an interest in the NTS propaganda he saw in her apartment and even borrowed her copy of the NTS's German-language publication *Deutsch-Russische Stossrichtung* ("The German-Russian Thrust").[52] Unfortunately for Schneider, the engineer was in fact "our GI [*Geheimer Informator* or secret informer] *Raucher* ['Smoker']." The Stasi left Schneider at freedom to meet with her NTS contact for a few months, no doubt hoping that her trips to West Berlin would produce further inroads into CIA activities there. Probably realizing that the case had exhausted itself, the Stasi arrested Schneider while she was en route to the West sector in early 1954.[53] Schneider's capture demonstrated a central weakness of the exile REDCAP operations: their reliance on a chain of intermediaries extending from the CIA and Russian émigrés via Germans to Soviet citizens. Each link proved vulnerable to the disruption and penetration measures of Soviet and GDR counterintelligence.

It may be that the exiles and the CIA were powerless to protect Schneider from the GDR's extensive net of informers or, indeed, the extensive KGB–MfS operations to detect enemy agents in East Germany during these years.[54] Yet MfS files reveal that the CIA-backed exiles, and perhaps particularly those of the NTS, also

[49] In this case, the NTS literature consisted of "self-printed inflammatory pamphlets" (*selbstgedruckte Hetzschriften*), so presumably it was spread by agents rather than by balloon. Staatssekretariat für Staatssicherheit Bezirksverwaltung Halle to Staatssekretariat für Staatssicherheit, Hauptabteilung II/1, December 21, 1954, in BStU, ZA, MfS-Allg. S 7/55, 000065.

[50] *Chetvertyi s'ezd Soiuza Bor'by za Osvobozhdenie Narodov Rossii (SBONR), Zakrytaia chast' 19–22 fevralia 1956 goda* (Munich: Verlag "Golos Naroda," 1958), 8.

[51] In addition to the episode described here, Schneider delivered to the NTS the insignia of mass organizations of the GDR, including the SED and the German-Soviet Friendship Association—hardly a high-value task. Schlussbericht, Berlin, April 20, 1954, in BStU, ZA, MfS-AU 357/54, Bd. I, 000121.

[52] Schlussbericht, 000120–000121. This publication is discussed in Chapter 11 in the context of émigré contacts with West German society.

[53] See Zwischenbericht, February 21, 1954, in BStU, ZA, MfS-AU 357/54, Bd. I, 00008–000012.

[54] S. N. Lebedev, *Ocherki istorii Rossiiskoi vneshnei razvedki*, vol. 5 (Moscow: Mezhdunarodnye Otnosheniia, 2003), 31.

bore responsibility for the frequent capture of their German agents. Without a doubt, the CIA–exile operations in Berlin were reckless and poorly thought out. Consider the case of Hans Schick, a house painter from Rostock who fled the GDR in 1951. Notably, the NTS recruited Schick through blackmail, with a stranger warning him that he would lose his refugee status should he refuse to work for the Solidarists.[55] The NTS sent Schick back to the East with the task of recruiting his friends as propaganda distributors. The hapless East German then received the assignment of strewing NTS leaflets from a moving S-Bahn train on the Friedrichstrasse in East Berlin. He was immediately spotted by a Stasi employee while carrying out his dangerous assignment and was arrested at the next station.[56]

As was the case with the ill-fated NTS infiltration operations, failure bred suspicion of Soviet penetration of the exile ranks. In particular, the exile operations in Berlin proved vulnerable to penetration agents infiltrated directly by KGB or MfS into the milieu of the émigrés.[57] Indeed, one important Soviet agent is known to have run REDCAP operations in the 1950s. Aleksandr Grigor'evich Orlov-Kopatskii earned his spot in the history of espionage as "Sasha," the Soviet agent whose existence spurred a bruising mole hunt within the CIA in the 1960s and 1970s.[58] Less widely known are his connections to the REDCAP operations. Apparently, Kopatskii was a Soviet spy who worked for a German intelligence service in World War II. After the war, Kopatskii worked for the Gehlen Organization for a time before being dropped, prompting him to take up with Soviet intelligence yet again in 1949. Probably on instructions from his Soviet handlers, Kopatskii joined SBONR's "combat detachment" in 1951, a CIA-funded espionage and propaganda outfit in divided Berlin.[59] Although the detachment was soon disbanded when CIA became convinced of the Vlasovites' "unsuitability for clandestine activity," Kopatskii continued to work as a contract agent in Berlin

---

[55] The threat was issued by a man claiming to act on behalf of the *Vereinigung Politischer Ostflüchtlinge* (League of Political Refugees from the East), an interest group representing refugees that had close ties to West Germany's ruling Christian Democratic Party. The unnamed individual claimed that Schick had traveled back to Rostock from the West, violating his refugee claim. Urteil, July 21, 1952, in BStU-ZA, MfS-AU 82/52, Bd. 2, 00065.

[56] Vernehmungsprotokoll, September 3, 1951, in BStU-ZA, MfS-AU 82/52, Bd. 2, 000018–000019. The file leaves unclear whether Schick was already under observation when he was arrested. Festnahmebericht, August 17, 1951, in BStU-ZA, MfS-AU 82/52, Bd. 1, 000007.

[57] For instance, the Berlin sector MfS office reported that the unidentified agent "Wolf" was "smuggled close" (*herangeschleust*) to TsOPE. Analyse und Plan zur weiteren Bearbeitung der ZOPE, March 23, 1956, in BStU, ZA, MfS-AOP 10286/62, Bd. I, 0173.

[58] The hunt for a mole with the code name "Sasha" was sparked by information provided by KGB defector Anatolii Mikhailovich Golitsyn. See David E. Murphy, "Sasha Who?", *Intelligence and National Security* 8, no. 1 (1993): 102–7, and "The Hunt for Sasha is Over," *CIRA Newsletter* 25, no. 3 (Fall 2000): 11–15. The identification of Kopatskii as "Sasha" comes from Christopher M. Andrew and Vasilii Mitrokhin, *The Mitrokhin Archive: The KGB in Europe and the West* (London: Allen Lane, 1999), 195–6, 230–2.

[59] See Kopatskii's "oath" in joining the organization. Obiazatel'stvo, September 10, 1951, in FSO, 01–034 Kromiadi-Kruzhin, kor. K-2 (marked 2-aia emig. polit., deiat., otchety, delovaia perepiska).

REDCAP operations for several years, using his position to betray an unclear but perhaps large number of German agents in the East.[60] Clearly, the East German recruits for the REDCAP enterprise faced danger and betrayal on all sides, victims of an intelligence game played at their expense.

Seducing the Enemy

The REDCAP operations, then, faced substantial problems in the form of East German and Soviet counterintelligence operations and amateurishness on the CIA–émigré side. But problems did not end there. Even those German agents who managed to go under the radar in the East faced the daunting challenge of contacting and building trust with Soviet personnel or soldiers, all with the aim of feeding them NTS or TsOPE anti-communist propaganda and calling on them to flee to the West. By reconstructing the situation facing Soviet citizens serving abroad, one can appreciate how tall an order facilitating defection would be.

Soviet citizens in military or civilian positions in East Germany had multiple reasons to rebuff REDCAP approaches. Most weighty among them was fear. Defectors knew they were putting their own lives in danger, for they would be tried for treason should the attempt at flight go awry or should their intentions be detected beforehand. And foremost in the minds of Soviet citizens contemplating defection was fear of reprisals against their family members who would remain in the USSR, as a 1954 report by an unnamed CIA officer who had worked on REDCAP missions conveyed. The targets of REDCAP approaches were well aware that Soviet law enshrined the principle that the immediate relatives of "traitors" shared their responsibility.[61]

A second set of considerations involved doubts about the people approaching the Soviet servitors (that is, the REDCAP operatives and their German intermediaries). Soviet citizens had no means of checking the bona fides of the Germans who offered to help them flee, or of the Russian émigrés who stood behind them. How could one be sure that the invitation to defect was not a provocation by the Soviet intelligence services? Even if one believed that the approach was genuine, potential defectors remained mistrustful of the powers whose asylum they would seek, fearing that US or British authorities might mistreat defectors or even hand

---

[60] Murphy, "The Hunt for Sasha is Over": 13. A. Balshov, head of SBONR Combat Organization to Council of Combat Organization, July 27, 1951, in FSO, 01–034 Kromiadi-Kruzhin, kor. K-2. Ironically, CIA suspicions of Kopatskii's loyalty were fed by his scattered accomplishments in REDCAP operations, a circumstance that indirectly suggests the poor record of defection operations. Murphy, Kondrashev, and Bailey, *Battleground Berlin*, 110–12.

[61] Su: The Inducement of Soviet Defections, report sent from [redacted] to Chief, SR, May 4, 1954, 15, in REDCAP. For an example, see Report 3, May 15, 1952, 2, in The Soviet Union as Reported by Former Soviet Citizens.

them back to the Soviet authorities—fears that Soviet propaganda efforts in the armed forces in Germany did everything possible to strengthen.[62]

Potential defectors had reason to worry about their prospects after defection, as well. As the CIA report noted, Soviet personnel abroad were "fearful of assassination or kidnapping by the Soviets if they can be located after their defection"—again, an apprehension the Soviet authorities sought to inflate through propaganda stressing "the omniscience, omnipotence, and omnipresence of the Soviet Intelligence Service."[63] Even if one leaves such perceived dangers aside, the future life of a potential defector in the West remained unclear. What material support might one receive from the US (or British) government, and how could one survive in the capitalist economy, which Soviet citizens were accustomed to perceive as "a vicious system of survival of the fittest"?[64] In sum, even a soldier or civilian with a desire to flee to the West had countless reasons not to act on it.

The difficulty of creating trust between the inducer and induced dictated the primary strategy employed in REDCAP operations: the exploitation of sexual relationships between Soviet personnel stationed in the Eastern zones of Germany or Austria and women from the surrounding societies. There was good reason for the CIA to embrace this approach. Military defeat and occupation led to extensive sexual relations between vanquisher and vanquished in postwar Germany and Austria. Alongside the widespread rape of German women by Soviet troops after victory there existed a sphere of at least nominally consensual romantic and sexual relationships across the national divide.[65] One might picture a spectrum of such amorous encounters according to their degree of seriousness, extending from prostitution, on one end, to the Soviet officers who established families with so-called "occupation wives," on the other.[66] The testimony of defectors offers some sense of the scope of the phenomenon, even if one makes allowances for hyperbole. A postwar captain who defected from the Soviet forces in Germany recalled that "almost every Soviet officer had ties (sviazi) with at least one German woman."[67]

---

[62] Sponge Report no. 53 (DS-616), February 3, 1955, 22, in NARA, RG 466 (HICOG), box 2 (hereinafter Peripheral Reporting Unit).

[63] Ibid., 14–20.

[64] Su: The Inducement of Soviet Defections, 17.

[65] As Barbara Stelzl-Marx notes, the "material asymmetry" between occupiers and the occupied made the line between voluntary and forced relationships unclear. Stelzl-Marx, Stalins Soldaten in Österreich: Die Innensicht der Sowjetischen Besatzung 1945–1955 (Munich: Böhlau Verlag, 2012), 496.

[66] See ibid., 490–524; Silke Satjukow, Besatzer: "Die Russen" in Deutschland 1945–1994 (Göttingen: Vandenhoeck & Ruprecht, 2008), 56–60, and Ingrid Bauer and Renate Huber, "Sexual encounters across (former) enemy lines," in Günter Bischof et al. (eds.) Sexuality in Austria (Piscataway, NJ: Transaction Publishers, 2007), 79–81.

[67] The Harvard Project on the Soviet Social System Online (hereinafter HPSSS), schedule A, vol. 27, case 527, 57–8.

The already mentioned Soviet anti-fraternization measures aimed to prevent and disrupt such cross-national relationships. From the late 1940s, Soviet authorities in Germany typically reacted to cases of amorous ties to Germans by redeploying the offending Soviet citizen to the USSR and demoting him in the service. Even casual contact was punished. In 1954, a border guard caught talking to a German girl while on duty was subjected to public shaming at a platoon meeting and given three days of solitary confinement.[68] Meanwhile, political officers in the Soviet army attempted to scare away the soldiers from German women, describing the latter as "fascists" and, not necessarily inaccurately in light of REDCAP, "spies of Anglo-American imperialists."[69] While the anti-fraternization measures were surely effective, Soviet military forces failed to stamp out romantic attachments between German women and Soviet citizens entirely. A private who deserted from Austria in 1953 recalled that perhaps 5 percent of soldiers fraternized with the local population, although "secretly and at night."[70] One can assume that considerably more officers, who enjoyed more freedom than their subordinates, did the same.

Sexual encounters were the main means by which the CIA sought to contact the Soviet armed forces. Then Berlin CIA chief Murphy claims that "at least 95 percent of the social contacts" between Soviet citizens and Germans of which his base became aware involved ties between Soviet men and German women, and the latter became the main recruits for REDCAP operations.[71] Presumably, the use of sex in the Berlin operations was a product of CIA tradecraft, but the Russian exiles were complicit in it; indeed, according to the MfS, some NTS and TsOPE operatives in Berlin had sexual relations with the German women they recruited.[72] Relevant in this regard was the patriarchal internal culture of the NTS, an organization in which few women participated—and those who did were viewed as matriarchal and refined "ladies of the old society."[73] Predictably, the spies of East Germany and the USSR used similar tactics as their opponents, recruiting German women who "associate[d] with" Soviet citizens on a regular basis in order to combat the émigré operations.[74] In this manner, women's bodies served as a battleground in an intelligence war in Germany and Austria.

A view of the place of German women in the exile operations emerges from the MfS case of Gertrude Weber, who was tried for anti-socialist activities in 1954.

---

[68] Sponge Report no. 52 (DS-615), December 7, 1954, 2, in Peripheral Reporting Unit.

[69] Interview Report no. 6, November 17, 1952, 4, in The Soviet Union as Reported by Former Soviet Citizens and HPSSS schedule A, vol. 27, case 527, 57–8.

[70] Sponge Report no. 53 (DS-616), March 2, 1955, 14, in Peripheral Reporting Unit and Interview Report no. 7, June 4, 1953, 9, in The Soviet Union as Reported by Former Soviet Citizens.

[71] Murphy, Kondrashev, and Bailey, *Battleground Berlin*, 299. On the use of women in the émigré REDCAP operations, see Vernehmungsprotokoll der Beschuldigten, February 23, 1952, in BStU, ZA, MfS-AU 357/54, Bd. II, 000034, and Analyse und Plan, 0173.

[72] On the TsOPE agent "Petrov," see Analyse und Plan, 0172.

[73] A. E. Levitin-Krasnov, *Iz drugoi strany: emigratsiia* (Parizh: Poiski, 1985), 99.

[74] Monatsbericht-Oktober-1955, 0292.

While a student at Humboldt University in East Berlin in 1952, Weber developed "intimate relations" with N. F. Lupenko, a Soviet Air Force Lieutenant—according to the investigation, already her second amorous relationship with a member of the Soviet armed forces. Weber's desire to defect to the West with Lupenko brought her into contact with the NTS, which promised to facilitate their flight.[75] When Lupenko returned to the USSR soon before their planned defection—and documents leave unclear whether this occurred by chance or because his ties to Weber had been discovered—the NTS recruited Weber as an agent.

Compared to that of Schneider (discussed above), Weber's work as an agent in the East was eventful and even turbulent. One evening, Sergeant F. G. Kravchuk, Lupenko's former supervisor in Germany, unexpectedly appeared at her apartment in Brandenburg an der Havel to deliver a letter from Lupenko, who was now serving outside Kiev. Soon Kravchuk began to frequent Weber's apartment, and she received an assignment from NTS to influence him in an anti-Soviet direction. Apparently she had success, for she handed Kravchuk NTS propaganda materials and even a letter from her Russian contact in West Berlin.[76] An apparent breakthrough came in June 1953, when Sergeant Kravchuk departed for leave in the USSR carrying a bag with a secret pouch containing NTS literature, a kit for writing in secret script, and a copy of the NTS program on a film negative that was hidden in a toothpaste tube.[77] Apparently, in Kiev Kravchuk met with Lupenko, whom he encouraged either to defect or to work for the NTS on Soviet soil.

The penetration of Soviet borders by an NTS agent, a rare occurrence for the period, did not yield concrete results. According to Weber, Lupenko had declared that defection was impossible and was noncommittal about creating an underground NTS cell, claiming that he would have to read the materials brought by Kravchuk before reaching a decision.[78] Meanwhile, Weber continued to work for the NTS, gathering intelligence on nearby military installations, establishing contact with other Soviet officers, and—in an assignment that speaks to the wider REDCAP strategy in the GDR—compiling a list of twelve women who were known to be in "friendly relations" with Soviet officers.[79]

---

[75] She received the phone number of the NTS Berlin office from the Investigating Committee of Free Jurists (*Untersuchungsausschuß Freiheitlicher Juristen* or UfJ), another controversial CIA-funded underground organization operating in East Germany. Anklageschrift, Der Staatsanwalt des Bezirkes I 284/54, July 27, 1954, in BStU, ZA, MfS-AU 410/54, Bd. II, 0135–6. On the checkered history of the UfJ's operations in the GDR, see Murphy, Kondrashev, and Bailey, *Battleground Berlin*, 112–26.

[76] On Weber's work recruiting Kravchuk for the NTS, see Vernehmungs-Protokoll der Beschuldigten, May 7, 1954, in BStU, ZA, MfS-AU 410/54, Bd. I, 0077–9.

[77] Vernehmungs-Protokoll der Beschuldigten, May 13, 1954, in BStU, ZA, MfS-AU 410/54, Bd. I, 0088.

[78] Ibid., 0091, 0097. A CIA report mentions one "NIKITA," a Soviet sergeant who had returned to the USSR and whose letter had been "received by his friend in the Soviet occupation forces." This might well be a reference to the Weber-Lupenko-Kravchuk case, although the Stasi file lists Lupenko as a lieutenant, not a sergeant. CSOB Progress Report for December 1952, 6 in AESAURUS, vol. 2, pt. 1.

[79] Anklageschrift, Der Staatsanwalt des Bezirkes I 284/54, July 27, 1954, in BStU, ZA, MfS-AU 410/54, Bd. II, 0134.

After her arrest, the Stasi investigators presented Weber as an anti-communist seductress who had long been using temptations of the flesh and her command of Russian to corrupt officers of the Soviet army.[80] Sexual relations were indeed a constant theme in Weber's case, and included the romantic relationship she allegedly had with her NTS handler in West Berlin.[81] Weber, who belonged to the German population forcefully expelled from East Prussian lands annexed by Poland at the end of the war, might well have been hostile to the Soviet Union. Nevertheless, one should treat the Stasi's picture of sexual–ideological subversion skeptically. Useful here is the view of Barbara Stelzl-Marx, who uses Soviet records to argue that Austrian women who worked for Western intelligence services were "inconspicuous women" (*unauffällige Frauen*) whose connection to the Cold War was largely coincidental.[82] In all likelihood, Weber's agreement to work for the NTS had much to do with the considerable earnings it brought her, which amounted to some 5,000 DM by the time of her arrest. The extent to which she had bettered her circumstances is conveyed by the valuables she listed carefully during interrogation: a new bicycle, a camera, a typewriter, clothes, and an alarm clock.[83] Rather than accurately describing Weber's life, the Stasi operatives' invocation of a sexualized anti-communism reflected their totalizing ideological vision of the enemy, the conspiratorial notion that the imperialists would stop at nothing to disrupt socialism.[84]

Whatever Weber's motivations were, her committed service to the NTS seems unquestionable. More doubtful was its effectiveness. The Weber file shows that the REDCAP operations frequently met with standoffish or hostile responses from the Soviet citizens who were their target. With the exception of Kravchuk and perhaps Lupenko, the Soviet citizens Weber contacted proved uninterested in or downright hostile toward her exile connections and their anti-communist propaganda. In 1953, Weber met with Soviet Captain Borisov, with whom, according to her testimony, she had been engaged in "an intimate relationship" before meeting Lupenko in 1951. When Weber told Borisov of "an anti-Soviet Russian group," he advised her to break ties with it immediately. And while Borisov borrowed from Weber an anti-Soviet novel published by the NTS's *Posev* publishing house— *Denis Bushuev* by second-wave writer S. S. Maksimov—he returned it unceremoniously a week later by throwing it through the window of her apartment and never spoke to Weber again.[85] Likewise, two Soviet officers she approached in

---

[80] Ibid., 0134.
[81] Ibid., 0136.
[82] Stelzl-Marx, *Stalins Soldaten in Österreich*, 489.
[83] Vernehmungsprotokoll, June 15, 1954, in BStU, ZA, MfS-AU 410/54, Bd. I, 0126.
[84] Mary Fulbrook, *Anatomy of a Dictatorship: Inside the GDR, 1949–1989* (New York: Oxford University Press, 1997), 24–6.
[85] Vernehmungsprotokoll, June 10, 1954, in BStU, ZA, MfS-AU 410/54, Bd. I, 0116. The one Soviet citizen other than Kravchuk whom Weber roped into NTS affairs, a Soviet doctor who had a "purely friendly" relationship with Weber, apparently did so out of a feeling of obligation. Through Weber's

1953 rebuffed her because, in Weber's estimation, they "had a positive attitude toward the Soviet Union."[86] Such cool reactions to Weber surely reflected the constant stream of Soviet invective against the émigrés in the Soviet press, which must have shaped soldiers' view of NTS "traitors" and "terrorists" in the West and driven home the dire consequences that might follow from interacting with German women (or men) tied to them.

The MfS arrested Weber in April 1954, roughly three years after her association with the NTS began. Although documents leave unclear how the Stasi had come onto her trail, several potential scenarios come to mind. Kravchuk, the mysterious sergeant who procured a letter from Weber's estranged lover in the USSR and then agreed to be recruited by Weber for the NTS, might well have been a Soviet plant. Just as likely was the possibility that Weber was spotted near the heavily surveilled NTS office in Berlin, which, inexplicably, she visited every four months to write reports on her activities.[87]

Regardless of how she fell into the Stasi's net, Weber's plight is suggestive of the wider limitations of REDCAP operations. While the overall record of the exiles' REDCAP operations is not entirely clear, sources leave no doubt that it was marginal. The total number of Soviet defections was small in the period: according to one source, Soviet military defections in particular numbered just forty-four persons from 1951 to 1958.[88] And several sources suggest that the émigrés, or the CIA in general, often played no role in spurring those defections that did take place. A January 1953 CIA report mentioned that the NTS had just three Soviet contacts in Berlin at the time.[89] Interrogations of defectors by US personnel also suggest that REDCAP-inspired defections were few and far between. Of the fifty-seven interviews of defectors located in the archives, only one case, which involved a Soviet officer serving in Austria who was passed Russian exile literature by "friends" from the local population, bore the clear contours of a REDCAP operation.[90] And a book coauthored by then Berlin Chief of Base David E. Murphy offers a negative view of the entire REDCAP enterprise in the city,

---

NTS-CIA contacts, the doctor acquired six million units of penicillin to make up for a large stockpile of the drug that had gone missing on his watch. Even then, the doctor refused to do more than provide the NTS with the numbers of several Soviet army units as well as copies of the magazine *Sovetskaia armiia* ("Soviet Army"). Vernehmungsprotokoll, May 5, 1954, in BStU, ZA, MfS-AU 410/54, Bd. I, 0072–0073.

---

[86] Notably, Weber heard later that one of them cursed the collective farms in discussions with his comrades. Ibid., 0118.

[87] See Vernehmungsprotokollen for May 3 and June 8, 1954, in BStU, ZA, MfS-AU 410/54, Bd. I, 0068, 0100.

[88] Riehle, "Early Cold War evolution of British and US defector policy": 15.

[89] Ibid., and Project AEVIRGIL Outline, 4.

[90] All the publications the officer received from his "Western friends in Austria" were connected to CIA operations: *Posev* (the NTS), *Svoboda* (TsOPE), and the Bulletin of the Institute for the Study of the History and Culture of the USSR. Sponge Defector Interrogation Report (Sponge no. 49, DS-602), October 25, 1954, 4, in Peripheral Reporting Unit.

stating that by mid-decade "it became accepted that is was useless for BOB [Berlin Operations Base] even to try to recruit and maintain East Germans in or near Soviet installations in East Germany."[91] The results of émigré-CIA efforts to recruit defectors in place via Germany were even bleaker: three of the four "NTS Berlin REDCAP recruits" who returned to the USSR from 1954 to 1957, including a navy lieutenant and an army captain, turned out to be under Soviet control, and might well have been Soviet intelligence agents dangled by the enemy.[92]

CIA officials at the time were unwilling to admit the ineffectiveness of the REDCAP operations, but their defense of them was unconvincing. For instance, in 1958 Murphy claimed that the émigré REDCAP operations had an *indirect* effect on defection, as they had encouraged spontaneous or "walk-in" defections of Soviet officials in West Berlin. In the previous few years, "virtually every defector" from the Soviet armed forces in East Germany had "been aware of the existence" of the NTS as well as of TsOPE, and such knowledge had exerted "some effect on their individual decisions to defect."[93] One should view this sanguine take on REDCAP's impact skeptically. Murphy might have been under pressure to depict REDCAP operations as not having been in vain. And the notion that NTS and TsOPE propaganda was what drove defections is flawed: As Chapter 9 will show, many defectors in the period were driven by motivations other than anti-communist beliefs, let alone inspiration gained from the pronouncements of NTS or TsOPE.

Why did CIA operatives and the exiles working under them refuse to acknowledge their inability to spur Soviet defections? For the exiles, it made sense to stress that the Russian people were virtually uniformly hostile to Soviet rule, and that "a total uprising is possible any day," as TsOPE operative G. A. Kurbatov put it in 1954.[94] As the émigrés understood, the viability of the NTS and TsOPE as instruments of political warfare depended on the perception that mass discontent existed among the Russian Soviet population. The CIA's ongoing support of REDCAP throughout the decade had a political logic, as well. As Wesley Wark identified in an analysis of defection policies pursued by the British Information Research Department (IRD) in the same period, defections bolstered the home front by providing a useful image of "a Red Army ready and waiting to hear the siren call of the West."[95] Similarly, the US defector strategy, which from its inception had treated defectors "more as propaganda opportunities than as

[91] Murphy, Kondrashev, and Bailey, *Battleground Berlin*, 256.
[92] Termination of Project AENOBLE, Memorandum from Chief, SR Division, October 13, 1959, in AESAURUS, vol. 3. pt. 1.
[93] See COB, Berlin, to COS, Germany, June 2, 1958 in AEVIRGIL, vol. 1.
[94] Bericht, betr: Grosskundgebung des Zentralvorstands der Nachkriegsemigranten aus der UdSSR in der Festhalle, April 8, 1954, in BStU-ZA, MfS-AOP 10286/62, Bd. I, 0259.
[95] Wesley K. Wark, "Coming in from the Cold: British Propaganda and Red Army Defectors," *International History Review* 9, no. 1 (1987): 71.

intelligence sources," had an essentially populist and barnstorming quality.[96] As Murphy writes with regard to REDCAP, "Americans love nothing better than a well-organized promotional campaign."[97] As happened with the NTS infiltration campaigns discussed in Chapter 7, the CIA defector-inducement program in Germany was as much a publicity stunt as an intelligence operation.

Ninety-Nine Exile Balloons

The REDCAP operations, with their murky affairs involving spies and lovers, coincided with a seemingly more straightforward action against the East: mass propaganda operations. The main means of sending propaganda to the East was the launching of hot-air balloons from West Berlin or along the German inter-zonal border, which were carried over the Iron Curtain by prevailing winds and dropped packets of anti-Soviet leaflets along their path.[98] The balloon operations were large-scale operations that encompassed propaganda workshops, print shops, and distribution teams. In 1959, TsOPE produced an extraordinary five million leaflets a month, while ordering twelve million more per month from commercial printers.[99] The sheer scale of the leaflet drops caused considerable trouble for East German authorities. In a single week of June 1954, local author-ities in the Thuringian district of Suhl confiscated 71,500 Russian-language leaflets, mostly from the NTS, and mobilized for the purpose the police, Special Command forces (*Sonderkommando*), and "voluntary helpers" from the civilian population.[100] For the administrators in East German towns and villages, the logistical hassles posed by the leaflet actions were perhaps a form of psychological harassment.

Unfortunately for the exiles, the possibility of delivering balloons to specific targets such as Soviet troop concentrations and barracks was slight. To be sure, TsOPE literature boasted of the organization's successes, such as the alleged distribution of six million leaflets to Soviet troops carrying out maneuvers in fall 1953—an operation which, according to CIA staff, was probably responsible for the "abrupt termination" of the exercises ten days ahead of schedule.[101] Nonethe-less, imperfect balloon technology made such direct hits rare. Unpredictable

[96] Riehle, "Early Cold War evolution of British and US defector policy": 15.

[97] Murphy, Kondrashev, and Bailey, *Battleground Berlin*, 239.

[98] See the description in Ia. A. Trushnovich, "NTS v poslevoennom Berline: probnyi shar," *Posev* no. 9 (1999), http://www.posev.ru/files/nts-about/ne9993.htm, accessed July 20, 2016. Alongside the balloons to the GDR, the CIA-funded émigrés also carried out "long-range" ballooning targeting the Soviet Union itself. See Chapter 11 of this book.

[99] Project report: TsOPE, no author, n.d. (1959), 2, in AEVIRGIL, vol. 1.

[100] Staatsekretariat für Staatssicherheit, Bezirksverwaltung Suhl to Staatssekretariat für Staatssicher-heit, Hauptabteilung II, June 3, 1954, in BStU-ZA, MfS-Allg. S 7/55.

[101] Emigration aus der Sowjetunion—Stimme des russischen Volkes von heute: Über den Zentral-verband der Nachkriegsemigranten aus der UdSSR, n.d. (no later than 1955), in BStU-ZA, MfS-AOP

climate conditions meant that the leaflets rarely fell where they were supposed to, instead littering farms and forests in nearby areas.[102] And while the enterprising émigrés developed wax-seal mechanisms meant to ensure the timed release of leaflets, huge numbers of leaflets often fell in a single spot; witness the peasant in the county of Weimar who discovered a 10-kilogram bundle of NTS leaflets in his fields.[103] Typically, local residents informed the authorities of the mysterious objects, and the police quickly descended on the scene to destroy them. One can say with confidence that the vast majority of printed material distributed to East Germany was never opened, let alone read by Soviet personnel who were its intended audience.

The inaccuracy of ballooning, of course, severely limited whatever impact the leaflet campaign might have had on the morale of Soviet soldiers in East Germany. The debriefings of Soviet defectors did, it is true, yield descriptions of several soldiers' encounters with the subversive paper from the West. A defector inter-viewed by State Department investigators in Germany recalled finding NTS leaflets near his military unit in 1952 that "so impressed him that he kept them folded up in his watch pocket for about six months, until they were worn to illegibility."[104] In the same year, a Ukrainian soldier in the GDR was in a class in map-reading when his platoon was "deluged" with leaflets that "came from nowhere." According to the source, "the soldiers picked up the leaflets and stuck them in their pockets," but were stopped by the platoon commander. In the barracks, however, one soldier allegedly passed around a few leaflets, prompting seditious talk among his comrades. Why did the defeated Germans live better than their Russian counterparts? More provocative still: "Stalin and his henchmen had stolen everything from the Russian people and turned them into beggars."[105] The defector who witnessed the scene claimed that the leaflets had inspired him to defect, galvanizing his longstanding bitterness over the lot of collective farmers in Ukraine.[106]

Even if the leaflets influenced at least a few of the Soviet soldiers who managed to read them, one should not exaggerate the impact of the airborne mass-

---

10286/62, Bd. I, 0143, and Project AEVIRGIL Outline, Chief, SR to Chief of Mission, Frankfurt, February 8, 1955, 20, in AEVIRGIL, vol. 1.

[102] Sponge Report no. 45 (DS-583), May 17, 1954, 5, in Peripheral Reporting Unit.

[103] Staatssekretariat für Staatssicherheit, Bezirksverwaltung Erfurt to Staatsekretariat für Staatssi-cherheit, Hauptabteilung II, June 18, 1954, in BStU, ZA, MfS-Allg. S 7/55.

[104] Notably, the leaflet that impressed the soldier showed the sophistication of the émigré propa-ganda. The leaflet in question featured a recent defector, Sergeant Nikifor Novoselchenko, who called on his comrades to follow his path to the West. See Sponge Report no. 48 (DS-601), September 7, 1954, 16, in Peripheral Reporting Unit. For the leaflet itself, see Moim tovarishcham iz 154-go otdel'nogo bataliona, March 7, 1952, in Bundesarchiv-Koblenz, B137, Akte 1019.

[105] The episode is described in Sponge Report no. 46 (DS-596), June 22, 1954, 21, in Peripheral Reporting Unit.

[106] Ibid., 4.

propaganda operations. As Chapter 9 will discuss in greater detail, interrogations of defectors are problematic sources, for they had an incentive to say what their American interlocutors wanted to hear—not least of which was affirmation that they had fled to the West for political reasons. And even if the few cases discussed above are accurate, they can hardly be taken as evidence for the overall effectiveness of the leaflet campaigns. Very few of the defectors screened by American interrogators mentioned having seen anti-Soviet leaflets, at least in those files that have been declassified, with State Department interrogators in Germany reporting that the Ukrainian soldier discussed above was the first defector they had met who had "actually read such a leaflet in its entirety."[107] Most soldiers must have kept their distance from the subversive propaganda, just as they did when approached by Germans and émigrés involved in the REDCAP operations.

The difficulty the CIA and exiles experienced in propagandizing Soviet citizens had an unintended result: the main consumers of the airborne Russian-language propaganda were actually East Germans. In recognition of this fact, most leaflets included, alongside Russian-language texts, messages in German calling on their readers to help redirect the subversive paper to its target. The TsOPE leaflet with which this chapter opened included a message in German that declared that "you can now associate with the Russians," and that doing so would "strengthen the friendship between German and Russian anti-communists."[108] The émigrés also sought to establish two-way communications with their German audience by providing the location of the organization's headquarters in West Berlin and addresses to which they could send letters. As with the REDCAP agent operations, the exiles' CIA-funded mass propaganda actions relied on the oppositional moods of East Germans.

The hope that leaflets alone would spur anti-Soviet fraternization between occupied and occupier was far-fetched. The East Germans, of course, understood that it was anything but risk-free to "associate with the Russians" in the ways the leaflets encouraged them to do; indeed, the MfS tracked down and punished some of the Germans who wrote to West Berlin.[109] Nevertheless, some "German friends" did read the leaflets, as letters received by CIA-exile offices in West Berlin confirmed. In 1957, a student in Jüterbog reported that "every time [he found] some of your leaflets, the yearning for freedom always wells up again in my heart."[110] Logically enough, the respondents were concerned with immediate

---

[107] Sponge Report no. 46, 23. Of the fifty-seven interrogation records consulted for this chapter, only five contained explicit mention of the suspects having read anti-Soviet propaganda (including the two mentioned above). One defector reported seeing anti-communist leaflets in German but not in Russian, suggesting a lack of connection to REDCAP operations. See Sponge Report 56 (DS-619), March 1, 1955, 4, in Peripheral Reporting Unit.

[108] Leaflet beginning "Deutscher Freund."

[109] See correspondence relating to the investigation of German letter writers in BStU, ZA, MfS-AOP 10286/62, Bd. I.

[110] Project Status Report, July 1957, 1, in AEVIRGIL, vol. 1.

political realities in the GDR rather than the cause of Russian liberation—indeed, the Germans probably had little idea about who the authors of the pamphlets were in the first place. Instructive was a letter from a worker who mailed to TsOPE a report on leaflets near a Soviet army maneuver area near Zeithain and thanked the Russians for promoting the cause of "freedom, justice and [German] reunification."[111] Regardless of the extent and nature of German responses, it is beyond doubt that the exile leaflet drops had more effect in fanning domestic discontent in the GDR than they did in influencing the Soviet personnel for whom they were intended.

The Germans who visited exile headquarters in West Berlin were even more useful than those who penned letters to the West sector. As Berlin chief Murphy put it, émigré balloon propaganda became useful "zonal advertising" to extend CIA intelligence coverage of the GDR.[112] In 1957, the NTS Berlin office averaged some 110 visitors per month, including 11 new visitors monthly.[113] While some visitors might have taken up roles in REDCAP operations, the vast majority came to West Berlin to exchange whatever information they could offer for money.

Determining the value of the many German informants who crossed over to the Western zone to meet with representatives of shadowy Russian organizations is difficult. TsOPE's CIA case officers acknowledged that "the nature of the sources" was the central shortcoming of the West Berlin-based intelligence-gathering, by which they surely meant the low-level status of the German informants.[114] Nevertheless, TsOPE's West Berlin office produced information that was valuable enough to be consumed by US army intelligence on such topics as the Soviet army's order of battle, the mood of its troops, and the overall situation in the Eastern zone.[115] In what might have appeared to be a hollow victory for the CIA, operations designed to disrupt Soviet forces in Germany and Austria morphed into an intelligence-gathering venture for which the émigrés acted mostly as conduits and cover.

* * *

The utilization of the exiles in Berlin dried up in the late 1950s, even before the erection of the Berlin Wall put a decisive end to it. By the start of the new decade,

---

[111] Action Reported by the Field, no author indicated, January 1–31, 1957, 2, in AEVIRGIL, vol. 1.

[112] Chief of Base, Berlin to Chief of Station, Germany, Su: Specific—AEVIRGIL Ballooning, etc., June 2, 1958, 3, in AEVIRGIL, vol. 1.

[113] These figures might include repeated visits by the same people, to say nothing about the possibility that they were inflated by the émigrés. The total monthly number for TsOPE visitors was fifty-eight in the same period. COB, Berlin to COS, Germany, Su: Aevirgil Ballooning, etc., June 2, 1958, 3, in AEVIRGIL, vol. 1.

[114] Memorandum: Provisional Review of Positive Intelligence Production from Project AERVIRGIL for the Period July 1, 1959 to June 10, 1960, from [ ] C/O AEVIRGIL to SR/3, June 11, 1960, in AEVIRGIL, vol. 2, and Questions asked of CADARZO (TsOPE staff member in Berlin), December 1959, in AEVIRGIL, vol. 2.

[115] Chief of Base, Berlin to Chief of Station, Germany, Su: Specific—AEVIRGIL Ballooning, etc., June 2, 1958, 3, in AEVIRGIL, vol. 1.

the REDCAP operations had yielded minimal results, whether measured by the recruitment of defectors or defectors in place. In 1962, the Chief of Frankfurt Operations Base reached the categorical conclusion that the use of TsOPE as an "intelligence collection mechanism," in particular for the recruitment of "legal" agents among Soviet personnel abroad, was "both dangerous and futile."[116] The failure of REDCAP stemmed from factors already familiar from Chapter 7's discussion of the "black" infiltration operations: the inexpert methods of the exile revolutionaries, the sophisticated spoiler strategies of Soviet counterintelligence, and the dangers of relying on multilayered proxies. And while the CIA officer did not mention it, the Berlin operations came at considerable human cost. German civilians who were unwise enough to take up with the Russian exiles—most of whom were women—bore the brunt of CIA failures on the operational front.

The Berlin operations, though, represented more than just another chapter in the unfolding story of exile and American failure in the clash of intelligence services in Germany. The myriad CIA activities in the divided German capital demonstrated the protean character of Russian émigré politics, its ability to adapt to disparate historical conditions and interests. While Russian anti-communist agendas did little to spur defections, they did underpin the estab-lishment of elaborate CIA operations in the intelligence cauldron of divided Germany. In the process, the exile cause took on forms fitting to the unstable situation in East Germany and Austria, characterized by the unpopularity of regimes propped up by Soviet occupation forces, the steady stream of German refugees to the West, and weak borders in divided Berlin and (to a lesser extent) Vienna, which offered unrivaled opportunities for spying and potential pathways for cross-bloc flight.

The unexpected directions of the Berlin operations demonstrate the trans-national nature of the exile political sphere. The range of cross-cultural relations that occurred under the aegis of émigré REDCAP was wide: CIA agents worked with Russian anti-communists, exiles recruited Germans residing in both halves of Berlin, and East German civilians (sometimes) contacted their Russian occupiers. Of course, these various relationships were often accompanied by deception, mercenary motives, and sexual intrigue. Yet the REDCAP interactions also involved the flow and crossing of ideas, as seen in the ways that Russian anti-communism resonated with East Germans discontented with their new commun-ist rulers and, to a far lesser extent, influenced the moods of servitors of the Soviet state and armed forces stationed abroad. To a degree sometimes ignored in American-, British-, or Russocentric intelligence history, the activities of spy

---

[116] Re: AEVIRGIL: New Operations Directive, Chief, Frankfurt Operations Base to Chief SR, Chief, EE, Chief of Station, Germany and Chief, Munich Operations Operations Base, April 17, 1962, in AEVIRGIL, vol. 2.

services became absorbed in the political and cultural frameworks of the societies and communities in which they functioned.[117]

The operations in Berlin did not exhaust the exiles' transnational exchanges across the Iron Curtain. For while the CIA had little luck in securing defections through REDCAP, a small stream of Soviet citizens *did* cross over into the West during the 1950s, regardless. The new arrivals fueled American and émigré hopes that anti-Soviet moods simmered under the surface in the USSR, while inserting new energies and interests into both American Cold War policies and Russian anti-communist circles in Germany.

[117] For a call to integrate culture into intelligence history, see Stephen Welch, "Political Culture: Approaches and Prospects," in Philip H. J. Davies and Kristian Gustafson (eds.), *Intelligence Elsewhere: Spies and Espionage outside the Anglosphere* (Washington, DC: Georgetown University Press, 2013), 13–26.

9

The Real Anti-Soviet Russians?

Soviet Defectors and the Cold War

"Former Soviet soldiers and officers who came to the free world because they no longer wanted to be instruments of Soviet despotism." Such was the characterization of the membership of the Central Representation of Postwar Emigrants (*Tsentral'noe ob'edinenie poslevoennykh emigrantov* or TsOPE), the CIA-created organization discussed in Chapter 8 in the context of defector-inducement operations. The defectors who made up the organization claimed to represent their co-nationals behind the Iron Curtain who rejected the "communist system of terror" and yearned for freedom.[1]

The exiles belonging to the secretive organization, however, looked quite different when they were examined up close. To Western observers and Russian exiles, the defectors arrived with unknown pasts in the Soviet Union and therefore aroused suspicion, even as their arrival was greeted as a sign of communism's failings. And the recent arrivals from the USSR often appeared to be less than principled cold warriors. A case in point was TsOPE member Leon Olschwang, an employee of the Soviet Military Administration who fled to West Berlin in 1949. The Americans recruited Olschwang for Cold War purposes, granting him work at the anti-communist journal *Ost-Probleme*, published by the Office of the US High Commissioner for Germany. Yet, according to a German source, Olschwang had been involved in black-market dealings meant to finance Soviet intelligence networks in West Germany. After defection, he rarely took part in TsOPE activities and earned a reputation as a "man without convictions" in émigré circles.[2]

The contrast between propaganda and reality in the case of Olschwang was common for Soviet defectors who entered US institutions for fighting the Cold War. In the geographical imagination of divided Europe, moving from one bloc to the other was an ideological act, one that was either equated with righteous protest (in the West) or betrayal (in the East). In part because of their presumed stance of opposition to communism, defectors were eagerly sought-out commodities for

---

[1] TsOPE letter to unnamed East German citizen, March 1954, in Bundesbeauftragte für die Unterlagen des Staatssicherheitsdienstes der ehemaligen Deutschen Demokratischen Republik, Zentralarchiv (BStU, ZA), MfS-AOP 10286/62, Bd. I, 0148.
[2] Betr: Olschwang, Leon, n.d., author not given (perhaps from the Bundesamt für Verfassungsschutz (BfV)), Bundesarchiv-Koblenz, B 137, Akte 1021.

Cold War Exiles and the CIA: Plotting to Free Russia. Benjamin Tromly, Oxford University Press (2019). © Benjamin Tromly.
DOI: 10.1093/oso/9780198840404.001.0001

American intelligence, military, and propaganda institutions in Europe. But as Olschwang's case suggested, defectors did not always live up to the ideological standards imposed on them. Indeed, all too often the encounter between the defector and American power brought disillusionment on both sides.

This chapter examines the defectors and their interaction with two intertwined forces: the US defector program and the Russian anti-communist diaspora. The CIA devoted significant resources to programs to receive and deploy defectors against their homeland—efforts, one should add, which are still poorly explored in literature on the Cold War.[3] However, the defectors who crossed into US control in Germany rarely fit the mode of dedicated cold warriors. Most defectors passed over the Iron Curtain for reasons that had little to do with ideology. Once abroad, defectors found themselves in trying circumstances, facing inadequate programs for their care and assimilation and experiencing difficulty adapting to very new circumstances. As a result, defectors typically proved to be of limited usefulness as agents of American Cold War agendas.

An overlapping problem was defectors' relationships to the exile political scene they encountered in Germany. The defectors constituted a new wave—or, given their small numbers, a mini-wave—in the already multifarious Russian political emigration. Anti-communist groups viewed the defectors as new recruits for the cause, and set out to organize and influence them. But it soon emerged that the émigré–defector encounter would be marked by disparate interests and dissimilar historical experiences, recalling the already-examined tensions between previous waves of exiles. Rather than shoring up the project of making an anti-Soviet Russia abroad, the defectors added an additional layer of discord to exile politics.

Defectors: Myth and Reality

The defector was an outsized figure in the Cold War West. As discussed in Chapter 8, the National Security Council adopted a policy aimed at employing defectors as strategic weapons in the Cold War, drawing on defectors' possession of up-to-date information from the USSR and their gravitas as opponents of communism. For media and public opinion as well, defectors presented a rare opportunity to peek behind the virtually impenetrable Iron Curtain of the late

---

[3] Most literature on defectors focuses on individuals rather than Agency programs. Cf. Boris Volodarsky, *Stalin's Agent: The Life and Death of Alexander Orlov* (Oxford and New York: Oxford University Press, 2015). Work that addresses defection in US Cold War plans includes Susan Carruthers, *Cold War Captives: Imprisonment, Escape, and Brainwashing* (Berkeley, CA: University of California Press, 2009), chs. 1–2 and, most recently, Kevin P. Riehle, "Early Cold War evolution of British and US defector policy and practice," *Cold War History*, online edn (2018): 1–19.

Stalin period. As a Swiss newspaper put it, finally people had appeared who "authentically told us what it is like 'over there.'"[4]

In embracing the potential psychological warfare capabilities of defectors, US policymakers were reacting to several high-profile examples of the phenomenon in the early postwar years. First came the 1944 defection of Viktor Andreevich Kravchenko, who absconded from the Soviet Purchasing Commission in Washington, DC. Kravchenko's 1946 memoir, *I Chose Freedom*, exposed the evils of collectivization and forced labor in Stalin's USSR and led to a libel trial against French communists dubbed the "trial of the century" in anti-communist circles.[5] Soon after Kravchenko's defection and just a few days after the end of World War II, the Military Intelligence cipher clerk Igor' Sergeevich Guzenko fled the Soviet embassy in Canada—a defection that would harden American attitudes toward communism by uncovering spy rings in Canada and the United States.[6] In 1948, Ol'ga Stepanovna Kasenkina, a teacher attached to Soviet diplomats in New York, jumped out of a third-floor window of the Soviet consulate in what was billed in the newspapers as a "leap to freedom."[7] Based on these widely fêted escapes, Washington policy elites determined that defectors were not just promising agents of intelligence and political warfare, but also offered the American public an easily consumed message about the moral superiority of the West. George F. Kennan's Policy Planning Staff credited "Kravchenko's book, Guzenko's testimony in Canada, and the defection of Kasenkina in New York" with doing more "to arouse the Western world to the realities of the nature of communist tyranny than anything else since the end of the war."[8]

The reality of defection, though, differed greatly from propaganda in the West. Discovering the true voices and motivations of defectors is no simple task given the ways in which they were represented, and presented themselves, in the Cold War. Defectors' stories about their own pasts, especially those that were published as memoirs in English and other Western languages, were highly politicized. Ghostwritten by American anti-communists—Isaac Don Levine wrote Kasenkina's—the memoirs followed standard "demands of the genre," most important of which was the presentation of defection as a quintessentially ideological act.[9] In these Cold War storylines, it is difficult to distinguish facts from propaganda.

---

[4] Emigration aus der Sowjetunion—Stimme des russischen Volkes von heute: Über den Zentralverband der Nachkriegsemigranten aus der UdSSR, n.d. (no later than 1955), in BStU-ZA, MfS-AOP 10286/62, Bd. I, 0140.

[5] Gary Kern, *The Kravchenko Case: One Man's War on Stalin* (New York: Enigma Books, 2007).

[6] Amy Knight, *How the Cold War Began: The Igor Gouzenko Affair and the Hunt for Soviet Spies* (New York: Carroll & Graf, 2005).

[7] Carruthers, *Cold War Captives*, 23–32.

[8] PPS 54: Policy Relating to Defection and Defectors from Soviet Power, June 28, 1949, 4, in NARA, RG 59, Records of the Policy Planning Staff, Microfiche 1171, card 62.

[9] On the authorship of Oksana Kasenkina's memoir *Leap to Freedom*, see Carruthers, *Cold War Captives*, 31. While drawing attention to the "demands of the genre," Kern nevertheless uses

The best sources for reconstructing the thinking of defectors are the records of interrogations carried out by intelligence agencies in the West. As secret documents produced for intelligence purposes, the interrogations avoid the memoirs' propagandistic nature; as records usually produced within months of the individual's arrival in the West, they are less shaped than memoirs by post-defection influences. Interrogations demonstrate that most defectors in the period were motivated, to a considerable degree, by non-ideological factors.[10] Certain repeating themes in the fifty-seven available interrogation files show that specific life situations were often behind an individual's motive to defect (see Figure 9.1). Consider the following cases: a high-ranking civilian in Austria who defected in 1954 after getting into a bar fight in Vienna and being picked up by Soviet military police; an army private in Germany who, feeling he was "picked on" by his superiors, "slugged" his platoon leader; and an army sergeant who defected in the late 1940s to marry a German girl, convinced that there could be no "happy future" for him or his bride-to-be in the Soviet bloc.[11] In all three scenarios, defection was an escape from expected punishment in the USSR rather than a

Superior Living Standards outside USSR	Romantic Attachments to Foreign Women	Listening to Foreign Radio	Victimization of Self or Family Members in USSR (Arrest, Collectivization)	Infractions during Service	Work Conditions prior to Defection
20 (35.1%)	18 (31.6 %)	18 (31.6%)	15 (26.3%)	14 (24.6%)	12 (21%)

Figure 9.1 Table of reasons cited for defection in fifty-seven defector interrogations.

Kravchenko's memoir uncritically. Kern, *The Kravchenko Case*, 6–10, 162. For a related discussion, see Jay Bergman, "The Memoirs of Soviet Defectors: Are They a Reliable Source about the Soviet Union?" *Canadian Slavonic Papers* 31, no. 1 (1989): 1–24.

---

[10] I accessed three incomplete sets of US government defector interviews: the lengthy "Overall Attitudinal Reports" (also evocatively called "Sponge reports") conducted by the Peripheral Reporting Unit, a team of State Department Russian specialists stationed in Germany; a series of interviews conducted by External Research Staff at the Department of State, which contain less sensitive information than Sponge reports; and a set of shorter reports on investigations of Soviet army deserters conducted by the US Army Counter Intelligence Corps (CIC). See NARA, RG 466 (HICOG), box 2 (hereinafter Peripheral Reporting Unit); Hoover Institution Library and Archives (hereinafter HILA), Office of External Research typescript: The Soviet Union as Reported by Former Soviet Citizens, External Research Staff, Office of Intelligence Research, Department of State (hereinafter The Soviet Union as Reported by Former Soviet Citizens); and NARA, RG 319, Entry 134A, ZC500670, 270/84/20/02, box 31 (hereinafter Soviet Army Deserters), vols. 1–2. I discuss these sources at greater length in "Ambivalent Heroes: Russian Defectors and American Power in the Early Cold War," *Intelligence and National Security* 33, no. 5 (2018): 642–58.
[11] Sponge report no. 47 (DS-593), August 19, 1954, 39, and Sponge report no. 52 (DS-615), December 7, 1954, both in Peripheral Reporting Unit; and Interview Report no. 11, May 1955, 1–2 in The Soviet Union as Reported by Former Soviet Citizens. Romantic attachments between Soviet soldiers and Austrian women are explored in Barbara Stelzl-Marx, *Stalins Soldaten in Österreich: die Innensicht der Sowjetischen Besatzung 1945–1955* (Vienna: Böhlau, 2012), 497–524. In general terms,

politically inspired voting with one's feet.[12] Whether they were fleeing political repression, the criminal justice system, military discipline, or an impending separation from a German lover, the defectors fled in desperation, convinced they had nothing to lose.

None of this means that political discontent was irrelevant to defection. Most defectors—including those who pointed to non-ideological factors to explain their flight—criticized the Soviet regime, often denouncing "Stalin and the other Soviet leaders in terms of unmeasured abuse."[13] Yet the interviews probably exaggerated the political and ideological motivations of defectors. As uprooted individuals who had committed treason against the Soviet state, defectors had good reason to "present testimony which will be pleasing to the interviewer." In practice, this meant "slant[ing] their statements" to stress their opposition to Soviet communism, as one interrogator noted.[14]

In light of such an incentive structure, the historian cannot be sure that the defectors actually held the anti-communist sentiments they articulated, let alone that they had thought this way at the time of defection. In a 1954 review of defection cases, a CIA officer involved with defector programs argued that individuals often "rationalize[d] their defections as stemming from ideological convictions" *post facto*, after arriving in the West.[15] Some defectors must have done this memory work subconsciously, reappraising their pasts in light of current realities in a process all too familiar to the practitioners of oral history.[16] Others were surely dissimulating. For instance, an interrogator cast doubt on the testimony of a border guard who fled from Soviet territory to Iran, suspecting that "more immediate and compelling" factors had been at work than the interviewee's vocal hatred of communism.[17] In light of these facts, one CIA officer was probably correct in arguing that "few of the defections of Soviets...can be attributed unequivocally and primarily to pure ideological motivation."[18] No less

---

the picture gained from interrogations is consistent with much fuller figures on defection to the British authorities. See Wesley K. Wark, "Coming in from the Cold: British Propaganda and Red Army Defectors," *International History Review* 9, no. 1 (1987): 72.

---

[12] It is also worthwhile to point out that the seemingly more ideological "victimization" category, in which I grouped interviews that mentioned persecution of the defector or his or her family members, sometimes involved flight from imminent arrest as well. An example is a military doctor who fled to West Berlin in the late 1940s because he feared that his identity as the son of an "enemy of the people" would be discovered. Interview Report no. 9, 1955, 2–3, in The Soviet Union as Reported by Former Soviet Citizens.

[13] Interview Report no. 2, February 1952, 3 in The Soviet Union as Reported by Former Soviet Citizens.

[14] Ibid.

[15] Su: The Inducement of Soviet Defections, report sent from [redacted] to Chief, SR, May 4, 1954, 2, in NARA, RG 319, Entry 134A, 230/86/26/02, box 60.

[16] Cf. Donald A. Ritchie, *Doing Oral History* (New York: Twayne Publishers, 1995).

[17] Sponge report no. 51 (DS-609), 3, in Peripheral Reporting Unit.

[18] Su: The Inducement of Soviet Defections, 3.

authoritative a figure than CIA director Allen Dulles agreed, stating at a 1953 NSC meeting that, for defectors, "human reasons have been the incentives, not high ideals."[19]

For some defectors, no doubt, expressions of anti-Soviet sentiment were sincere. Even in these cases, though, the defectors' anti-communist expressions rarely attained the articulate character that American interrogators hoped to hear. Frequently, defectors' opposition to communism rested on the basic conviction that life was better abroad than at home. A common refrain was the shock they had experienced in discovering that the vanquished and occupied Germans lived better than the Soviet people did.[20] Comparing living standards in Germany and the USSR made one "increasingly discontented with Russian life," as an army geologist who fled the GDR in the early 1950s put it. He contrasted Germany, where "even ordinary people lived in clean homes and had such luxuries as guest homes and gardens," to Moscow, which he found "poor and miserable" during his leave in 1948.[21] Defectors from rural backgrounds drew even starker contrasts, often citing impressions gained from visiting their families in the impoverished postwar Soviet countryside.[22] Adding to such ideologically sensitive comparisons was the considerable privilege that some high-ranking Soviet personnel enjoyed in Germany in the chaotic months immediately after the war, which for some officers entailed acquiring cars and hiring servants.[23] For such soldiers and civilians, the West was a coveted land of plenty, but not necessarily an object of ideological solidarity.

The picture of defectors that emerges from interrogation records, then, is that of a group driven above all by self-preservation and self-advancement.[24] There is nothing surprising here for the student of Soviet history. As Stephen Kotkin has argued, Stalin-era Soviet citizens approached ideology instrumentally, "speaking

[19] Record of Meeting of the Ad Hoc Committee on NSC 143, March 30, 1953, in Foreign Relations of the United States (hereinafter FRUS), 1952–1954, vol. VIII: Eastern Europe, Soviet Union, Eastern Mediterranean, doc. 77.

[20] On the tangled political loyalties of World War II veterans, see Mark Edele, "More Than Just Stalinists: the Political Sentiments of Victors, 1945–1953," in Juliane Fürst (ed.), Late Stalinist Russia: Society between Reconstruction and Reinvention (London and New York: Routledge, 2006), 167–91, and Elena Zubkova, Russia after the War: Hopes, Illusions, and Disappointments, 1945–1957 (Armonk, NY: M.E. Sharpe, 1998), 25–6.

[21] Interview Report no. 5, September 2, 1952, 1, in The Soviet Union as Reported by Former Soviet Citizens.

[22] Interview Report no. 6, November 17, 1952, 2, in The Soviet Union as Reported by Former Soviet Citizens.

[23] Interview report no. 14, August 1955, 17, in The Soviet Union as Reported by Former Soviet Citizens. On the illegal and semi-legal activities of Soviet officers and officials in Germany, see Norman M. Naimark, The Russians in Germany: A History of the Soviet Zone of Occupation, 1945–1949 (Cambridge, MA: Belknap Press of Harvard University Press, 1995), 173–5.

[24] Here I agree with Nigel West, who has argued that Soviet defectors were typically "opportunists seeking to better their own circumstances." See his Games of Intelligence: The Classified Conduct of International Espionage (London: Weidenfeld & Nicolson, 1989), 98.

Bolshevik" in order to get by amidst the unstable conditions of Stalin's rule.[25] Even the defectors' willingness to rewrite their biographies had a Stalin-era precedent in citizens' strategies of evading a coercive and unpredictable party state.[26] The problem was that defectors' preoccupation with "immediate problems of survival," as one interrogator put it somewhat dismissively, often came into tension with American expectations that they would be committed to the liberation of their homeland from Soviet rule.[27] In turn, the disconnect between American plans and defector realities made an inauspicious background for the defectors' experiences in West Germany and their relationships to US power.

Defectors as Objects of Government Planning and Philanthropy

Defectors were unsure of what to expect when they crossed into US custody. Although those fleeing dangerous situations might have given little thought to the matter, some border-crossers arrived in the West with high expectations of a comfortable existence. Often, such ambitions were the product of Cold War radio propaganda. Broadcasts of the US-funded Voice of America and Radio Liberation featured recently arrived defectors, who appealed directly to their compatriots with glowing descriptions of how they had been received in the West.[28]

Defectors optimistic about their prospects in the West were often disappointed. The first reality defectors experienced was internment in an army camp—typically in Camp King near Oberursel, used by the Nazis during the war to interrogate captured Allied air pilots—and weeks of interrogation, often by representatives of numerous agencies who asked the same questions ad nauseam.[29] After this trying process, American intelligence officials divided their subjects into two broad categories. Defectors deemed useful—which meant those with various desirable traits such as clear bona fides, knowledge of sensitive matters from past work, anti-Soviet commitments, a degree of education, and administrative experience—were well situated to find work in the CIA or other US-backed Cold War institutions.

The remaining defectors, mainly low-level soldiers or service personnel, had the unenviable fate of being released to the West German authorities. With doubtful career prospects, poor or non-existent language skills beyond Russian or other

[25] Stephen Kotkin, *Magnetic Mountain: Stalinism as a Civilization* (Berkeley: University of California Press, 1995), 220.
[26] Sheila Fitzpatrick, *Tear Off the Masks! Identity and Imposture in Twentieth-Century Russia* (Princeton: Princeton University Press, 2005).
[27] Sponge report no. 54 (DS-610), February 11, 1955, 20, in Peripheral Reporting Unit.
[28] Cf. Kern, *The Kravchenko Case*, 363.
[29] Boris Volodarsky, *Nikolai Khokhlov ("Whistler"): Self-Esteem with a Halo* (Vienna and London: Borwall Verlag, 2005), 47.

Soviet languages, and no experience of living outside the USSR and its satellite states, these defectors faced uncertain futures. In the best-case scenario, they would receive an unemployment subsidy from the German government—which, however, was barely sufficient for survival. And even this outcome was far from guaranteed, as the old émigré socialist Vasilii Federovich Butenko explained. The Germans hardly wanted to support "their former enemies," the Red Army soldiers "who had passed over Eastern Germany with fire, sword and unheard-of violence." Often unable to obtain work and forced to live in displaced persons (DP) camps, the defectors became enveloped by "inactivity, hopelessness, chronic and despair-inducing poverty."[30]

Policymakers in Washington soon grew concerned about the morale of the relatively small collectivity of defectors from the Soviet bloc languishing in West Germany and elsewhere.[31] As Secretary of State John Foster Dulles explained in a 1953 memorandum, the "inadequate conditions and general neglect" experienced by recent defectors in the West gave Soviet propaganda a ready-made issue to exploit.[32] The situation was all the more damaging for US political-warfare projects. As a 1951 NSC directive intoned, if the US government hoped to benefit from defection—both by employing defectors for "intelligence or operational purposes" and by incentivizing future waves of cross-bloc migration—it had to provide them with "personal and economic security," which was necessary to "feel that there is a place for them in a free society."[33]

In part to alleviate their troubled position in the West, Washington adopted a multipronged strategy for utilizing defectors in the early 1950s. One aspect of the plan was a projected Volunteer Freedom Corps, a "Cold War army" consisting of military units recruited from Eastern bloc escapees.[34] The same legislation that authorized the Volunteer Freedom Corps, the so-called Kirsten Amendment to the 1951 Mutual Security Act, also set in motion the Escapee Program (USEP). The program directed funds toward the reception of "escapees" from communist countries who were now located in Germany, Austria, Italy, Greece, and Turkey, with the goal of resettling substantial numbers of them outside Europe.

---

[30] V. F. Butenko to R. R. Abramovich, May 8, 1953, in Columbia University Rare Book and Manuscript Library, Bakhmeteff Archive of Russian and East European History and Culture, Vasilii Fedoseevich Butenko Papers (hereinafter Butenko Papers), box 1, fol. 1.

[31] Precise numbers of defectors are lacking. The US Psychological Study Board estimated in late 1951 that 12,000 people had fled the Soviet bloc as a whole since 1945, a figure that excluded Germans and Yugoslavs. Psychological Operations Plan for Soviet Orbit Escapees Phase A, December 20, 1951, in CREST: General CIA Records, Document Number (FOIA) /ESDN (CREST): CIA-RDP80R01731R003200030002-6.

[32] Secretary of State to certain Diplomatic and Consular Offices, January 31, 1952, in FRUS, 1952–1954, vol. VIII, doc. 64.

[33] National Security Council Intelligence Directive no. 13: Exploitation of Soviet and Satellite Defectors outside the United States, January 19, 1950, 1, in CREST: Creating Global Intelligence, Document Number (FOIA) /ESDN (CREST): 50dde104993247d4d8392344.

[34] On the initiative and its denouement, see James Jay Carafano, "Mobilizing Europe's Stateless: America's Plan for a Cold War Army," *Journal of Cold War Studies* 1, no. 2 (1999): 61–85.

Here was a bold agenda to deal with defectors already in the Western orbit and to prepare for eagerly anticipated future population outflows from the Soviet bloc. Too bold, in fact. A "Cold War army" recruited from Eastern bloc defectors never came into existence, largely due to opposition from America's European allies.[35] Equally damaging was President Harry Truman's failure to convince Congress to liberalize immigration policies. The McCarran–Walter Act of 1952 posed particular barriers to the entry of the often undocumented East European defectors.[36] In turn, these policy shortcomings placed undue strain on the Escapee Program, which had a limited mandate to provide supplemental aid to escapees in Europe and elsewhere and could not remove the escapees from the demoralizing environment of the DP camps. In fact, the USEP probably worsened morale in the camps by mandating privileges for escapees that were not accessible to the rest of the displaced population.[37]

The USEP also suffered from design flaws. The escapee program's indirect administrative structure, according to which private, non-profit voluntary agencies released aid on the basis of government contracts, proved cumbersome. American onlookers were critical of the two US-based contracted organizations specifically authorized to work among the Russian defectors: the Tolstoy Foundation and the American Friends of Russian Freedom (AFRF). The first organization, headed by Aleksandra L'vovna Tolstaia, the dynamic daughter of the great writer Lev Nikolaevich Tolstoi, had been active for years in organizing aid to Russian DPs and facilitating their emigration to the United States. In contrast, the AFRF was a recent invention, the brainchild of high-society American patriots who grew concerned about the lot of escapees in Europe when stories about them reached the pages of the American press.[38] Both charitable organizations, critics alleged, developed overly "grandiose ideas" for helping the population of Russian defectors in Germany, while refusing to cooperate with each other to bring them about.[39] The two organizations were also hampered by a chronic lack of funds—a reflection of the enormity of the escapee problem to be tackled, to be sure, but perhaps also a result of profligate and unwieldy management.[40]

---

[35] Carafano, "Mobilizing Europe's Stateless."

[36] Ibid. Carruthers, *Cold War Captives*, 78–9.

[37] Ibid., 78.

[38] Eva Jollis to Eugene Lyons, n.d., in Stuart A. Rose Manuscript, Archives, and Rare Book Library, Emory University, Isaac Don Levine Papers (hereinafter Levine Papers), box 9. The organization, whose original name was Friends of Fighters for Russian Freedom, would come to occupy a durable role in CIA defector programs. See Richard Cummings, "CIA and Defectors from the USSR, Part One: Project CAMANTILLA: The American Friends of Russian Freedom (AFRF)," *Cold War Vignettes*, June 2, 2018, https://coldwarradios.blogspot.com/, accessed June 11, 2018.

[39] Memorandum for the Files, Su: Miscellaneous Notes—Trip to Frankfurt and Bonn, September 12–14, 1952, Joseph T. Kendrick, Jr, Peripheral Reporting Unit, US High Commissioner for Germany, 5, in Georgetown University Archives and Special Collections, Robert F. Kelley Papers, box 5, fol. 1.

[40] In 1955, Allen Dulles reported to his CIA deputies that the Tolstoy Foundation was "about to go under again," and resolved to send its request for funding to Nelson Rockefeller. Deputies Meeting,

The two charitable organizations also collided with the politics of the Russian diaspora. The Tolstoy Foundation alienated some exiles and also Americans with its nationalist and Orthodox mission, which treated welfare for refugees as an exercise in saving Christian souls and restoring historic Russia.[41] For her part, Tolstaia was an ardent monarchist with close connections to far-right political circles in New York and Europe.[42] Eugene Lyons, the first leader of the American Committee for Liberation from Bolshevism, Inc. (Amcomlib), kept his distance from the Tolstoy Foundation on the conviction that any link to it would do the organization "no good" in its relations with the different exile groupings.[43] Clearly, charity for defectors was bound up with diasporic political divides, reproducing the pattern by which American anti-communists became entangled with the internal politics of their Russian émigré clients.

As a result of its myriad problems, the USEP had a limited impact on the life situations of defectors in Germany and Austria. In early 1955, the head of the CIA SR (Soviet Russia) Division noted that "poverty and hopelessness" were still common for most defectors in Germany, and stated that the situation represented "a propaganda blot on the record of the West."[44] Worst of all, evidence emerged that defectors in West Germany represented an unstable element and even a security risk. As one defector explained, the uprooted and trying existence of defectors led them to "moral decline," marked by a drift to the black market, theft, drinking, and banditry.[45]

A striking example of the failure of US policies toward the defectors was the Munich "Friendship House," a reception center for new escapees opened by AFRF with much fanfare in 1951. Envisaged as a symbol of American friendship for the Russian people, by 1957 the Friendship House had "degenerated" into a "place of refuge" for "criminal or shady emigres of various nationalities," including professional criminals from the East bearing colorful underworld nicknames such as "the Monk" (Semen Maksimov) and "One-Armed" (Gennadii Alekseev). Even more concerning was evidence that there existed "a direct connection between the

April 18, 1955, in CREST: General CIA Records, Document Number (FOIA) /ESDN (CREST): CIA-RDP80B01676R002300170021-8.

---

[41] For the Tolstoy Foundation's religious mission, see Rockefeller Archive Center, Ford Foundation records, East European Fund, Series IV: Grant Files, box 11, Tolstoy Foundation, Literature. See also Paul B. Anderson, "The Tolstoy Foundation," *Russian Review*, no. 1 (1958): 60–6.

[42] See the Paris journal *Russkaia mysl'* in Review of the Émigré Press, no. 6, March 19, 1953, 2, in Levine Papers, box 14. The foundation's European representative was Bolko Freiherr von Richthofen, an archeologist who had penned anti-Semitic and anti-Slavic works in Nazi Germany. Bernd Stöver, *Die Befreiung vom Kommunismus: amerikanische Liberation Policy im Kalten Krieg 1947–1991* (Cologne: Böhlau, 2002), 328.

[43] Eugene Lyons to Isaac Don Levine, May 16, 1952, in Levine Papers, box 8.

[44] Project AEVIRGIL outline, Chief, SR to Chief of Mission, Frankfurt, February 8, 1955, 4, 8, in NARA, RG 263, Entry ZZ-19, 230/86/25/04, box 25, AEVIRGIL (hereinafter AEVIRGIL), vol. 4.

[45] Konspekt doklada o polozhenii poslevoennykh bezhentsev iz Sovetskogo Soiuza, nakhodiashchikhsia v zapadnoi Germanii, V. M. Denisov, November 24, 1952, 3–4, in Butenko Papers, box 6.

émigré criminal undergroup [*sic*] and Soviet agents." Several convicted or suspected Soviet agents had lived in the House of Friendship or had been friends of its inhabitants, including six individuals who redefected to the USSR in mid-decade.[46] The transformation of a flagship institution of American philanthropy for Russian refugees into a base for organized crime and Soviet espionage showed how little USEP had alleviated the disoriented and demoralized state of defectors in Germany.

Defector-bandits and defector-spies were an embarrassing deviation from propaganda depicting heroic escapees who cherished freedom and plenty in the West. So too were the increasing numbers of defectors who, comparing Western propaganda with realities on the ground, grew disillusioned with the societies they had entered. In a particularly harsh variation on this theme, a defector opined that the poor treatment of defectors showed that "the governments of Western and American peoples do not want to live in friendship and peace with our peoples." Going further, he saw the iniquities suffered by the defectors as no less than "a foreshadowing" of how the Americans would treat Russians as occupiers after a future war.[47] One can understand the psychological state that drove defectors to such conclusions. For defectors who had crossed over after listening to radio broadcasts promising a good life in the West, the "suspicion, mistrust," and "unemployment" they encountered after their crossing were a rude awakening.[48]

The resentful mindset of some defectors also reflected the tremendous risks and sacrifices they had made. The defectors were well aware that their illegal passage to the West had harmed friends, family members, or co-workers who had remained at home.[49] A case in point was an engineer who had crossed over to West Berlin in 1949. When he was interviewed for the Harvard Project on the Soviet Social System two years later, the defector, now unemployed, "looked with suspicion, condescension, [and] contempt" at his interlocutor. His hostility, it would seem, was rooted in an overwhelming sense of guilt and disappointment:

> The crossing of our people over to the West is no easy thing, they risk their lives. Each one is covered with the bodies of Russian people, who were their friends and their parents, their relatives.[50]

[46] Cover letter, Richard M. Christenson, Chief of Base, Munich, to Chief, IO, September 11, 1957, 2, in AEVIRGIL, vol. 2. The list of individuals under suspicion included A. G. Orlov-Kopatskii, the Soviet spy discussed in Chapter 8.

[47] Konspekt doklada o polozhenii, 2. While the speaker, V. M. Denisov, for reasons to be explained, was not a typical defector, there is no reason to think that his sentiments were out of touch with wider opinion among the defectors.

[48] Notes on the first meeting of the All-German Congress of Postwar Emigrants from the USSR, V. F. Butenko, November 11, 1952 in Butenko Papers, box 6.

[49] Vladislav Krasnov, *Soviet Defectors: The KGB Wanted List* (Stanford, CA: Hoover Institution Press, 1985), 77–8, 232 n. 13. See also Peer De Silva, *Sub Rosa: The CIA and the Uses of Intelligence* (New York: Times Books, 1978), 64.

[50] The Harvard Project on the Soviet Social System Online (hereinafter HPSSS), schedule A, vol. 17, case 337, 2, 58.

The defector's response conveyed a characteristic dilemma of the Cold War defector. Western propaganda depicted flight from communism as heroic, but it might also be construed as treason, against not only one's homeland but also one's loved ones in the USSR. In light of such troubling reflections, the lot of the typical defector in the West—calculated exploitation by intelligence services followed by neglect and indifference—was surely devastating. Little wonder that some defectors decided that the West was no better than the communist dictatorship they had fled.

The Defector–Émigré Encounter

The defectors' generally unheroic origins, their mixed motives, and their skeptical or even hostile attitudes toward their hosts formed an inauspicious context for their involvement in the Cold War. While rolling out USEP and encouraging new waves of defectors, the US government was also developing ways to utilize them against their homeland. The Escapee Program emerged from a wider "Psychological Operations Plan for Soviet Orbit Escapees" constructed by the Psychological Strategy Board, a committee established by the Truman administration. "Phase A" of the plan addressed the reception and care of escapees already in the West, while "Phase B" aimed at spurring more defections and utilizing them as part of "national psychological strategy." A major component of Phase B was the utilization of defectors in unconventional warfare, including psychological operations, the creation of "émigré groups," and even the formation of guerilla units made up of East Europeans.[51] The plan offered scope for the development of CIA projects utilizing defectors.

A clear question arose for the CIA: how would political projects for defectors differ from already existing operations the Agency pursued with Russian exiles? The CIA might have preferred to deal with Russian defectors and exiles as totally separate entities, but such a course of action was impossible. Defectors often became associated with émigré communities, particularly with activists of the existing anti-communist exile organizations, once they arrived in Germany or elsewhere. Naturally, exiles were interested in the new arrivals from the USSR, who provided a base of potential recruits, a crucial source of information on conditions in the homeland and an audience for émigré ideologies. And the defectors, who often could not communicate in German or other languages spoken in the West, typically found themselves psychologically or even materially

---

[51] Documentation on the implementation of Phase B remains classified. Attachment B: Absorption of Escapees through Utilization in Intelligence and Psychological Programs, December 20, 1951, 1, in CREST: General CIA Records, Document Number (FOIA) /ESDN (CREST): CIA-RDP80R01731R003200030004-4. See also the description in Carruthers, *Cold War Captives*, 260 n. 73.

dependent on established exile communities abroad.[52] As a result, the interaction between postwar defectors and their co-nationals already in the West impacted exile politics and American political-warfare plans alike.

The view of Americans was crucial for the defector–émigré encounter. In the common view of US officials, a hierarchy existed within the communities of Russians and other former Soviet citizens in the West, according to which political relevance was inversely proportional to time spent abroad. Defectors were particularly valuable not only due to the intelligence on the USSR they could provide but also thanks to their ability to express "the true wishes and hopes of the Russian people," which made them superior recruits for psy-war operations of all kinds.[53] However, defectors were "rapidly wasting assets," for their knowledge of the closed society of the enemy and, more widely, their legitimacy as "truth tellers" lessened steadily over time.[54] In fact, the Russian exiles had already witnessed this law of diminishing returns in action. Just as CIA planners and officers favored second-wave exiles over first-wavers, each postwar defector—invariably greeted as "a fresh person from over there" (svezhii chelovek ottuda)—dulled the credentials of the second-wave exiles as interpreters of Soviet realities and mouthpieces for Russian public opinion abroad.[55]

The Americans' differentiation between defectors and exiles fed into the mutual relations between the two cohorts of Russians. Typically, the defectors remained critical of the exile communities in which they became engaged. Internalizing the American perspective that they were the more genuine articulators of Russian opinion, defectors presented themselves as "representatives of the wide popular masses" of the USSR, not émigrés "in the usual sense."[56] Defectors were particularly dismissive of émigré political organizations, which one likened to "dry earth... that falls apart if you drop it."[57] To some extent, such contempt for the unruly politics of the diaspora reflected the fact that defectors had only ever known a country where the will of the ruling party reigned supreme. On a more basic level, the defectors spurned Russian anti-communism abroad on the conviction that they understood better what the Soviet people wanted.

---

[52] Notably, émigrés had played roles in high-profile defections, including those of Kravchenko (D. Iu. Dalin) and Kasenkina (A. L. Tolstaia). Carruthers, Cold War Captives, 26–31, and Kern, The Kravchenko Case, 46–50.

[53] PPS 54: Policy Relating to Defection and Defectors from Soviet Power, 4. See also the cogent discussion of the advantages of defectors for US psy-war projects in Aufzeichnung, Betr: Die Emigration aus der Sowjetunion und den von ihr beherrschten Gebieten, Ref. Scholl and von Staden, November 19, 1956, 2, in AA-PA B12 455. The quotation is from Vermerk, Betr: Die Tätigkeit des TOLSTOY FOUNDATION für die Nachkriegsemigration, February 16, 1955, in AA-PA, B12, 455.

[54] TROY Report, cited in Carruthers, Cold War Captives, 75.

[55] The quotation belongs to the memoir of one defector who recalled his own "authority" as a defector. I. V. Ovchinnikov, Na pereput'iakh Rossii (Moscow: Informatsionno-ekspertnaia gruppa "Panorama," 1995), 106.

[56] Emigration aus der Sowjetunion: 137.

[57] Interview Report no. 8, 1953, 35, in The Soviet Union as Reported by Former Soviet Citizens.

The exiles' views of the defectors were especially ambivalent. The political activists abroad needed the recent defectors, in large part because of the attention Americans and other foreigners paid to the recent transplants from the Soviet orbit. Even leaving aside American attitudes, the exiles themselves recognized that recent defectors provided the best window on Soviet-Russian public opinion that existed outside the Soviet bloc. Insofar as the defectors better represented the current Russia than they did, the exiles sought to win them over for their own organizations, a move one document described as strengthening émigrés' "living connection with the homeland."[58]

While courting defectors, the exiles remained critical of them. Paradoxically, defectors' Sovietness, in the general sense of being current products of the Soviet order, made them both attractive and suspicious to Russian exiles. Doubts were particularly rife with regard to defectors who had previously occupied high-ranking positions in the Soviet system, whom exiles sometimes suspected of being Soviet plants.[59] (Recall the cold shoulder some exiles gave to N. E. Khokhlov, the KGB assassin whose defection was discussed in Chapter 7.) The defector was a dangerous figure for the same reason that he or she was a politically promising one—notably, an echo of the ways that many first-wave exiles had greeted the supposedly "red" second wave years before.

The defectors' image in the emigration also suffered from the way they had arrived there. Previous cohorts of émigré political activists were defined (in word if not in deed) by struggle against the Soviet state, either in the Russian Civil War or in World War II. By contrast, defection was an act of flight and therefore a potentially awkward starting point for the image of anti-communist fighters. One exile leader, Union for the Struggle for the Liberation of the Peoples of Russia (SBONR) head Georgii Il'ich Antonov, stressed that defectors were "envoys of their people," not "runaways from under the Iron Curtain"—an assertion that suggested the existence of debate on the issue.[60] No doubt to avoid unwanted associations of betrayal or cowardice, the CIA chose for TsOPE the designation "postwar emigrants" over the alternatives of *perebezhchiki* ("defectors," "deserters") or *bezhentsy* ("refugees," "fugitives").

Distinct from the question of fight versus flight were the defectors' and exiles' differing views of the Soviet and Russian past. Postwar defectors often took pride in having fought on the Soviet side in World War II, an echo of the general patriotic upsurge in the USSR during and after the war. As TsOPE propaganda declared, "Love of country" had inspired defectors first to fight against Nazi rule

---

[58] Memorandum o polozhenii poslevoennykh bezhentsev (proekt), no author given—perhaps V. F. Butenko, n.d., 1, in Butenko Papers, box 6.

[59] See the excerpt from *Russkaia mysl'* in Review of the Russian Émigré Press, vol. 3, no. 43, November 2, 1955, 4, in Levine Papers, box 15.

[60] Tezisy vystupleniia na 1-m s'ezde poslevoennoi emigratsii iz SSSR, G. A. Antonov, November 14, 1952, 3, in Butenko Papers, box 6.

and then to oppose communist tyranny.[61] Such a position collided with the historical memories of most of the second-wave exiles, whose political identity was inextricably tied to the collaborationist Vlasov movement. In this manner, the defectors rekindled tensions over World War II and collaboration that had marked the Vlasovites' engagement in the Cold War, as explored in Chapter 3.

The exiles and defectors, then, were tied to each other in an awkward embrace, with mutual interests commingling with suspicion and jealousies. The complexity of defector–émigré interactions was at work in the political career of the most important Russian defector of the period, Grigorii Petrovich Klimov. A high-ranking engineer of the Soviet Military Administration who spoke fluent German and English, Klimov quickly entered the public spotlight in the West after he fled to West Berlin in 1948. Immediately after his arrival in West Germany, the NTS helped Klimov "in every way," publishing his memoir at *Posev* publishing house and organizing his German lecture tour. However, Klimov resisted the Solidarists' blandishments.[62] Klimov had little interest in the NTS's ideology, but perhaps a more important consideration was the fact the he had lucrative employment opportunities outside the émigré organizations.[63] By 1950 Klimov had taken up work with A. M. Mil'rud, the US military intelligence agent whose involvement in promoting the Russian exile right was discussed in Chapter 4. Mil'rud and Klimov assembled a group of defectors with literary talent to publish anti-communist propaganda, including a satirical journal called *Satirikon*. With a direct link to US intelligence, Klimov had little need to work through the Solidarists, who were, after all, only clients of the agency—and only partly trusted ones at that.[64]

Mil'rud and Klimov were soon at the center of a bruising conflict involving defectors, different parts of the émigré anti-communist scene, and their American backers. In 1952, the CIA launched a project (cryptonym: AEVIRGIL) to create an organization of Russian defectors spearheaded by Klimov and a circle of defectors surrounding him. Simultaneously, the left wing of the Russian emigration, grouped in the League of Struggle for People's Freedom in New York, sought to organize recent defectors themselves. The leftists had good reason to court defectors: they had virtually no followers in Europe, and they had been unable to forge a close connection to the Vlasovites, as Chapter 3 discussed.[65] D. Iu. Dalin and B. I. Nikolaevskii cultivated ties with a group of defectors residing in

[61] Emigration aus der Sowjetunion: 138.

[62] Memorandum on the Congress of Postwar Emigres, no author indicated (a "person who is familiar with the background of the whole post-war refugee movement"), January 22, 1953, 1–2, in Levine Papers, box 8. The book, serialized in *Reader's Digest* in 1953, was published as Grigorii Klimov, *The Terror Machine: The Inside Story of the Soviet Administration in Germany* (London: Faber & Faber, 1953) in English and *Berliner Kreml* (Cologne: Verlag Rote Weissbücher, 1953) in German.

[63] Cf. Grigorii Klimov, *Otkrovenie*, chs. 1–2, at http://g-klimov.info/, accessed July 11, 2017. Klimov's recollections of émigré politics are unreliable sources, for reasons to be addressed at the end of the chapter.

[64] Memorandum on the Congress of Postwar Emigres, 2 in Levine Papers, box 8.

[65] Ibid., 1.

Hamburg that was led unofficially by Major Vasilii Mikhailovich Denisov. The Hamburg circle reportedly included "regular military men, former Party workers who escaped to the West for personal reasons, and a few former workers in the organs of state security."[66] Apparently, the Mensheviks driven from Russia by Lenin found common ground with such former Stalinists, and several of the defectors even contributed pieces to the Menshevik publication *Sotsialisticheskii vestnik*.[67] Here was a fine example that émigré politics made strange bedfellows.

In the confusing situation that emerged, the Russian defectors in Germany had divided into two hostile camps, one affiliated with the rightist Klimov in Munich and another based around Denisov in Hamburg. When Amcomlib leader Eugene Lyons tried to reconcile them by inviting allies of Klimov and Denisov to his home in New York, his dinner guests almost came to blows.[68] Complicating matters further, the sparring defectors had different connections to US power. If Klimov was tied directly to the CIA via Mil'rud, Denisov and the old socialists had reason to hope for Amcomlib support for their gambit to organize recent defectors. The clash over defectors coincided with the brief existence of the Coordinating Center for Anti-Bolshevik Struggle (KTsAB), the united-front organization that the League played a key role in creating. The indefatigable émigré operator Nikolaevskii pressured his Amcomlib backers to forge a "Division of Postwar Defectors" in KTsAB.[69]

The defector conflict crested in November 1952 in Munich. Apparently heading off a similar event in the works within KTsAB, Mil'rud and Klimov—who was under "fairly tight KUBARK [CIA] control" at the time—gathered a "Congress of Postwar Emigrants from the USSR."[70] The congress was hardly a well-managed affair. Many speakers vented their dissatisfaction with the poor lot of defectors in Germany, expressions of anger that Klimov tried to counter with the argument that creating a "fighting alliance" with the West would bring about an improvement in their treatment.[71] More disruptive still, defectors affiliated with the Denisov group arrived from Hamburg and put up a spirited resistance—so strong, in fact, that Mil'rud felt compelled to intervene in the congress to restore order. If the financing of a large defectors' conference by the virtually unknown Mil'rud were not suspicious enough, his meddling in the proceedings exposed the fact that the meeting was not the "all-émigré affair" it purported to be.[72]

[66] Ibid.
[67] Review of the Émigré Press, no. 2, January 20, 1953, 1–3, in Levine Papers, box 15.
[68] The individuals were the Klimov ally Lev Volkov-Malakhov and the Hamburg defector Miroshnikov. Memorandum from Eugene Lyons, su: Organizations of the "New Fugitives," February 13, 1952, in Levine Papers, box 9.
[69] Apparently, S. P. Mel'gunov and other Russian exiles in KTsAB opposed the League's defector project. V. F. Butenko to R. R. Abramovich, May 8, 1953, 1 in Butenko Papers, box 1.
[70] Vystuplenie V. Butenko na konferentsii poslevoennykh emigrantov v kachestve predstavitelia Koordinatsionnogo Tsentra, 1 in Butenko Papers, box 6, and AEVIRGIL Project Review, no author indicated, March, 15–April 30, 1962, 3, in AEVIRGIL, vol. 2.
[71] Notes on the first meeting.
[72] Status Report on Project AEVIRGIL, 2.

The interference of an intelligence operative in the congress was an awkward start to the CIA's Russian defector project. Although the conveners of the congress demanded that participants remain silent about what had transpired, news about the congress quickly spread throughout the press of Russia abroad, producing heated debate.[73] Exiles tied to KTsAB were livid at what they saw as a right-wing coup in the defector community. Writing in *Sotsialisticheskii vestnik*, Menshevik stalwart Rafael Abramovich retold a list of grievances that surely came to him from the Denisov camp: Mil'rud and Klimov had stacked the conference in their favor, given the floor only to their own supporters, and even resorted to "bribery, home searches, intimidation, and threats of action by American and German police" against the Hamburg group. Challenging the code of silence about such matters, Abramovich hinted at the role of US intelligence agencies, which he called "organizations whose names are known to the Lord alone," in arranging the congress. He also criticized Amcomlib for letting the congress proceed—and, implicitly, for failing to protect the interests of the League and the other organizations committed to the united-front project.[74] Clearly, Abramovich was trying to pressure Amcomlib into taking his side, hoping to pit one set of American cold warriors against another.

Abramovich misread the situation in Washington. The CIA was firmly in charge of defector matters, not Amcomlib—which, in any case, faced heightened scrutiny in Washington at the time due to the turmoil of the united-front campaign. Meanwhile, Russian émigré publications admonished Abramovich almost unanimously, no doubt out of fear that by exposing the role of US intelligence officers in the congress in all but name, he ran the risk of ending American patronage of exiles altogether.[75]

As it turned out, Abramovich's and Nikolaevskii's courtship of defectors was a flawed endeavor in a more basic sense. Well before Mil'rud's defector congress met, the League's ally V. M. Denisov had acted unpredictably, most notably by making "a sharp attack on Socialism and the Mensheviks" at one meeting of the united-front negotiations.[76] Butenko, a leader of the New York League, admired Denisov as a "clever" and "tough guy (*krepkii muzhik*)," yet grew exasperated by his constant pleas for money.[77] The meaning of Denisov's erratic behavior and perhaps also of the intransigence of his small group of allies became clear only in

[73] V. F. Butenko to M. E. Veinbaum, November 24, 1952, in Butenko Papers, box 6.
[74] Review of the Émigré Press, no. 2, January 20, 1953, 1–3, in Levine Papers, box 15.
[75] See the account in the SBONR publication *Golos naroda* in Review of the Émigré Press, no. 3, January 29, 1953, 1–2, in Levine Papers, box 15. While much of the centrist émigré press supported the American defector congress, Abramovich's criticism—strangely enough—was repeated on the émigré right, which expressed "delight" in emphasizing that the new organization was "a tool of American intelligence." Status Report on Project AEVIRGIL, 2.
[76] Memorandum on the Congress of Postwar Emigres, 1.
[77] V. F. Butenko to R. R. Abramovich, May 8, 1953, in Butenko Papers, box 1, and V. F. Butenko to V. M. Denisov, December 20, 1952, in ibid.

1955, when he was arrested crossing from the Soviet to the British zone of Germany with false documents and a large sum of money.[78] Denisov was a Soviet agent tasked with spurring infighting in the émigré scene, and he had played the role with skill. So embarrassing was the Denisov episode that Nikolaevskii and the other Mensheviks—political warriors from the time of the tsars—gave up politics entirely in its wake and retreated to their intellectual work.[79] The entry of defectors to the anti-communist scene had replicated damaging trends all too familiar from other episodes of American–émigré collaboration: inter-emigration infighting, American lack of coordination, poorly kept secrets, and Soviet moles.

America's Defector Party

Despite the fiasco in Munich, the CIA pressed ahead with its defector initiative. In fact, CIA officials in Germany were optimistic that TsOPE, the product of the ill-starred defector congress, would be an effective instrument against the Soviet state—or, at least, that it would prove more useful than the Russian émigré groups that the Agency supported as psy-war outfits (see Figure 9.2). One source of their bullish attitude was the tight control the CIA held over TsOPE. From the outset, the organization's leaders were made "witting" to the CIA's role, and therefore understood that American support "should be fairly quickly terminated if the group should choose to go off on some tangent not acceptable to the case-officer [sic] and his organization."[80] Even more important in the CIA's attitude toward TsOPE was the belief that defectors, armed with insights about the Soviet system and deriving moral stature from having defied it, would prove particularly effective at conducting psychological warfare against their homeland. As a CIA officer involved in the project explained, TsOPE would allow "today's Russian" to speak "to his brothers" across the Iron Curtain—a scenario that supposedly offered unique opportunities to foment anti-communist moods on the Soviet home front.[81]

The CIA's sanguine take on TsOPE was exaggerated, as already suggested by the underwhelming outcomes of the organization's Berlin operations discussed in Chapter 8. The outfit's distinctive features—its tight subordination to the CIA and its defector composition—carried unintended consequences as well as benefits. Thanks to American control, it is true, TsOPE avoided the painful internal fissures that plagued virtually every exile group in the 1950s. Quite simply, the CIA

---

[78] Review of the Russian Émigré Press, vol. 3, no. 46, November 30, 1955, 2, in Levine Papers, box 15.

[79] See Review of the Russian Émigré Press, vol. 4, no. 4, March 19, 1956, 2–4, in Levine Papers, box 9.

[80] Status Report on Project AEVIRGIL, 2, and Revised Project Outline: AEMANGO, no author indicated, February 15, 1954, 4, in AEVIRGIL, vol. 1.

[81] Status Report on Project AEVIRGIL, 8.

Figure 9.2 Members of the Central Representation of Postwar Emigrants (TsOPE), the CIA's organization of Soviet defectors. In the center is the organization's original leader, Grigorii Petrovich Klimov. CIA officials heralded TsOPE as an entity that could influence the Soviet public and as an answer to the chaos of exile politics.

Source: Der Bundesbeauftragte für die Unterlagen des Staatssicherheitsdienstes der ehemaligen DDR.

refused to let ideological questions become a bone of contention within the organization. In its first few years, the organization articulated little in the way of unifying political principles apart from a general desire to "throw the rascals out" of the Kremlin, as a CIA case officer put it succinctly. When TsOPE did adopt a program in 1954, it was so "extremely broad and extremely liberal" that virtually no émigré could find issue with it.[82]

Close CIA control and the resulting ideological amorphousness, however, were mixed blessings. It was an open secret in émigré circles that TsOPE worked directly for the CIA. Surprisingly, speakers at a 1957 TsOPE meeting in Berlin went so far as to "hint that they were somehow tied to the intelligence services of the West," according to an East German informant present at the event.[83] There can be no doubt that the open secret of TsOPE's CIA birthright was a source of weakness and demoralization for the organization. In the opinion of one defector who abandoned the organization, the exiles grouped in TsOPE were

[82] Ibid., 11.
[83] Bericht über die Versammlung der ZOPE, no author indicated, March 18, 1957, in BStU, MfS-AOP 10286/62, Bd. I, 0250.

"mercenaries" (*naemniki*) whose political activity was limited to following orders from above.[84] CIA agents were also aware of the problem. Closely scrutinized by the Americans and not permitted to develop its own agenda, TsOPE remained a "passive and politically meaningless collection of émigrés," as the CIA's Munich Chief of Base acknowledged.[85] Why should defectors devote their energies to an organization that was a mere "front or façade" for operations conducted by intelligence agents?[86]

TsOPE's reliance on defectors was also a double-edged sword. The CIA had difficulty finding enough defectors to operate TsOPE, whose membership was a mere 200 persons in West Germany in 1955 (including a smaller number of paid operatives).[87] One problem was that the number of Soviet defections actually decreased in Germany throughout the 1950s, despite the resources invested in the REDCAP operations to induce flight. Making matters worse, those defectors who did arrive in the West were mostly Soviet soldiers, "young lads with very little schooling and no significant leadership qualities"—perhaps useful as one-off sources of information but hardly promising as operatives of an anti-communist organization.[88] Making matters worse, virtually all the TsOPE leaders had defected from 1945 to 1948, and therefore were passing through the life cycle from defectors to exilés described above. In fact, TsOPE's staffing problem became so serious that it was forced to outsource its operations to Russian exiles belonging to other anti-communist organizations.[89] Soon the CIA had bowed to the reality that the organization's distinctive "concept" of representing defectors was becoming "more fiction than fact."[90] In 1956, TsOPE changed its name to the Central Representation of *Political* (rather than Postwar) Emigrants, a move that allowed the organization to keep its acronym but represented an implicit admission that it no longer represented recent defectors.

The CIA also discovered that many defectors were less than fully committed anti-communists. On display was the defectors' commitment to self-advancement, which, as discussed above, was frequently made evident in the conditions of defection itself. The defectors who joined TsOPE often did so in order to improve their life chances in a challenging new environment. The organization's CIA handlers recognized that improving the "material lot" of TsOPE members was "a most important aspect of the situation" facing it.[91]

[84] Ovchinnikov, *Na pereput'iakh Rossii*, 95.
[85] Chief of Base, Munich to Chief, SR, January 28, 1957, 3, in AEVIRGIL, vol. 1.
[86] Status Report on Project AEVIRGIL, 4.
[87] Status Report and Plans for Future Development of AEVIRGIL, Chief of Base, Munich to Chief, SR, November 7, 1955, 6, in AEVIRGIL, vol. 1, and Review of the Russian Émigré Press, vol. 5, no. 2, January 25, 1957, 4, in Levine Papers, box 15.
[88] Status Report and Plans, 7.
[89] What we have in AEVIRGIL, no author indicated (CIA officer in Germany), n.d. (after February 1961), 2, in AEVIRGIL, vol. 1.
[90] Status Report on Project AEVIRGIL, 8.
[91] Ibid., 9.

Accordingly, the CIA officers did extensive "welfare" work for TsOPE, which involved exerting pressure on the relevant USEP organizations to "get help for a particularly needy individual or family" in the organization's orbit.[92] The fact that TsOPE's handlers spent so much time attending to its members' everyday needs reflected the ongoing difficulties facing the defectors, to be sure, but also suggested the limits of the exiles' drive to battle the Soviet state.

The defectors' questionable commitment to fighting the Cold War—at least in the ways the CIA directed them to—became clear when the issue of emigration from Europe arose. When the 1953 Refugee Relief Act offered DPs new opportunities to emigrate to the United States, many TsOPE leaders announced their intention to leave as soon as possible. On one level, there was nothing surprising or damning in the fact that defectors made for the exits: their lives in Germany were unstable, and fear of war on the European continent made them dread their fate should West Germany be overrun by the Soviet army. Moreover, one should not read the eagerness of TsOPE figures to leave the continent as a sign that their anti-communism was somehow artificial. However, the desire to pursue a new life as far as possible from their vengeful homeland sat uncomfortably with the organization's anti-communist militancy and its Eastern orientation.[93] In defiance of American expectations, the defectors acted more like refugees fleeing their homeland than exiles devoted to liberating it.

The emigration of TsOPE figures to the United States threatened to strip the organization of cadres for operations on the all-important German front. Worse yet, the departure of several TsOPE leaders to the United States called into doubt the viability of the organization itself, so much so that CIA officers even sought to bring back several TsOPE figures from the United States to Europe as Agency employees.[94] Exit for the United States was also problematic because of what became of defectors and exiles when they arrived there. The move often meant the end of defectors' anti-communist careers, and not only because strict limits on the CIA's ability to operate stateside deprived the émigré anti-communist scene of funding. In the United States, exiles typically became concerned with "earning their daily bread" in a new and trying environment rather than fighting against a Soviet enemy that now seemed far away.[95]

A case in point was Petr Afanas'evich Pirogov, a Soviet airman who landed his plane in the US zone of Austria in 1948 in a widely publicized defection. After immigrating to the United States in 1949, Pirogov found work, bought a small house in rural Alexandria—he experienced the "greatest desire to build when you

---

[92] Ibid.
[93] Action Reported by the Field, Chief of Base, Munich to Chief, SR, September 1957, 2, in AEVIRGIL, vol. 1.
[94] Emigration of Key AEVIRGIL Personnel, Chief, SR to Chief of Base, Munich, and Chief of Station, December 27, 1956, 1–3, in AEVIRGIL, vol. 1.
[95] Chief, SR to Chief of Base, Munich, January 22, 1957, 3, in AEVIRGIL, vol. 1.

understand it is for yourself"—and started a family with an émigré of Ukrainian background.[96] But this immigrant idyll was deceptive. A judge rejected his application for citizenship in 1955 under the terms of the Internal Security Act; its stipulation that immigrants spend ten years outside "totalitarian" organizations disqualified Pirogov, who had been a member of the Young Communist League like most Soviet citizens of his generation.[97] Behind the scenes, Pirogov also lost favor with the CIA, the organization that had helped him immigrate to the United States and even paid for his house. In 1954, the CIA appointed him as the head of an embryonic American chapter of TsOPE. However, Pirogov was inactive in his role—he only "came to life" in the organization "when he would collect his monthly $300.00"—and was dropped unceremoniously by the CIA in 1956 when he demanded a raise.[98]

Klimov, the founder of TsOPE, went off script in American exile in more dramatic fashion than Pirogov. In 1954, Klimov immigrated to the United States, where he continued to work for the CIA. For instance, he was at the center of the propaganda effort surrounding one of the most publicized defection cases of the period: the decision of nine Soviet sailors from the tanker *Tuapse*, seized by the Republic of China in 1954, to move to the United States rather than return home.[99] Soon after, however, Klimov severed his ties with TsOPE, "denouncing it roundly in the process."[100] In 1956, a CIA officer and a psychologist visited Klimov amid concerns that he was becoming "preoccupied with the subject of sexual aberrations" and making some "scurrilous and bizarre accusations against some of his former colleagues."[101] Although the document does not offer details, Klimov's later activities provide some clues. In 1971 Klimov wrote a forward to the second edition of his book about his escape from the Soviet bloc. While making angry complaints about his treatment by CIA officers, whom he called "gangsters," Klimov articulated some decidedly "bizarre accusations." American intelligence officials were sadists and latent homosexuals, he alleged—a notion he developed into a theory that "degenerates rule the world," which he spread on the Internet along with anti-Semitic diatribes before his death in 2007.[102]

* * *

The reasons for Klimov's transformation from trusted CIA asset to unhinged conspiracy theorist remain obscure. However, his exit from the CIA orbit hinted

---

[96] Director, Radio Programming Support Division to Howland Sargaent, November 7, 1955, in Levine Papers, box 8.

[97] Clayton L. Burwell to Howland Sargaent, n.d. (late 1955), in Levine Papers, box 8.

[98] Chief, SR, to Chief of Base, Munich, January 22, 1957, 3, in AEVIRGIL, vol. 1.

[99] Peter Kihss, "Red Agents Here Accost Refugees: But Seamen Having Asylum from Soviet are said to Resist Pleas to Return," *The New York Times*, January 14, 1956: 2.

[100] Aevirgil Project Review, in AEVIRGIL, vol. 2.

[101] Project Status Report, no author indicated, June 1957, 2, in AEVIRGIL vol. 1.

[102] Tsena svobody: dopolnenie k 2-mu izdaniiu, http://g-klimov.info/, accessed June 15, 2016, and Degenerates Rule the World! Klimov Interview, https://groups.google.com/forum/#!topic/alt. privacy.anon-server/7RfJNXmTlRQ, accessed June 15, 2016.

at the psychological toll exacted on Soviet defectors by lives spent at the whim of forces beyond their control. In the experience of many defectors, the ordeal of a risky flight—preceded and triggered, often, by menacing circumstances in the Soviet bloc—gave way to a frightening, unsettled, and impoverished existence in the West. They had to grapple with the question of whether their betrayal of the Soviet state, and perhaps also of the specific people they left behind, had been justified. Making matters worse, defectors often felt that they had been exploited and deceived by the Western governments and officials under whose custody they had placed themselves. Given all this, one can hardly wonder why defectors proved unenergetic cold warriors, at least according to the standards imposed by CIA agents.

Flesh-and-blood defectors, though, were overshadowed by their propagandistic representation. Indeed, the notion of the defector harbored in the Cold War West—as a figure who abandoned the communist bloc for principled reasons, and who devoted himself or herself to fighting communism from abroad—was more fiction than reality. As seen in political operations discussed in Chapter 7, the US defector program relied on the projection and manipulation of narratives for mass opinion—in this case, the act of Cold War border-crossing, with its symbolism and easily appreciated moral valence.

The gap between ideal and reality characterized the entry of defectors into exile communities in Germany, as well. The arrival of defectors was celebrated by US policymakers but also by the Russian diaspora, for they had the reputation of being more genuine anti-Soviet Russians than their co-nationals abroad. Such expectations proved hollow. In some ways, the defectors took their place as yet another wave—or, given their very small numbers, a mini-wave—in the ongoing shaping of Russia abroad. Like previous groups of exiles that had washed up on distant shores, the defectors brought their own agendas to the anti-communist milieu and found themselves entangled in political struggles and debates across generational lines. And similar to the second wave years before, the defectors were courted by Cold War institutions and émigré anti-communists but also sometimes distrusted by them. In one sense, though, the defectors differed from the other exiles in their political engagements. More so than the first two waves, the defectors resembled refugees who wanted nothing more than to resettle as far away from Soviet power as possible.

The defectors could not revive the fortunes of the anti-communist Russian émigrés in the ways expected of them. Even worse, the identity of defectors increasingly came into question among the anti-communist Russians. In mid-decade, the Soviet government instituted a new campaign designed to make traffic across the Iron Curtain more of a two-directional affair. Just as the United States and its allies embraced defectors from the East, the Soviet side sought to facilitate movement in the other direction. The emergence of counter- or re-defection as an instrument of Soviet policy would pose an existential threat to Russian anti-communist organizations.

PART IV

THE END OF THE AFFAIR

The Decline of Émigré Anti-Communism

10

"All Will Be Forgiven"

The Soviet Campaign for Return to the Homeland

"Don't you wonder why all of a sudden a hurriedly thrown-together committee has said such touching words about us, former Soviet citizens living abroad?" The letter, published in an émigré journal in 1955, was addressed simply to "Kostia," who had been reading a Russian-language publication, *Za vozvrashchenie na rodinu!* ("For Return to the Homeland!"), released by the Soviet-sponsored Committee for Return to the Homeland. From its headquarters in East Berlin, the new committee published "touching" descriptions of the life that awaited displaced Soviet citizens who returned home, replete with accounts of satisfying work, happiness with being reunited with one's people, and reunions with long-estranged family and friends. The author warned Kostia not to fall victim to "beautifully chosen words" which represented "terrible lies." Return to the hated Soviet regime was "a beautiful trap from which you will never escape."[1]

A few years after Stalin's death, the collective leadership in the Kremlin turned to a task it had failed to complete a decade before: the repatriation of Soviet citizens abroad. In contrast to the postwar precedent of involving Western governments in forced repatriation in areas under their administration, the Soviet government now sought to convince the second-wave exiles, as well as smaller numbers of postwar defectors, to return to the USSR voluntarily. At first glance, the Soviet plan to lure exiles back to the USSR might appear to have been a realistic prospect. Stalin was dead, communism was undergoing a path toward liberalization, and, most important of all, Soviet power now promised that its wayward sons and daughters would be integrated into Soviet society with their sins forgotten.

Such were the origins of the letter to Kostia, which appeared in a publication of the Vlasovite Union for the Struggle for the Liberation of the Peoples of Russia (SBONR) devoted to counteracting the new Soviet repatriation campaign. Whether it was a genuine letter to a friend or merely a propaganda piece written for publication, the message for Kostia conveyed the threat that the return campaign posed to Russian anti-communists abroad. It conceded that living conditions were "severe" in the West, and that "bread bought in foreign lands

---

[1] "My nuzhny na zapade (pis'mo drugu)," *Nash Otvet*, biulleten' No. 1, May 1955, in Archiv der Forschungsstelle Osteuropa-Bremen (hereinafter FSO), 01–034 Kromiadi-Kruzhin, kor. 1.

Cold War Exiles and the CIA: Plotting to Free Russia. Benjamin Tromly, Oxford University Press (2019). © Benjamin Tromly.
DOI: 10.1093/oso/9780198840404.001.0001

was bitter." But Kostia must remember that "his ten-year stay here in the West gave a singular witness testimony" to the free world about the nature of communism, the "archenemy of humanity." In other words, Kostia must retain faith in the anti-communist mission despite the sorry lot of life abroad—and, the letter implied, defy the temptation to believe the Soviet state's "beautifully chosen words" about life in the USSR.[2]

What little literature exists on the repatriation campaign of the 1950s presents it as a stark failure for the Soviet government. Most Soviet exiles in Europe and elsewhere, it is rightly pointed out, stayed put in exile, rejecting the prospect of living under a regime they hated and refusing to believe promises that the returnees would not be subject to repression in the USSR.[3] This argument has some merit but is incomplete. For the Soviet side, the return campaign did not achieve its direct aim of bringing large numbers of bodies across the Iron Curtain, but it went much further toward an ancillary goal: destabilizing anti-communist exiles in the West. This chapter argues that the campaign was a Soviet offensive in the ongoing political war fought by the two superpowers within the Russian exile milieu. The Committee for Return, also known as the "Mikhailov Committee" after its head, general-major and former prisoner of war N. F. Mikhailov, functioned as cover for Soviet intelligence activities in the West, particularly for KGB efforts to locate, surveil, and contact Soviet citizens abroad.[4] Moreover, the campaign targeted anti-communist exiles, utilizing offers of return as a means of demoralizing and dividing the anti-Soviet émigré milieu. To take the letter as an example, whether or not Kostia succumbed to the "beautiful trap" thought to be set for him, the Return Committee's activities created a sense of doubt and mistrust among the exiles, who feared that someone from among their ranks might break ranks and side with the Soviet government.

Despite its disruptive effects on émigré anti-communism, the return campaign had unanticipated consequences for Soviet power. It pushed exiles and their American patrons together, a development that was the opposite of KGB agendas toward exiles in the period. In particular, the American Committee for Liberation from Bolshevism, Inc. (Amcomlib), which had undergone a bruising split with the exiles during the united-front campaign, now sought to rebuild bridges with the Russian émigré political organizations in order to counteract the return

---

[2] Ibid.

[3] Simo Mikkonen, "Mass Communications as a Vehicle to Lure Russian Émigrés Homeward," in *Journal of International and Global Studies* 2, no. 2 (2011): 45–61, http://www.lindenwood.edu/jigs/docs/volume2Issue2/essays/1-20.pdf, accessed July 20, 2015. See also I. A. Luneva, "Fenomen 'nevozvrashchentsev' v propagandistskoi voine SBONR protiv Sovetskogo Soiuza," *Vestnik Nizhegorodskogo gosudarstvennogo universiteta im. N. I. Lobachevskogo*, Seriia "Istoiriia. Politologiia. Mezhdunarodnye otnosheniia," ed. 1 (2003): 557–64.

[4] One reflection of the predominance of intelligence activity in the campaign is the fact that records in Russian archives pertaining to the Return Committee remain classified. Mikkonen, "Mass Communications as a Vehicle."

campaign. Thus, the redefection campaign continued the self-sustaining dynamic of the émigré political scene, in which an offensive by one superpower's spy agencies provoked a response from those of the other.

The Return Campaign as "Psy-Op"

If the appearance of the Mikhailov Committee marked a stark new challenge to the Russian exiles, it also represented a basic continuity in official Soviet views of them. Stalin's successors inherited the dictator's neuralgic view of the diaspora as a breeding ground for anti-Soviet conspiracies and therefore maintained the goal of repatriating its former citizens. A new approach to the exile problem emerged among the post-Stalin leadership, which was searching for solutions to Stalin-era problems in many spheres. In a 1954 memorandum that catalyzed the repatriation campaign, KGB head Ivan Aleksandrovich Serov stressed the danger that displaced Soviet citizens could be utilized against the USSR in the event of war in Europe.[5] Of course, the fact that Russian exiles were backed by the United States made the old business of counteracting exile anti-communists especially urgent.

That repatriation was connected to events from a decade earlier was immediately apparent. The opening steps of the return campaign seemed to recall the events of 1945. Prior to Konrad Adenauer's 1955 trip to Moscow, Soviet premier Nikolai Aleksandrovich Bulganin called for Soviet citizens in Germany to be returned to the USSR, in contravention of their status as refugees.[6] Bulganin's demand threw Soviet exiles in Germany, Russian and non-Russian alike, into a panic. Perhaps, they worried, the Federal Republic of Germany (FRG) would agree to a forcible repatriation of former Soviet citizens in Germany in exchange for the return of German prisoners of war still languishing in the USSR since World War II, whose release the Adenauer government was eager to secure.[7]

Such fears were inflated. There would be no repeat of forced repatriation, both because the FRG had granted the Soviet DPs remaining in the country legal asylum and because the Cold War context made such a course of action inconceivable.[8] Nevertheless, exiles' fears were easy to understand, as the repatriation campaign of a decade before remained fresh in their minds. Even if it ran up

[5] Andrei Artizov, *Reabilitatsiia—kak eto bylo: Dokumenty Prezidiuma TsK KPSS i drugie materialy* (Moscow: Mezhdunar. fond Demokratiia, 2000), 406, n. 54.

[6] *Za vozvrashchenie na rodinu*, no. 12 (October 1955): 1.

[7] Aufzeichnung, Betr: Repatriierung von sowjetischen Staatsangehörigen, no author indicated (Ministry of Foreign Affairs), October 13, 1956, in Auswärtiges Amt-Politisches Archiv (hereinafter AA-PA), B12, Akte 454, and "Ostaemsia, chtoby borot'sia," Munich, 1956, no author indicated, 13, in FSO, 01–034 Kromiadi-Kruzhin, kor. 1.

[8] Correspondence between the foreign ministries of the FRG and the USSR makes these points clear. See AA-PA, B12, Akte 454.

against West German opposition, the return campaign was a painful reminder to the exiles of their insecurity.

At roughly the same time, the Soviet government unleashed a propaganda campaign for return that was massive and sophisticated. From its office in East Berlin, the Committee for Return to the Homeland delivered Russian-language broadcasts over East German radio, printed a journal, and also organized personal contacts between exiles and Soviet citizens. Across these different media and means of contact, the Mikhailov Committee's message to exiles followed a fairly consistent pattern. Presenting a Manichaean divide between exile and the USSR, it called on the émigré to "tear himself out of the slough of the emigration and return to his sunny native shores."[9] To drive home this message, the committee touted a decree of the Council of Ministers, which determined that returnees could travel to the USSR free of charge and would receive work and housing upon their arrival.[10] Buttressing these promises of deliverance were glowing accounts of Soviet life, along with songs and poems which had "but one aim – to evoke the greatest possible homesickness in the listener," as an Amcomlib review of the committee's radio broadcasts put it.[11]

As the Soviet leadership surely understood, not even the most persuasive propaganda could undo the exiles' fear that they would be targeted after their return, a conviction that was particularly widely held among the former collaborators who dominated the émigré political scene. To confront this dilemma, the Soviet leaders adopted legislation to demonstrate that the homeland would welcome exiles with open arms, regardless of their histories of opposition to it. Such was the origin of the 1955 Supreme Soviet decree "on the Amnesty of Soviet Citizens who collaborated with the occupiers during the Great Patriotic War of 1941–1945." The measure amnestied Soviet citizens who had served in the national legions and other units of the Wehrmacht in ranks up to the senior officer personnel. Citizens who had committed "serious crimes against the Soviet government" during the war were not to be amnestied en masse—although, if they "surrendered themselves (iavilis' s povinnoi)" to Soviet authorities they would receive reduced sentences of exile to distant parts of the country for terms of up to five years.

---

[9] Review of Return to the Homeland Radio, no. 3, September 8, 1955, in Stuart A. Rose Manuscript, Archives, and Rare Book Library, Emory University, Isaac Don Levine Papers (hereinafter Levine Papers), box 15. On Manichaean constructions in Soviet propaganda, see Richard Stites, "Heaven and Hell: Soviet Propaganda Constructs the World," in Gary D. Rawnsley (ed.), Cold-War Propaganda in the 1950s (New York: St. Martin's Press, 1999), 85–103.

[10] V. N. Zemskov, "'Vtoraia emigratsiia' i otnoshenie k nei rukovodstva SSSR, 1947–1955," in Iu. A. Poliakov et al. (eds.), Istoriia rossiiskogo zarubez'hia: emigratsiia iz SSSR-Rossii, 1941–2001 gg.: sbornik stat'ei (Moscow: Rossiiskaia akademiia nauk, Institut rossiiskoi istorii, 2007), 86.

[11] Review of Return to the Homeland Radio, Amcomlib, August 25–September 5, 1955, 2, in Levine Papers, box 15.

Going further, the decree held out the possibility that even the most guilty traitors and war criminals—leaders in Axis "repressive organs" and propaganda organizations and individuals who had been "drawn into anti-Soviet organizations" after the war—might escape punishment entirely if they "redeemed themselves through patriotic activity in favor of the Homeland."[12] Indeed, the Soviet authorities offered an example of just such forgiveness when two NTS agents, N. I. Iakuta and M. P. Kudriavtsev, sent as part of the Carcass infiltration operations discussed in Chapter 7, were captured on Soviet soil in 1954. Rather than being executed for treason as the previous set of detained agents had been a year before, the two exiles allegedly were forgiven and allowed to lead full lives as Soviet citizens.[13]

The apparatus of persuasion and legislative incentives aimed at the exiles was elaborate. However, spurring the return of exiles was not the only purpose of the campaign, which was also a psychological-warfare operation against émigré anticommunism and its American backers. The return campaign targeted exiles active in anti-Soviet organizations as well as Amcomlib operations that had consolidated in mid-decade—of course, the subgroup of exiles that one would expect to be least likely to move back to the USSR. Indeed, the return campaign can be seen as a Soviet answer to Amcomlib. In what was perhaps a backhanded tribute, the Committee for Return was structured along the same lines as the American Committee. While claiming to be a non-governmental, civic organization—its operating budget, improbably enough, was said to consist of donations from patriotic exiles who had already made the trek back to the USSR–the Mikhailov Committee was in fact a cover for Soviet intelligence services.[14] Just as US government support of Amcomlib was an open secret in émigré circles, so too was state control of the Return Committee; so flimsy was the latter's cover as an independent body that it mailed materials to exiles directly from the Soviet embassy in East Berlin.[15]

The return campaign aimed at the *razlozhenie* ("dissolution" or "corruption") of the anti-Soviet emigration, a term in the Chekist lexicon that referred to the

[12] A. A. Fabrichnikov and I. A. Ovchinnikov, *Ispol'zovanie vozmozhnostei sovetskogo komiteta po kul'turnym sviaziam s sootechestvennikami za rubezhom v razvedyvatel'noi rabote*, uchebnoe posobie (Moscow: Komitet gosudarstvennoi bezopasnosti pri Sovete Ministrov SSSR, 1968), 12, https://www.thedailybeast.com/the-kgb-papers-here-are-the-originals, accessed January 3, 2018, and "Ukaz ot 17 sentiabria 1955 goda, Ob amnistii sovetskikh grazhdan, sotrudnichavshikh s okkupantami v period Velikoi Otechestvennoi Voiny 1941–1945 gg.," *Vedomosti verkhovnogo soveta SSSR* no. 17 (1955): 345.
[13] David C. S. Albanese, "'It Takes a Russian to Beat a Russian': the National Union of Labor Solidarists, Nationalism, and Human Intelligence Operations in the Cold War," *Intelligence and National Security* 32, no. 6 (2017): 789.
[14] See *Nash Otvet*, bulleten' no. 16, April 16, 1956, 2, in FSO, 01–034 Kromiadi-Kruzhin, kor. 1, and Komitet "Vozvrashchenie na Rodinu," report by R. Wraga (evidently for French intelligence), n.d. (1955), in Hoover Institution Library and Archives, Ryszard Wraga Papers, box 4, fol. 9.
[15] Vermerk, Ministerial Advisor for the Ministry for All-German Affairs, February 23, 1956, in Bundesarchiv-Koblenz (hereinafter BA), B 137, Akte 1021.

weakening of a target organization or population through the promotion of its internal disarray and demoralization.[16] The gathering of intelligence on exiles for the campaign was a form of harassment in its own right. Break-ins at the offices of political organizations, camp administrations, and even state institutions tied to Russian exiles were common in West Germany, and exiles assumed, probably often correctly, that they were the work of Soviet agents pursuing the return campaign.[17] And exiles were shaken up when they received mail from the Return Committee at their current addresses and under their original Soviet names.[18] (Second-wave exiles, the reader will recall, had usually adopted new identities to avoid repatriation to the USSR.)

A more insidious psychological tool in the return campaign was the exploitation of personal relationships. Exiles received appeals to come home not just from official mouthpieces but also from long-separated family members and friends in the USSR. Whether carried over the airwaves of the committee's radio facilities or in letters—which mysterious strangers delivered directly to the doorstep of an exile's home—contact from loved ones served political warfare functions.[19] Exiles, and particularly those who were determined to stay abroad at all costs, found familiar voices from their past lives emotionally unnerving. What did Andrei Voloshchuk feel when his wife, daughter, and neighbor called upon him to return home to his native village of Pesok in Ukraine, "telling him of their happy life and promising full forgiveness"?[20] And what was the emotional impact on another exile when his mother in Tatarstan said she hoped to see her son again before she died?[21]

Apart from eliciting sadness and guilt, the campaign's use of Soviet citizens evoked fear. The exiles' relatives who talked about their happy lives in the USSR, whether honestly or not, were obviously operating under official oversight. As Radio Liberation official James Critchlow explained, the émigré contacted by a relative in the Soviet Union would wonder how the latter was "coerced or cajoled" by the KGB into taking part, and what consequences for them might follow if he or she rebuffed the advance.[22] In 1957, the Homeland Committee paper and radio addressed an appeal for return to the second-wave NTS activist

[16] Artizov, *Reabilitatsiia—kak eto bylo*, 406.

[17] Cf. Oleg Burevestnikov, "Blatnoi general," n d., 2, in FSO, 01–034 Kromiadi-Kruzhin, kor. 1.

[18] *Nash otvet*, SBONR publication, biulleten' no. 1, May 1955, 3, in FSO, 01–034 Kromiadi-Kruzhin, kor. 1.

[19] Mikkonen, "Mass Communications as a Vehicle."

[20] Review of Return to the Homeland Radio, Amcomlib, August 25–September 5, 1955, 1–2 in Levine Papers, box 15.

[21] R. V. Dautova, "Iz istorii radiopropagandy vozvrashcheniia 'nevozvrashchentsev' v gody 'Khrushchevskoi Ottepeli,'" *Vestnik Cheliabinskogo gosudarstvennogo universiteta*, vyp. 30 (2010): 50, http://cyberleninka.ru/article/n/iz-istorii-radiopropagandy-vozvrascheniya-nevozvraschentsev-v-gody-hruschevskoy-ottepeli, accessed March 30, 2016.

[22] James Critchlow, *Radio Hole-in-the-head/Radio Liberty: An Insider's Story of Cold War Broadcasting* (Washington, DC: American University Press, 1995), 58.

Aleksandr Semenovich Parfenov-Svetov from his wife and son in the USSR.[23] An Amcomlib official noted that a photograph in *For Return to the Homeland* showed the two family members with faces "tragic with fear and anxiety." If the gloomy expressions cast doubt on the voluntary nature of their appeal to Svetov, one wonders if the move was not deliberate. What better way to signal that his family members were essentially hostages?[24] While Svetov would remain in the West and continue his activities in the NTS, the Amcomlib reviewer predicted that his "balance will have been shaken" now that he was aware that his family was "under careful surveillance."[25]

While the specific operational angle taken with regard to Svetov is unclear, there is no doubt that the return campaign was operating in dual registers, evoking a positive view of Soviet life while also conveying messages about the vulnerability of the exiles and their loved ones at home. Telling in this regard was the fact that the return campaign coincided with a spate of violent measures carried out by Soviet spies against selected exiles, including the already discussed 1954 abduction of NTS leader A. R. Trushnovich—significantly, in this context, a kidnapping operation masquerading as voluntary return to the USSR.[26] Apart from such relatively rare reprisals, Soviet intelligence operatives also subjected the exiles to more routine forms of intimidation. Exiles received phone calls and letters with death threats, had unnerving contact with Russian-speaking strangers on the street, and were followed by agents on foot.[27] The goals of Soviet foreign intelligence in pursuing such harassment were clear to exiles at the time. If the campaign could not spark a mass exodus to the USSR, at least it could "disturb one's calm life and thereby deprive the emigration of the ability to pursue political work..."[28]

The Spectacle of Return

The nature of the return campaign as a psychological-warfare operation was nowhere clearer than in the handling of those exiles who did decide to re-defect

---

[23] During the war, Svetov worked as a propagandist in the Nazi Propaganda Ministry and was an ROA member. Igor' Petrov (ed.), "Vustrau," *Live Journal*, August 22, 2014, https://labas. livejournal. com/1078806.html, accessed June 30, 2018.

[24] The Bolsheviks had a long tradition of taking hostages for political gain. See Vladimir N. Brovkin, *The Bolsheviks in Russian Society: The Revolution and the Civil Wars* (New Haven: Yale University Press, 1997), 222–4.

[25] Review of Return to the Homeland Press and Radio, June 3, 1957, 3, in Levine Papers, box 12.

[26] *Organizovannoe pokushenie na emigratsiiu* (Munich: Izdanie SBONR, 1956) in FSO, 01–034 Kromiadi-Kruzhin, kor. 1. See also Memorandum on Radio Liberation, no author indicated, May 16, 1954, 3, in Georgetown University Archives and Special Collections, Robert F. Kelley Papers, box 5, fol. 3. The Trushnovich abduction is discussed in Chapter 7.

[27] Pamiatka emigranta: kak uberech' sebia ot sovetskoi agentury, SBONR, May 1956, 2–5, in FSO, 01–034 Kromiadi-Kruzhin, kor. 1.

[28] Ibid., 3.

to the USSR, and especially those who had been active in anti-communist circles in Germany. According to the KGB, from 1955 to 1959 the Mikhailov Committee affected the repatriation of 84 "agents of foreign spy services," 98 "traitors", and 105 "participants of anti-Soviet emigrant organizations" to the USSR. (One imagines that, while not specified, these categories were overlapping.)[29] The Mikhailov Committee exploited such defections to disrupt the émigré organizations they left behind and the American institutions with which they were involved.

That some anti-communist exiles could be lured home is hardly surprising. Even ardent anti-communists in exile dreamed of returning to Russia, especially as they lacked virtually all contact with the Soviet population. Most exiles experienced "severe" everyday conditions in Germany and found that "bread bought in foreign lands was bitter," to recall the Kostia letter which opened this chapter. The Vlasovite and former NTS member Gregorii Petrovich Telegin-Kondrashov returned to the USSR in 1956 out of desperation: he and his wife in Germany were divorced, his attempt at immigration to the United States had stalled, he had a "spot on his lungs," and he had been passed over for a promotion at the Labor Service Company, a labor scheme for stateless persons in Europe under the US Army. In a letter to his former wife after his departure to the East, he explained that "he had contemplated suicide but lacked the nerve so he intended to return to Russia which amounted to the same thing."[30]

Kondrashov's fatalism did not stop him from sending glowing reports to the West on his new life in the USSR, both in Return Committee propaganda and in letters to his exile friends. Without a doubt, such an abrupt transformation was testimony to the dependence of returners on the Mikhailov Committee and, more importantly, the intelligence officers who stood behind it. The decree of 1955, it will be recalled, established that World War II collaborators and émigré anti-communists could avoid juridical responsibility for their crimes if they proved willing to "redeem themselves through patriotic activity." Conversely, refusal to cooperate could result in charges of anti-Soviet activity, which carried sentences in camps or even execution. In practice, a clear incentive structure pushed exiles willing to return to take part in the "patriotic movement" of the Return Committee, as a KGB training manual put it.[31]

According to the quid pro quo that dominated the return campaign, exiles who took up the call to return contributed to Soviet propaganda and intelligence

[29] Fabrichnikov and Ovchinnikov, *Ispol'zovanie vozmozhnostei sovetskogo komiteta*, 12.

[30] Kondraschow, Gregorij, Agent Report, Refugee Relief Act, June 11, 1956 in NARA, RG 319, Entry 134B, XE328980, box 442, Gregorij Kondraschow. For similar cases of redefection driven by trying circumstances, see Soviet Re-Defection Program, CIC intelligence report, n.d., 3, 5, in ibid. NTS leader V. M. Baidalakov insinuated in his biography that Telegin-Kondrashov was a Soviet agent, a charge that is not substantiated by information in his CIC file. Viktor Mikhailovich Baidalakov, *Da vozvelichits'ia Rossiia, da pogibnut nashi imena: vospominaniia predsedatelia NTS: 1930–1960 gg.* (Moscow: Avuar Konsalting, 2002), 71.

[31] Fabrichnikov and Ovchinnikov, *Ispol'zovanie vozmozhnostei sovetskogo komiteta*, 12.

operations both before and after crossing the Iron Curtain. While the inaccessible status of most Soviet intelligence sources leaves the details obscure, one can establish the range of redefectors' assignments: writing letters that called on friends and co-workers in exile to follow one's path to the East, providing intelligence to the Soviets, and, contributing pieces to the committee's newspaper or radio once they had crossed over to East Berlin (or sometimes after arriving in the USSR). By all accounts, the redefectors carried out the orders they were given to the letter, a reflection of the tight control intelligence officials held over them.

The place of intelligence activities in the return campaign was apparent in the case of Aleksei Goltiakov-Kurganov. A second-wave exile who had allegedly "avoided military service" in the USSR and "came to Germany," Kurganov hardly seemed to be a likely candidate for repatriation.[32] Like so many exiles, however, Kurganov became disillusioned with life in exile. Constantly unemployed while living as a DP in Fulda, Kurganov expressed to friends his "hatred for the West, especially the USA, and sympathy for Russia" (surely, the USSR).[33] In 1953, Kurganov wrote to the Soviet Military Liaison Mission in Frankfurt asking for news of his family and expressed his willingness to return, even if it meant being "tried by a Soviet court for betrayal of my country."[34] Evidently, the Mikhailov Committee realized that it could exploit Kurganov's desire to return home. Soon after meeting with Soviet officers, Kurganov told a friend that "he intended to collect as much information as possible on the West German Government and the US Occupational Forces and offer it to Soviet Intelligence."[35] Presumably in pursuit of this goal, Kurganov joined the NTS and took up work for the *Posev* publishing house.[36] In 1955, perhaps in recognition of his efforts, the Soviet Return Committee greeted him in East Berlin, where he dutifully denounced his fellow exiles in the pages of *For Return to the Homeland*.[37]

One should not imagine that every redefection proceeded as smoothly as Kurganov's apparently did. In particular, Soviet state-security operatives were not bound by the implicit exchange of service for forgiveness that was central to the return campaign. In 1955, Ivan Vasil'evich Ovchinnikov, an intelligence official in the Main Intelligence Directorate (GRU) involved in radio communications, fled to West Berlin. As his memoir shows, Ovchinnikov defected, in part,

---

[32] Report, Headquarters, 66th CIC Group, n.d. (1955 or later), in NARA, RG 319, Entry 134B, H8005052, box 446, Aleksej Kurganow (hereinafter Kurganow).

[33] Ibid.

[34] This letter was intercepted by US authorities. See translated letter, Alekseej Kurganow, December 8, 1953, in Kurganow.

[35] Report, H. M. Nielsen, 66th CIC Group, May 3, 1955, in Kurganow.

[36] Report from unnamed BfV agent, October–November 1952, in Kurganow. Once in the Soviet bloc, returners were interrogated at length about their contacts in anti-communist circles. Cf. nachal'nik 6 otdela gl. Upr. KGB polk. Grigorenko pri SM SSSR and nachal'nik 3 otdeleniia KGB Polsholikov to zam. nachal'nika 2 upravleniia KGB pri SM USSR G. M. Zhivaga, 2 July 1957, in Haluzevyi derzhavnyi arkhiv Sluzhby Bezpeky Ukrainy fond 1, opys 1, sprava 176711–2, Grigorenko. Thanks to Joshua Sanborn for this source.

[37] HQ 66th CIC Group Bad Cannstatt to AC of S G-2 USAREUR, n.d., in Kurganow.

out of fear that his origins as the son of a repressed kulak had been detected.[38] However, Ovchinnikov soon came to regret his risky escape. Sharing Kurganov's bitterness toward exile existence and Americans, Ovchinnikov fell under the influence of E. N. Artsiuk, the fanatically nationalistic and anti-Semitic old exile and probable Soviet spy discussed in Chapter 2.[39] While he initially joined the émigré anti-communist political scene with enthusiasm, becoming a member of the CIA defector organization TsOPE (the Central Representation of Postwar Emigrants) and then working for a time at Radio Liberation, Ovchinnikov soon became convinced that all the exiles associated with the Americans were "Russophobes, Jews" or "Soviet spies."[40] Ovchinnikov decided that he would return to the homeland after Khrushchev defeated the "Anti-Party Group" of Stalin-era leaders in 1957, a move he interpreted as a sign that the USSR would finally have a "Russian national government" free of Jewish influence.[41] Arriving in East Berlin in 1958, Ovchinnikov was arrested, charged with treason, and sentenced to death, commuted later to ten years in the camps.[42]

Redefection, then, was a phenomenon closely managed by Soviet intelligence and state security organs. In fact, it seems entirely possible to suggest that some returners were actually longstanding intelligence agents brought back to the Soviet bloc under the guise of returners.[43] And in all cases of re-defection, tight control over the returners gave Soviet intelligence abundant opportunities for political actions against the Russian anti-communists in the West. For instance, it was hardly accidental that the redefection of prominent anti-communists—which, according to the typical scenario, involved the abrupt conversion of enemies of Soviet power into loyal and repentant Soviet subjects—created confusion in the communities they left behind. Frenzied questioning gripped the émigré press. Had he or she returned voluntarily or been kidnapped? Had the returner been working for the enemy all along? Should one trust the statements made by repatriates on the other side of the Iron Curtain or were they "Soviet falsification" dictated by KGB agents, as an émigré publication posited with regard to the post-return pieces penned by defector and anti-communist writer Boris Ol'shanskii?[44] The returner's

---

[38] I. V. Ovchinnikov, *Na pereput'iakh Rossii* (Moscow: Informatsionno-ekspertnaia gruppa "Panorama," 1995), 69–73.

[39] Ibid., 92–3.

[40] Ibid., 218.

[41] Ibid., 140.

[42] Ibid.

[43] A state official in West Germany posited that the 1955 redefection of V. P. Vasilaki, the émigré discussed as a probable Soviet agent in Chapter 2, was staged—perhaps in order to give the Mikhailov Committee a tangible first victory in its campaign. G. von Mende to Dr. Bräutigam, Auswärtiges Amt, Betr: Ukrainischer Re-Emigrant Wladimir Petrowitsch Wassilakij, April 29, 1955, in AA-PA, B 12, Akte 455.

[44] See the account of *Novoe slovo* in Review of the Russian Émigré Press, vol. 4, no. 22, 1956, 4, in Levine Papers, box 15.

sudden and total passage across geographical and ideological borders left the exiles in disarray.

CIA intelligence officers in Germany also had difficulty making sense of the redefectors' motivations for departure. A security officer detached to Radio Liberation wondered whether Ovchinnikov and Viktor Il'inskii, another recent defector and fellow radio employee who made his way to the East in 1959, were Soviet plants from the beginning or "simply homesick young men who felt they had made a mistake in fleeing to the West."[45] In fact, such doubts about the individuals who returned East on the premise that "all will be forgotten" were the inevitable byproduct of the methods employed by the Mikhailov campaign: the covert approaches to exiles by intelligence agents, the use of potential returners as intelligence sources, and the propagandistic accounts attributed to them after they arrived in East Berlin. On one level, the stories of repentant anti-communists must have seemed unbelievable: what self-respecting anti-communist, one would ask, could undergo such a humiliating transformation? The Soviet script was impenetrable, creating a lingering sense of ambiguity.

Sowing confusion and distrust among the exiles and their CIA backers was not the only psychological objective of the operations that returned anti-communists to the USSR. The return campaign also sought to use redefectors from the anti-communist scene such as Ovchinnikov and Il'inskii to weaken the ties between exiles and the Americans who sponsored their anti-communist activities. Upon arrival in the East, returners lashed out at their former patrons, calling Amcomlib and Radio Liberation "a nest of spies," as one returner put it in an article in the central Soviet press.[46] Such verbal assaults served multiple purposes. If CIA officers and Amcomlib employees were forced to witness the "betrayal and weakness" of exiles they had previously patronized, they might reach the conclusion that working with exiles in general was not worth the effort.[47] Following this logic, the redefectors strove to embarrass their American patrons in any way possible, with redefector V. P. Vasilaki exaggerating in his mea culpa from East Berlin the extent to which he had been close to Amcomlib officials.[48]

The redefectors' relentless attacks on Amcomlib sought to influence mass opinion in the Russian diaspora, as well. In the writings of the returners, US officials sponsoring Russian anti-communists appear as sadistic brutes,

[45] Critchlow, Radio Hole-in-the-head/Radio Liberty, 58. See also CIA analysis of Ovchinnikov's redefection in Security Officer, Munich, to Assistant to the President, November 5, 1959, 1, in NARA, RG 263, Entry ZZ-19, 250/86/26/01, QKACTIVE (henceforth QKACTIVE), box 55, vol. 4.

[46] G. Oleinik, "A Nest of Spies," Izvestiia, December 21, 1956, translated by Amcomlib in Levine Papers, box 15.

[47] See the cogent explanation of this point by a Ukrainian émigré in Der bolschewistische Wühl-versuch gegen die Emigration, Dmytro Andriewsky, April 29, 1955, 2, in AA-PA, B 12, Akte 455.

[48] "Vozvrashenets Vasiliaki: glava Amerikanskogo Komiteta shchitaet ego sovetskim agentom," Novoe russkoe slovo, April 9, 1955.

functionaries of an "American Gestapo" that terrorized the exiled Russians.[49] In one account, Amcomlib employees in Germany sold helpless displaced Russians overseas like slaves.[50] Even if some exiles surely were skeptical of such lurid stories about exploitation at the hands of the US authorities, the returners' railing against the Americans might have constituted effective propaganda. After all, many exiles had some basis for animosity toward the Americans, either for personal reasons (bitterness over one's treatment in the West) or political ones (such as American courtship of Soviet minorities and suspicion over US diplomatic overtures to the USSR following Stalin's death). The propaganda did not have to be believable to undermine the reputation of the Americans in the diaspora. In fact, the very spectacle of Russian anti-communists' denouncing their former patrons drove home the fact that the Americans were unable to prevent their clients from defecting—or, worse yet, that they had failed to detect Soviet agents in their midst. Without a doubt, the KGB hoped that such undermining of the prestige of the Americans would dampen émigrés' willingness to work for US interests.[51]

The Return Campaign attacked the exile political organizations even more virulently than the Americans who stood behind them. Exile anti-communists, a Mikhailov Committee appeal to exiles maintained, had sold "their country, their honor and their conscience," delivering "helpless people" to the Americans in order to "satisfy their whims and their depravity."[52] The Return Committee also provided examples of the exiles' lavish lifestyles. Apparently, Fedor Tarasovich Lebedev-Tarasov of TsOPE acquired a villa illegally, while Grigor Saaruni, the leader of the Armenian Fighters for Freedom, drove "around in a car and pays 250 marks for his apartment."[53] Against the backdrop of émigré hardship, luxurious lifestyles funded by intelligence work might indeed have seemed like "depravity."

The Mikhailov Committee also used the personal touch in its efforts to undermine the Russian political activists in Germany, much as it did in utilizing exiles' family members in its propaganda. Just before crossing the Iron Curtain, redefectors left written messages to friends or colleagues remaining in the West that encouraged them to renounce exile and follow their path to the homeland. If such exit letters followed the overall narrative of national deliverance and homecoming featured in the return propaganda, they also carried a more intimate tone and better reflected the experiences of the redefectors than did the set pieces in *For Return to the*

[49] In the Torture Chambers of the American Intelligence Service: I. V. Ovchinnikov tells about Peter Moroz's tragedy, translation from *Za Vozvrashchenie na Rodinu* no. 25 (320), March 1959, 4, in QKACTIVE, box 56, vol. 5.

[50] Review of the Russian Émigré Press, vol. 3, no. 46, November 30, 1955, in Levine Papers, box 15.

[51] G. von Mende to Dr. Bräutigam.

[52] Appeal of the Committee for Return to the Homeland mailed to exiles in Munich, forwarded by Gerhard von Mende, June 10, 1955, in AA-PA, B 12, Akte 455.

[53] Review of Return to the Homeland Press and Radio, no. 12, December 13, 1955, Radio Liberation, 1, in Levine Papers, box 15.

Homeland. In a letter left for the old émigré Aleksei Alekseevich Orlov, who worked as an announcer at Radio Liberation, Ovchinnikov declared that he had finally "extricated himself from the kingdom of darkness" and the "filth into which we were dragged and in which we were drowning"—an accurate description, his memoirs suggest, of Ovchinnikov's perception of exile at the time.[54]

Orlov's reaction to this letter is unknown, although the fact that Radio Liberation came into possession of it suggests that he might not have been sympathetic to the appeals of his departed acquaintance. Some exiles receiving such exit letters saw them as the handiwork of Soviet spies, not as earnest appeals from friends. For instance, White émigré Nikolai Iakovlevich Galai, then head of the Munich Institute for the Study of the USSR, responded to the parting letter he received from the returner Mikhail Kolosov with the charge that he was either a "Soviet agent or someone without moral substance."[55] Yet such hostile reactions are hard to interpret, as exiles working for the Americans had a vested interest in renouncing the returners. Surely, missives from the redefectors sometimes struck a chord with the exiles who received them. Ovchinnikov's description of life "in a strange country, torn away from his homeland, in the position of a man deprived of rights, humiliated and homeless" corresponded to the perceptions many Soviet exiles and especially recent defectors held of their lot.[56] Despite the role of Soviet intelligence agencies in handling returners, their statements and letters both expressed and capitalized on real tensions in the Russian colony in Germany.

Like all effective propaganda, the return campaign merged fact and fiction. The campaign conveyed criticisms of exile life that were quite commonly held by exiles. At the same time, the propaganda campaign forced returners into a carefully orchestrated crossing of Cold War ideological lines. By returning to the USSR, exiles created a spectacle of human degradation tailored to American and émigré audiences. If active anti-Soviet exiles were driven to *this*—abandoning the cause, betraying their companions abroad, and obsequiously mouthing platitudes about Soviet life—then resistance to the Soviet regime was surely a fool's errand.

The Struggle for Georgii Il'ich Antonov

The story of one exile anti-communist, SBONR leader G. I. Antonov, demonstrates the myriad ways in which the return campaign struck at the Russian exiles and their American patrons. A former colonel in the Red Army who had fought in Vlasov's forces, Antonov headed SBONR following its bruising split in 1953 and

---

[54] Ivan Ovchinnikov to Alexis Orlov, November 4, 1958, in QKACTIVE, box 55, vol. 4. In his memoir, Ovchinnikov describes Orlov as a mentor and ideological companion. Ovchinnikov, *Na pereput'iakh Rossii*, 116–17.

[55] N. Galai, "M. Kolosovu," in *Privet Rodine!*, 27.

[56] In the Torture Chambers of the American Intelligence Service.

then helped to bring about its reunification—a rarity in an émigré milieu where ruptures were far more common than reconciliations.[57] If anyone would seem to be immune to the advances of the return campaign, it was Antonov.

All the more disturbing, then, were rumors that swept Russian Munich in 1958 that Antonov was considering relocating to the USSR, and was in ongoing contact with Soviet agents. The CIA's investigation of the affair gave some indication of the situation that had brought an anti-communist leader to the brink of ideological betrayal. Antonov's position in SBONR's leadership, we learn, had come into question, perhaps because the organization had failed to regain its previous level of effectiveness or Amcomlib patronage. Added to this, Antonov was "a weak person, a heavy drinker, and not adverse [sic] to females of questionable reputation," according to CIA sources.[58] As a broken man with a fading political career, Antonov constituted a suitable target for the Soviet sirens of return.

The Soviet approach to Antonov drew on the strongest lever the Mikhailov Committee had over the exiles: relatives in the USSR. In 1958, Antonov received a letter from a stranger who was supposedly a friend of his long-estranged daughter living in Leningrad. The letter invited Antonov to reunite with his daughter at the upcoming Brussels World Fair, which she was apparently going to visit as a Soviet delegate.[59] Antonov had "broken down" when shown a picture of his daughter, as "he had been told that she and his wife had perished in a wartime bombing attack and [Antonov] had long since ceased to think of himself as part of a family."[60] Soon Antonov's colleagues grew concerned. In its propaganda against the return campaign, SBONR's leadership implored its cadres not to respond to the Mikhailov Committee's offers to establish contact with family members in the USSR, and even to leave letters from them unopened. Acting otherwise, SBONR warned, would only threaten entrapment or blackmail for the émigré involved, while exposing his or her loved ones in the USSR to manipulation.[61] In other words, Antonov had failed to live up to the demands SBONR made of its members—a stark reminder of the low state of morale among all exiles in the period as well as the vulnerability of even the most committed anti-communists to the approaches of Soviet agents.

The CIA investigation offered a vivid picture of Antonov's emotional upheaval, but left many questions unanswered. Antonov's own descriptions of the affair were particularly confusing. The SBONR leader "felt that there was no longer

---

[57] On the SBONR split and the united-front project, see Chapter 6.

[58] A. Melbardis, Asst. to Director of Émigré Relations to Amcomlib Security Officer, no date (1958), 2, in QKACTIVE, box 55, vol. 4.

[59] Dispatch, Chief of Base, Munich to Chief, IO, December 29, 1958, 2, in QKACTIVE, box 55, vol. 4.

[60] Memorandum for the Record, author not indicated, sent from Chief of Base, Munich to Chief, IO, on February 3, 1959, 2, in QKACTIVE, box 56, vol. 5.

[61] Nash otvet, biulleten' no. 16 (April 1956): 7 and S. Iu. Volk, "Proshu poniat' nizhesleduiushchee...," in Privet Rodine!, 23.

anything left for him in the West during the relatively few remaining years of his life," according to a CIA contact, and supposedly even spoke to émigré friends "in hopeful terms about the treatment that might be afforded him should he return to the Soviet Union."[62] On the other hand, Antonov agreed with Robert Dreher, a CIA official detailed to Amcomlib, that the letters were "undoubtedly a provocation by the Return to the Homeland Committee" designed to paralyze SBONR.[63] The eventual outcome of the Antonov affair was equally ambiguous: Antonov did not redefect, but he did experience a "nervous breakdown."[64]

If breaking the spirit of Antonov was one objective of the Soviet advances, a broader goal was to weaken SBONR and the émigré anti-communists. Not surprisingly, rumors that a respected anti-Soviet leader was considering return roiled the SBONR leadership. V. P. Chernetskii-Zarudnyi, tasked by the exile organization to investigate the Antonov situation, came to the damning conclusion that Antonov had been blackmailed by Soviet agents. The SBONR Central Bureau then closed ranks behind its embattled leader, accusing the hapless Chernetskii of slandering Antonov and pursuing the breakdown of the organization—charges for which they had no evidence.[65] In this manner, a mysterious letter from Leningrad had sparked an internal crisis in the émigré political milieu.

The Antonov affair also took its toll on Amcomlib. The American Committee and its CIA funders were deeply concerned lest the "loss" of Antonov, "either through re-defection or discreditation [sic]," bring an end to SBONR as "an effective political instrument."[66] Yet the Americans remained in the dark about Antonov's situation. Alex Melbardis, Amcomlib Assistant Director of Émigré Relations, thought that Antonov had more contact with Soviet authorities than he admitted to and might even be under their control. By contrast, Dreher refused to offer a clear position on the affair—at least, apart from making the cryptic comment that "there appears to be much more to this case than meets the eye."[67] Given this confusion, Amcomlib struggled to find a suitable response. Should Amcomlib support the troubled SBONR leader or treat him with circumspection, preparing for the day when he would appear in East Berlin and denounce his

---

[62] Dispatch, Chief of Base, 2.
[63] Ibid. and Memorandum for the Record. On Dreher's role in Amcomlib, see Isaac Patch, *Closing the Circle: A Buckalino Journey around Our Time* (Wellesley, MA: Wellesley College Printing Services, 1996), 233–4.
[64] Otkrytoe pis'mo chlenam Rukovokiashchego Soveta Soiuza Bor'by za Osvobozhdenie Narodov Rossii i vsem chlenam SBONR, V. Chernetskii, n.d., 6, in FSO, 01–034 Kromiadi-Kruzhin, kor. 2.
[65] In a lengthy "open letter" to SBONR, Chernetskii provided extensive documentation for his position that SBONR had refused to deal with the Antonov case in an objective manner. Otkrytoe pis'mo chlenam Rukovokiashchego Soveta. For countercharges against Chernetskii, see Protokol zasedaniia Tsentral'nogo Biuro i TsKK SBONR, May 21, 1960, in FSO, 01–034 Kromiadi-Kruzhin, kor. 2.
[66] Memorandum for the Record, 2.
[67] Ibid., 3.

American patrons? Faced with this dilemma, Amcomlib sought to take a middle position. Robert F. Kelley, then Amcomlib representative in Munich, reasoned that the committee should offer the SBONR leader "all possible aid and sympathy" without making "any unusual or obvious moves which ANTONOV might distort after his possible re-defection."[68] As was so often the case when dealing with Soviet penetration of the exile organizations, the CIA seemed to be playing defense without knowing the rules of the game.

The problems the Antonov affair posed for the CIA and its front organization were hardly an isolated case. With the growth of Radio Liberation, Amcomlib found itself in charge of a large émigré clientele in Germany—a "sprawling monster" full of "varied characters," a 1953 CIA report called it—that was the target of persistent harassment by Soviet intelligence agents.[69] Remarkably, the CIA was not in a position to keep track of all the Soviet approaches to exiles in Amcomlib's employ, let alone to pursue a cogent strategy toward countering them. In 1961, a CIA staff member responded to an inquiry about Soviet advances toward one émigré employee almost dismissively, explaining that "the mere reporting to Headquarters of the numerous letters, telephone calls and visits received by our employees which stem from Soviet attempts to disaffect them would in itself be [a] full time job."[70] The repatriation campaign and the widespread Soviet contact operations it entailed constituted a permanent strain on Amcomlib's émigré enterprise, even if relatively few exiles actually crossed over the Iron Curtain.

Losing the Exiles? The Return Campaign and American Power

The efforts of the Mikhailov Committee came into force at a low point for the fortunes of the anti-communist Russians in Europe. The American attempts to unite Soviet exiles in a political center had fallen apart, prompting Amcomlib to take control of the institutions that were slated to come under the émigrés' authority (see Chapter 6). Adding to the general mood of pessimism that prevailed in anti-communist exile circles in mid-decade were the improved diplomatic relations between the United States and the USSR. Faced with the lowered temperature of the Cold War in the years immediately following Stalin's death, émigré anti-communists of all stripes feared that the West was losing the war

---

[68] Ibid., 4.

[69] Prist Visit to Europe, March 9–24, 1953, Chief of Base, Munich to Chief EE, April 3, 1953, 5, in QKACTIVE, box 55, vol. 1.

[70] Memorandum, Re: Attached and Prior Traffic re. Wolfgang KOEHLER, November 8, 1961, 1, in QKACTIVE, box 55, vol. 4.

against international communism and might, in a fit of naïveté and weakness, make peace with it.[71]

The sorry state of Russian anti-communism in mid-decade set the tone for US responses to the Soviet redefection campaign. The CIA saw the efforts of the Mikhailov Committee—which, we have seen, targeted exiles working for its many projects—as a considerable threat to its interests and deserving of a concerted response. The Committee for Return's attempts to divorce the exiles from US influence might, if unchecked, deplete manpower the CIA relied on for psy-war enterprises. Indeed, this danger was not hypothetical. For example, in the late 1950s, the Agency blocked a TsOPE operative from participation in Berlin operations when it became known that his brother in the USSR was "trying to encourage" the émigré's return.[72] As already seen, Soviet harassment of Amcomlib's exile employees was even more common. In a wider sense, the at least ostensibly voluntary movement of Russians to the USSR called into question the US programs to incite, manage, and publicize defections from the Soviet bloc. If the escape of East bloc citizens to the West helped to solidify the division of Europe and the world into democratic and totalitarian halves, the movement of bodies in the opposite direction might call this moral-ideological geography into question.

For these reasons, the return campaign spurred a re-engagement of Amcomlib with the Russian exiles. To be sure, Amcomlib did not return to its previous practice of granting monthly subsidies to émigré political organizations. Instead, the American Committee adopted a limited and selective strategy of funding "practical projects" proposed by any exiles "of a democratic persuasion."[73] By keying funding to specific actions, Amcomlib leaders hoped, the committee would capitalize on émigré anti-communism while keeping its distance from the exiles' internal disputes. The role of the return campaign in spurring this limited rapprochement was made clear by the nature of the "practical projects" funded, which included holding rallies and publishing pamphlets and brochures attacking the Mikhailov Committee.[74]

Whatever were its limitations, Amcomlib's renewed interest in the exiles did revive its relationships with the political organizations. In fact, the committee's approach to funding individual émigré initiatives had the advantage of widening

---

[71] Presse-spiegel der russischen Exilpresse, 15.8-31.8 54, 1, in BA, B 137, Akte 1019. For astute observations about the hard-line stances of Russian émigrés on US–Soviet relations in the period, see A. V. Antoshin, *Rossiiskie emigranty v usloviiakh "kholodnoi voiny" (seredina 1940-kh-seredina-1960-kh gg.)* (Ekaterinburg: Izd. Ural'skogo universiteta, 2008), 455–6, 464, 496, 504, 508–9.

[72] Action Reported by the Field, July 8, 1959, in AEVIRGIL, vol. 1.

[73] Howland Sargaent to Spencer Williams, November 5, 1954, in Levine Papers, box 8.

[74] As part of this shift, Amcomlib created its own Russian-language journal, *Nashe obshchee delo* ("Our Common Cause"), whose purpose was to promote "an understanding of and support for the policies of the United States and its allies" in the emigration. The American Committee for Liberation, Inc., The President's Annual Report to the Board of Trustees, November 15, 1960, 21 in Levine Papers, box 9.

the range of groups that Amcomlib could engage. For the first time, Amcomlib established contact with some monarchist organizations that held a strong position in the Russian community of New York yet had been left in the cold during the united front.[75] For their part, many anti-communist activists proved willing to re-engage with the "little uncles" (*diadushki*), as exiles disparagingly called the Americans.[76] Although SBONR leaders feared "losing face" by working with Amcomlib—recalling, of course, the accusations of national treachery that the exiles who participated in the united front had faced—they also understood that the Americans remained indispensable patrons of their anti-communist cause.[77] Ironically, the return campaign, which sought to pry apart émigrés from their American patrons, had actually driven them together.

Renewed Amcomlib–émigré cooperation produced an aggressive counter-propaganda drive against the Mikhailov Committee. As suggested by the "Kostia" letter with which this chapter opened, the basic approach of the anti-return agitation urged exiles not to believe the promises of the Mikhailov Committee, which were a ploy to "put to sleep" the exiles.[78] Once on the other side of the Iron Curtain, the propagandists warned exile readers, they would be subjected to the incarceration and exploitation inflicted on previous waves of repatriates—a warning conveyed in Figure 10.1. To some extent, the exiles were playing fast and loose with the facts. As suggested by the case of Ovchinnikov, a minority of émigrés were indeed "tricked" into return, and then tried for state crimes.[79] Yet while returnees to the USSR sometimes experienced local-level discrimination and special scrutiny from security organs, they seem to have been reintegrated into Soviet life to a significant degree.[80]

Whether the exile anti-communists—or, for that matter, their Amcomlib backers—believed their own propaganda remains unclear. Like most ideologues, they rarely went off script. Beyond doubt, however, is the overly simplistic language of national betrayal the anti-communists imposed on the phenomenon of return. In this view, Mikhailov himself was a "criminal general" who staffed his

---

[75] Review of the Russian Émigré Press, no. 44, December 31, 1954, 4, in Levine Papers, box 15. Another sign of Amcomlib's new ideological flexibility was the committee's funding of a leaflet campaign and anti-return rally in Munich carried out by the Coordinating Center for the Liberation of the Peoples of Russia (*Koordinatsionnyi Tsentr Osvobozhdeniia Narodov Rossii* or KTsONR), the Russian-dominated rump born of the united front negotiations with which the Americans had clashed just months before. Vermerk, Betr: die gegenwartige Situation in kzonr, Dr. Schulte, abt. 6, April 29, 1955, 1, in AA-PA, B 12, Akte 455.

[76] Protokol zasedaniia tsentral'nogo komiteta SBONR, February 25, 1955, 2, in FSO, 01–034 Kromiadi-Kruzhin, kor. 1.

[77] Ibid.

[78] *Organizovannoe pokushenie na emigratsiiu*, 7–8.

[79] Compare with Zemskov, "'Vtoraia emigratsiia' i otnoshenie k nei," 89.

[80] Fabrichnikov and I. A. Ovchinnikov, *Ispol'zovanie vozmozhnostei sovetskogo komiteta*, 12, and Dautova, "Iz istorii radiopropagandy vozvrashcheniia 'nevozvrashchentsev'": 49.

Figure 10.1 Émigré propaganda against the Soviet return campaign from a publication of the exile group SBONR. *My vernulis' domoi!* ("We have returned home!") also spells out the acronym for the Soviet Ministry of Internal Affairs. A caption appearing alongside the image made the point even blunter by declaring that the Soviet Union is a "giant concentration camp" and calling on exiles to ignore the blandishments of the Committee for Return to the Homeland.

Source: Archiv der Forschungsstelle Osteuropa an der Universität Bremen.

committee with former Gestapo agents and black-marketeers.[81] Exiles who returned to the USSR were not only foolish but guilty of "full betrayal" to the emigration and to the true Russia the Bolsheviks had enslaved.[82] Likewise, the exiles did everything they could to discredit the individual repatriates, no doubt to forestall the stigma of having lost cadres to the enemy. For instance, SBONR alleged that one returner had opened a shop in Munich to sell off looted

---

[81] Burevestnikov, "Blatnoi general," 3–5. It is true that Soviet state security showed a willingness to employ former SS figures. See Perry Biddiscombe, "The Problem with Glass Houses: The Soviet Recruitment and Deployment of SS Men as Spies and Saboteurs," *Intelligence and National Security* 15, no. 3 (2000): 131–45.

[82] *Organizovannoe pokushenie*, 7–8.

belongings from Jewish victims of the Holocaust.[83] In its condemnation of the enemy, the exiles' propaganda resembled the return campaign it meant to discredit, with the traitor-returnee appearing as the mirror image of the common Soviet trope of the depraved émigré anti-communist.

The CIA-funded propaganda against return was considerably more substantive when it came to refuting specific claims made by the Mikhailov Committee. In particular, the exiles had little difficulty challenging the Soviet claim, discussed above, that exiles were being held hostage by the West German government through "moral pressure, intimidation, persecution and even violent acts."[84] When *For Return to the Homeland* described the extreme poverty of the DP Bogalin family, the SBONR publication *Svoboda* ("Freedom") responded cleverly by publishing a picture of the same family—everyone plump, well dressed, and smiling.[85]

An elaborate approach to debunking the return campaign was what might be called "returner escapee" accounts. In 1955, TsOPE organized a mass meeting in Munich directed against the Mikhailov Committee's activities. The speakers, DPs Leonid Khorevich, Boris Serebriakov, and the couple Evgenii Nemov and Liudmila Nemova, had apparently taken up the appeal for return, traveled to East Berlin, and then fled back to West Germany. As the speakers explained, they had believed the Mikhailov Committee's promises of a good life and "forgiveness" in the USSR, in part because of their postwar experiences of "lack of constant work, a difficult life in camps, and a longing for one's native land that is common to every émigré."[86] However, the returners were immediately disillusioned by their treatment in East Berlin, where they were subjected to interrogations about their émigré contacts, fed ghostwritten texts to deliver over Committee for Return radio and tasked with conducting undefined activities in the West before leaving Germany, with the suggestion that refusal to cooperate demonstrated a failure to "expiate their sins" toward the homeland.[87] Convinced that the Mikhailov Committee was a mere "organ" of the KGB and fearing for their future—apparently, they were to be escorted East by a military convoy and were not told of their final point of destination—the returners fled back to West Berlin.[88]

---

[83] *Nash Otvet*, builleten' no. 16, April 16, 1956, 3, in FSO, 01–034 Kromiadi-Kruzhin, kor. 1. Notably, Amcomlib also tried to distance itself from returners with whom it had been associated. Cf. O vozvrashchenii poslevoennogo emigranta M. Kolosova v sovetskuiu zonu, Amcomlib, no date (late 1955), 1–3, in FSO, 01–034 Kromiadi-Kruzhin, kor. 1.

[84] Telegram from Moscow to Foreign Ministry, Bonn, August 29, 1956, 1, in AA-PA, B 12, Akte 450.

[85] *Privet Rodine!*, 38–9.

[86] *Amnistiia 1955 goda – ocherednaia fal'shivka "kollektivnogo rukovodstva": Pokazaniia vozvrativshikhsia vozvrashchentsev na sobranii 8 oktiabria 1955 goda* (Munich: Izd. Svobodnyi golos, 1955), 3, in FSO, 01–034 Kromiadi-Kruzhin, kor. 1.

[87] Ibid., 11–20.

[88] Ibid., 1–2.

The Soviets alleged that the CIA staged the entire saga of the Nemovs and the others from start to finish, a claim that available sources can neither prove nor disprove.[89] What is clear is that the counter-return narrative—that the return campaign was designed to lure unsuspecting exiles to the East, where they were manipulated and mistreated—was widely shared in émigré anti-communist circles.[90] Indeed, it corresponded with the experiences of many Russian exiles, who viewed the current Soviet gambit for repatriation through the lens of their own traumatic histories of persecution, evasion of repatriation, and fear of Soviet retribution. And even if the returner-escapees *were* plants as the Soviets claimed, the picture they drew of the Mikhailov Committee's function as cover for intelligence operations was basically accurate. Like all good propaganda, the returner-escapee genre included a dose of truth.

Exile counter-propaganda against the return campaign served a wider purpose than punching holes in the claims made by the Soviet side. It showed that the exiles could fight back against the Soviet regime's new plan to unwind the emigration. The stream of redefectors was very small, as the Mikhailov Committee confirmed indirectly by providing "confused data on the returners, repeating the same names several times in different disguises" in order to create the illusion that a mass exodus was underway.[91] Accordingly, the exiles could claim with at least some justification that they were winning the fight with the Soviet regime, at least on one front. The mere rhetoric of victory provided a gain of sorts in the world of psychological warfare, in which perceptions and even emotional states were the stuff of political contestation.

If the exiles' propaganda activities received an unexpected boost from the otherwise devastating return campaign, so too did the internal affairs of the Russian community in West Germany. As discussed in Chapter 2, political divisions among the exiles had hindered the consolidation of a viable civic organization for Russian refugees that could act as an intermediary with the West German state. The clear and immediate threat posed by the return campaign, however, provided an impetus for the exiles—true, already a quite small population by mid-decade thanks to migration from Europe—to create a viable representative organization.[92] Perhaps inevitably, the National Representation of the Russian Emigration (NATsPRE) was a creature of the Cold War. Despite its ostensibly apolitical

[89] *Amnistiia 1955 goda*, 3. See also Review of Return to the Homeland, no. 12, December 13, 1955, 1, in Levine Papers, box 15.

[90] Tellingly, right-wing newspapers that routinely attacked TsOPE and Amcomlib covered the Nemov story without inserting critical comment. On coverage in the monarchist publications *Nasha Strana* and *Rossiia*, see Review of the Russian Émigré Press, vol. III, no. 42, October 26, 1955, 6, in Levine Papers, box 15.

[91] Review of Return to the Homeland Radio, November18–December 8, 1955, 3, in Levine Papers, box 15.

[92] A 1954 German Foreign Ministry document estimated a population of just 15,000 Russian exiles in Germany, of whom 7,000 had registered with NATsPRE. Ausarbeitung über die russische Emigration, March 1954, 30 in AA-PA, B 12, Akte 455. Andrew Janco estimates that there were 20,000 Soviet

mandate of representing the "legal, social, and national-cultural matters of the Russian emigration in its entirety," NATsPRE drew leaders from the ranks of the political émigrés and funding, it would seem, from the CIA.[93] German officials posited simply that NATsPRE was "supported by the Americans," while the organization's chairman, F. T. Lebedev, was a leader of TsOPE, the exile outfit that was under close Agency control.[94]

The return campaign jolted NATsPRE into action. The organization responded to Soviet diplomatic pressure over repatriation by petitioning the West German government for protection and action to improve exiles' job prospects—exactly the kind of grassroots lobbying that is so important to exile groups, and which the hyper-politicized life of the Russians in Germany had previously prevented.[95] A German observer of a NATsPRE congress in 1956, himself a Baltic German who had had been involved in the Vlasov project during the war, made the barbed and stereotype-laden comment that it was "the first meeting of Russians" he had witnessed "that proceeded in an organized and disciplined way."[96] Clearly, political divides had given way to the imperative of dissuading exiles from returning to the USSR—which, ultimately, meant preserving Russian communities abroad. The solidification of NATsPRE was another unintended consequence of the return campaign, as the rapidly shrinking Russian exile population in Germany finally came to act as a more cohesive community.

*   *   *

Was the campaign for return to the homeland a successful endeavor for the Soviet state? The ostensible results of the repatriation campaign, it is safe to say, were underwhelming. An estimated 10,000 exiles returned from 1954 to 1959, but the largest groups of repatriates came from less assimilated exile communities in South America, which actually included few of the Soviet citizens of the second wave who constituted the campaign's main target.[97] In a tacit acknowledgment of its failure to induce mass return, the Soviet leadership shifted gears in 1960, redefining the

Russians in the FRG at the start of 1952. See "Soviet 'Displaced Persons' in Europe, 1941–1951," PhD diss., University of Chicago, 2012, 136.

[93] Betr: Delegation der nazpre Walter von Conradi, Büro für heimatvertriebene Ausländer to von Dellingshausen, BMG, June 25, 1956, in BA, B 137, Akte 1021.
[94] Ibid., and Schreiben der Nationalen Vertretung der russischen Emigranten in der Bundesrepublik Deutschland (NATsPRE) e. V. vom 30 April 1956, von Staden, in AA-PA, B 12, Akte 455.
[95] Resolution der Tagung der Russischen Emigranten angenommen in München am 15 April 1956, in BA, B 137, Akte 1021.
[96] The speaker was Eduard von Dellingshausen, the cousin of Ewert von Dellingshausen, the official responsible for ties with émigrés in the Federal Ministry of Intra-German Affairs. Vermerk, betr: Delegationkongress der Russischen Emigranten in der Bundesrepublik vom 14–18 April 1956, von Dellingshausen, in BA, B 137, Akte 1021.
[97] Soviet Activities against the Emigration, no author indicated, January 4, 1962, 1 in AEVIRGIL, box 25, vol. 1.

Committee for Return to the Homeland by adding "and Cultural Ties with Compatriots" to its title.[98] As its new name suggested, the committee now focused on influencing exiles *in situ* rather than pursuing their movement to the USSR—a revised mission that was advanced by funding pro-Soviet émigré groups, arranging cultural and social programs, and facilitating the travel of exiles to the USSR. In a sense, the revamping of the Mikhailov Committee was a concession to reality: the Soviet state was unable to uproot the Russian diaspora in Europe.

It would be a mistake, however, to dismiss the return campaign as a failure. If its ostensible purpose of luring large numbers of exiles back home was perhaps implausible, it proved to be an effective instrument for weakening anti-communist organizations abroad. The redefection of a select number of prominent anti-communists embarrassed and befuddled the exiles and their American backers. Less tangible but equally significant was the psychological effect on the many exiles who remained but emerged from the campaign compromised or unnerved by advances from the Soviet authorities. The best example was the pitiful Antonov, whose ambiguous entanglements with the return campaign sparked an internal crisis in the émigré anti-communist milieu, even though he remained in the West.

Although the return campaign disrupted the anti-communist exile organizations, it also demonstrated the self-sustaining character of the Russian émigré political struggle. The very real threat to émigré anti-communism posed by the Mikhailov Committee and the spies organized under its cover spurred counter-reactions that were unforeseen by and undesirable to Soviet leaders. Amcomlib reforged relationships with exiles that had been badly disrupted in previous years, leading to a robust propaganda counterattack against the repatriation drive. Moreover, the Russian emigration began to organize itself more effectively than before.

In a wider perspective, the return campaign revealed that the Soviet government, much like its American opponent, had difficulty marshalling the exiles as effective instruments of great-power policy. In the propaganda letter with which this chapter opened, the émigré Kostia was warned that the return campaign was "a beautiful trap from which you will never escape." Placing these words in a different context, the exiles as a whole were perhaps a "beautiful trap," a diaspora that seemed ripe for exploitation by the superpowers but proved nearly impossible to control. So long as the intelligence agencies of both superpowers held a stake in the Russian exile milieu, one might posit, they would remain in a shifting state of gridlock, with the CIA pouring its seemingly endless resources into it, while the Soviet side replied with crafty countermeasures. Ultimately, the decisive break in the émigré anticommunists' fortunes came from an unexpected quarter: the Americans' West German allies, whose territory had been the exiles' main staging ground.

---

[98] Ibid.

11

Unreliable Allies

The German Crucible and Russian Anti-Communism

In 1957, the American Committee for Liberation from Bolshevism (Amcomlib) decided to hold an event marking the fortieth anniversary of the October Revolution. The committee turned to Russian exile organizations in Germany to provide a noisy counterpunch to the fanfare with which Moscow commemorated October 1917. Unfortunately for both sides, the anti- commemoration rehashed the competing national claims that had plagued the united-front campaign a few years before, as non-Russian exiles boycotted the event and even distributed anti-Russian propaganda while it was taking place.[1]

While the debacle surrounding the October Revolution confirmed the toxic nature of exile national questions, it also saw a challenge to the exiles emerge from a relatively new source: the West German state. The government of the Federal Republic (FRG) took a negative view of the exiles' plan to mark the fortieth anniversary. Walter Hallstein, State Secretary in the Foreign Ministry and the country's senior diplomat, urged all government ministries to decline and even leave unanswered invitations to the émigré events. The Federal Republic maintained diplomatic relations with the USSR, Hallstein noted, and "the anniversary of the October Revolution is celebrated as their national holiday."[2] When the closely CIA-controlled Central Representation of Postwar Emigrants (TsOPE) staged its own commemoration of the date in the symbolic space of Congress Hall in West Berlin, German statesmen again worried about the event's impact on relations with the Soviet Union. In particular, federal authorities viewed the Berlin meeting, a crowded event for which British troops provided the security detail, as an "unnecessary provocation" of the USSR.[3]

---

[1] Munich Meetings Commemorating the 40th Anniversary of the Bolshevik Revolution, Chief, SR, to Chief, Munich Base, February 3, 1958, 1–4, in National Archives and Records Administration (NARA), RG 263, Entry ZZ-19, 250/86/26/01, QKACTIVE (hereinafter QKACTIVE), box 55, vol. 1.

[2] Walter Hallstein to federal ministries, Betr: Empfang antikommunistischer Exilorganisationen aus der Sowjetunion anlässlich des 40. Jahrestages der bolschewistischen Oktoberrevolution am 7. November 1917 im Bergischen Hof, Bonn, November 6, 1957, in Auswärtiges Amt-Politisches Archiv (AA-PA), B 12, Akte 451.

[3] Director to chief, Munich base, re: DTDORIC QKACTIVE, November 14, 1957, in QKACTIVE, box 55, vol. 1. On the meeting, which featured speeches by Hungarian, Polish, and Bulgarian exiles, see Bericht über die Veranstaltung der ZOPE in der Berliner Kongresshalle am 7. November 1957, no author indicated, in Bundesarchiv-Koblenz (BA), B 137, Akte 1021.

Cold War Exiles and the CIA: Plotting to Free Russia. Benjamin Tromly, Oxford University Press (2019). © Benjamin Tromly.
DOI: 10.1093/oso/9780198840404.001.0001

That the West German government would oppose the activities of CIA-backed anti-communist organizations was counterintuitive. First as an occupied land and then as the United States' foremost ally in Europe, West Germany was the essential base for anti-communist covert operations in Europe, including those involving Russian émigrés. Moreover, the Federal Republic had anti-communism in its genetic material, so to speak, as its very existence reflected the decision to ally with the capitalist West instead of seeking reunification through accommodation with fellow Germans to the East. For these reasons, the Russians pursuing the liberation of the homeland might appear to be the natural allies of West Germans struggling against the USSR's German satellite state. The long existence of a Russian community in Germany and the role of World War II collaborators in the CIA's Russian enterprises made such a coalition all the more plausible.[4]

This chapter explores the changing position of the Russian exiles in West Germany, the essential base for CIA Soviet operations in the 1950s (though hardly the only country in which exiles operated). In contrast to existing accounts that present the relationship between the CIA and the West German government as basically harmonious in the 1950s, it demonstrates that the position of Russian exiles in Germany was uncertain from the outset and deteriorated over the course of the decade.[5] Recognizing their vulnerability in Germany, the Russian émigrés and their CIA backers engaged in a campaign to sell their cause to the elites and public of West Germany, an effort that the CIA saw as a means of protecting its assets in the Federal Republic and also of strengthening the anti-communist resolve of its crucial European ally. The exile public-relations campaign aimed at West German public opinion had some effect, as German anti-communists of various kinds established ties with the two main CIA-supported organizations in the Federal Republic, TsOPE and the National Labor Alliance (NTS).

The German "front" of the Federal Republic, however, proved to be more complicated political terrain than the exiles and their US backers hoped, particularly after the FRG gained sovereignty and established diplomatic relations with the USSR in 1955. In part, old animosities between Germans and Russians made the cross-cultural alliance of anti-communists fragile. Even more important were the security and diplomatic considerations that Hallstein cited in his criticism of émigré counter-commemorations of the October Revolution. At the

---

[4] Karl Schlögel, *Russische Emigration in Deutschland 1918 bis 1941: Leben im Europäischen Bürgerkrieg* (Berlin: Akademie Verlag, 1995), and Robert C. Williams, *Culture in Exile: Russian Emigres in Germany, 1881–1941* (Ithaca, NY: Cornell University Press, 1972).

[5] Compare with Bernd Stöver, *Die Befreiung vom Kommunismus: amerikanische Liberation Policy im Kalten Krieg 1947–1991* (Cologne: Böhlau, 2002), 333–40. Stefan Creuzberger offers a more nuanced account, stressing disagreements between the CIA and the Federal Ministry of Intra-German Affairs (*Bundesministerium für gesamtdeutsche Fragen*), caused in part by American secretiveness. However, he sees a basic confluence of interest between the two sides in the pursuit of psychological warfare. See his *Kampf für die Einheit: Das Gesamtdeutsche Ministerium und die Politische Kultur des Kalten Krieges 1949–1969* (Düsseldorf: Droste, 2008), 197–223.

center of Cold War tensions and war scares in the period and exposed to constant pressure from Soviet diplomats, West German policymakers came to see the Russian exile cause as an "unnecessary provocation." In a wider sense, the cooling of West German bureaucrats toward CIA–émigré operations demonstrated the assertive nature of the security policies of the newly sovereign German state, which should be seen as a factor in the complex US–FRG alliance politics of the period.

A Transnational Charm Offensive: Russian Anti-Communists and West German Elites

CIA operatives were not naïve about their position in West Germany. To be sure, so long as the country was under allied occupation, the Agency and its various assets enjoyed a virtually free field of action in the Western zone. Yet the Americans' gradual transfer of sovereignty to Germans after the creation of the FRG in 1949 made it obvious that eventually the CIA would need the goodwill of the West German state.[6] For their part, Russian exiles were well aware that their German hosts might choose to constrain their anti-communist activities. Political emigrations are always at the mercy of local circumstances and interests, and Russian émigrés of the first wave still remembered interwar experiences of being censored, restricted, or even deported from countries of exile based on shifting political winds.[7]

The Russian exiles and their US patrons set out to secure their long-term position in the FRG through an extensive program of publicity directed at the host society. TsOPE was engaged in a range of activities that demonstrated the CIA's determination to sell the anti-communist cause to the policy elite and the wider public of the Federal Republic. The organization published a bimonthly German-language publication called *Die Freie Rundschau* ("The Free Review") geared to German elites, and it held regular seminars on Soviet affairs that brought together Russian exiles and Germans.[8] TsOPE also courted West German government circles, the real arbiters of the CIA's future in Germany. By 1955, as the exiles' CIA case officers reported, several TsOPE leaders had "made pilgrimages

---

[6] On concerns about German sovereignty with regard to Radio Liberation, see State Department Views of RL Broadcasting, February 11, 1953, in History and Public Policy Program Digital Archive at the Woodrow Wilson Center, Radio Free Europe, and Radio Liberty: Cold War International History Project e-Dossier no. 32 (hereinafter Radio Free Europe and Radio Liberty).

[7] Cf. Marc Raeff, *Russia Abroad: a Cultural History of the Russian Emigration, 1919–1939* (New York: Oxford University Press, 1990), 38.

[8] Renewal Project AEVIRGIL, no author indicated, n.d. (1959), 4, in National Archives and Records Administration (NARA), RG 263, Entry ZZ-19, 230/86/25/04, box 25, AEVIRGIL (hereinafter AEVIRGIL), vol. 1.

to Bonn and have developed useful contacts in the Kaiser Ministry [the Federal Ministry of Intra-German Affairs or *Bundesministerium für gesamtdeutsche Fragen*, BMG] and elsewhere."[9]

The National Labor Alliance pursued a more aggressive and controversial agenda in the Federal Republic. Much like its efforts to engage US power after the war (see Chapter 4), the NTS used subterfuge to pursue influence in German elites and public opinion. Central to NTS activities were its conferences at the *Posev* publishing house, annual meetings to which politicians, intellectuals, and public figures from Germany and other Western countries were invited. NTS leaders used these events to deliver party-line reports on the organization's supposed revolutionary exploits.[10] Yet the meetings' sponsorship by the Solidarist publishing house gave them an appearance of scholarly neutrality. Evidently, the gambit worked: a German diplomat helped the NTS contact invitees to a 1956 *Posev* conference on the logic that attendance would not amount to support for the activities of the NTS.[11]

The utilization of ostensibly non-partisan fronts was also the crux of the Solidarists' most ambitious foray into German society: the Freedom League for German-Russian Friendship (*Freiheitsbund für Deutsch-Russische Freundschaft*). Styled as a response to Soviet friendship fronts of the period, the Freedom League set out to win the "moral, psychological and political" support of German society for the Russian struggle against communism.[12] The Freedom League recruited prominent Germans, giving the endeavor an air of cultural diplomacy. The Initiative Group that established the organization included prominent Germans such as Hilde Körber, a star of the silver screen since the time of Hitler, and Berlin's popular socialist mayor, Ernst Reuter, who opened the organization's inaugural rally in the Berlin Opera Hall in 1951.[13] Nevertheless, the endeavor was under the firm control of the Solidarists, whose representatives or fellow travelers were the only Russians involved in the organization.[14] According to a CIA official

[9] Status Report on Project AEVIRGIL, no author indicated, n.d. (1955), 5 in AEVIRGIL, vol. 1.

[10] See E. Romanov, Delo revoliutsii v Rossii i zadachi novogo etapa, doklad na rasshirennom redaktsionnom soveshchanii "Poseva," September 13, 1954, Columbia University Rare Book and Manuscript Library, Bakhmeteff Archive of Russian and East European History and Culture, Boris Sapir Papers, Series VI: Papers of Boris L'vovich Gurevich, box 63.

[11] Berndt von Staden, Auswärtiges Amt to Baron Hahn, Bundeszentrale für Heimatdienst, May 17, 1956, in AA-PA, B 12, Akte 455.

[12] Arbeitsbericht des Freiheitsbunds für Deutsch-Russische Freundschaft, November 1, 1951, 1, in Stuart A. Rose Manuscript, Archives, and Rare Book Library, Emory University, Isaac Don Levine Papers (henceforth Levine Papers), box 9.

[13] See Aufruf, Freiheitsbund für Deutsch-Russische Freundschaft, n.d., in Hoover Institution Library and Archives (hereinafter HILA), Nicolaevsky Collection, series 205, box 266, fol. 20, and Die russische und russlandische Emigration, O. E. H. Becker, n d., 11, in BA, B 137, Akte 1019.

[14] Its first chairman was A. R. Trushnovich, the head of NTS Berlin operations at the time, whose 1954 abduction from Berlin was discussed in Chapter 7. Dr. Alexander Rudolf Truschnowitsch, Kurzer Lebenslauf, 5, in BA, B137, Akte 1019.

in Germany, the NTS hoped that the friendship initiative would constitute "an additional organization for their operational needs" and provide "sorely needed funds to carry on their activities."[15]

The NTS's German outreach faced serious hurdles. Any effort to bring together Russians and Germans after World War II was a fraught exercise. Distrust of all things Russian was widespread in West Germany, rooted in recent memories of the Eastern Front, the brutality of Soviet troops on German soil, and the flight of many Germans from Eastern Europe (and later the GDR).[16] To counteract these associations, the League stressed that the Russian nation stood in opposition to Soviet rule.[17] A German representative of the Friendship League called on his co-nationals to distinguish between "the Russian people," which had a "culture of a Western type," and "Soviet power," which was hostile to all progress.[18] Of course, the positing of a firm distinction between Russian and Soviet was the essential premise of the émigrés' Cold War activities. It was also an attempt to impart on Russia the status of a *Kulturnation*, thereby counteracting longstanding German stereotypes of "the Russian character" as primitive, childlike, and fanatical, notions that continued to dominate public discourse in the early Federal Republic.[19]

A more subtle aspect of the Freedom League's propaganda was its appeal to German nationalism, and particularly to narratives of victimhood. Like Russians, the German nation from 1933 to 1945 was "the victim and tool of a totalitarian system," the Freedom League asserted.[20] In this narrative, both Germans under the Nazi regime and Soviet-ruled Russians had been "cut off" from the outside world and made "helpless" by terror. And similarly to postwar Russian anti-communists, anti-Hitler "insurgents" (*povstantsy* in Russian) had carried on their struggle "without the support of the free world, which did not try to distinguish Germans from Nazis to a sufficient degree."[21] In short, the Germans and Russians had been doubly maligned, both by totalitarianism—which was presented as a foreign parasite on the nation—and by Westerners who blamed

---

[15] Memorandum, Su: DTLINEN, author and recipient redacted, April 13, 1951, 3, in NARA, RG 263, Entry ZZ-19, 230/86/25/05, box 32, DTLINEN (hereinafter DTLINEN), vol. 1.
[16] Vejas G. Liulevicius, *The German Myth of the East: 1800 to the Present* (Oxford and New York: Oxford University Press, 2009), 171–219.
[17] Aufruf.
[18] Betr: Versammlung in der Funkhallen in Westberlin, April 6, 1954, no author indicated, in BStU, MfS AOP 10286/62, Bd. I, 0265.
[19] Peter Jahn, "Facing the Ostfront: The Other War in German Memory," in Karl Schlögel (ed.), *Russian-German Special Relations in the Twentieth Century: A Closed Chapter?* (Oxford: Berg Publishers, 2006), 124–5.
[20] Freiheit durch Freundschaft, Gründungskundgebung des Freiheitsbundes für Deutsch-Russische Freundschaft, 1951, 2 in NARA, RG 466.4 (HICOG), box 6, Berlin Element-Classified Subject Files, 1949–1953, Po-Pr (hereinafter Berlin Element).
[21] Ibid.

them collectively for it. Here was a propaganda line designed to appeal to a German public embittered by defeat, occupation, and denazification.[22]

The CIA's patronage of exile public relations in Germany, it is true, provided a rare postwar space for confronting the two countries' recent history of bloodshed and animosity. But the small-scale German–Russian émigré national reconciliation that emerged had a distinctly illiberal form, as its participants on both sides—who shared anti-communist beliefs and wartime pasts associated with the German war effort in World War II—unified around anti-Western values and narratives of national suffering. Here is a stark reminder that transnational encounters are not necessarily "progressive and co-operative in character."[23]

The Freedom League for German–Russian Friendship soon underwent an internal crisis over money and control, the likes of which so often plagued exile initiatives. Ironically, the attempt at a right-wing German–Russian rapprochement had been underwritten by the United States. The central figure in the Freedom League was Rainer Hildebrandt, an anti-communist intellectual who was also the leader of the Combat Group against Inhumanity (*Kampfgruppe gegen Unmenschlichkeit* or KgU), a CIA-backed group whose attempts to subvert communist rule in the GDR made it as controversial an organization as the NTS.[24] Perhaps unbeknown to the Solidarists—and certainly without the knowledge of most of the Germans who lent their names to its cause—Hildebrandt had drawn on CIA-KgU channels to launch the friendship endeavor.

The confused money flows underpinning the friendship undertaking—with two CIA assets, the NTS and KgU, creating a political front apparently on their own initiative—soon became embroiled in scandal. An October 1951 meeting of KgU leaders and the Freedom League's Board of Directors turned on Hildebrandt, presenting him with an extensive list of accusations: drawing on KgU funds for "unauthorized purposes," attempting to turn the Friendship Society into "an intelligence gathering organization," and interacting with two known East German spies. More remarkable still, Hildebrandt was accused of having fabricated his biography as a "resistance fighter and concentration camp victim" for the sake of his "world-wide advertised activities."[25] The KgU and Freedom League promptly dropped him from their ranks, a consequence of which was the latter organization's loss of funding through CIA-KgU channels. In addition, the Hildebrandt affair yielded embarrassing public disclosures, such as *Der*

---

[22] On victim narratives in postwar West Germany, see Robert G. Moeller, *War Stories: The Search for a Usable Past in the Federal Republic of Germany* (Berkeley: University of California Press, 2001).

[23] Patricia Clavin, "Defining Transnationalism," *Contemporary European History* 14, no. 4 (2005): 424.

[24] The best documented account is Enrico Heitzer, *Die Kampfgruppe gegen Unmenschlichkeit (KgU): Widerstand und Spionage im Kalten Krieg 1948-1959* (Cologne: Böhlau Verlag, 2014).

[25] Security Information, Su: Boudreau's forced leave from DTLINEN, CIA case officer to Chief of Mission, Germany, November 9, 1951, 1-2, in DTLINEN, vol. 1, and Heitzer, *Die Kampfgruppe gegen Unmenschlichkeit*, 63–6.

Spiegel's false report that the Russian exiles had forced him out of the Friendship Society after discovering his contact with the Counter Intelligence Corps.[26] The scandal surrounding Hildebrandt was a manifestation of a problem that had long troubled the Americans' interactions with Russian exiles. American political-warfare efforts involved intermediaries or "cut-outs," such as the Gehlen Organization and even Amcomlib that frequently proved to be independent-minded, poorly controlled, and unable to mask their ties to intelligence agencies.

The Hildebrandt affair was a blow to the NTS's "German line," but not a fatal one. The Freedom League for German-Russian Friendship quickly reconstituted itself, focusing its efforts on organizing anti-communist lectures at universities and other institutions.[27] More importantly, the BMG stepped in to support NTS diplomacy toward the host country.[28] For instance, the NTS drew on funds from both the Kaiser Ministry and the CIA to publish a German-language journal bearing the strikingly martial title *Deutsch-Russische Stossrichtung* ("The German-Russian Thrust"), which was distributed to the West German political elite.[29] The new arrangement suited both the Germans and the exiles. For the BMG, support for émigré publishing offered it a rare path to influence vis-à-vis CIA-supported groups in Germany.[30] From the exile perspective, BMG support offered a platform for appealing directly to a German audience and fed hopes of more extensive German backing of NTS activities.

Establishing what the wider German public made of the German-language propaganda of the NTS and TsOPE is difficult. As the Freedom League's initial recruitment drive showed, some German academics, writers, and even entertainers admired the Russians driven from their homeland, seeing them as "men who had experienced and understood communism" and therefore had earned the moral authority to edify Germans on the subject.[31] In all likelihood, some German readers were swayed by the NTS journal's assertion that the German question was inseparable from the Russian one—that is, that Germany could be reunited only after the Kremlin, the "Strategic High Bastion" of international communism, was toppled.[32] Harry Pohl, a West Berliner who became an NTS operative in the late

---

[26] "So etwas wie Feme," no author indicated, *Der Spiegel*, November 19, 1952: 14.

[27] Die russische und russländische Emigration, 11. See also Hans-Erich Volkmann, "Die politischen Hauptströmungen in der russischen Emigration nach dem Zweiten Weltkrieg," *Osteuropa* no. 4 (1965): 246–7.

[28] V. D. Poremskii to K. V. Boldyrev, September 27, 1951, in Archiv der Forschungsstelle Osteuropa an der Universität Bremen (hereinafter FSO), 01–098 Tarasova, kor. 41.

[29] Vermerk, June 17, 1951, in BA, B 137, Akte 1020.

[30] On the BMG's efforts to influence CIA psy-war operations in the early 1950s, see a letter from unidentified CIA case official "Waterfield" in Germany to "Mike" in the United States, May 10, 1951, 1–3, in DTLINEN, vol. 1, and Creuzberger, *Kampf für die Einheit*, 213–14.

[31] Von Dellingshausen to Fedor Arnol'd, November 8, 1956, BA, B 137, Akte 1021.

[32] *Deutsch-Russische Stossrichtung*, no. 2 (1952): 3, in BA, B 137, Akte 1020.

1950s, recalled that he was drawn to the Russian organization on the logic that struggling against the GDR itself, a mere satellite state, was "pointless."[33]

The Russian public relations campaign seems to have had its greatest success among German youth. In 1955 the leaders of TsOPE forwarded to BMG officials some letters they received from young German readers of its German-language publication *Der Antikommunist*. Harmut Ratalsky of the Göttingen District Branch of the CDU Youth Union wrote to G. P. Klimov praising his "gripping" book *The Berlin Kremlin*. Ratalsky asked Klimov for materials in order to prepare for an upcoming debate with a young communist; he was especially eager to find an answer to the communist claim that West Germans were responsible for the division of the country.[34] Klimov's stature as an anti-communist authority among some German youth perhaps resulted from the 1953 feature film *Weg ohne Umkehr* (released in English as *No Way Back*), which drew on Klimov's semi-autobiographical novel about a Soviet engineer who defects to the West after discovering the inhumanity of communism.[35] Such letters showed that the exiles had tapped into the anti-communist convictions among young Germans, as suggested by the wish of one reader that the Russian exiles would promptly send the leaders of the Soviet "giant empire" (*Riesenreich*) "to hell."[36]

Yet the émigré propaganda faced skeptical responses in German public opinion, where the attempt to champion a Russianness distinct from Soviet power often fell on deaf ears. In 1952, a State Department official in Munich expressed skepticism about the Friendship League, opining that "the Germans have been taught for so long to hate the Russian people that any change of line will now confuse them and be pointless."[37] The Friendship League's German head, historian O. E. H. Becker, made the same point in a more diplomatic manner. Due to the "totally false policy of the National Socialists" toward Russia during the war, he explained, Germans' view of Russia was still marked by what he called a certain "psychological stress."[38]

---

[33] See an interview with Pohl in Liudmila Klimovich, "Po tu storonu sovetskoi vlasti: k istorii Narodno-trodovogo soiuza," *Neprikosnovennyi zapas*, no. 5/67 (May 2009), http://magazines.russ.ru/nz/2009/5/kl12.html, accessed July 5, 2018.

[34] Hartmut J. H. Ratalsky to Grigorii Klimov, April 3, 1956, in BA, B 137, Akte 1021. See also a similar request for anti-communist arguments on German division that reached TsOPE from a Student Working Group for all-German Relations in an unspecified institution. Horst Hellwig to Fedor Arnold, February 7, 1956, BA, B 137, Akte 1021.

[35] *Weg ohne Umkehr*, dir. Victor Vicas, Hamburg: Occident Film Produktion, 1953.

[36] Julie Krull to Grigorii Klimov, March 2, 1955, in BA, B 137, Akte 1021.

[37] Memorandum for the Files, Su: Miscellaneous Notes—Trip to Frankfurt and Bonn, September 12–14, 1952, Joseph T. Kendrick, Jr, Peripheral Reporting Unit, US High Commissioner for Germany [USHCG], 5, in Georgetown University Archives and Special Collections, Robert F. Kelley Papers (hereinafter Kelley Papers), box 5, fol. 1. The accumulation of mutual German-Russian enmities is conveyed in Michael David-Fox, Peter Holquist, and Alexander Martin (eds.), *Fascination and Enmity: Russia and Germany as Entangled Histories, 1914–1945* (Pittsburgh: University of Pittsburgh, 2012).

[38] O. E. H. Becker, Waffen der Psychologie, February 4, 1952, in BStU, MfS AOP 10286/62, Bd. I, 0262.

The content of the exiles' German propaganda suggested the difficulty of confronting divisive German and Russian national narratives and memories. Instead of launching a joint German–Russian "Thrust" against the USSR as the publication's title suggested, the Solidarists and their German allies often found themselves fighting what they perceived as anti-Russian slights in German officialdom and society. In 1951, the Freedom League complained to US authorities about propaganda posters that had been distributed in East Berlin during the World Festival of Youth and Students earlier that year (which probably originated with the Kaiser Ministry). The posters featured an imposing Soviet soldier with the slogan "*Von / Iwan Raus!*" or "Ivan Out!" in Russian and German—evidently a response to the German communist propaganda slogan "Ami go home"—on the grounds that it nurtured hatred of Russians.[39] Later that year, *Deutsch-Russische Stossrichtung* criticized a recently released documentary film about the Soviets in Germany, *Kreuzweg der Freiheit* ("Crossroads of Freedom"). German writer Günther Birkenfeld complained that the film saddled Russians with collective guilt for the crimes committed against Germans in the final stages of World War II and beyond and depicted Russians as "Untermenschen-Asians."[40] Such heated protests were telling. In both cases, the NTS and their German partners protested against the conflation of Soviet power and the Russian people in the German imagination. The defensiveness of their reactions suggested how persistent and deep-rooted the association was.

The exiles' brand of anti-communism would seem to have had the most potential appeal among the rightist fringe of German politics. Indeed, German supporters of the Freedom League included far-rightist law professor and former Luftwaffe officer Friedrich August Freiherr von der Heydte and historian Bolko Karl Ernst Gotthard Freiherr von Richthofen, whom an Amcomlib contact described as "an ardent Nazi."[41] To some extent, émigré contacts with far-right figures were unsurprising given the Solidarists' own involvement with the interwar far right and wartime collaboration. Yet the NTS's German line was not unassailable even among the German right. For instance, the NTS was able to cultivate only rudimentary ties with the organizations of German expellees (*Landsmannschaften*), powerful interest groups that lobbied for the liberation of their lost East European homelands from communism.[42] Presumably, the political

[39] Manifest, Freedom Union for Russian Friendship, July 20, 1951, in Berlin Element.

[40] *Deutsch-Russische Stossrichtung*, no. 1 (1951): 3, in BA, B 137, Akte 1020.

[41] Von Richthofen was a National Socialist from 1933 and an employee of the Institute for the Study of the Jewish Question and Ancestral Heritage. Kurt Hirsch, *Rechts von der Union. Personen, Organisationen, Parteien seit 1945: Ein Lexikon* (Munich: Knesebeck & Schuler, 1989), 429 (on von Richthofen) and 385–6 (on von der Heydte). The characterization of von Richthofen from 1952 is from Dr. Peter Scheibert, Professor of Russian History at Cologne University. Memorandum for the Files, Su: Miscellaneous Notes, 6.

[42] A report of the Freedom League for German-Russian Friendship from early 1954 states that it had only "contact" with the Homeland Association of East Prussia (*Landsmannschaft Ostpreußen*). Notably, the League's limited ties with the *Landsmannschaften* contrasted with the organization's joint

activists of the expelled population had little inclination to ally themselves with Russians of any political coloration—a reminder of just how awkward the marriage of Russian and German national narratives remained. As A. R. Trushnovich, the central figure for the NTS's German initiatives, conceded, "Of all friendships," the one between Germans and Russians was "the most difficult."[43]

Tepid Supporters: Russian Anti-Communism and the German State

The most important audience for Russian exile propaganda was the German political elite, not the general public. As already mentioned, the CIA wanted to create an environment conducive to the ongoing operation of its multifaceted political warfare operations in the FRG. For the NTS, ambitions vis-à-vis German power went further. As reported by Ryszard Wraga, an intelligence agent with close contacts with the NTS, the Solidarists remained skeptical of the Americans, who seemed to be unable "to deal with the Bolsheviks in political terms" or to create "a general anti-Bolshevik front." In this perspective, the Solidarists saw ties to West German state structures as a means to offset their dependence on the United States in the present, while also laying the groundwork for the organiza-tion's future activities should American power one day recede from the contin-ent.[44] The Solidarists hoped for a postwar revival of German anti-communist *Drang nach Osten*, only now pursued in alliance with the Russian people.

The NTS leaders were soon disabused of their German ambitions. Most officials of the emergent West German state thought it too risky to dabble in Russian exile politics and instead left the task to the Americans. In 1952, NTS leader K. V. Boldyrev approached the US-managed West Berlin radio station RIAS (*Rundfunk im amerikanischen Sektor*) with a plan to use its airwaves to target Soviet soldiers in East Germany with anti-Soviet propaganda. RIAS's German employees rejected the suggestion due to "fundamental considerations." When Boldyrev brought the matter to Bonn, Foreign Ministry official Oskar Kossman

---

activities with moderate conservative organizations such as the Frankfurt Economic-Political Society (*Wirtschaftspolitische Gesellschaft von 1947 e.V.*) and the federalist Europa-Union. Tätigkeitsbericht von Januar 1952-Dezember 1953, S. Padiukow, 1–3, in BA, B 137, Akte 1020. On the influence of the Homeland Associations in West Germany, see Perrti Ahonen, *After the Expulsion: West Germany and Eastern Europe, 1945–1990* (New York: Oxford University Press, 2003).

[43] Gespräch zwischen Jochen Wimmer und Vertretern des Freiheitsbundes für Deutsch-Russische Freundschaft, 3 in BA, B 137, Akte 1020.
[44] NTS, report (evidently for French intelligence), n d. in HILA, Ryszard Wraga Papers (hereinafter Wraga Papers), box 4, fol. 6. The NTS was persistent in pursuing closer West German ties, as seen in a 1955 approach to the BMG that the latter saw as a bid for financial support. Notiz, Ref: Dr. Peckert, May 16, 1955, in AA-PA, B12, Akte 455.

clarified that the Federal Republic would not stand in the way of NTS plans, explaining simply in an accompanying note that the organization was operating "on behalf of the Americans."[45] At the same time, Kossman explained to Boldyrev the source of the German RIAS employees' opposition: Germany had "just recently lost a war," and it would be hard to win over Germans for actions that "led in a direction that is uncertain and out of our control."[46] Clearly, war memories heightened the Germans' appreciation of the dangerous situation in Europe, spurring opposition to exile operations. As a BMG official explained in a review of the émigré press, Germans and other Europeans hoped for peace out of a fear of nuclear war—and what he referred to as the prospect of England being "blown off the face of the earth"—and were appalled by the exiles' conviction that a "great decisive confrontation" with the USSR was inevitable.[47] For Kossman and other FRG officials, the need to go along with the intelligence operations of the country's vital American ally conflicted with their resistance to risky schemes of political subversion against the Soviet behemoth.

The exile cause seemed to have better prospects with the Ministry for Intra-German Affairs, the body that helped to fund the émigrés' publicity efforts in West German society. The BMG's remit of seeking German reunification through fighting communism as well as its embrace of American-style psychological warfare seemed to hold out the prospect of an alliance between German and Russian anti-communists.[48] The West Germans drew on the expertise of Russia experts who had experience working with exiles during World War II, most notably Otto Bräutigam and Gerhard von Mende, former officials in Rosenberg's Reich Ministry for the Occupied Eastern Territories.[49] The BMG also had a fitting point person for dealing with the exiles in Ewert Freiherr von Dellingshausen, whose commitment to fighting communism had its origins in the expulsion of his Baltic German aristocratic family by the Bolsheviks.[50]

BMG patronage, however, fell short of exile expectations. With a few exceptions, the Kaiser Ministry limited its support of the exiles to activities geared toward a West German audience, such as the German-language NTS and TsOPE

---

[45] Aufzeichnung, Betr. Prof Boldyreff, Ref. Dr. Kossman, October 6, 1952, in AA-PA, B 10, Akte 1.910.

[46] Ibid.

[47] Presse-Spiegel 1.7 bis 15.7 1954, 1 in BA, B 137, Akte 1019.

[48] Creuzberger, Kampf für die Einheit, 205–8.

[49] Bräutigam had championed the formation of Cossack military units, while von Mende had been the head of the Caucasus division at the ministry. Henry C. Newton, Col. Inf. To Colonel C. F. Fritzsche, Asst. Deputy Director of Intelligence, Hqs, European Command, April 23, 1947, 3–4, in NARA, RG 263, Entry ZZ-18, 230/86/23/06, box 88, Gerhard von Mende, vol. 1.

[50] Stefan Creuzberger, "Ewert von Dellingshausen (1909–1996): Ein baltendeutscher Antikommunist im Dienste der 'Psychologischen Kriegsführung,'" in Helmut Müller-Enbergs and Armin Wagner (eds.), Spione und Nachrichtenhändler: Geheimdienst-Karrieren in Deutschland 1939–1989 (Berlin: Ch. Links Verlag, 2016), 224.

publications mentioned above.[51] In all likelihood, the Kaiser Ministry's decision to limit its involvement with the exiles to home-front propaganda reflected the BMG's national mission. If Russian émigrés' activities in furthering "education about Bolshevism" in West Germany fit the ministry's mandate, their activities directed against the USSR did not.[52] Just as important, BMG officials held a sober view of the Russian exiles. A report to the BMG from writer O. E. H. Backer of the Freedom League for German-Russian Friendship—someone who might be expected to stress the exiles' importance—dwelled on the tendency of émigré endeavors to "degenerate into fragmentation."[53] Such a verdict was only strengthened by the political fiasco of Amcomlib's united front, which BMG observed closely from the sidelines.[54] Based on these observations, the All-German Ministry decided to keep a distance from the exiles, convinced that associating closely with any émigré grouping would mean carrying responsibility for its actions and draw the Germans into internal exile squabbles.[55]

Even if the officials of the Kaiser Ministry had wanted to offer more robust support of the Russian exiles, the wider political situation in the nascent FRG would have given them pause. The period saw Konrad Adenauer moving the rump German state toward the Western alliance amid the volatile conditions of ongoing occupation, war scares, and domestic division over the path to reunification of the country. In the early postwar years, the opposition German socialists (*Sozialdemokratische Partei Deutschlands* or SPD) prioritized reunification over the Cold War, adopting a platform that William Hitchcock summarizes as "Germany united, all foreign occupiers out, and a return to the German people of their full sovereign rights."[56] The embattled status of Adenauer's *Westpolitik* made anti-communist projects such as support of anti-communist exiles a risky proposition. The political danger posed by the exiles became apparent at a meeting of the Bundestag Committee for All-German Questions in 1951, where a debate emerged about the NTS's CIA-funded mobile radio operation, Radio Free Russia, in West Germany. SPD representative Nils Schmid called it "intolerable

---

[51] A notable exception to the BMG's focus on domestic propaganda was its agreement to fund the publishing of mini-copies of TsOPE's *Die Freie Rundschau* for distribution in the GDR. Von Dellingshausen to Klimov, April 5, 1955, in BA, B 137, Akte 1021, and Stöver, *Die Befreiung vom Kommunismus*, 333.

[52] Von Dellingshausen to Gumbel, Republic Chancellor's Office, May 28, 1954, 2, in BA, B 137, Akte 1019. Discrediting communism in West Germany was a crucial domestic component of von Dellingshausen's conception of psychological warfare. Creuzberger, *Kampf für die Einheit*, 156–60.

[53] Die russische und russländische Emigration, O. E. H. Backer, n.d. (1952–1953), in BA, B137, Akte 1018.

[54] For evidence that the BMG followed the twists and turns of the united-front campaign closely, see Kirk zur russischen Frage, Presse- und Informationsamt der Bundesregierung, May 28, 1952, in BA, B137, Akte 1018.

[55] Vermerk, betr: russische Organisationen, May 9, 1953, in BA, B137, Akte 1021.

[56] William Hitchcock, *The Struggle for Europe: The Turbulent History of a Divided Continent, 1945–2002* (New York: Anchor, 2004), 148.

that uncontrolled broadcasts should occur on German soil."[57] The freewheeling anti-communist activities of the NTS appeared here not only as dangerous adventurism given West-East tensions but also as a reminder of the limits of German sovereignty. In this context, news of covert US financial support for the Solidarists had the potential to cause serious embarrassment for Adenauer, not least by buttressing the SPD charge that the West German government was a puppet of the occupying powers.

The mistrust of the West German state toward the CIA-funded exile organizations intensified with the suppression of the workers' revolt in the GDR by Soviet troops in 1953. As recounted in Chapter 8, the CIA actually expanded its operations in divided Berlin, or at least those related to émigrés, after the failed uprising. But attitudes in Bonn were quite different. Although Adenauer sought to utilize anti-communist sentiments generated by the East German uprising for political ends, the FRG government shied away from more provocative US covert actions in the wake of the revolt, including a campaign to deliver food to East Germans.[58] More broadly, much of the West German press had responded negatively to Eisenhower's overheated liberation rhetoric in the 1952 US presidential elections and sometimes held it responsible for sparking the East Berlin revolt—sentiments that might well have been shared by Adenauer himself.[59]

The cool attitude toward CIA political warfare in the Federal Republic presented a threat to the Russian groups that were its active agents. Anticipating political fallout from the failed 1953 revolt, the NTS went into damage-control mode. The Solidarists' *Deutsch-Russische Stossrichtung* sought to keep alive its assurances about impending revolution in the USSR by claiming that the Soviet soldiers tasked with putting down the workers' revolt had sympathized with the protestors, sometimes shooting in the air instead of at German workers. "Ivan is with us," the East German demonstrators had supposedly concluded.[60] To drive the point home, the NTS was involved in popularizing—and quite possibly

[57] Notably, the BMG's von Dellingshausen offered the committee a highly distorted view of the Russian organization as standing "close to communist ideology" and having been active "above all" in the United States during the war. One suspects that such a misleading description of the NTS was an effort to make the émigré organization acceptable to the skeptical SPD delegates. Andreas Biefang, ed. and comp., *Der Gesamtdeutsche Ausschuss: Sitzungsprotokolle des Ausschusses für Gesamtdeutsche Fragen des Deutschen Bundestages 1949–1953*, Quellen zur Geschichte des Parlamentarismus und der Politischen Parteien, Vierte Reihe, Deutschland Seit 1945: Bd. 12 (Düsseldorf: Droste, 1998), 170. See also Stöver, *Die Befreiung vom Kommunismus*, 329. On SPD skepticism of the BMG, see Creuzberger, *Kampf für die Einheit*, 200.

[58] On Adenauer's attempt to regain the initiative on the German question in the wake of the June revolt and its limits, see Valur Ingimundarson, "The Eisenhower Administration, the Adenauer Government, and the Political Uses of the East German Uprising in 1953," *Diplomatic History* 20, no. 3 (1996): 407–8.

[59] For an elaboration of this argument, see Steven Brady, *Eisenhower and Adenauer: Alliance Maintenance under Pressure, 1953–1960* (Lanham, MD: Lexington Books, 2010), 60.

[60] "Die Lehren eines Aufstandes: Statt 'Iwan raus' – 'Iwan mit uns,'" *Deutsch-Russische Stossrichtung*, number not indicated (1953): 1, in BA, B137, Akte 1020.

concocting—a story about forty-one Soviet soldiers who had been shot for refusing to follow orders during the German revolt.[61]

While asserting that Russian soldiers in Germany were on the brink of insubordination, the NTS also sought to convey an understanding of West German concerns over the revolt in the East. In October 1953, the Solidarists sent to BMG a recent exchange of letters published in *Posev* between its editor, E. R. Ostrovskii-Romanov, and an active duty Soviet officer in the East, named simply "S. I." (The mysterious Soviet officer, one suspects, might have been a literary invention.) In *Posev*, Romanov had inveighed against the Western powers for failing to support the rebels in East Berlin, asking provocatively with whom they would side in the case of a future revolt in the Soviet bloc, "the oppressors or the oppressed"? However, "S. I." responded with a defense of US inaction, claiming that sending American tanks into East Berlin would have started an all-out war.[62] The NTS's reason for sending the exchange of letters to the editor to the BMG— and quite possibly the decision to publish it in the first place—was to convey the exiles' willingness to fall in line with the more cautious foreign policy of the West German government.

If the NTS was seeking to show restraint, the strategy worked, at least with regard to the BMG officials who were most closely associated with the Russian groups. After discussing the *Posev* exchange of letters with NTS leader V. D. Poremskii, von Dellingshausen stated that the contact had been useful for the purpose of "coordinat[ing] all tactical measures of psychological warfare" in the future, particularly in light of "fundamental errors" US radio stations had made in broadcasting to the Eastern bloc.[63] The NTS, an organization hardly known for political moderation, had gone some way in dissociating itself from the perceived reckless behavior of the United States before and during the Berlin crisis.

The NTS's approach to the Kaiser Ministry might have been an effective bit of émigré diplomacy, but it did not alter the limited prospects for exile anti-communism within the West German state. In fact, during the exchange von Dellingshausen explicitly reaffirmed the Kaiser Ministry's policy of avoiding "too obvious ties with any groups of the emigration."[64] The relationship returned to the status quo, according to which the BMG allowed the CIA-backed Russian exiles to function in Germany but offered only limited funding for their German-language periodicals. With hopes for a greater German role dashed, Russian exiles became

[61] On the controversy over the case, see Hans Halter, "Volksaufstand vom 17. Juni 1953: Die Legende von den toten Russen," *Der Spiegel*, June 16, 2003, http://www.spiegel.de/politik/de utschland/volksaufstand-vom-17-juni-1953-die-legende-von-den-toten-russen-a-253126.html, accessed July 19, 2018.
[62] Eine unangenehme Frage, NTS report submitted to von Dellingshausen, October 1953, 2, in BA, B137, Akte 1018.
[63] Vermerk, von Dellingshausen to Jacob Kaiser, October 15, 1953, 1–2, in BA, B137, Akte 1018.
[64] Ibid., 1.

reconciled to the fact that the FRG could only ever hold "second place" to the United States in their plans and activities.[65] This situation was not ideal from the émigré point of view, but at least it allowed scope for ongoing anti-communist activities in Germany.

Open Skies? The Federal Republic Asserts Control

Wider developments in the Cold War would soon undermine German toleration of the exiles' activities. Three mid-decade developments in the Cold War intervened to destabilize the exiles' position in West Germany: the Federal Republic's attainment of nearly full sovereignty in the Bonn–Paris Agreements of 1955, the advent of Soviet–West German diplomatic relations following Adenauer's visit to Moscow later the same year, and the mass instability that erupted in Poland and Hungary in late 1956. Taken together, these shifts made German officials increasingly reluctant to remain benevolent onlookers of CIA-backed exile political warfare operations.

The Federal Republic's establishment of diplomatic relations with the USSR proved particularly damaging to the exile groups active in Germany. The mutual recognition agreement between the two countries did not call into question the basic anti-communist stance of West Germany, for Adenauer began talks with the Soviets only after successfully integrating the FRG into the Western bloc.[66] Nevertheless, the Russian exiles were virtually unanimous in rejecting Adenauer's move. In the view of virtually all active Russian anti-communists, the death of Stalin and the Kremlin's measured steps toward liberalization changed nothing about the Soviet regime, which was still bent on world domination and continued to oppress the Soviet population in the USSR.[67] Given these realities, they argued, signing treaties with the USSR was naïve and even self-destructive—the equivalent of forming "a united front with polygamists against polygamy," as the influential Menshevik Rafael Abramovich put it.[68] And as some exiles probably sensed, the possibility of rapprochement between the superpowers cast into limbo the CIA's political-warfare operations upon which émigré anti-communism relied.[69]

[65] Presse-Spiegel der russischen Exilpresse, 1.7 bis 15.7 1954, 1 in BA, B137, Akte 1019.

[66] Vladislav M. Zubok, *A Failed Empire: The Soviet Union in the Cold War from Stalin to Gorbachev* (Chapel Hill: University of North Carolina Press, 2007), 108.

[67] Aleksei Antoshin, *Rossiiskie emigranty v usloviiakh "kholodnoi voiny" (seredina 1940-kh–seredina-1960-kh gg.)* (Ekaterinburg: Izd. Ural'skogo universiteta, 2008), 259–62.

[68] Review of the Russian Émigré Press, vol. 3, no. 37, September 19, 1955, 5, in Levine Papers, box 15. Abramovich's words are drawn from André Liebich, *From the Other Shore: Russian Social Democracy after 1921* (Cambridge, MA: Harvard University Press, 1997), 300.

[69] For a sign that CIA operatives were unsure of the future of psy-war programs against the USSR, see Status Report on Project AEVIRGIL, no author indicated, n.d. (1955), 1 in AEVIRGIL, vol. 1.

Worse still from the exiles' point of view, mutual recognition between the two countries created a new instrument with which the Soviets could harass their émigré opponents. In recent years, the Soviet government had launched diplomatic protests against many governments on whose territory the NTS and TsOPE were active, from the United Kingdom to Greece.[70] Diplomatic relations with West Germany now offered the Soviets a chance to place pressure on the exiles in their man European base. Moreover, the Soviet government was able to wield a specific policy instrument with regard to the exiles in Germany: the repatriation of Soviet citizens that was the topic of Chapter 10. Already at the 1955 Adenauer–Bulganin meetings in Moscow, the Soviets sought to create "reciprocity" between the repatriation of German POWs from the USSR (which Adenauer was seeking to achieve) and that of Soviet citizens in West Germany. The Germans rejected this linkage point-blank, denying Moscow's claim that the exiles from the USSR wished to be repatriated and defending their right to asylum.[71] Yet the Soviets continued to press the FRG on the repatriation issue in the following years, sending the Adenauer government lists containing thousands of Soviet citizens allegedly "abducted" during the war and kept in West Germany by force—many of whom, the German diplomats pointed out incredulously, had long since emigrated overseas.[72] Far from being an exercise in futility, the "constant efforts of the Soviets to activate the 'repatriation complex,'" as one German diplomat called it, formed a mechanism for applying pressure on the FRG regarding the long-resented German protection of Soviet exile groups.[73]

The Soviet government also utilized its new diplomatic relationship to protest the exiles' anti-communist activities, clearly with the goal of raising the political costs Germans paid for providing refuge and giving a free hand to the CIA exile assets. The central focus in the Soviets' pressure campaign against the exiles were their previously discussed operations to carry propaganda to both the GDR and the Soviet Union by hot-air balloon.[74] In the first half of the 1950s, the West German state tolerated the balloon operations, with the BMG even intervening to help the CIA when unforeseen problems arose. When Russian speakers asked befuddled employees of the German weather service for information on prevailing wind patterns at a height of 5,000 meters—making the improbable statement that the data was needed to conduct "experiments"—Jacob Kaiser instructed them to

---

[70] See Boldyrev, "Reaction of the Soviet Government" and Soviet Section, F.O.R.D., May 29, 1954, in NAUK, FO 371/111795/C560762.

[71] Entwurf, ref. von Welen to Staatssekretaär Hans von Lex, n. d. (1956), 1 in AA-PA, B 12, Akte 450.

[72] Telegram from Moscow to Foreign Ministry, August 29, 1956, in AA-PA, B 12, Akte 450, and Text der Erklärung Oberländers in deutscher Korrespondenz, October 1, 1955, 2, in AA-PA, B 12, Akte 455.

[73] Entwurf, ref. von Welen.

[74] See Chapter 8.

grant the request.[75] A more serious exposure of the propaganda balloons came a year later when Maria Probst, Bundestag delegate from the Christian Social Union, wrote to the BMG asking for information on mysterious pieces of paper bearing Russian type that had fallen in the wooded hills of her district of Bavaria.[76] After communicating with his contact in the NTS, von Dellingshausen wrote to Probst that the leaflets, which described the Trushnovich case and "the Meaning of the NTS," had fallen in West German territory mistakenly. Significantly, von Dellingshausen informed Probst that his ministry kept "no direct contacts with the NTS"—a disingenuous statement that revealed the ministry's desire to avoid responsibility for the émigrés' activities.[77]

The CIA–exile balloon operations came under increased scrutiny with the establishment of Soviet–West German diplomatic relations. Particularly controversial were the long-distance balloons, which littered the USSR with hostile propaganda; the KGB seized over 56,000 NTS leaflets across regions from Ukraine to Siberia in the first six months of 1956 alone.[78] Against the backdrop of uncertainty within the post-Soviet bloc, the collective leadership in the Kremlin ramped up pressure against the CIA-backed groups carrying out the propaganda operations.[79] In particular, the Soviet leaders protested to Adenauer during his landmark trip to Moscow, and not without result. In September 1955, CIA headquarters ordered a temporary suspension of the propaganda ballooning to the USSR, citing a "Bulganin/Adenauer discussion of leaflets allegedly launched from the German Federal Republic into the USSR."[80] Evidently, Adenauer's desire to improve relations with the USSR had convinced the United States to curtail the CIA operation.

The Soviet victory on ballooning was short-lived, as the operations resumed shortly after Adenauer's trip. Again, the Soviets tried to turn the West German government against the intelligence operations of their great-power patron, this

---

[75] Bundesminister für Verkehr to Bundesminister für gesamtdeutsche Fragen, December 17, 1953, 1, in BA, B137, Akte 1018.

[76] Dr. Maria Probst to von Dellingshausen, July 28, 1954, and von Dellingshausen to Probst, n.d., in BA, B137, Akte 1019.

[77] Vermerk, Bundesminister Jakob Kaiser, August 20, 1954, in BA, B137, Akte 1019.

[78] Russian State Archive of Contemporary History (Rossiiskii gosudarstvennyi arkhiv noveishei istorii, RGANI) f. 5, op. 30, d. 141, ll. 54–6.

[79] Rob Hornsby, *Protest, Reform and Repression in Khrushchev's Soviet Union* (New York: Cambridge University Press, 2013), 84, 164. On Soviet fears over domestic order in 1956, see Mark Kramer, "The Soviet Union and the 1956 Crises in Hungary and Poland: Reassessments and New Findings," *Journal of Contemporary History* 33, no. 2 (1998): 195–8.

[80] Excerpted copy from the USSR and Eastern European Soviet Dominated areas for the USSR Territory, February 7, 1956, 2, in NARA, RG 263, Entry ZZ-19, 230/86/25/02, box 11, AERODYNAMIC: OPERATIONS, vol. 13 (CIA Project tied to ZP/UHVR, Ukrainian Supreme Liberation Council) and AEVIRGIL status report, Chief of Base, Munich to Chief, SR, November 7, 1955, 5 in AEVIRGIL, vol. 1. David Murphy, the head of CIA Berlin operations at the time, recalled that "Western restraint" placed limits on the ballooning operations of the period. David E. Murphy, Sergei A. Kondrashev, and George Bailey, *Battleground Berlin: CIA vs. KGB in the Cold War* (New Haven, CT: Yale University Press, 1997), 113.

time by claiming that the balloons posed a threat to civilian aviation.[81] The FRG Foreign Ministry and Ministry of Transport drafted a request to the US embassy to stop the balloons—a move the CIA managed to head off by contacting Hans Glöbke, Director of the Federal Chancellery and the Agency's main contact in Adenauer's government.[82] However, the *coup de grâce* for the long-range balloons came soon thereafter, as the United States canceled balloons to the USSR during the Hungarian Revolution. Although the US decision reflected a determination to avoid dangerous moves during a time of high geopolitical tension, relations with West Germany might well have contributed to the willingness to jettison the project.[83]

The strains over ballooning were only one sign of the new scrutiny to which the Federal Republic subjected the exiles. In 1956, the NTS undertook quixotic actions aimed at intensifying the instability in Poland and Hungary. After the Poznań riots in July 1956, the exiled Polish leader Stanisław Mikołajczyk complained to State Department officials about "a Polish language leaflet which the Russian émigré NTS organization had sent into Poland and which appeared to speak for the Free Poles although it had no right to do so."[84] More remarkable still, during the Hungarian Revolution the NTS's radio broadcast a Hungarian-language message ostensibly from an "extraordinary council" of the Association of Hungarian Former Servicemen in the West, which offered armed help to the insurgents.[85] Documents that would shed light on these apparent false-flag operations have not been declassified, although one might posit that such reckless attempts to exploit unrest in the bloc fit into the CIA-NTS strategy of provocation discussed in Chapter 7.[86] Unquestionable, however, was the German perception that the NTS actions were dangerous.

Making matters worse for the Germans was the fact that the NTS's provocative activities often involved the West German government directly. In the wake of the Hungarian Revolution, NTS activities gave rise to several high-profile scandals in which the West German government was forced to intervene: an NTS member was stopped by Austrian police in Innsbruck en route to the Hungarian border

---

[81] A. P. Stolypin, *Na sluzhbe Rossii: ocherki po istorii NTS* (Frankfurt: Posev, 1986), ch. 13.

[82] Frankfurt to Director, November 6, 1956, in NARA, RG 263, Entry ZZ-18, 230/86/22/06, box 25, Hans Glöbke. See also Chief of Station, Germany to Chief, SR and Chief, EE, June 5, 1958, in AEVIRGIL, vol. 1.

[83] Arch Puddington, *Broadcasting Freedom: the Cold War Triumph of Radio Free Europe and Radio Liberty* (Lexington: University Press of Kentucky, 2000), 111.

[84] Memorandum of a Conversation, Department of State, Washington, July 20, 1956, in *Foreign Relations of the United States*, 1955–1957, vol. XXV: Eastern Europe, document 84.

[85] Other Hungarian-Language Radios, October 30, 1956, in Radio Free Europe and Radio Liberty.

[86] Adding to the confusion about the NTS's activities during the Polish and Hungarian events is a declassified KGB document that makes the unbelievable claim that the NTS's main leaders were carrying out "active subversive activity" from within Hungarian territory. See Orientirovka Osobogo otdela Iuzhnoi gruppy voisk, November 27, 1956, reproduced in part in Vladimir Tol'ts, "Vengriia-56 po materialam KGB i MVD SSSR," Raznitsa vo vremeni, Radio Svoboda, http://www.svoboda.org/content/transcript/24404513.html, accessed October 10, 2018.

carrying print propaganda in Hungarian; another was assaulted by Soviet sailors while throwing leaflets onto their ship in the Hamburg port; and émigré activists besieged a tour of the Leningrad Symphony Orchestra to West Germany.[87] Such encounters with the CIA-funded exiles, and the NTS most of all, compelled German officials to engage in embarrassing diplomatic exchanges with the USSR and other countries.

The exiles' attempts to exploit instability in the East—and the unwelcome entanglements produced by them—sparked a backlash in the halls of power in Bonn. In December 1956, veteran German diplomat Wolfgang von Welck submitted a memorandum on the need to "find a solution" to the "social and political problems" of the Soviet emigration, citing their "unwanted actions" during the Hungarian crisis. He stopped short of advising that exile political groups be banned on German soil entirely, a move that he saw as not "opportune" for relations with the United States and hardly enforceable in any case. Instead, von Welck recommended imposing "strict control" over militant émigré organizations, starting with the NTS, and promoted the idea that they should redirect their "political center of gravity" to the United States in the future.[88] In short, the anticommunist exiles had become "compromising" for the German government and should be shunted off to the United States—the country that funded them, after all—at the first opportunity.[89] Clearly, such a position had become possible only after the advent of West German sovereignty and diplomatic relations with the USSR.

Von Welck's hard line was never fully implemented. Yet after the Hungarian Revolution, West German authorities became increasingly assertive in limiting the scope of the various covert operations involving the exiles. In September 1957, a Soviet captain complained that his ship was pelted with NTS leaflets while passing through the North Sea to Baltic Sea Canal. In response, the Ministry of the Interior proclaimed that it would "work toward" stopping the "propaganda activity of NTS in shipping areas of Kiel-Holtenau in the future," even while recognizing that it could find no legal basis for intervening.[90] Fear of embarrassing confrontations

---

[87] On these episodes, see BfV to Ministerial Advisor Dr. Toyka, Internal Ministry, January 1957, in AA-PA, B 12, Akte 450 (Austrian arrest); Mangold, German Consulate in Innsbruck to Foreign Ministry, Betr: Haftsache, June 6, 1957, in BA, B 137, Akte 1018 (Hamburg port incident); Betr: Antikommunistische Propaganda gegenüber den Mitgliedern des Leningrader Sinfonie-Orchesters, Embassy of the Federal Republic in Moscow to Foreign Ministry, Bonn, September 6, 1957, in AA-PA, B 12, Akte 451 (symphony incident).

[88] Aufzeichnung, Betr: Die Problematik der aus dem Machtbereich der Sowjetunion stammenden Emigration, von Welck, December 1956, 1–4 in AA-PA, B 12, Akte 450. After speaking to von Welck, Bernd von Staden of the Russian Department suggested that the propaganda and radio broadcasting of the NTS should be halted entirely, a move that was not taken. Betr: Die Problematik der aus dem Machtbereich der Sowjetunion stammenden Emigration, B. von Standen to Karl Herman Knoke and Günther Scholl, January 1957, in AA-PA, B 12, Akte 450.

[89] Entwurf, ref. von Welck to Staatssekretaär Hans von Lex, n.d. (1956), 1, in AA-PA, B 12, Akte 450.

[90] Ministry of the Interior to Foreign Ministry, October 17, 1957, in AA-PA, B 12, Akte 451.

with the Soviets eclipsed whatever stock of goodwill the anti-communist Russians had built up among West German officials.

The CIA's longstanding partners in West Germany were also shifting their priorities. The BMG was less willing than before to act as troubleshooter for CIA operations, a shift probably related to its adoption of a "more careful and less spectacular" approach to political warfare toward the end of the decade.[91] Meanwhile, the CIA and the exile organizations now had to deal with emergent West German intelligence services, namely the BfV or Federal Office for the Protection of the Constitution (*Bundesamt für Verfassungsschutz*) and the Federal Intelligence Service (*Bundesnachrichtendienst* or BND), an outgrowth of the Gehlen Organization.[92] If Reinhard Gehlen's organization had asserted its prerogatives vis-à-vis the CIA while still dependent on the United States, the BND took a much more assertive stance once it had become a national intelligence service.[93] For instance, the BND attempted to recruit a TsOPE leader as an informant in the late 1950s, a move that must have exasperated the CIA officers in Germany.[94] Clearly, the advent of West German sovereignty brought a severe challenge to the CIA operations, adding a degree of resolve to state structures at the same moment when diplomatic considerations seemed to dictate a position of restraint.

Rising tensions between the FRG and the CIA Russian operations came to a head in the late 1950s, with the propaganda balloons—this time, the so-called "short range" balloons directed at Soviet troops stationed in East Germany—again emerging as the point of dispute. In defense of these operations, an official of the CIA SR Division stressed (in a revealing statement) that after the end of ballooning to the USSR in mid-decade the airborne shipment of leaflets to Soviet forces in the GDR constituted its only propaganda operation targeting Soviet citizens directly.[95] Accordingly, the CIA pursued a protracted struggle to protect its GDR-bound balloons from increasingly skeptical West German politicians and officials. Such a position ran up against tensions in the Cold War, as Khrushchev's 1958 ultimatum over Western access to Berlin heightened West German security concerns. In the same year, the CIA Berlin Chief of Base reported that in the German government there was "a considerable body of opinion opposed to the activities of the émigré groups," and he predicted an imminent end to the project.[96]

---

[91] Creuzberger, *Kampf für die Einheit*, 220.

[92] Renewal of Project AEVIRGIL, FY-1962, 7 in AEVIRGIL, vol. 1.

[93] For clashes over Gehlen's aggressive pursuit of contacts with other spy services, see Christoph Franceschini, Thomas Wegener Friis, and Erich Schmidt-Eenboom, *Spionage unter Freunden: Partnerdienstbeziehungen und Westaufklärung der Organisation Gehlen und des BND* (Berlin: Chr. Links Verlag, 2017), 28–32.

[94] Renewal of Project AEVIRGIL.

[95] Chief of Station, Germany to Chief, SR, and Chief, EE, June 5, 1958, in AEVIRGIL, vol. 1.

[96] Chief of Base, Berlin to Chief of Station, Germany, Su: Specific—AEVIRGIL Ballooning, etc., June 2, 1958, 3, in AEVIRGIL, vol. 1.

Pushback over the balloon operations called into question the CIA's role in the wider US–West German relationship. The Berlin Chief of Base continued to press for the continuation of the ballooning operations, urging his superiors to intercede with senior figures of the Adenauer government, as they had before.[97] However, CIA headquarters acknowledged that the Germans had good reason to be displeased with the exile activities on their territory. The issue was not just that the NTS and TsOPE were carrying out provocative acts. By "denying U. S. responsibility" for the émigré organizations, the head of the CIA Eastern Europe (EE) Division pointed out, the Americans were making the "obvious inference the Germans are responsible."[98] By forcing their German ally to take the blame for its operations, the CIA official acknowledged, the Agency was harming bilateral relations with the United States' most important ally on the European continent.

Diplomatic considerations eventually won out over the plans of covert operators. CIA ballooning into the Eastern bloc ceased entirely in March 1960, which caused a wider retreat of CIA–exile activity from West Berlin; the erection of the Berlin Wall a year later brought the final closure of the exile offices in the city.[99]

In 1968, an East German State Security document claimed that Soviet and GDR "active measures" had undermined the CIA–émigré operations in Germany, especially by encouraging the population of West Germany and West Berlin to "take a stand" against them.[100] The Soviet diplomatic and covert efforts to curtail the exile operations in Germany—which went so far as restricting the sale of hydrogen gas in Berlin to starve the balloons of fuel—surely had some effect in restraining the CIA operations. While the Soviets might have applied pressure, sources suggest that the West German government pursued its own security concerns in restraining noxious CIA operations on its territory.[101]

West German arguments against CIA operations in the Federal Republic also helped to shape decision-making in Washington. Even some CIA officers had come around to the argument that exile activities were an unjustified "irritant to the Soviets at a time when the political situation in Berlin is becoming more tense," as an SR Division employee described the soon-to-be-closed TsOPE office in West Berlin.[102] To some extent, West Germany had imposed its security

---

[97] Ibid. In 1956, TsOPE had saved its ballooning operations from suspension by federal authorities by winning the favor of foreign ministry official Berndt von Staden. Vermerk, Betr: Ballonaktionen der russischen Emigrantenorganisation ZOPE, LF von Staden, May 24, 1956, in AA-PA, B12, Akte 455.

[98] Director to Frankfurt Hqs., Berlin, Bonn, and Munich, October 24, 1957, in AEVIRGIL, vol. 1.

[99] Renewal of Project AEVIRGIL, FY-1962, no author indicated, n.d. (1961), 1–2, in AEVIRGIL, vol. 1.

[100] Auskunftsbericht über den sogenannten "Nationalen Bund der Schaffenden Russischen Solidaristen," Hauptabteilung II, 1968, in Bundesbeauftragte für die Unterlagen des Staatssicherheitsdienstes der ehemaligen Deutschen Demokratischen Republik, Zentralarchiv, MfS-AFO 1187, 000094.

[101] TsOPE (Union of Political Emigrants from the USSR), no author indicated (SR Division), n.d. (1959), 2, in AEVIRGIL, vol. 1.

[102] Chief, SR/3 to Chief, SR, Su: Budget for Project AEVIRGIL for FY-1962, June 7, 1961, in AEVIRGIL, vol. 2.

priorities on its superpower ally, a development that provides a curious parallel to the GDR's pressuring of the USSR over the Berlin question in the same years.[103]

* * *

The exiles' German dreams were severely deflated by the loss of the Berlin loophole and the general tightening of West German state control vis-à-vis CIA affairs. At the same time, the expansion of CIA "legal" espionage (meaning spying done under official cover), a result of the end of the USSR's Stalin-era isolation and the "lessening urgency of ground requirements" in line with nuclear deterrence, further lowered the relevance of exile operations.[104]

The consequences of the new situation were not long in coming. In 1963, the CIA stopped subsidizing and dissolved TsOPE. The decision stemmed from infighting in the TsOPE leadership, which was perhaps promoted by Soviet active measures (in this case, the release of documents showing that TsOPE leader Mikhail Dziuba had been a secret-police agent in the interwar USSR). But the essential context of TsOPE's demise was the CIA's inability to find a suitable replacement for the organization's Berlin operations.[105] The NTS survived, but the loss of its Berlin operations reduced the size and CIA funding of the organization.[106] In the 1960s, the NTS spent much energy soliciting voluntary contributions, including "donations in kind," from wealthy Westerners to supplement reduced levels of support from the CIA and perhaps other intelligence services.[107] Meanwhile, the NTS operations in other European countries suffered from problems analogous to those in Germany: the difficulty of reaching arrangements with state authorities and Soviet pressure.[108] The deterioration of the CIA–émigré

[103] On the GDR's influence on the USSR during the Berlin crisis of the late 1950s, see Hope Harrison, "Driving the Soviets up the Wall: A Super-Ally, a Superpower, and the Building of the Berlin Wall, 1958-61," *Cold War History* 1, no. 1 (2000): 53–74.

[104] Moreover, the use of overflights and then satellites to gather intelligence on the USSR decreased the value of human intelligence on military targets more generally. Harry Rositzke, "America's Secret Operations: A Perspective," *Foreign Affairs* 53, no. 2 (1975): 336.

[105] Request for the Renewal and Termination of Project AEVIRGIL—Fiscal Years 1963 and 1964, 2–3, Munich Operations Base, SR Division to Deputy Director (Plans), March 26, 1963, in AEVIRGIL, vol. 2. Information on the compromising of Dziuba comes from the KGB defector and archivist Vasilii Mitrokhin; available CIA documents do not provide confirmation of the story. History and Public Policy Program Digital Archive at the Woodrow Wilson Center, The Mitrokhin Archive: The Chekist Anthology, Association of the United Postwar Immigrants, fol. 52, at https://digitalarchive.wil soncenter.org/document/113609, accessed December 12, 2018.

[106] According to the KGB, which was surely in the know, the NTS's membership depleted from the postwar high of 800 to some 120–50 in the late 1960s. A. A. Fabrichnikov and I. A. Ovchinnikov, *Ispol'zovanie vozmozhnostei sovetskogo komiteta po kul'turnym sviaziam s sootechestvennikami za rubezhom v razvedyvatel'noi rabote*, uchebnoe posobie (Moscow: Komitet gosudarstvennoi bezopasnosti pri Sovete Ministrov SSSR, 1968), 6.

[107] The source for this claim was a German translator who worked closely with TsOPE and NTS before being arrested by the East German security forces. Vernehmungsprotokoll des Beschuldigten, September 22, 1961, BStU, MfS GH 9/62, Bd. 1, 000121.

[108] Diplomaticheskaia storona organizatsionnoi raboty, n.d., no author indicated, in FSO, 01–098 Tarasova, kor. 5 b. n. See also an account of the 1960 expulsion of NTS activists from Belgian ports in Evgenii Drevinskii, "My zhertvenno sluzhili Rossii," in V. A. Senderov (ed. and comp.), *Ot zarubezh'ia do Moskvy: Narodno-Trudovoi Soiuz (NTS) v vospominaniiakh i dokumentakh 1924-2014* (Moscow: Posev, 2014), 310.

nexus within West Germany and elsewhere demonstrated that the exiles were at the whim of larger historical forces: public opinion (and particularly German mistrust of Russians), shifting cross-bloc diplomacy, and, most important, the dangers of the second Berlin crisis of the late 1950s.

An unexpected development was the entanglement of CIA–Russian exiles activities with US–West German relations in the 1950s. Scholarship attributes strains in the alliance to the potential for rapprochement between the super-powers, which, along with Adenauer's perception that the Americans were "falling behind in the race for world mastery," led the West Germans to worry about the dangers of dependence on the United States.[109] The growing assertiveness of the Adenauer government vis-à-vis the Russian exiles demonstrates that another source of tension in the US–West German relationship was at work in the period.[110] Particularly after receiving sovereignty, West Germany acted to con-strain actions pursued by its cross-Atlantic patron that seemed to pose a threat to stability in Europe. More surprising still, in pursuing this line the West Germans factored in bilateral ties with the Soviet Union. German interests took precedence over the demands of American covert operators, a reminder of how US "consen-sual hegemony" in Western Europe allowed for the assertiveness of its European allies.[111]

The exiles' interactions with West Germans were important in another context: that of Russian and German historical memories. The CIA provided a space for transnational cooperation between German and Russian anti-communists, albeit of a heavily conservative bent. More pronounced than common interests, however, was a fundamental historical–ideological rift that divided the Russian anti-communists from the West Germans. The Russians' goal of liberating the homeland had its origins in the great ideological conflicts of the Russian Civil War and World War II. In contrast, by the end of the decade the West European powers and also the United States had come to view the bipolarity of the continent as a source of stability, however imperfect and painfully gained. In a pan-European perspective, the exiles appeared out of place, representatives of a recent past that Europeans in the postwar years were all too happy to forget.

---

[109] Gordon A. Craig, "Konrad Adenauer and the United States," in Reiner Pommerin (ed.), The American Impact on Postwar Germany (Providence, RI: Berghahn, 1995), 8. The challenges facing the alliance during the limited détente after Stalin's death is a core theme of Brady, Eisenhower and Adenauer.

[110] Recent works that present other independent ambitions in German security policies in the 1950s and 1960s are Giles Scott-Smith, Western Anti-Communism and the Interdoc Network: Cold War Internationale (New York: Palgrave Macmillan, 2012), and Mathilde von Bülow, West Germany, Cold War Europe and the Algerian War (Cambridge and New York: Cambridge University Press, 2016).

[111] Charles Maier, "Hegemony and Autonomy within the Western Alliance," in Melvyn P. Leffler and David S. Painter (eds.), Origins of the Cold War: An International History (New York: Routledge, 2005), 154–74.

Conclusion

Russian émigré activities took place in crowded meeting halls, in Bavarian hotels, in Frankfurt print shops, in posh New York office buildings, at balloon launch sites in German forests, and in the more intimate setting of safe houses in West Berlin. In the late 1950s, the émigrés' struggle to free Russia found a new setting: tourist centers in Western Europe. With the slow opening up of the USSR after Stalin's death, the CIA increasingly focused its human-intelligence operations on the exploitation of different forms of cross-bloc movement such as tourism, travel by official delegations, and academic exchanges.[1] As part of this shift, the Agency's Russian assets were tasked with carrying out "contact operations" in which they met and cultivated Soviet travelers abroad—interactions meant primarily as a form of psychological warfare but that might also produce contacts for intelligence purposes. CIA hopes that the contact operations would become "the bread and butter of worthwhile émigré activities in the West" explain the significant size of the endeavor: apparently, operatives of the CIA-controlled Central Representation of Postwar Emigrants (TsOPE) "met almost all Soviets visiting Germany" in 1961 and many travelers in France, Belgium, Italy, and Austria as well.[2]

The exiles came face to face with Soviet Russians—and the results were often disheartening. Merely establishing contact with groups of well-vetted and tightly surveilled Soviet travelers was challenging enough.[3] Soviet tourists spent their free time shopping for goods that were unavailable at home, and they usually had little appetite for social contact of any kind. They were especially apprehensive about the mysterious Russian speakers who approached them, especially given the warnings they received from their KGB handlers about the dangers of the machinations of "fascists" and "White Guardists" in the West.[4]

---

[1] A textbook of the KGB academy discusses the involvement of Western spy services in cross-bloc communications. V. M. Chebrikov, *Istoriia Sovetskikh organov gosudarstvennoi bezopasnosti: uchebnik* (Moscow: Vysshaia Krasnoznamennaia Shkola Komiteta Gosudarstvennoi Bezopasnosti pri Sovete Ministrov SSSR imeni F.E. Dzerzhinskogo, 1977), 493.

[2] AEVIRGIL 1 and Radio Rome, Chief of Base, Munich to Chief, SR, January 29, 1958, 1, in NARA, RG 263, Entry ZZ-19, box 25, 230/86/25/04, AEVIRGIL (hereinafter AEVIRGIL), vol. 1 and TsOPE Report, no author indicated, January 4, 1962, in AEVIRGIL, vol. 1.

[3] On Soviet measures to prevent travelers' contact with émigrés, see AEVIRGIL Project Review, no author indicated, March 15–April 30, 1962, 2, in AEVIRGIL, vol. 2. See also Anne E. Gorsuch, *All This Is Your World: Soviet Tourism at Home and Abroad after Stalin* (Oxford and New York: Oxford University Press, 2011), 126–7.

[4] SUMMARY=AEVIRGIL CONTACT INFORMATION, Post Brussels Fair-June 1959, no author indicated, in AEVIRGIL, Vol. 1. For the impact of such ideological preparation of Soviet travelers, see Aprel', n.d. (1956 or 1957), 1, in Archiv der Forschungsstelle Osteuropa an der Universität Bremen (hereinafter FSO), 01–098 Tarasova, kor. 5 b. n. See also the recollections of an NTS operative in Andrei

Cold War Exiles and the CIA: Plotting to Free Russia. Benjamin Tromly, Oxford University Press (2019). © Benjamin Tromly.
DOI: 10.1093/oso/9780198840404.001.0001

Even when the exiles managed to interact with Soviet citizens in a more private setting, the results were usually disappointing. A vast gulf in life experiences, culture, and ideology existed between the émigré political operatives and the Soviet citizens they approached on the streets of Paris, Rome, or Munich. The challenges were conveyed in a report written by longstanding leader of the National Labor Alliance (NTS) K. V. Boldyrev on a three-day trip to contact Soviet tourists in Naples in 1957. The cosmopolitan old émigré was clearly repulsed by the Soviet travelers and offered a biting depiction of their uncultured hunt for material goods, their moral outrage over bikinis worn on the beach, and, above all, signs of their orthodox Marxist–Leninist views, which became obvious from the "sighs, 'ohs,' and declamations" the tourists let out when being shown the house where Soviet writer Maksim Gor'kii had once lived in exile.[5] The only tourist Boldyrev was able to engage in extended political discussion, a young engineer from Leningrad, asserted that the USSR had put the Stalinist past firmly behind it and reacted with incredulity to the NTS postulate that revolution was inevitable.[6] Boldyrev did not hide his discouragement, breaking with the NTS tradition of claiming that Solidarist ideology held a magnetic appeal for Soviet citizens.

"Operation Tourist" underscored a crucial problem for Russian exile politics in the Cold War: the elusive nature of national legitimacy. The essential underpinning of the exiles' anti-Soviet activities in the West was the assumption that Russians in the USSR were hostile to communism. Proving to interested parties in the West that the exiles' ardent anti-communism typified sentiments widely held within the Soviet populace, however, was no easy matter. With the Iron Curtain proving almost impenetrable in the years before Stalin's death, Soviet public opinion remained virtual terra incognita for observers in the Cold War West. In this situation, establishing their own national credentials—their ability to speak for Soviet Russians—became the central preoccupation for émigré politicians.

The pursuit of national legitimacy took place in the inherently challenging political situation of exile. Most immediately, the Russian exiles depended on state bureaucracies in the West, and spy services most of all, whose permission and financing were necessary for conducting anti-Soviet initiatives (though hard-won). Another crucial audience for national claims was the Russian diaspora itself. The Russian anti-communist organizations relied on recruits from their

---

Vasil'ev, "Tret'ia Grazhdanskaia," in V. A. Senderov (ed. and comp.), *Ot zarubezh'ia do Moskvy: Narodno-Trudovoi Soiuz (NTS) v vospominaniiakh i dokumentakh 1924–2014* (Moscow: Posev, 2014), 266–9.

[5] Vstrechi s sovetskimi turistami v Italii 2–4 iiulia 57 g., K. V. Boldyrev, 1 in FSO, 01–098 Tarasova, kor. 46.
[6] Ibid., 14.

own communities, people willing to undertake anti-Soviet activities which were often risky and held little promise of yielding an immediate impact. Moreover, as this book has stressed, the wider diaspora was badly divided in generational, cultural, and political terms. Complicating matters further, the two audiences for exile anti-communism were interconnected. In a conundrum faced by all political exiles, an émigré group that lacked membership in the wide diaspora would have a hard time attracting foreign backers, and vice versa.[7] Indeed, a major difficulty of pursuing émigré politics was the need to develop political legitimacy among disparate populations and interests—and, at least in the Russian case, to do so without a tangible legal or traditional claim to political authority, such as the existence of a government in exile.[8]

Luckily for them, the exiles' anti-communist politics found an agreeable political environment in Western Europe during the early Cold War. In the early 1950s, the US government sought out assets abroad for its rapidly expanding constellation of covert operations against the USSR and global communism more generally. Beyond pragmatic considerations, many influential American anti-communists held the "liberationist" stance that exiles represented the aspirations of the Russian masses in the USSR, a position that reflected a simplistic view of Russian history as a story of oppression and resistance. The Amcomlib (American Committee for Liberation from Bolshevism) project provided the most uncompromising iteration of this view, as it set out to institutionalize an émigré political center as the basis for a future anti-communist Russian-Soviet polity. The united-front approach created a wide opening for exiles to pass their ideologies and historical memories to their American patrons, perhaps the best example of which was the prevalence in the US security establishment of the view that the collaborationist Vlasov movement was a useful precedent for countering Soviet power in the Cold War. Certainly, the CIA's Russian actions of the period relied on vibrant transnational flows of anti-communist ideas.[9]

Despite their important place in US political warfare plans against the USSR, the Russians were compelled to craft their political tactics in response to the challenges of exile. The Russian political activists, as this book has shown, confronted the challenge of building up political capital in the Cold War West with energy and often creativity. Through crafting propaganda and establishing political connections, the exiles sought to convince foreign constituencies that the Russian people was anti-communist and that the émigré organizations could voice

---

[7] The fullest comparative treatment of the distinct shape of exile politics is Yossi Shain, *The Frontier of Loyalty: Political Exiles in the Age of the Nation-state* (Middletown, CT: Wesleyan University Press, 1989), 50–70.

[8] Yossi Shain (ed.), *Governments-in-exile in Contemporary World Politics* (New York: Routledge, 1991).

[9] See Luc Van Dongen, Stéphanie Roulin, and Giles Scott-Smith (eds.), *Transnational Anti-Communism and the Cold War: Agents, Activities, and Networks* (Basingstoke: Palgrave Macmillan, 2014).

their sentiments. To bolster their claims, the émigré politicians pointed to Soviet attacks against them as evidence of their own current and potential political influence in Russia, an approach that sometimes involved finding victory in the jaws of defeat. According to a Soviet source, TsOPE leader G. P. Klimov once planted a bomb in the office of his own organization in order to boost its reputation in the West—a story that, while quite possibly false, is nonetheless illustrative of the perverse incentives involved in émigré political life.[10] The exiles also fought viciously amongst themselves for political influence within the diaspora, a practice fueled by clashing ideological programs and old feuds. The very nature of émigré existence made aggressive, disingenuous, and often cynical political practices the norm, dulling the best intentions and selfless actions of many exiles.

In the course of the 1950s, the weakness of the exiles' roles as mouthpieces and potential leaders of the Russian people became clear. For the American adherents of Russian liberation in Amcomlib, hopes that the exiles and their brand of nationalism would become an effective weapon against the USSR foundered on the tenacity of émigré divides along generational, ideological, and cultural lines. As Chapter 5 discussed, the far-reaching united front program turned into a forum for Russians and their counterparts from Soviet minority nations to clash over an imagined map of post-Soviet Eurasia, while the wider Russian diaspora looked on in disgust. As a result, the exiles' national identities, and particularly the imperial complex that characterized them, lost its appeal for the CIA and other US institutions fighting the Cold War. The failure of the united front not only placed limits on the émigrés' participation in US projects, but—adding insult to injury for the Russians—provided wider scope for CIA and Amcomlib to work with their non-Russian counterparts, including their archenemies in the Ukrainian diaspora.[11]

CIA operations pursued through the NTS and TsOPE saw a similar trajectory of disappointing outcomes and US withdrawal, albeit for different reasons than in the political-center debacle. The émigrés' setbacks on the operational front in Germany had much to do with the persistent and resourceful efforts of Soviet counterintelligence and state-security operatives to discredit, penetrate, and otherwise disrupt their activities. As seen in Chapter 7, operations to infiltrate NTS members into the USSR ended in fiasco, while the defector-inducement efforts in Berlin also had negligible results, at least apart from easing the collection of intelligence from East Germans (see Chapter 8). The US defector program held out the promise of

---

[10] K. K. Cherezov, *Maska NTS, ili NTS bez maski* (Berlin: Izd. Sovetskogo komiteta po kul'turnym sviaziam s sootechestvennikami za rubezhom, 1965), 54.

[11] A wider study of exile national problems and US policy remains to be written. For the enduring though shifting CIA backing of Ukrainian exiles, see Taras Kuzio, "U.S. Support for Ukraine's Liberation during the Cold War: A Study of Prolog Research and Publishing Corporation," *Communist and Post-Communist Studies* (2012), at doi:10.1016/j.postcomstud.2012.02.007, accessed June 3, 2014.

improving the Agency's anti-Soviet operations by drawing on a new mini-wave of Russian exiles who were better informed about Soviet conditions and more representative of current Russian-Soviet culture than its predecessors. Yet the creation of a pliant defector organization in TsOPE offered only limited improvement for Agency operations in Germany. Given their marginal results, the CIA Russian operations were already vulnerable when new external challenges emerged in the mid- to late 1950s, namely the Soviet return campaign and West German efforts to head off provocative CIA operations during the second Berlin crisis.

By the early 1960s, émigré anti-communism was a shadow of its former self. The major groupings of first-wave exiles had given way to the political and then numerical decline of its members, including the Mensheviks and other socialists who had grouped in the left-wing League of Struggle for the People's Freedom. The Vlasovite Council for the Liberation of the Peoples of Russia was only intermittently active in North America or Germany.[12] As Chapter 11 discussed, the CIA dissolved TsOPE, previously their prized émigré accomplishment, in 1963, a move that caused the exiles' "deep disappointment."[13] The only émigré outfit able to continue the struggle actively was the NTS, an organization whose far-right complexion, probable penetration by Soviet moles, and conflictual past with Amcomlib made it an unnatural CIA asset. Despite the tenacity with which the NTS would continue its activities, illusions about the exiles' ability to influence Soviet society were greatly diminished in American halls of power.

The story of Russian political life abroad, then, was one of ambitions and disappointments, as the exposure of exiles' lack of national legitimacy eroded their positions within US structures for combatting the USSR. Yet Russian émigré politics was also a transnational affair whose significance ranged far beyond its immediate accomplishments and, indeed, its temporal and geographical confines. Three such wider contexts deserve further discussion: CIA tactics, proxy battles of the Cold War, and contemporary Russian political developments.

Naturally, the adventures and travails of Russian exiles speak to the methods of the CIA that was their patron. Indeed, the flawed outcomes of intelligence operations examined in this book were as much the responsibility of US policy-makers and intelligence officers as they were reflective of problems specific to exiles. It bears repeating that the overall record of CIA human intelligence toward the Soviet bloc in the early Cold War was poor, which in itself suggests that problems far broader than the peculiarities of Russian émigré politics were at

[12] The Emigration in North America, 1960, B. E. Kuniholm, Director, Political Affairs Division, Amcomlib, 7, in Levine Papers, box 11.
[13] On the reaction of TsOPE members, see Obrashchenie, G. A. Khomiakov, March 3, 1963, in Arkhiv Doma russkogo zarubezh'ia im. A. Solzhenitsyna, f. 155 (zhurnal "Mosty." Khomiakov Gennadii Andreevich) and Interim Status Report, March 27, 1963, 2, in NARA, RG 263, Entry ZZ-19, 239/86/25/04, box 25, AEVIRGIL, vol. 3. I thank Pavel Tribunskii for access to the first source.

work.[14] Indeed, examining the CIA's involvement with the Russians reveals serious flaws of design and execution.

The CIA used Russian exiles as covert proxies in a political war against communism. Previous literature has shown that such an approach involved the US government with groups and individuals harboring political ideals that were foreign to American notions of democracy and holding compromising records of wartime collaboration.[15] While this book's treatment of the NTS confirms these problems, it also underscores the political and operational difficulties posed by the US approach to practicing psychological warfare through proxy groups.[16] Predictably, exile anti-communist groups tapped for US support remained committed to their own ideological programs for overthrowing communism and chafed at demands to act in accordance with the wishes and tradecraft practices of a foreign intelligence service. In fact, émigré groups sought to use American monetary support to pursue their own goals. Moreover, the CIA had difficulty controlling the politics of its Russian clients, a phenomenon that was on display in the united-front project. As Chapter 5 points out, the political center empowered the émigré groups as representatives of the Russian nation, thereby allowing the exiles to wield their American sponsors' liberation rhetoric against them. At root, this situation reveals that the CIA pursued a confused line toward the exiles, treating them not only as intelligence assets but also as legitimate political movements, an "uneasy pairing" of functions that proved a recipe for misunderstanding and dissention.[17]

A no less important problem for the CIA's interactions with the exiles was the difficulty of covering its tracks. The rule of maintaining plausible deniability, universally understood as essential for covert action, was observed mostly in the breach. The appearance of foreign money in the ranks of the impecunious Russian political émigrés was hard to conceal, and sloppy security arrangements and Soviet infiltration among the exiles made it an open secret which émigré groups enjoyed CIA funding. The fact that the invisible hand of the CIA was plain to see

---

[14] This wider point is made forcefully in Matthew W. Aid, "The National Security Agency and the Cold War," in Matthew W. Aid and Cees Wiebes (eds.), *Secrets of Signals Intelligence during the Cold War and beyond* (London and Portland, OR: Frank Cass, 2001), 30–1.

[15] Richard Breitman and Norman J. W. Goda, *In Hitler's Shadow: Nazi War Criminals, U.S. Intelligence, and the Cold War* (Washington, DC: National Archives and Records Administration, 2010).

[16] Here the case of Russian exiles corresponds to problems plaguing the CIA's false-front operations, as analyzed in Hugh Wilford, *The Mighty Wurlitzer: How the CIA Played America* (Cambridge, MA: Harvard University Press, 2008).

[17] On the danger of "lumping 'noisy' action missions with secret intelligence operations," see Harry Rositzke, "America's Secret Operations: A Perspective," *Foreign Affairs* 53, no. 2 (1975): 344. Notably, British intelligence officials criticized the CIA for "consider[ing] the groups which they were exploiting not only from an intelligence standpoint but also politically." CIA (OSO & OPC)/State Department Talks with SIS/Foreign Office: VI. Russian Emigre Groups, April 24, 1951, 1–2, in National Archives and Records Administration (NARA), RG 263, Entry ZZ-19, 230/86/25/02, box 13, AERODYNAMIC: OPERATIONS, vol. 20.

had damaging consequences. It produced embarrassing flaps and much fodder for Soviet propaganda, perhaps most glaringly in the exposure of US involvement in the united front (see Chapter 5) and in the Americans' feeble attempts to claim innocence when Carcass agents were seized in the USSR (see Chapter 7). Less directly, exiles' awareness of foreign backing produced strains within their own organizations. As was on display in the splits of both the NTS and the Union for the Struggle for the Liberation of the Peoples of Russia (SBONR), CIA money stirred the petty jealousies of émigré leaders and also incited patriotic backlash among exiles who considered it axiomatic that Russians wage a struggle against communism free of foreign designs.

The CIA, it is true, learned from its mistakes. In the course of the 1950s, the US moved away from its aggressive covert operations toward the Soviet bloc, especially the illegal infiltration of agents into Soviet territory. In their place, the United States adopted a more gradualist—and less inflammatory—strategy of "cultural infiltration" in the USSR and its satellite states.[18] As seen in Chapter 6, this shift produced a volte-face at Radio Liberation, which now eschewed its "émigré voice" approach in favor of American-style news broadcasting to the Soviet Union.[19] While the more combative aspect of CIA covert operations against the USSR did not disappear entirely, the new mode of political warfare had little need for the staunchly anti-communist and nationalist Russian exiles.

Despite its eventual curtailment, the US government's engagement of Russian anti-communist exiles was a serious undertaking that absorbed considerable resources. From the narrow viewpoint of intelligence history, the CIA Russian exile operations show the difficulty of utilizing political movements for covert action, especially when they rely on fractious or closed communities such as the Russian diaspora.[20] In a wider perspective, they underscore the danger of risky covert operations for US foreign policy. Indeed, the eventual exposure of CIA operations similar to those discussed in this book in the 1960s and 1970s caused a major backlash in American society, contributing to the advent of greater congressional oversight over the national security state.[21]

---

[18] The classic study is Walter L. Hixson, *Parting the Curtain: Propaganda, Culture, and the Cold War, 1945–1961* (New York: St. Martin's Press, 1997).

[19] One sign of this shift was the replacement of the term "political or psychological warfare" with the euphemism "information policy." For evaluations of the impact of Radio Liberty, see A. Ross Johnson and R. Eugene Parta, *Cold War Broadcasting: Impact on the Soviet Union and Eastern Europe: A Collection of Studies and Documents* (Budapest and New York: Central European University Press, 2010).

[20] In particular, one should doubt the assumption that "operations involving propaganda or aid to individuals or organizations" are "low-visibility" in nature, as stated in Jeffrey T. Richelson, *The U.S. Intelligence Community* (Boulder, CO: Westview Press, 2016), 468. An enlightening discussion of the justification and limits of secret operations in the period by a CIA veteran is Rositzke, "America's Secret Operations": 343–5.

[21] Loch K. Johnson, "Congressional Supervision of America's Secret Agencies: The Experience and Legacy of the Church Committee," *Public Administration Review* 64, no. 1 (2004): 3–14.

The case of the Russian exiles is also instructive for considering the broader phenomenon of proxy conflicts in the Cold War. In his rebuttal of George F. Kennan's famous "X" article in *Foreign Affairs* that laid out a justification for containing the Soviet Union, journalist Walter Lippmann objected that the new policy was a "strategic monstrosity" that "could be implemented only by recruiting, subsidizing and supporting a heterogeneous array of satellites, clients, dependents and puppets."[22] Lippmann's warning was prescient, as the decades that followed saw the Cold War played out in proxy wars across the globe.[23] The basic Cold War logic of pursuing proxy conflicts—they were an alternative to hot war between the superpowers, which would probably lead to nuclear Armageddon—meant that their brunt was often borne by other peoples or nations. Yet precisely because they were fought with only limited involvement of the superpowers, Cold War proxy wars often developed in ways that Washington and Moscow could not dictate. As Pierre Grosser has put it, in proxy clashes the "alleged puppets were less victims than puppeteers" in their own right, a fact that made the global Cold War multilayered and even "kaleidoscopic."[24]

Russian exile politics constituted a Cold War proxy conflict of a distinct sort: the competition of spy services within a diasporic community. Yet the battles involving Russian exiles followed roughly the same model as a proxy war, with superpowers financing and manipulating, more or less successfully, subordinate actors. From the American point of view, the major appeal of covert operations such as those pursued by the exiles was that they constituted a "relatively low cost weapon" for fighting communism (in terms of American lives and economic sacrifice), a rationale analogous to that surrounding proxy wars.[25] And just as victims of Cold War military engagements were often neither American nor Soviet, the casualties of the spy wars in Berlin, at least as they concerned the exile operations, were typically exiles or citizens of East Germany. The Russian exile milieu suggests that the Cold War was sometimes fought in Europe in ways that resembled its military manifestations elsewhere around the globe.

The politics of the Russian diaspora produced some of the complicated dynamics of militarized proxy wars, as well. As explored at length in these pages, the émigré sphere operated in a byzantine political environment occupied not only by CIA officers and their Soviet counterparts but also by West Germans and other West Europeans. One Soviet defector described the Russian political world as "a

---

[22] This is drawn from Walter L. Hixson, *George F. Kennan: Cold War Iconoclast* (New York: Columbia University Press, 1989), 74.

[23] Odd Arne Westad, *The Global Cold War: Third World Interventions and the Making of our Times* (Cambridge and New York: Cambridge University Press, 2007).

[24] Pierre Grosser, "Looking for the Core of the Cold War, and Finding a Mirage?" *Cold War History* 15, no. 2 (2015): 246–7.

[25] Elizabeth E. Anderson, "The Security Dilemma and Covert Action: The Truman Years," *International Journal of Intelligence and Counter Intelligence* 11, no. 4 (1998): 409.

real labyrinth of political struggle where it was not so easy to find an entry or exit."[26] Russian anti-communist circles encapsulated the wider complexity of power relations in the international Cold War order, and especially the ways that global conflict played out in subsidiary "cold wars," as Volker Berghahn describes them.[27] And as these auxiliary struggles frequently crossed national lines—as they did in the Russian case—they underscore the need to examine transnational flows of ideas and memories in Cold War studies.

The last context for émigré politics, and the one that was all-important for the exiles themselves, is Russian history. In a direct sense, the exiles involved with the CIA in the 1950s seemed to have had little relevance for future developments in their homeland. No doubt, for most exiles discussed in this book involvement with US power in the 1950s was a brief phase sandwiched between longer periods of political irrelevance. In some cases, the anti-communist exiles managed to trans-late their Cold War activities into careers in the United States: N. I. Nikolaevskii worked on his massive archives at the Hoover Institution before his death in 1966, K. V. Boldyrev taught at Georgetown University's School of Foreign Service until retirement, and N. E. Khokhlov extended his mysterious reputation by becoming an expert on parapsychology at California State University, San Bernardino. No doubt with rich memories and probably a degree of regret, the exiles were compelled to put down roots in their places of sojourn.

The NTS continued its mission. There is a lack of serious scholarly work on NTS's activities during the long period of stagnation in the USSR (from the 1960s to 1985), including the publication abroad of the writings of Soviet citizens (*samizdat*) and the smuggling of literature across the Iron Curtain (carried out largely by Western travelers to the Soviet Union).[28] In all likelihood, the NTS had a limited impact on late Soviet public opinion, and indeed the organization aroused the suspicions of several Soviet human rights activists (the so-called dissidents).[29] During the upheaval of Soviet collapse from 1989 to 1991, the NTS, now led by Soviet citizens, began to operate openly in Russia and was even involved in mobilizing strikers and organizing independent political organizations.[30] Yet one

---

[26] I. V. Ovchinnikov, *Na pereput'iakh Rossii* (Moscow: Informatsionno-ekspertnaia gruppa "Pano-rama," 1995), 88.

[27] Volker R. Berghahn, *America and the Intellectual Cold Wars in Europe: Shepard Stone between Philanthropy, Academy, and Diplomacy* (Princeton, NJ: Princeton University Press, 2001).

[28] For one of many propagandistic accounts, see A. P. Stolypin, *Na sluzhbe Rossii: ocherki po istorii NTS* (Frankfurt am Main: Posev, 1986), chs. 14–15. For files pertaining to NTS operations to prepare and debrief Western tourists to the Soviet Union in the 1970s ("Operation Walrus") and contact operations abroad, see Hoover Institution Library and Archives, George Miller-Kurakin papers, box 1.

[29] Robert Horvath, *The Legacy of Soviet Dissent: Dissidents, Democratisation and Radical Nationalism in Russia* (London and New York: RoutledgeCurzon, 2005), 59, 90. More surprisingly, the Russian nationalist movement that emerged in the late Soviet period seems to have had little contact with anti-communist exiles. See Nikolai Mitrokhin, *Russkaia partiia: dvizhenie russkikh natsionalistov v SSSR, 1953–1985* (Moscow: Novoe Literaturnoe Obozrenie, 2003).

[30] See Rostislav Evdokimov Papers, Hoover Institution Library and Archives.

can hardly maintain that anti-communist exiles made a major contribution to the collapse of the Soviet system.

The Solidarists and other anti-communist exiles also found that they had little role in the post-Soviet Russia they had so long envisioned. Plans to elect NTS delegates to the Russian Duma in the 1990s fell flat, and exile politicians remained marginal figures in post-Soviet Russian politics.[31] For the most part, the NTS has survived through the ongoing existence of the *Posev* publishing house, which has specialized in works meant to rehabilitate the organization's reputation by obscuring its collaborationist past and its close association with American power.[32]

Although the exiles had little direct impact on recent Russian history, their politics are nevertheless useful for understanding it. The exiles active in the 1950s sought to both imagine and shape Russia's post-Soviet future, and their experiments in political scheming are illuminating given the actual experiences of transition from communism in the former Soviet Union. In fact, when the non-communist Russia of which the exiles dreamed came to fruition in the 1990s, it quickly became mired in problems that had been familiar to the émigrés decades before.

Nowhere is this clearer than with regard to the crucial national question. Exactly as the Russian exiles in the 1950s feared would happen, the end of Soviet socialism in the 1980s and early 1990s unraveled the Russian empire. With the support of American diplomacy, the fifteen Soviet republics gained independence, forcing Russia to retreat to its current-day borders, which are comparable to those of the seventeenth century. As exile politics of the 1950s foreshadowed, Russia's loss of its empire has proven a highly painful and complex matter. Indeed, the legacy of multiethnic empire should be seen as central to Russian politics and foreign policy in the twenty-first century, as the resurgence of Russian power in the post-Soviet space under Putin makes clear.[33]

Another post-Soviet dilemma presaged by émigré politics is the contested nature of historical memory in Russia, and particularly the difficulty of confronting the violent ruptures that marked its twentieth-century experience. As was the case for Russia abroad in the 1950s, post-Soviet Russia has been divided over national history. Moreover, émigré legacies live on in today's Russia, and for good

---

[31] Vladimir Tol'ts, "NTS: vchera, segodnia i?...," Raznitsa vo vremeni, Radio Svoboda, May 15, 2010, at https://www.svoboda.org/a/2044124.html, accessed December 12, 2018. The activities of former exiles in post-Soviet Russia is a topic yet to be explored. For NTS perspectives, see Senderov (ed. and comp.), *Ot zarubezh'ia do Moskvy*, 335–68.

[32] For a sense of post-1991 NTS historical narratives, see the comments of its members in "NTS: vchera, segodnia i?...."

[33] Serhii Plokhy, *Lost Kingdom: The Quest for Empire and the Making of the Russian Nation, from 1470 to the Present* (New York: Basic Books, 2017), 299–346; Marlene Laruelle, "National Identity and the Contested Nation," in Richard Sakwa, Henry Hale, and Stephen White (eds.), *Developments in Russian Politics*, 9th edn (London: Red Globe Press, 2019), 67–79.

reason: the exiles incubated ideologies and political movements that the Bolsheviks had largely swept from Soviet territory, including social democracy, neofascism, and monarchism. Once the void left by the collapse of Soviet communism allowed Russians to think about their pasts without the constraints of Marxism–Leninism, the various ideological alternatives presented by the exiles took on new life. In recent years, the Putin state itself has turned to the émigré legacy, namely that of the White exiles, to find substance for its increasingly conservative and anti-Western vision of Russia.[34] Vladimir Vladimirovich Putin himself has spoken admiringly of Ivan Aleksandrovich Il'in, a White émigré thinker whose embrace of fascist ideas, and specifically the need to forge a "national elite," had inspired the NTS.[35]

Yet the political forces of the Russian diaspora hardly provide a clear legacy for national identity or historical memory in contemporary Russia. Indeed, the Putin regime has not "reintegrate[d] the White émigré past into the national master narrative" of the state in a full way, as doing so would clash with the Soviet backgrounds and outlook of its leaders.[36] The pro-Soviet bent in Russian historical consciousness is particularly strong with regard to the "Great Patriotic War," and attempts by some contemporary Russian historians to depict Vlasov's collaborationist movement in a more sympathetic light have met with harsh reactions from state bureaucrats and war veterans.[37] Given the ongoing clash of Soviet and White narratives, the only firm conclusion one can reach is that émigré political movements of the past century will continue to provide raw material for the construction of national identity and historical memory in Russia.

The final and, at the time of writing, most urgent reflection of émigré politics of the 1950s concerns US–Russian relations. Echoes of anti-communist exile politics are present in the current historical moment, during a standoff between the two countries which some have likened to a new Cold War. As in the 1950s, the United States has attempted to influence politics in the former Soviet bloc, including Russia itself, albeit now through the broad and non-clandestine nexus of policies

[34] Brian D. Taylor, *The Code of Putinism* (New York: Oxford University Press, 2018), 12–22.
[35] For discussion of Il'in and the NTS, see "NTS—The Russian Solidarist Movement," RNAL Research Paper, US Department of State External Research Staff, Series 3, no. 76, January 10, 1951, 6–9. An NTS obituary for Il'in avoids the question of European fascism, as does a recent scholarly article. Roman Redlikh, "Pamiati I. A. Il'ina," *Posev* no. 3 (454), January 16, 1955, and V. P. Izvergina, "I. A. Il'in i ideologiia Belogo dvizheniia," *Regionologiia* no. 1 (2012), at http://regionsar.ru/ru/node/887, accessed December 21, 2018.
[36] Marlene Laruelle, "In search of Putin's philosopher: Why Ivan Ilyin is not Putin's Ideological Guru," *Intersection: Russia/Europe/World,* March 3, 2017, at http://intersectionproject.eu/article/politics/search-putins-philosopher, accessed December 27, 2018. For a treatment that exaggerates Il'in's contemporary influence on Putinism, see Timothy Snyder, "God is a Russian," *The New York Review of Books,* April 5, 2018.
[37] Mark Edele, "Fighting Russia's History Wars: Vladimir Putin and the Codification of World War II," *History & Memory* 29, no. 2 (2017): 90–124.

known as "democracy promotion." Kremlin leaders have seen these efforts not only as violations of national sovereignty but also, amid the outbreak of "colored revolutions" in the Soviet space, as an existential threat.[38] Moreover, the Russian government has retaliated by turning to non-conventional methods of struggle rooted in Cold War intelligence practices, professionally updated for the digital age.[39] Indeed, Russia's meddling in the 2016 US presidential election has made the American public wary (and sometimes fearful) of Russian influence in a way not seen for decades, spurring the emergence of a cottage industry of journalistic works on the Kremlin's weaving of conspiracies and employment of "active measures."[40] In short, the toxic international landscape that sustained émigré political plotting during the early Cold War—a US foreign policy driven by the promotion of an assertive liberal internationalism and a Russian one characterized by a siege mentality—has re-emerged some seventy years later.

The anti-communist exiles themselves, however, are no longer here to witness the current confrontation. To be sure, conflict over Russia's future has again spilled beyond the country's borders. Russia justified the 2014 annexation of Crimea and intervention in East Ukraine, in part, on the ideological construct of a "Russian world," drawing widespread attention to the political sentiments of Russian minorities in countries across the globe. Moreover, the Russian government has launched a new effort to attract its wayward citizens home, reviving a term with an obvious 1950s pedigree by referring to Russians abroad as potential "returners" (vozvrashchentsy).[41] And some opponents of the current Russian government have sought to organize their struggle from abroad, most notably the formerly imprisoned oligarch Mikhail Khodorkovskii.[42] Nevertheless, a sizable community of political exiles, understood as people stranded outside of their country for political reasons who aspire to revolutionary changes within it, no longer exists. And as astute observers of the US–Russia relationship have pointed out, the ideological bipolarity of the Cold War world order is itself a thing of the past.[43] The Russian exiles were political warriors, living in a world of cataclysms, broken lives, and zero-sum ideological alternatives. We should empathize with them but take hope in the fact that their era has passed.

[38] Taylor, The Code of Putinism, 17, 27, 166–94.

[39] Robert D. Blackwill and Philip H. Gordon, Containing Russia: How to Respond to Moscow's Intervention in U.S. Democracy and Growing Geopolitical Challenge (New York: Council on Foreign Relations, 2018), 6–18.

[40] Cf. Evan Osnos et al., "New Cold War: What lay behind Russia's interference in the 2016 election—and what lies ahead?" The New Yorker, March 6, 2017.

[41] On Russians abroad as "returners," see Boris Volodarsky, Nikolai Khokhlov ("Whistler"): Self-Esteem with a Halo (Vienna and London: Borwall Verlag, 2005), 60. See also Michael Weiss, "The KGB Playbook for Turning Russians Worldwide into Agents," The Daily Beast, 29 December 29, 2017, at https://www.thedailybeast.com/the-kgb-playbook-for-turning-russians-worldwide-into-agents, accessed January 2, 2018.

[42] Masha Gessen, "The Putin Nemesis Plotting a Post-Putin Russia," Vanity Fair, July 11, 2016.

[43] Stephen M. Walt, "I Knew the Cold War. This is No Cold War," Foreign Policy, March 12, 2018, at https://foreignpolicy.com/2018/03/12/i-knew-the-cold-war-this-is-no-cold-war/, accessed April 1, 2018.

Bibliography

Archives and Online Repositories Consulted

Archive of the Research Center for East European Studies at the University of Bremen (*Archiv der Forschungsstelle Osteuropa an der Universität Bremen*, FSO).

- 01–098 Tarasova; 01–106 Rahr; 01–044 Poremsky; 01–034 Kromiadi-Kruzhin.

Central Intelligence Agency (CIA), Freedom of Information Act (FOIA) Electronic Reading Room. https://www.cia.gov/library/readingroom/home. *Last accessed November 1, 2018.*

- CIA Historical Collection; Crafting an Intelligence Community: Papers of the First Four DCIs; CREST: 25-Year Program Archive; CREST: Creating Global Intelligence; CREST: General CIA Records; History Staff, Central Intelligence Agency; Special Collection: Intelligence, Policy, and Politics: The DCI, the White House, and Congress; *Studies in Intelligence.*

Columbia University Rare Book and Manuscript Library, Bakhmeteff Archive of Russian and East European History and Culture.

- Boris Sapir Papers; Mikhail Mikhailovich Karpovich Correspondence; Vasilii Fedoseevich Butenko Papers; Viktor Mikhailovich Baidalakov Manuscript and Printed Materials, 1950–1966; Vladimir Mikhailovich Zenzinov Papers.

Department of Special Collections and University Archives, Stanford University Libraries.

- National Alliance of Russian Solidarists: Correspondence and Photographs, 1930–1982 (M1909).

Federal Archives, Koblenz, Germany (*Bundesarchiv-Koblenz*).

- B 137: Federal Ministry of Intra-German Affairs (*Bundesministerium für gesamtdeutsche Fragen*), West Germany; B 206: Federal Intelligence Service (*Bundesnachrichtendienst* -Digitalisierte Bestände).

Federal Commissioner for the Records of the State Security Service of the former German Democratic Republic, Central Archive (*Bundesbeauftragte für die Unterlagen des Staatssicherheitsdienstes der ehemaligen Deutschen Demokratischen Republik, Zentralarchiv* BStU, ZA).

Foreign Relations of the United States, Office of the Historian. https://history.state.gov/historicaldocuments. *Last accessed November 1, 2018.*

Georgetown University Archives and Special Collections.

- Robert F. Kelley Papers; Victor M. Baydalakoff Collection.

Harvard Project on the Soviet Social System Online, Widener Library, Harvard University. https://library.harvard.edu/collections/hpsss/index.html. *Last accessed November 1, 2018.*

History and Public Policy Program Digital Archive at the Woodrow Wilson Center. https://digitalarchive.wilsoncenter.org. *Last accessed November 14, 2018.*

- Radio Free Europe and Radio Liberty: Cold War International History Project e-Dossier no. 32; The Mitrokhin Archive: The Chekist Anthology.

Hoover Institution Library and Archives (HILA).

- Aleksei Milrud Papers; Arch Puddington Collection; Boris I. Nicolaevsky Collection; Boris V. Prianishnikov Papers; Constantin W. Boldyreff Papers; George Miller-Kurakin papers; Ivan Alekseevich Kurganov Papers, John O. Koehler Papers; Nikolai Evgen'evich Khokhlov Papers; RFE/RL corporate records; Rostislav Evdokimov Papers; Ryszard Wraga Papers; The Soviet Union as Reported by Former Soviet Citizens, External Research Staff, Office of Intelligence Research, Department of State.

International Institute of Social History Archive, Amsterdam.

- Boris L'vovich Dvinov Papers.

National Archives and Records Administration II, College Park, MD.

- Military Agency Records–Records of US Occupation Headquarters, WWII (Record Group 260); Records of the Army Staff (Record Group 319), Entry 134A: Security Classified Intelligence and Investigative Dossiers - Impersonal Files and Entry 134B: Security Classified Intelligence and Investigative Dossiers - Personal Files; Records of the Central Intelligence Agency (Record Group 263): Entry ZZ-18 (CIA Name Files-Second Release); Entry ZZ-19 (CIA Subject Files-Second Release); Records of the Policy Planning Staff (Record Group 59); Records of the US High Commissioner for Germany [HICOG] (Record Group 466).

Political Archive of the Foreign Ministry, Berlin (*Auswärtiges Amt–Politisches Archiv*, AA–PA).

Records of the Federal Bureau of Investigation:

- Nicholas Bevad, Alexander Kerensky, Boris Nicolaevsky.

Rockefeller Archive Center, Ford Foundation records.

- Ford Foundation records, East European Fund.

Russian State Archive of Contemporary History (*Rossiiskii gosudarstvennyi arkhiv noveishei istorii*, RGANI).

- Fond 5, opis' 30: General Department of the Central Committee of the Communist Party of the Soviet Union; Fond 89: Trial of the Communist Party of the Soviet Union.

Sectoral State Archive of the Security Service of Ukraine (*Haluzevyi derzhavnyi arkhiv Sluzhby Bezpeky Ukrainy*).
Seeley G. Mudd Manuscript Library, Princeton University.

- Louis Fischer Papers; George F. Kennan Papers.

Stuart A. Rose Manuscript, Archives, and Rare Book Library, Emory University.

- Isaac Don Levine Papers.

The National Archives of the United Kingdom (NAUK).

- Foreign Office 371: Political Departments, General Correspondence.

Primary Source Journals and Magazines

Bor'ba: Tsentral'nyi organ Soiuza Bor'by za Osvobozhdenie Narodov Rossii (SBONR), Munich.

Der Spiegel, Hamburg.

Deutsch-Russische Stossrichtung: Informationsbriefe und Diskussionsbeiträge des NTS in Deutschland, Frankfurt am Main and Berlin.

Die Freie Rundschau: Zeitschrift für aktive Freiheitspolitik, Munich.

Life Magazine, New York.

Look, Des Moines.

Nabat: Vestnik natsional'no-patrioticheskoi pravoi demokraticheskoi mysli Rossiiskoi Emigratsii, Munich.

Nashe obshchee delo, Munich.

Nash otvet, Munich.

Newsweek, New York.

Novoe russkoe slovo, New York.

Novyi zhurnal, New York.

Posev: obshchestvenno-politicheskii zhurnal, Frankfurt am Main.

Rossiiskii democrat: organ "Soiuza bor'by za svobodu Rossii", Paris.

Russian Review, New York.

The Commercial and Financial Chronicle, San Francisco.

The New Leader, New York.

Za Rossiiu, Frankfurt am Main.

Za vozvrashchenie na rodinu, Berlin.

Published Memoirs, Letters and Archival Documents

Aleksandrov, K. M., ed. *Pod nemtsami: vospominaniia, svidetel'stva, dokumenty*. St. Petersburg: Skriptorium, 2011.

Artizov, Andrei. *Reabilitatsiia—kak eto bylo: Dokumenty Prezidiuma TsK KPSS i drugie materialy*. Moscow: Mezhdunar. fond Demokratiia, 2000.

Artizov, A. N. et al., eds. *Vlasov: istoriia predatel'stva*, tom 1–2. Moscow: ROSSPEN, 2015.

Avtorkhanov, Abdurakhman. *O sebe i vremeni: memuary*. Moscow: Dika-M, 2003.

Baidalakov, Viktor Mikhailovich. *Da vozvelichits'ia Rossiia, da pogibnut nashi imena: vospominaniia predsedatelia NTS: 1930–1960 gg*. Moscow: Avuar Konsalting, 2002.

Biefang, Andreas, ed. and comp. *Der gesamtdeutsche Ausschuss: Sitzungsprotokolle des Ausschusses für gesamtdeutsche Fragen des Deutschen Bundestages 1949–1953*. Quellen zur Geschichte des Parlamentarismus und der politischen Parteien, Vierte Reihe. Deutschland Seit 1945: Bd. 12. Düsseldorf: Droste, 1998.

Budnitskii, O. V. and G. S. Zelenina, ed. and comp. *Svershilos'-prishli Nemtsy! ideinyi kollaboratsionizm v SSSR v period Velikoi Otechestvennoi Voiny*. Moscow: ROSSPEN, 2014.

Burke, Michael. *Outrageous Good Fortune*. Boston: Little, Brown, 1984.

Chebrikov, V. M. *Istoriia Sovetskikh organov gosudarstvennoi bezopasnosti: uchebnik*. Moscow: Vysshaia Krasnoznamennaia Shkola Komiteta Gosudarstvennoi Bezopasnosti pri Sovete Ministrov SSSR imeni F. E. Dzerzhinskogo, 1977.

Cherezov, K. K. *Maska NTS, ili NTS bez maski.* Berlin: Izd. Sovetskogo komiteta po kul'turnym sviaziam s sootechestvennikami za rubezhom, 1965.

Chetvertyi s'ezd Soiuza Bor'by za Osvobozhdenie Narodov Rossii (SBONR), Zakrytaia chast' 19–22 fevralia 1956 goda. Munich: Verlag "Golos Naroda," 1958.

Chikarleev, Iu. *Tragediia NTS: epizod tainoi voiny.* New York: International University Book Exchange Service, 1987.

Coffin, William Sloane. *Once to Every Man: a Memoir.* New York: Atheneum, 1977.

Critchlow, James. *Radio Hole-in-the-head/Radio Liberty: An Insider's Story of Cold War Broadcasting.* Washington, DC: American University Press, 1995.

Critchfield, James H. *Partners at the Creation: The Men behind Postwar Germany's Defense and Intelligence Establishments.* Annapolis, MD: Naval Institute Press, 2003.

Critchfield, James H. "The Early History of the Gehlen Organization and its Influence on the Development of a National Security System in the Federal Republic of Germany." In Bungert, Heike et al., eds. *Secret Intelligence in the Twentieth Century.* London: Frank Cass, 2003, 159–66.

Degenerates Rule the World! Klimov Interview. https://groups.google.com/forum/#!topic/alt.privacy.anon-server/7RfJNXmTlRQ. *Last accessed June 15, 2016.*

De Silva, Peer. *Sub Rosa: The CIA and the Uses of Intelligence.* New York: Times Books, 1978.

Divnich, E. I. *NTS, nam pora obiasnit'sia!* (New York: Izd. "Sootechestvenniki," 1968).

Dorba, Ivan. *Svoi sredi chuzhikh: v omute istiny.* Moscow: Veche, 2012.

Dvinov, Boris L. *Vlasovskoe dvizhenie v svete dokumentov (s prilozheniem sekretnykh dokumentov).* New York: publisher not identified, 1950.

Fabrichnikov, A. A. and I. A. Ovchinnikov. *Ispol'zovanie vozmozhnostei sovetskogo komiteta po kul'turnym sviaziam s sootechestvennikami za rubezhom v razvedyvatel'noi rabote. Uchebnoe posobie.* Moscow: Komitet gosudarstvennoi bezopasnosti pri Sovete Ministrov SSSR, 1968. https://www.thedailybeast.com/the-kgb-papers-here-are-the-originals. *Last accessed January 3, 2018.*

Fischer, George Uri. *Insatiable: A Story of my Nine Lives.* Philadelphia: unpublished ms., 2000.

Fischer, Louis and Boris A. Yakovlev, eds. *Thirteen Who Fled.* New York: Harper, 1949.

Flam, Liudmila, ed. *Sud'by pokoleniia 1920-1930-kh godov v emigratsii: ocherki i vospominaniia.* Moscow: Russkii put', 2006.

Gehlen, Reinhard. *The Service: The Memoirs of General Reinhard Gehlen.* New York: World Pub., 1972.

Gul', Roman. *Ia unes Rossiiu: apologiia emigratsii,* 3 vols. New York: "Most," 1981.

Guzevich, D. Iu., et al., ed. and comp. "Russkaia emigratsiia vo Frantsii v 1940-e, 1 chast': Politseiskii otchet 1948 goda 'La colonie russe de Paris' ('Russkaia koloniia v Parizhe')." *Diaspora,* t. 8 (2007): 341–655.

Iakovlev, N. N. *CIA Target, the USSR.* Moscow: Progress Publishers, 1982.

Kalugin, Oleg. *Spymaster: My Thirty-Two Years in Intelligence and Espionage Against the West.* New York: Basic Books, 2009.

Karpov, V. S. et al., eds. *V poiskakh istiny: puti i sud'by vtoroi emigratsii, sbornik statei i dokumentov.* Moscow: Rossiiskii gos. Gumanitarnyi universitet, 1997.

Kennan, George F. *Memoirs, 1925–1950.* Boston: Little, Brown, 1967.

Kennan, George F. *Memoirs, 1950–1963.* Boston: Little, Brown, 1972.

Kiselev, A. F. *Politicheskaia istoriia russkoi emigratsii, 1920–1940 gg.: dokumenty i materialy.* Moscow: Vlados, 1999.

Klimov, Grigorii. *Berliner Kreml.* Cologne: Verlag Rote Weissbücher, 1953.

Klimov, Grigorii. *Pesn' pobeditelia*. Krasnodar: Peresvet, 2004. http://g-klimov.info/klimov-pp/. *Last accessed April 22 2016.*

Konstantinov, D. V. *Cherez tunnel' 20-go stoletiia*. Moscow, IAI RGGU, 1997.

Kozlov, V. A. and S. V. Mironenko, eds. *58–10: nadzornye proizvodstva prokuratury SSSR po delam ob antisovetskoi agitatsii i propagande: annatirovannyi katolog, mart 1953–1991*. Moscow: Mezhdunarodnyi fond "Demokratiia," 1999.

Kromiadi, Konstantin. *Za zemliu, za voliu*. San Francisco: "Globus," 1980.

Kuznetsov, B. M. *V ugodu Stalina: gody 1945–1946*. London, ON: Izdatel'stvo SBONR, 1968.

Levine, Isaac Don. *Eyewitness to History: Memoirs and Reflections of a Foreign Correspondent for Half a Century*. New York: Hawthorn Books, 1973.

Levitin-Krasnov, A. E. *Iz drugoi strany: emigratsiia*. Parizh: Poiski, 1985.

Lyons, Eugene. *Assignment in Utopia*. New York: Harcourt, Brace, 1937.

Lyons, Eugene. *Our Secret Allies: The Peoples of Russia*. New York: Duell, Sloan and Pearce, 1953.

Mosely, Philip E. "Boris Nicolaevsky: The American Years." In Boris I. Nicolaevsky et al., *Revolution and Politics in Russia: Essays in Memory of B. I. Nicolaevsky*. Bloomington, IN: Indiana University Press, 1973.

"NTS—The Russian Solidarist Movement." RNAL Research Paper, US Department of State External Research Staff, Series 3, no. 76, January 10, 1951.

Ostermann, Christian, ed. "Implementing 'Roll-back': NSC 158." *Newsletter of the Society of Historians of American Foreign Relations* 26, no. 3 (1996): 1–7.

Ovchinnikov, I. V. *Na pereput'iakh Rossii*. Moscow: Informatsionno-ekspertnaia gruppa "Panorama," 1995.

Patch, Isaac. *Closing the Circle: A Buckalino Journey around Our Time*. Wellesley, MA: Wellesley College Printing Services, 1996.

Pervyi s'ezd SBONR: materialy sekretariata s'ezda. Munich: Izdatel'stvo Bor'ba, 1950.

Petrov, Igor', with Oleg Beyda. "Pervyi god plena polkovnika Nerianina," pts. 1–2, *Live Journal*, 2015. http://labas.livejournal.com/1097511.html. *Last accessed July 1, 2017.*

Pirozhkova, Vera. *Poteriannoe pokolenie: vospominaniia o detstve i iunosti*. St. Petersburg: Zhurnal Neva, 1998.

Poremskii, V. D. *Strategiia antibol'shevitskoi emigratsii: izbrannye stat'i, 1934–1997*. Moscow: Posev, 1998.

Prianishnikov, B. V. *Novopokolentsy*. Silver Spring, MD: Multilingual Typesetting, 1986.

Romanov, Evgenii. *V bor'be za Rossiiu: vospominaniia*. Moscow: Golos, 1999.

Romanov, Evgenii. "Zametki o soiuze." *Za Rossiiu*, nos. 335–6 (2001). http://ntsrs.ru/content/zametki-o-soyuze. *Last accessed July 17, 2014.*

Rositzke, Harry. "America's Secret Operations: A Perspective." *Foreign Affairs* 53, no. 2 (1975): 334–51.

Rositzke, Harry. *The KGB: The Eyes of Russia*. Garden City, NY: Doubleday, 1981.

Ruffner, Kevin C., ed. *Forging an Intelligence Partnership: CIA and the Origins of the BND, 1945–1949*, vol. II. CIA History Staff, Center for the Study of Intelligence, European Division 1999). http://www.foia.cia.gov. *Last accessed February 24, 2016.*

Senderov, V. A., ed. and comp. *Ot zarubezh'ia do Moskvy: Narodno-Trudovoi Soiuz (NTS) v vospominaniiakh i dokumentakh 1924–2014*. Moscow: Posev, 2014.

Slavinsky, Michel. *Ombres sur le Kremlin: une voix libre se fait entendre derrière le Rideau de fer*. Paris: La Table Ronde, 1973.

Sosin, Gene. *Sparks of Liberty: An Insider's Memoir of Radio Liberty*. University Park, PA: Pennsylvania State University Press, 1999.

Stepashin, S. V. and V. P. Iampol'skii, eds. *Organy gosudarstvennoi bezopasnosti SSSR v Velikoi otechestvennoi voine: sbornik dokumentov*, vol. 4, pt. 1. Moscow: Kniga i biznes, 1995.

Stepashin, S. V. and V. P. Iampol'skii, eds. *Organy gosudarstvennoi* bezopasnosti *SSSR v Velikoi otechestvennoi voine: sbornik dokumentov*, vol. 5, pt. 1. Moscow: Kuchkovo pole, 2007.

Stolypin, A. P. *Na sluzhbe Rossii: ocherki po istorii NTS*. Frankfurt am Main: Posev, 1986.

Sudoplatov, Pavel et al. *Special Tasks: The Memoirs of an Unwanted Witness, a Soviet Spymaster*. Boston: Little, Brown, 1994.

Tol'ts, Vladimir. "NTS: vchera, segodnia i? . . . ," Raznitsa vo vremeni, Radio Svoboda, May 15, 2010. At https://www.svoboda.org/a/2044124.html. *Last accessed December 12, 2018.*

Tol'ts, Vladimir. "Vengriia-56 po materialam KGB i MVD SSSR." Raznitsa vo vremeni, Radio Svoboda, November 26, 2011. http://www.svoboda.org/content/transcript/24404513.html. *Last accessed October 10, 2018.*

Troitskii, Nikolai. *Ty, moe stoletie-*. Moscow: Institut politicheskogo i voennogo analiza, 2006.

Trushnovich, Ia. A. "NTS v poslevoennom Berline: probnyi shar." *Posev* no. 9 (1999). http://www.posev.ru/files/nts-about/ne9993.htm. *Last accessed July 20, 2016.*

"Ukaz ot 17 sentiabria 1955 goda. Ob amnistii sovetskikh grazhdan, sotrudnichavshikh s okkupantami v period Velikoi Otechestvennoi Voiny 1941–1945 gg." *Vedomosti verkhovnogo soveta SSSR*, no. 17 (1955): 342–50.

Varshavskii, V. S. *Nezamechennoe pokolenie*. New York: Izd-vo im. Chekhova, 1956.

Wasson, R. Gordon. "A Second Look at Some Popular Beliefs about Russia." *The Commercial and Financial Chronicle* 173 (Feb. 1951): 819–22.

Weiss, Michael, ed. "The KGB Playbook for Turning Russians Worldwide into Agents." *The Daily Beast*, December 29, 2017. https://www.thedailybeast.com/the-kgb-playbook-for-turning-russians-worldwide-into-agents. *Last accessed January 2, 2018.*

Young, George Gordon. *The House of Secrets*. New York: Duell, Sloan, and Pearce, 1959.

Secondary Sources

Aarons, Mark and John Loftus. *Ratlines: How the Vatican's Nazi Networks Betrayed Western Intelligence to the Soviets*. London: William Heinemann, 1991.

Abraham, Richard. *Alexander Kerensky: The First Love of the Revolution*. New York: Columbia University Press, 1987.

"Across and Beyond: Rethinking Transnational History." *Kritika* 17, no. 4 (2016): 715–21.

Ahonen, Pertti. *After the Expulsion: West Germany and Eastern Europe, 1945–1990*. Oxford and New York: Oxford University Press, 2003.

Aid, Matthew W. "The National Security Agency and the Cold War." In Matthew W. Aid and Cees Wiebes, eds. *Secrets of Signals Intelligence during the Cold War and beyond*. London and Portland, OR: Frank Cass, 2001.

Albanese, David C. S. "In Search of a Lesser Evil: Anti-Soviet Nationalism and the Cold War." PhD thesis, Northeastern University, 2015.

Albanese, David C. S. "'It Takes a Russian to Beat a Russian': the National Union of Labor Solidarists, Nationalism, and Human Intelligence Operations in the Cold War." *Intelligence and National Security* 32, no. 6 (2017): 782–96.

Aldrich, Richard J. *The Hidden Hand: Britain, America, and Cold War Secret Intelligence.* New York: Overlook, 2002.

Aleksandrov, K. M. *Protiv Stalina: Vlasovtsy i vostochnye dobrovol'tsy vo vtoroi mirovoi voine: sbornik statei i materialov.* St. Petersburg: Iunventa, 2003.

Aleksandrov, K. M. *Mify o Generale Vlasove.* Moscow: Posev, 2010.

Anderson, Elizabeth E. "The Security Dilemma and Covert Action: The Truman Years." *International Journal of Intelligence and Counter Intelligence* 11, no. 4 (1998): 403–27.

Andrew, Christopher M. and Vasilii Mitrokhin. *The Mitrokhin Archive: The KGB in Europe and the West.* London: Allen Lane, 1999.

Andreyev, Catherine. *Vlasov and the Russian Liberation Movement: Soviet Reality and Émigré Theories.* Cambridge and New York: Cambridge University Press, 1987.

Andreyev, Catherine, and Ivan Savický. *Russia Abroad: Prague and the Russian Diaspora, 1918–1938.* New Haven: Yale University Press, 2004.

Antoshin, A. V. "Rossiiskaia emigratsiia i germanskii vopros v 1945–1961 gg." *Ural'skii vestnik mezhdunarodnykh issledovanii,* ed. 3. Ekaterinburg: Izd-o Ural'skogo universiteta, 2005, 168–76.

Antoshin, A. V. "Men'sheviki v emigratsii posle Vtoroi mirovoi voiny." *Otechestvennaia istoriia* no. 1 (2007): 102–15.

Antoshin, A. V. "Rossiiskaia emigratsiia i apogeia 'kholodnoi voiny.'" In Iu. A. Poliakov et al., eds. *Istoriia rossiiskogo zarubez'hia: emigratsiia iz SSSR-Rossii, 1941–2001 gg.: sbornik stat'ei.* Moscow: Rossiiskaia akademiia nauk, Institut rossiiskoi istorii, 2007, 92–102.

Antoshin, A. V. *Rossiiskie emigranty v usloviiakh "kholodnoi voiny" (seredina 1940-kh-seredina-1960-kh gg.).* Ekaterinburg: Izd. Ural'skogo universiteta, 2008.

Antoshin, A. V. *Russkii Parizh za Sovetskii Soiuz? Ideinye iskaniia russkikh emigrantov vo Frantsii (vtoraia polovina 1940-kh gg.).* Ekaterinburg: Izd. Ural'skogo universiteta, 2017.

Bauer, Ingrid, and Renate Huber. "Sexual encounters across (former) Enemy Lines." In Günter Bischof et al., eds. *Sexuality in Austria.* Piscataway, NJ: Transaction Publishers, 2007, 65–101.

Berghahn, Volker R. *America and the Intellectual Cold Wars in Europe: Shepard Stone between Philanthropy, Academy, and Diplomacy.* Princeton, NJ: Princeton University Press, 2001.

Bergman, Jay. "The Memoirs of Soviet Defectors: Are They a Reliable Source about the Soviet Union?" *Canadian Slavonic Papers* 31, no. 1 (1989): 1–24.

Beyda, Oleg. "'Iron Cross of the Wrangel's Army': Russian Emigrants as Interpreters in the Wehrmacht." *Journal of Slavic Military Studies* 27, no. 3 (2014): 430–48.

Beyda, Oleg. "'Re-Fighting the Civil War': Second Lieutenant Mikhail Aleksandrovich Gubanov," *Jahrbücher für Geschichte Osteuropas* 66, no. 2 (2018): 245–73.

Beyda, Oleg and Igor Petrov. "The Soviet Union." In David Stahel, ed. *Joining Hitler's Crusade: European Nations and the Invasion of the Soviet Union, 1941.* Cambridge and New York: Cambridge University Press, 2018, 369–425.

Biddiscombe, Perry. "The Problem with Glass Houses: The Soviet Recruitment and Deployment of SS Men as Spies and Saboteurs." *Intelligence and National Security* 15, no. 3 (2000): 131–45.

Blackwill, Robert D., and Philip H. Gordon. *Containing Russia: How to Respond to Moscow's Intervention in U.S. Democracy and Growing Geopolitical Challenge.* New York: Council on Foreign Relations, 2018.

Bolkhovitinov, N. N. *Russkie uchenye-emigranty (G. V. Vernadskii, M. M. Karpovich, M. T. Florinskii) i stanovlenie Rusistiki v SShA.* Moscow: ROSSPEN, 2005.

Borhi, László. "Rollback, Liberation, Containment, or Inaction? U.S. Policy and Eastern Europe in the 1950s." *Journal of Cold War Studies* 1, no. 3 (1999): 67–110.

Bower, Tom. *The Perfect English Spy: Sir Dick White and the Secret War, 1935–1990.* New York: St. Martin's Press, 1995.

Brady, Steven. *Eisenhower and Adenauer: Alliance Maintenance under Pressure, 1953–1960.* Lanham, MD: Lexington Books, 2010.

Brandenburger, David. *National Bolshevism: Stalinist Mass Culture and the Formation of Modern Russian National Identity, 1931–1956.* Cambridge, MA: Harvard University Press, 2002.

Breitman, Richard, and Norman J. W. Goda. *In Hitler's Shadow: Nazi War Criminals, U.S. Intelligence, and the Cold War.* Washington, DC: National Archives and Records Administration, 2010.

Brook-Shepard, Gordon. *The Storm Birds: Soviet Post-War Defectors.* London: Weidenfeld & Nicolson, 1989.

Brovkin, Vladimir N. *The Bolsheviks in Russian Society: The Revolution and the Civil Wars.* New Haven, CT: Yale University Press, 1997.

Brubaker, Rogers. "Nationhood and the National Question in the Soviet Union and Post-Soviet Eurasia: An Institutional Account." *Theory and Society* 23, no. 1 (1994): 47–78.

Budnitskii, O. V. *Den'gi russkoi emigratsii: kolchakovskoe zoloto, 1918–1957* (Moscow: Novoe Literaturnoe Obozrenie, 2008).

Budnitskii, O. V. "The Great Patriotic War and Soviet Society: Defeatism, 1941–42." *Kritika* 15, no. 4 (2014): 767–97.

Bülow, Mathilde von. *West Germany, Cold War Europe and the Algerian War.* Cambridge and New York: Cambridge University Press, 2016.

Burbank, Jane. *Intelligentsia and Revolution: Russian Views of Bolshevism, 1917–1922.* New York and Oxford: Oxford University Press, 1989.

Burds, Jeffrey. "Agentura: Soviet Informants' Networks & the Ukrainian Underground in Galicia, 1944–48." *East European Politics & Societies* 11, no. 1 (1996): 89–130.

Burds, Jeffrey. *The early Cold War in Soviet West Ukraine, 1944–1948.* Pittsburgh, PA: Russian and East European Studies Program, University of Pittsburgh, 2001.

Burton, Bob. *Dictionary of Espionage and Intelligence: Over 800 Phrases Used in International and Covert Espionage.* New York: Skyhorse Publishing, 2014.

Carafano, James Jay. "Mobilizing Europe's Stateless: America's Plan for a Cold War Army." *Journal of Cold War Studies* 1, no. 2 (1999): 61–85.

Carpenter, Kirsty, and Philip Mansel, eds. *The French Émigrés in Europe and the Struggle against Revolution, 1789–1814.* New York: St. Martin's Press, 1999.

Carruthers, Susan L. "Between Camps: Eastern Bloc 'Escapees' and Cold War Borderlands." *American Quarterly* 57, no. 3 (2005): 911–42.

Carruthers, Susan L. *Cold War Captives: Imprisonment, Escape, and Brainwashing.* Berkeley, CA: University of California Press, 2009.

Ceplair, Larry. *Anti-Communism in Twentieth-Century America: A Critical History.* Santa Barbara, CA: Praeger, 2011.

Chester, Eric Thomas. *Covert Network: Progressives, the International Rescue Committee, and the CIA.* Armonk, NY: M.E. Sharpe, 1995.

Chuev, S. G. *Spetssluzhby Tret'ego Reikha*, books 1–2. Moscow: Neva, 2003.

Clavin, Patricia. "Defining Transnationalism." *Contemporary European History* 14, no. 4 (2005): 421–39.

Cohen, Robin. *Global Diasporas: an Introduction.* Hoboken: Taylor & Francis, 1997.

Corke, Sarah-Jane. *US Covert Operations and Cold War Strategy: Truman, the CIA and Secret Warfare*. London: Routledge, 2007.

Costello, John, and Oleg Tsarev. *Deadly Illusions*. New York: Crown, 1993.

Coudenys, Wim. "Russian Collaboration in Belgium During World War II: The Case of Jurij L. Vojcehovskij." *Cahiers Du Monde Russe* 43, no. 2/3 (2002): 479–514.

Craig, Gordon A. "Konrad Adenauer and the United States." In Reiner Pommerin, ed. *The American Impact on Postwar Germany*. Providence, RI: Berghahn, 1995, 1–14.

Creuzberger, Stefan. "Ewert von Dellingshausen (1909–1996): Ein baltendeutscher Antikommunist im Dienste der 'Psychologischen Kriegsführung." In Helmut Müller-Enbergs and Armin Wagner, eds. *Spione und Nachrichtenhändler: Geheimdienst-Karrieren in Deutschland 1939–1989*. Berlin: Ch. Links Verlag, 2016, 208–28.

Creuzberger, Stefan. *Kampf für die Einheit: Das Gesamtdeutsche Ministerium und die Politische Kultur des Kalten Krieges 1949–1969*. Düsseldorf: Droste, 2008.

Cummings, Richard H. *Cold War Radio: the Dangerous History of American Broadcasting in Europe, 1950–1989*. Jefferson, NC: McFarland & Co., 2009.

Cummings, Richard H. "CIA and Defectors from the USSR, Part One: Project CAMANTILLA: The American Friends of Russian Freedom (AFRF)." *Cold War Vignettes*, June 2, 2018. https://coldwarradios.blogspot.com/. *Last accessed June 11, 2018.*

Dallin, Alexander. *German Rule in Russia, 1941–1945: A Study of Occupation Policies*. London and New York: Macmillan; St. Martin's Press, 1957.

Dallin, David J., and Boris I. Nicolaevsky. *Forced Labor in Soviet Russia*. New Haven: Yale University Press, 1947.

Dautova, R. V. "Iz istorii radiopropagandy vozvrashcheniia 'nevozvrashchentsev' v gody 'Khrushchevskoi Ottepeli."" *Vestnik Cheliabinskogo gosudarstvennogo universiteta*, vyp. 30 (2010), http://cyberleninka.ru/article/n/iz-istorii-radiopropagandy-vozvrascheniya-nevozvraschentsev-v-gody-hruschevskoy-ottepeli. *Last accessed March 30, 2016.*

David-Fox, Michael, Peter Holquist, and Alexander Martin, eds. *Fascination and Enmity: Russia and Germany as Entangled Histories, 1914–1945*. Pittsburgh: University of Pittsburgh Press, 2012.

Diamond, Sigmund. *Compromised Campus: The Collaboration of Universities with the Intelligence Community, 1945–1955*. New York: Oxford University Press, 1992.

Dorril, Stephen. *MI6: Inside the Covert World of Her Majesty's Secret Intelligence Service*. New York: Free Press, 2000.

Drobiazko, S. I. *Pod znamenami vraga: antisovetskie formirovaniia v sostave Germanskikh Vooruzhennkh Sil, 1941–1945*. Moscow: EKSMO, 2004.

Dvinov, Boris L. *Politics of the Russian Emigration*. Santa Monica, CA: Rand Corp., 1955.

Edele, Mark. "More Than Just Stalinists: the Political Sentiments of Victors, 1945–1953." In Juliane Fürst, ed. *Late Stalinist Russia: Society between Reconstruction and Reinvention* (London and New York: Routledge, 2006), 167–91.

Edele, Mark. "Fighting Russia's History Wars: Vladimir Putin and the Codification of World War II." *History & Memory* 29, no. 2 (2017): 90–124.

Edele, Mark. *Stalin's Defectors: How Red Army Soldiers became Hitler's Collaborators, 1941–1945*. New York and Oxford: Oxford University Press, 2017.

Elliot, Mark R. "Andrei Vlasov: Red Army General in Hitler's Service." *Military Affairs* 46, no. 2 (1982): 84–7.

Elliot, Mark R. *Pawns of Yalta: Soviet Refugees and America's Role in their Repatriation* (Urbana, IL: University of Illinois Press, 1982).

Emel'ianov, Iu. N. S. P. *Mel'gunov: v Rossii i emigratsii*. Moscow: Editorial URSS, 1998.

Engerman, David C. "William Henry Chamberlin and Russia's Revolt against Western Civilization." *Russian History* 26, no. 1 (1999): 45–64.

Engerman, David C. *Know Your Enemy: The Rise and Fall of America's Soviet Experts.* New York and Oxford: Oxford University Press, 2011.

Epstein, Julius. *Operation Keelhaul: the Story of Forced Repatriation from 1944 to the Present.* Old Greenwich, CT: Devin-Adair, 1973.

Fainsod, Merle. "Controls and Tensions in the Soviet System." *The American Political Science Review* 44, no. 2 (1950): 266–82.

Farmer, Sarah Bennett. *Martyred Village: Commemorating the 1944 Massacre at Oradour-sur-Glane.* Berkeley: University of California Press, 1999.

Fel'shtinksii, Iu. G., and G. I. Cherniavskii. *Cherez veka i strany: B. I. Nikolaevskii. Sub'da men'shevika, istorika, sovetologa, glavnogo svidetelia epokhal'nykh izmenenii v zhizni Rossii pervoi poloviny XX veka.* Moscow: Izd. Tsentr-poligraf, 2012.

Ferris, John. "Coming in from the Cold War: the historiography of American intelligence, 1945–1990." In Michael J. Hogan, ed. *America in the World: The Historiography of American Foreign Relations since 1941.* Cambridge and New York: Cambridge University Press, 1995.

Fischer, George, ed. *Russian Émigré Politics.* New York: Free Russia Fund, 1951.

Fitzpatrick, Sheila. *Tear Off the Masks! Identity and Imposture in Twentieth-Century Russia.* Princeton: Princeton University Press, 2005.

Foglesong, David S. "Roots of 'Liberation': American Images of the Future of Russia in the Early Cold War, 1948–1953." *The International History Review* 21, no. 1 (1999): 57–79.

Foglesong, David S. *America's Secret War against Bolshevism: U.S. Intervention in the Russian Civil War, 1917–1920.* Raleigh: University of North Carolina Press, 2001.

Foglesong, David S. *The American Mission and the "Evil Empire": The Crusade for a "Free Russia" since 1881.* New York: Cambridge University Press, 2007.

Franceschini, Christoph, Thomas Wegener Friis, and Erich Schmidt-Eenboom. *Spionage unter Freunden: Partnerdienstbeziehungen und Westaufklärung der Organisation Gehlen und des BND.* Berlin: Chr. Links Verlag, 2017.

Fulbrook, Mary. *Anatomy of a Dictatorship: Inside the GDR, 1949–1989.* New York: Oxford University Press, 1997.

Fulbrook, Mary. *A History of Germany, 1918–2014: The Divided Nation.* Chichester, UK: Wiley-Blackwell, 2014.

Gaddis, John Lewis. *George F. Kennan: An American Life.* New York: Penguin Press, 2011.

Gaddis, John Lewis. *The Long Peace: Inquiries into the History of the Cold War.* New York and Oxford: Oxford University Press, 1989.

Gessen, Masha. "The Putin Nemesis Plotting a Post-Putin Russia." *Vanity Fair*, July 11, 2016.

Gieseke, Jens, and David Burnett. *The History of the Stasi: East Germany's Secret Police, 1945–1990.* New York: Berghahn Books, 2014.

Gilbert, James L. et al. *In the Shadow of the Sphinx: A History of Army Counterintelligence.* Belvoir, VA: History Office, Office of Strategic Management and Information, US Army Intelligence and Security Command, 2005. http://permanent.access.gpo.gov/lps103181/GPO_Army_318-530.pdf. *Last accessed February 27, 2016.*

Glad, John. *Russia Abroad: Writers, History, Politics.* Tenafly, NJ, and Washington, DC: Hermitage Publishers & Birchbark Press, 1999.

Glebov, Sergei. "The Mongol–Bolshevik Revolution: Eurasianist Ideology in Search for an Ideal Past." *Journal of Eurasian Studies* 2, no. 2 (2011): 103–14.

Goloseeva, A. A. "Sotsial'no-politicheskaia pozitsiia eserov v gody Vtoroi mirovoi voiny (po materialam emigrantskoi pressy v SShA)." *Klio* no. 10 (106) (2015): 33–40.

Gorsuch, Anne E. *All This Is Your World: Soviet Tourism at Home and Abroad after Stalin.* Oxford and New York: Oxford University Press, 2011.

Grant, Natalie. "Deception on a Grand Scale." *International Journal of Intelligence and Counterintelligence* 1, no. 4 (1986): 51–77.

Grose, Peter. *Operation Rollback: America's Secret War behind the Iron Curtain.* Boston: Houghton Mifflin, 2000.

Gross, Jan T. "Themes for a Social History of War Experience and Collaboration." In István Deák et al., eds. *The Politics of Retribution in Europe: World War II and Its Aftermath.* Princeton, NJ: Princeton University Press, 2000, 15–35.

Grosser, Pierre. "Looking for the Core of the Cold War, and Finding a Mirage?" *Cold War History* 15, no. 2 (2015): 245–52.

Hardeman, Hilde. *Coming to Terms with the Soviet Regime: The "Changing Signposts" Movement among Russian Emigrés in the Early 1920s.* DeKalb: Northern Illinois University Press, 1994.

Harrison, Hope. "Driving the Soviets up the Wall: A Super-Ally, a Superpower, and the Building of the Berlin Wall, 1958–61." *Cold War History* 1, no. 1 (2000): 53–74.

Haslam, Jonathan. *Near and Distant Neighbors: A New History of Soviet Intelligence.* New York: Farrar, Straus and Giroux, 2015.

Heitzer, Enrico. *Die Kampfgruppe gegen Unmenschlichkeit (KgU): Widerstand und Spionage im Kalten Krieg 1948–1959.* Cologne: Böhlau Verlag, 2014.

Hermiston, Roger. *The Greatest Traitor: The Secret Lives of Agent George Blake.* London: Aurum Press, 2013.

Heuser, Beatrice. "Covert Actions within British and American Concepts of Containment, 1948–1951." In Richard J. Aldrich, ed. *British Intelligence, Strategy and the Cold War, 1945–1951.* London: Routledge, 1992, 65–84.

Himka, John-Paul. "War Criminality: A Blank Spot in the Collective Memory of the Ukrainian Diaspora." *Spaces of Identity* 5, no. 1 (2005): 9–24.

Hirsch, Kurt. *Rechts von der Union. Personen, Organisationen, Parteien seit 1945: Ein Lexikon.* Munich: Knesebeck & Schuler, 1989.

Hixson, Walter L. *George F. Kennan: Cold War Iconoclast.* New York: Columbia University Press, 1989.

Hixson, Walter L. *Parting the Curtain: Propaganda, Culture, and the Cold War, 1945–1961.* New York: St. Martin's Press, 1997.

Holian, Anna. *Between National Socialism and Soviet Communism: Displaced Persons in Postwar Germany.* Ann Arbor: University of Michigan Press, 2011.

Hornsby, Robert. *Protest, Reform and Repression in Khrushchev's Soviet Union.* Cambridge: Cambridge University Press, 2013.

Horvath, Robert. *The Legacy of Soviet Dissent: Dissidents, Democratisation and Radical Nationalism in Russia.* London and New York: RoutledgeCurzon, 2005.

Hosking, Geoffrey A. *Russia: People and Empire, 1552–1917.* Cambridge, MA: Harvard University Press, 1997.

Hosking, Geoffrey A. *Rulers and Victims: the Russians in the Soviet Union.* Cambridge, MA: Harvard University Press, 2006.

Iakunin, Mikhail, and D. Iu. Guzevich. *Zakat Rossiiskoi emigratsii vo Frantsii v 1940-e gody: istoriia i pamiat'.* Paris-Novosibirsk: Assosiatsiia "Zarubezhnaia Rossiia," 2012.

Immerman, Richard H. *The Hidden Hand: A Brief History of the CIA.* Chichester, England: Wiley-Blackwell, 2014.

Ingimundarson, Valur. "The Eisenhower Administration, the Adenauer Government, and the Political Uses of the East German Uprising in 1953." *Diplomatic History* 20, no. 3 (1996): 381–410.

Izvergina, V. P. "I. A. Il'in i ideologiia Belogo dvizheniia." *Regionologiia* no. 1 (2012). http://regionsar.ru/ru/node/887. *Last accessed December 21, 2018.*

Jahn, Peter. "Facing the Ostfront: The Other War in German Memory." In Karl Schlögel (ed.), *Russian-German Special Relations in the Twentieth Century A Closed Chapter?* Oxford: Berg Publishers, 2006, 119–31.

Janco, Andrew Paul. "Soviet 'Displaced Persons' in Europe, 1941–1951." PhD diss., University of Chicago, 2012.

Janco, Andrew Paul. "'Unwilling': The One-Word Revolution in Refugee Status, 1940–51." *Contemporary European History* 23, no. 3 (2014): 429–46.

Johnson, A. Ross. *Radio Free Europe and Radio Liberty: The CIA Years and Beyond.* Washington, DC: Woodrow Wilson Center Press, 2010.

Johnson, A. Ross, and R. Eugene Parta. *Cold War Broadcasting: Impact on the Soviet Union and Eastern Europe: A Collection of Studies and Documents.* Budapest and New York: Central European University Press, 2010.

Johnson, Loch K. "Congressional Supervision of America's Secret Agencies: The Experience and Legacy of the Church Committee." *Public Administration Review* 64, no. 1 (2004): 3–14.

Johnston, Robert H. "The Great Patriotic War and the Russian Exiles in France." *Russian Review* 35, no. 3 (1976): 303–21.

Johnston, Robert H. *New Mecca, New Babylon: Paris and the Russian Exiles, 1920–1945.* Kingston: McGill-Queen's University Press, 1988.

Karpenko, Sergei. *Mezhdu Rossiei i Stalinym: rossiiskaia emigratsiia i vtoraia mirovaia voina.* Moscow: RGGU, 2004.

Kellogg, Michael. *The Russian Roots of Nazism: White Émigrés and the Making of National Socialism, 1917–1945.* Cambridge, UK, and New York: Cambridge University Press, 2004.

Kern, Gary. *The Kravchenko Case: One Man's War on Stalin.* New York: Enigma Books, 2007.

Kind-Kovács, Friederike. "Voices, letters, and literature through the Iron Curtain: exiles and the (trans)mission of radio in the Cold War." *Cold War History* 13, no. 2 (2013): 193–219.

Klimovich, Liudmila. "Po tu storonu sovetskoi vlasti: k istorii Narodno-troduvogo soiuza." *Neprikosnovennyi zapas*, no. 5/67 (May 2009). http://magazines.russ.ru/nz/2009/5/kl12.html. *Last accessed July 22, 2018.*

Klimovich, Liudmila. "Narodno-trudovoi soiuz rossiiskikh solidaristov: rannye stranitsy istorii." *Neprikosnovennyi zapas*, no. 91 (May 2013). http://www.nlobooks.ru/node/4018. *Last accessed August 5, 2015.*

Knight, Amy W. *How the Cold War Began: The Igor Gouzenko Affair and the Hunt for Soviet Spies.* New York: Carroll & Graf, 2005.

Kodin, E. V. *'Garvardskii Proekt'.* Moscow: ROSSPEN, 2003.

Kodin, E. V. "Nikolai Troitskii: ot Simbirskogo povstantsa do direktora Miunkhenskogo instituta po izucheniiu SSSR." *Novyi Istoricheskii Vestnik* 37, no. 3 (2013): 148–67.

Kodin, E. V. *Miunkhenskii institut po izucheniiu istorii i kul'tury SSSR, 1950–1972 gg.: evropeiskii tsentr sovetologii?* Smolensk: Izd-o SmolGU, 2016.

Koestler, Arthur. *Bricks to Babel: A Selection from 50 Years of His Writings, Chosen and with New Commentary by the Author*. New York: Random House, 1981.

Kolpakidi, Aleksandr and Dmitri Prokhorov. *KGB: Spetsoperatsii sovetskoi razvedki*. Moscow: AST, 2000.

Kotkin, Stephen. *Magnetic Mountain: Stalinism as a Civilization*. Berkeley: University of California Press, 1995.

Kovalev, B. N. *Kollaboratsionizm v Rossii v 1941–1945 gg.: tipy i formy*. Novgorod: Novgorodskii Gosudarstvennyi Universitet imeni Iaroslava Mudrogo, 2009.

Kowalczuk, Ilko-Sascha, and Stefan Wolle. *Roter Stern über Deutschland: Sowjetische Truppen in der DDR*. Berlin: Links, 2001.

Krasnov, Vladislav. *Soviet Defectors: The KGB Wanted List*. Stanford, CA: Hoover Institution Press, 1985.

Kristof, Ladis K. "B. I. Nicolaevsky: The Formative Years." In *Boris I. Nicolaevsky et al., Revolution and Politics in Russia: Essays in Memory of B.I. Nicolaevsky*. Bloomington, IN: Indiana University Press, 1973, 5–32.

Krivosheev, S. A. *KGB protiv NTS*. Moscow: Trovant, 2015.

Kuhlmann-Smirnov, Anne. " 'Stiller als Wasser, Tiefer als Gras': Zur Migrationgeschichte der Russischen Displaced Persons in Deutschland nach dem Zweiten Weltkrieg." *Arbeitspapiere und Materialien—Universität Bremen*, no. 68, Forschungsstelle Osteuropa an der Universität Bremen, 2005.

Kulyk, Volodymyr. "Ukrainian displaced persons in Germany and Austria after the Second World War." In Karen Schönwälder et al, eds. *European Encounters: Migrants, Migration, and European Societies since 1945*. Burlington, VT: Ashgate, 2003, 214–37.

Kurilla, I. I. *Zakliatye druz'ia: Istoriia mnenii, fantazii, kontaktov, vzaimo(ne)ponimania Rossii i SShA*. Moscow: Novoe literaturnoe obozrenie, 2018.

Kurilla, I. I., and V. Iu. Zhuravleva, eds. *Russian/Soviet Studies in the United States, Amerikanistika in Russia: Mutual Representations in Academic Projects*. Lanham: Lexington Books, 2016.

Kuropas, Myron B. "Fighting Moscow from Afar: Ukrainian Americans and the Evil Empire." In Ieva Zake, ed., *Anti-communist Minorities in the U.S.: Political Activism of Ethnic Refugees* (New York: Palgrave Macmillan, 2009, 43–66.

Kutakov, Andrei, and Sebastian Stopper. *Nelegal'nyi Briansk, 1941–1943. Nelegal'naia deiatel'nost' razlichnykh sil v okkupirovannykh Brianske i Ordzhonikidzegrade s 6 oktiabria 1941 po 17 sentabria 1943*. Briansk: "klub liubitelei rodnogo kraia," 2014.

Kuzio, Taras. "U.S. Support for Ukraine's Liberation during the Cold War: A Study of Prolog Research and Publishing Corporation." *Communist and Post-Communist Studies* no. 45 (2012): 51–64. DOI:10.1016/j.postcomstud.2012.02.007. *Last accessed June 3, 2014*.

Larres, Klaus. "Eisenhower and the First Forty Days after Stalin's Death: The Incompatibility of Détente and Political Warfare." *Diplomacy & Statecraft* 6, no. 2 (1995): 431–69.

Laruelle, Marlene. "In search of Putin's philosopher: Why Ivan Ilyin is not Putin's Ideological Guru." *Intersection: Russia/Europe/World*, March 3, 2017, at http://intersectionproject.eu/article/politics/search-putins-philosopher. *Last accessed December 27, 2018*.

Laruelle, Marlene, ed. *Entangled Far Rights: A Russian-European Intellectual Romance in the Twentieth Century*. Pittsburgh: University of Pittsburgh Press, 2018.

Laruelle, Marlene. "National Identity and the Contested Nation." In Richard Sakwa, Henry Hale, and Stephen White, eds. *Developments in Russian Politics*, 9th edn. London: Red Globe Press, 2019, 67–79.

Laville, Helen, and Hugh Wilford, eds. *The US Government, Citizen Groups and the Cold War: The State-private Network*. London: Routledge, 2012.

Lebedev, S. N. *Ocherki istorii Rossiiskoi vneshnei razvedki*, vol. 5. Moscow: Mezhdunarodnye Otnosheniia, 2003.

Liebich, André. *From the Other Shore: Russian Social Democracy after 1921*. Cambridge, MA: Harvard University Press, 1997.

Liebich, André. "Mensheviks Wage the Cold War." *Journal of Contemporary History* 30, no. 2 (1995): 247–64.

Liulevicius, Vejas G. *The German Myth of the East: 1800 to the Present*. Oxford and New York: Oxford University Press, 2009.

Livak, Leonid. "The Two Solitudes of Russia Abroad: Russian and Russian-Jewish Writers in the Aftermath of World War II." Paper presented at the National Convention of the Association for Slavic, East European, and Eurasian Studies, Philadelphia, PA, November 2015.

Lohr, Eric. *Russian Citizenship from Empire to Soviet Union*. Cambridge, MA: Harvard University Press, 2012.

Long, Stephen. "Strategic Disorder, the Office of Policy Coordination and the Inauguration of US Political Warfare against the Soviet Bloc, 1948–50." *Intelligence & National Security* 27, no. 4 (2012): 459–87.

Long, Stephen. *The CIA and the Soviet Bloc: Political Warfare, the Origins of the CIA and Countering Communism in Europe*. New York: I. B. Tauris, 2014.

Luneva, I. A. "Fenomen 'nevozvrashchentsev' v propagandistskoi voine SBONR protiv Sovetskogo Soiuza." *Vestnik Nizhegorodskogo gosudarstvennogo universiteta im. N. I. Lobachevskogo*. Seriia "Istoiriia. Politologiia. Mezhdunarodnye otnosheniia," edn 1 (2003): 557–64.

Lynn, Katalin Kádár, ed. *The Inauguration of Organized Political Warfare: Cold War Organizations sponsored by the National Committee for a Free Europe/Free Europe Committee*. Saint Helena, CA: Helena History Press, 2013.

Maddrell, Paul. "British Intelligence through the Eyes of the Stasi: What the Stasi's Records Show about the Operations of British Intelligence in Cold War Germany." *Intelligence and National Security* 27, no. 1 (2012): 46–74.

Maddrell, Paul. "The Western Secret Services, the East German Ministry of State Security and the Building of the Berlin Wall." *Intelligence and National Security* 21, no. 5 (2006): 829–47.

Magnúsdóttir, Rósa. *Enemy Number One: The United States of America in Soviet Ideology and Propaganda, 1945–1959*. New York: Oxford University Press, 2019.

Maier, Charles. "Hegemony and Autonomy within the Western Alliance." In Melvyn P. Leffler and David S. Painter, eds. *Origins of the Cold War: An International History*. New York: Routledge, 2005, 154–74.

Makarov, V. G. "Poruchik SD. Nikolai Rutchenko-Rutych i ego nepredskazuemoe proshloe." *Rodina*, no. 3 (2007): 83–7.

Malia, Martin E. *Russia under Western Eyes: From the Bronze Horseman to the Lenin Mausoleum*. Cambridge, MA: Belknap Press of Harvard University Press, 1999.

Manchester, Laurie. "Repatriation to a Totalitarian Homeland: The Ambiguous Alterity of Russian Repatriates from China to the USSR." *Diaspora: A Journal of Transnational Studies* 16, no. 3 (2007): 353–88.

Manchester, Laurie. "How Statelessness Can Force Refugees to Redefine Their Ethnicity: What can be Learned from Russian Émigrés Dispersed to Six Continents in the Inter-war Period?" *Immigrants & Minorities* 34, no. 1 (2016): 70–91.

Martin, Terry. *The Affirmative Action Empire: Nations and Nationalism in the Soviet Union, 1923–1939*. Ithaca and London: Cornell University Press, 2001.

Massie, Robert K. *The Romanovs: The Final Chapter*. New York: Ballantine, 1996.

Massip, Mirey. *Istina – doch' vremeni. Alexandr Kazem-Bek i russkaia emigratsiia na zapade*. Moscow: Iazyki slavianskoi kul'tury, 2010.

Mazower, Mark. *Dark Continent: Europe's Twentieth Century*. New York: Vintage Books, 2000.

Mazower, Mark. *Hitler's Empire: How the Nazis Ruled Europe*. New York: Penguin Press, 2008.

Mazurkiewicz, Anna. "'Join, or Die' – The Road to Cooperation among East European Exiled Political Leaders in the United States, 1949–1954." *Polish American Studies* 69, no. 2 (2012): 5–43.

Mazurkiewicz, Anna, ed. *East Central Europe in Exile*, vols. 1–2. Newcastle upon Tyne, UK: Cambridge Scholars Publishing, 2013.

Merridale, Catherine. *Ivan's War: The Red Army 1939–45*. London: Faber, 2005.

Mickelson, Sig. *America's Other Voice: The Story of Radio Free Europe and Radio Liberty*. New York: Praeger, 1983.

Mikkonen, Simo. "Mass Communications as a Vehicle to Lure Russian Émigrés Homeward." In *Journal of International and Global Studies* 2, no. 2 (2011): 45–61. http://www.lindenwood.edu/jigs/docs/volume2Issue2/essays/1-20.pdf. *Last accessed July 20, 2015.*

Mikkonen, Simo. "Exploiting the Exiles: Soviet Émigrés in U.S. Cold War Strategy." *Journal of Cold War Studies* 14, no. 2 (2012): 98–127.

Miller, Matthew Lee. *The American YMCA and Russian Culture: The Preservation and Expansion of Orthodox Christianity, 1900–1940*. Lanham: Lexington Books, 2013.

Mitrokhin, Nikolai. *Russkaia partiia: dvizhenie russkikh natsionalistov v SSSR, 1953–1985*. Moscow: Novoe Literaturnoe Obozrenie, 2003.

Mitrovich, Gregory. *Undermining the Kremlin: America's Strategy to Subvert the Soviet Bloc, 1947–1956*. Ithaca, NY: Cornell University Press, 2000.

Mnukhin, L. A. et al. *Rossiiskoe zarubezh'e vo Frantsii: 1919–2000: biograficheskii slovar'*. Moscow: Dom-muzei Mariny Tsvetaevoi, 2008.

Moeller, Robert G. *War Stories: The Search for a Usable past in the Federal Republic of Germany*. Berkeley: University of California Press, 2001.

Mooney, Jadwiga E. Pieper, and Fabio Lanza, eds. *De-centering Cold War History: Local and Global Change*. London and New York: Routledge, 2013.

Morgan, Ted. *A Covert Life: Jay Lovestone, Communist, Anti-communist, and Spymaster*. 1st ed. New York: Random House, 1999.

Mumford, Andrew. *Proxy Warfare*. Oxford: Wiley, 2013.

Murphy, David E. "Sasha Who?" *Intelligence and National Security* 8, 1 (1993): 102–7.

Murphy, David E. "The Hunt for Sasha is Over." *CIRA Newsletter* 25, no. 3 (Fall 2000): 11–15.

Murphy, David E., Sergei A. Kondrashev, and George Bailey. *Battleground Berlin: CIA vs. KGB in the Cold War*. New Haven: Yale University Press, 1997.

Naimark, Norman M. *The Russians in Germany: A History of the Soviet Zone of Occupation, 1945–1949*. Cambridge, MA: Belknap Press of Harvard University Press, 1995.

Nitoburg, E. L. *Russkie v SShA: Istoriia i sub'dby*. Moscow: Nauka, 2005.

O'Connell, Charles T. "The Munich Institute for the Study of the USSR: Origin and Social Composition." *The Carl Beck Papers in Russian and East European Studies*, no. 808. Pittsburgh, 1992.

Okorokov, A. V. *Antisovetskie voinskie formirovaniia v gody Vtoroi mirovoi voiny: monografiia*. Moscow: Voennyi Universitet, 2000.

Okulov, Andrei. "Polupravda s Lubianki." *Posev* no. 4 (1615) (2012): 23–6.

Okulov, Andrei. *V bor'be za Beluiu Rossiiu: Kholodnaia grazhdanskaia voina*. Moscow: Veche, 2013.

Osgood, Kenneth. "Hearts and Minds: The Unconventional Cold War." *Journal of Cold War Studies* 4, no. 2 (2002): 85–107.

Osgood, Kenneth. *Total Cold War: Eisenhower's Secret Propaganda Battle at Home and Abroad*. Lawrence: University of Kansas, 2006.

Osnos, Evan, et al. "New Cold War: What lay behind Russia's interference in the 2016 election—and what lies ahead?" *The New Yorker*, March 6, 2017.

Ostermann, Christian. "US Intelligence and the GDR: The Early Years." In Heike Bungert et al., eds. *Secret Intelligence in the Twentieth Century*. London: Frank Cass, 2003, 128–46.

Pahl, Magnus. *Hitler's Fremde Heere Ost: German Military Intelligence on the Eastern Front, 1942–45*, trans. Derik Hammond. Solihull, UK: Helion & Company Ltd, 2016.

Peterson, Jody Lee. *Ideology and Influence Robert F. Kelley and the State Department 1926–1937*. PhD diss., Washington State University, 1998.

Petrov, Igor'. "Rol' russkikh istorikov-emigrantov v stanovlenii 'rossievedcheskoi traditsii' v Velikobritanii." In O. B. Vasilevskaia, ed. *Kul'turnoe i nauchnoe nasledie rossiiskoi emigratsii*. Moscow: Russkii put', 2002, 254–64.

Petrov, Igor'. "Vneshnepoliticheskoe vedomstvo NSDAP: vzgliad iznutri." *Live Journal*, December 1, 2012. https://labas.livejournal.com/. *Last accessed June 30, 2018*.

Petrov, Igor'. "Odin agent i try razvedki: avtobiografiia A. F. Chikalova i kommentarii k nei." *Live Journal*, December 31, 2013. https://labas.livejournal.com/1052599.html. *Last accessed June 30, 2018*.

Petrov, Igor'. "Tainstvennoe izcheznovanie maiora Chikalova." *Live Journal*, July 14, 2016. https://labas.livejournal.com/1152407.html. *Last accessed June 30, 2018*.

Petrov, Igor', and Andrei Martynov. "'Neprigliadnaia kartina kulis vlasovskogo dvizheniia': Mikhail Samygin i ego kniga." In A. Martynov, ed. *Istoriia otechestvennoi kollaboratsii: materialy i issledovaniia*. Moscow: Staraia Basmannaia, 2017, 25–36.

Plokhy, Serhii. *The Man with the Poison Gun: A Cold War Spy Story*. New York: Basic Books, 2016.

Plokhy, Serhii. *Lost Kingdom: The Quest for Empire and the Making of the Russian Nation, from 1470 to the Present*. New York: Basic Books, 2017.

Polian, P. M. *Deportiert nach Hause: Sowjetische Kriegsgefangene im 'Dritten Reich' und ihre Repatriierung*. Munich and Vienna: Oldenbourg, 2001.

Polian, P. M. *Zhertvy dvukh diktatur: zhizn', trud, unizhenie i smert' sovetskikh voennoplennykh i ostarbaiterov na chuzhbine i na rodine*. Moscow: ROSSPEN, 2002.

Popov, A. V. "Miunkhenskii institut po izucheniiu istorii i kul'tury SSSR i vtoraia emigratsiia." *Novyi istoricheskii vestnik* 10, no. 1 (2004): 54–70.

Powers, Richard Gid. *Not without Honor: The History of American Anticommunism*. New York: Free Press, 1995.

Prados, John. *Safe for Democracy: The Secret Wars of the CIA*. Chicago: Ivan R. Dee, 2006.

Puddington, Arch. *Broadcasting Freedom: The Cold War Triumph of Radio Free Europe and Radio Liberty*. Lexington: University Press of Kentucky, 2000.

Radchenko, Yuri. "'We Emptied our Magazines into Them': The Ukrainian Auxiliary Police and the Holocaust in Generalbezirk Charkow, 1941–1943." *Yad Vashem Studies* 41, no. 1 (2013): 63–98.

Raeff, Marc. *Russia Abroad: A Cultural History of the Russian Emigration, 1919–1939.* New York: Oxford University Press, 1990.

Rawnsley, Gary D. "The Campaign of Truth: A Populist Propaganda." In Gary D. Rawnsley, ed. *Cold-War Propaganda in the 1950s.* New York: St. Martin's Press, 1999, 31–46.

Rein, Leonid. *The Kings and the Pawns: Collaboration in Byelorussia.* New York: Berghahn Books, 2011.

Richelson, Jeffrey T. *The U.S. Intelligence Community.* Boulder, CO: Westview Press, 2016.

Riehle, Kevin P. "Early Cold War evolution of British and US defector policy and practice." *Cold War History*, online edn (2018): 1–19.

Ritchie, Donald A. *Doing Oral History.* New York: Twayne Publishers, 1995.

Robinson, Paul. *The White Russian Army in Exile, 1920–1941.* Oxford: Clarendon Press, 2002.

Rudling, Per Anders. "Historical Representation of the Wartime Accounts of the Activities of the OUN–UPA (Organization of Ukrainian Nationalists—Ukrainian Insurgent Army)." *East European Jewish Affairs* 36, no. 2 (2006): 163–89.

Ruffner, Kevin Conley. "A Controversial Liaison Relationship: American Intelligence and the Gehlen Organization, 1945–49." *Studies in Intelligence* (1997), CIA History Staff. http://www.foia.cia.gov/. *Last accessed February 23, 2016.*

Ruffner, Kevin Conley. "*Eagle and Swastika*: CIA and Nazi War Criminals and Collaborators." Draft Working Paper, History Staff, Central Intelligence Agency, Washington, DC, April 2003. http://www.foia.cia.gov/. *Last accessed June 4, 2014.*

Satiukow, Silke. *Besatzer: "Die Russen" in Deutschland 1945–1994.* Göttingen: Vandenhoeck & Ruprecht, 2008.

Schlögel, Karl, ed. *Der Grosse Exodus: Die Russische Emigration und Ihre Zentren, 1917 bis 1941.* Munich: C. H. Beck, 1994.

Schwartz, Lowell. *Political Warfare against the Kremlin: US and British Propaganda Policy at the Beginning of the Cold War.* Basingstoke and New York: Palgrave Macmillan, 2009.

Scott, James C. *Domination and the Arts of Resistance: Hidden Transcripts.* New Haven, CT: Yale University Press, 2008.

Scott-Smith, Giles. *Western Anti-Communism and the Interdoc Network: Cold War Internationale.* New York: Palgrave Macmillan, 2012.

Shain, Yossi. *The Frontier of Loyalty: Political Exiles in the Age of the Nation-state.* Middletown, CT: Wesleyan University Press, 1989.

Shmelev, Anatol. "Gallipoli to Golgotha: Remembering the Internment of the Russian White Army at Gallipoli, 1920–3." In Jenny Macleod (ed.), *Defeat and Memory: Cultural Histories of Military Defeat in the Modern Era.* Basingstoke and New York: Palgrave Macmillan, 2008, 193–215.

Simpson, Christopher. *Blowback: America's Recruitment of Nazis and its Effects on the Cold War.* New York: Weidenfeld & Nicolson, 1988.

Smith, Scott B. *Captives of Revolution: The Socialist Revolutionaries and the Bolshevik Dictatorship, 1918–1923.* Pittsburgh, PA: University of Pittsburgh Press, 2011.

Snyder, Timothy. "God is a Russian." *The New York Review of Books*, April 5, 2018.

Statiev, Alexander. *The Soviet Counterinsurgency in the Western Borderlands.* Cambridge and New York: Cambridge University Press, 2010.

Stelzl-Marx, Barbara. *Stalins Soldaten in Österreich: Die Innensicht der Sowjetischen Besatzung 1945–1955*. Munich: Böhlau Verlag, 2012.

Stephan, John J. *The Russian Fascists: Tragedy and Farce in Exile, 1925–1945*. New York: Harper & Row, 1978.

Stephan, Robert W. *Stalin's Secret War: Soviet Counterintelligence against the Nazis, 1941–1945*. Lawrence: University of Kansas Press, 2004.

Stites, Richard. "Heaven and Hell: Soviet Propaganda Constructs the World." In Gary D. Rawnsley, ed. *Cold-War Propaganda in the 1950s*. New York: St. Martin's Press, 1999, 85–103.

Stöcker, Lars Fredrik. *Bridging the Baltic Sea: Networks of Resistance and Opposition during the Cold War Era*. Lanham, Maryland: Lexington Books, 2018.

Stöver, Bernd. *Die Befreiung vom Kommunismus: Amerikanische Liberation Policy im Kalten Krieg 1947–1991*. Cologne: Böhlau, 2002.

Suny, Ronald Grigor. *The Revenge of the Past: Nationalism, Revolution, and the Collapse of the Soviet Union*. Stanford, CA: Stanford University Press, 1993.

Taylor, Brian D. *The Code of Putinism*. New York: Oxford University Press, 2018.

Taylor, Philip M. "Through a Glass Darkly? The Psychological Climate and Psychological Warfare of the Cold War." In Gary D. Rawnsley, ed. *Cold-War Propaganda in the 1950s*. New York: St. Martin's Press, 1999, 225–42.

Thorwald, Jürgen. *The Illusion: Soviet Soldiers in Hitler's Armies*. New York: Harcourt Brace Jovanovich, 1975.

Thurston, Robert W., and Bernd Bonwetsch, eds. *The People's War: Responses to World War II in the Soviet Union*. Urbana, IL: University of Illinois Press, 2000.

Tribunskii, P. A. "Fond Forda, Fond 'Svobodnaia Rossiia,' Vostochno-Evropeiskii Fond i Sozdanie 'Izdatel'stva imeni Chekhova.'" *Ezhegodnik Doma Russkogo zarubezhiia imeni Aleksandra Solzhenitsyna 2014–2015*, Moscow, 2015, 577–600.

Tromly, Benjamin. "Ambivalent Heroes: Russian Defectors and American Power in the Early Cold War." *Intelligence and National Security* 33, no. 5 (2018): 642–58.

Tsurganov, Iu. S. *Neudavshiiasia revansh: belaia emigratsiia vo vtoroi mirovoi voine*. Moscow: Intrada, 2001.

Ul'iankina, T. I. *'Dikaia istoricheskaia polosa…' sud'by Rossiiskoi nauchnoi emigratsii v Evrope (1940–1950)*. Moscow: ROSSPEN, 2010.

Van Dongen, Luc, Stéphanie Roulin, and Giles Scott-Smith, eds. *Transnational Anti-Communism and the Cold War: Agents, Activities, and Networks*. Basingstoke: Palgrave Macmillan, 2014.

Volkmann, Hans-Erich. "Die politischen Hauptströmungen in der russischen Emigration nach dem Zweiten Weltkrieg." *Osteuropa* no. 4 (1965): 242–52.

Volkov, S. V. *Russkaia voennaia emigratsiia: izdatel'skaia deiatel'nost'*. Moscow: "Pashkov Dom," 2008.

Volodarsky, Boris. *Nikolai Khokhlov ("Whistler"): Self-Esteem with a Halo*. Vienna and London: Borwall Verlag, 2005.

Volodarsky, Boris. *Stalin's Agent: The Life and Death of Alexander Orlov*. Oxford and New York: Oxford University Press, 2015.

Walt, Stephen M. "I Knew the Cold War. This Is No Cold War." *Foreign Policy*, March 12, 2018. https://foreignpolicy.com/2018/03/12/i-knew-the-cold-war-this-is-no-cold-war/. *Last accessed April 1, 2018*.

Wark, Wesley K. "Coming in from the Cold: British Propaganda and Red Army Defectors." *International History Review* 9, no. 1 (1987): 48–72.

Watt, D. Cameron. "The Proper Study of Propaganda." *Intelligence and National Security* 15, no. 4 (2000): 143–63.

Weeks, Theodore R. *Nation and State in Late Imperial Russia: Nationalism and Russification on the Western Frontier, 1863–1914.* DeKalb, IL: Northern Illinois University Press, 1996.

Weiss, Claudia. "Russian Political Parties in Exile." *Kritika* 5, no. 1 (2004): 219–32.

Weiss, Michael. "The KGB Playbook for Turning Russians Worldwide into Agents." *The Daily Beast*, December 29, 2017. https://www.thedailybeast.com/the-kgb-playbook-for-turning-russians-worldwide-into-agents. *Last accessed January 2, 2018.*

Welch, Stephen. "Political Culture: Approaches and Prospects." In Philip H. J. Davies and Kristian Gustafson, eds. *Intelligence Elsewhere: Spies and Espionage outside the Anglosphere* Washington, DC: Georgetown University Press, 2013, 13–26.

West, Nigel. *Games of Intelligence: The Classified Conduct of International Espionage.* London: Weidenfeld & Nicolson, 1989.

West, Nigel. *Historical Dictionary of Cold War Counterintelligence.* Lanham, MD: Scarecrow Press, 2007.

Westad, Odd Arne. *The Global Cold War: Third World Interventions and the Making of our Times.* Cambridge and New York: Cambridge University Press, 2007.

Whitaker, Reg. "Cold War Alchemy: How America, Britain and Canada transformed Espionage into Subversion." *Intelligence and National Security* 15, no. 2 (2000): 177–210.

Wilford, Hugh. *The Mighty Wurlitzer: How the CIA Played America.* Cambridge, MA: Harvard University Press, 2008.

Williams, Robert C. "European Political Emigrations: A Lost Subject." *Comparative Studies in Society and History* 12, no. 2 (1970): 140–8.

Williams, Robert C. *Culture in Exile: Russian Emigres in Germany, 1881–1941.* Ithaca, NY: Cornell University Press, 1972.

Wyman, Mark. *DP: Europe's Displaced Persons, 1945–1951.* Philadelphia: Balch Institute Press, 1988.

Yergin, Daniel. *Shattered Peace: The Origins of the Cold War and the National Security State.* Boston: Houghton Mifflin, 1977.

Zake, Ieva. ed. *Anti-communist Minorities in the U.S.: Political Activism of Ethnic Refugees.* New York: Palgrave Macmillan, 2009.

Zemskov, V. N. "K voprosy o repatriatsii sovetskikh grazhdan, 1944–1951." *Istoriia SSSR,* no. 4 (1990): 26–41.

Zemskov, V. N. "'Vtoraia emigratsiia' i otnoshenie k nei rukovodstva SSSR, 1947–1955." In Iu. A. Poliakov et al., eds. *Istoriia rossiiskogo zarubez'hia: emigratsiia iz SSSR-Rossii, 1941–2001 gg.: sbornik stat'ei.* Moscow: Rossiiskaia akademiia nauk, Institut rossiiskoi istorii, 2007, 63–91.

Zhukov, Dmitrii, and Ivan Kovtun. "Boris Khol'mston-Smyslovskii i NTS: Istoriia sotrudnichestva i protivostoianiia." In A. Martynov, ed. *Istoriia otechestvennoi kollaboratsii: materialy i issledovaniia.* Moscow: Staraia Basmannaia, 2017, 297–338.

Zubkova, Elena. *Russia after the War: Hopes, Illusions, and Disappointments, 1945–1957.* Armonk, NY: M.E. Sharpe, 1998.

Zubok, Vladislav M. *A Failed Empire: The Soviet Union in the Cold War from Stalin to Gorbachev.* Chapel Hill: University of North Carolina Press, 2007.

Index